DISABILITY LAW
CASES AND MATERIALS

Second Edition

■ ■ ■

Stephen F. Befort
Gray, Plant, Mooty, Mooty, and Bennett Professor of Law
University of Minnesota Law School

Nicole Buonocore Porter
Professor of Law
University of Toledo College of Law

for

THE LABOR LAW GROUP

AMERICAN CASEBOOK SERIES®

American Casebook Series is a trademark registered in the U.S. Patent and Trademark Office.

© 2017 THE LABOR LAW GROUP
© 2021 THE LABOR LAW GROUP
      444 Cedar Street, Suite 700
      St. Paul, MN 55101
      1-877-888-1330

West, West Academic Publishing, and West Academic are trademarks of West Publishing Corporation, used under license.

Printed in the United States of America

ISBN: 978-1-64708-486-8

PREFACE

The study of disability law is the study of how the lives of individuals with disabilities interact and intersect with various institutions—including places of employment, educational institutions, governmental services and benefits, and places of public accommodation. At each point of intersection, disability law addresses the rights and responsibilities of the individual with a disability and the institution. This book covers the three primary federal statutes that govern these interactions—the Americans with Disabilities Act (ADA), Section 504 of the Rehabilitation Act, and the Individuals with Disabilities Education Act (IDEA).

We have three objectives for this book. First, because the majority of litigation that takes place under the ADA is employment litigation, we sought to provide an in-depth coverage of disability law in the employment context. We do this by providing two chapters on employment—one that covers the foundational concepts and a second chapter that covers some of the specialized topics that arise in disability employment cases. These chapters are summarized below. Our second objective was to provide a robust coverage of recent cases that have been decided since the ADA Amendments Act of 2008 went into effect. The ADA Amendments Act dramatically broadened the interpretation of the definition of "disability." Of course, our chapter on the definition of disability includes recent cases exploring the broadened interpretation of the definition of disability. But we have also incorporated many post-Amendments cases throughout the casebook. Finally, our third objective was to provide practical problems and thought-provoking questions to test students' understanding of the materials covered and spark classroom discussion. Below is a summary of each chapter's coverage.

Chapter 1: Introduction

Chapter 1 introduces the topic of disability discrimination by first discussing the historical systemic discrimination experienced by individuals with disabilities and the rise of the disability rights movement. The chapter then proceeds to examine the status of individuals with disabilities under the Equal Protection clause of the U.S. Constitution. Finally, Chapter 1 briefly describes the coverage and basic requirements of the Americans with Disabilities Act.

Chapter 2: Definition of Disability

Chapter 2 covers the definition of disability under the ADA, which was the subject of the majority of ADA litigation before the ADA was amended in 2008. After describing the three-prong structure of the definition of disability under the ADA (and the Rehabilitation Act), the chapter briefly covers the Supreme Court's narrow interpretation of "disability" under the original ADA, before the 2008 Amendments were passed. It then describes the ADA Amendments Act's provisions before turning to cases decided after the Amendments that interpret the new provisions. Chapter 2 then provides a very brief section on the "record of" prong of the definition of disability. Finally, this chapter addresses the interpretation of the "regarded as" prong, both before and after the ADA Amendments Act.

Chapter 3: Employment Discrimination—Title I of the ADA

Chapter 3 is the primary chapter on disability discrimination in employment, covering Title I of the ADA. It begins with a discussion of the prima facie case in disability discrimination cases. The chapter then turns to the hallmark of ADA employment cases—the qualified individual inquiry and the reasonable accommodation provision. In addition to describing the general concept of reasonable accommodation, this chapter includes coverage of: reassignment to a vacant position; accommodating the "structural norms" of the workplace (the hours, shifts, schedules, etc.); and the interactive process. Chapter 3 then covers employers' defenses, including: the undue hardship defense; qualification standards; and the direct threat defense.

Chapter 4: Employment Discrimination—Contextual Applications

Chapter 4 takes a closer look at employment discrimination by focusing on several recurring contexts. Topics include: illegal drug and alcohol use, mental impairments, and associational discrimination. The chapter then explores the ADA's treatment of medical examinations and inquiries and the interplay between the ADA and the Family and Medical Leave Act. The chapter concludes by discussing procedures and remedies in employment cases and by presenting an excerpt from an article asking the provocative question as to whether the ADA is working as intended.

Chapter 5: Government Services—Title II of the ADA

Chapter 5 presents material on Title II of the ADA, which applies to governmental entities and services. The chapter begins by exploring Title II coverage. The chapter then addresses what constitutes discrimination for Title II purposes, with particular attention given to the issues of access versus content and segregated services. Other issues covered by this chapter are: civic participation, zoning, physical accessibility, and licensing rules. The chapter ends with a brief section on Title II enforcement and remedies.

Chapter 6: Public Accommodations—Title III of the ADA

Chapter 6 covers Title III of the ADA, which applies to places of public accommodation. After providing the main statutory provisions, the chapter addresses reasonable modifications that are sought at places of public accommodation (including a new case regarding service animals) and accessibility issues that arise in places of public accommodation. Chapter 6 then covers examinations and courses, including testing accommodations. Chapter 6 also provides a section on Title III's coverage of insurance policies. Finally, the chapter ends with a section on remedies, including standing, "serial litigation," and the statute of limitations.

Chapter 7: Education

Chapter 7 is the chapter on education and covers Titles II and III of the ADA, Section 504 of the Rehabilitation Act, and the Individuals with Disabilities Education Act. This chapter is organized into two main parts— higher education followed by primary/secondary education. The higher education part includes a section on admissions and then a section on the issue of academic deference, especially as it applies in academic dismissal cases. Finally, the higher education part covers the issue of waiver of degree requirements. The primary/secondary education part begins with the standard for a Free Appropriate Public Education under the IDEA. This part then turns to mainstreaming, related services, and the "stay-put" provision in discipline cases. We then cover the issue of private school reimbursement and the procedures and remedies applicable to the IDEA. Finally, the chapter ends with a section on the relevance of the ADA and Section 504 of the Rehabilitation Act in primary and secondary education.

STEPHEN F. BEFORT
NICOLE BUONOCORE PORTER

December 2020

ACKNOWLEDGMENTS AND PERMISSIONS

The authors gratefully acknowledge the permissions granted to enable the reprinting of the following copyrighted materials:

Chapter 1

Jonathan C. Drimmer, *Cripples, Overcomers, and Civil Rights: Tracing the Evolution of Federal Legislation and Social Policy for People with Disabilities*, 40 UCLA Law Review 1341 (1003).

Lawrence O. Gostin, *The Americans with Disabilities Act at 25: The Highest Expression of American Values*, 313 Journal of the American Medical Association 2231 (2015).

Chapter 2

Stephen F. Befort, *An Empirical Examination of Case Outcomes Under the ADA Amendments Act*, 70 Washington and Lee Law Review 2027 (2013).

Chapter 3

Mark Weber, *Unreasonable Accommodation and Due Hardship*, 62 Florida Law Review 1119 (2010).

Nicole Buonocore Porter, *Martinizing Title I of the Americans with Disabilities Act*, 47 Georgia Law Review 527 (2013).

Stephen F. Befort, *Accommodating an Employee's Commute to Work Under the ADA: Reasonable, Preferential, or Both?*, 63 Drake Law Review 739 (2015).

Chapter 4

Randal I. Goldstein, *Mental Illness in the Workplace after* Sutton v. United Airlines, 86 Cornell Law Review 927 (2001).

Sharona Hoffman, *Settling the Matter: Does Title I of the ADA Work?*, 59 Alabama Law Review 305 (2007–2008).

For the second edition of this casebook, Professor Befort would like to thank Molly Fischl for research assistance and the University of Minnesota Law School for research support. Professor Porter would like to thank the University of Toledo College of Law for providing summer research support.

FOREWORD

The Labor Law Group had its origins in the desire of scholars to produce quality casebooks for instruction in labor and employment law. Over the course of its existence, the hallmarks of the Group have been collaborative efforts among scholars, informed by skilled practitioners, under a cooperative nonprofit trust in which royalties from past work finance future meetings and projects.

At the 1946 meeting of the Association of American Law Schools, Professor W. Willard Wirtz delivered a compelling paper criticizing the labor law coursebooks then available. His remarks so impressed those present that the Labor Law Roundtable of the Association organized a general conference on the teaching of labor law to be held in Ann Arbor in 1947. The late Professor Robert E. Mathews served as coordinator for the Ann Arbor meeting, and several conferees agreed to exchange proposals for sections of a new coursebook that would facilitate training exemplary practitioners of labor law. Beginning in 1948, a preliminary mimeographed version was used in seventeen schools; each user supplied comments and suggestions for change. In 1953, a hardcover version was published under the title *Labor Relations and the Law*. The thirty-one "cooperating editors" were so convinced of the value of multicampus collaboration that they gave up any individual claims to royalties. Instead, those royalties were paid to a trust fund to be used to develop and "provide the best possible materials" for training students in labor law and labor relations. The Declaration of Trust memorializing this agreement was executed November 4, 1953, and remains the Group's charter.

The founding committee's hope that the initial collaboration would bear fruit has been fulfilled. Under Professor Mathews's continuing leadership, the Group's members produced *Readings on Labor Law* in 1955 and *The Employment Relation and the Law* in 1957, edited by Robert Mathews and Benjamin Aaron. A second edition of *Labor Relations and the Law* appeared in 1960, with Benjamin Aaron and Donald H. Wollett as coeditors of the book and cochairs of the Group, and a third edition was published in 1965, with Jerre S. Williams at the helm.

In June 1969 the Group, now chaired by William P. Murphy, sponsored a conference to reexamine the labor law curriculum. Practitioners and full-time teachers, including nonmembers as well as members of the Group, attended the meeting, held at the University of Colorado. In meetings that followed the conference, the Group decided to reshape its work substantially. It restructured itself into ten task forces, each assigned a unit of no more than two hundred pages on a discrete topic such as employment discrimination or union-member relations. An individual teacher could then choose two or three of these units as the material around which to build a particular course. This multiunit approach dominated the Group's work throughout much of the 1970s under Professor Murphy and his successor as chair, Herbert L. Sherman, Jr.

As the 1970s progressed and teachers refined their views about what topics to include and how to address them, some units were dropped from the series while others increased in scope and length. Under Professor Sherman's leadership, the Group planned a new series of six enlarged books to cover the full range of topics taught by labor and employment law teachers. Professor James E. Jones, Jr., was elected chair in 1978, and he shepherded to completion the promised set of six full-size, independent casebooks. The Group continued to reevaluate its work and eventually decided that it was time to convene another conference of law teachers.

In 1984 the Group, now chaired by Robert Covington, sponsored another general conference to discuss developments in the substance and teaching of labor and employment law, this time in Park City, Utah. Those discussions and a subsequent working session led to the conclusion that the Group should devote principal attention to three new conventional length coursebooks, one devoted to employment discrimination, one to union-management relations, and one to the individual employment relationship. In addition, work was planned on more abbreviated coursebooks to serve as successors to the Group's earlier works covering public employment bargaining and labor arbitration.

In 1989, with Alvin Goldman as chair, the Group met in Breckenridge, Colorado, to assess its most recent efforts and develop plans for the future. In addition to outlining new coursebook projects, the Group discussed ways to assist teachers of labor and employment law in their efforts to expand conceptual horizons and perspectives. In pursuit of the latter goals it cosponsored, in 1992, a conference held at the University of Toronto Faculty of Law at which legal and nonlegal specialists examined alternative models of corporate governance and their impact on workers.

When Robert J. Rabin became chair in 1996, the Group and a number of invited guests met in Tucson, Arizona, to celebrate the imminent fiftieth anniversary of the Group. The topics of discussion included the impact of the global economy and of changing forms of representation on the teaching of labor and employment law, and the impact of new technologies of electronic publishing on the preparation of teaching materials. The Group honored three of its members who had been present at the creation of the Group, Willard Wirtz, Ben Aaron, and Clyde Summers. The Group next met in Scottsdale, Arizona, in December 1999, to discuss the production of materials that would more effectively bring emerging issues of labor and employment law into the classroom. Among the issues discussed were integration of international and comparative materials into the labor and employment curriculum and the pedagogical uses of the World Wide Web.

Laura J. Cooper became chair of the Group in July 2001. In June 2003, the Group met in Alton, Ontario, Canada. The focus there was on "labor law on the edge"—looking at doctrinal synergies between workplace law and other legal and social-science disciplines—and "workers on the edge"—exploring the legal issues of highly compensated technology workers, vulnerable immigrant employees, and unionized manufacturing employees threatened by foreign competition. The Group also heard a report from its study of the status of the teaching of labor and employment law in the nation's law schools and discussed the implications of the study for the Group's future projects. Members of the Group began work on the casebook on international labor law at this meeting. During Professor Cooper's term, the Group also finished its popular reader *Labor Law Stories*, which examines the stories behind many of the most important American labor law cases.

In July 2005, Kenneth G. Dau-Schmidt became the chair of the Labor Law Group. Shortly after his election, the Group held a meeting in Chicago with nationally recognized practitioners to discuss how best to teach students about the practice of labor law in the new global economy of the information age. The outline that resulted from this meeting served as the basis for *Labor Law in the Contemporary Workplace*. Following the Chicago meeting, the Group met several times to work on new editions of its books and develop new projects: June 2006 in Saratoga Springs, New York; June 2007 in St. Charles, Illinois; and June 2010 in Arrowhead, California. Group projects that grew out of or benefited from these meetings include *International Labor Law: Cases and Materials on Workers' Rights in the Global Economy* and *A Concise Hornbook on Employment Law*. The Group also hosted: a November 2007 symposium on the problems of low-wage workers, the proceedings of which were published in the *Minnesota Law Review*; a February 2009 symposium on the American Law Institute's Proposed Restatement of Employment Law, the proceedings of which were published in the *Employee Rights and Employment Policy Journal*; and a November 2010 symposium on labor and employment law policies under the Obama administration, the proceedings of which were published in the *Indiana Law Journal*.

Marion Crain became chair of the Group at the beginning of 2011. That same year, the Group sponsored a one-day conference on the crisis confronting public-sector employment, the proceedings of which were published in the *ABA Journal of Labor and Employment Law*. In 2011 the Group also hosted a meeting of experts in Chicago to consider the ongoing Restatement of Employment Law project. In June 2012, the Group met in Asheville, North Carolina, and approved the formation of an editorial policy committee charged with establishing policies to ensure that the

Group's products continue to reflect its tradition of close collaboration and high standards. The Asheville meeting served as the genesis for a labor arbitrator training workshop for academics in Chicago in December 2012. In February 2013, the Group cosponsored a symposium at the University of California-Irvine School of Law on alternatives to the Wagner Act and employment law models of workplace protection. The proceedings of the conference, called "Re-imagining Labor Law: Building Worker Collectivities After the NLRA," were published in the *UC Irvine Law Review*. In June 2014, the Group met in Ithaca, New York and conducted a lively educational program.

Steve Befort and Melissa Hart became Co-Chairs of the Group at the beginning of 2015. In that year, Group members voted to approve a partnership between the Group and the Chicago-Kent Law School to oversee the publication of the *Employee Rights and Employment Policy Journal*. In November 2016, the Group hosted a third conference on the American Law Institute's Restatement of Employment Law. This conference was held at Indiana University-Bloomington and its proceedings were published in the *Employee Rights and Employment Policy Journal*. The Group met in Los Angeles, California in December 2016 and in Denver Colorado in June 2018. Melissa Hart stepped down as Co-Chair of the Group in December 2017 after being appointed a Justice on the Colorado Supreme Court. In 2019, the Group renegotiated its agreement with Chicago-Kent and the Group obtained authority to appoint a co-editor of the journal and to sponsor periodic symposia which would generate articles for publication in the journal. The Group appointed Noah Zatz to the co-editor position. Jeff Hirsch took over as Chair of the Group in 2020.

At any one time, roughly twenty-five to thirty members are actively engaged in the Group's work; this has proven to be a practical size, given the challenges of communication and logistics. Coordination and editorial review of the projects are the responsibility of the executive committee, whose members are the successor trustees of the Group. Governance is by consensus; votes are taken only to elect trustees and to determine whom to invite to join the Group. Since 1953, more than eighty persons have worked on Group projects; in keeping with the original agreement, none has ever received anything more than reimbursement of expenses.

The Labor Law Group has ten books in print. West has published *Public Sector Employment: Cases and Materials* (Third Edition) by Martin H. Malin, Ann C. Hodges, Joseph E. Slater, and Jeffrey M. Hirsch; *Principles of Employment Law* by Peggie R. Smith, Ann C. Hodges, Susan J. Stabile, and Rafael Gely; *Labor Law in the Contemporary Workplace* (Third Edition) by Kenneth G. Dau-Schmidt, Martin H. Malin, Roberto L. Corrada, Christopher David Ruiz Cameron, and Catherine L. Fisk; *International Labor Law: Cases and Materials on Workers' Rights in the*

Global Economy by James Atleson, Lance Compa, Kerry Rittich, Calvin William Sharpe, and Marley S. Weiss; *Labor Law, Collective Bargaining in a Free Society* (Seventh Edition) by Dennis Nolan, Richard Bales, and Rafael Gely; *Disability Law: Cases and Materials* (Second Edition) by Stephen F. Befort and Nicole Buonocore Porter; *Employment Discrimination Law: Cases and Materials on Equality in the Workplace* (Tenth Edition) by Maria L. Ontiveros, Roberto L. Corrada, Michael Selmi, Nicole Buonocore Porter, and Marcia L. McCormick; *ADR in the Workplace* (Fourth Edition) by Laura J. Cooper, Dennis R. Nolan, Richard A. Bales, Stephen F. Befort, Lise Gelernter, and Michael Z. Green; and *Legal Protection for the Individual Employee* (Fifth Edition) by Kenneth G. Dau-Schmidt, Matthew W. Finkin and Robert N. Covington. Foundation Press also has published *Labor Law Stories*, edited by Laura J. Cooper and Catherine L. Fisk.

Stephen F. Befort is the Gray, Plant, Mooty, Mooty, and Bennett Professor of Law at the University of Minnesota Law School. Professor Befort teaches courses in Employment Law, Employment Discrimination, Disability Law, Labor Law, Alternative Dispute Resolution, and a seminar on Advanced Topics in Labor and Employment Law. He has authored six books and more than 50 articles on labor and employment subjects. He is the past Co-Editor of the ABA Journal on Labor and Employment Law and a fellow of the American College of Labor and Employment Lawyers. He has served as Chair of the U.S. Branch of the International Society for Labor Law and Social Security and as Chair of the Labor Law Group. He is an active arbitrator and mediator, and he is a member of the National Academy of Arbitrators.

Nicole Buonocore Porter is a Professor of Law at the University of Toledo College of Law. Professor Porter teaches courses in Disability Law, Employment Discrimination, Education Law, Feminist Legal Theory, Contracts, and Criminal Law. She has published over 40 articles and four books (including this one) focusing primarily on the employment rights of women and individuals with disabilities. Professor Porter began her teaching career at Saint Louis University School of Law and was a visiting professor at University of Denver Sturm College of Law and the University of Iowa College of Law. She is the Secretary of the Executive Committee of the Labor Law Group. In 2018, she was one of three professors who was selected for a university-wide award for outstanding faculty scholarship.

THE EXECUTIVE COMMITTEE

JEFFREY HIRSCH (CHAIR)
RUBEN GARCIA (TREASURER)
NICOLE BUONOCORE PORTER (SECRETARY)
STEPHEN BEFORT

CHARLOTTE GARDEN

CYNTHIA NANCE

CÉSAR F. MARZAN ROSADO

NOAH ZATZ

THE LABOR LAW GROUP

Members

Steven D. Anderman
University of Essex

Rachel Arnow-Richman
University of Florida

Harry W. Arthurs
York University (Emeritus)

James B. Atleson
State University of New York–Buffalo (Emeritus)

Dianne Avery
State University of New York–Buffalo (Emerita)

Richard A. Bales
Ohio Northern University

Stephen Befort
University of Minnesota

Adele Blackett
McGill University

Alfred W. Blumrosen
Rutgers University (Emeritus)

Christopher David Ruiz Cameron
Southwestern Law School

Lance Compa
Cornell University

Laura Cooper
University of Minnesota (Emerita)

Roberto L. Corrada
University of Denver

Robert N. Covington
Vanderbilt University (Emeritus)

Jeffrey Hirsch
University of North Carolina

Ann C. Hodges
University of Richmond (Emerita)

Alan Hyde
Rutgers University–Newark

Pauline T. Kim
Washington University–St. Louis

Thomas C. Kohler
Boston College

Brian A. Langille
University of Toronto

Stephen Lee
University of California–Irvine

Orly Lobel
University of San Diego

Deborah Malamud
New York University

Martin H. Malin
Illinois Institute of Technology
Chicago–Kent College of Law

Marcia McCormick
St. Louis University

Mordehai Mironi
University of Haifa

Robert B. Moberly
University of Arkansas

Charles J. Morris
Southern Methodist University (Emeritus)

Cynthia Nance
University of Arkansas–Fayetteville

Peggie R. Smith
Washington University–St. Louis

Susan J. Stabile
University of St. Thomas

Katherine V. W. Stone
University of California–Los Angeles

Lea S. VanderVelde
University of Iowa

Laura Weinrib
Harvard University

June Weisberger
University of Wisconsin–Madison (Emerita)

Marley Weiss
University of Maryland

Michael Wishnie
Yale University

Noah Zatz
University of California–Los Angeles

SUMMARY OF CONTENTS

———

PREFACE V

ACKNOWLEDGMENTS AND PERMISSIONS IX

FOREWORD XI

THE LABOR LAW GROUP XVII

TABLE OF CASES XXXIII

Chapter 1. Introduction 1
A. Systemic Discrimination and the Disability Rights Movement 2
B. Models of Disability Interpretation 4
C. Constitutional Status 7
D. Introduction to the Americans with Disabilities Act 18

Chapter 2. Definition of Disability Under the Americans with Disabilities Act 23
A. Actual Disability 23
B. Record of Disability 69
C. Regarded as Disabled 70
D. Post-ADAAA Summary 82

Chapter 3. Employment Discrimination 89
A. Plaintiff's Prima Facie Case 89
B. Qualified Individual with a Disability 104
C. Reasonable Accommodation Mandate 119
D. Undue Hardship 193
E. Qualification Standards 206
F. Direct Threat 218

Chapter 4. Employment Discrimination: Contextual Applications 237
A. Illegal Drug and Alcohol Use 237
B. Mental Impairments 253
C. Associational Discrimination 257
D. Medical Examinations and Inquiries 280
E. Special Issues 297
F. Family and Medical Leave Act 302
G. Procedures and Remedies 321
H. Is the ADA Working? 325

Chapter 5. Government Services: Title II of the ADA 329
A. Background and Statutory Language 329
B. Coverage 330

C. Access/Content Distinction 338
D. Integration 347
E. Civic Participation 361
F. Zoning 367
G. Accessibility 382
H. Licensing Rules 397
I. A Note on Enforcement and Remedies 416

Chapter 6. Public Accommodations: Title III of the ADA 419
A. Statutory Provisions 419
B. Reasonable Modifications 421
C. Accessibility 457
D. Examinations and Courses 476
E. Insurance 489
F. Remedies 501

Chapter 7. Education 525
A. Higher Education 525
B. Primary/Secondary Education 591

INDEX 683

TABLE OF CONTENTS

PREFACE V

ACKNOWLEDGMENTS AND PERMISSIONS IX

FOREWORD XI

THE LABOR LAW GROUP XVII

TABLE OF CASES XXXIII

Chapter 1. Introduction 1
A. Systemic Discrimination and the Disability Rights Movement 2
    A Brief History of the Disability Rights Movement 2
B. Models of Disability Interpretation 4
    Jonathan C. Drimmer, Cripples, Overcomers, and Civil Rights:
        Tracing the Evolution of Federal Legislation and Social Policy
        for People with Disabilities 5
C. Constitutional Status 7
    City of Cleburne v. Cleburne Living Center 7
    Notes and Questions 17
D. Introduction to the Americans with Disabilities Act 18
    Lawrence O. Gostin, The Americans with Disabilities Act at 25: The
        Highest Expression of American Values 18
    Notes and Questions 21

**Chapter 2. Definition of Disability Under the Americans with
    Disabilities Act** 23
A. Actual Disability 23
    1. Statutory Definition 23
    2. Defining Disability 23
        Bragdon v. Abbott 23
        Notes and Questions 33
    3. Pre-Amendments Narrowing Definition of Disability 34
        Sutton v. United Air Lines, Inc. 34
        Notes and Questions 44
        Toyota Motor Mfg., Ky., Inc. v. Williams 47
        Notes and Questions 50
    4. ADA Amendments Act of 2008 51
        a. Summary of Statutory Provisions 51
        b. Post-ADAAA Cases 53
            Feldman v. Law Enforcement Associates Corp. 53
            Notes and Questions 59
            Alston v. Park Pleasant, Inc. 62
            Notes and Questions 65
B. Record of Disability 69

C.　Regarded as Disabled.. 70
　　1.　Pre-Amendments Interpretation....................................... 70
　　　　Sutton v. United Air Lines, Inc. 71
　　　　Notes and Questions 73
　　2.　ADAAA's "Regarded as" Provisions................................. 74
　　3.　Post-ADAAA "Regarded as" Caselaw 75
　　　　Nunies v. Hie Holdings, Inc. 75
　　　　Notes and Questions 80
D.　Post-ADAAA Summary.. 82
　　Stephen F. Befort, An Empirical Examination of Case Outcomes
　　　　Under the ADA Amendments Act 82
　　Notes and Questions 86

Chapter 3. Employment Discrimination................................... 89
A.　Plaintiff's Prima Facie Case 89
　　Monroe v. Indiana Department of Transportation 91
　　Notes and Questions 101
B.　Qualified Individual with a Disability 104
　　1.　General Requirements 104
　　　　Keith v. County of Oakland 105
　　　　Notes and Questions 113
　　2.　Judicial Estoppel 114
　　　　Cleveland v. Policy Management Systems Corporation 114
　　　　Notes and Questions 119
C.　Reasonable Accommodation Mandate 119
　　1.　Statutory Language and EEOC Regulations.................... 119
　　2.　General Concept 120
　　　　Vande Zande v. State of Wisconsin Department of
　　　　　　Administration.. 120
　　　　Notes and Questions 127
　　3.　Defining "Reasonable".. 128
　　　　a.　Excerpt from Mark Weber, *Unreasonable Accommodation*
　　　　　　and Due Hardship, 62 FLA. L. REV. 1119 (2010) 128
　　　　b.　Excerpt from Nicole Porter, *Martinizing Title I of the*
　　　　　　Americans with Disabilities Act, 47 GA. L. REV. 527
　　　　　　(2013).. 129
　　4.　Reassignment to a Vacant Position................................. 131
　　　　U.S. Airways, Inc. v. Barnett.. 131
　　　　Notes and Questions 142
　　　　Huber v. Wal-Mart Stores, Inc. 144
　　　　Equal Employment Opportunity Commission v. United Airlines,
　　　　　　Inc. 146
　　　　Notes and Questions 147
　　5.　Accommodating the Structural Norms of the Workplace 148
　　　　a.　Leaves of Absence... 149
　　　　　　García-Ayala v. Lederle Parenterals, Inc.......................... 149
　　　　　　Severson v. Heartland Woodcraft, Inc............................. 156

Notes and Questions... 160
    b. Working from Home 163
        Equal Employment Opportunity Commission v. Ford
            Motor Company.. 163
        Mosby-Meachem v. Memphis Light, Gas & Water
            Division... 171
        Notes and Questions... 177
    c. Schedules and Shifts 180
  6. Accommodation Mandate: Affirmative Action or Anti-
      Discrimination? 183
      Stephen F. Befort, Accommodating an Employee's Commute to
          Work Under the ADA: Reasonable, Preferential, or Both?.... 183
      Notes and Questions 185
  7. Interactive Process 185
      Barnett v. U.S. Air, Inc. 185
      Notes and Questions 192
D. Undue Hardship... 193
    Reyazuddin v. Montgomery County, Maryland 194
    Notes and Questions 205
E. Qualification Standards.. 206
    Bates v. United Parcel Service, Inc.. 207
    Notes and Questions 217
F. Direct Threat 218
    Bragdon v. Abbott.. 219
    Hutton v. Elf Atochem North America, Inc. 225
    Notes and Questions 233

Chapter 4. Employment Discrimination: Contextual
Applications 237
A. Illegal Drug and Alcohol Use... 237
    Zenor v. El Paso Healthcare System....................................... 238
    Raytheon Co. v. Hernandez 247
    Notes and Questions 251
B. Mental Impairments 253
    Doyal v. Oklahoma Heart, Inc.. 253
    Randal I. Goldstein, Mental Illness in the Workplace After Sutton v.
        United Airlines 255
    Notes and Questions 256
C. Associational Discrimination.. 257
    Den Hartog v. Wasatch Academy.. 257
    Dewitt v. Proctor Hospital 274
    Notes and Questions 279
D. Medical Examinations and Inquiries....................................... 280
    Leonel v. American Airlines, Inc. 282
    Owusu-Ansah v. Coca-Cola Co. 288
    Notes and Questions 293
    The COVID-19 Pandemic.. 295

E.   Special Issues 297
     1.   Retaliation.. 297
     2.   Disparate Impact.. 299
     3.   Harassment.. 301
F.   Family and Medical Leave Act 302
     Caldwell v. Holland of Texas, Inc.. 305
     Diaz v. Fort Wayne Foundry Corp. 314
     Notes and Questions 318
     Interplay with ADA.. 320
G.   Procedures and Remedies.. 321
     1.   Jurisdiction 321
     2.   Agency Enforcement.. 322
     3.   Private Litigation Enforcement.. 323
     4.   Remedies 323
          Notes and Questions 325
H.   Is the ADA Working? 325
     Sharona Hoffman, Settling the Matter: Does Title I of the ADA
          Work?.. 325
     Notes and Questions 327

Chapter 5. Government Services: Title II of the ADA 329
A.   Background and Statutory Language... 329
B.   Coverage.. 330
     Pennsylvania Department of Corrections v. Yeskey.................. 330
     Notes and Questions 333
     Reyazuddin v. Montgomery County, Maryland 335
     Notes and Questions 338
C.   Access/Content Distinction.. 338
     Alexander v. Choate.. 338
     Notes and Questions 346
D.   Integration.. 347
     Olmstead v. L.C. ex rel. Zimring 347
     Notes and Questions 360
E.   Civic Participation... 361
     Galloway v. Superior Court 361
     Notes and Questions 366
F.   Zoning.. 367
     Wisconsin Community Services, Inc. v. City of Milwaukee 367
     New Directions Treatment Services v. City of Reading............ 375
     Notes and Questions 381
G.   Accessibility 382
     Bardon v. City of Sacramento... 382
     Notes and Questions 384
     National Federation of the Blind v. Lamone 386
     Notes and Questions 396
H.   Licensing Rules 397
     Applicants v. Texas State Board of Law Examiners................. 397

U.S. Department of Justice, Civil Rights Division, Re: The United
States' Investigation of the Louisiana Attorney Licensure
System Pursuant to the Americans with Disabilities Act 407
Civil Rights Trustees, News Release: Department of Justice
Reaches Agreement with the Louisiana Supreme Court to
Protect Bar Candidates with Disabilities 415
    Notes and Questions 415
I.   A Note on Enforcement and Remedies 416
    1.   Statutory Synchronicity 416
    2.   Enforcement Procedures 416
    3.   Remedies 417

Chapter 6. Public Accommodations: Title III of the ADA.................. 419
A.   Statutory Provisions.. 419
B.   Reasonable Modifications 421
    PGA Tour, Inc. v. Martin 421
    Notes and Questions 436
    Aikins v. St. Helena Hospital 439
    Notes and Questions 445
    Matheis v. CSL Plasma, Inc. 446
    Notes and Questions 455
C.   Accessibility 457
    Kennedy v. Omegagas & Oil, LLC 458
    Notes and Questions 465
    Gil v. Winn Dixie Stores, Inc. 469
    Notes and Questions 475
D.   Examinations and Courses 476
    1.   Statutory Provisions and Regulations 476
    2.   Testing Accommodations 478
        Enyart v. National Conference of Bar Examiners, Inc. 478
        Notes and Questions 488
E.   Insurance 489
    Fletcher v. Tufts University 489
    Notes and Questions 500
F.   Remedies... 501
    1.   Statutory Provisions... 501
    2.   Standing... 502
        Naiman v. New York University 502
        Notes and Questions 505
    3.   Serial Litigation.. 506
        Molski v. Evergreen Dynasty Corp. 506
        Notes and Questions 521
    4.   Statute of Limitations 523

Chapter 7. Education.. 525
A.   Higher Education 525
    1.   Introduction/Statutory Coverage... 525

2. Admissions 526
    a. Pre-Admission Inquiries.. 526
    b. Qualified Individual with a Disability 526
        Southeastern Community College v. Davis 527
        Notes and Questions.. 532
3. Dismissal/Academic Deference 535
    Zukle v. Regents of the University of California 536
    Wong v. Regents of the University of California 544
    Notes and Questions 554
    Halpern v. Wake Forest University Health Sciences.................... 557
    Notes and Questions 565
4. Waiver of Degree Requirements... 567
    Guckenberger v. Boston University ("Guckenberger I").............. 567
    Guckenberger v. Boston University ("Guckenberger II") 584
    Notes and Questions 590
B. Primary/Secondary Education.. 591
  1. Individuals with Disabilities Education Act ("IDEA")................... 591
    a. Free Appropriate Public Education 592
        Board of Education of the Hendrick Hudson Central
            School District, Westchester County v. Rowley 592
        Notes and Questions.. 607
        Endrew F. v. Douglas County School District Re-1............... 609
        Notes and Questions.. 617
    b. Mainstreaming (Least Restrictive Environment) 620
        Sacramento City Unified School District v. Rachel H........... 620
        Hartmann v. Loudoun County Board of Education 625
        Notes and Questions.. 634
    c. Related Services... 635
        Cedar Rapids Community School District v. Garret F........... 635
        Notes and Questions.. 643
    d. Discipline/Stay-Put Provision 643
        Honig v. Doe.. 643
        Notes and Questions.. 652
    e. Private School Reimbursement 654
        Florence County School District Four v. Carter.................... 654
        Notes and Questions.. 658
    f. Procedures and Remedies 661
        Schaffer v. Weast.. 661
        Notes and Questions.. 668
  2. ADA and Rehabilitation Act in Primary/Secondary Education 670
    Fry v. Napolean Community Schools 670
    Notes and Questions 680

INDEX.. 683

TABLE OF CASES

The principal cases are in bold type.

A.H. by Holzmueller v. Illinois High
    School Association, 438
AARP v. United States Equal
    Employment Opportunity
    Commission, 295
Access Now, Inc. v. Southwest
    Airlines, Co., 473
Aikins v. St. Helena Hospital, 439,
    504, 505
Aka v. Washington Hospital Center,
    147
Alaska Dept. of Environmental
    Conservation v. EPA, 666
Albertson's, Inc. v. Kirkingburg, 44,
    64, 207
Alboniga v. School Bd. of Broward
    Cty., 671
Alexander v. Choate, 338, 359, 373,
    391, 533, 671
Alexiadis v. New York College of
    Health Professions, 33
Allied Stores of Ohio, Inc. v. Bowers,
    15
Alston v. Park Pleasant, Inc., 62
Anchor v. O'Toole, 174
Anderson v. Block, 323
Anderson v. Liberty Lobby, Inc., 198
Applicants v. Texas State Board of
    Law Examiners, 397
Argenyi v. Creighton U., 534
Arlington Central School District v.
    Murphy, 669
Arnold v. Wilder, 174
Ashcroft v. Iqbal, 54
AT&T Mobility LLC v. Concepcion,
    325
Azzam v. Baptist Healthcare
    Affiliates, Inc., 182
Baert v. Euclid Beverage, Ltd., 190
Baird v. Rose, 103
Ballard v. Chicago Park District, 319
Bardon v. City of Sacramento, 382
Barlia v. MWI Veterinary Supply, Inc.,
    62
Barnes v. Gorman, 324, 417
Barnes v. Northwest Iowa Health
    Center, 70
Barnett v. U.S. Air, Inc., 185
Bates v. United Parcel Service,
    Inc., 207
Baughman v. Walt Disney World
    Company, 437

Bay Area Addiction Research and
    Treatment, Inc. v. City of Antioch,
    376
Beck v. University of Wis. Bd. of
    Regents, 189
Berardelli v. Allied Servs. Inst. of
    Rehab., Med., 448
Bircoll v. Miami-Dade County, 334
Blatt v. Cabela's Retail, Inc., 68
Bledsoe v. Palm Beach Cnty. Soil &
    Water Conservation Dist., 336
BNSF Ry Co. v. EEOC, 294
Board of Ed. of Hendrick Hudson
    Central School Dist.,
    Westchester Cty. v. Rowley, 592,
    609, 615, 645, 661, 670
Board of Trustees of the Univ. of Ala.
    v. Garrett, 336, 338
Bogner v. Wackenhut Corp., 182
Bogovich v. Sandoval, 417
Boots v. Northwestern Mutual Life
    Ins., 499
Borkowski v. Valley Central School
    Dist., 127, 143
Botosan v. Paul McNally Realty, 519
Bragdon v. Abbott, 23, 67, **219,** 352,
    379
Bray v. Town of Wake Forest, 62
Brian S. v. Vance, 663
Brickers v. Cleveland Bd. of Educ.,
    167
Brown v. Board of Education, 644
Brown v. District of Columbia, 360
Brumfield v. City of Chicago, 336
Bryant v. Madigan, 333
Buchanan v. City of Antonio, 103
Budhun v. Reading Hospital and
    Medical Center, 81
Bultemeyer v. Fort Wayne Community
    Schools, 192
Burks v. Wis. Dep't. of Transp., 99
Burlington Northern & Santa Fe
    Railroad v. White, 297
Bush v. Donahoe, 81
Butler v. Evans, 643
Byrne v. Avon Prods., Inc., 156
C.M., In re, 334
Caldwell v. Holland of Texas, Inc.,
    305
Carmona v. Southwest Airlines Co., 57

Carparts Distribution Center, Inc. v.
Automotive Wholesaler's Ass'n. of
New England, 499
Carr v. Reno, 125
Carroll Towing Co., United States v.,
122
Casias v. Wal-Mart Stores, Inc., 252
Castellano v. City of New York, 491
**Cedar Rapids Community School
District v. Garret F., 635**
Cehrs v. Northeast Ohio Alzheimer's
Research Center, 161
Chevron U.S.A. Inc. v. Natural Res.
Def. Council, Inc., 337, 352, 393,
484, 640
Chevron U.S.A., Inc. v. Echazabal, 234
Circuit City Stores, Inc. v. Adams, 325
Clackamas Gastroenterology
Associates, P.C., 322
Clark v. Virginia Bd. of Bar
Examiners, 412, 413, 414
**Cleburne, City of v. Cleburne
Living Center, 7**
**Cleveland v. Policy Management
Systems Corporation, 114**
Cloe v. City of Indianapolis, 299
Colas v. City of University of New
York, 62
Coleman v. Court of Appeals of
Maryland, 320
Collings v. Longview Fibre Co., 244
Colorado Cross Disability Coalition v.
Hermanson Family Ltd.
Partnership, 464, 467
Colwell v. Rite Aid Corp., 181
Conners v. Maine Med. Ctr., 491
Conroy v. New York Department of
Correctional Services, 294
Constantine v. Rectors & Visitors of
George Mason Univ., 390
Contract Mgmt., Inc. v. Rumsfeld, 484
Cook v. State of Rhode Island, Dept. of
Mental Health, Retardation, and
Hospitals, 68
Corbin v. Town of Palm Beach, 299
Cravens v. BlueCross & Blue Shield of
Kansas City, 148
Criado v. IBM Corp., 152
D.B. ex rel. Elizabeth B. v. Esposito,
618
D.L. ex rel. K.L. v. Balt. Bd. of Sch.
Comm'rs, 198
Dalton v. ManorCare of W. Des
Moines, 318
Dandridge v. Williams, 223
De Long v. Hennessey, 511
Deal v. Hamilton Cty. Bd. of Educ.,
618
DeBacker v. City of Moline, 67

DeLeo v. City of Stamford, 504
**Den Hartog v. Wasatch Academy,
257**, 276, 278
Department of Housing & Urban Dev.
v. Rucker, 337
Detsel v. Board of Ed. of Auburn
Enlarged City School Dist., 637
DeVries v. Fairfax County Sch. Bd.,
628
Dewitt v. Proctor Hospital, 274
**Diaz v. Fort Wayne Foundry
Corp., 314**
DiCarlo v. Potter, 175
Dicksey v. New Hanover Sheriff's
Department, 182
Disabled in Action v. Board of
Elections in City of New York, 397
Doe v. Maher, 648, 649
Doe v. New York University, 533
Doe v. Region 13 Mental Health-
Mental Retardation Comm'n, 533
Donahue v. Consol. Rail Corp., 232
Doukas v. Metropolitan Life Ins. Co.,
499
Doyal v. Oklahoma Heart, Inc., 253
Duvall v. County of Kitsap, 417
Dwyer v. Cappell, 449
Earll v. eBay, Inc., 472
EEOC v. Amego, Inc., 151
EEOC v. AutoZone, Inc., 179
EEOC v. CNA Ins. Cos., 493
EEOC v. Exxon Corp., 216, 234
**EEOC v. Ford Motor Company,
163**, 175
EEOC v. Humiston-Keeling, Inc., 144
EEOC v. LHC Group, Inc, 179
EEOC v. R.J. Gallagher Co., 64
EEOC v. Resources for Human
Development, 68
EEOC v. St. Joseph's Hosp., 147
EEOC v. Staten Island Savings Bank,
493
EEOC v. STME, LLC, 82
EEOC v. United Airlines, Inc., 146
EEOC v. Watkins Motor Lines, Inc.,
68
EEOC v. Yellow Freight Sys., Inc., 167
El-Hajj v. Fortis Benefits Ins. Co., 493
Ellenberg v. New Mexico Military
Institute, 680
Elwell v. Okla. ex rel. Bd. of Regents
of the Univ. of, Okla., 336
**Endrew F. v. Douglas County
School District Re-1, 609**, 618
**Enyart v. National Conference of
Bar Examiners, Inc., 478**
Eshelman v. Patrick Industries, Inc.,
81

Exby-Stolley v. Board of County Commissioners, 179
Federal Election Comm'n v. Wis. Right to Life, Inc., 482
Feldman v. Law Enforcement Associates Corp., 53
Felix v. Wisconsin Dep't. of Transp., 98, 102
Fenny v. Dakota, Minnesota & Eastern Railroad, 179
Ferguson v. City of Phoenix, 417
Fjellestad v. Pizza Hut of America, Inc., 190
Fleck v. Wilmac Corp., 163
Fletcher v. Tufts University, 489
Florence County School District Four v. Carter, 654
Flowers v. Southern Regional Physician Services, 301
Ford v. Schering-Plough Corp., 472
Forest Grove School District v. T.A., 660, 661
Foster v. Arthur Andersen, LLP, 103
Fox v. Costco Wholesale Corp., 301
Fox v. General Motors, 301
Francis v. City of Meriden, 68
Franklin v. Murphy, 518
Friends of the Earth, Inc. v. Laidlaw Envtl. Servs. (TOC), Inc., 462, 466
Frontiero v. Richardson, 9
Fry v. Napolean Community Schools, 670
Furgess v. Pennsylvania Dep't of Corrections, 333
Gallagher v. San Diego Unified Port Dist., 298
Galloway v. Superior Court, 361
Garcia v. Lawn, 482
García-Ayala v. Lederle Parenterals, Inc., 134, 149
Gates v. Caterpillar, Inc., 99
Gathright-Dietrich v. Atlanta Landmarks, Inc., 463
Gaul v. Lucent Technologies, Inc., 63
Gebser v. Lago Vista Independent School Dist., 642
Gentry v. East West Partners Club Management Co. Inc., 104
Gil v. Winn Dixie Stores, Inc., 469
Gilmer v. Interstate/Johnson Lane Corp., 325
Gogos v. AMS Mechanical Systems, Inc., 62
Gohier v. Enright, 334
Gomez v. Bang & Olufsen Am., Inc., 473
Gorman v. Bartch, 417
Graves v. Finch Pruyn & Co., Inc., 161
Greenleaf's Lessee v. Birth, 665

Gregory v. Ashcroft, 330
Grimes v. U.S. Postal Serv., 246
Gross v. FBL Financial Services, Inc., 103, 298
Guckenberger v. Boston University ("Guckenberger I"), 567
Guckenberger v. Boston University ("Guckenberger II"), 584
Gunter v. Bemis Co., 323
Hainze v. Richards, 334
Halpern v. Wake Forest University Health Sciences, 199, 394, 557
Haneke v. Mid-Atlantic Capital Mgmt., 55
Harper v. C.R. England, Inc., 97
Hartmann v. Loudoun County Board of Education, 625
Haulbrook v. Michelin N. Am. Inc., 54
Hazen Paper Co. v. Biggins, 278
Heatherly v. Portillo's Hot Dogs, Inc., 62
Hendricks-Robinson v. Excel Corp., 134
Henry v. Jones, 99
Hodgens v. General Dynamics Corp., 308, 312
Hoepfl v. Barlow, 504
Hoffman v. Carefirst of Fort Wayne, Inc., 57, 60
Holly v. Clairson Industries, LLC, 180
Holt v. Olmsted Twp. Bd. of Trustees, 182
Homes v. Alive Hospice, Inc., 66
Honig v. Doe, 643
Hooper v. Proctor Health Care Inc., 95
Horgan v. Simmons, 33
Huber v. Wal-Mart Stores, Inc., 144, 147
Humphrey v. Memorial Hospitals Ass'n, 163, 178
Hutton v. Elf Atochem North America, Inc., 225
Hwang v. Kansas State Univ., 161
International Brotherhood of Teamsters v. United States, 207
Irving Independent School Dist. v. Tatro, 637, 640
Iwata v. Intel Corp., 491
J.D. by Doherty v. Colonial Williamsburg Foundation, 62
Jackson v. Franklin County School Board, 649
Jennings v. Alexander, 340
Jernigan v. Bellsouth Telecommunications, LLC, 206
Johnson v. Cleveland City Sch. Dist., 175

Johnson v. K Mart Corp., 494
Jones v. Calvert Group, Ltd., 323
JSK by and through JK v. Hendry
    Cty. Sch. Bd., 618
Kallail v. Alliant Energy Corporate
    Services, Inc., 182
Karraker v. Rent-A-Center, Inc., 294
Katz v. City Metal Co., 103
Kayla N., In re, 334
Keith v. County of Oakland, 105
Kennedy v. Dresser Rand Co., 152
**Kennedy v. Omegagas & Oil, LLC,
458**
Kidwell v. Florida Comm'n on Human
    Relations, 473
Kieffer v. CPR Restoration & Cleaning
    Services, LLC, 163
Kim v. Potter, 70
Kimber v. Thiokol Corp., 493
Kinney v. Yerusalim, 385
Kintz v. United Parcel Service, Inc.,
    299
Kiphart v. Saturn Corp., 175
Knutson v. Schwan's Home Service,
    113
Kolstad v. American Dental Ass'n, 324
Kowitz v. Trinity Health, 192
Krauel v. Iowa Methodist Med. Ctr.,
    493
L.J. by N.N.J. v. School Board of
    Broward County, 618
Lamb v. Qualex, Inc., 206
Lane v. Riverview Hosp., 98
Langon v. Dept. of Health & Human
    Services, 125, 178
Larimer v. International Business
    Machines Corp., 275, 278
Law v. United States Postal Service,
    125
Lee v. City of Columbus, 294
Lentini v. Calif. Ctr. for the Arts,
    Escondido, 452
**Leonel v. American Airlines, Inc.,
282**
Levorsen v. Octapharma Plasma, Inc.,
    449
Lewis v. Humboldt Acquisition Corp.,
    104
Lewis v. Kmart Corp., 493
Lintemuth v. Saturn Corp., 300
Little v. FBI, 566
Lopez v. Pac. Mar. Ass'n, 300
Los Angeles, City of v. Lyons, 503
Lucas v. Forty-Fourth General
    Assembly of Colorado, 13
Lujan v. Defenders of Wildlife, 503
Lyons v. England, 323
Lyons v. Legal Aid Society, 181

M.B. ex rel. Berns v. Hamilton Se.
    Sch., 618
Mach Mining, LLC v. E.E.O.C., 323
Mancini v. City of Providence by and
    through Lombardi, 66
Mannie v. Potter, 301
Manuel v. Westlake Polymers Corp.,
    318
Mary Jo C. v. N.Y. State & Local Ret.
    Sys., 336
Mary T. v. School Dist. of
    Philadelphia, 643
Massachusetts Board of Retirement v.
    Murgia, 9
**Matheis v. CSL Plasma, Inc., 446,
448**
Matsushita Elec. Indus. Co. v. Zenith
    Radio Corp., 171
Matthews v. Jefferson, 417
Mayle v. City of Chicago, 456
Mays v. Principi, 146
McDaniel v. Mississippi Baptist
    Medical Center, 242
McDonnell Douglas Corp. v. Green, 90,
    96, 249, 265, 315, 452
McKenzie v. Benton, 234
McLaughlin v. Florida, 9
McNely v. Ocala Star-Banner Corp.,
    103
Medical Society of New Jersey v.
    Jacobs, 412
Menkowitz v. Pottstown Mem'l Med.
    Ctr., 336
Meritor Savings Bank, FSB v. Vinson,
    301
Miller v. Hersman, 161
Mills v. Board of Education of District
    of Columbia, 599, 644, 650, 651, 664
Mobley v. Allstate Ins. Co., 178
Modderno v. King, 493
**Molski v. Evergreen Dynasty
Corp., 506**
Molski v. Foley Estates Vineyard and
    Winery, LLC, 467
Molski v. Kahn Winery, 522
Molski v. M.J. Cable, Inc., 519
Molski v. Mandarin Touch Rest., 507,
    508, 510
Molski v. Rapazzini Winery, 511, 519,
    520
Monette v. Elec. Data Sys. Corp., 148,
    209
**Monroe v. Indiana Department of
Transportation, 91**
Morgan v. Hilti, Inc., 316
Morgan v. Joint Admin. Bd.,
    Retirement Plan of the Pillsbury,
    Co., and, others, 472
Morriss v. BNSF Ry. Co., 68, 82

Morton v. United Parcel Service, Inc., 207

Mosby-Meachem v. Memphis Light, Gas & Water Division, 171

Moser v. Ind. Dep't. of Corr., 97

Moss v. Harris County Constable Precinct One, 161

Munoz v. Echosphere, L.L.C., 58, 59

Murphy v. United Parcel Service, 44

Murray v. Mayo Clinic, 104

MX Group v. City of Covington., 378

Myers v. Hose, 152, 163

Naiman v. New York University, 502

National Ass'n of the Deaf v. Netflix, Inc., 472

National Credit Union Admin. v. First Nat. Bank & Trust Co., 640

National Fed'n of the Blind v. Scribd Inc., 472

National Fed'n of the Blind v. Target Corp., 474

National Federation of the Blind v. Lamone, 386

Natofsky v. City of New York, 104

Neely v. Rutherford County School, 637

Nevada Dept. of Human Resources v. Hibbs, 320

New Directions Treatment Services v. City of Reading, 375

Niece v. Fitzner, 417

Noffsinger v. SSC Niantic Operating Co., 252

Norton v. Assisted Living Concepts, Inc., 59

Nunes v. Wal-Mart Stores, Inc., 153, 161, 231

Nunies v. Hie Holdings, Inc., 75

O.S. v. Fairfax Cty. Sch. Bd., 618

O'Brien v. Werner Bus Lines, Inc., 503

O'Connor v. PCA Family Health Plan, Inc., 319

Oehmeke v. Medtronic, Inc., 59, 64

Ohio Civil Rights Commission v. Case Western Reserve University, 534

Olinger v. United States Golf Assn., 425

Olmstead v. L.C. ex rel. Zimring, 347, 494

Oneok, Inc. v. Learjet, Inc., 395

Orr v. Wal-Mart Stores, Inc., 46

Ortiz v. Werner Enter., Inc., 96

Oswalt v. Sara Lee Corp., 318

Owusu-Ansah v. Coca-Cola Co., 288

Palmer College of Chiropractic v. Davenport Civil Rights Commission, 534

Parker v. Columbia Pictures Indus., 103

Parker v. Metro. Life Ins. Co., 336, 472, 493

Pedigo v. P.A.M. Transp., Inc., 103

Pennhurst State School and Hospital v. Halderman, 641

Pennsylvania Assn. for Retarded Children v. Commonwealth, 599, 645, 664

Pennsylvania Department of Corrections v. Yeskey, 330, 431

Petition & Questionnaire for Admission to Rhode Island Bar, In re, 414

PGA Tour, Inc. v. Martin, 129, 392, 421, 448

Pickern v. Holiday Quality Foods, Inc., 523

Pierce v. District of Columbia., 333

Plyler v. Doe, 8

Polk v. Cent. Susquehanna Intermediate Unit 16, 618

Pollard v. E.I. DuPont De Nemours & Co., 324, 325

Pollard v. High's of Baltimore, Inc., 56

Power v. University of North Dakota School of Law, 534

Price v. City of Fort Wayne, 308, 316, 318

Proctor v. UPS, 297

Ragsdale v. Wolverine World Wide, Inc., 319

Ralph v. Lucent Technologies, Inc., 151, 153

Randall v. United Petroleum Transports, Inc., 81

Rauen v. U.S. Tobacco Mfg. L.P., 167

Raytheon Co. v. Hernandez, 247, 299

Regan v. Faurecia Automotive Seating, Inc., 181

Regents of the Univ. of Michigan v. Ewing, 554

Rehrs v. Iams Co., 182

Reinhardt v. Albuquerque Pub. Sch. Bd. of Educ., 298

Rendon v. Valleycrest Prods., 473

Republican Party v. Martin, 54

Reyazuddin v. Montgomery County, Maryland, 194, 335

Rice v. Sunrise Express, Inc., 319

Richardson v. Chicago Transit Authority, 68

Richter v. Advance Auto Parts, Inc., 323

Robert v. Board of County Com'rs of Brown County, Kans., 161

Roberts v. City of Chi., 95

Robles v. Domino's Pizza, LLC, 475
Rogers v. Dep't of Health & Envtl. Control, 335
Roncker v. Walter, 624
Rorrer v. City of Stow, 169
Rose v. Home Depot USA, Inc., 55
S-1 v. Turlington, 649
Sacramento City Unified School District v. Rachel H., 620
Safir v. United States Lines, Inc., 507
Samper v. Providence St. Vincent Medical Center, 148
Samson v. Federal Express Corporation, 114
San Antonio Independent School Dist. v. Rodriguez, 15, 604
Scavetta v. Dillon Companies, Inc., 66
Schaffer v. Weast, 661
Scherr v. Marriott International, Inc., 523
School Bd. of Nassau County, Florida v. Arline, 45, 71, 220, 224, 272, 362, 378
School Comm. of Burlington v. Department of Ed. of Mass., 655, 658
Schweiker v. Wilson, 8
Scruggs v. Pulaski County, Ark., 161
Serwatka v. Rockwell Automation, Inc., 95, 104
Severson v. Heartland Woodcraft, Inc., 156
Shafer v. Preston Memorial Hospital Corp., 244
Shaver v. Indep. Stave Co., 301
Shell v. Burlington Northern Santa Fe Railway Co., 82
Siefken v. Village of Arlington Heights, 268
Silguero v. CSL Plasma, Inc., 449, 455
Silk v. Board of Trustees of Moraine Valley Community College, District No. 524, 81
Silk v. City of Chicago, 301
Sjöstrand v. Ohio State University, 534
Skerski v. Time Warner Cable Co., 113
Skidmore v. Swift & Co., 352
Skinner v. Oklahoma ex rel. Williamson, 16
Smith v. Ameritech, 167
Smith v. Midland Brake, Inc., 144, 147, 188, 192
Smith v. Robinson, 670, 672
Soileau v. Guilford of Maine, Inc., 298
Southeastern Community College v. Davis, 341, 362, 527

Spector v. Norwegian Cruise Line Ltd., 437
St. Mary's Honor Center v. Hicks, 316
Staley v. Gruenberg, 298
Stinson v. United States, 393
Sullivan v. Vallejo City Unified School Dist., 671
Summers v. Altarum Institute, Corp., 60, 81
Sutton v. United Air Lines, Inc., 34, 71
T.M., In re, 334
Teahan v. Metro-North Commuter R.R. Co., 241
Tellis v. Alaska Airlines, Inc., 319
Tennessee v. Lane, 338, 394
Tesone v. Empire Marketing Strategies, 66
Thorson v. Gemini, Inc., 318
Tompkins v. United Healthcare of New England, 499
Toyota Motor Mfg., Ky., Inc. v. Williams, 47, 56
Trans World Airlines, Inc. v. Hardison, 137
Tucker v. Bay Shore Union Free School Dist., 655
Tucker v. Mo. Dept. of Soc. Servs., 182
Turco v. Hoechst Celanese Corp., 182, 232
Tyndall v. National Educ. Ctrs., Inc., 125, 264, 566
U.S. Airways, Inc. v. Barnett, 128, 131, 145, 146, 160, 199, 200, 206, 373
University of Texas Southwestern Medical Center v. Nassar, 103, 298
Valdez v. Minnesota Quarries, Inc., 81
Vande Zande v. State of Wisconsin Department of Administration, 120, 170
Victoria L. v. District School Bd. of Lee County, Fla., 649
Waddell v. Valley Forge Dental Associates, Inc, 233
Walters v. Metropolitan Educational Enterprises, Inc., 321
Walton v. Mental Health Ass'n., 63, 301
Walton v. U.S. Marshals Serv., 78
Washington v. Indiana High School Athletic Association, 439
Watson v. City of Miami Beach, 291
Weaving v. City of Hillsboro, 67
Welch v. Level 3 Communications, LLC, 80
Weyer v. Twentieth Century Fox Film Corp., 472

Williams v. AT&T Mobility Services
LLC, 176
Williamson v. Lee Optical of
Oklahoma, Inc., 15
Willis v. Conopco, 192
Wilson v. Dollar Gen. Corp., 67, 199
Winnie v. Infectious Disease
Associates, P.A., 161
**Wisconsin Community Services,
Inc. v. City of Milwaukee, 367**
**Wong v. Regents of the University
of California, 544**
Wood v. Green, 163
Wynne v. Tufts University School of
Medicine, 533, 554, 555, 582
**Zenor v. El Paso Healthcare
System, 238**
Zimmerman v. Or. Dep't of Justice,
336
Zobel v. Williams, 12
**Zukle v. Regents of the University
of California, 536**

DISABILITY LAW
CASES AND MATERIALS

Second Edition

CHAPTER 1

INTRODUCTION

■ ■ ■

Individuals with disabilities[1] constitute approximately 20% of the United States population. In spite of these numbers, disabled people have long experienced societal discrimination resulting in less access to education, meaningful jobs, and social interaction.

With the enactment of the Americans with Disabilities Act (ADA) in 1990, efforts to redress disability discrimination have moved beyond a welfare approach to embrace a civil rights model. Under the ADA, employers, governmental entities, and most private businesses may not discriminate against individuals with disabilities. In some instances, these entities may even have an obligation to provide accommodations that enable the participation of individuals with disabilities.

As the most recently enacted federal civil rights law, the ADA provides an exciting and challenging area of study and practice. The adoption of the ADA triggered a deluge in new charges filed with the Equal Employment Opportunity Commission. In addition, the imprecision of many ADA provisions also spawned considerable interpretive confusion and more than twenty Supreme Court decisions. The Supreme Court's response included a string of decisions narrowing the ADA's reach. Congress, in turn, overrode those interpretations and reinvigorated the statute by enacting the ADA Amendments Act of 2008 (ADAAA).

The fact that Congress was able to pass the ADAAA illustrates the broad and unique constituency that supports disability rights. In other areas of labor and employment law, political divisions have made legislative reform virtually impossible. Yet, in the arena of disability law, representatives of the disability rights movement and the business community came together to forge a breakthrough compromise that became the ADAAA. Whether this legislation launches a new era of civil rights enforcement for individuals with disabilities or is blunted by renewed judicial resistance is one of the plot lines this book examines.

While the principal focus of this book is the ADA, it also explores other federal laws such the Rehabilitation Act of 1973 and the Individuals with Disabilities in Education Act. As you read the cases and materials in this book, think about whether these laws should be enforced robustly—like

---

[1] Throughout this casebook, the authors strive to use people-first terminology, such as referring to "individuals with disabilities" rather than "disabled individuals." Most Americans with disabilities believe that this language is more respectful and less objectifying.

those combating race and sex discrimination—in order to overcome the ingrained history of socially-constructed, disability-based discrimination. Alternatively, consider whether these laws should be more limited in application to reflect the fact that some of the obstacles faced by the disabled—unlike those based on race and sex—go beyond stereotypical antipathy to encompass actual physical and mental limitations on capabilities.

A. SYSTEMIC DISCRIMINATION AND THE DISABILITY RIGHTS MOVEMENT

A BRIEF HISTORY OF THE DISABILITY RIGHTS MOVEMENT
Anti-Defamation League (2005)

People with disabilities have had to battle against centuries of biased assumptions, harmful stereotypes, and irrational fears. The stigmatization of disability resulted in the social and economic marginalization of generations of Americans with disabilities, and like many other oppressed minorities, left people with disabilities in a severe state of impoverishment for centuries.

In the 1800s, people with disabilities were considered meager, tragic, pitiful individuals unfit and unable to contribute to society, except to serve as ridiculed objects of entertainment in circuses and exhibitions. They were assumed to be abnormal and feeble-minded, and numerous persons were forced to undergo sterilization. People with disabilities were also forced to enter institutions and asylums, where many spent their entire lives. The "purification" and segregation of persons with disability were considered merciful actions, but ultimately served to keep people with disabilities invisible and hidden from a fearful and biased society.

The marginalization of people with disabilities continued until World War I when veterans with disabilities expected that the U.S. government provide rehabilitation in exchange for their service to the nation. In the 1930s the United States saw the introduction of many new advancements in technology as well as in government assistance, contributing to the self-reliance and self-sufficiency of people with disabilities.

* * *

In the 1940s and 1950s, disabled World War II veterans placed increasing pressure on government to provide them with rehabilitation and vocational training. World War II veterans made disability issues more visible to a country of thankful citizens who were concerned for the long-term welfare of young men who sacrificed their lives to secure the safety of the United States.

Despite these initial advancements made towards independence and self-reliance, people with disabilities still did not have access to public transportation, telephones, bathrooms and stores. Office buildings and worksites with stairs offered no entry for people with disabilities who sought employment, and employer attitudes created even worse barriers. Otherwise talented and eligible people with disabilities were locked out of opportunities for meaningful work.

By the 1960s, the civil rights movement began to take shape, and disability advocates saw the opportunity to join forces alongside other minority groups to demand equal treatment, equal access and equal opportunity for people with disabilities. The struggle for disability rights has followed a similar pattern to many other civil rights movements—challenging negative attitudes and stereotypes, rallying for political and institutional change, and lobbying for the self-determination of a minority community.

Disability rights activists mobilized on the local level demanding national initiatives to address the physical and social barriers facing the disability community. Parent advocates were at the forefront, demanding that their children be taken out of institutions and asylums, and placed into schools where their children could have the opportunity to engage in society just like children who were not disabled.

In the 1970s, disability rights activists lobbied Congress and marched on Washington to include civil rights language for people with disabilities into the 1972 Rehabilitation Act. In 1973, the Rehabilitation Act was passed, and for the first time in history, civil rights of people with disabilities were protected by law.

The Rehabilitation Act of 1973 (Section 504) provided equal opportunity for employment within the federal government and in federally funded programs, prohibiting discrimination on the basis of either physical or mental disability. Section 504 of the Rehabilitation Act also established the Architectural and Transportation Barriers Compliance Board, mandating equal access to public services (such as public housing and public transportation services) to people with disabilities, and the allocation of money for vocational training.

In 1975, the Education for All Handicapped Children Act was passed to guarantee equal access to public education for children with disabilities. This act of legislation specified that every child had a right to education, and mandated the full inclusion of children with disabilities in mainstream education classes, unless a satisfactory level of education could not be achieved due to the nature of the child's disability.

The Education for All Handicapped Children Act was renamed in 1990 to the Individuals with Disabilities Education Act (IDEA), which further elaborated on the inclusion of children with disabilities into regular classes, but also focused on the rights of parents to be involved in the educational decisions affecting their children. IDEA required that an Individual Education Plan be designed with parental approval to meet the educational needs of a child with a disability.

In the 1980s, disability activists began to lobby for a consolidation of various pieces of legislation under one broad civil rights statute that would protect the rights of people with disabilities, much like the 1964 Civil Rights Act had achieved for Black Americans. The Civil Rights Act of 1964 prohibited discrimination on the basis of race, religion, national origin, or gender, but people with disabilities were not included under such protection.

After decades of campaigning and lobbying, the Americans with Disabilities Act (ADA) was passed in 1990, and ensured the equal treatment and equal access of people with disabilities to employment opportunities and to public accommodations. The ADA intended to prohibit discrimination on the basis of disability in: employment, services rendered by state and local governments, places of public accommodation, transportation, and telecommunications services.

Under the ADA, businesses were mandated to provide reasonable accommodations to people with disabilities (such as restructuring jobs or modifying work equipment), public services could no longer deny services to people with disabilities (such as public transportation systems), all public accommodations were expected to have modifications made to be accessible to people with disabilities, and all telecommunications services were mandated to offer adaptive services to people with disabilities. With this piece of legislation, the U.S. government identified the full participation, inclusion and integration of people with disabilities in all levels of society.

While the signing of the ADA placed immediate legislative demands to ensure equal access and equal treatment of people with disabilities, deep-rooted assumptions and stereotypical biases were not instantly transformed with the stroke of a pen. People with disabilities still face prejudice and bias with the stereotypical portrayal of people with disabilities in the movies and in the media, physical barriers to schools, housing and to voting stations, and lack of affordable health care. The promise of the ADA is yet to be fully realized, but the disability rights movement continues to make great strides towards the empowerment and self-determination of Americans with disabilities.

B. MODELS OF DISABILITY INTERPRETATION

For many of the early years described in the above history, public policy and legislation relating to individuals with disabilities were premised on a medical model of disability. Under this view, individuals having impairments suffered from a medical deficiency that needed to be cured or pitied. But a social or civil rights model eventually emerged, which recognizes that disability results from societal attitudes and responses directed toward such individuals. These concepts and their importance are discussed in the following excerpt.

JONATHAN C. DRIMMER, CRIPPLES, OVERCOMERS, AND CIVIL RIGHTS: TRACING THE EVOLUTION OF FEDERAL LEGISLATION AND SOCIAL POLICY FOR PEOPLE WITH DISABILITIES
40 UCLA L. REV. 1341, 1349–59 (1993)

Both the medical and social pathology interpretations . . . function under the assumption that something within the individual with a disability is wrong and must be fixed. This locates the "problem" within the individual with a disability, stigmatizing and labeling that person with a status of physiological inferiority. According to many sociologists, the major problem faced by people with disabilities is learning to conquer not their own physical handicaps, but social stigma. Most commentators think that "stigmatizing actions harm the individual in two ways: They inflict psychological injury by assaulting a person's self-respect and human dignity, and they brand the individual with a sign that signals her inferior status to others and designates her as an outcast." With regard to the latter effect of stigma, the "dominant group has systematically used stigmatizing labels against" people with disabilities and has developed a social system of laws, practices, and cultural mores that devalues people with disabilities, treating them as different from, and inferior to, the norm. The laws and practices effectively define people with disabilities as inferior, exclude people with disabilities from society, and rationalize such treatment as justified and natural.

As to the psychological damage of stigma, the true harm comes when a person with a disability accepts the values developed by a society that labels disability as a sign of inferiority. With society continually reinforcing these beliefs through the law, cultural practice, and a denial of participation for people with disabilities, it is difficult for a person with a disability not "to accept at least part of the version of their identities imposed by the stigma." For these people the "injurious effects of stigmatizing inequalities are both psychological and tangible. It hurts to confront, day after day, the denial of your individual humanity."

* * *

The civil rights model is based largely on the civil rights movement of the 1950s and 1960s and views society, rather than the individual with a disability, as defective. In the civil rights model, the barriers facing the disabled community do not result solely from physical limitations, but from social standards created by an ablist society, from historic oversight of the disabled population, and from the fears and prejudice from centuries of discrimination. In this model, the legal status of people with disabilities-like their social status-reflects underlying social attitudes and assumptions concerning disability.

Above all, the civil rights model attempts to unmask the false objectivity that allows society to label some of its members "disabled" and treat those citizens as less than equal. Although society seeks to define and classify a person as having a disability using "rational," sociological, and often scientific bases—laws and labels are often based upon these definitions—ultimately it is impossible to render an accurate, objective definition of "disability." The only precise answer to the question "What is a disability?" is "I know it when I see it." In other words, the concept of "disability" is culturally defined, the product of an artificial labelling process. Furthermore, society not only creates these false classifications, but it proceeds to form a set of negative assumptions about the disabled population. The physical or mental limitations of people with disabilities generally play a small role in determining these assumptions. Rather, the judgments usually result from a variety of considerations closely tied to societal attitudes that are frequently erroneous or misconceived. They may include far-ranging inputs, such as "public imaginings about what the inherent physical limitations must be; public solicitude about the safety to be achieved by keeping the disabled out of harm's way; public feelings of protective care and custodial security . . . and public aversion to the sight of them and the conspicuous reminder of their plight."

The civil rights model attacks these misconceptions. Although the model recognizes physical and mental differences, it does not support the use of these differences to create hierarchical structures of superiority and inferiority upon which societal participation is premised. Limitations on the full participation of people with disabilities are not natural, unavoidable, or insulated results of physical or mental impairments. The limitations result directly from characteristics of and decisions made by society. Thus, the civil rights model places much more weight on the social and economic handicaps of having a disability than the actual physical restrictions.

* * *

Most federal policy to this point [in 1993] has favored the medical and social pathology models, focusing on using experts to help people with disabilities overcome what are considered individual problems and enter mainstream society in search of validation by able-bodied peers. In the last [thirty] years, however, policies have begun to incorporate the civil rights model, and there has been a shift toward removing physical and attitudinal barriers that have precluded the full participation of people with disabilities in society. Despite this movement toward a civil rights view of disability, the medical and social pathology interpretations continue to influence social policy, and thus the view of inferiority that has dominated the treatment of people with disabilities remains.

C. CONSTITUTIONAL STATUS

The Supreme Court has established three levels of scrutiny for purposes of equal protection analysis under the U.S. Constitution. They are: a) strict scrutiny for legislative classifications based on race which may be sustained only by a showing that such classification serves a compelling governmental interest, b) intermediate scrutiny for gender-based classifications which require the demonstration of a substantial governmental interest, and c) low-level scrutiny for other categories, such as age, which are presumed valid so long as they serve a rational basis. In determining the appropriate level of scrutiny, the Court looks to such factors as the history of purposeful discrimination, unfair stereotyping, the immutability of the characteristic, and the lack of political power to affect legislative change. The following case presents the issue of the appropriate level of scrutiny for legislation that classifies on the basis of one category of individuals with disabilities—those having intellectual development impairments.

CITY OF CLEBURNE V. CLEBURNE LIVING CENTER
473 U.S. 432, 105 S.Ct. 3249 (1985)

JUSTICE WHITE delivered the opinion of the Court.

A Texas city denied a special use permit for the operation of a group home for the mentally retarded, acting pursuant to a municipal zoning ordinance requiring permits for such homes. The Court of Appeals for the Fifth Circuit held that mental retardation[2] is a "quasi-suspect" classification and that the ordinance violated the Equal Protection Clause because it did not substantially further an important governmental purpose. We hold that a lesser standard of scrutiny is appropriate, but conclude that under that standard the ordinance is invalid as applied in this case.

I

In July 1980, respondent Jan Hannah purchased a building at 201 Featherston Street in the city of Cleburne, Texas, with the intention of leasing it to Cleburne Living Center, Inc. (CLC), for the operation of a group home for the mentally retarded. It was anticipated that the home would house 13 retarded men and women, who would be under the constant supervision of CLC staff members. The house had four bedrooms and two baths, with a half bath to be added. CLC planned to comply with all applicable state and federal regulations.

[2 The term "mental retardation" has now been replaced in common usage by the descriptor "intellectual disability."]

The city informed CLC that a special use permit would be required for the operation of a group home at the site, and CLC accordingly submitted a permit application. In response to a subsequent inquiry from CLC, the city explained that under the zoning regulations applicable to the site, a special use permit, renewable annually, was required for the construction of "[h]ospitals for the insane or feeble-minded, or alcoholic [sic] or drug addicts, or penal or correctional institutions." The city had determined that the proposed group home should be classified as a "hospital for the feebleminded." After holding a public hearing on CLC's application, the City Council voted 3 to 1 to deny a special use permit.

CLC then filed suit in Federal District Court against the city and a number of its officials, alleging, *inter alia,* that the zoning ordinance was invalid on its face and as applied because it discriminated against the mentally retarded in violation of the equal protection rights of CLC and its potential residents. [T]he District Court held the ordinance and its application constitutional. Concluding that no fundamental right was implicated and that mental retardation was neither a suspect nor a quasi-suspect classification, the court employed the minimum level of judicial scrutiny applicable to equal protection claims.

The Court of Appeals for the Fifth Circuit reversed, determining that mental retardation was a quasi-suspect classification and that it should assess the validity of the ordinance under intermediate-level scrutiny. Because mental retardation was in fact relevant to many legislative actions, strict scrutiny was not appropriate. . . . Applying the test that it considered appropriate, the court held that the ordinance was invalid on its face because it did not substantially further any important governmental interests. The Court of Appeals went on to hold that the ordinance was also invalid as applied. Rehearing en banc was denied with six judges dissenting in an opinion urging en banc consideration of the panel's adoption of a heightened standard of review.

II

The Equal Protection Clause of the Fourteenth Amendment commands that no State shall "deny to any person within its jurisdiction the equal protection of the laws," which is essentially a direction that all persons similarly situated should be treated alike. *Plyler v. Doe,* 457 U.S. 202, 216, 102 S.Ct. 2382, 2394 (1982). Section 5 of the Amendment empowers Congress to enforce this mandate, but absent controlling congressional direction, the courts have themselves devised standards for determining the validity of state legislation or other official action that is challenged as denying equal protection. The general rule is that legislation is presumed to be valid and will be sustained if the classification drawn by the statute is rationally related to a legitimate state interest. *Schweiker v. Wilson,* 450 U.S. 221, 230, 101 S.Ct. 1074, 1080 (1981). When social or economic legislation is at issue, the Equal Protection Clause allows the States wide latitude and the Constitution presumes that even improvident decisions will eventually be rectified by the democratic processes.

The general rule gives way, however, when a statute classifies by race, alienage, or national origin. These factors are so seldom relevant to the achievement of any legitimate state interest that laws grounded in such considerations are deemed to reflect prejudice and antipathy—a view that those in the burdened class are not as worthy or deserving as others. For these reasons and because such discrimination is unlikely to be soon rectified by legislative means, these laws are subjected to strict scrutiny and will be sustained only if they are suitably tailored to serve a compelling state interest. *McLaughlin v. Florida*, 379 U.S. 184, 192, 85 S.Ct. 283, 288 (1964).

Legislative classifications based on gender also call for a heightened standard of review. That factor generally provides no sensible ground for differential treatment. "[W]hat differentiates sex from such nonsuspect statuses as intelligence or physical disability ... is that the sex characteristic frequently bears no relation to ability to perform or contribute to society." *Frontiero v. Richardson*, 411 U.S. 677, 686, 93 S.Ct. 1764, 1770 (1973).

We have declined, however, to extend heightened review to differential treatment based on age:

> "While the treatment of the aged in this Nation has not been wholly free of discrimination, such persons, unlike, say, those who have been discriminated against on the basis of race or national origin, have not experienced a 'history of purposeful unequal treatment' or been subjected to unique disabilities on the basis of stereotyped characteristics not truly indicative of their abilities." *Massachusetts Board of Retirement v. Murgia,* 427 U.S. 307, 313, 96 S.Ct. 2562, 2567 (1976).

The lesson of *Murgia* is that where individuals in the group affected by a law have distinguishing characteristics relevant to interests the State has the authority to implement, the courts have been very reluctant, as they should be in our federal system and with our respect for the separation of powers, to closely scrutinize legislative choices as to whether, how, and to what extent those interests should be pursued. In such cases, the Equal Protection Clause requires only a rational means to serve a legitimate end.

III

Against this background, we conclude for several reasons that the Court of Appeals erred in holding mental retardation a quasi-suspect classification calling for a more exacting standard of judicial review than is normally accorded economic and social legislation. First, it is undeniable, and it is not argued otherwise here, that those who are mentally retarded have a reduced ability to cope with and function in the everyday world. Nor are they all cut from the same pattern: as the testimony in this record indicates, they range from those whose disability is not immediately evident to those who must be constantly cared for. They are thus different, immutably so, in relevant respects, and the States' interest in dealing with and providing for them is plainly a legitimate one. How this large and diversified group is to be treated under the law is a difficult and often a technical matter, very much a task for legislators guided by qualified professionals and not by the perhaps ill-informed opinions of the judiciary. Heightened scrutiny inevitably involves substantive judgments about legislative decisions, and we doubt that the predicate for such judicial oversight is present where the classification deals with mental retardation.

Second, the distinctive legislative response, both national and state, to the plight of those who are mentally retarded demonstrates not only that they have unique problems, but also that the lawmakers have been addressing their difficulties in a manner that belies a continuing antipathy or prejudice and a corresponding need for more intrusive oversight by the judiciary. Thus, the Federal Government has not only outlawed discrimination against the mentally retarded in federally funded programs, see § 504 of the Rehabilitation Act of 1973, 29 U.S.C. § 794, but it has also provided the retarded with the right to receive "appropriate treatment, services, and habilitation" in a setting that is "least restrictive of [their] personal liberty." In addition, the Government has conditioned federal education funds on a State's assurance that retarded children will enjoy an education that, "to the maximum extent appropriate," is integrated with that of nonmentally retarded children. Education of the Handicapped Act, 20 U.S.C. § 1412(5)(B). The Government has also facilitated the hiring of the mentally retarded into the federal civil service by exempting them from the requirement of competitive examination. See 5 CFR § 213.3102(t) (1984). The State of Texas has similarly enacted legislation that acknowledges the special status of the mentally retarded by conferring certain rights upon them, such as "the right to live in the least restrictive setting appropriate to [their] individual needs and abilities," including "the right to live ... in a group home." Mentally Retarded Persons Act of 1977, Tex.Rev.Civ.Stat., Art. 5547–300, § 7.

Such legislation thus singling out the retarded for special treatment reflects the real and undeniable differences between the retarded and others. That a civilized and decent society expects and approves such legislation indicates that governmental consideration of those differences in the vast majority of situations is not only legitimate but also desirable. It may be, as CLC contends, that legislation designed to benefit, rather than disadvantage, the retarded would generally withstand examination under a test of heightened scrutiny. The relevant inquiry, however, is whether heightened scrutiny is constitutionally mandated in the first instance. Even assuming that many of these laws could be shown to be substantially related to an important governmental purpose, merely requiring the legislature to justify its efforts in these terms may lead it to refrain from acting at all. Much recent legislation intended to benefit the retarded also assumes the need for measures that might be perceived to disadvantage them. The Education of the Handicapped Act, for example, requires an "appropriate" education, not one that is equal in all respects to the education of nonretarded children; clearly, admission to a class that exceeded the abilities of a retarded child would not be appropriate. Similarly, the Developmental Disabilities Assistance Act and the Texas Act give the retarded the right to live only in the "least restrictive setting" appropriate to their abilities, implicitly assuming the need for at least some restrictions that would not be imposed on others. Especially given the wide variation in the abilities and needs of the retarded themselves, governmental bodies must have a certain amount of flexibility and freedom from judicial oversight in shaping and limiting their remedial efforts.

Third, the legislative response, which could hardly have occurred and survived without public support, negates any claim that the mentally retarded are politically powerless in the sense that they have no ability to attract the attention of the lawmakers. Any minority can be said to be powerless to assert direct control over the legislature, but if that were a criterion for higher level scrutiny by the courts, much economic and social legislation would now be suspect.

Fourth, if the large and amorphous class of the mentally retarded were deemed quasi-suspect for the reasons given by the Court of Appeals, it would be difficult to find a principled way to distinguish a variety of other groups who have perhaps immutable disabilities setting them off from others, who cannot themselves mandate the desired legislative responses, and who can claim some degree of prejudice from at least part of the public at large. One need mention in this respect only the aging, the disabled, the mentally ill, and the infirm. We are reluctant to set out on that course, and we decline to do so.

Doubtless, there have been and there will continue to be instances of discrimination against the retarded that are in fact invidious, and that are properly subject to judicial correction under constitutional norms. But the appropriate method of reaching such instances is not to create a new quasi-suspect classification and subject all governmental action based on that classification to more searching evaluation. Rather, we should look to the likelihood that governmental action premised on a particular classification is valid as a general matter, not merely to the specifics of the case before us. Because mental retardation is a characteristic that the government may legitimately take into account in a wide range of decisions, and because both State and Federal Governments have recently committed themselves to assisting the retarded, we will not presume that any given legislative action, even one that disadvantages retarded individuals, is rooted in considerations that the Constitution will not tolerate.

Our refusal to recognize the retarded as a quasi-suspect class does not leave them entirely unprotected from invidious discrimination. To withstand equal protection review, legislation that distinguishes between the mentally retarded and others must be rationally related to a legitimate governmental purpose. This standard, we believe, affords government the latitude necessary both to pursue policies designed to assist the retarded in realizing their full potential, and to freely and efficiently engage in activities that burden the retarded in what is essentially an incidental manner. The State may not rely on a classification whose relationship to an asserted goal is so attenuated as to render the distinction arbitrary or irrational. See *Zobel v. Williams,* 457 U.S. 55, 61–63, 102 S.Ct. 2309, 2313–2314 (1982). Furthermore, some objectives—such as "a bare . . . desire to harm a politically unpopular group, are not legitimate state interests. Beyond that, the mentally retarded, like others, have and retain their substantive constitutional rights in addition to the right to be treated equally by the law.

IV

We turn to the issue of the validity of the zoning ordinance insofar as it requires a special use permit for homes for the mentally retarded. We inquire first whether requiring a special use permit for the Featherston home in the circumstances here deprives respondents of the equal protection of the laws. If it does, there will be no occasion to decide whether the special use permit provision is facially invalid where the mentally retarded are involved, or to put it another way, whether the city may never insist on a special use permit for a home for the mentally retarded in an R-3 zone. This is the preferred course of adjudication since it enables courts to avoid making unnecessarily broad constitutional judgments.

The constitutional issue is clearly posed. The city does not require a special use permit in an R-3 zone for apartment houses, multiple dwellings, boarding and lodging houses, fraternity or sorority houses, dormitories, apartment hotels, hospitals, sanitariums, nursing homes for convalescents or the aged (other than for the insane or feebleminded or alcoholics or drug addicts), private clubs or fraternal orders, and other specified uses. It does, however, insist on a special permit for the Featherston home, and it does so, as the District Court found, because it would be a facility for the mentally retarded. May the city require the permit for this facility when other care and multiple-dwelling facilities are freely permitted?

It is true, as already pointed out, that the mentally retarded as a group are indeed different from others not sharing their misfortune, and in this respect they may be different from those who would occupy other facilities that would be permitted in an R-3 zone without a special permit. But this difference is largely irrelevant unless the Featherston home and those who would occupy it would threaten legitimate interests of the city in a way that other permitted uses such as boarding houses and hospitals would not.

Because in our view the record does not reveal any rational basis for believing that the Featherston home would pose any special threat to the city's legitimate interests, we affirm the judgment below insofar as it holds the ordinance invalid as applied in this case.

The District Court found that the City Council's insistence on the permit rested on several factors. First, the Council was concerned with the negative attitude of the majority of property owners located within 200 feet of the Featherston facility, as well as with the fears of elderly residents of the neighborhood. But mere negative attitudes, or fear, unsubstantiated by factors which are properly cognizable in a zoning proceeding, are not permissible bases for treating a home for the mentally retarded differently from apartment houses, multiple dwellings, and the like. It is plain that the electorate as a whole, whether by referendum or otherwise, could not order city action violative of the Equal Protection Clause, *Lucas v. Forty-Fourth General Assembly of Colorado,* 377 U.S. 713, 736–737, 84 S.Ct. 1459, 1473–1474 (1964), and the City may not avoid the strictures of that Clause by deferring to the wishes or objections of some fraction of the body politic.

Second, the Council had two objections to the location of the facility. It was concerned that the facility was across the street from a junior high school, and it feared that the students might harass the occupants of the Featherston home. But the school itself is attended by about 30 mentally retarded students, and denying a permit based on such vague, undifferentiated fears is again permitting some portion of the community to validate what would otherwise be an equal protection violation. The other objection to the home's location was that it was located on "a five hundred year flood plain." This concern with the possibility of a flood, however, can hardly be based on a distinction between the Featherston home and, for example, nursing homes, homes for convalescents or the aged, or sanitariums or hospitals, any of which could be located on the Featherston site without obtaining a special use permit. The same may be said of another concern of the Council-doubts about the legal responsibility for actions which the mentally retarded might take. If there is no concern about legal responsibility with respect to other uses that would be permitted in the area, such as boarding and fraternity houses, it is difficult to believe that the groups of mildly or moderately mentally retarded individuals who would live at 201 Featherston would present any different or special hazard.

Fourth, the Council was concerned with the size of the home and the number of people that would occupy it. The District Court found, and the Court of Appeals repeated, that "[i]f the potential residents of the Featherston Street home were not mentally retarded, but the home was the same in all other respects, its use would be permitted under the city's zoning ordinance." Given this finding, there would be no restrictions on the number of people who could occupy this home as a boarding house, nursing home, family dwelling, fraternity house, or dormitory. The question is whether it is rational to treat the mentally retarded differently. It is true that they suffer disability not shared by others; but why this difference warrants a density regulation that others need not observe is not at all apparent. . . . In the words of the Court of Appeals, "[t]he City never justifies its apparent view that other people can live under such 'crowded' conditions when mentally retarded persons cannot." 726 F.2d, at 202.

In the courts below the city also urged that the ordinance is aimed at avoiding concentration of population and at lessening congestion of the streets. These concerns obviously fail to explain why apartment houses, fraternity and sorority houses, hospitals and the like, may freely locate in the area without a permit. So, too, the expressed worry about fire hazards, the serenity of the neighborhood, and the avoidance of danger to other residents fail rationally to justify singling out a home such as 201 Featherston for the special use permit, yet imposing no such restrictions on the many other uses freely permitted in the neighborhood.

The short of it is that requiring the permit in this case appears to us to rest on an irrational prejudice against the mentally retarded, including those who would occupy the Featherston facility and who would live under the closely supervised and highly regulated conditions expressly provided for by state and federal law.

The judgment of the Court of Appeals is affirmed insofar as it invalidates the zoning ordinance as applied to the Featherston home. The judgment is otherwise vacated, and the case is remanded.

JUSTICE MARSHALL, with whom JUSTICE BRENNAN and JUSTICE BLACKMUN join, concurring in the judgment in part and dissenting in part.

The Court holds that all retarded individuals cannot be grouped together as the "feebleminded" and deemed presumptively unfit to live in a community. Underlying this holding is the principle that mental retardation *per se* cannot be a proxy for depriving retarded people of their rights and interests without regard to variations in individual ability. With this holding and principle I agree. The Equal Protection Clause requires attention to the capacities and needs of retarded people as individuals.

I cannot agree, however, with the way in which the Court reaches its result or with the narrow, as-applied remedy it provides for the city of Cleburne's equal protection violation. The Court holds the ordinance invalid on rational-basis grounds and disclaims that anything special, in the form of heightened scrutiny, is taking place. Yet Cleburne's ordinance surely would be valid under the traditional rational-basis test applicable to economic and commercial regulation. In my view, it is important to articulate, as the Court does not, the facts and principles that justify subjecting this zoning ordinance to the searching review—the heightened scrutiny—that actually leads to its invalidation. Moreover, in invalidating Cleburne's exclusion of the "feebleminded" only as applied to respondents, rather than on its face, the Court radically departs from our equal protection precedents. Because I dissent from this novel and truncated remedy, and because I cannot accept the Court's disclaimer that no "more exacting standard" than ordinary rational-basis review is being applied, I write separately.

I

At the outset, two curious and paradoxical aspects of the Court's opinion must be noted. First, because the Court invalidates Cleburne's zoning ordinance on rational-basis grounds, the Court's wide-ranging discussion of heightened scrutiny is wholly superfluous to the decision of this case.

* * *

Second, the Court's heightened-scrutiny discussion is even more puzzling given that Cleburne's ordinance is invalidated only after being subjected to precisely the sort of probing inquiry associated with heightened scrutiny. To be sure, the Court does not label its handiwork heightened scrutiny, and perhaps the method employed must hereafter be called "second order" rational-basis review rather than "heightened scrutiny." But however labeled, the rational basis test invoked today is most assuredly not the rational-basis test of *Williamson v. Lee Optical of Oklahoma, Inc.*, 348 U.S. 483, 75 S.Ct. 461 (1955), *Allied Stores of Ohio, Inc. v. Bowers*, 358 U.S. 522, 79 S.Ct. 437 (1959), and their progeny. . . .

II

I have long believed the level of scrutiny employed in an equal protection case should vary with "the constitutional and societal importance of the interest adversely affected and the recognized invidiousness of the basis upon which the particular classification is drawn." *San Antonio Independent School District v. Rodriguez,* 411 U.S. 1, 99, 93 S.Ct. 1278, 1330 (1973) (MARSHALL, J., dissenting). When a zoning ordinance works to exclude the retarded from all residential districts in a community, these two considerations require that the ordinance be convincingly justified as substantially furthering legitimate and important purposes.

First, the interest of the retarded in establishing group homes is substantial. The right to "establish a home" has long been cherished as one of the fundamental liberties embraced by the Due Process Clause. . . .

Second, the mentally retarded have been subject to a "lengthy and tragic history," of segregation and discrimination that can only be called grotesque. During much of the 19th century, mental retardation was viewed as neither curable nor dangerous and the retarded were largely left to their own devices. By the latter part of the century and during the first decades of the new one, however, social views of the retarded underwent a radical transformation. Fueled by the rising tide of Social Darwinism, the "science" of eugenics, and the extreme xenophobia of those years, leading medical authorities and others began to portray the "feeble-minded" as a "menace to society and civilization . . . responsible in a large degree for many, if not all, of our social problems." A regime of state-mandated segregation and degradation soon emerged that in its virulence and bigotry rivaled, and indeed paralleled, the worst excesses of Jim Crow. Massive custodial institutions were built to warehouse the retarded for life; the aim was to halt reproduction of the retarded and "nearly extinguish their race." Retarded children were categorically excluded from public schools, based on the false stereotype that all were ineducable and on the purported need to protect nonretarded children from them. State laws deemed the retarded "unfit for citizenship."

Segregation was accompanied by eugenic marriage and sterilization laws that extinguished for the retarded one of the "basic civil rights of man"— the right to marry and procreate. *Skinner v. Oklahoma ex rel. Williamson,* 316 U.S. 535, 541, 62 S.Ct. 1110, 1113 (1942). Marriages of the retarded were made, and in some States continue to be, not only voidable but also often a criminal offense. The purpose of such limitations, which frequently applied only to women of child-bearing age, was unabashedly eugenic: to prevent the retarded from propagating. To assure this end, 29 States enacted compulsory eugenic sterilization laws between 1907 and 1931.

Prejudice, once let loose, is not easily cabined. As of 1979, most States still categorically disqualified "idiots" from voting, without regard to individual capacity and with discretion to exclude left in the hands of low-level election officials. Not until Congress enacted the Education of the Handicapped Act, 20 U.S.C. § 1400 *et seq.,* were "the door[s] of public education" opened wide to handicapped children. But most important, lengthy and continuing isolation of the retarded has perpetuated the ignorance, irrational fears, and stereotyping that long have plagued them.

In light of the importance of the interest at stake and the history of discrimination the retarded have suffered, the Equal Protection Clause requires us to do more than review the distinctions drawn by Cleburne's zoning ordinance as if they appeared in a taxing statute or in economic or commercial legislation. The searching scrutiny I would give to restrictions on the ability of the retarded to establish community group homes leads me to conclude that Cleburne's vague generalizations for classifying the "feeble-minded" with drug addicts, alcoholics, and the insane, and excluding them where the elderly, the ill, the boarder, and the transient are allowed, are not substantial or important enough to overcome the suspicion that the ordinance rests on impermissible assumptions or outmoded and perhaps invidious stereotypes.

III

In its effort to show that Cleburne's ordinance can be struck down under no "more exacting standard . . . than is normally accorded economic and social legislation," the Court offers several justifications as to why the retarded do not warrant heightened judicial solicitude. These justifications, however, find no support in our heightened-scrutiny precedents and cannot withstand logical analysis. . . .

* * *

For the retarded, just as for Negroes and women, much has changed in recent years, but much remains the same; out-dated statutes are still on the books, and irrational fears or ignorance, traceable to the prolonged social and cultural isolation of the retarded, continue to stymie recognition of the dignity and individuality of retarded people. Heightened judicial scrutiny of action appearing to impose unnecessary barriers to the retarded is required in light of increasing recognition that such barriers are inconsistent with evolving principles of equality embedded in the Fourteenth Amendment.

The fact that retardation may be deemed a constitutional irrelevancy in *some* circumstances is enough, given the history of discrimination the retarded have suffered, to require careful judicial review of classifications singling out the retarded for special burdens. Although the Court acknowledges that many instances of invidious discrimination against the retarded still exist, the Court boldly asserts that "in the vast majority of situations" special treatment of the retarded is "not only legitimate but also desirable." That assertion suggests the Court would somehow have us calculate the percentage of "situations" in which a characteristic is validly and invalidly invoked before determining whether heightened scrutiny is appropriate. But heightened scrutiny has not been "triggered" in our past cases only after some undefined numerical threshold of invalid "situations" has been crossed. An inquiry into constitutional principle, not mathematics, determines whether heightened scrutiny is appropriate. Whenever evolving principles of equality, rooted in the Equal Protection Clause, require that certain classifications be viewed as *potentially* discriminatory, and when history reveals systemic unequal treatment, more searching judicial inquiry than minimum rationality becomes relevant.

NOTES AND QUESTIONS

1. *Equal protection analysis.* Do you agree with Justice White that distinctions based on mental retardation, now termed intellectual disabilities, should not be afforded heightened scrutiny? In thinking about the factors relevant to equal protection analysis, *i.e.*, the history of purposeful discrimination, unfair stereotyping, the immutability of the characteristic, and political powerlessness, do you think that being disabled is more like race, sex, or age?

2. *The diversity of impairments.* One of the reasons given by Justice White for ostensibly adopting rational basis scrutiny in *Cleburne* is that

individuals with disabilities constitute a "large and diversified group," having a variety of differing impairments that generate varying degrees of antipathy and prejudice. What does he mean by this observation and how crucial should this be for constitutional analysis? In what ways do the diversity of impairments grouped together under the disability umbrella pose challenges for a uniform statutory response to disability discrimination?

3. *Rational basis.* Is Justice Marshall correct in asserting that the *Cleburne* ordinance "would be valid under the traditional rational-basis test applicable to economic and commercial regulation?" How does Justice White justify striking down the ordinance in spite of applying purported rational-basis analysis?

D. INTRODUCTION TO THE AMERICANS WITH DISABILITIES ACT

LAWRENCE O. GOSTIN, THE AMERICANS WITH DISABILITIES ACT AT 25: THE HIGHEST EXPRESSION OF AMERICAN VALUES
313 J. AM. MED. ASS'N 2231 (2015)

Twenty-five years ago, on July 26, 1990, President George H. W. Bush signed the Americans with Disabilities Act (ADA), a historic moment when the polity gave voice to the nation's highest ideals. The ADA enshrined in law a social promise of equality and inclusion into all facets of life, while offering an inspiring model that much of the world would come to embrace. As a civil rights law coming in the wake of racial and gender equality legislation, the ADA has had profound symbolic meaning and real-world effects. Its promise of full participation in life stood in marked contrast to the often impenetrable social and physical barriers that individuals with disabilities faced regarding inclusion in the workplace and public spaces. In sponsoring the ADA, Senator Edward Kennedy described life for persons with disabilities as an "American apartheid." . . .

Like all major pieces of civil rights legislation, the ADA did not emerge in a vacuum. Rather, it was the culmination of decades of groundwork laid by disability rights advocates—an exceptionally diverse and innovative group of individuals and organizations.

Advocacy groups representing a wide spectrum of individuals with disabilities campaigned for civil rights legislation. Prior to the ADA, the movement's most important success was the passage of the 1973 Rehabilitation Act (and, after additional struggle, the implementing regulations issued in 1977). Section 504 of that act proscribed discrimination and required affirmative accommodations to enable persons with disabilities to participate in employment and other life activities. The act's major limitation, however, was that it applied only to recipients of federal funding. With this new legal tool, activists began targeting institutions that impeded their full access, especially public transportation. They achieved remarkable success, convincing major cities such as San Francisco and New York to make their transit systems accessible.

By the 1980s, the disability rights movement had matured, bringing together an array of groups working toward a single goal—comprehensive antidiscrimination legislation. Rallying around slogans such as "Nothing About Us Without Us," disability rights organizations came together to advocate for the ADA.

Certainly, the movement had diverse, sometimes conflicting, aims. For example, individuals using wheelchairs wanted to reduce the impediment of sidewalk curbs, while individuals with vision impairments relied on curbs to sense the boundary between the sidewalk and the street. There was also tension, still existing today, between the need for special accommodations and the rejection of "any special help that might let [the public] conclude that [persons with disabilities] are inferior." . . .

Understanding the ADA

Definition of Disability

The ADA prohibits discrimination against persons on the basis of disability in employment, state and local government, public accommodations, commercial facilities, transportation, and telecommunications. Perhaps the most important and litigated element of the ADA involved the definition of "disability," as this determines which individuals the law will actually protect.

An individual can be included within the definition of "disability" in three different ways: by (a) having a physical or mental impairment that substantially limits one or more major life activities; (b) having a record of such an impairment; or (c) being regarded as having such an impairment. The last two criteria in the definition provide protection if an individual has a history of a disability (e.g., cancer that is in remission), or if the individual is perceived as having a disability. The latter is meant to counter discrimination due to assumptions or stereotypes (e.g., a gay man falsely presumed to be infected with HIV).

The concepts of "substantial limitation" and "major life activities" were particularly contentious. Courts and regulators interpreted these concepts narrowly, reducing the scope and reach of the ADA over time. The Supreme Court redefined "substantial limitation" to mean one that "prevents or severely restricts" a major life activity. The high court also narrowly construed the concept of "major life activity" to encompass only activities of "central importance to most people's daily lives." This resulted in a high and unreasonable threshold for gaining the protection of the ADA, even excluding a man diagnosed with mental retardation. [O]verall the Supreme Court's record on the ADA has been mixed, sometimes expanding coverage for persons with disabilities but at other times restricting coverage.

In 2008, Congress passed the Americans with Disabilities Act Amendments Act (ADAAA), specifically replacing the Court's narrow interpretation of the law, making clear that courts and employers should apply a broad standard when determining whether an individual is "disabled." The ADAAA instructs courts to provide protection "to the maximum extent permitted" and provides a nonexhaustive list of "major life activities," which include caring for oneself, performing manual tasks, seeing, hearing, eating, sleeping, walking, standing, lifting, bending, speaking, breathing, learning, reading, concentrating, thinking, communicating, and working. The ADAAA sought to shift legal discourse away from semantics, refocusing on the ADA's original intent—eliminating discriminatory conduct. The breadth of the definition of disability even enables the ADA to serve as a tool to protect against the misuse of genetic information. This protection is particularly important with increased use of genetic testing and the evolving science of genomics in health care.

The ADAAA also clarified that the ameliorative effects of mitigating measures, such as prosthetic devices or medication for epilepsy, are irrelevant in determining whether the statute protects an individual. Before the ADAAA, several Supreme Court decisions had stated that in establishing whether an individual has a disability, courts must consider the effects of any "mitigating" or "corrective treatment." Now, with the exception of eyeglasses and contact lenses, any medications or devices such as hearing aids or mobility devices that may compensate for disability are not relevant in determining whether a person is protected by the ADA.

Employment

Title I of the ADA prohibits discrimination in the workplace and requires employers with 15 or more employees to provide qualified individuals with disabilities an equal opportunity to benefit from the full range of employment-related opportunities available to others. An employer who is aware of an employee's disability must provide "reasonable accommodations," so long as they do not impose an "undue hardship" on the employer. "Undue hardship" sets a high bar, requiring the employer to demonstrate that accommodating the disability would incur an inordinate level of difficulty or expense.

Before the ADA, employers frequently required job applicants to complete detailed medical questionnaires. [T]he ADA places strict limitations on what questions an employer may ask and when medical examinations can be required, based on the stage of employment. For example, at a job interview an employer cannot inquire about the existence or nature of an individual's disability. Furthermore, the ADA restricts the types of medical examinations or inquiries the employer can make once the individual is employed and requires that all medical information be kept confidential.

Public Services

Title II of the ADA prohibits disability discrimination across all activities of state and local government and requires public entities to provide persons with disabilities equal opportunity to benefit from government programs and services. The scope of protection is broad, including ensuring nondiscriminatory policies, practices, and procedures. Narrow exceptions apply when accommodations would fundamentally alter the nature of the service, program, or activity being provided or would result in undue financial and administrative burdens. The act also sets accessibility standards for new construction and alterations to existing buildings.

Furthermore, Title II requires public transportation authorities to ensure accessibility of buses and rail cars, as well as stations, unless it would result in an undue burden. In places where public transportation is not accessible, other types of transportation must be provided.

Public Accommodations

Title III prohibits disability discrimination by "public accommodations," private entities that offer certain types of public services (e.g., hospitals, physicians' offices, restaurants, retail stores, pharmacies, schools). Public accommodations must ensure that any new or altered construction is accessible; that, wherever reasonably possible, barriers are removed from existing buildings; and that policies and practices are nondiscriminatory.

NOTES AND QUESTIONS

As you proceed through this book and your disability law class, several common themes and questions will arise. Both now and at the end of your study, we encourage you to reflect on the following questions:

1.   Although the Rehabilitation Act and the ADA are modeled after other civil rights statutes, they are different in very significant ways. What are those differences and do you agree with them?

2.   One of the goals of all of the disability statutes we will study is to increase the integration of individuals with disabilities into all aspects of society. Why is this an important goal? How do the statutes attempt to accomplish this goal? Are those methods effective in doing so?

3.   Throughout this course, you will see courts weighing the rights of individuals with disabilities against the rights of institutions—employers, government entities, places of public accommodation. Do courts weigh these interests similarly for all of these institutions? Put another way, are some institutions given more deference than others? If so, why? Do you think that some institutions *should* be given more deference than others?

4.   Another area of frequent conflict is that between individuals with disabilities and individuals who are not disabled. How does this conflict manifest itself in various contexts? Do you think the courts properly weigh these interests in the contexts in which this conflict arises?

CHAPTER 2

DEFINITION OF DISABILITY UNDER THE AMERICANS WITH DISABILITIES ACT

■ ■ ■

A. ACTUAL DISABILITY

1. STATUTORY DEFINITION

The Americans with Disabilities Act defines "disability" as:

(A) a physical or mental impairment that substantially limits one or more major life activities of such individual;

(B) having a record of such an impairment; or

(C) being regarded as having such an impairment.

42 U.S.C. § 12102(1). This chapter will address the first prong of the definition of disability (the "actual disability prong") before very briefly turning to the "record of" prong, and then discussing the "regarded as" prong.

2. DEFINING DISABILITY

The following case, *Bragdon v. Abbott*, provides the basic framework for analyzing whether someone has a "disability" as defined in the ADA. Shortly after this case, the Supreme Court started to narrowly interpret the definition of disability. Excerpts of those cases are provided below. Because Congress was dissatisfied with the narrow interpretation of disability, Congress amended the ADA in 2008. ADA Amendments Act of 2008, Pub. L. No. 110–325, 122 Stat. 3553 (2008). The Amendments' provisions and cases interpreting the new provisions are provided *infra* Section A.4.

BRAGDON V. ABBOTT
524 U.S. 624, 118 S.Ct. 2196 (1998)

JUSTICE KENNEDY delivered the opinion of the Court.

We address in this case the application of the Americans with Disabilities Act of 1990 (ADA) to persons infected with the human immunodeficiency virus (HIV). We granted certiorari to review, first, whether HIV infection is a disability under the ADA when the infection has not yet progressed to the so-called symptomatic phase; and, second, whether the Court of

Appeals, in affirming a grant of summary judgment, cited sufficient material in the record to determine, as a matter of law, that respondent's infection with HIV posed no direct threat to the health and safety of her treating dentist. [Ed. Note: The second issue is discussed in Chapter 3.]

Respondent Sidney Abbott (hereinafter respondent) has been infected with HIV since 1986. When the incidents we recite occurred, her infection had not manifested its most serious symptoms. On September 16, 1994, she went to the office of petitioner Randon Bragdon in Bangor, Maine, for a dental appointment. She disclosed her HIV infection on the patient registration form. Petitioner completed a dental examination, discovered a cavity, and informed respondent of his policy against filling cavities of HIV-infected patients. He offered to perform the work at a hospital with no added fee for his services, though respondent would be responsible for the cost of using the hospital's facilities. Respondent declined.

Respondent sued petitioner under state law and § 302 of the ADA, 42 U.S.C. § 12182, alleging discrimination on the basis of her disability. The state-law claims are not before us. Section 302 of the ADA provides:

> "No individual shall be discriminated against on the basis of disability in the full and equal enjoyment of the goods, services, facilities, privileges, advantages, or accommodations of any place of public accommodation by any person who . . . operates a place of public accommodation." § 12182(a).

The term "public accommodation" is defined to include the "professional office of a health care provider." § 12181(7)(F).

A later subsection qualifies the mandate not to discriminate. It provides:

> "Nothing in this subchapter shall require an entity to permit an individual to participate in or benefit from the goods, services, facilities, privileges, advantages and accommodations of such entity where such individual poses a direct threat to the health or safety of others." § 12182(b)(3).

[Upon the parties' cross-motions for summary judgment, the district court ruled in favor of the plaintiffs, holding that respondent's HIV infection was a disability under the ADA. The Court of Appeals affirmed.]

II

We first review the ruling that respondent's HIV infection constituted a disability under the ADA. The statute defines disability as:

> "(A) a physical or mental impairment that substantially limits one or more of the major life activities of such individual;

> "(B) a record of such an impairment; or

"(C) being regarded as having such an impairment." § 12102(2).[3]

We hold respondent's HIV infection was a disability under subsection (A) of the definitional section of the statute. In light of this conclusion, we need not consider the applicability of subsections (B) or (C).

Our consideration of subsection (A) of the definition proceeds in three steps. First, we consider whether respondent's HIV infection was a physical impairment. Second, we identify the life activity upon which respondent relies (reproduction and childbearing) and determine whether it constitutes a major life activity under the ADA. Third, tying the two statutory phrases together, we ask whether the impairment substantially limited the major life activity. In construing the statute, we are informed by interpretations of parallel definitions in previous statutes and the views of various administrative agencies which have faced this interpretive question.

A

The ADA's definition of disability is drawn almost verbatim from the definition of "handicapped individual" included in the Rehabilitation Act of 1973, 29 U.S.C. § 706(8)(B). . . . Congress' repetition of a well-established term carries the implication that Congress intended the term to be construed in accordance with pre-existing regulatory interpretations. In this case, Congress did more than suggest this construction; it adopted a specific statutory provision in the ADA directing as follows:

> "Except as otherwise provided in this chapter, nothing in this chapter shall be construed to apply a lesser standard than the standards applied under title V of the Rehabilitation Act of 1973 or the regulations issued by Federal agencies pursuant to such title." 42 U.S.C. § 12201(a).

The directive requires us to construe the ADA to grant at least as much protection as provided by the regulations implementing the Rehabilitation Act.

1

The first step in the inquiry under subsection (A) requires us to determine whether respondent's condition constituted a physical impairment. The Department of Health, Education and Welfare (HEW) issued the first regulations interpreting the Rehabilitation Act in 1977. The regulations are of particular significance because, at the time, HEW was the agency responsible for coordinating the implementation and enforcement of § 504 of that statute. Section 504 prohibits discrimination against individuals with disabilities by recipients of federal financial assistance. The HEW

[3 Eds. Note: Before the ADA was amended, the definition of disability appeared in section 12102(2). However, after the Amendments, as noted above, the definition of disability is in subsection (1).]

regulations, which appear without change in the current regulations issued by the Department of Health and Human Services, define "physical or mental impairment" to mean:

"(A) any physiological disorder or condition, cosmetic disfigurement, or anatomical loss affecting one or more of the following body systems: neurological; musculoskeletal; special sense organs; respiratory, including speech organs; cardiovascular; reproductive, digestive, genito-urinary; hemic and lymphatic; skin; and endocrine; or

"(B) any mental or psychological disorder, such as mental retardation, organic brain syndrome, emotional or mental illness, and specific learning disabilities." 45 CFR § 84.3(j)(2)(i) (1997).

In issuing these regulations, HEW decided against including a list of disorders constituting physical or mental impairments, out of concern that any specific enumeration might not be comprehensive. The commentary accompanying the regulations, however, contains a representative list of disorders and conditions constituting physical impairments, including "such diseases and conditions as orthopedic, visual, speech, and hearing impairments, cerebral palsy, epilepsy, muscular dystrophy, multiple sclerosis, cancer, heart disease, diabetes, mental retardation, emotional illness, and . . . drug addiction and alcoholism."

* * *

HIV infection is not included in the list of specific disorders constituting physical impairments, in part because HIV was not identified as the cause of AIDS until 1983. HIV infection does fall well within the general definition set forth by the regulations, however.

The disease follows a predictable and, as of today, an unalterable course. Once a person is infected with HIV, the virus invades different cells in the blood and in body tissues. Certain white blood cells, known as helper T-lymphocytes or CD4+ cells, are particularly vulnerable to HIV. The virus attaches to the CD4 receptor site of the target cell and fuses its membrane to the cell's membrane. HIV is a retrovirus, which means it uses an enzyme to convert its own genetic material into a form indistinguishable from the genetic material of the target cell. The virus' genetic material migrates to the cell's nucleus and becomes integrated with the cell's chromosomes. Once integrated, the virus can use the cell's own genetic machinery to replicate itself. Additional copies of the virus are released into the body and infect other cells in turn. Although the body does produce antibodies to combat HIV infection, the antibodies are not effective in eliminating the virus.

The virus eventually kills the infected host cell. CD4+ cells play a critical role in coordinating the body's immune response system, and the decline in their number causes corresponding deterioration of the body's ability to fight infections from many sources. Tracking the infected individual's CD4+ cell count is one of the most accurate measures of the course of the disease.

The initial stage of HIV infection is known as acute or primary HIV infection. In a typical case, this stage lasts three months. The virus concentrates in the blood. The assault on the immune system is immediate. The victim suffers from a sudden and serious decline in the number of white blood cells. There is no latency period. Mononucleosis-like symptoms often emerge between six days and six weeks after infection, at times accompanied by fever, headache, enlargement of the lymph nodes (lymphadenopathy), muscle pain (myalgia), rash, lethargy, gastrointestinal disorders, and neurological disorders. Usually these symptoms abate within 14 to 21 days. HIV antibodies appear in the bloodstream within 3 weeks; circulating HIV can be detected within 10 weeks.

After the symptoms associated with the initial stage subside, the disease enters what is referred to sometimes as its asymptomatic phase. The term is a misnomer, in some respects, for clinical features persist throughout, including lymphadenopathy, dermatological disorders, oral lesions, and bacterial infections. Although it varies with each individual, in most instances this stage lasts from 7 to 11 years. The virus now tends to concentrate in the lymph nodes, though low levels of the virus continue to appear in the blood. It was once thought the virus became inactive during this period, but it is now known that the relative lack of symptoms is attributable to the virus' migration from the circulatory system into the lymph nodes. The migration reduces the viral presence in other parts of the body, with a corresponding diminution in physical manifestations of the disease. The virus, however, thrives in the lymph nodes, which, as a vital point of the body's immune response system, represents an ideal environment for the infection of other CD4+ cells. Studies have shown that viral production continues at a high rate. CD4+ cells continue to decline an average of 5% to 10% (40 to 80 cells/mm3) per year throughout this phase.

A person is regarded as having AIDS when his or her CD4+ count drops below 200 cells/mm3 of blood or when CD4+ cells comprise less than 14% of his or her total lymphocytes. During this stage, the clinical conditions most often associated with HIV, such as *pneumocystis carninii* pneumonia, Kaposi's sarcoma, and non-Hodgkins lymphoma, tend to appear. In addition, the general systemic disorders present during all stages of the disease, such as fever, weight loss, fatigue, lesions, nausea, and diarrhea, tend to worsen. In most cases, once the patient's CD4+ count drops below 10 cells/mm3, death soon follows.

In light of the immediacy with which the virus begins to damage the infected person's white blood cells and the severity of the disease, we hold it is an impairment from the moment of infection. As noted earlier, infection with HIV causes immediate abnormalities in a person's blood, and the infected person's white cell count continues to drop throughout the course of the disease, even when the attack is concentrated in the lymph nodes. In light of these facts, HIV infection must be regarded as a physiological disorder with a constant and detrimental effect on the infected person's hemic and lymphatic systems from the moment of infection. HIV infection satisfies the statutory and regulatory definition of a physical impairment during every stage of the disease.

2

The statute is not operative, and the definition not satisfied, unless the impairment affects a major life activity. Respondent's claim throughout this case has been that the HIV infection placed a substantial limitation on her ability to reproduce and to bear children. Given the pervasive, and invariably fatal, course of the disease, its effect on major life activities of many sorts might have been relevant to our inquiry. Respondent and a number of *amici* make arguments about HIV's profound impact on almost every phase of the infected person's life. In light of these submissions, it may seem legalistic to circumscribe our discussion to the activity of reproduction. We have little doubt that had different parties brought the suit they would have maintained that an HIV infection imposes substantial limitations on other major life activities.

From the outset, however, the case has been treated as one in which reproduction was the major life activity limited by the impairment. It is our practice to decide cases on the grounds raised and considered in the Court of Appeals and included in the question on which we granted certiorari. We ask, then, whether reproduction is a major life activity.

We have little difficulty concluding that it is. As the Court of Appeals held, "[t]he plain meaning of the word 'major' denotes comparative importance" and "suggest[s] that the touchstone for determining an activity's inclusion under the statutory rubric is its significance." Reproduction falls well within the phrase "major life activity." Reproduction and the sexual dynamics surrounding it are central to the life process itself.

While petitioner concedes the importance of reproduction, he claims that Congress intended the ADA only to cover those aspects of a person's life which have a public, economic, or daily character. The argument founders on the statutory language. Nothing in the definition suggests that activities without a public, economic, or daily dimension may somehow be regarded as so unimportant or insignificant as to fall outside the meaning of the word "major." The breadth of the term confounds the attempt to limit its construction in this manner.

As we have noted, the ADA must be construed to be consistent with regulations issued to implement the Rehabilitation Act. Rather than enunciating a general principle for determining what is and is not a major life activity, the Rehabilitation Act regulations instead provide a representative list, defining the term to include "functions such as caring for one's self, performing manual tasks, walking, seeing, hearing, speaking, breathing, learning, and working." 45 CFR § 84.3(j)(2)(ii) (1997). As the use of the term "such as" confirms, the list is illustrative, not exhaustive.

These regulations are contrary to petitioner's attempt to limit the meaning of the term "major" to public activities. The inclusion of activities such as caring for one's self and performing manual tasks belies the suggestion that a task must have a public or economic character in order to be a major life activity for purposes of the ADA. On the contrary, the Rehabilitation Act regulations support the inclusion of reproduction as a major life activity, since reproduction could not be regarded as any less important than working and learning. Petitioner advances no credible basis for confining major life activities to those with a public, economic, or daily aspect. In the absence of any reason to reach a contrary conclusion, we agree with the Court of Appeals' determination that reproduction is a major life activity for the purposes of the ADA.

3

The final element of the disability definition in subsection (A) is whether respondent's physical impairment was a substantial limit on the major life activity she asserts. The Rehabilitation Act regulations provide no additional guidance.

Our evaluation of the medical evidence leads us to conclude that respondent's infection substantially limited her ability to reproduce in two independent ways. First, a woman infected with HIV who tries to conceive a child imposes on the man a significant risk of becoming infected. The cumulative results of 13 studies collected in a 1994 textbook on AIDS indicates that 20% of male partners of women with HIV became HIV-positive themselves, with a majority of the studies finding a statistically significant risk of infection.

Second, an infected woman risks infecting her child during gestation and childbirth, *i.e.,* perinatal transmission. Petitioner concedes that women infected with HIV face about a 25% risk of transmitting the virus to their children. Published reports available in 1994 confirm the accuracy of this statistic.

Petitioner points to evidence in the record suggesting that antiretroviral therapy can lower the risk of perinatal transmission to about 8%. The United States questions the relevance of the 8% figure, pointing to regulatory language requiring the substantiality of a limitation to be assessed without regard to available mitigating measures. We need not resolve this dispute in order to decide this case, however. It cannot be said as a matter of law that an 8% risk of transmitting a dread and fatal disease to one's child does not represent a substantial limitation on reproduction.

The Act addresses substantial limitations on major life activities, not utter inabilities. Conception and childbirth are not impossible for an HIV victim but, without doubt, are dangerous to the public health. This meets the definition of a substantial limitation. The decision to reproduce carries economic and legal consequences as well. There are added costs for antiretroviral therapy, supplemental insurance, and long-term health care for the child who must be examined and, tragic to think, treated for the infection. The laws of some States, moreover, forbid persons infected with HIV to have sex with others, regardless of consent.

In the end, the disability definition does not turn on personal choice. When significant limitations result from the impairment, the definition is met even if the difficulties are not insurmountable. For the statistical and other reasons we have cited, of course, the limitations on reproduction may be insurmountable here. Testimony from the respondent that her HIV infection controlled her decision not to have a child is unchallenged. In the context of reviewing summary judgment, we must take it to be true. We agree with the District Court and the Court of Appeals that no triable issue of fact impedes a ruling on the question of statutory coverage. Respondent's HIV infection is a physical impairment which substantially limits a major life activity, as the ADA defines it. In view of our holding, we need not address the second question presented, *i.e.,* whether HIV infection is a *per se* disability under the ADA.

B

Our holding is confirmed by a consistent course of agency interpretation before and after enactment of the ADA. Every agency to consider the issue under the Rehabilitation Act found statutory coverage for persons with asymptomatic HIV.

* * *

Every court which addressed the issue before the ADA was enacted in July 1990, moreover, concluded that asymptomatic HIV infection satisfied the Rehabilitation Act's definition of a handicap. We are aware of no instance prior to the enactment of the ADA in which a court or agency ruled that HIV infection was not a handicap under the Rehabilitation Act.

* * *

We find the uniformity of the administrative and judicial precedent construing the definition significant. When administrative and judicial interpretations have settled the meaning of an existing statutory provision, repetition of the same language in a new statute indicates, as a general matter, the intent to incorporate its administrative and judicial interpretations as well. The uniform body of administrative and judicial precedent confirms the conclusion we reach today as the most faithful way to effect the congressional design.

* * *

CHIEF JUSTICE REHNQUIST, with whom JUSTICE SCALIA and JUSTICE THOMAS join, . . . concurring in the judgment in part and dissenting in part.

* * *

It is important to note that whether respondent has a disability covered by the ADA is an individualized inquiry. The Act could not be clearer on this point: Section 12102(2) states explicitly that the disability determination must be made "with respect to an individual." Were this not sufficiently clear, the Act goes on to provide that the "major life activities" allegedly limited by an impairment must be those "of such individual." § 12102(2)(A).

* * *

Petitioner does not dispute that asymptomatic HIV-positive status is a physical impairment. I therefore assume this to be the case, and proceed to the second and third statutory requirements for "disability."

According to the Court, the next question is "whether reproduction is a major life activity." That, however, is only half of the relevant question. As mentioned above, the ADA's definition of a "disability" requires that the major life activity at issue be one "of such individual." § 12102(2)(A). The Court truncates the question, perhaps because there is not a shred of record evidence indicating that, prior to becoming infected with HIV, respondent's major life activities included reproduction (assuming for the moment that reproduction is a major life activity at all). At most, the record indicates that after learning of her HIV status, respondent, whatever her previous inclination, conclusively decided that she would not have children. There is absolutely no evidence that, absent the HIV, respondent would have had or was even considering having children. Indeed, when asked during her deposition whether her HIV infection had in any way impaired her ability to carry out any of *her* life functions, respondent answered "No." It is further telling that in the course of her entire brief to this Court, respondent studiously avoids asserting even once that reproduction is a major life activity *to her*. To the contrary, she argues that the "major life activity" inquiry should not turn on a particularized assessment of the circumstances of this or any other case.

But even aside from the facts of this particular case, the Court is simply wrong in concluding as a general matter that reproduction is a "major life activity." Unfortunately, the ADA does not define the phrase "major life activities." But the Act does incorporate by reference a list of such activities contained in regulations issued under the Rehabilitation Act. The Court correctly recognizes that this list of major life activities "is illustrative, not exhaustive," but then makes no attempt to demonstrate that reproduction is a major life activity in the same sense that "caring for one's self, performing manual tasks, walking, seeing, hearing, speaking, breathing, learning, and working" are.

Instead, the Court argues that reproduction is a "major" life activity in that it is "central to the life process itself." In support of this reading, the Court focuses on the fact that " 'major' " indicates " 'comparative importance,' " ignoring the alternative definition of "major" as "greater in quantity, number, or extent." It is the latter definition that is most consistent with the ADA's illustrative list of major life activities.

No one can deny that reproductive decisions are important in a person's life. But so are decisions as to who to marry, where to live, and how to earn one's living. Fundamental importance of this sort is not the common thread linking the statute's listed activities. The common thread is rather that the activities are repetitively performed and essential in the day-to-day existence of a normally functioning individual. They are thus quite different from the series of activities leading to the birth of a child.

But even if I were to assume that reproduction *is* a major life activity of respondent, I do not agree that an asymptomatic HIV infection "substantially limits" that activity. The record before us leaves no doubt that those so infected are still entirely able to engage in sexual intercourse, give birth to a child if they become pregnant, and perform the manual tasks necessary to rear a child to maturity. While individuals infected with HIV may choose not to engage in these activities, there is no support in language, logic, or our case law for the proposition that such voluntary choices constitute a "limit" on one's own life activities.

The Court responds that the ADA "addresses substantial limitations on major life activities, not utter inabilities." I agree, but fail to see how this assists the Court's cause. Apart from being unable to demonstrate that she is utterly unable to engage in the various activities that comprise the reproductive process, respondent has not even explained how she is less able to engage in those activities.

Respondent contends that her ability to reproduce is limited because "the fatal nature of HIV infection means that a parent is unlikely to live long enough to raise and nurture the child to adulthood." But the ADA's definition of a disability is met only if the alleged impairment substantially "limits" (present tense) a major life activity. 42 U.S.C. § 12102(2)(A). Asymptomatic HIV does not presently limit respondent's ability to perform any of the tasks necessary to bear or raise a child. Respondent's argument, taken to its logical extreme, would render every individual with a genetic marker for some debilitating disease "disabled" here and now because of some possible future effects.

In my view, therefore, respondent has failed to demonstrate that any of her major life activities were substantially limited by her HIV infection.

NOTES AND QUESTIONS

1. *Not a per se disability.* The Court holds that the plaintiff is disabled in this case but refuses to hold that asymptomatic HIV is a *per se* disability. Is it clear from the opinion what an individual with HIV must prove in order to demonstrate that she is disabled? In other words, accepting the majority's conclusion that HIV can substantially limit the major life activity of reproduction, does an individual plaintiff have to prove that her HIV is what precluded her from reproducing? Are men infected with HIV disabled under the majority's analysis? Note that the dissent criticizes the majority's decision because the majority did not require the plaintiff to prove that she was planning on having children before learning she was HIV positive. What evidence should be sufficient in these cases? Should the plaintiff be able to simply assert that, post-HIV diagnosis, she is definitely not going to have children? Or should she also have to demonstrate that she had planned to have children before the HIV diagnosis? Similarly, would a priest or a nun, who have taken vows of celibacy, be able to prove that he or she is disabled if infected with HIV?

2. *Other major life activities?* The majority states that because of "HIV's profound impact on almost every phase of the infected person's life," "it may seem legalistic to circumscribe our discussion to the activity of reproduction. We have little doubt that had different parties brought the suit, they would have maintained that an HIV infection imposes substantial limitations on other major life activities." Do you agree with the Court that other major life activities would be affected by a person's asymptomatic HIV? If so, which major life activities?

3. *Medical advances.* The introduction of anti-retroviral therapy has changed HIV infection from a death sentence to a largely manageable disease. The widespread use of these drugs in the United States has resulted in a 40% drop in annual deaths and a thirteen-year increase in life expectancy.

4. *HIV after the ADA Amendments Act of 2008.* As is discussed below, the ADA Amendments Act of 2008 have made it much easier for an individual to prove that she is disabled under the ADA. This includes those who are HIV positive. *See, e.g.,* Horgan v. Simmons, 704 F.Supp.2d 814, 819 (N.D. Ill. 2010) (holding that HIV may constitute a disability after the ADAAA); Alexiadis v. New York College of Health Professions, 891 F.Supp.2d 418, 428–29 (E.D.N.Y. 2012) (same).

3. PRE-AMENDMENTS NARROWING
DEFINITION OF DISABILITY

SUTTON V. UNITED AIR LINES, INC.

527 U.S. 471, 119 S.Ct. 2139 (1999)

JUSTICE O'CONNOR delivered the opinion of the Court.

I

Petitioners are twin sisters, both of whom have severe myopia. Each petitioner's uncorrected visual acuity is 20/200 or worse in her right eye and 20/400 or worse in her left eye, but "[w]ith the use of corrective lenses, each ... has vision that is 20/20 or better." Consequently, without corrective lenses, each "effectively cannot see to conduct numerous activities such as driving a vehicle, watching television or shopping in public stores," but with corrective measures, such as glasses or contact lenses, both "function identically to individuals without a similar impairment."

In 1992, petitioners applied to respondent for employment as commercial airline pilots. They met respondent's basic age, education, experience, and Federal Aviation Administration certification qualifications. After submitting their applications for employment, both petitioners were invited by respondent to an interview and to flight simulator tests. Both were told during their interviews, however, that a mistake had been made in inviting them to interview because petitioners did not meet respondent's minimum vision requirement, which was uncorrected visual acuity of 20/100 or better. Due to their failure to meet this requirement, petitioners' interviews were terminated, and neither was offered a pilot position.

In light of respondent's proffered reason for rejecting them, petitioners ... alleged that due to their severe myopia they actually have a substantially limiting impairment or are regarded as having such an impairment, and are thus disabled under the Act.

The District Court dismissed petitioners' complaint for failure to state a claim upon which relief could be granted. Because petitioners could fully correct their visual impairments, the court held that they were not actually substantially limited in any major life activity and thus had not stated a claim that they were disabled within the meaning of the ADA. The court also determined that petitioners had not made allegations sufficient to support their claim that they were "regarded" by respondent as having an impairment that substantially limits a major life activity. . . . Employing similar logic, the Court of Appeals for the Tenth Circuit affirmed the District Court's judgment.

The Tenth Circuit's decision is in tension with the decisions of other Courts of Appeals. We granted certiorari, and now affirm.

II

The ADA prohibits discrimination by covered entities, including private employers, against qualified individuals with a disability. Specifically, it provides that no covered employer "shall discriminate against a qualified individual with a disability because of the disability of such individual in regard to job application procedures, the hiring, advancement, or discharge of employees, employee compensation, job training, and other terms, conditions, and privileges of employment." 42 U.S.C. § 12112(a). A "qualified individual with a disability" is identified as "an individual with a disability who, with or without reasonable accommodation, can perform the essential functions of the employment position that such individual holds or desires." § 12111(8). In turn, a "disability" is defined as:

> "(A) a physical or mental impairment that substantially limits one or more of the major life activities of such individual;

> "(B) a record of such an impairment; or

> "(C) being regarded as having such an impairment." § 12102(2).

Accordingly, to fall within this definition one must have an actual disability (subsection (A)), have a record of a disability (subsection (B)), or be regarded as having one (subsection (C)).

The parties agree that the authority to issue regulations to implement the Act is split primarily among three Government agencies. According to the parties, the EEOC has authority to issue regulations to carry out the employment provisions in Title I of the ADA, §§ 12111–12117, pursuant to § 12116. The Attorney General is granted authority to issue regulations with respect to Title II, subtitle A, §§ 12131–12134, which relates to public services. Finally, the Secretary of Transportation has authority to issue regulations pertaining to the transportation provisions of Titles II and III. See § 12149(a). Moreover, each of these agencies is authorized to offer technical assistance regarding the provisions they administer.

No agency, however, has been given authority to issue regulations implementing the generally applicable provisions of the ADA, see §§ 12101–12102, which fall outside Titles I–V. Most notably, no agency has been delegated authority to interpret the term "disability." § 12102(2). Justice BREYER's contrary, imaginative interpretation of the Act's delegation provisions is belied by the terms and structure of the ADA. The EEOC has, nonetheless, issued regulations to provide additional guidance regarding the proper interpretation of this term. After restating the definition of disability given in the statute, the EEOC regulations define the three elements of disability: (1) "physical or mental impairment," (2) "substantially limits," and (3) "major life activities." ... Because both parties accept these regulations as valid, and determining their validity is not necessary to decide this case, we have no occasion to consider what deference they are due, if any.

The agencies have also issued interpretive guidelines to aid in the implementation of their regulations. For instance, at the time that it promulgated the above regulations, the EEOC issued an "Interpretive Guidance," which provides that "[t]he determination of whether an individual is substantially limited in a major life activity must be made on a case by case basis, without regard to mitigating measures such as medicines, or assistive or prosthetic devices." 29 CFR pt. 1630, App. § 1630.2(j). The Department of Justice has issued a similar guideline. See 28 CFR pt. 35, App. A, § 35.104. Although the parties dispute the persuasive force of these interpretive guidelines, we have no need in this case to decide what deference is due.

III

With this statutory and regulatory framework in mind, we turn first to the question whether petitioners have stated a claim under subsection (A) of the disability definition, that is, whether they have alleged that they possess a physical impairment that substantially limits them in one or more major life activities. Because petitioners allege that with corrective measures their vision "is 20/20 or better," they are not actually disabled within the meaning of the Act if the "disability" determination is made with reference to these measures. Consequently, with respect to subsection (A) of the disability definition, our decision turns on whether disability is to be determined with or without reference to corrective measures.

Petitioners maintain that whether an impairment is substantially limiting should be determined without regard to corrective measures. They argue that, because the ADA does not directly address the question at hand, the Court should defer to the agency interpretations of the statute, which are embodied in the agency guidelines issued by the EEOC and the Department of Justice. These guidelines specifically direct that the determination of whether an individual is substantially limited in a major life activity be made without regard to mitigating measures.

* * *

We conclude that respondent is correct that the approach adopted by the agency guidelines—that persons are to be evaluated in their hypothetical uncorrected state—is an impermissible interpretation of the ADA. Looking at the Act as a whole, it is apparent that if a person is taking measures to correct for, or mitigate, a physical or mental impairment, the effects of those measures—both positive and negative—must be taken into account when judging whether that person is "substantially limited" in a major life activity and thus "disabled" under the Act. Justice STEVENS relies on the legislative history of the ADA for the contrary proposition that individuals should be examined in their uncorrected state. Because we decide that, by its terms, the ADA cannot be read in this manner, we have no reason to consider the ADA's legislative history.

Three separate provisions of the ADA, read in concert, lead us to this conclusion. The Act defines a "disability" as "a physical or mental impairment that *substantially limits* one or more of the major life activities" of an individual. § 12102(2)(A). Because the phrase "substantially limits" appears in the Act in the present indicative verb form, we think the language is properly read as requiring that a person be presently—not potentially or hypothetically—substantially limited in order to demonstrate a disability. A "disability" exists only where an impairment "substantially limits" a major life activity, not where it "might," "could," or "would" be substantially limiting if mitigating measures were not taken. A person whose physical or mental impairment is corrected by medication or other measures does not have an impairment that presently "substantially limits" a major life activity. To be sure, a person whose physical or mental impairment is corrected by mitigating measures still has an impairment, but if the impairment is corrected it does not "substantially limi[t]" a major life activity.

The definition of disability also requires that disabilities be evaluated "with respect to an individual" and be determined based on whether an impairment substantially limits the "major life activities of such individual." § 12102(2). Thus, whether a person has a disability under the ADA is an individualized inquiry.

The agency guidelines' directive that persons be judged in their uncorrected or unmitigated state runs directly counter to the individualized inquiry mandated by the ADA. The agency approach would often require courts and employers to speculate about a person's condition and would, in many cases, force them to make a disability determination based on general information about how an uncorrected impairment usually affects individuals, rather than on the individual's actual condition. For instance, under this view, courts would almost certainly find all diabetics to be disabled, because if they failed to monitor their blood sugar levels and administer insulin, they would almost certainly be substantially limited in one or more major life activities. A diabetic whose illness does not impair his or her daily activities would therefore be considered disabled simply because he or she has diabetes. Thus, the guidelines approach would create a system in which persons often must be treated as members of a group of people with similar impairments, rather than as individuals. This is contrary to both the letter and the spirit of the ADA.

The guidelines approach could also lead to the anomalous result that in determining whether an individual is disabled, courts and employers could not consider any negative side effects suffered by an individual resulting from the use of mitigating measures, even when those side effects are very severe. This result is also inconsistent with the individualized approach of the ADA.

Finally, and critically, findings enacted as part of the ADA require the conclusion that Congress did not intend to bring under the statute's protection all those whose uncorrected conditions amount to disabilities. Congress found that "some 43,000,000 Americans have one or more physical or mental disabilities, and this number is increasing as the population as a whole is growing older." § 12101(a)(1). This figure is inconsistent with the definition of disability pressed by petitioners.

Although the exact source of the 43 million figure is not clear, . . . the 43 million figure reflects an understanding that those whose impairments are largely corrected by medication or other devices are not "disabled" within the meaning of the ADA. . . .

* * *

. . . Had Congress intended to include all persons with corrected physical limitations among those covered by the Act, it undoubtedly would have cited a much higher number of disabled persons in the findings. That it did not is evidence that the ADA's coverage is restricted to only those whose impairments are not mitigated by corrective measures.

The dissents suggest that viewing individuals in their corrected state will exclude from the definition of "disab[led]" those who use prosthetic limbs, or take medicine for epilepsy or high blood pressure. This suggestion is incorrect. The use of a corrective device does not, by itself, relieve one's disability. Rather, one has a disability under subsection (A) if, notwithstanding the use of a corrective device, that individual is substantially limited in a major life activity. For example, individuals who use prosthetic limbs or wheelchairs may be mobile and capable of functioning in society but still be disabled because of a substantial limitation on their ability to walk or run. The same may be true of individuals who take medicine to lessen the symptoms of an impairment so that they can function but nevertheless remain substantially limited. . . . The use or nonuse of a corrective device does not determine whether an individual is disabled; that determination depends on whether the limitations an individual with an impairment *actually* faces are in fact substantially limiting.

Applying this reading of the Act to the case at hand, we conclude that the Court of Appeals correctly resolved the issue of disability in respondent's favor. As noted above, petitioners allege that with corrective measures, their visual acuity is 20/20, and that they "function identically to individuals without a similar impairment." In addition, petitioners concede that they "do not argue that the use of corrective lenses in itself demonstrates a substantially limiting impairment." Accordingly, because we decide that disability under the Act is to be determined with reference to corrective measures, we agree with the courts below that petitioners have not stated a claim that they are substantially limited in any major life activity.

* * *

JUSTICE GINSBURG, concurring.

I agree that 42 U.S.C. § 12102(2)(A) does not reach the legions of people with correctable disabilities. The strongest clues to Congress' perception of the domain of the Americans with Disabilities Act of 1990 (ADA), as I see it, are legislative findings that "some 43,000,000 Americans have one or more physical or mental disabilities," § 12101(a)(1), and that "individuals with disabilities are a discrete and insular minority," persons "subjected to a history of purposeful unequal treatment, and relegated to a position of political powerlessness in our society," § 12101(a)(7). These declarations are inconsistent with the enormously embracing definition of disability petitioners urge. As the Court demonstrates, the inclusion of correctable disabilities within the ADA's domain would extend the Act's coverage to far more than 43 million people. And persons whose uncorrected eyesight is poor, or who rely on daily medication for their well-being, can be found in every social and economic class; they do not cluster among the politically powerless, nor do they coalesce as historical victims of discrimination. In short, in no sensible way can one rank the large numbers of diverse individuals with corrected disabilities as a "discrete and insular minority." I do not mean to suggest that any of the constitutional presumptions or doctrines that may apply to "discrete and insular" minorities in other contexts are relevant here; there is no constitutional dimension to this case. Congress' use of the phrase, however, is a telling indication of its intent to restrict the ADA's coverage to a confined, and historically disadvantaged, class.

JUSTICE STEVENS, with whom JUSTICE BREYER joins, dissenting.

When it enacted the Americans with Disabilities Act of 1990 (ADA or Act), Congress certainly did not intend to require United Air Lines to hire unsafe or unqualified pilots. Nor, in all likelihood, did it view every person who wears glasses as a member of a "discrete and insular minority." Indeed, by reason of legislative myopia it may not have foreseen that its definition of "disability" might theoretically encompass, not just "some 43,000,000 Americans," but perhaps two or three times that number. Nevertheless, if we apply customary tools of statutory construction, it is quite clear that the threshold question whether an individual is "disabled" within the meaning of the Act—and, therefore, is entitled to the basic assurances that the Act affords—focuses on her past or present physical condition without regard to mitigation that has resulted from rehabilitation, self-improvement, prosthetic devices, or medication. One might reasonably argue that the general rule should not apply to an impairment that merely requires a nearsighted person to wear glasses. But I believe that, in order to be faithful to the remedial purpose of the Act, we should give it a generous, rather than a miserly, construction.

There are really two parts to the question of statutory construction presented by this case. The first question is whether the determination of disability for people that Congress unquestionably intended to cover should focus on their unmitigated or their mitigated condition. If the correct answer to that question is the one provided by eight of the nine Federal Courts of Appeals to address the issue, and by all three of the Executive agencies that have issued regulations or interpretive bulletins construing the statute—namely, that the statute defines "disability" without regard to ameliorative measures—it would still be necessary to decide whether that general rule should be applied to what might be characterized as a "minor, trivial impairment." I shall therefore first consider impairments that Congress surely had in mind before turning to the special facts of this case.

I

* * *

The ADA's definition provides:

> "The term 'disability' means, with respect to an individual—

> "(A) a physical or mental impairment that substantially limits one or more of the major life activities of such individual;

> "(B) a record of such an impairment; or

> "(C) being regarded as having such an impairment." 42 U.S.C. § 12102(2).

The three parts of this definition do not identify mutually exclusive, discrete categories. On the contrary, they furnish three overlapping formulas aimed at ensuring that individuals who now have, or ever had, a substantially limiting impairment are covered by the Act.

An example of a rather common condition illustrates this point: There are many individuals who have lost one or more limbs in industrial accidents, or perhaps in the service of their country in places like Iwo Jima. With the aid of prostheses, coupled with courageous determination and physical therapy, many of these hardy individuals can perform all of their major life activities just as efficiently as an average couch potato. If the Act were just concerned with their present ability to participate in society, many of these individuals' physical impairments would not be viewed as disabilities. . . .

The sweep of the statute's three-pronged definition, however, makes it pellucidly clear that Congress intended the Act to cover such persons. The fact that a prosthetic device, such as an artificial leg, has restored one's ability to perform major life activities surely cannot mean that subsection (A) of the definition is inapplicable. Nor should the fact that the individual considers himself (or actually is) "cured," or that a prospective employer considers him generally employable, mean that subsections (B) or (C) are inapplicable. But under the Court's emphasis on "the present indicative verb form" used in subsection (A), that subsection presumably would not apply. . . .

. . . Subsection (B) of the definition, in fact, sheds a revelatory light on the question whether Congress was concerned only about the corrected or mitigated status of a person's impairment. If the Court is correct that "[a] 'disability' exists only where" a person's "present" or "actual" condition is substantially impaired, there would be no reason to include in the protected class those who were once disabled but who are now fully recovered. Subsection (B) of the Act's definition, however, plainly covers a person who previously had a serious hearing impairment that has since been completely cured. Still, if I correctly understand the Court's opinion, it holds that one who *continues to wear* a hearing aid that she has worn all her life might not be covered—fully cured impairments are covered, but merely treatable ones are not. The text of the Act surely does not require such a bizarre result.

The three prongs of the statute, rather, are most plausibly read together not to inquire into whether a person is currently "functionally" limited in a major life activity, but only into the existence of an impairment—present or past—that substantially limits, or did so limit, the individual before amelioration. This reading avoids the counterintuitive conclusion that the ADA's safeguards vanish when individuals make themselves more employable by ascertaining ways to overcome their physical or mental limitations.

To the extent that there may be doubt concerning the meaning of the statutory text, ambiguity is easily removed by looking at the legislative history. . . . The Committee Reports on the bill that became the ADA make it abundantly clear that Congress intended the ADA to cover individuals who could perform all of their major life activities only with the help of ameliorative measures.

* * *

All of the Reports, indeed, are replete with references to the understanding that the Act's protected class includes individuals with various medical conditions that ordinarily are perfectly "correctable" with medication or treatment.

In addition, each of the three Executive agencies charged with implementing the Act has consistently interpreted the Act as mandating that the presence of disability turns on an individual's uncorrected state. . . .

The EEOC's Interpretive Guidance provides that "[t]he determination of whether an individual is substantially limited in a major life activity must be made on a case by case basis, without regard to mitigating measures such as medicines, or assistive or prosthetic devices." 29 CFR pt. 1630, App. § 1630.2(j) (1998). The EEOC further explains:

> "[A]n individual who uses artificial legs would . . . be substantially limited in the major life activity of walking because the individual is unable to walk without the aid of prosthetic devices. Similarly, a diabetic who without insulin would lapse into a coma would be substantially limited because the individual cannot perform major life activities without the aid of medication."

The Department of Justice has reached the same conclusion. . . .

In my judgment, the Committee Reports and the uniform agency regulations merely confirm the message conveyed by the text of the Act— at least insofar as it applies to impairments such as the loss of a limb, the inability to hear, or any condition such as diabetes that is substantially limiting without medication. The Act generally protects individuals who have "correctable" substantially limiting impairments from unjustified employment discrimination on the basis of those impairments. The question, then, is whether the fact that Congress was specifically concerned about protecting a class that included persons characterized as a "discrete and insular minority" and that it estimated that class to include "some 43,000,000 Americans" means that we should construe the term "disability" to exclude individuals with impairments that Congress probably did not have in mind.

II

The EEOC maintains that, in order to remain allegiant to the Act's structure and purpose, courts should always answer "the question whether an individual has a disability . . . without regard to mitigating measures that the individual takes to ameliorate the effects of the impairment." Brief for United States et al. as *Amici Curiae* 6. "[T]here is nothing about poor vision," as the EEOC interprets the Act, "that would justify adopting a different rule in this case."

If a narrow reading of the term "disability" were necessary in order to avoid the danger that the Act might otherwise force United to hire pilots who might endanger the lives of their passengers, it would make good sense to use the "43,000,000 Americans" finding to confine its coverage. There is, however, no such danger in this case. If a person is "disabled" within the meaning of the Act, she still cannot prevail on a claim of discrimination unless she can prove that the employer took action "because of" that impairment, 42 U.S.C. § 12112(a), and that she can, "with or without reasonable accommodation, . . . perform the essential functions" of the job of a commercial airline pilot. Even then, an employer may avoid liability if it shows that the criteria of having uncorrected visual acuity of at least 20/100 is "job-related and consistent with business necessity" or if such vision (even if correctable to 20/20) would pose a health or safety hazard. §§ 12113(a) and (b).

This case, in other words, is not about whether petitioners are genuinely qualified or whether they can perform the job of an airline pilot without posing an undue safety risk. The case just raises the threshold question whether petitioners are members of the ADA's protected class. It simply asks whether the ADA lets petitioners in the door in the same way as the Age Discrimination in Employment Act of 1967 does for every person who is at least 40 years old, and as Title VII of the Civil Rights Act of 1964 does for every single individual in the work force. Inside that door lies nothing more than basic protection from irrational and unjustified discrimination because of a characteristic that is beyond a person's control. Hence, this particular case, at its core, is about whether, assuming that petitioners can prove that they are "qualified," the airline has any duty to come forward with some legitimate explanation for refusing to hire them because of their uncorrected eyesight, or whether the ADA leaves the airline free to decline to hire petitioners on this basis even if it is acting purely on the basis of irrational fear and stereotype.

* * *

III

The Court does not disagree that the logic of the ADA requires petitioners' visual impairments to be judged the same as other "correctable" conditions. Instead of including petitioners within the Act's umbrella, however, the Court decides, in this opinion and its companion, to expel all individuals who, by using "measures [to] mitigate [their] impairment[s]," are able to overcome substantial limitations regarding major life activities. . . .

The Court claims that this rule is necessary to avoid requiring courts to "speculate" about a person's "hypothetical" condition and to preserve the Act's focus on making "individualized inquiries" into whether a person is disabled. . . . And, I suspect, the Court has been cowed by respondent's persistent argument that viewing all individuals in their unmitigated state will lead to a tidal wave of lawsuits. None of the Court's reasoning, however, justifies a construction of the Act that will obviously deprive many of Congress' intended beneficiaries of the legal protection it affords.

The agencies' approach, the Court repeatedly contends, "would create a system in which persons often must be treated as members of a group of people with similar impairments, rather than individuals, [which] is both contrary to the letter and spirit of the ADA." The Court's mantra regarding the Act's "individualized approach," however, fails to support its holding. I agree that the letter and spirit of the ADA is designed to deter decisionmaking based on group stereotypes, but the agencies' interpretation of the Act does not lead to this result. Nor does it require courts to "speculate" about people's "hypothetical" conditions. Viewing a person in her "unmitigated" state simply requires examining that individual's abilities in a different state, not the abilities of every person who shares a similar condition. It is just as easy individually to test petitioners' eyesight with their glasses on as with their glasses off.

* * *

IV

Occupational hazards characterize many trades. The farsighted pilot may have as much trouble seeing the instrument panel as the nearsighted pilot has in identifying a safe place to land. The vision of appellate judges is sometimes subconsciously obscured by a concern that their decision will legalize issues best left to the private sphere or will magnify the work of an already-overburdened judiciary. Although these concerns may help to explain the Court's decision to chart its own course—rather than to follow the one that has been well marked by Congress, by the overwhelming consensus of circuit judges, and by the Executive officials charged with the responsibility of administering the ADA—they surely do not justify the Court's crabbed vision of the territory covered by this important statute.

Accordingly, although I express no opinion on the ultimate merits of petitioners' claim, I am persuaded that they have a disability covered by the ADA. I therefore respectfully dissent.

NOTES AND QUESTIONS

1. *The* Sutton *trilogy.* The Supreme Court decided two other cases the day it decided *Sutton.* In *Murphy v. United Parcel Service,* 527 U.S. 516, 119 S.Ct. 2133 (1999), the plaintiff was a mechanic for UPS who had high blood pressure. Because of his high blood pressure, he failed the medical exam for Department of Transportation ("DOT") certification, which was required because his mechanic job necessitated that he occasionally drive the trucks he was repairing. The Court applied the mitigating measures rule it had just announced in *Sutton* and held that, in determining whether Murphy had a disability under the Act, he should be viewed in his mitigated state, *i.e.,* with the medication he takes for his blood pressure. Because the medication lowers his high blood pressure, the Court held that he was not disabled. *Id.* at 519–21.

In *Albertson's, Inc. v. Kirkingburg,* 527 U.S. 555, 119 S.Ct. 2162 (1999), the third case, the Court considered whether the plaintiff's monocular vision constituted a disability. The plaintiff in this case, similar to the plaintiff in the *Murphy* case, had a job that required DOT certification. The plaintiff had been certified as a driver, but after a leave of absence because of a workplace injury, he was required to undergo a fitness-for-duty physical exam. The doctor noted that Kirkingburg had monocular vision and therefore did not meet the vision requirement for DOT certification. Even though he did not have eyeglasses or other assistive devices to help with his vision, the Court elaborated on its mitigating measures rule, stating that courts should not only consider artificial assistive devices but should also consider how Kirkingburg's brain can mitigate his vision impairment by developing techniques to cope with his monocular vision. *Id.* at 558–59, 565–66.

2.   *The* Sutton *majority's interpretation of the statute.* Putting aside the policy issue for now, does the majority's opinion make sense as a matter of statutory interpretation? The majority focuses on two statutory mandates operating in tandem; first, the requirement for an "individualized" inquiry; and second, the requirement that courts should consider the individual in his or her present state. This analysis seems to make sense. After all, why should courts consider someone in a hypothetical state? Although it might be easy to consider the Sutton sisters in their unmitigated state (they could simply take off their eyeglasses), it is not as easy with other impairments and their corresponding mitigating measures. If a court were to consider someone who controls his diabetes with insulin in an unmitigated state, does that mean that the court would require that individual to stop controlling his diabetes for some period of time? Obviously not. Instead, a court would hear testimony from the individual's doctor regarding his condition if the diabetes were not being controlled. This hypothetical analysis seems to be what troubles the majority.

But what about this passage in Justice Steven's dissent?

> If the Court is correct that "[a] 'disability' exists only where" a person's "present" or "actual" condition is substantially impaired, there would be no reason to include in the protected class those who were once disabled but who are now fully recovered. Subsection (B) of the Act's definition, however, plainly covers a person who previously had a serious hearing impairment that has since been completely cured. See *School Bd. of Nassau Cty. v. Arline,* 480 U.S. 273, 281 (1987). Still, if I correctly understand the Court's opinion, it holds that one who *continues to wear* a hearing aid that she has worn all her life might not be covered—fully cured impairments are covered, but merely treatable ones are not. The text of the Act surely does not require such a bizarre result.

Is there a suitable response to the dissent's concern? Does it make sense to protect someone who has a record of a disability (had a disability that is fully cured) but not to protect someone who currently has an impairment, albeit one that is mitigated?

3.   *Should there be a hierarchy of impairments? Sutton* adopts a one-size-fits-all rule with respect to mitigating measures. That is, mitigating measures must be taken into account regardless of the impairment at issue. But is there an argument that all impairments should not be treated the same with respect to the impact of mitigating measures? For example, assume that mitigating measures can ameliorate the limitations resulting from each of the following impairments: (1) poor but fully correctable eyesight, (2) diabetes, (3) lost limb, and (4) depression. Which of these impairments do you consider to be most worthy of being considered a disability under the ADA? Or the least? Why?

4. *Was* Sutton *the right case to challenge the mitigating measures rule?* The attorneys in *Sutton* acknowledged that the Sutton sisters had an uphill battle. Many disability rights advocates thought that *Sutton* was the "wrong case to pursue at the Supreme Court level" because it required the twins to take the "relatively extreme position that mitigating measures must be disregarded in each and every ADA case." Stephen F. Befort, *The Story of* Sutton v. United Air Lines, Inc.: *Narrowing the Reach of the Americans with Disabilities Act*, at 343 *in* EMPLOYMENT DISCRIMINATION STORIES (Joel Wm. Friedman, Ed. 2006). Certainly, because the twins had fully correctable vision when wearing ordinary contacts or glasses, they were not very sympathetic plaintiffs. Do you think the Court would have come to a different conclusion if the plaintiffs had a more stigmatizing or serious impairment?

5. *The effect of the mitigating measures rule on an employer's obligation to accommodate an employee.* In *Sutton*, the Court says diabetes should not be considered a disability if it is mitigated by insulin. If an employee has diabetes that is controlled by insulin and/or a proper eating regimen, presumably that employee needs to take time during the day to test his blood sugar, eat proper meals, and possibly inject himself with insulin. However, if such an employee is not considered disabled under the ADA, then the employer is not obligated to accommodate this employee by giving him regular breaks during the day to properly manage his diabetes. *See, e.g.,* Orr v. Wal-Mart Stores, Inc., 297 F.3d 720 (8th Cir. 2002) (holding that a pharmacist who was fired for taking a half-hour lunch break to manage his diabetes was not disabled because he did so well managing his diabetes with insulin and diet). Did the Court give sufficient consideration to this possible scenario?

6. *The importance of the 43 million figure.* The Court found significant that the preamble to the ADA states that "some 43,000,000 Americans have one or more physical or mental disabilities, and this number is increasing as the population as a whole is growing older." 42 U.S.C. § 12101(a)(1). The Court stated: "Because it is included in the ADA's text, the finding that 43 million individuals are disabled gives content to the ADA's terms, specifically the term 'disability.' Had Congress intended to include all persons with corrected physical limitations among those covered by the Act, it undoubtedly would have cited a much higher number of disabled persons in the findings. That it did not is evidence that the ADA's coverage is restricted to only those whose impairments are not mitigated by corrective measures." Is the Court's reasoning persuasive? From reading the statutory text, did Congress intend the 43 million figure to be a floor or a ceiling? The majority considers it a ceiling, although the specific language states that the number is increasing as the population ages. Justice Ginsburg agreed that the 43 million figure was significant. She reasoned that the 43 million figure along with the language in the statute's preamble that "individuals with disabilities are a discrete and insular minority," is evidence that Congress intended the protected class under the ADA to be narrowly interpreted.

7. *Minority group approach.* Scholars have referred to Justice Ginsburg's position as the "minority group" approach to disability. *See, e.g.,*

Kevin Barry, *Toward Universalism: What the ADA Amendments Act of 2008 Can and Can't Do for Disability Rights*, 31 BERKELEY J. EMP. & LAB. L. 203, 246–47 (2010) (stating that Justice Ginsburg's position—that non-stigmatizing impairments, like fully correctable myopia and high blood pressure, should not be considered disabilities—reflects the minority group approach). The minority group approach to disability defines those who are disabled as a discrete, identifiable group "whose impairments subject them to systematic disadvantages in society." *Id.* at 213. Under this approach, only those who have stigmatized impairments should be protected by the ADA. Do you agree with this approach?

Below, beginning in part 4 of this section, is a discussion of the significant changes made to the interpretation of the definition of disability under the ADA Amendments Act. Some have argued that the Amendments have gone from a minority group model to a more universal approach to defining disability. *See, e.g.,* Barry, *supra*, at 251–77 (referring to the ADA Amendments Act as "The March Toward Universalism"). One indication of Congress's intent in this regard is that Congress removed the 43 million figure, and it removed the statement in the preamble of the ADA that states that those with disabilities are a "discrete and insular minority." *Id.* at 254.

After the *Sutton* trilogy of cases, the lower courts began applying the mitigating measures rule quite vigorously. Courts found all kinds of impairments to *not* be disabilities under the statute. Impairments such as: monocular vision, diabetes, cancer, multiple sclerosis, hypertension, learning disabilities, depression, AIDS, epilepsy, cerebral palsy, intellectual disabilities, and other were all found to not be disabilities under the ADA. *See* sources cited in Nicole Buonocore Porter, *The New ADA Backlash*, 82 TENN. L. REV. 1, 11 (2014). In many of these cases, the courts simply granted summary judgment to the employers on the coverage question, holding that the plaintiff did not have a disability under the statute; thus, there was no reason to decide the merits of the plaintiff's case. In addition to the mitigating measures rule, the Court struck a final blow against ADA plaintiffs in *Toyota Motor Mfg., Ky., Inc. v. Williams*, excerpted below.

TOYOTA MOTOR MFG., KY., INC. V. WILLIAMS
534 U.S. 184, 122 S.Ct. 681 (2002)

Excerpted Facts:

[The plaintiff worked on an assembly line at petitioner's automobile manufacturing plant in Georgetown, Kentucky. Her duties included work with pneumatic tools, which eventually caused pain in respondent's hands, wrists, and arms. She was diagnosed with bilateral carpal tunnel syndrome and bilateral tendinitis and placed on permanent work restrictions that precluded her from (1) lifting more than 20 pounds; (2) engaging in constant repetitive extension of her wrists or elbows; (3) performing overhead work; or (4) using vibratory or pneumatic tools. Although the employer modified her duties, she eventually filed a claim under the Kentucky Workers' Compensation Act.

When she returned from a medical leave related to her injuries, she was assigned to a team in Quality Control Inspection Operations (QCIO), which was responsible for four tasks: (1) "assembly paint"; (2) "paint second inspection"; (3) "shell body audit"; and (4) "ED surface repair." She initially only had to perform the first two of these tasks, and she had no problem with those tasks. Eventually, however, the employer announced that it wanted QCIO employees to be able to rotate through all four of the QCIO processes, one of which required the plaintiff to hold her hands and arms up around shoulder height for several hours at a time. Shortly thereafter, the plaintiff began to experience pain in her neck and shoulders, and was diagnosed with myotendinitis bilateral periscapular, an inflammation of the muscles and tendons around both of her shoulder blades; myotendinitis and myositis bilateral forearms with nerve compression causing median nerve irritation; and thoracic outlet compression, a condition that causes pain in the nerves that lead to the upper extremities. The plaintiff asked for an accommodation—to only have to perform the first two tasks that did not exacerbate her condition. The employer refused, and eventually terminated the plaintiff, citing her poor attendance record.

The plaintiff filed a lawsuit under the ADA, basing her claim that she was "disabled" under the ADA on the ground that her physical impairments substantially limited her in (1) manual tasks; (2) housework; (3) gardening; (4) playing with her children; (5) lifting; and (6) working, all of which, she argued, constituted major life activities under the Act. The employer filed a motion for summary judgment, which the district court granted, stating that she was not disabled.

The plaintiff appealed all but the gardening, housework, and playing-with-children rulings. The Court of Appeals for the Sixth Circuit reversed the District Court's ruling on whether the plaintiff was disabled at the time she sought an accommodation.]

JUSTICE O'CONNOR delivered the opinion of the Court.

* * *

III

The question presented by this case is whether the Sixth Circuit properly determined that respondent was disabled under subsection (A) of the ADA's disability definition at the time that she sought an accommodation from petitioner. 42 U.S.C. § 12102(2)(A). The parties do not dispute that respondent's medical conditions, which include carpal tunnel syndrome, myotendinitis, and thoracic outlet compression, amount to physical impairments. The relevant question, therefore, is whether the Sixth Circuit correctly analyzed whether these impairments substantially limited respondent in the major life activity of performing manual tasks.

Answering this requires us to address an issue about which the EEOC regulations are silent: what a plaintiff must demonstrate to establish a substantial limitation in the specific major life activity of performing manual tasks.

Our consideration of this issue is guided first and foremost by the words of the disability definition itself. "[S]ubstantially" in the phrase "substantially limits" suggests "considerable" or "to a large degree." See Webster's Third New International Dictionary 2280 (1976). The word "substantial" thus clearly precludes impairments that interfere in only a minor way with the performance of manual tasks from qualifying as disabilities.

"Major" in the phrase "major life activities" means important. "Major life activities" thus refers to those activities that are of central importance to daily life. In order for performing manual tasks to fit into this category—a category that includes such basic abilities as walking, seeing, and hearing—the manual tasks in question must be central to daily life. If each of the tasks included in the major life activity of performing manual tasks does not independently qualify as a major life activity, then together they must do so.

That these terms need to be interpreted strictly to create a demanding standard for qualifying as disabled is confirmed by the first section of the ADA, which lays out the legislative findings and purposes that motivate the Act. See 42 U.S.C. § 12101. When it enacted the ADA in 1990, Congress found that "some 43,000,000 Americans have one or more physical or mental disabilities." § 12101(a)(1). If Congress intended everyone with a physical impairment that precluded the performance of some isolated, unimportant, or particularly difficult manual task to qualify as disabled, the number of disabled Americans would surely have been much higher.

We therefore hold that to be substantially limited in performing manual tasks, an individual must have an impairment that prevents or severely restricts the individual from doing activities that are of central importance to most people's daily lives. The impairment's impact must also be permanent or long term.

* * *

IV

* * *

... [T]he Court of Appeals appears to have disregarded the very type of evidence that it should have focused upon. It treated as irrelevant "[t]he fact that [respondent] can ... ten[d] to her personal hygiene [and] carr[y] out personal or household chores." Yet household chores, bathing, and brushing one's teeth are among the types of manual tasks of central importance to people's daily lives, and should have been part of the assessment of whether respondent was substantially limited in performing manual tasks.

... [A]ccording to respondent's deposition testimony, even after her condition worsened, she could still brush her teeth, wash her face, bathe, tend her flower garden, fix breakfast, do laundry, and pick up around the house. The record also indicates that her medical conditions caused her to avoid sweeping, to quit dancing, to occasionally seek help dressing, and to reduce how often she plays with her children, gardens, and drives long distances. But these changes in her life did not amount to such severe restrictions in the activities that are of central importance to most people's daily lives that they establish a manual task disability as a matter of law. On this record, it was therefore inappropriate for the Court of Appeals to grant partial summary judgment to respondent on the issue of whether she was substantially limited in performing manual tasks, and its decision to do so must be reversed. . . .

Accordingly, we reverse the Court of Appeals' judgment granting partial summary judgment to respondent and remand the case for further proceedings consistent with this opinion.

NOTES AND QUESTIONS

1. *Making sense of* Toyota. The *Toyota* decision was unanimous. All of the justices (including Justices Breyer and Stevens, who dissented in *Sutton*) signed on to the Court's very broad language, stating that the definition of disability needs to be "interpreted strictly to create a demanding standard for qualifying as disabled." The Court also stated that to be "substantially limited in performing manual tasks, an individual must have an impairment that prevents or severely restricts the individual from doing activities that are of central importance to most people's daily lives." Justices Stevens and Breyer dissented in *Sutton*, arguing that the definition of disability does not need to be given a narrow construction. So why did they sign on to the opinion in *Toyota*? Did the nature of plaintiff's impairment have something to do with the Court's unanimous decision? In other words, is carpal tunnel so common and considered so minor that it is laughable to consider it a disability? If not, then what else might explain why Justices Stevens and Breyer agree with the decision in *Toyota*?

2. Toyota *aftermath.* In conjunction with the mitigating measures rule announced in *Sutton*, the *Toyota* decision led to a dramatic narrowing of the class of individuals who were protected by the ADA. Only those with the most severe disabilities would be considered disabled under the Act, but yet many of those individuals could not meet another criteria of the statute—that they were "qualified" for the job. This led to many scholars commenting that the ADA was protecting only those who are disabled "just enough," thereby excluding many individuals who need the protection of the ADA. *See, e.g.,* Matthew Diller, *Judicial Backlash, the ADA, and the Civil Rights Model*, 21 BERKELEY J. EMP. & LAB. L. 19, 29 (2000); Chai R. Feldblum, Kevin Barry, &

Emily A. Benfer, *The ADA Amendments Act of 2008*, 13 TEX. J. ON C.L. & C.R. 187, 218–20 (2008) (citing to many cases where the plaintiffs were held not disabled enough to be protected by the Act but apparently too disabled to work); Bradley A. Areheart, *When Disability Isn't "Just Right": The Entrenchment of the Medical Model of Disability and the Goldilocks Dilemma*, 83 IND. L. J. 181, 181 (2008) ("The Supreme Court's interpretation of the Americans with Disabilities Act (ADA) has forced people with disabilities into a Goldilocks dilemma—they are either too disabled or not disabled enough. And thus far, very few have been 'disabled just right.' "). The ADA Amendments Act was enacted to reverse this line of restrictive decisions.

4.   ADA AMENDMENTS ACT OF 2008

On September 25, 2008, President Bush signed into law the ADA Amendments Act of 2008, Pub. L. No. 110–325, 122 Stat. 3553 (2008) ("ADAAA" or "Amendments"). The goal of the Amendments was to overturn the Court's restrictive interpretations of the definition of disability. *Id.* § 2(a)(4)–(6) (disagreeing with the *Sutton* trilogy of cases and the *Toyota* decision, and stating that as a result of these decisions, "lower courts have incorrectly found in individual cases that people with a range of substantially limiting impairments are not people with disabilities").

a.   Summary of Statutory Provisions

The Amendments did not change the basic definition of disability—a physical or mental impairment that substantially limits one or more major life activities. 42 U.S.C. § 12102(1)(A). Instead, the Amendments include several rules of construction to help courts interpret the definition of disability.

Broad Construction

Overruling the Supreme Court's decision in *Toyota* that the ADA needs to be strictly construed in order to "create a demanding standard for qualifying as disabled," the Amendments state that the definition of disability "shall be construed in favor of broad coverage of individuals under this chapter, to the maximum extent permitted by the terms of this chapter." 42 U.S.C. § 12102(4)(A).

Mitigating Measures

Expressly overruling *Sutton*'s mitigating measures rule, the Amendments state that the "determination of whether an impairment substantially limits a major life activity shall be made without regard to the ameliorative effects of mitigating measures." 42 U.S.C. § 12102(4)(E)(i). However, the Amendments do allow courts to consider the ameliorative effects of ordinary eyeglasses or contact lenses. 42 U.S.C. § 12102(4)(E)(ii).[4]

---

[4]   Although not relevant to this chapter on the definition of disability, the Amendments do state that if an employer uses a qualification standard based on *uncorrected* vision, the employer

Substantially Limits

Recall that in *Toyota*, the Court stated that, in order to be considered "substantially limited" in a major life activity, an "individual must have an impairment that *prevents or severely restricts* the individual from doing activities that are of central importance to most people's daily lives. The impairment's impact must also be permanent or long term." Congress did not specifically define "substantially limits" in the ADA Amendments Act, but instead deferred to the EEOC to do so, stating that the "term 'substantially limits' shall be interpreted consistently with the findings and purposes of the ADA Amendments Act of 2008." 42 U.S.C. § 12102(4)(B). Pursuant to this mandate, the EEOC issued regulations further elaborating on the definition of disability, generally, and the "substantially limits" standard, specifically. With respect to the latter, the EEOC's regulations state that the term "substantially limits" shall be construed "broadly in favor of expansive coverage, to the maximum extent permitted by the terms of the ADA." Furthermore, "substantially limits" is not meant to be a "demanding standard." 29 C.F.R. § 1630.2(j)(1)(i). More specifically, the regulations state:

> (ii) An impairment is a disability within the meaning of this section if it substantially limits the ability of an individual to perform a major life activity as compared to most people in the general population. An impairment need not prevent, or significantly or severely restrict, the individual from performing a major life activity in order to be considered substantially limiting. Nonetheless, not every impairment will constitute a disability within the meaning of this section.

> (iii) The primary object of attention in cases brought under the ADA should be whether covered entities have complied with their obligations and whether discrimination has occurred, not whether an individual's impairment substantially limits a major life activity. Accordingly, the threshold issue of whether an impairment "substantially limits" a major life activity should not demand extensive analysis.

The Amendments also make clear that if an impairment substantially limits one major life activity, it "need not limit other major life activities in order to be considered a disability." 42 U.S.C. § 12102(4)(C). Finally, the Amendments state that an "impairment that is episodic or in remission is a disability if it would substantially limit a major life activity when active." 42 U.S.C. § 12102(4)(D).

---

must justify the standard as being job related and consistent with business necessity. 42 U.S.C. § 12113(c).

Major Life Activities

Under the original ADA, the term "major life activities" was only defined in the regulations, and not the statute itself. Thus, there was a great deal of litigation over whether an activity counted as a "major life activity." In the Amendments, Congress provided a non-exhaustive list of major life activities, including several that were not listed in the EEOC's prior definition (additions in the Amendments are in *italics*): "caring for oneself, performing manual tasks, seeing, hearing, *eating, sleeping, walking, standing, lifting, bending,* speaking, breathing, learning, *reading, concentrating, thinking, communicating,* and working." 42 U.S.C. § 12102(2)(A).

Significantly, Congress also defined "major life activity" to include "the operation of a major bodily function, including, but not limited to, functions of the immune system, normal cell growth, digestive, bowel, bladder, neurological, brain, respiratory, circulatory, endocrine, and reproductive functions." 42 U.S.C. § 12102(2)(B).

The next section provides two representative cases where courts have had to grapple with some of the new interpretive provisions in the ADAAA.

b. Post-ADAAA Cases

FELDMAN V. LAW ENFORCEMENT ASSOCIATES CORP.
779 F.Supp.2d 472 (E.D.N.C. 2011)

W. EARL BRITT, SENIOR DISTRICT JUDGE.

This matter is before the court on . . . motion to dismiss filed by defendants Law Enforcement Associates Corporation ("LEA"), Anthony Rand ("Rand"), James J. Lindsay ("Lindsay"), Joseph A. Jordan ("Jordan") and Paul Briggs ("Briggs"), and . . . John H. Carrington ("Carrington"). . . .

I. FACTUAL AND PROCEDURAL HISTORY

LEA . . . is a manufacturer of security and surveillance equipment used by local, state, federal and international law enforcement agencies and by public and private companies. . . . Plaintiffs Paul H. Feldman ("Feldman") and Martin L. Perry ("Perry") were employees of LEA. Feldman was LEA's President for almost twenty years. Perry was employed by LEA for nine years and was LEA's Director of Sales for three years. From approximately 2003 until 3 December 2009, Feldman and Perry were also directors of the corporation. The other three members of LEA's Board of Directors ("Board") during the time period relevant to this case were defendants Rand, Lindsay and Jordan.

[Eds. Note: The lengthy statement of facts has been substantially redacted to include only the facts relevant to the plaintiffs' ADA claims.]

* * *

In or around late August 2009, both Feldman and Perry suffered from separate medical conditions that required brief hospitalizations and forced them out of work for a period of time. Plaintiffs allege that their medical conditions substantially limited their ability to work, and, as a result, they both sought reasonable accommodations for their disabilities. Plaintiffs further allege that their requests were disregarded and that they were discharged from their employment. Feldman's employment was terminated on 27 August 2009, and Perry's employment was allegedly terminated on 23 September 2009.

* * *

Plaintiffs initially filed separate complaints, but they subsequently filed a consolidated complaint on 16 April 2010. Plaintiffs filed a first amended complaint on 7 June 2010 and raise the following claims: (1) claims under the Americans with Disabilities Act (Feldman and Perry against LEA) . . . . Defendants filed the instant motions to dismiss on 21 June 2010.

II. DISCUSSION

A motion to dismiss pursuant to Federal Rule of Civil Procedure 12(b)(6) "tests the sufficiency of a complaint" but "does not resolve contests surrounding the facts, the merits of a claim, or the applicability of defenses." *Republican Party v. Martin,* 980 F.2d 943, 952 (4th Cir.1992). In order to survive a Rule 12(b)(6) motion to dismiss, the complaint must contain "sufficient factual matter, accepted as true, to 'state a claim to relief that is plausible on its face.'" *Ashcroft v. Iqbal,* 556 U.S. 662, 129 S.Ct. 1937, 1949 (2009). . . .

A. *Americans with Disabilities Act Claims*

Both plaintiffs assert claims against LEA for violations of the Americans with Disabilities Act ("ADA"), 42 U.S.C. § 12101 *et seq.* The ADA prohibits discrimination "against a qualified individual on the basis of disability in regard to . . . terms, conditions, and privileges of employment." 42 U.S.C. § 12112(a) (2011). Here, each plaintiff brings two separate claims under the ADA: (1) a claim for wrongful discharge and (2) a claim for failure to accommodate.

In a wrongful discharge case under the ADA, a plaintiff establishes a *prima facie* case by demonstrating that "(1) he is within the ADA's protected class; (2) he was discharged; (3) at the time of his discharge, he was performing the job at a level that met his employer's legitimate expectations; and (4) his discharge occurred under circumstances that raise a reasonable inference of unlawful discrimination." *Haulbrook v. Michelin N. Am., Inc.,* 252 F.3d 696, 702 (4th Cir.2001).

In a failure to accommodate case, a plaintiff establishes a *prima facie* case by showing (1) that he was an individual who had a disability within the meaning of the statute; (2) that the employer had notice of his disability;

(3) that with reasonable accommodation he could perform the essential functions of the position; and (4) that the employer refused to make such accommodations. *Haneke v. Mid-Atlantic Capital Mgmt.*, 131 Fed.Appx. 399, 400 (4th Cir.2005).

Here, Perry alleges that he had a neurological episode in 1990 that was diagnosed as Multiple Sclerosis ("MS"). At that time, his symptoms included vertigo, slurred speech and double vision. These symptoms gradually resolved over the course of several months. In 2004, while employed by LEA, Perry suffered a second MS episode that temporarily caused complete left-side paralysis and permanently caused weakness on his left side. Perry's MS episode in 2004 caused him to miss time from work at LEA, and LEA knew that MS had caused Perry's absence.

On 27 August 2009, the day of Feldman's discharge from LEA, Perry suffered from a stress-induced "flare up" of symptoms related to his MS. This exacerbation of Perry's MS symptoms caused him to be hospitalized for several days. On three occasions after his MS flare up, requests for medical leave were made to LEA on Perry's behalf. Despite these requests, on 23 September 2009, "LEA terminated Perry's employment as Director of Sales, falsely claiming that Perry had 'abandoned' his job."

With respect to Feldman's ADA claims, he alleges that he suffered from a Transient Ischemic Attack ("TIA"), also known as a "mini-stroke" or "warning stroke," on 26 August 2009. As a result of the TIA, Feldman was hospitalized for two days and required "an additional several weeks" to recover before he was able to work again. While hospitalized for this medical condition, Feldman made a request through his attorney, asking that Rand, Lindsay and Jordan reschedule a Board meeting that had been previously scheduled for 27 August 2009. Rand, acting for the Board and LEA, refused to reschedule the Board meeting. Rand, Lindsay and Jordan, acting on behalf of LEA, subsequently terminated Feldman's employment during the 27 August 2009 Board meeting.

1.   *Whether Plaintiffs are Disabled Under the Recently Amended ADA*

Plaintiffs' ADA claims for wrongful discharge and for failure to make a reasonable accommodation both require a showing that plaintiffs were "disabled" within the meaning of the ADA. *Rhoads*, 257 F.3d at 387. LEA contends that plaintiffs have failed to make the required showing because their impairments were temporary and not severe. "The question of whether a plaintiff is disabled under the ADA, 'and therefore can bring a claim under the statute, is a question of law for the court, not a question of fact for the jury.'" *Rose v. Home Depot USA, Inc.*, 186 F.Supp.2d 595, 608 (D.Md.2002).

The ADA defines "disability" with respect to an individual as "(A) a physical or mental impairment that substantially limits one or more major life activities of such individual; (B) a record of such an impairment; or (C) being regarded as having such an impairment. . . ." 42 U.S.C. § 12102(1) (2011). Here, there is no dispute that plaintiffs are proceeding under the first prong of the disability definition.

In 2002, the United States Supreme Court held that an impairment rises to the level of a disability only if its impact is "permanent or long term." *Toyota Motor Mfg., Ky., Inc. v. Williams,* 534 U.S. 184, 198, 122 S.Ct. 681, 151 L.Ed.2d 615 (2002). Accordingly, under Fourth Circuit precedent, temporary, non-chronic impairments have generally not constituted disabilities. *See, e.g., Pollard v. High's of Baltimore, Inc.,* 281 F.3d 462, 468–69 (4th Cir.2002) (recuperation from back surgery was a temporary impairment that did not qualify as a substantially limiting disability under the ADA). While the presumption existed that temporary impairments did not qualify as disabilities under the ADA, the Fourth Circuit determined that temporary impairments required a case-by-case evaluation. *Id.* at 468. A temporary impairment could be so severe or have a duration so long that to classify it as "temporary" would be improper. *Id.* at 469.

However, subsequent to the decision of the United States Supreme Court in *Toyota Motor,* Congress passed the Americans with Disabilities Act Amendments Act of 2008 ("ADAAA"), which became effective on 1 January 2009. In the ADAAA, Congress rejected the unduly restrictive approach established in *Toyota Motor* for analyzing whether a plaintiff suffers from a disability for purposes of the ADA. *Id.,* § 2(b)(5). As a result, Congress mandated in the ADAAA that the definition of disability is to be construed "in favor of broad coverage of individuals . . . to the maximum extent permitted" by the law. 42 U.S.C. § 12102(4)(A).

Although the ADAAA left the ADA's three-category definition of "disability" intact, significant changes were made regarding how these categories are to be interpreted. For example, with respect to the definition of actual disability found in 42 U.S.C. § 12102(1)(A), the ADAAA expanded the list of "major life activities." As a result, examples of "major life activities" now include "caring for oneself, performing manual tasks, seeing, hearing, eating, sleeping, walking, standing, lifting, bending, speaking, breathing, learning, reading, concentrating, thinking, communicating, and working." 42 U.S.C. § 12102(2)(A). In addition, Congress instructed that the term "substantially limits," which is also found in 42 U.S.C. § 12102(1)(A), "shall be interpreted consistently with the findings and purposes of the [ADAAA]." 42 U.S.C. § 12102(4)(B).

Noting that the courts had "created an inappropriately high level of limitation necessary to obtain coverage under the ADA," the ADAAA states that "it is the intent of Congress that the primary object of attention in cases brought under the ADA should be whether entities covered under the ADA have complied with their obligations. . . ." § 2(b)(5). As a result, "the question of whether an individual's impairment is a disability under the ADA should not demand extensive analysis." *Id.*

As previously mentioned, the ADAAA went into effect on 1 January 2009. The Fourth Circuit Court of Appeals and most other courts have held that the ADAAA does not apply retroactively. As a result, there is now a lack of case law relating to the interpretation of the ADAAA. However, since the alleged discriminatory action in this case occurred during August and September 2009, there is no dispute that the ADAAA applies to plaintiffs' claims.[3]

LEA argues that even under the ADAAA, plaintiffs have failed to allege sufficient facts to show that they each had a disability. The court disagrees. Drawing all inferences in plaintiffs' favor, it is certainly plausible under the ADAAA that both plaintiffs had a physical impairment that constitutes a disability. With respect to Perry, such a conclusion is consistent with the language of the ADAAA. Perry alleges that he suffered an episodic MS flare up on 27 August 2009. Here, the ADAAA clearly provides that "[a]n impairment that is episodic or in remission is a disability if it would substantially limit a major life activity when active." 42 U.S.C. § 12102(4)(D). Thus, the ADAAA "make[s] it easier for a plaintiff with an episodic condition ... to establish that he is an 'individual with a disability.'" *Carmona v. Southwest Airlines Co.*, 604 F.3d 848, 855 (5th Cir.2010). Because none of the parties appear to dispute that MS, when active, constitutes a disability, this court finds that Perry has sufficiently stated a claim that he was disabled under the ADAAA. *Cf. Hoffman v. Carefirst of Fort Wayne, Inc.*, 737 F.Supp.2d 976, 985–86 (N.D.Ind.2010) (finding that the clear wording of 42 U.S.C. § 12102(4)(D) rendered plaintiff's renal cancer, which was in remission, a disability under the ADAAA).

Furthermore, the Equal Employment Opportunity Commission ("EEOC") has issued a Notice of Proposed Rulemaking to implement the ADAAA. *See* Proposed Rules, Regulations To Implement the Equal Employment Provisions of the Americans with Disabilities Act, As Amended, 74 Fed. Reg. 48431 (Sept. 23, 2009) (to be codified at 29 C.F.R. Part 1630). The proposed regulations provide examples of impairments that will consistently meet the definition of a disability. In discussing this concept, the EEOC explains:

> Interpreting the definition of disability broadly and without extensive analysis as required under the [ADAAA], some types of impairments will consistently meet the definition of disability. Because of certain characteristics associated with these impairments, the individualized assessment of the limitations on

---

[3] LEA contends that it has cited ADAAA case law to supports its arguments. However, all of the cases cited by LEA, even those cases decided after the effective date of the ADAAA, involved alleged discrimination that took place before the ADAAA went into effect. Because the ADAAA has been found not to apply retroactively to pre-amendment conduct, pre-ADAAA case law was applied in these actions. As a result, the cases cited by LEA carry little, if any, precedential weight with respect to the issue of whether the plaintiffs in this case were disabled under the ADAAA.

a person can be conducted quickly and easily, and will consistently result in a determination that the person is substantially limited in a major life activity.

Id. at 48441 (to be codified at 29 C.F.R. § 1630.2(j)(5)(i)). The proposed regulations then list MS as an impairment that will consistently meet the definition of disability. *Id.* (to be codified at 29 C.F.R. § 1630.2(j)(5)(i)(G) (MS "substantially limit[s] major life activities including neurological functions, walking, performing manual tasks, seeing, speaking, or thinking")). Thus, the court's conclusion that Perry has sufficiently alleged a disability is bolstered by the interpretative guidance of the EEOC.

LEA also contends that Perry did not have a disability because he was able to engage in many activities in spite of his alleged impairment, such as leaving the house, going to doctor appointments, and contacting a lawyer. It may not even be necessary to consider this argument given that the court has already found that Perry's episodic impairment falls within the clear language of 42 U.S.C. § 12102(4)(D). In any event, the language of the ADAAA also addresses this issue. It provides that "[a]n impairment that substantially limits one major life activity need not limit other major life activities in order to be considered a disability." 42 U.S.C. § 12102(4)(C). Here, the complaint alleges that Perry's impairment was so severe that he was unable to work for period of time. "Working" is considered to be a major life activity under the ADAAA. 42 U.S.C. § 12102(2)(A). Thus, the complaint sufficiently alleges that Perry's impairment "substantially limit[ed] a major life activity." 42 U.S.C. § 12102(1)(A).

The court will now consider whether Feldman has sufficiently alleged a disability for the purposes of his ADA claims. Feldman states that he suffered from a TIA, also known as a "mini-stroke" or "warning stroke," on 26 August 2009. As a result of the TIA, Feldman was hospitalized for two days and required "an additional several weeks" to recover before he was able to work again. As conceded in plaintiffs' complaint, the symptoms of a TIA "last a relatively short time." Unlike Perry's MS, Feldman's impairment is non-chronic, and there is no allegation that the residual effects of the TIA were permanent. Feldman admits that it may have been "a close question" as to whether he was disabled under pre-ADAAA law. However, he contends that under the ADAAA, his status as an individual with a disability is "beyond question."

The ADAAA does not explicitly overturn the finding in *Toyota Motor* that temporary disabilities do not qualify for ADA protection. *See Munoz v. Echosphere, L.L.C.*, No. 09–CV–0308–KC, 2010 WL 2838356, at *12 (W.D.Tex. July 15, 2010). However, as previously noted, the ADAAA states that the definition of disability is to be construed "in favor of broad coverage of individuals . . . to the maximum extent permitted" by the law. 42 U.S.C. § 12102(4)(A). Accordingly, even if Feldman's TIA "only temporarily limited [his] ability to work, the stringent requirements of *Toyota Motor* may be rejected by the amended statute in favor of a more inclusive standard." *Munoz,* 2010 WL 2838356, at *12.

In addition, the proposed EEOC regulations address this issue. "Temporary, non-chronic impairments of short duration with little or no residual effects (such as the common cold, seasonal or common influenza, a sprained joint, minor and non-chronic gastrointestinal disorders, or a broken bone that is expected to heal completely) usually will not substantially limit a major life activity." 74 Fed. Reg. at 48443 (to be codified at 29 C.F.R. § 1630.2(j)(8)). Here, while the duration of Feldman's impairment may have been relatively short, the effects of the impairment were significant. The amended complaint demonstrates the severity of Feldman's impairment. Feldman alleges that a TIA "produces stroke-like symptoms[,]" and that a TIA occurs when "a blood clot temporarily clogs an artery, and part of the brain does not get the blood it needs." He also alleges that while he suffered the effects of the TIA, he was substantially limited in his ability to perform "multiple major life activities." As a result, the court finds that a TIA is not comparable to a common cold, a sprained joint, or any of the other examples listed in the proposed EEOC regulations. Thus, at this early stage of the proceedings, the court is unwilling to say that Feldman has failed to sufficiently allege that he had a disability. The court concludes that both Perry and Feldman have alleged sufficient facts to show that they suffered from a disability under the ADA.

* * *

III. CONCLUSION

Based on the foregoing reasons, the motion to dismiss filed by LEA, Rand, Lindsay, Jordan and Briggs is . . . DENIED IN PART. . . . The claims remaining in this case are (1) both plaintiffs' ADA claims for wrongful discharge and failure to accommodate . . . .

NOTES AND QUESTIONS

1.   *Impairments that are episodic or in remission.* The court in *Feldman* does a good job of explaining and following the provision in the ADAAA regarding impairments that are episodic or in remission. That provision states that: "an impairment that is episodic or in remission is a disability if it would substantially limit a major life activity when active." 42 U.S.C. § 12102(4)(D). Thus, because plaintiff Perry had a flare-up related to his multiple sclerosis (MS), and because the court assumed that his MS would be a disability when active (during the flare-up), it is still considered a disability even when it's not active.

The other common use of this provision is cancer that has gone into remission. Several courts have held that cancer that is in remission can still be considered a disability. *See, e.g.,* Oehmke v. Medtronic, Inc., 844 F.3d 748 (8th Cir. 2016) (holding that cancer in remission is a disability); Norton v. Assisted Living Concepts, Inc., 786 F.Supp.2d 1173, 1185 (E.D. Tex. 2011) (holding that renal cancer even when in remission is a disability because, when active, it substantially limited normal cell growth); Hoffman v. Carefirst of Fort Wayne, Inc., 737 F.Supp.2d 976, 985–86 (N.D. Ind. 2010) (finding that the clear wording of 42 U.S.C. § 12102(4)(D) rendered plaintiff's renal cancer, which was in remission, a disability under the ADAAA). Do you understand why Congress included this provision? In other words, why should an individual be considered disabled under the ADA if the individual is not currently (at the time of the adverse action) experiencing a substantial limitation of a major life activity? Although it's certainly possible to imagine a scenario where an employer has discriminated against employees because of cancer in remission or the relapsing-remitting form of MS, such employees should be able to succeed even if they were not considered actually disabled. They should be able to succeed under the regarded as prong of disability, which will be discussed, *infra*. But one benefit to an actual disability claim (as opposed to a regarded as claim) is that employees pursuing a claim under the actual disability prong of the definition of disability are entitled to seek reasonable accommodations for their disabilities. Does someone whose cancer is in remission *need* an accommodation?

2.   *Short-term impairments.* In *Feldman*, the court also discussed the post-ADAAA law regarding short-term impairments. Contrary to the language in *Toyota* that impairments must be permanent or long-term to qualify as disabilities, the Amendments contain no such qualification, at least with respect to the actual disability prong of the definition. As will be discussed below, there is an exception for coverage under the "regarded as" prong for impairments that are "transitory and minor." 42 U.S.C. § 12102(3)(B). The EEOC has issued regulations that make clear that this transitory and minor exception only applies to the "regarded as" prong, and not the actual disability prong of the definition. 29 C.F.R. § 1630.2(j)(1)(ix)–(j)(2). Accordingly, the court in *Feldman* held that plaintiff Feldman's transient ischemic attack (mini-stroke) that caused a brief hospitalization followed by a few weeks of leave could be a disability under the amended ADA. Other courts agree that short-term impairments can be disabilities if sufficiently severe. *See, e.g.,* Summers v. Altarum Institute, Corp. 740 F.3d 325, 333 (4th Cir. 2014) (holding that impairments that are temporary, such as the plaintiff's broken legs, are not excluded from the ADA's coverage).

3.   *Major bodily functions.* The court in *Feldman* says that the parties agreed that plaintiff Perry's MS would be a disability when active. Is it clear to you why that is? The facts indicate that Perry had a "flare-up" related to his MS and that this flare-up caused him to be hospitalized for a few days. That certainly sounds serious but the court does not specify which of Perry's major life activities were substantially limited. The most straightforward way to prove that MS is a disability when active is to use the addition in the Amendments of "major bodily functions" as major life activities. As stated earlier, the amended ADA defines "major life activities" to include "the operation of a major bodily function, including but not limited to, functions of the immune system, normal cell growth, digestive, bowel, bladder, neurological, brain, respiratory, circulatory, endocrine, and reproductive

functions." 42 U.S.C. § 12102(2)(B). MS affects a person's neurological function. It is an auto-immune disease where the person's immune system attacks the myelin sheath surrounding nerves in the central nervous system, creating lesions on the brain. These lesions interrupt signals between the brain and other parts of the body, causing neurological flare-ups, which can be numbness, weakness, paralysis, blindness, and other symptoms. *See* https:// www.nationalmssociety.org/What-is-MS/Definition-of-MS. Accordingly, even if Perry's flare-up had been relatively mild, it would still have substantially limited his neurological function.

This "major bodily functions" provision is significant because it means that an impairment can be considered a disability even when it does not have an effect that is visible to others. Prior to the Amendments, it was difficult for plaintiffs to establish that diseases such as cancer, diabetes, hypertension, and many others were disabilities because they did not necessarily cause a substantial limitation on a major life activity, when that phrase was defined to only include activities such as walking, seeing, hearing, breathing, etc. In other words, before the ADAAA, only external manifestations of impairments would allow the condition to be considered a disability. But after the ADAAA, even if an impairment has no external manifestation, it can still be considered a disability if the impairment causes a substantial limitation on some internal bodily function. The list of major bodily functions tracks the impairments (mostly diseases) that courts had previously determined were not disabilities under the pre-Amendments ADA. Thus, cancer affects normal cell growth; HIV affects the immune system; multiple sclerosis affects neurological functions, etc.

4. *The ADAAA is not retroactive.* In footnote 3 of the opinion, the court notes that many of the cases cited by the defendant, *even cases decided after the ADAAA went into effect*, do not have precedential value for the case at hand. That is because the ADAAA does not apply retroactively. Accordingly, even if a case is decided *after* the Amendments went into effect, the court would still have to apply the pre-Amendments law if the facts of the case occurred *before* January 1, 2009, the date the ADAAA went into effect. Unfortunately, this distinction is often lost on litigants and courts. *See* Robert Iafolla, *6th Circuit Weighs Broader Disability Definition of ADA Amendments,* BLOOMBERG LAW DAILY LABOR REPORT (Jan. 28, 2020) (discussing a case where the court relied on cases applying pre-ADAAA rules).

5. *Pregnancy and "lifting" as a major life activity.* In addition to the "major bodily functions" provision, the Amendments also expanded the list of "major life activities." As one example of this expansion, prior to the Amendments, most courts held that lifting was not a major life activity, but it is now listed as a major life activity in the statute. Although there are many individuals with back, hip, or knee injuries that might be able to claim a substantial limitation on the major life activity of lifting, one unique context where the addition of lifting has had a significant effect is on women who have lifting restrictions because they are pregnant. Prior to the Amendments, most courts held that pregnancy was not a disability. But with the addition of

"lifting" to the list of major life activities, more courts have held that pregnancy can be a disability. *See, e.g.,* Heatherly v. Portillo's Hot Dogs, Inc., 958 F.Supp.2d 913, 920–21 (N.D. Ill. 2013) (plaintiff's pregnancy constitutes a disability given her inability to lift heavy objects); Bray v. Town of Wake Forest, 2015 WL 1534515, at *11 (E.D.N.C. April 6, 2015) (plaintiff had enough evidence to establish that her pregnancy was a disability when she had three doctors' notes advising her to not lift more than 20 pounds, in addition to other restrictions); Colas v. City of University of New York, 2019 WL 2028701, at *4 (E.D.N.Y. May 7, 2019) (sufficient evidence to demonstrate that plaintiff's pregnancy-related complications substantially limited her ability to lift). *See also* Nicole Buonocore Porter, *Accommodating Pregnancy Five Years After Young v. UPS: Where We Are & Where We Should Go,* __ St. Louis U. J. Health L. & Pol'y __ (forthcoming 2021) (exploring pregnancy as a disability after the ADAAA).

6. *A sample of mitigating measures cases.* As discussed earlier, one of Congress's goals in amending the ADA was to overturn the *Sutton* Court's rule that the disability inquiry should be made considering the ameliorative effects of mitigating measures. The ADAAA now states that "determination of whether an impairment substantially limits a major life activity shall be made without regard to the ameliorative effects of mitigating measures." 42 U.S.C. § 12102(4)(E)(i). Since the Amendments went into effect, there have been several cases decided where the rule regarding mitigating measures made a difference in the result. For instance, courts have found the following impairments to be disabilities:

- **Gluten sensitivity managed by avoiding eating gluten.** J.D. by Doherty v. Colonial Williamsburg Foundation, 925 F.3d 663, 670–71 (4th Cir. 2019).

- **Thyroid disorder partially controlled with medication.** Barlia v. MWI Veterinary Supply, Inc., 721 F. App'x 439, 446–47 (6th Cir. 2018).

- **Chronic high blood pressure lowered by medication.** Gogos v. AMS Mechanical Systems, Inc., 737 F.3d 1170, 1173 (7th Cir. 2013).

Alston v. Park Pleasant, Inc.
679 Fed. Appx. 169 (3d Cir. 2017)

Restrepo, Circuit Judge.

Joanie Alston appeals the District Court's grant of summary judgment to Park Pleasant, Inc., her former employer, in her suit for employment discrimination under the Americans with Disabilities Act ("ADA") and the Pennsylvania Human Relations Act. . . . We will affirm.

I

As we write solely for the benefit of the parties, we set out only the facts necessary for the discussion that follows. In August 2011, Alston was hired by Park Pleasant, Inc., to be the Director of Nursing at its eponymously-named adult care facility. Initially, Alston's supervisor was Nancy Kleinberg, with whom Alston had personal rapport and from whom Alston received positive work reviews. In February 2012, Kleinberg was promoted, and her role as Alston's supervisor was filled by Carmella Kane. Kane and Alston clashed almost immediately, and repeatedly, although the parties dispute the extent and underlying causes of the conflict. Alston discussed with both Kane and Kleinberg that she was unhappy with her role after Kleinberg's promotion.

On June 21, 2012, Alston, Kleinberg, Kane, and HR director Sonjii West had a meeting in which Kane explained to Alston that Alston's performance was not meeting expectations, and the group laid out an improvement plan for Alston. Five days after that meeting, Alston missed work to have a biopsy, an absence for which she gave advance notice. On July 12, she was diagnosed with early-stage DCIS, a type of breast cancer.

Alston's relationship with her supervisors at Park Pleasant continued to deteriorate. By late July, Kleinberg and Kane instituted weekly meetings at which Alston's duties and performance were discussed and memorialized. Park Pleasant terminated Alston in early August of 2012.

* * *

In her initial complaint against Park Pleasant, Alston alleged discrimination on the bases of age, race, color, and disability. . . .

The District Court granted Park Pleasant summary judgment on all of Alston's claims . . . . Alston has appealed only the District Court's grant of summary judgment as to her claim of discrimination on the basis of disability . . . .

II

In assessing a claim of employment discrimination under the ADA, courts employ the *McDonnell Douglas* burden-shifting framework. *Walton v. Mental Health Ass'n of Se. Pa.*, 168 F.3d 661, 667–68 (3d Cir. 1999). To overcome a motion for summary judgment, a plaintiff alleging employment discrimination under the ADA must make a prima facie case with three elements. A plaintiff must demonstrate "(1) he is a disabled person within the meaning of the ADA; (2) he is otherwise qualified to perform the essential functions of the job, with or without reasonable accommodations by the employer; and (3) he has suffered an otherwise adverse employment decision as a result of discrimination." *Gaul v. Lucent Technologies, Inc.*, 134 F.3d 576, 580 (3d Cir. 1998). . . .

The District Court granted summary judgment to Park Pleasant, finding that Alston failed to prove that she had a disability. The parties do not dispute that Alston was diagnosed with DCIS, a form of breast cancer. At issue is whether Alston produced enough evidence to create a genuine issue of material fact as to whether her DCIS qualified as a disability under the ADA.

Under the ADA, "disability" is defined as "(A) a physical or mental impairment that substantially limits one or more of the major life activities of [an] individual; (B) a record of such an impairment; or (C) being regarded as having such an impairment." 42 U.S.C. § 12102(1). "For purposes of [defining disability under § 12102(1)], a major life activity . . . includes the operation of a major bodily function, including but not limited to, functions of the immune system [and] normal cell growth. . . ." 42 U.S.C. § 12102(2)(B).

Those definitions incorporate amendments to the ADA enacted in 2009 as part of the ADA Amendments Act ("ADAAA"). The ADAAA broadened the scope of ADA coverage by expanding the definition of disability to include a range of symptoms—such as reduced immune functioning or abnormal cell growth—characteristic of cancer and other diseases. Regulations implementing the ADAAA reflect that intention, as well. 29 C.F.R. § 1630.2(j)(3)(iii) ("[A]pplying the principles set forth in [ ] this section, it should easily be concluded that . . . cancer substantially limits normal cell growth."). In subsequent decisions addressing cancer as a qualifying disability, courts have interpreted the updated statute and regulations in accord with the intent behind the ADAAA. *Compare EEOC v. R.J. Gallagher Co.*, 181 F.3d 645, 653–54 (5th Cir. 1999) (declining to hold cancer to be an ADA-qualifying disability prior to ADAAA), *with Oehmke v. Medtronic, Inc.*, 844 F.3d 748, 756 (8th Cir. 2016) (agreeing, after the ADAAA, that cancer is an impairment qualifying as a disability because "the functioning of one's immune system is a major life activity").

We agree that cancer can—and generally will—be a qualifying disability under the ADA. Nevertheless, "[t]he determination of whether an impairment substantially limits a major life activity requires an individualized assessment." 29 C.F.R. § 1630.2(j)(1)(iv). Although the ADAAA makes the individualized assessment "particularly simple and straightforward" for diseases like cancer, 29 C.F.R. § 1630.2(j)(3)(ii), an individualized assessment must still take place. To undertake that individualized assessment, courts have required some evidence of the plaintiff's substantial limitation—even when the limitation seems self-evident in context. *Albertson's, Inc. v. Kirkingburg*, 527 U.S. 555, 566, 119 S.Ct. 2162 (1999) (holding that although vision-impaired individuals may not have "an onerous burden" in demonstrating disability and "ordinarily will meet the [ADA]'s definition of disability," they must still offer evidence of "limitation in terms of their own experience").

Here, Alston has never claimed at any stage of this litigation that her DCIS limited any substantial life activity, including immune system function or normal cell growth. In her initial complaint, Alston's sole reference to her disability was to note that "[t]he termination decision occurred within weeks after Alston had been diagnosed with breast cancer and had taken leave to undergo a diagnostic medical procedure," and that "[a]fter Park Pleasant became aware of Alston's serious health issues, the criticisms of her ratcheted up." There was no reference anywhere in the complaint to limitations of any kind.

At her deposition, Alston averred that she was not substantially limited in any major life activity, including her work, her ability to drive, or her ability to take care of herself or her household. At oral argument before the District Court, her counsel stated that Alston "has not claimed that she had any limitations in her activities." Even in her "motion to amend findings of fact and judgment or, in the alternative, motion for reconsideration," Alston did not reference abnormal cell growth, reduced immune function, or any other substantial limits on a major life activity to make out the qualifying disability element of a prima facie case. Instead, she simply stated that "an individual who has been diagnosed with cancer which is in remission qualifies as an individual with a disability." Because she has not offered evidence as to any limits on any major life activity, Alston has failed to make out an element of her prima facie case, and so her discrimination claim fails.

IV

For the foregoing reasons, we will affirm the District Court's grant of summary judgment to Park Pleasant . . . .

NOTES AND QUESTIONS

1. *Disclaiming disability.* The court in *Alston* recognizes that cancer should ordinarily be considered a disability, based on the EEOC regulations that list several impairments that should easily be determined a disability. *See* 29 C.F.R. § 1630.2(j)(3)(iii) (referring to cancer as one impairment that should easily be considered a disability because it substantially limits normal cell growth, which is a major bodily function that constitutes a major life activity in the statute). Nevertheless, the court held that the plaintiff was not disabled because she did not specifically allege that she was substantially limited in a major life activity, and in her deposition, she "averred that she was not substantially limited in any major life activity, including her work, her ability to drive, or her ability to take care of herself or her household." And yet, it does not appear that there is any evidence that the plaintiff's cancer was affecting her differently than how cancer normally operates. In other words, if cancer should ordinarily be considered a disability because it substantially limits normal cell growth, was the plaintiff's only mistake in not pleading that her cancer substantially limited normal cell growth? Or would the plaintiff still have lost because she stated in her deposition that she was not limited in any

major life activities? Should a plaintiff's denial of the significance of her impairment be used against her? Why or why not?

2.   *Failure to use ADAAA's most helpful provisions.* If the plaintiff lost in *Alston* simply because she failed to argue that her cancer substantially limited her normal cell growth, why did her lawyer fail to make this argument? As it turns out, plaintiffs and their lawyers often fail to take advantage of the most straightforward way to prove that their impairments are disabilities. For most diseases, the most straightforward way of arguing that they constitute disabilities is the major bodily functions provision. And yet, in Professor Porter's article exploring all of the cases where plaintiffs lost on the disability issue from 2014 to 2018 (the second five-year period after the ADAAA went into effect), she noted that plaintiffs failed to use the major bodily functions provision in 34 of the 210 cases she identified as incorrectly decided. *See* Nicole Buonocore Porter, *Explaining "Not Disabled" Cases Ten Years After the ADAAA: A Story of Ignorance, Incompetence, and Possibly Animus*, 26 GEO. J. POVERTY L. & POL'Y 383, 392, 401–02 (2019) (hereinafter "Porter, *Not Disabled*") (citing to cases involving impairments such as diabetes (endocrine system), stroke (brain function), hypertension (circulatory function), mental illnesses (brain function)).

3.   *Need for medical evidence.* In *Alston*, the court criticized the plaintiff for failing to allege or argue that she was substantially limited in the major bodily function of normal cell growth. However, can a plaintiff (assuming that the plaintiff is not a doctor) testify about what is occurring inside her body? Some courts have said no to this and there is a debate about whether medical evidence is required to prove a disability. *Compare* Tesone v. Empire Marketing Strategies, 942 F.3d 979, 998–99 (10th Cir. 2019) (holding that the district court erred in requiring plaintiff to present medical expert testimony to establish that her back injury was a disability because a back injury is something a jury can understand without the necessity of expert testimony), *and* Mancini v. City of Providence by and through Lombardi, 909 F.3d 32, 39, 41–42 (1st Cir. 2018) (stating that whether medical evidence is necessary to support a disability claim must be made on a case by case basis and that obvious impairments like a knee injury or a missing limb should not require medical evidence; thus, plaintiff's knee injury did not require medical evidence), *with* Homes v. Alive Hospice, Inc., 2015 WL 459330, at *4 (M.D. Tenn. Feb. 3, 2015) (holding that because plaintiff did not present medical evidence that she actually had been diagnosed with MS or how her alleged MS limited any major life activities, her disability claim failed). *See also* 29 C.F.R. § 1630.2(j)(1)(v) ("The comparison of an individual's performance of a major life activity to the performance of the same major life activity by most people in the general population usually will not require scientific, medical, or statistical evidence.").

In one case, the plaintiff was apparently caught in a catch-22 when trying to prove that her impairment (rheumatoid arthritis) substantially limited her major bodily functions. In *Scavetta v. Dillon Companies, Inc.*, 569 F. App'x 622 (10th Cir. 2014), the plaintiff argued that her rheumatoid arthritis (RA) substantially limited two major bodily functions, immune and musculoskeletal functions. At trial, plaintiff's doctor described RA as an auto-immune disorder and explained how the disease attacks the joints, causing pain, stiffness, swelling and fatigue. Denying the plaintiff's request to include a jury instruction on the major bodily functions provision, the trial court stated that the doctor's testimony focused on the general progression of the disease and not specifically on the plaintiff's condition; however, there was no indication that the plaintiff's RA did not comport with the usual progression of the disease. The court then noted that the plaintiff's testimony could not be used to support a jury instruction on the major bodily functions provision because it only focused on her daily activities and not how her disease affected her major bodily functions. *Id.* at 623–26. What the court seemed to miss is that the plaintiff (who was not a doctor) would not have been qualified to testify as to how her RA affected her immune or musculoskeletal systems. Given the EEOC's regulation (quoted above) that medical evidence should not ordinarily be required, should courts insist on medical evidence to establish that diseases such as MS, cancer, or diabetes are disabilities? Why or why not?

4.   *Continued consideration of mitigating measures.* Despite the Amendments specifically overturning the *Sutton* Court's holding that impairments should be viewed considering mitigating measures, some courts continue to get this wrong. In Professor Porter's survey of the 2014–2018 cases, she identified eight cases where courts erroneously considered the plaintiff's mitigating measures when determining disability. Porter, *Not Disabled, supra,* at 404–05; *see, e.g.,* Weaving v. City of Hillsboro, 763 F.3d 1106, 1112 (9th Cir. 2014) (holding plaintiff's ADHD was not a disability, and specifically mentioning that Weaving had "developed compensatory mechanisms that helped him overcome ADHD's impediments"); DeBacker v. City of Moline, 78 F.Supp.3d 916, 924 (C.D. Ill. 2015) (holding that plaintiff's depression was not a disability because his medication ameliorated the effects of the depression); Wilson v. Dollar General Corp., 122 F.Supp.3d 460, 465 (W.D. Va. 2015) (holding that plaintiff's monocular vision is not a disability because his brain compensated for his limitation).

5.   *Continued debates.* Despite the fact that the Amendments have been instrumental in many more impairments being found disabilities, debate remains about a couple of impairments.

a.   *Obesity.* Recall that the definition of disability requires three steps: (1) find an impairment; (2) identify the major life activity that the impairment affects; and (3) link the two together by determining if the impairment substantially limits the major life activity. *See* Bragdon v. Abbott, 524 U.S. 624 (1998). The first step of identifying the impairment is usually the easiest step and is rarely challenged. The one exception to this is obesity. Courts are split regarding whether obesity, even morbid obesity, constitutes an impairment. Some courts hold that obesity, without evidence of an underlying physiological cause, is not an impairment. The debate is partially over the meaning of the EEOC's guidance interpreting the definition of impairment:

> It is important to distinguish between conditions that are impairments and physical, psychological, environmental, cultural, and economic characteristics that are not impairments. The definition of the term "impairment" does not include physical characteristics such as eye color, hair color, left-handedness, or height, *weight*, or muscle tone that are within "normal" range and are not the result of a physiological disorder.

29 C.F.R. pt. 1630, app. § 1630.2(h) (emphasis added). Courts disagree on the meaning of this provision. Some courts, including the Second, Sixth, Seventh, and Eighth Circuits, interpret this language to mean that a physical characteristic like weight will only qualify as an impairment if it is *both* outside a normal range *and* the result of a physiological disorder. *See* Richardson v. Chicago Transit Authority, 926 F.3d 881 (7th Cir. 2019); Morriss v. BNSF Ry. Co., 817 F.3d 1104, 1108–13 (8th Cir.), *cert. denied*, 137 S. Ct. 256 (2016); EEOC v. Watkins Motor Lines, Inc., 463 F.3d 436, 441–43 (6th Cir. 2006); Francis v. City of Meriden, 129 F.3d 281, 286–87 (2d Cir. 1997).

On the other side, courts interpret the EEOC's quoted language above to mean that only when weight is within a normal range does it need to be the result of a physiological disorder to be considered a disability. Someone whose weight is outside of normal range, such as someone who is morbidly obese, could be considered disabled even absent a physiological cause of the obesity. *See, e.g.*, Cook v. State of Rhode Island, Dept. of Mental Health, Retardation, and Hospitals, 10 F.3d 17, 23 (1st Cir. 1993); EEOC v. Resources for Human Development, 827 F.Supp. 2d 688 (E.D. La. 2011). Should obesity be considered an impairment, and assuming it substantially limits a major life activity, a disability? How is it similar to other disabilities? How is it different?

b.   *Gender dysphoria.* The ADA specifically excludes from coverage "homosexuality and bisexuality," 42 U.S.C. § 12211(a); and "transvestism, transsexualism, . . . [and] gender identity disorders not resulting from physical impairments . . . ." 42 U.S.C. § 12211(b)(1). In recent years, there has been some debate about whether gender dysphoria should be considered a disability under the ADA. One recent district court interpreted the above exclusion provision narrowly so as not to include the plaintiff's gender dysphoria, and therefore allowed gender dysphoria to be considered a disability. *See* Blatt v. Cabela's Retail, Inc., 2017 WL 2178123 (E.D. Pa. May 18, 2017). The court interpreted the exclusionary phrase "gender identity disorders" narrowly to refer only to the condition of identifying with a different gender, and not to include the plaintiff's gender dysphoria, which "substantially limits her major life activities of interacting with others, reproducing, and social and occupational functioning." *Id.* at *4. For a critical assessment of the exclusions and a discussion of other cases challenging the constitutionality of the exclusion, see Jennifer L. Levi & Kevin M. Barry, *Transgender Tropes & Constitutional Review,* 37 YALE L. & POL'Y REV. 589, 618–27 (2019).

6. *Winning the battle but losing the war.* In the aftermath of the ADAAA, many disability scholars suspected that once courts could no longer use the definition of disability to limit coverage of the ADA, they might begin using the merits of the case (including the qualified inquiry) to limit the reach of the ADA. *See, e.g.,* Nicole Buonocore Porter, *The New ADA Backlash,* 82 TENN. L. REV. 1 (2014). The evidence is mixed regarding whether caselaw since the Amendments reveals that courts are headed towards another backlash against the ADA. *See id.* at 67 (stating that there is no evidence that courts are using the qualified inquiry to limit the protection of the Act). *But see* Stephen F. Befort, *An Empirical Examination of Case Outcomes under the ADA Amendments Act,* 70 WASH. & LEE L. REV. 2027, 2055 (2013) (finding that the percentage of employer summary judgment wins on the qualified issue jumped from 47% prior to the Amendments to 69% after the Amendments); Michelle A. Travis, *Disqualifying Universality Under the Americans with Disabilities Act Amendments Act,* 2015 MICH. ST. L. REV. 1689, 1697 (arguing that the essential functions component of the qualified test has become the critical source for undermining the ADAAA).

B. RECORD OF DISABILITY

The statute provides that the term disability includes: (A) a physical or mental impairment that substantially limits one or more major life activities; (B) *a record of such an impairment*; or (C) being regarded as having such an impairment. 42 U.S.C. § 12102(1).

The "record of" prong is primarily used if an individual has a "history of, or has been misclassified as having a mental or physical impairment that substantially limits one or more major life activities." 29 C.F.R. § 1630.2(k)(1). The principle of this provision is to protect individuals who have recovered from a prior substantially limiting impairment but who do not presently have an impairment severe enough to constitute an actual disability within the meaning of the ADA. S. Rep. No. 93–1297, at 38–39 (1974) (The protection of the "record of" prong extends to "persons who have recovered—in whole or in part—from a handicapping condition, such as mental or neurological illness, a heart attack, or cancer and to persons who were classified as handicapped (for example, as mentally ill or mentally retarded). . . ."); H.R. Rep. No. 101–485(II), at 52 (1990) (The "record of" prong was designed "to protect individuals who have recovered from a physical or mental impairment which previously substantially limited them in a major life activity."). The regulations implementing the ADA state that the definition should be "construed broadly to the maximum extent permitted by the ADA and should not demand extensive analysis." 29 C.F.R. § 1630.2(k)(2). Before the Amendments, the "record of" prong was used very infrequently. After the Amendments, the broad interpretation of the actual disability prong under the ADAAA makes it unlikely that this prong will gain much traction. Specifically, the addition of the provision regarding impairments that are in remission—"an impairment that is episodic or in remission is a disability if it would substantially limit a major life activity when active"—means that individuals who might have needed to use the record of prong can now use the actual disability prong.

Another issue that was often litigated under the "record of" prong is whether individuals who have a record of a disability are entitled to reasonable accommodations. The regulations implementing the ADA state that they are: "An individual with a record of a substantially limiting impairment may be entitled, absent undue hardship, to a reasonable accommodation if needed and related to the past disability. For example, an employee with an impairment that previously limited, but no longer substantially limits, a major life activity may need leave or a schedule change to permit him or her to attend follow-up or "monitoring" appointments with a health care provider." 29 C.F.R. § 1630.2(k)(3). However, before the Amendments, many courts held that employers do *not* need to accommodate individuals with a record of a disability. *See, e.g.,* Barnes v. Northwest Iowa Health Center, 238 F.Supp.2d 1053 (N.D. Iowa 2002); Kim v. Potter, 460 F.Supp.2d 1194 (D. Haw. 2006). What do you think about this issue? Should individuals who only meet the "record of" prong of the definition of disability be entitled to reasonable accommodations? Why or why not?

C. REGARDED AS DISABLED

1. PRE-AMENDMENTS INTERPRETATION

The original ADA defined disability as: (A) a physical or mental impairment that substantially limits one or more major life activities; (B) a record of such an impairment; or (C) *being regarded as having such an impairment.* 42 U.S.C. § 12102(1).

The first Supreme Court case to interpret the "regarded as" provision was the *Sutton* case, discussed earlier. In *Sutton,* the plaintiffs brought their claim under both the actual disability prong and the regarded as prong of the definition of disability. With regard to their regarded as claim, they argued that their employer, United Airlines, regarded them as substantially limited in the major life activity of working. Below is the Court's discussion of this claim.

SUTTON V. UNITED AIR LINES, INC.
527 U.S. 471, 119 S.Ct. 2139 (1999)

JUSTICE O'CONNOR delivered the opinion of the Court.

* * *

Our conclusion that petitioners have failed to state a claim that they are actually disabled under subsection (A) of the disability definition does not end our inquiry. Under subsection (C), individuals who are "regarded as" having a disability are disabled within the meaning of the ADA. See § 12102(2)(C). Subsection (C) provides that having a disability includes "being regarded as having," § 12102(2)(C), "a physical or mental impairment that substantially limits one or more of the major life activities of such individual," § 12102(2)(A). There are two apparent ways in which individuals may fall within this statutory definition: (1) a covered entity mistakenly believes that a person has a physical impairment that substantially limits one or more major life activities, or (2) a covered entity mistakenly believes that an actual, nonlimiting impairment substantially limits one or more major life activities. In both cases, it is necessary that a covered entity entertain misperceptions about the individual—it must believe either that one has a substantially limiting impairment that one does not have or that one has a substantially limiting impairment when, in fact, the impairment is not so limiting. These misperceptions often "resul[t] from stereotypic assumptions not truly indicative of . . . individual ability." See 42 U.S.C. § 12101(7). See also *School Bd. of Nassau Cty. v. Arline,* 480 U.S. 273, 284, 107 S.Ct. 1123 (1987) ("By amending the definition of 'handicapped individual' to include not only those who are actually physically impaired, but also those who are regarded as impaired and who, as a result, are substantially limited in a major life activity, Congress acknowledged that society's accumulated myths and fears about disability and disease are as handicapping as are the physical limitations that flow from actual impairment"). . . .

There is no dispute that petitioners are physically impaired. Petitioners do not make the obvious argument that they are regarded due to their impairments as substantially limited in the major life activity of seeing. They contend only that respondent mistakenly believes their physical impairments substantially limit them in the major life activity of working. To support this claim, petitioners allege that respondent has a vision requirement that is allegedly based on myth and stereotype. Further, this requirement substantially limits their ability to engage in the major life activity of working by precluding them from obtaining the job of global airline pilot, which they argue is a "class of employment." . . .

Standing alone, the allegation that respondent has a vision requirement in place does not establish a claim that respondent regards petitioners as substantially limited in the major life activity of working. By its terms, the

ADA allows employers to prefer some physical attributes over others and to establish physical criteria. An employer runs afoul of the ADA when it makes an employment decision based on a physical or mental impairment, real or imagined, that is regarded as substantially limiting a major life activity. Accordingly, an employer is free to decide that physical characteristics or medical conditions that do not rise to the level of an impairment—such as one's height, build, or singing voice—are preferable to others, just as it is free to decide that some limiting, but not *substantially* limiting, impairments make individuals less than ideally suited for a job.

* * *

When the major life activity under consideration is that of working, the statutory phrase "substantially limits" requires, at a minimum, that plaintiffs allege they are unable to work in a broad class of jobs. Reflecting this requirement, the EEOC uses a specialized definition of the term "substantially limits" when referring to the major life activity of working:

> "significantly restricted in the ability to perform either a class of jobs or a broad range of jobs in various classes as compared to the average person having comparable training, skills and abilities. The inability to perform a single, particular job does not constitute a substantial limitation in the major life activity of working."
> § 1630.2(j)(3)(i).

The EEOC further identifies several factors that courts should consider when determining whether an individual is substantially limited in the major life activity of working, including the geographical area to which the individual has reasonable access, and "the number and types of jobs utilizing similar training, knowledge, skills or abilities, within the geographical area, from which the individual is also disqualified." §§ 1630.2(j)(3)(ii)(A), (B). To be substantially limited in the major life activity of working, then, one must be precluded from more than one type of job, a specialized job, or a particular job of choice. If jobs utilizing an individual's skills (but perhaps not his or her unique talents) are available, one is not precluded from a substantial class of jobs. Similarly, if a host of different types of jobs are available, one is not precluded from a broad range of jobs.

Because the parties accept that the term "major life activities" includes working, we do not determine the validity of the cited regulations. We note, however, that there may be some conceptual difficulty in defining "major life activities" to include work, for it seems "to argue in a circle to say that if one is excluded, for instance, by reason of [an impairment, from working with others] . . . then that exclusion constitutes an impairment, when the question you're asking is, whether the exclusion itself is by reason of handicap." Indeed, even the EEOC has expressed reluctance to define "major life activities" to include working and has suggested that working be viewed as a residual life activity, considered, as a last resort, *only* "[i]f an individual is not substantially limited with respect to *any other* major life activity." 29 CFR pt. 1630, App. § 1630.2(j) (1998).

Assuming without deciding that working is a major life activity and that the EEOC regulations interpreting the term "substantially limits" are reasonable, petitioners have failed to allege adequately that their poor eyesight is regarded as an impairment that substantially limits them in the major life activity of working. They allege only that respondent regards their poor vision as precluding them from holding positions as a "global airline pilot." Because the position of global airline pilot is a single job, this allegation does not support the claim that respondent regards petitioners as having a *substantially limiting* impairment. See 29 CFR § 1630.2(j)(3)(i) (1998) ("The inability to perform a single, particular job does not constitute a substantial limitation in the major life activity of working"). Indeed, there are a number of other positions utilizing petitioners' skills, such as regional pilot and pilot instructor to name a few, that are available to them.

* * *

NOTES AND QUESTIONS

1. *Ways to prove "regarded as."* The Court in *Sutton* describes two ways that a covered entity might regard an individual as disabled: "(1) a covered entity mistakenly believes that a person has a physical impairment that substantially limits one or more major life activities, or (2) a covered entity mistakenly believes that an actual, nonlimiting impairment substantially limits one or more major life activities." An example of the first method is if an employer mistakenly believes one of its employees has HIV. An example of the second is an employee who has high blood pressure that the employer mistakenly believes causes a substantial limitation on a major life activity. The EEOC, in its regulations implementing the original ADA, articulated a third method—if the individual has an impairment that is substantially limiting because of the attitude of others. For instance, if an employee has a prominent facial scar that causes no limitation on that employee's major life activities but the employer terminates her because of the negative reactions of customers, this is an example of this third method. *See* 29 C.F.R. pt. 1630, app. A § 1630.2(*l*) (1997).

2. *Major life activity of working.* Before the ADA Amendments Act, many of the cases that addressed the "regarded as" prong were cases where the plaintiff claimed that her employer regarded her as substantially limited in the major life activity of working. This was because it is often difficult to prove that an employer regarded the plaintiff as being substantially limited in other major life activities. For instance, if the evidence demonstrated that the plaintiff had been successfully treated for cancer, and the employer refused to promote the plaintiff for that reason, how would the plaintiff prove that the employer believed she was substantially limited in a major life activity? Before the addition of the "major bodily functions" provision in the Amendments, it is

unlikely that the plaintiff could prove that her employer regarded her as substantially limited in any major life activity besides working. Prior to the Amendments, the list of major life activities (listed in EEOC regulations, and not in the statute itself) were: caring for oneself, performing manual tasks, seeing, hearing, walking, speaking, breathing, learning, and working. Especially if an individual's cancer is in remission, a plaintiff would be hard-pressed to argue successfully that her employer regarded her as being substantially limited in these other major life activities. Thus, under the original statute, most plaintiffs who brought "regarded as" claims argued that their employers regarded them as being substantially limited in the major life activity of working. Of course, this argument was a difficult one to make because, as seen in *Sutton*, the plaintiff had to prove that her employer regarded her as being unable to perform a "broad class of jobs" in order to demonstrate that her employer regarded her as being substantially limited in the major life activity of working. For an interesting discussion and critique of the single-job requirement as it applies to the pre-ADAAA regarded as prong of the definition of disability, see Arlene B. Mayerson, *Restoring Regard for the "Regarded As" Prong: Giving Effect to Congressional Intent*, 42 VILL. L. REV. 587 (1997).

3.   *The difficulty in proving "regarded as" disabled.* In addition to the narrow interpretation of the major life activity of working, plaintiffs also had difficulty proving their regarded as claims because these claims required them to have information about the decisionmaker's state of mind that was hard to acquire. In other words, it was not enough to prove that the employer knew of the plaintiff's impairment—for example, knew the plaintiff had diabetes. After *Sutton*, the plaintiff had to prove that the employer believed that the diabetes caused a substantial limitation on a major life activity. Thus, assuming the lack of any "smoking gun" evidence, the plaintiff would have to get the decisionmaker to testify (in a deposition or at trial) that he believed that the plaintiff's diabetes substantially limited one or more of the plaintiff's major life activities. Any well-counseled employer's witness will easily avoid making such a statement. Thus, before the ADAAA, winning "regarded as" claims was very difficult. *See generally* Mayerson, *supra,* at 593–98 (discussing the history of the "regarded as" prong, and criticizing the courts' requirement that plaintiff prove that the defendant-employer regarded her as being substantially limited in a major life activity); Stephen F. Befort, *Let's Try This Again: The ADA Amendments Act of 2008 Attempts to Reinvigorate the "Regarded As" Prong of the Statutory Definition of Disability*, 2010 UTAH L. REV. 993, 1008–09.

2.   ADAAA'S "REGARDED AS" PROVISIONS

Under the Amendments, an individual is "regarded as having such an impairment" if "the individual establishes that he or she has been subjected to an action prohibited under this chapter because of an actual or perceived physical or mental impairment *whether or not the impairment limits or is perceived to limit a major life activity.*" 42 U.S.C. § 12102(3)(A) (emphasis added). This language is very significant, as it negates the need for the plaintiff to prove that her employer believes she is substantially limited in a major life activity. As long as the plaintiff can prove that a prohibited action was taken because of her impairment (or perceived impairment), she meets the statutory definition. This provision more closely aligns the ADA with other civil rights statutes, like Title VII, which prohibits discrimination because of status in a protected group. *Cf.* Kevin Barry, *Toward Universalism: What the ADA Amendments Act of 2008 Can and Can't Do for Disability Rights*, 31 BERKELEY J. EMP. & LAB. L. 203, 218 (2010) (stating that those who argued for a universal approach to disability believe that the Act ought to protect everyone who experiences discrimination based on an impairment much like the Civil Rights Act of 1964 protects everyone who experiences discrimination based on race, religion, sex, or national origin).

However, as a compromise to this very broad coverage under the "regarded as" prong, Congress inserted two limiting provisions. First, the "regarded as" provision does not "apply to impairments that are transitory and minor" and a transitory impairment is defined as an "impairment with an actual or expected duration of 6 months or less." *Id.* § 12102(3)(B). And second, Congress clarified that reasonable accommodations are not required for a plaintiff who only meets the definition of disability under the regarded as prong. Specifically, the statute states that a covered entity "need not provide a reasonable accommodation or a reasonable modification to policies, practices, or procedures to an individual who meets the definition of disability in section 3(1) solely under subparagraph (C) of such section." 42 U.S.C. § 12201(1)(h).

3. POST-ADAAA "REGARDED AS" CASELAW

NUNIES V. HIE HOLDINGS, INC.
908 F.3d 428 (9th Cir. 2018)

TASHIMA, CIRCUIT JUDGE:

In 2008, Congress enacted the ADA Amendments Act ("ADAAA"), which broadened the definition of disability under the Americans with Disabilities Act ("ADA"), 42 U.S.C. §§ 12101 *et seq.* As relevant to this appeal, the ADAAA expanded the scope of the ADA's "regarded-as" definition of disability. We have not opined on this issue in the ten years since the ADAAA was enacted and some district courts have mistakenly continued to apply the narrower pre-ADAAA definition of regarded-as disability. We now write to clarify this issue.

Plaintiff-appellant Herman Nunies was a delivery driver for HIE Holdings, Inc. ("HIE"). Nunies claims that he injured his shoulder and wanted to transfer to a part-time, less-physical warehouse job. The requested transfer was approved and all set to go through until Nunies told HIE about his shoulder injury. Two days after Nunies allegedly informed HIE about his injury, the company rejected his transfer request and forced him to resign. Nunies brought a disability discrimination suit against HIE under the ADA and state law, arguing that HIE terminated him because of his shoulder injury. HIE moved for summary judgment, which the district court granted.

Applying the standard set forth in the ADAAA, we hold that the district court erred in concluding, as a matter of law, that Nunies was not regarded-as disabled. . . . We reverse and remand.

BACKGROUND

1. Factual Background

HIE is in the business of the purchase, sale, and distribution of food products for residential and commercial use. Nunies was a five-gallon delivery driver for the company in Kauai. His primary duties included operating HIE's company vehicle; loading, unloading, and delivering five-gallon water bottles; and occasionally assisting in the warehouse. The position required lifting and carrying a minimum of 50 pounds and other physical tasks.

Sometime in mid-June 2013, Nunies wanted to transfer from his full-time delivery driver position to a part-time warehouse position. The parties dispute the motivation for this switch. Nunies attributes his desire to switch to the pain he had developed in his left shoulder. HIE—through a supervisor, Victor Watabu—contends that Nunies wanted to transfer so that he could focus on his independent side-business. To effectuate the transfer, Nunies found a part-time warehouse employee, Sidney Aguinaldo, to swap positions.

Watabu contacted HIE's Honolulu office because that office needed to approve the Nunies-Aguinaldo swap. According to Watabu, the Honolulu office "tentatively" approved the switch pending resolution of some pay and duties questions. Nunies asserts that on June 14, 2013, Watabu told him that the switch had been approved.

Next, Nunies states that on June 17, 2013, he notified his operations manager and Watabu that he was having shoulder pain. HIE disputes that it was aware of Nunies' shoulder injury. However, on a later-filed "Employer's Report of Industrial Injury," an HIE HR official noted that Nunies first reported the injury on June 17.

The parties agree that on June 19, Watabu told Nunies that HIE would not extend the part-time warehouse position to him and that Nunies' last day would be July 3. Nunies argues that there were no discussions after June 14 about reaching an agreement until, on June 19, Watabu said "[y]ou gotta resign" because "[y]our job no longer exists because of budget cuts." HIE's termination report, dated June 27, 2013, states that the "type" of Nunies' separation was "resignation," and that the reason for the separation was that the "part-time position [was] not available." However, on June 24, 2013, Watabu emailed his HIE colleagues, on an email chain about Nunies' last day of employment, and asked, "can you scan a copy for a job opening for a part-time warehouseman ad[?]" Nunies saw an ad for the position in the newspaper on June 26, 2013, one day before HIE completed Nunies' termination report.

Following an MRI on July 29, 2013, Nunies was diagnosed with supraspinatus tendinitis/partial tear of his left shoulder. By September 2014, medical reports concluded that the injury had been resolved.

2. Procedural Background

Nunies brought suit on April 6, 2015, alleging that HIE violated the ADA and Hawaii's employment discrimination law, by discriminating against him because of his disability. HIE moved for summary judgment on all claims, arguing that: . . . Nunies could not establish a prima facie case of disability discrimination because he was not "disabled," not a "qualified individual," and did not suffer an "adverse employment action." The district court granted HIE summary judgment on all of Nunies' claims.

* * *

[T]he district court concluded that Nunies did not have a "disability" under the ADA. Even though Nunies only argued in his briefs that HIE regarded him as having a disability, the district court also considered whether he had an "actual," or a "record" disability. As to actual disability, the district court concluded that Nunies had not established that his shoulder injury "substantially limited" any "major life activity." The district court also found that Nunies did not establish a record of impairment. Finally, the district court concluded that Nunies had not established that HIE regarded him as having a disability because Nunies did not come forward with any evidence that HIE subjectively believed that Nunies was substantially limited in a major life activity.

Nunies timely appealed.

STANDARD OF REVIEW

This court reviews an order granting summary judgment *de novo*.

DISCUSSION

1. Waiver

[Eds. Note: The court first addressed whether Nunies had waived his "regarded as" claim, ultimately holding that he had not waived it.]

2. Disability

To set forth a prima facie disability discrimination claim, a plaintiff must establish that: (1) he is disabled within the meaning of the ADA; (2) he is qualified (i.e., able to perform the essential functions of the job with or without reasonable accommodation); and (3) the employer terminated him because of his disability.

"The term 'disability' means, with respect to an individual—(A) a physical or mental impairment that substantially limits one or more major life activities of such individual; (B) a record of such an impairment; or (C) being regarded as having such an impairment." 42 U.S.C. § 12102(1)(A)–(C). The ADA does not define "physical or mental impairment," but the Equal Employment Opportunity Commission's ("EEOC") regulations define physical impairment as "[a]ny physiological disorder or condition . . . affecting one or more body systems, such as . . . musculoskeletal . . . ." 29 C.F.R. § 1630.2(h)(1).

The regarded-as and actual disability prongs of the definition are at issue on appeal.

A. Regarded-as

Under the ADAAA,

> An individual meets the requirement of "being regarded as having such an impairment" if the individual establishes that he or she has been subjected to an action prohibited under this chapter because of an actual or perceived physical or mental impairment *whether or not the impairment limits or is perceived to limit a major life activity.*

42 U.S.C. § 12102(3)(A) (emphasis added). Prior to the ADAAA, to sustain a regarded-as claim, the plaintiff had to "provide evidence that the employer subjectively believe[d] that the plaintiff [was] substantially limited in a major life activity." *Walton v. U.S. Marshals Serv.*, 492 F.3d 998, 1006 (9th Cir. 2007) (relying in part on the interpretation of regarded-as in *Sutton*, which the ADAAA explicitly superseded).

The ADA excludes individuals from regarded-as coverage if the impairment is both transitory (i.e., expected to last six months or less) and minor (which the statute does not define). 42 U.S.C. § 12102(3)(B).

Here, the district court cited the ADAAA definition of regarded-as, but relied on pre-ADAAA caselaw to hold that Nunies did not establish coverage. Specifically, the district court concluded "that Plaintiff has not sustained his burden of presenting direct evidence that Defendant *subjectively believed that Plaintiff is substantially limited in a major life activity.*" Based on the plain language of the ADAAA, it was error for the district court to require Nunies to present evidence that HIE believed that Nunies was substantially limited in a major life activity.

Applying the correct law, and viewing the evidence in the light most favorable to the non-moving party, we conclude that Nunies established a genuine issue of material fact as to whether HIE regarded him as having a disability. A reasonable jury could conclude that HIE effectively terminated Nunies "because of" its knowledge of Nunies' shoulder injury.

Nunies proffered evidence that Watabu told him that the transfer to the part-time position was fully approved on June 14. On June 17, Nunies informed Watabu and his operations manager that he was having shoulder pain. Then, on June 19, Nunies learned that he would not receive the transfer and that he had to resign. When Nunies asked why, Watabu told him that the part-time job no longer existed because of budget cuts. Nevertheless, because HIE advertised an opening for the exact same position just days afterwards, it reasonably can be inferred that the position clearly still existed.

Put simply, there is evidence in the record that everything was going swimmingly for Nunies in terms of transferring to the part-time position until he informed HIE that he had shoulder pain. Once HIE learned of the shoulder pain, it rescinded the offer, and forced Nunies to resign. Further, there is evidence that HIE misrepresented to Nunies that the position was no longer available because shortly thereafter the company was looking to hire someone for the same position. From these facts, on summary judgment, it would be reasonable to infer that HIE forced Nunies to resign "because of" his shoulder injury.

HIE's arguments to the contrary are not convincing. First, HIE correctly points out that the regarded-as definition of disability does not apply to "transitory and minor" impairments. 42 U.S.C. § 12102(3)(B). Citing this provision, HIE contends that "Nunies' report of 'shoulder pain' would not be sufficient to convince a reasonable jury that Nunies had a physical impairment expected to last six months or longer, or that HIE regarded him as such." However, HIE errs by placing the burden on Nunies to show that his impairment was not transitory or minor. As *Amicus* EEOC points out, the "transitory and minor" exception is an affirmative defense, and "[a]s such, the employer bears the burden of establishing the defense." *See* 29 C.F.R. pt. 1630, app. § 1630.2(*l*); *id.* at § 1630.15(f). HIE offered no evidence to sustain its burden that Nunies' actual or perceived injury was "transitory and minor."

Second, HIE's attacks on Nunies' evidence on summary judgment are irrelevant to the analysis. HIE asserts that Nunies' "uncorroborated report of 'shoulder pain' is made more suspect" by an allegedly contradictory statement from Nunies. But, Nunies' statement is not contradictory and, more fundamentally, whether Nunies' evidence is suspect is a question for a jury, not one to be resolved on summary judgment. Likewise, we reject HIE's contention that its newspaper advertisement was irrelevant to whether the company regarded Nunies as disabled. Evidence that HIE lied to Nunies about the availability of the part-time position raises the reasonable inference that the company withdrew its transfer offer to Nunies based on an illicit reason. Considering that Nunies had informed the company two days earlier that he was hurt, a reasonable jury could connect those dots.

All in all, considering the broader definition of regarded-as disability under the ADAAA, and viewing the evidence in the light most favorable to Nunies, the district court erred in granting of summary judgment to HIE on this issue.

* * *

[Eds. Note: The court's discussion of the actual disability prong, holding that there was sufficient evidence that the plaintiff's shoulder injury was an actual disability, has been omitted.]

CONCLUSION

The judgment of the district court is . . . REVERSED, and the case is REMANDED for further proceedings consistent with this opinion. . . .

NOTES AND QUESTIONS

1.   *The new "regarded as" prong.* Recall that, under *Sutton*, the plaintiff would have to prove that the defendant regarded him as being substantially limited in a major life activity. Under the Amendments, the burden is much easier. Now the plaintiff only must demonstrate that he or she has been subjected to an adverse employment action "because of an actual or perceived physical or mental impairment whether or not the impairment limits or is perceived to limit a major life activity." In the context of the *Nunies* case, this means that it does not matter whether the plaintiff's supervisors believed that his shoulder injury substantially limited any major life activity. The plaintiff only needed to demonstrate that they fired him because of his shoulder injury.

Unlike the court in *Nunies*, some courts have struggled to apply this provision correctly. For instance, in *Welch v. Level 3 Communications, LLC,* 2017 WL 2306443 (E.D. Mich. May 26, 2017), the plaintiff had multiple sclerosis (MS) and suffered from seizures. The court cited to the correct law but then stated that even though the employer knew about the plaintiff's MS and her seizures, it was not aware about problems these impairments caused. *Id.* at *5. The court noted that the employer "certainly knew that she . . . had a driving restriction because of her MS and her seizure disorder." However, the court held that plaintiff could not show that her employer regarded her as disabled merely by pointing to the portion of the record where the employer admitted it was aware of plaintiff's medical restrictions. *Id.* at *5. The fact that the employer knew that the plaintiff had MS and a seizure disorder and took an adverse action because of those impairments should have been enough for plaintiff's regarded as claim to survive. *See* Porter, *Not Disabled, supra* at 408–09 (discussing regarded as claims where the court arrived at the wrong result).

2.   *Transitory and minor exception.* As stated above, the "regarded as" provision does not "apply to impairments that are transitory and minor. A transitory impairment is an impairment with an actual or expected duration

of 6 months or less." *Id.* § 12102(3)(B). As the court notes in *Nunies*, this provision is an affirmative defense; thus, the employer has the burden of proof.

Most courts recognize that transitory and minor are separate standards and both must be met. *See, e.g.,* Silk v. Board of Trustees of Moraine Valley Community College, District No. 524, 46 F.Supp.3d 821, 829–30 (N.D. Ill. 2014) (holding that plaintiff's regarded as claim survives because, even though plaintiff was only hospitalized for a short duration, he needed bypass surgery, which is indicative of a serious impairment); Bush v. Donahoe, 964 F.Supp.2d 401, 422–23 (W.D. Pa. 2013) (holding that an ankle/foot sprain that required a walking cast/boot for almost six months was transitory and minor but noting that the parties had erroneously assumed that because it was transitory, it was also minor). But some courts get this wrong and conflate the two inquiries. *See, e.g.,* Randall v. United Petroleum Transports, Inc., 131 F.Supp.3d 566, 572 (W.D. La. 2015) (holding that plaintiff's seizure disorder that prevented him from driving was transitory and minor, without ever discussing the minor prong of the defense); Eshelman v. Patrick Industries, Inc., 2018 WL 3219497, at *4 (E.D. Pa. July 2, 2018) (holding that plaintiff's impairment, which involved surgery to remove a nodule on his lung followed by several months of leave to recover from surgery and a severe upper respiratory infection was transitory and minor, but never discussing how surgery to remove a nodule on one's lung is a minor impairment).

"Transitory" is defined in the statute but "minor" is not. Some examples of impairments that courts held were *both* transitory *and* minor include: H1N1 flu, *see* Valdez v. Minnesota Quarries, Inc., 2012 WL 6112846, at *3 (D. Minn., Dec. 10, 3012); broken finger, *see* Budhun v. Reading Hospital and Medical Center, 765 F.3d 245, 259 (3d Cir. 2014); and ankle/foot sprain that involved wearing a walking cast/boot for almost six months, *see Bush,* 964 F.Supp.2d at 422–23. Finally, it is important to remember that this limitation does not apply to the actual disability prong of the definition and the effects of an impairment that are expected to last fewer than six months can be substantially limiting within the meaning of the ADA. *See, e.g.,* Summers v. Altarum Institute, Corp., 740 F.3d 325, 333 (4th Cir. 2014) (holding that temporary impairments are not excluded from the actual disability prong).

3.   *No reasonable accommodations under the "regarded as" prong.* As stated above, as a compromise to the broadened coverage for the "regarded as" prong, Congress added a limitation that specifies that employees are not entitled to reasonable accommodations if they only meet the definition of disability under the "regarded as" prong. Can you think of a situation in which a "regarded as" plaintiff might need a reasonable accommodation in order to be able to perform the essential functions of a job? *See* Stephen F. Befort, *Let's Try This Again: The ADA Amendments Act of 2008 Attempts to Reinvigorate the "Regarded As" Prong of the Statutory Definition of Disability,* 2010 UTAH L. REV. 993, 1023–24 (discussing this issue).

4.   *Predictive disabilities.* Imagine that an employer refuses to hire an employee not because of a current impairment or disability, but because the employer is concerned that some characteristic of the individual makes it more

likely that the individual will develop other medical conditions. If the individual actually had those medical conditions, the ADA would prohibit the employer from refusing to hire the individual (assuming the applicant was qualified and absent some defense). Is it unlawful for the employer to refuse to hire this individual because it predicts that the individual will be disabled in the future?

This issue was recently discussed in *Shell v. Burlington Northern Santa Fe Railway Co.*, 941 F.3d 331 (7th Cir. 2019). In *Shell*, the employer refused to hire the plaintiff "solely because it believed his obesity presented an unacceptably high risk that he would develop certain medical conditions that would suddenly incapacitate him on the job." *Id.* at 333. Specifically, the conditions the employer was concerned about included sleep apnea, diabetes, and heart disease, and that the onset of these conditions is unpredictable, leading to a concern that a debilitating health episode might cause the employee to lose consciousness while operating dangerous equipment. *Id.* at 334. As discussed earlier, in the Seventh Circuit, obesity is not an impairment (unless it has a physiological cause) so the plaintiff tried to base his disability claim on the medical conditions that the employer feared he would develop—sleep apnea, diabetes, and heart disease. *Id.* at 335. But the court noted that the risk of future impairment is not the same thing as a current impairment, and therefore the employer did not regard him as having an impairment. *Id.* at 336. *See also* Morriss v. BNSF Ry. Co., 817 F.3d 1104, 1113 (8th Cir. 2016) (under similar facts as the *Shell* case, the court held that basing an employment decision on the perception that someone might become disabled does not constitute discrimination under the regarded as prong); EEOC v. STME, LLC, 938 F.3d 1305 (11th Cir. 2019) (concluding that the disability definition does not cover the case where an employer fears that someone will become ill in the future; in this case, the employer believed that the plaintiff would contract Ebola because she had plans to travel to Ghana). What do you think of these cases? Should it be *lawful* for an employer to take an adverse action against an individual because it believes that individual will become disabled even though it would be *unlawful* to take such an action if the individual actually had the feared disability? At least one scholar has argued that this type of predictive discrimination should be unlawful. *See generally* Sharona Hoffman, *What Genetic Testing Teaches About Predictive Health Analytics Regulation*, 98 N.C. L. Rev. 123 (2019).

D. POST-ADAAA SUMMARY

Stephen F. Befort, An Empirical Examination of Case Outcomes Under the ADA Amendments Act
70 Wash & Lee L. Rev. 2027 (2013)

This Article undertakes an empirical examination of how the ADAAA has impacted actual case outcomes. The recent reported cases provide a unique opportunity for such an examination because, with the ADAAA not retroactively applicable to cases pending prior to its effective date, courts have been simultaneously deciding cases under both the pre-amendment and post-amendment standards. This study examines all reported federal court summary judgment decisions arising under Title I of the ADA for a forty-month period extending from January 1, 2010 to April 30, 2013. The study coded these pre-ADAAA and post-ADAAA decisions for both disability standing determinations and for rulings on whether the plaintiff is qualified for the job in question.

★ ★ ★

A Closer Look at Three Assumptions

A principal objective of this study is to determine empirically whether the ADAAA is fulfilling three core assumptions widely held at the time of its passage. [T]hese three assumptions are as follows:

1) That the ADAAA will result in fewer summary judgment rulings finding that plaintiffs lack standing as covered individuals with a disability,

2) That the amendments will result in more cases being decided on the basis of whether the plaintiff is a qualified individual with or without a reasonable accommodation, and

3) That the amendments will result in higher overall win rates for ADA plaintiffs.

Assumption #1—Fewer Summary Judgment
Rulings Denying Disability Status

The federal district court data provides strong support for this assumption. While the district courts granted summary judgment to the employer in 74.4% of the pre-amendment outcomes addressing disability status, the employer win rate in the post-amendment cases dropped to 45.9%. This data, accordingly, show a 28.5 percentage point decline in pro-employer summary judgment rulings.

Disability Status—Cumulative Totals Comparison

	Pre-Amendment		Post-Amendment	
	Number of Claims	Percentage	Number of Claims	Percentage
S/J for Ee	1	.9	3	8.1
S/J for Er	87	74.4	17	45.9
S/J for Er Denied	29	24.8	17	45.9
Total	117	100	37	100

B.   Assumption #2—An Enhanced Focus on Qualified Status

A second commonly-held assumption about the likely effect of the ADAAA was that the amendments would refocus ADA litigation on issues of discrimination as opposed to issues of standing, resulting in more cases being decided on the basis of whether the plaintiff is qualified for the job with or without a reasonable accommodation. The data set out in the table [below] provides significant support for this assumption. The table shows that the percentage of summary judgment rulings on the qualified status issue as compared to all summary judgment rulings jumped from 28.2% in the pre-amendment outcomes to 47.1% in the post-amendment outcomes.

Issue for Summary Judgment

	Pre-Amendment		Post-Amendment	
	Number of Claims	Percentages	Number of Claims	Percentages
Disability Status	117	71.8	37	52.9
Qualified Status	46	28.2	33	47.1
Total	163	100	70	100

* * *

In sum, the post-amendment decisions also provide support for the second commonly-held ADAAA assumption, namely that the amendments would focus more attention on whether a plaintiff is qualified for the job with or without a reasonable accommodation, and less attention on the issue of whether the plaintiff is an individual with a disability. By placing a greater emphasis on the merits of a claim and less on the question of standing, the ADAAA has recast disability discrimination litigation in a manner more akin to litigation under Title VII.

C.   Assumption #3—Higher Win Rates for ADA Plaintiffs

The third and final assumption concerning the ADAAA's likely effect was that it would result in greater overall wins for plaintiffs in ADA lawsuits. The logic was that if a greater proportion of plaintiffs survived summary judgment motions with respect to standing, a subset of this larger cohort also would go on to experience more favorable outcomes by litigation's end.

The database generated in this study does not directly capture overall wins and losses. Instead, it tallies outcomes on summary judgment motions relating to disability status and qualified status. What this study captures, accordingly, is rulings that can be characterized as either plaintiff-loss outcomes or as plaintiff-survives-to-litigate-another-day outcomes. . . .

One way of measuring this data is to compare summary judgment outcomes on disability status and qualified status motions. . . .

This comparison does not reveal a clear overall path in this instance because the post-amendment outcomes with respect to these two types of summary judgment issues trend in opposite directions. Summary judgment rulings favorable to employers on the disability status issue, as expected, show a marked downward trend among the post-amendment decisions.

In contrast, employers thus far have achieved more favorable outcomes in the post-amendment rulings on the qualified status issue. In the pre-amendment decisions, courts granted summary judgment to employers in 47.9% of the outcomes, but this figure jumped to 69.7% in the post-amendment outcomes, representing a more than 21 percentage point increase.

Qualified Status Cumulative Totals Comparison

	Pre-Amendment		Post-Amendment	
	Number of Claims	Percentages	Number of Claims	Percentages
S/J for Er	22	47.9	23	69.7
S/J for Er Denied	24	52.2	10	30.3
Total	46	100	33	100

This data suggests that the more plaintiff-friendly outcomes engineered by the ADAAA with respect to disability status are being partially offset by more employer-friendly outcomes with respect to qualified status. These results also provide some support for those commentators who have expressed concerns that the courts could once again undermine congressional efforts to establish a national mandate against disability discrimination.

This rather rough comparison of proportional changes, however, masks the transformative impact of the ADAAA in two ways. First, it does not take into account the fact that the database contains far more summary judgment rulings as to disability status than it does summary judgment rulings as to qualified status. Indeed, almost two-thirds of the summary judgment rulings in this data set (66.1%) involve disability status issues. As such, looking only at percentage changes does not capture the fact that each percentage point change in disability status outcomes has approximately two times the numeric clout than a percentage point change in qualified status outcomes.

Second, the above comparison analyzes claim outcomes rather than case outcomes. Quantifying claim outcomes has the advantage of generating data with respect to the type of disability status prong asserted and the type of summary judgment motion being decided. But this data, even though rich in detail, do not provide an accurate depiction of case outcomes. . . .

A more meaningful way to compare losers and survivors is to focus on numerical case outcomes. The table [below] depicts such a comparison. The table shows that plaintiffs survived summary judgment motions in 41 out of 127 pre-amendment cases coded for this study. This translates to a survival rate of 32.3%. In the set of post-amendment decisions, plaintiffs survived in 22 of the reported 55 cases. The survival rate for plaintiffs in these post-amendment cases rose to 40%, which is equivalent to 7.7 percentage points higher than in the pre-amendment decisions.

Case Loss and Survivor Outcomes

	Pre-Amendment		Post-Amendment	
	Number of Cases	Percentages	Number of Cases	Percentages
Plaintiff Loss	86	67.7	33	60.0
Plaintiff Survives	41	32.3	22	40.0
	127	100	55	100

The data set out in [this] table shows that the positive gains made by plaintiffs in post-amendment disability status rulings more than made up for the greater frequency of negative outcomes in the post-amendment qualified status rulings. While a 7.7 increase in percentage points does not represent a "radical" change, it does corroborate the assessment of Professor Samuel Bagenstos that the ADAAA "is a worthy effort that is likely to make things somewhat better" for ADA plaintiffs. This data, accordingly, support the assumption that the ADAAA will assist plaintiffs in achieving higher overall win rates in disability discrimination cases.

NOTES AND QUESTIONS

1.   Professor Befort contends that the ADA Amendments Act has made the ADA operate more like Title VII. What does he mean by this statement and do you agree?

2.   *Qualified inquiry.* A major finding of this empirical study is that ADA Amendments Act's more favorable formula for determining disability status has been partially offset by an increase in court decisions finding plaintiffs not to be qualified. While this preliminary data may or may not be indicative of a

long-term trend, what factors might lead to an increase in employer wins at the summary judgment stage on the qualified issue?

3.   *Disability status cases 2014–2018.* Professor Befort's article analyzed post-ADAAA cases that were decided up until April 30, 2013. In 2019, Professor Porter set out to analyze the cases discussing the issue of disability status in the second five-year period after the ADA went into effect, 2014–2018. That research resulted in 976 federal cases where the court discussed the issue of disability. Of those 976, Porter found 210 cases that she believed were wrongly decided. Porter, *Not Disabled, supra* at 385. Some of the errors made by litigants, their lawyers, and courts have been discussed throughout this chapter. But the most surprising finding of all was the number of opinions that did not mention the ADA Amendments Act at all. With respect to the actual disability prong, Porter discovered a shocking 54 cases where the court cited to absolutely no post-ADAAA statutory authority or caselaw, despite the fact that the ADAAA would very likely have changed the result of the case. *Id.* at 393–95 (discussing cases that involved plaintiffs with pretty severe impairments, such as one plaintiff who used a walker to walk, another who had multiple sclerosis that caused significant mobility limitations, and another who had a seizure disorder). Courts were also seemingly unaware of the ADAAA in cases under the "regarded as" prong of the definition of disability. In her dataset, Porter discovered 34 cases where courts cited and relied on the old regarded as rule, and did not cite to the very significant changes Congress made to the regarded-as prong in the ADAAA. *Id.* at 397–98.

How can this result be explained? Presumably, if the court is not mentioning the ADAAA, neither did the attorneys in their briefs. And federal judges usually have judicial clerks (often recent law graduates with top-notch credentials) whose job it is to supplement the litigants' briefs by doing their own research and analysis. How is it possible that all of those lawyers (a minimum of four lawyers on every case, unless the plaintiff was pro se) missed the very significant fact that the ADA was substantially amended in 2008? And perhaps more importantly, what can be done about it? As Porter suggests in her article, it is clear more education is needed. *Id.* at 410. As you likely have concluded from this chapter, the law surrounding the definition of disability is complicated, but not always reaching the correct analysis under the ADAAA's new provisions is quite different from not being aware that the ADA was amended at all. How can we fix *that* problem?

CHAPTER 3

EMPLOYMENT DISCRIMINATION

■ ■ ■

As indicated in Chapter 1, the ADA is divided into several titles. Title I of the ADA is the employment discrimination title. The general anti-discrimination provision states:

(a) General rule. No covered entity shall discriminate against a qualified individual on the basis of disability in regard to job application procedures, the hiring, advancement, or discharge of employees, employee compensation, job training, or other terms, conditions, and privileges of employment.

42 U.S.C. § 12112. The term "discriminate" includes several provisions, including the most prominent—the reasonable accommodation provision, which states that discrimination includes:

(A) not making reasonable accommodations to the known physical or mental limitations of an otherwise qualified individual with a disability who is an applicant or employee, unless such covered entity can demonstrate that the accommodation would impose an undue hardship on the operation of the business of such covered entity. . . .

42 U.S.C. § 12112(b)(5). An employer's obligation to provide reasonable accommodations is what makes the ADA unique, and will be discussed below.

First, however, this chapter addresses the situation where an employee is claiming discrimination because of an actual or perceived disability, but is not seeking a reasonable accommodation. In other words, how does a plaintiff prove discrimination when the plaintiff believes she suffered an adverse employment action because of her employer's animus against her actual or perceived disability?

A. PLAINTIFF'S PRIMA FACIE CASE

Burden-Shifting Framework: *McDonnell Douglas v. Green*

In many cases, the ADA is simply an anti-discrimination statute. For instance, an employee's supervisor might have recently discovered that the employee is HIV positive or that the employee has a non-visible impairment, such as cancer, diabetes, high blood pressure, or multiple sclerosis. If that supervisor subsequently terminates the employee or fails to promote him to a position for which he believes he was qualified, the employee might assume that the adverse employment action was *because of* his disability. However, without a "smoking gun," proving causation can be difficult. When deciding causation issues under the ADA, courts rely on the famous United States Supreme Court opinion in *McDonnell Douglas v. Green*, 411 U.S. 792 (1973), which was a race discrimination case brought under Title VII of the Civil Rights Act of 1964. In that case, the Supreme Court held that when relying on circumstantial evidence to prove discrimination, a court should employ a three-step "burden-shifting framework."

First, the plaintiff has the burden to prove his prima facie case, specifically that he:

1.   Belongs to a protected class;

2.   Is qualified for the position;

3.   Suffered an adverse employment action; and

4.   Was either replaced by someone outside of his protected class or was treated less favorably than someone similarly situated but in a different protected class.

Assuming the plaintiff meets this burden, the burden (only the burden of production, not the burden of persuasion, as later explained by the Court) shifts to the defendant-employer to articulate a legitimate, non-discriminatory reason for the adverse employment action. This is a very easy burden because, assuming there is no employment contract, the default rule in almost all states is employment is "at-will," which means that an employer can terminate an employee for good reason, bad reason, or no reason at all. Because of this at-will presumption, employers can give almost any non-discriminatory reason to meet this very easy burden.

The burden then shifts back to the plaintiff to prove (by a preponderance of the evidence) that the defendant's articulated reason is not the real reason, and is instead a pretext for discrimination. This is most often accomplished by demonstrating that the defendant treated the plaintiff less favorably than someone who was similarly situated but in a different protected class. Thus, for instance, imagine that an African-American employee and a white employee both engaged in the same behavior—not showing up for work without notice for a certain number of days. If the black employee is terminated and the white employee is merely given a verbal reprimand, this would be persuasive evidence that the defendant's articulated reason for terminating the black employee— missing work without notice—is not the true reason, but rather, race discrimination was the real reason for the termination. Of course, if there were other differences between the two employees, this different treatment would not be as compelling. The *Monroe* case below discusses the burden-shifting framework in the context of an ADA case.

MONROE V. INDIANA DEPARTMENT OF TRANSPORTATION
871 F.3d 495 (7th Cir. 2017)

WILLIAMS, CIRCUIT JUDGE.

Jeff Monroe worked for the Indiana Department of Transportation ("INDOT") for just over twenty-one years. In January 2013, after seven or eight of Monroe's subordinates went to Monroe's supervisor, Terry George, to complain about Monroe's treatment of them, INDOT conducted an investigation of Monroe's conduct. During the investigation, Monroe disclosed that recently he had been diagnosed with Post Traumatic Stress Disorder ("PTSD"). After completing the investigation, INDOT discharged Monroe for creating a hostile and intimidating work environment. Monroe then sued INDOT and its Commissioner alleging various claims, including that he was terminated "on the basis of" or "solely because of" his mental disability in violation of the Americans With Disabilities Act ("ADA") and Section 504 of the Rehabilitation Act. The district court granted defendants' motion for summary judgment. Monroe now appeals, claiming that he provided sufficient evidence that INDOT's proffered reason for discharging him was pretextual and that INDOT treated similarly situated non-disabled employees more favorably than they treated him. Because we find there is not a genuine issue of material fact regarding either of Monroe's contentions, we affirm the district court.

I.   BACKGROUND

Monroe began working for INDOT on January 6, 1992 and continued his employment until he was terminated on February 4, 2013. The last position Monroe held with INDOT was unit foreman on the night shift, from 8 p.m. until 6 a.m. Monroe supervised fourteen regular employees and four seasonal employees. As part of his job, Monroe had the difficult task of helping to clean up human remains after traffic accidents. He also witnessed a co-worker die after a work-related accident.

Monroe faced challenging circumstances outside of his work for INDOT as well. He had served in combat in the Gulf War. In late 2012 Monroe's sister, who had lived with him, died of cancer. While employed at INDOT, Monroe also worked a second job as a stagehand. He testified that near the end of his employment with INDOT, he was not sleeping well and had become irritable and easily upset.

In December 2012, Monroe spoke with his supervisor George and told him that he was stressed, burned out, could not sleep, and that he wanted to be transferred to a day shift position. In January 2013, after George did not get back to him, Monroe met with George and George's supervisor, J.D. Brooks. Monroe again requested to be transferred to the day shift, but was told that no position was available.

On January 7, 2013, George completed a performance review for Monroe in which he gave Monroe an overall performance rating of "Exceeds

Expectations" for 2012. Monroe had received the same rating from other supervisors for 2010 and 2011 as well.

A. January 24, 2013 Incident

On the evening of January 24, 2013, Monroe arrived for his usual 8 p.m. to 6 a.m. shift. During a safety briefing, Monroe informed his subordinates that some of them would have to go to another unit to help prepare some equipment for a predicted overnight snowfall. According to Monroe, crew members Johnny Perkins and Josh McClung objected and complained about doing other peoples' work. Perkins told Monroe he did not respect the crew and Monroe responded that respect had to be earned. Monroe then dropped his clipboard on the desk, said, "f*** this," and told his crew leader Danny Wise to take over.

Monroe went into his office to calm down and then asked Perkins to meet him in the wash bay, which was an area with more privacy. Monroe contends that Perkins tried to fight him in the wash bay but that he would not fight and instead told Perkins to come to his house so they could discuss why Perkins wanted to fight all the time.

The next day, January 25, after they had completed their shift, seven or eight of Monroe's subordinates went to speak to George about Monroe's treatment of them. When George heard the nature of the employees' complaints, he called in his supervisor, J.D. Brooks. Brooks in turn called in Jeff Neuman, Human Resources Manager of the Greenfield District, to listen to the employees' concerns. The employees stated that Monroe screamed at them, treated them with no respect, threatened to terminate them, and publicly ridiculed one employee who had a hearing impairment. After listening to the employees' statements, it was decided that Neuman would conduct an investigation into their complaints.

B. Investigation of Complaints Against Monroe

On Sunday, January 27, 2013, George called Monroe at home to let him know that some complaints had been made and that he needed to attend a meeting in George's office the next day. During the conversation, Monroe told George that he had been given a preliminary diagnosis of PTSD.

On January 28, Monroe met with George, Brooks, and Neuman, although George left soon after the meeting began. Monroe was told that an investigation of complaints made about him would be conducted. He was offered the choice of either taking vacation or moving to a different location during the investigation. Monroe chose to take vacation. During the meeting, Monroe told Brooks and Neuman that he had spoken to a therapist who believed he had PTSD.

Also on January 28, seven of the original employees who met with George, Brooks, and Neuman on January 25 each gave written statements about Monroe. Several said that at the January 24 safety briefing Monroe had cursed at the crew, called them names, yelled, and threatened to fight Perkins. Several also said that Monroe's yelling, threatening to fire employees, and belittling employees had been going on for quite some time. Edward (Eddie) Sellers, the employee with a hearing impairment, said that Monroe made him feel bad for asking Monroe to repeat an assignment when Sellers did not hear him initially, that Monroe told him he should wear a "bell-tone" referring to Sellers' "lack of hearing," and that Monroe disciplined him like a child.

On January 29, Monroe was interviewed about the allegations made against him. Monroe stated he had PTSD and depression that affected his sleep. He said not getting sleep caused him to get frustrated easily, although he denied using profanity or blowing up on January 24. He said, "I don't handle Eddie [Sellers] like I should—[I] talk[ ] real slow to him."

As the investigation continued, a number of other employees and former employees were also interviewed regarding their experiences with Monroe. The eleven current crew members reporting to Monroe that had not already given written statements were interviewed and only three had primarily positive things to say about him. The rest had either mixed or mostly negative comments including that Monroe was testy, intimidating, volatile, demeaning, militaristic, and disrespectful. Some also reported that Monroe threatened their jobs and that he made fun of Sellers. Eight former employees were also interviewed. A few said they never had a problem with Monroe, but others said working for Monroe was stressful, that he would have outbursts and be demeaning, and that he used military methods to get the work done.

When the investigation was completed, Neuman, Brooks, George, and Brandye Hendrickson, who was then District Deputy Commissioner, met to discuss what action to take. According to Neuman, they believed "it wasn't clear whether the diagnosis [of PTSD] was legitimate or not . . ." because Monroe obtained the diagnosis right after a number of employees had complained about him and because Monroe did not produce documentation or even explain where he had gotten the diagnosis. The attendees at the meeting unanimously agreed that Monroe should be terminated. Monroe was discharged on February 4, 2013 for "consistently exhibit[ing] hostile and intimidating behavior in the execution of [his] responsibilities to the employees . . . assigned to [his] supervision."

C. INDOT's Treatment of Other Employees

Monroe identified three INDOT employees who also had instances of inappropriate conduct and were not fired. Monroe testified that in 2009 or 2010 an employee named Jim Patrick supervised five unit foremen, including Monroe. Monroe stated that four of the five unit foremen complained that Patrick was belittling and undermining his subordinates. According to Monroe, Patrick was not officially demoted, but his supervisory authority was taken away.

Between 2007 and 2009, Jeff Wilson, a unit foreman, was reprimanded, placed on a performance improvement plan, and given a poor performance rating for various shortcomings, including mistreating his subordinates. In 2010, Wilson was demoted for creating a hostile work environment for his employees. In 2014, when Wilson yelled at his former supervisor about a performance rating Wilson had received, he was given the option to resign or be discharged. He chose to resign.

The third employee identified by Monroe, Jim Branson, was disciplined for acting unprofessionally in February 2012 when he told two co-workers to "get away from the f***ing truck" he wanted to drive. According to Monroe, during the incident Branson also threw down a squeegee, cursed, and stomped his feet. Branson was given a three-day suspension for that infraction. In May 2013, George demoted Branson from the position of unit foreman after he "put his hands" on a co-worker. The document memorializing Branson's demotion stated that he had engaged in "[r]epeated and consistent inappropriate conduct in performing management and supervisory duties which have resulted in diminished ability to effectively manage the operations and personnel of the Indianapolis Sub-District."

D. INDOT's Employees Become At-Will Employees

Before July 1, 2011, INDOT employees were considered "non-merit employees." As such, they could appeal suspensions, demotions, and terminations imposed on them and INDOT would need to show "just cause" for the discipline to be upheld. On July 1, 2011, Indiana state law changed and INDOT employees became "unclassified employees." An unclassified employee "is an employee at will . . ." and "may be dismissed, demoted, disciplined, or transferred for any reason that does not contravene public policy." Ind. Code § 4–15–2.2–24. INDOT employees may still appeal discipline, such as discharge, however INDOT no longer has to show "just cause" for its disciplinary actions. Instead, the burden is now on the former employee to establish that "a public policy exception to the employment at will doctrine was the reason for the employee's discharge." Ind. Code Ann. § 4–15–2.2–42.

E. Proceedings in the District Court

Monroe filed suit against defendants on February 20, 2014 alleging, among other claims, that his discharge constituted disability discrimination . . . in violation of the ADA, as amended, and the Rehabilitation Act. Monroe requested damages, reinstatement, and front pay if reinstatement was not available.

On March 31, 2016, the district court granted defendants' motion for summary judgment. With regard to Monroe's discriminatory termination claim, the district court found that Monroe did not show that INDOT's proffered reason for discharging Monroe was pretextual and he did not identify a similarly situated non-disabled employee who was treated more favorably than he was treated. . . . Monroe now appeals the district court's decision to grant defendants' motion for summary judgment on his discriminatory discharge claim. . . .

II. ANALYSIS

We review the district court's decision to grant defendants' motion for summary judgment *de novo*. . . .

A. Standard for Analyzing ADA and Rehabilitation Act Claims

The ADA, as amended, provides, "No covered entity shall discriminate against a qualified individual on the basis of disability in regard to . . . discharge of employees . . ." 42 U.S.C. § 12112(a). "To prove a violation of § 12112(a), a plaintiff must show that: (1) he is disabled; (2) he is otherwise qualified to perform the essential functions of the job with or without reasonable accommodation; and (3) the adverse job action was caused by his disability." *Roberts v. City of Chi.*, 817 F.3d 561, 565 (7th Cir. 2016). To establish the third prong and survive summary judgment, a plaintiff must show a genuine issue of material fact exists regarding whether his disability was the "but for" reason for the adverse action, in this case termination. *Serwatka v. Rockwell Automation, Inc.*, 591 F.3d 957, 962 (7th Cir. 2010).

In *Serwatka* we held that "a plaintiff complaining of discriminatory discharge under the ADA must show that his or her employer would not have fired him but for his actual or perceived disability; proof of mixed motives will not suffice." *Id.* However, this holding applies to the language of the ADA before it was amended by the ADA Amendments Act ("ADAAA"). One of the changes made to the statute under the ADAAA was to change the language from prohibiting employers from discriminating "because of" a disability to prohibiting employers from discriminating "on the basis of" a disability. We noted in *Serwatka*, and in other cases since then, that it is an open question whether the change from "because of" to "on the basis of" changes the "but for" causation standard. *Id.* at 961 n.1; *see also Roberts*, 817 F.3d at 565 n.1; *Hooper v. Proctor Health Care Inc.*, 804 F.3d 846, 853 n. 2 (7th Cir. 2015). Like the parties in *Roberts* and *Hooper*, the parties in this case have not argued that another causation standard should apply, so we will continue to apply the "but for" causation standard.

To show that disability discrimination was the "but for" reason for the termination, a plaintiff can use either direct or circumstantial evidence. Direct evidence would be an admission that the defendant fired the plaintiff on the basis of his disability. Circumstantial evidence may include

> (1) suspicious timing; (2) ambiguous statements or behavior towards other employees in the protected group; (3) evidence,

statistical or otherwise, that similarly situated employees outside of the protected group systematically receive better treatment; and (4) evidence that the employer offered a pretextual reason for an adverse employment action.

Bunn, 753 F.3d at 684.

Some of our previous decisions have referred to this method of proof as the "direct method" of proving disability discrimination. *See, e.g., Hooper*, 804 F.3d at 853; *Bunn* 753 F.3d at 683. In *Hooper* and *Bunn* we noted that a plaintiff may also proceed under the "indirect method" of proving disability discrimination by employing the burden-shifting method established in *McDonnell-Douglas Corp. v. Green*, 411 U.S. 792, 93 S.Ct. 1817 (1973). *See Hooper*, 804 at 853; *Bunn*, 753 F.3d at 685. However, since deciding *Hooper* and *Bunn*, we have tried to move away from the many multifactored tests in employment discrimination cases and decide, when considering the evidence as a whole, "whether the evidence would permit a reasonable factfinder to conclude that the plaintiff's race, ethnicity, sex, religion, or other proscribed factor caused the discharge . . ." *Ortiz v. Werner Enter., Inc.*, 834 F.3d 760, 765 (7th Cir. 2016). As will be discussed below, in this case, regardless of the method of proof used, we find there is not sufficient evidence to create a genuine issue of fact that Monroe's disability was the "but for" cause of his discharge.

* * *

Monroe asserts that the district court should not have granted defendants' motion for summary judgment on his discriminatory discharge claims because he has sufficient evidence that INDOT's asserted reason for discharging him—that he created a hostile and intimidating working environment for his subordinates—is pretextual, and because he has put forth sufficient evidence that similarly situated non-disabled employees were treated better than he was treated. We disagree with both of Monroe's contentions.

B. Reason for Discharge Not Pretextual

Monroe claims that the district court improperly ignored evidence he submitted to support his claim that INDOT's proffered reason for its termination of Monroe is pretextual. Specifically, Monroe points to the following issues he believes establish pretext: (1) he received positive performance evaluations for the three years leading up to his termination and therefore he could not have "consistently" exhibited hostile and intimidating behavior; (2) INDOT made a misstatement in its EEOC position statement and indicated that all the employees who were at the January 24 safety briefing complained about Monroe the next day; (3) INDOT made inconsistent statements during discovery regarding whether George told Neuman and Brooks about Monroe's PTSD; and (4) the decision makers discussed Monroe's PTSD before deciding to terminate him. We do not find that these issues, alone or in combination, are sufficient to establish pretext.

"In determining whether an employer's stated reason [for discharge] is pretextual, the question is not whether the employer's stated reason was inaccurate or unfair, but whether the employer honestly believed the reason it has offered to explain the discharge." *Harper v. C.R. England, Inc.*, 687 F.3d 297, 311 (7th Cir. 2012). "Pretext involves more than just faulty reasoning or mistaken judgment on the part of the employer; it is [a] lie, specifically a phony reason for some action." *Argyropoulos*, 539 F.3d at 736. The issues cited by Monroe in no way show that the legitimate nondiscriminatory reason offered by INDOT for Monroe's discharge was a lie or a sham to cover up discriminatory motives.

Although it is undisputed that Monroe received performance evaluations of "Exceeds Expectations" for three years before his discharge, including his last evaluation which was completed less than one month before his discharge, this does not show that INDOT's reason for discharge was pretextual. George was not aware of Monroe's continued and serious mistreatment of his subordinates before seven or eight of them came to him to complain about Monroe on January 25. When that group came to his office, he took appropriate steps, including involving his supervisor Brooks and Neuman from Human Resources. Neuman conducted an extensive investigation, interviewing not only all of Monroe's current subordinates, but contacting former employees as well. Many current and former employees confirmed the complaints made by the original group of employees who had come to George's office on January 25, including that Monroe "consistently" exhibited hostile and intimidating behavior for many months, or perhaps even longer.

It is unfortunate that George did not have the information from the investigation when he filled out Monroe's performance evaluation in early January 2013. However, it is not altogether surprising given that many employees said that Monroe threatened to discharge them and one employee mentioned that when he had complained before he faced retaliation. In summary, Monroe's earlier positive evaluations do not call into question INDOT's proffered reason for discharge. "Certainly earlier evaluations cannot, by themselves, demonstrate the adequacy of performance at the crucial time when the employment action is taken." *Moser v. Ind. Dep't. of Corr.*, 406 F.3d 895, 901 (7th Cir. 2005).

Similarly, the misstatement INDOT made in the position statement it submitted to the EEOC was not sufficient to establish pretext. In its position statement INDOT indicated that only seven employees were present at Monroe's safety briefing on January 24, and that all seven employees went to George's office to complain about Monroe after their shift ended on January 25. In fact, Monroe supervised eighteen employees so, if none was absent, presumably there were eighteen employees at the safety briefing and not all of them went to complain to George on January 25. While it is more compelling to say that all employees at a meeting went to complain about their supervisor after the meeting, it is not insignificant that seven or eight of eighteen employees went to complain. In short, INDOT's erroneous statement, while careless, is not significant enough to create a genuine issue of fact regarding whether INDOT's proffered reason for Monroe's discharge was pretextual. *See Lane v. Riverview Hosp.*, 835 F.3d 691, 697 (7th Cir. 2016) (erroneously telling EEOC that decision maker was not aware of an allegation against a comparator is not sufficient to support an inference of discrimination when there was no other evidence "corroborating unlawful intent").

The issue of whether George told Brooks and Neuman about Monroe's PTSD is similarly insignificant. George testified that he did not tell Brooks and Neuman about Monroe's PTSD, and Neuman testified that George did tell him that Monroe said he had PTSD. However, this disagreement is irrelevant because it is undisputed that Monroe himself told Brooks and Neuman about his PTSD during their meetings on January 28 and January 29. Monroe cannot establish pretext by pointing to a disagreement between two defense witnesses regarding an insignificant detail.

Finally, the fact that the decision makers discussed Monroe's statement that he had PTSD during the meeting at which they decided to discharge him does not establish that their stated reason for discharge was a pretext for discrimination. According to Neuman, the decision makers discussed whether Monroe actually had PTSD, given the fortuitous timing of his disclosure and given Monroe's failure to submit any documentation from a health care provider confirming the diagnosis. It is illogical for Monroe to argue that the discussion here about whether he had PTSD shows an intent to discriminate against him because he had PTSD.

Moreover, even if the decision makers believed Monroe had PTSD, and that his PTSD caused him to not be able to sleep and to be volatile toward his subordinates, this still would not establish pretext. "[A]n employer may, consistent with the ADA and the Rehabilitation Act, terminate an employee for inappropriate behavior even when that behavior is precipitated by the employee's disability . . ." *Felix v. Wisconsin Dep't. of Transp.*, 828 F.3d 560, 574 (7th Cir. 2016).

In summary, the issues raised by Monroe, neither individually nor in combination, establish that INDOT's stated reason for Monroe's discharge is pretextual. Monroe cannot establish pretext by pointing to a positive performance evaluation filled out before an extensive investigation revealed his misconduct toward his subordinates. Similarly, highlighting a relatively minor misstatement in an EEOC position statement or a disagreement among defense witnesses about an irrelevant detail cannot establish pretext. Finally, the fact that the decision makers questioned the veracity of Monroe's statement that he had PTSD in no way supports the contention that INDOT's stated reason for discharging Monroe was a lie meant to cover up disability discrimination.

C. Monroe's Comparators Are Not Similarly Situated

Monroe identified three non-disabled INDOT employees, Jim Patrick, Jeff Wilson, and Jim Branson, who Monroe contends engaged in misconduct similar to his and were not discharged. Monroe asserts that INDOT's failure to discharge the non-disabled employees shows that his discharge was "on the basis of" . . . his disability. We agree with the district court that none of the three comparators named by Monroe was similarly situated to him and therefore they cannot be used by Monroe to create a genuine issue of fact regarding whether Monroe's disability was the "but for" . . . cause of his termination.

"In order for an individual to be similarly situated to the plaintiff, the plaintiff must show that the individual is 'directly comparable to her [or him] in all material respects.'" *Burks v. Wis. Dep't. of Transp.*, 464 F.3d 744, 751 (7th Cir. 2006). "The similarly situated inquiry is a flexible, common-sense one that asks, at bottom, whether 'there are enough common factors . . . to allow for a meaningful comparison in order to divine whether intentional discrimination was at play.'" *Henry v. Jones*, 507 F.3d 558, 564 (7th Cir. 2007). Generally, a plaintiff must show that his comparators "dealt with the same supervisor, were subject to the same standards and had engaged in similar conduct without such differentiating or mitigating circumstances as would distinguish their conduct or the employer's treatment of them." *Gates v. Caterpillar, Inc.*, 513 F.3d 680, 690 (7th Cir. 2008).

Jim Patrick was not similarly situated to Monroe for a number of reasons. First, Monroe submitted very little evidence regarding Patrick's misdeeds. Monroe testified at his deposition that four out of five foremen supervised by Patrick complained about Patrick for "belittling" his subordinates and "undermining" them by changing the work plans at the last minute. Monroe did not give any details regarding what Patrick said or did to "belittle" his subordinates and he did not say for how long the behavior had been occurring. Based on this sparse description, Monroe failed to establish that Patrick's behavior was at all comparable to Monroe's behavior of creating a hostile and intimidating work environment over a period of months (or perhaps even longer) that included targeting an employee because of his hearing impairment.

Another reason Patrick was not similarly situated to Monroe is because none of the supervisors involved in Monroe's discharge was involved in the decision to take away Patrick's supervisory responsibilities in 2009 or 2010. . . .

An additional reason why both Patrick and Jeff Wilson were not similarly situated to Monroe is because at the time Patrick and Wilson engaged in misconduct arguably similar to Monroe's and were not fired, before July 1, 2011, INDOT employees could be discharged only if INDOT could show "just cause" for the discharge. After July 1, 2011, all INDOT employees became "unclassified" or "at will" employees. So, after July 1, 2011, INDOT no longer had to show "just cause" for discipline. Instead, an INDOT employee could successfully appeal a discharge only if the employee could show that "a public policy exception to the employment at will doctrine was the reason for the employee's discharge." Ind. Code Ann. § 4–15–2.2–42. As George noted in his affidavit, "during the last few years INDOT has taken a much firmer stance on issues involving negative and hostile behaviors in the workplace and mistreatment of subordinates."

Jeff Wilson is a perfect example of this "firmer stance." Between 2007 and 2010, Wilson received a written reprimand, was placed on a performance improvement plan, and was ultimately demoted for various shortcomings including mistreatment of subordinates and creating a hostile work environment. He was not discharged during that time period. However, in 2014, when he angrily approached a former supervisor and yelled at him about a performance review, Wilson was given the option to resign or be discharged. In summary, because Patrick and Wilson engaged in misconduct arguably similar to Monroe's misconduct before the standard for appealing discipline changed from "just cause" to "at will," Patrick and Wilson cannot be deemed similarly situated to Monroe.

* * *

The only comparator identified by Monroe who engaged in misconduct arguably similar to Monroe's misconduct after July 1, 2011 and who was not fired was Jim Branson. However, upon closer inspection, it is evident that Branson's misconduct was not as egregious as Monroe's and therefore the two employees are not similarly situated. As discussed above, Branson was disciplined in 2012 for telling two co-workers to "get away from the f***ing truck" he wanted to drive, throwing down a squeegee, and stomping his feet. In 2013, he was demoted after a co-worker stated that Branson "put his hands on" him. The wording used in Branson's demotion document ("[r]epeated and consistent inappropriate conduct in performing management and supervisory duties") sounds similar to the wording used in Monroe's termination letter ("consistently exhibit[ing] hostile and intimidating behavior in the execution of [his] responsibilities to the employees . . . assigned to [his] supervision"). Yet, the conduct of the two men was quite distinguishable.

While we agree that a supervisor swearing at a co-worker or putting his hands on a co-worker is serious misconduct, these were apparently two individual incidents occurring over a year apart. In contrast, according to many of Monroe's current and former subordinates, Monroe created a hostile and abusive work environment for his subordinates over a lengthy period of time, including targeting an employee with a hearing disability.

Monroe's behavior was so extreme that it culminated in many of his subordinates going to Monroe's supervisor and stating that they could no longer work under Monroe. In summary, while neither Branson nor Monroe acted in an appropriate manner for a supervisor, Monroe has not submitted sufficient evidence to show that Branson's failings were comparable to his own failings. Therefore, the district court was correct to grant defendants' motion for summary judgment.

III. CONCLUSION

The judgment of the district court is AFFIRMED.

NOTES AND QUESTIONS

1.   *Methods of proving intentional discrimination.* Although we will spend most of this chapter discussing the ways in which the ADA is different from other anti-discrimination statutes, this first case demonstrates that intentional discrimination under the ADA is proven in much the same way that it is proven under other anti-discrimination statutes, such as Title VII. As the court in *Monroe* notes, intentional discrimination can be proven by direct or indirect evidence. In the context of this case, direct evidence would be something like a supervisor (near the time of termination) stating: "Monroe's PTSD scares me. I don't want someone like that working here. Let's terminate him." Perhaps surprisingly, statements like this are often made in the disability context (much more often than in the context of race discrimination). Supervisors often make stereotypical comments about an employee's actual or perceived disability. However, as the rest of this chapter discusses, the employer might argue that the employee with the disability was not qualified or that the employer has a right to terminate him because his disability causes him to be a danger to other employees (called the "direct threat" defense, discussed *infra*). Without such a defense, the direct evidence above would be sufficient to prove intentional discrimination. But without such direct evidence, the plaintiff has to prove his case using indirect or circumstantial evidence.

2.   *Proving a case with circumstantial evidence.* As discussed before the *Monroe* case, courts generally follow Title VII's *McDonnell Douglas* burden-shifting framework in ADA cases. The first step is proving the prima facie case. Although different courts state it differently, the formulation used in *Monroe* has become increasingly common: (1) he is disabled; (2) he is otherwise qualified to perform the essential functions of the job with or without reasonable accommodation; and (3) the adverse job action was caused by his disability. The Seventh Circuit has moved away from the traditional burden-shifting framework where, after the plaintiff establishes the prima facie case, the employer would articulate a legitimate non-discriminatory reason and then the plaintiff would have to prove that the employer's reason was a pretext for discrimination. The Seventh Circuit's approach basically moves the plaintiff's final burden in the burden-shifting framework up to the prima facie case.

Ultimately, the court notes, the inquiry is whether the plaintiff can establish that his disability caused his termination.

As the court states, plaintiffs can prove *causation*—that the disability caused the adverse employment action—using the following types of circumstantial evidence: (1) suspicious timing; (2) ambiguous statements or behavior towards other employees in the protected group; (3) evidence, statistical or otherwise, that similarly situated employees outside of the protected group systematically receive better treatment; and (4) evidence that the employer offered a pretextual reason for an adverse employment action.

3. *Analyzing* Monroe. The plaintiff in *Monroe* points to two common ways of proving that the employer's reason for terminating him was pretextual—inconsistent statements or explanations offered by the employer's witnesses, and comparators, non-disabled employees who were treated more favorably. Two of Monroe's arguments merit further discussion. The first is the fact that Monroe's supervisor evaluated him as "exceeds expectations" for three years prior to his termination, including the latest evaluation just one month before his termination. This is a very common fact pattern in employment discrimination lawsuits. Supervisors often have a difficult time being critical in evaluations. In this case, the employer's explanation was that the supervisor had been unaware of how Monroe had been treating his subordinates, in part because Monroe allegedly threatened his subordinates with termination if they reported him. Do you agree with the court's decision to ignore this evidence? Or is the positive evaluation one month before his termination suspicious enough that Monroe's case should have gone to a jury?

The other primary argument that Monroe made to try to prove his termination was discriminatory was to point to comparators, non-disabled coworkers who received more favorable treatment than Monroe. Using comparators to prove causation is very common in discrimination cases (although less common under the ADA than Title VII). But as the court noted in *Monroe*, the comparators need to be similar in all material respects. "Generally, a plaintiff must show that his comparators 'dealt with the same supervisor, were subject to the same standards and had engaged in similar conduct without such differentiating or mitigating circumstances as would distinguish their conduct or the employer's treatment of them.'" Do you agree with the court's explanations for why the three comparators were not similarly situated enough to Monroe? Why or why not?

4. *Misconduct not excused.* The court stated in *Monroe* that even if the employer believed Monroe had PTSD, that would still not protect Monroe from termination. As the court noted: "[A]n employer may, consistent with the ADA and the Rehabilitation Act, terminate an employee for inappropriate behavior even when that behavior is precipitated by the employee's disability . . ." Felix v. Wisconsin Dep't. of Transp., 828 F.3d 560, 574 (7th Cir. 2016). This scenario arises quite frequently, and the issue is often one of timing. If an employee requests an accommodation *before* the employee has engaged in misconduct or violated the employer's rules, the employer is likely obligated to provide one. But if the employee waits until he has already engaged in misconduct, the

employer is not obligated to provide an accommodation that would erase or excuse that misconduct.

Imagine an employee has narcolepsy (a sleeping disorder where the person may fall asleep suddenly, with no warning). If the employee asks the employer for an accommodation—perhaps a short leave of absence to get the disability under control through medication or other treatment—the employer would likely be obligated to provide such an accommodation. However, if the employee does not seek an accommodation but then falls asleep on the job, which is a violation of the employer's rules, the employer would have the right to terminate the employee. In this case, if Monroe had asked for an accommodation for his PTSD before he began treating his subordinates poorly, he might have been entitled to one. But the employer here was within its rights to terminate Monroe for the abusive behavior of his subordinates, even if his behavior was caused by his disability. What do you think of this distinction? Should employees who engage in misconduct or violate the employers' rules because of their disabilities be given a second chance before they are terminated or otherwise disciplined?

5.   *Mixed motive vs. but-for causation.* The court in *Monroe* briefly discusses the standard of causation applicable in ADA discrimination cases. There is still a debate (albeit a narrowing one) over whether the ADA requires "but-for" causation, or will allow a plaintiff to proceed on a "mixed-motive" theory. The mixed-motive theory, first announced in *Price Waterhouse* (a sex discrimination case) and then codified in the Civil Rights Act of 1991, only requires that a plaintiff prove her protected characteristic was a "motivating factor" for the defendant's adverse employment action, even if other factors also motivated the defendant. Price Waterhouse, 490 U.S. at 258; 42 U.S.C. § 2000e–2(m). Because this statutory mixed-motive provision only modified Title VII, and not the other employment discrimination statutes, the U.S. Supreme Court subsequently held that the mixed-motive analysis does not apply to age discrimination claims brought pursuant to the Age Discrimination in Employment Act. Gross v. FBL Financial Services, Inc., 557 U.S. 167, 174–76 (2009). Four years later, the Court also held that the mixed-motive standard does not apply when a plaintiff is suing under the anti-retaliation provision of Title VII. *See* University of Texas Southwestern Medical Center v. Nassar, 570 U.S. 338, 133 S.Ct. 2517, 2534 (2013).

The Supreme Court has not yet weighed in on whether an ADA plaintiff can proceed under a mixed-motive theory or must utilize the more difficult "but-for" causation test. Lower courts have reached mixed results. Before the *Gross* and *Nassar* decisions, most courts held that plaintiffs could proceed under a mixed-motive theory. *See, e.g.,* Parker v. Columbia Pictures Indus., 204 F.3d 326, 337 (2d Cir. 2000); Baird v. Rose, 192 F.3d 462, 470 (4th Cir. 1999); Foster v. Arthur Andersen, LLP, 168 F.3d 1029, 1033–34 (7th Cir. 1999); McNely v. Ocala Star-Banner Corp., 99 F.3d 1068, 1076 (11th Cir. 1996); Katz v. City Metal Co., 87 F.3d 26, 33 (1st Cir. 1996); Buchanan v. City of Antonio, 85 F.3d 196, 200 (5th Cir. 1996); Pedigo v. P.A.M. Transp., Inc., 60 F.3d 1300, 1301 (8th Cir. 1995). However, since the Supreme Court's opinions in *Gross* and *Nassar*, most courts have held that the more stringent "but-for" causation standard is appropriate for ADA cases rather than the more lenient "mixed-motive" standard. *See, e.g.*, Murray v. Mayo Clinic, 934 F.3d 1101, 1105–07 (9th Cir. 2019) (applying but-for causation standard to ADA claim, overturning its prior precedent); Lewis v. Humboldt Acquisition Corp., 681 F.3d 312, 321 (6th Cir. 2012) (same); Serwatka v. Rockwell Automation, Inc., 591 F.3d 957, 962 (7th Cir. 2010) (same). The court in *Monroe* briefly discusses whether the change in language in the ADAAA from "because of" to "on the basis of" a disability is significant. In other words, did Congress intend to change the standard required to prove causation in ADA cases after the Amendments? The court in *Monroe* refuses to address this question because neither party contested the use of the but-for causation standard. This question was addressed more directly in a couple of cases, with the courts holding that the change from "because of" to "on the basis of" is not meaningful and therefore, the but-for causation standard still applies. *See, e.g.*, Natofsky v. City of New York, 921 F.3d 337, 349–50 (2d Cir. 2019), *cert. denied*, 140 S.Ct. 2668 (2020); Gentry v. East West Partners Club Management Co. Inc., 816 F.3d 228, 235–36 (4th Cir. 2016).

B. QUALIFIED INDIVIDUAL WITH A DISABILITY

1. GENERAL REQUIREMENTS

Title I of the ADA defines a "qualified individual" as:

... an individual who, with or without reasonable accommodation, can perform the essential functions of the employment position that such individual holds or desires. For purposes of this subchapter, consideration shall be given to the employer's judgment as to what functions of a job are essential, and if an employer has prepared a written description before advertising or interviewing applicants for the job, this description shall be considered evidence of the essential functions of the job.

42 U.S.C. § 12111(8).

The regulations contain the following definitions:

(m) The term *"qualified,"* with respect to an individual with a disability means that the individual satisfies the requisite skill, experience, education and other job-related requirements of the employment position such individual holds or desires, and who, with or without reasonable accommodation, can perform the essential functions of such position.

(n) Essential functions.

(1) In general. The term essential functions means the fundamental job duties of the employment position the individual with a disability holds or desires. The term

"essential functions" does not include the marginal functions of the position.

29 C.F.R. § 1630.2.

KEITH V. COUNTY OF OAKLAND
703 F.3d 918 (6th Cir. 2013)

GRIFFIN, CIRCUIT JUDGE:

Plaintiff Nicholas Keith, a deaf individual, filed the instant action alleging that defendant Oakland County discriminated against him on the basis of disability in violation of the Americans with Disabilities Act ("ADA"), 42 U.S.C. § 12101, *et seq.,* and the Rehabilitation Act of 1973 ("Rehabilitation Act"), 29 U.S.C. § 794, *et seq.,* when it failed to hire him as a lifeguard. The district court granted Oakland County's motion for summary judgment. For the reasons that follow, we hold that genuine issues of material fact exist regarding whether Keith is otherwise qualified to be a lifeguard at Oakland County's wave pool, with or without reasonable accommodation. Accordingly, we reverse the district court's judgment and remand for further proceedings consistent with this opinion.

Keith has been deaf since his birth in 1980. When wearing an external sound transmitter, he can detect noises through his cochlear implant, such as alarms, whistles, and people calling for him. Because he is unable to speak verbally, he communicates using American Sign Language ("ASL").

In 2006, Keith enrolled in Oakland County's junior lifeguard training course. Oakland County provided an ASL interpreter to relay verbal instructions to him. The interpreter did not assist Keith in executing lifesaving tasks. Keith successfully completed the course.

In 2007, Keith enrolled in Oakland County's lifeguard training program. Candidates must pass a basic swim test to participate in the training. During training, candidates are taught how to enter the water, scan the water for distressed swimmers, execute basic saves, respond to spinal injuries, and perform CPR. With the assistance of an ASL interpreter to communicate verbal instructions, Keith successfully completed the training.

Having received his lifeguard certification, Keith applied for a lifeguard position at Oakland County's wave pool. The job announcement required applicants to be at least sixteen years old and pass Oakland County's water safety test and lifeguard training program. The application also contained the following condition of employment: "All persons hired by Oakland County must take and pass a medical examination from a county-appointed physician, at no cost to the applicant."

Katherine Stavale is Oakland County's recreation specialist. She contacted her supervisors to ask if she could offer Keith the position. She explained that Keith had requested an ASL interpreter to be present at staff meetings and further classroom instruction. Having received no objection, Stavale extended Keith an offer of employment, conditioned upon a pre-employment physical. In an email, Stavale told Keith, "you passed training and you did a good job, so we would like to offer you a part-time position as a lifeguard." Stavale asked him to contact her to set up a meeting to complete his paperwork and schedule his orientation sessions.

Shortly thereafter, Keith was examined by Dr. Paul Work, D.O. When Dr. Work entered the examination room, he looked at Keith's medical history and stated, "He's deaf; he can't be a lifeguard." Keith's mother asked Dr. Work, "Are you telling me you're going to fail him because he's deaf?" Dr. Work responded, "Well, I have to. I have a house and three sons to think about. If something happens, they're not going to sue you, they're not going to sue the county, they're going to come after me."

In his report, Dr. Work described Keith as "physically sound except for his deafness." Dr. Work did not believe that Keith could function independently as a lifeguard, but he thought that he could be a valuable member of a team if properly integrated and monitored. Dr. Work approved Keith's employment as a lifeguard if his deafness was *"constantly* accommodated." However, he did not say whether Keith could, in fact, be safely accommodated, and he expressed doubt that accommodation would always be adequate.

Having learned the results of the physical, Stavale placed Keith's employment on hold and contacted Wayne Crokus, the client manager at Ellis & Associates. Ellis is a group of aquatic safety and risk management consultants that provides guidance to Oakland County regarding its water park facilities and lifeguard training program. Oakland County follows Ellis's methodologies to train and test candidates for its lifeguard openings, but Ellis is not directly involved in the certification and employment of Oakland County's lifeguards. Oakland County is responsible for licensing and hiring its lifeguards.

Stavale told Crokus that she had trained and hired as a lifeguard a profoundly deaf individual. In response, Crokus expressed concern about whether a deaf individual could perform effectively as a lifeguard. He suggested to Stavale that a job-task analysis be done to determine whether Keith could perform the job with or without accommodation. Crokus has a background in aquatic safety and lifeguard training, but he has no education or experience regarding the ability of deaf people to work as lifeguards, and he did not conduct any research into the issue upon learning about Keith. He never communicated with Keith, never observed Keith during training, and never spoke with Dr. Work. . . .

After these discussions, Stavale prepared a six-page outline setting forth the accommodations that she believed could successfully integrate Keith, and she sent it to Crokus for feedback. Stavale explained:

    1.   Keith will carry laminated note cards in the pocket of his swim trunks to communicate with guests in non-emergency situations.

    2.   Keith does not need to hear to recognize and rescue a distressed swimmer; experience reveals that distressed swimmers do not cry out for help.

    3.   Keith will use his whistle and shake his head "no" to enforce pool rules.

    4.   Keith will briefly look at other lifeguards on duty when scanning his zone to see if they enter the pool for a save.

    5.   Because Keith cannot use the megaphone or radio, another lifeguard will have this responsibility when Keith is working.

    6.   Keith will not work the slide rotation, which should not be a problem because this is one of the favorite rotations and many lifeguards like to work more than one slide rotation.

    7.   The Emergency Action Plan ("EAP") will be modified, regardless of whether Keith is scheduled. To initiate the EAP, lifeguards will be required to signal with a fist in the air, opening and closing it like a siren. This will accommodate Keith and improve the effectiveness of the EAP for the entire team.

Crokus questioned Stavale on several of these accommodations and remained concerned about Keith's ability to function effectively as a lifeguard. He stated, "without 100 percent certainty that [the proposed accommodations] would always be effective, I don't think you could safely have [Keith] on the stand by himself." Ultimately, Stavale and her supervisors decided to revoke the offer of employment. . . .

Keith filed a complaint in the district court alleging violations of the ADA and the Rehabilitation Act. Oakland County moved for summary judgment, arguing that Keith is not "otherwise qualified" to be a lifeguard at its wave pool because he cannot effectively communicate with other lifeguards, patrons, emergency personnel, and injured persons. Further, Oakland County argued that hiring an additional lifeguard as an interpreter is an unreasonable accommodation.

Keith responded that he is "otherwise qualified" for the position and Oakland County revoked the offer of employment based on unfounded fear and speculation. According to Keith, he would require an interpreter only during staff meetings and further classroom instruction, which he argued is a reasonable accommodation. Keith also complained that Oakland County failed to make an individualized inquiry regarding his ability to perform the job or engage in an interactive process to determine whether he could be reasonably accommodated.

As evidence of his qualifications for the position, Keith provided the testimony of several experts. Anita Marchitelli has worked with deaf people in the area of lifeguarding and aquatics for more than thirty years. She is a certified lifeguard training instructor with the American Red Cross in the areas of lifeguarding, water safety, and CPR. She is also an associate professor in the physical education and recreation department at Gallaudet University, the only liberal arts university in the world dedicated to serving the needs of deaf individuals. She has certified more than 1,000 deaf lifeguards through the American Red Cross programs. According to Marchitelli, there have been no reported incidents of drowning or near drowning of any individuals over whom a deaf lifeguard was responsible. It is her professional opinion that the ability to hear is unnecessary to enable a person to perform the essential functions of a lifeguard. In her affidavit, Marchitelli notes that the world record for most lives saved is held by a deaf man, Leroy Colombo, who saved over 900 lives in his lifeguarding career.

Sheri Garnand is a deaf lifeguard certified by the American Red Cross. It is her professional opinion that the ability to hear is unnecessary to enable a person to perform the essential functions of a lifeguard. According to Garnand, distressed swimmers exhibit visual signs of distress, which a deaf person scanning his or her assigned area can detect. She believes that deaf lifeguards do not require accommodation to perform the essential functions of a lifeguard; in her opinion, an ASL interpreter is unnecessary.

Dr. Colleen Noble is a physician specializing in pediatric neurodevelopmental disabilities and has worked with hearing impaired individuals for over thirty years. It is Dr. Noble's opinion that deaf individuals have the potential to be excellent lifeguards. She stated that, in a noisy swimming area, recognizing a potential problem is almost completely visually based. Further, she said that individuals who become deaf before age three have better peripheral vision than hearing individuals. It is her opinion that Keith meets the criteria to become a lifeguard and his deafness should neither disqualify him nor require constant accommodation.

Addressing Oakland County's motion for summary judgment, the district court first concluded that Dr. Work failed to make an individualized inquiry regarding whether Keith's disability disqualified him from working as a lifeguard at Oakland County's wave pool. Nonetheless, the court determined that Oakland County, the ultimate decision-maker, made an individualized inquiry regarding Keith's abilities. The district court also determined that Keith failed to show that he could perform the essential communication functions of a lifeguard with or without reasonable accommodation. As such, the district court reasoned that any failure by Oakland County to engage in the interactive process regarding whether Keith could be accommodated did not establish a violation of the ADA.

Accordingly, it granted summary judgment in favor of Oakland County. In this appeal, Keith argues that the district court erred when it concluded as a matter of law that (1) Oakland County made an individualized inquiry regarding Keith's abilities; (2) he is unqualified to be a lifeguard at Oakland County's wave pool; (3) accommodating Keith would be unreasonable; and (4) any failure to engage in the interactive process was inconsequential because no reasonable accommodation was possible.

* * *

III.

The ADA makes it unlawful for an employer to "discriminate against a qualified individual on the basis of disability." 42 U.S.C. § 12112(a). The ADA defines "discriminate" to include the failure to provide reasonable accommodation to an otherwise qualified individual with a disability, unless doing so would impose an undue hardship on the employer's business. *Id.* § 12112(b)(5). To establish a prima facie case, a plaintiff must show that he is disabled and otherwise qualified for the position, either with or without reasonable accommodation. Once the plaintiff establishes a prima facie case, the burden shifts to the defendant to show that accommodating the plaintiff would impose an undue hardship on the operation of its business.

The parties do not dispute that Keith is disabled within the meaning of the ADA or that Oakland County rescinded the offer of employment because of his disability. . . .

A. Individualized Inquiry

As a threshold matter, "[t]he ADA mandates an individualized inquiry in determining whether an [applicant's] disability or other condition disqualifies him from a particular position." A proper evaluation involves consideration of the applicant's personal characteristics, his actual medical condition, and the effect, if any, the condition may have on his ability to perform the job in question. This follows from the ADA's underlying objective: "people with disabilities ought to be judged on the basis of their abilities; they should not be judged nor discriminated against based on unfounded fear, prejudice, ignorance, or mythologies; people ought to be judged on the relevant medical evidence and the abilities they have." The ADA requires employers to act, not based on stereotypes and generalizations about a disability, but based on the actual disability and the effect that disability has on the particular individual's ability to perform the job.

The district court properly determined that Dr. Work failed to make an individualized inquiry. After Dr. Work entered the examination room and briefly reviewed Keith's file, he declared, "He's deaf; he can't be a lifeguard." Dr. Work made no effort to determine whether, despite his deafness, Keith could nonetheless perform the essential functions of the position, either with or without reasonable accommodation. Indeed, Dr. Work has no education, training, or experience in assessing the ability of deaf individuals to work as lifeguards. Dr. Work's cursory medical examination is precisely the type that the ADA was designed to prohibit. . . .

In addition, although not addressed by the district court, we question whether Ellis, through its representatives, made an individualized inquiry regarding Keith's ability to perform the job. Ellis's representatives never spoke with Dr. Work, they never met Keith, and they never allowed Keith an opportunity to demonstrate his abilities. Although knowledgeable in aquatic safety, they have no education, training, or experience regarding the ability of deaf individuals to work as lifeguards. Indeed, the representatives testified that they could not provide an opinion regarding Keith's ability to perform the essential functions of the position without seeing him in the actual work environment with the proposed accommodations in place. It is also concerning that, when corresponding with Stavale about ways to incorporate Keith into the lifeguard team, an Ellis representative asked whether Keith would be able to perform perfectly "100 percent of the time." As Stavale acknowledged, that is an impossible standard to expect of any lifeguard. Individuals with disabilities cannot be held to a higher standard of performance than non-disabled individuals. *See* 42 U.S.C. § 12112(b)(3)(A) (prohibiting employers from "utilizing standards, criteria, or methods of administration . . . that have the effect of discrimination on the basis of disability").

Nonetheless, the district court concluded that Oakland County, the ultimate decision-maker, made an individualized inquiry. We do not disagree with this conclusion. Keith's abilities were observed during lifeguard training, accommodations were proposed to integrate Keith into the lifeguard team, and both staff and management were on board with the plan to hire Keith. That being the case, we question what changed? Did Oakland County alter its assessment based on Dr. Work's report and the advice of Ellis's representatives? If so, did Oakland County's individualized inquiry satisfy the ADA's mandate? Because it strikes us as incongruent with the underlying objective of the ADA for an employer to make an individualized inquiry only to defer to the opinions and advice of those who have not, we direct the district court to consider these questions on remand.

B. "Otherwise Qualified"

Whether the ability to hear is an essential function of a lifeguard position has not been addressed by this court and, as far as we can tell, no court has squarely addressed it. . . .

Without any authority directly on point, we turn to the statutory text and accompanying regulations for guidance on the issue whether a deaf individual may be considered "otherwise qualified" for lifeguarding within the meaning of the ADA. We begin with the language of the statute itself.

We may also rely on the regulations interpreting the ADA, which we assume are valid unless contested.

As defined in the statute, an individual is "otherwise qualified" if he or she can perform the "essential functions" of the job with or without reasonable accommodation. 42 U.S.C. § 12111(8). The ADA instructs, "consideration shall be given to the employer's judgment as to what functions of a job are essential, and if an employer has prepared a written description before advertising or interviewing applicants for the job, this description shall be considered evidence of the essential functions of the job." *Id.* According to the regulations, "essential functions" refer to job duties that are "fundamental" rather than "marginal." 29 C.F.R. § 1630.2(n)(1). A job function may be considered essential because: (1) the position exists to perform that function; (2) there are a limited number of employees available among whom the performance of that job function can be distributed; or (3) the function is highly specialized so that the incumbent in the position is hired for his or her expertise or ability to perform the particular function. *Id.* § 1630.2(n)(2). Factors to consider when determining whether a job function is essential to the position include: (1) the employer's judgment; (2) the written job description; (3) the amount of time spent performing the function; (4) the consequences of not requiring performance of the function; (5) the work experience of past incumbents of the position; and (6) the current work experience of incumbents in similar jobs. *Id.* § 1630.2(n)(3). Whether a job function is essential is a question of fact that is typically not suitable for resolution on a motion for summary judgment.

In this case, Stavale testified regarding the need for lifeguards to effectively communicate while on the job. As Oakland County's representative, her judgment is entitled to deference. Further, the job announcement indicates that summer lifeguards are required to supervise water activities, enforce safety rules, maintain water areas, and teach swim lessons. To the extent that these job duties necessarily require communication, the description provides evidence that communicating is an essential function of being a lifeguard at Oakland County's wave pool. For the purposes of our analysis, this much can be presumed.

With regard to supervising water activities and lifesaving, Keith has presented evidence from which a jury could reasonably find that he can communicate effectively despite his deafness. Like other lifeguards, Keith can adhere to the "10/20 standard of zone protection," a scanning technique taught to lifeguards in which they must scan their entire zone every ten seconds and be able to reach any part of their zone within twenty seconds. This method is purely visual. Further, by passing Oakland County's lifeguard training program and earning his lifeguard certification, Keith demonstrated his ability to detect distressed swimmers, which several experts testified is almost completely visually based.

In addition to communicating with distressed swimmers, there is evidence that Keith can effectively communicate with other lifeguards during lifesaving. Because he cannot hear another lifeguard's whistle blow before going in for a save, as a modest modification, he could briefly look at the other lifeguards when scanning his zone.

Likewise, Keith has presented evidence that he can enforce safety rules. Verbal enforcement is usually impractical in a noisy water park, and most lifeguards rely on their whistle and various physical gestures, including shaking their head "no" for patrons to stop engaging in horseplay, motioning their hand backward for a patron to get behind the red line, and signaling the number one with their finger for "one person per tube." Keith can use these same methods of enforcement.

Keith has also presented evidence that he can communicate effectively during emergencies with a modification to the EAP. To activate the EAP, lifeguards would signal with a fist in the air, opening and closing their fist in repetition. According to Stavale, this would improve the EAP for everyone, not just Keith. It would allow other lifeguards and staff to see the EAP visually if they are not in a position to hear it. Once activated, other lifeguards who are required to maintain their position would put their fist in the air and make the same signal.

Further, Keith has presented evidence that he can respond to patrons who approach him, at least at a level that may be considered *essential* for a lifeguard. He would carry a few laminated note cards in the pocket of his swim trunks with basic phrases such as, "I am deaf. I will get someone to assist you. Wait here." He can also provide first aid in situations in which he can see the ailment requiring attention. Although there may be situations in which verbal communication is necessary, attendants are posted throughout the water park to assist patrons with basic needs and inquiries, suggesting that this is not an essential function of lifeguards, or at least reasonable minds could differ on this point. In addition, staff members are required to respond whenever a whistle is blown to signal a save.

Perhaps the most compelling evidence that Keith is "otherwise qualified" comes from his experts who have knowledge, education, and experience regarding the ability of deaf individuals to serve as lifeguards. They all opine that the ability to hear is unnecessary to enable a person to perform the essential functions of a lifeguard. The world record for most lives saved is held by a deaf man, Leroy Colombo, who saved over 900 lives in his lifeguarding career. One also cannot ignore that the American Red Cross certifies deaf lifeguards, and Gallaudet University, the only liberal arts university in the world dedicated to serving the needs of deaf individuals, has a lifeguard certification program.

In light of this evidence, we hold that reasonable minds could differ regarding whether Keith is "otherwise qualified" because he can perform the essential communication functions of a lifeguard. The district court erred when it decided that Keith's deafness disqualified him from the position as a matter of law. . . .

NOTES AND QUESTIONS

1.   *Individualized inquiry.* Why must an employer undertake an individualized inquiry in determining whether an applicant or employee is qualified for the job in question? Since the *Keith* court found that the County of Oakland engaged in an individualized inquiry, why is the court nonetheless concerned that the County may not have fulfilled its obligation?

2.   *Essential functions.* Assume that the County of Oakland's job description for the lifeguard position lists the following as required job capabilities: the ability to swim, the ability to pull a body of up to 150 pounds out of the water, the ability to enforce pool rules, the ability to communicate, and the ability to hear. Which of those are essential functions? How do the concepts of "essential functions" and "qualification standards" differ? Qualification standards are discussed in Section E of this chapter.

3.   *Reasonable accommodation.* The ADA states that an individual may establish that he or she is "qualified" with or without reasonable accommodation. Would either of the following likely constitute a reasonable accommodation: a) providing Keith with a full-time assistant with hearing capabilities, or b) providing Keith with a sign-language interpreter for staff meetings?

4.   *Marginal functions.* An employer need not excuse the nonperformance of an essential function, but has a duty to reallocate a marginal function that an individual is unable to perform. What might be a marginal function of the lifeguard position?

5.   Larry Skerski is a cable service technician with an anxiety disorder that inhibits his ability to work at heights. For three years he was excused from overhead work on ladders and poles even though such work constituted 50% of the tasks that technicians performed. A new supervisor demanded that Skerski resume overhead work. In considering whether overhead work is an essential function of the job, what is the impact of: a) the fact that eight other technicians are available to perform such work, and b) the fact that Skerski did not perform such work for the preceding three year period? *See* Skerski v. Time Warner Cable Co., 257 F.3d 273 (3d Cir. 2001).

6.   *Deference to employer judgment.* The extent to which a court will defer to an employer's judgment as to essential functions may be determinative as to whether an employee is deemed qualified for the job. In *Knutson v. Schwan's Home Service,* 711 F.3d 911 (8th Cir. 2013), a home delivery products employer required employees serving as location general managers to comply with Department of Transportation (DOT) standards applicable to over-the-road drivers of trucks weighing more than 10,000 pounds. Knutson argued that DOT certification should not be viewed as an essential function of the manager position since he seldom was required to drive a delivery truck. The Eighth

Circuit Court of Appeals deferred to the employer's judgment that a manager's ability to drive delivery trucks on occasion positively correlated with productivity and found Knutson not to be qualified for the manager position.

In a case with similar facts, a FedEx delivery facility in Fort Myers, Florida required mechanics to comply with DOT certification requirements applicable to commercial motor vehicle drivers who transport property or passengers in interstate commerce. Samson, a mechanic who was unable to meet DOT standards because of his diabetes, maintained that DOT certification should not be an essential function of the mechanic position because he seldom test-drove trucks and almost never across state lines. The Eleventh Circuit, in *Samson v. Federal Express Corporation*, 746 F.3d 1196 (11th Cir. 2014), declined to defer to the employer's judgment and overturned the district court's grant of summary judgment to the employer, finding a fact question on the essential function issue.

Which approach is preferable?

2. JUDICIAL ESTOPPEL

CLEVELAND V. POLICY MANAGEMENT SYSTEMS CORPORATION
526 U.S. 795, 119 S.Ct. 1597 (1999)

JUSTICE BREYER delivered the opinion of the Court.

The Social Security Disability Insurance (SSDI) program provides benefits to a person with a disability so severe that she is "unable to do [her] previous work" and "cannot . . . engage in any other kind of substantial gainful work which exists in the national economy." § 223(a) of the Social Security Act, as set forth in 42 U.S.C. § 423(d)(2)(A). This case asks whether the law erects a special presumption that would significantly inhibit an SSDI recipient from simultaneously pursuing an action for disability discrimination under the Americans with Disabilities Act of 1990 (ADA), claiming that "with . . . reasonable accommodation" she could "perform the essential functions" of her job. 42 U.S.C. § 12111(8).

We believe that, in context, these two seemingly divergent statutory contentions are often consistent, each with the other. Thus pursuit, and receipt, of SSDI benefits does not automatically estop the recipient from pursuing an ADA claim. Nor does the law erect a strong presumption against the recipient's success under the ADA. Nonetheless, an ADA plaintiff cannot simply ignore her SSDI contention that she was too disabled to work. To survive a defendant's motion for summary judgment, she must explain why that SSDI contention is consistent with her ADA claim that she could "perform the essential functions" of her previous job, at least with "reasonable accommodation."

I

After suffering a disabling stroke and losing her job, Carolyn Cleveland sought and obtained SSDI benefits from the Social Security Administration (SSA). She has also brought this ADA suit in which she claims that her former employer, Policy Management Systems Corporation, discriminated against her on account of her disability. . . .

On September 22, 1995, the week before her SSDI award, Cleveland brought this ADA lawsuit. She contended that Policy Management Systems had "terminat[ed]" her employment without reasonably "accommodat[ing] her disability." She alleged that she requested, but was denied, accommodations such as training and additional time to complete her work. And she submitted a supporting affidavit from her treating physician. The District Court did not evaluate her reasonable accommodation claim on the merits, but granted summary judgment to the defendant because, in that court's view, Cleveland, by applying for and receiving SSDI benefits, had conceded that she was totally disabled. And that fact, the court concluded, now estopped Cleveland from proving an essential element of her ADA claim, namely, that she could "perform the essential functions" of her job, at least with "reasonable accommodation." 42 U.S.C. § 12111(8).

The Fifth Circuit affirmed the District Court's grant of summary judgment.

The court wrote:

> "[T]he application for or the receipt of social security disability benefits creates a *rebuttable* presumption that the claimant or recipient of such benefits is judicially estopped from asserting that he is a 'qualified individual with a disability.' "

We granted certiorari in light of disagreement among the Circuits about the legal effect upon an ADA suit of the application for, or receipt of, disability benefits. . . .

II

The Social Security Act and the ADA both help individuals with disabilities, but in different ways. The Social Security Act provides monetary benefits to every insured individual who "is under a disability." 42 U.S.C. § 423(a)(1). The Act defines "disability" as an "inability to engage in any substantial gainful activity by reason of any . . . physical or mental impairment which can be expected to result in death or which has lasted or can be expected to last for a continuous period of not less than 12 months." § 423(d)(1)(A). The individual's impairment, as we have said, must be "of such severity that [she] is not only unable to do [her] previous work but cannot, considering [her] age, education, and work experience, engage in any other kind of substantial gainful work which exists in the national economy. . . ." § 423(d)(2)(A).

The ADA seeks to eliminate unwarranted discrimination against disabled individuals in order both to guarantee those individuals equal opportunity and to provide the Nation with the benefit of their consequently increased productivity. See, *e.g.*, 42 U.S.C. §§ 12101(a)(8),(9). The ADA prohibits covered employers from discriminating "against a qualified individual with a disability because of the disability of such individual." § 12112(a). The ADA defines a "qualified individual with a disability" as a disabled person "who . . . can perform the essential functions" of her job, including those who can do so only "with . . . reasonable accommodation." § 12111(8). . . .

The case before us concerns an ADA plaintiff who both applied for, and received, SSDI benefits. It requires us to review a Court of Appeals decision upholding the grant of summary judgment on the ground that an ADA plaintiff's "represent[ation] to the SSA that she was totally disabled" created a "rebuttable presumption" sufficient to "judicially esto[p]" her later representation that, "for the time in question," with reasonable accommodation, she could perform the essential functions of her job. The Court of Appeals thought, in essence, that claims under both Acts would incorporate two directly conflicting propositions, namely, "I am too disabled to work" and "I am not too disabled to work." And in an effort to prevent two claims that would embody that kind of factual conflict, the court used a special judicial presumption, which it believed would ordinarily prevent a plaintiff like Cleveland from successfully asserting an ADA claim.

In our view, however, despite the appearance of conflict that arises from the language of the two statutes, the two claims do not inherently conflict to the point where courts should apply a special negative presumption like the one applied by the Court of Appeals here. That is because there are too many situations in which an SSDI claim and an ADA claim can comfortably exist side by side.

For one thing, as we have noted, the ADA defines a "qualified individual" to include a disabled person "who . . . can perform the essential functions" of her job *with reasonable accommodation.*" * * *

By way of contrast, when the SSA determines whether an individual is disabled for SSDI purposes, it does *not* take the possibility of "reasonable accommodation" into account, nor need an applicant refer to the possibility of reasonable accommodation when she applies for SSDI. The omission reflects the facts that the SSA receives more than 2.5 million claims for disability benefits each year; its administrative resources are limited; the matter of "reasonable accommodation" may turn on highly disputed workplace-specific matters; and an SSA misjudgment about that detailed, and often fact-specific matter would deprive a seriously disabled person of the critical financial support the statute seeks to provide. The result is that an ADA suit claiming that the plaintiff can perform her job *with* reasonable accommodation may well prove consistent with an SSDI claim that the plaintiff could not perform her own job (or other jobs) *without* it.

For another thing, in order to process the large number of SSDI claims, the SSA administers SSDI with the help of a five-step procedure that embodies a set of presumptions about disabilities, job availability, and their interrelation. The SSA asks:

> *Step One:* Are you presently working? (If so, you are ineligible.) See 20 CFR § 404.1520(b).

> *Step Two:* Do you have a "severe impairment," *i.e.,* one that "significantly limits" your ability to do basic work activities? (If not, you are ineligible.) See § 404.1520(c).

> *Step Three:* Does your impairment "mee[t] or equa[l]" an impairment on a specific (and fairly lengthy) SSA list? (If so, you are eligible *without more.*) See §§ 404.1520(d), 404.1525, 404.1526.

> *Step Four:* If your impairment does not meet or equal a listed impairment, can you perform your "past relevant work?" (If so, you are ineligible.) See § 404.1520(e).

> *Step Five:* If your impairment does not meet or equal a listed impairment and you cannot perform your "past relevant work," then can you perform other jobs that exist in significant numbers in the national economy? (If not, you are eligible.) See §§ 404.1520(f), 404.1560(c).

The presumptions embodied in these questions—particularly those necessary to produce Step Three's list, which, the Government tells us, accounts for approximately 60 percent of all awards, grow out of the need to administer a large benefits system efficiently. But they inevitably simplify, eliminating consideration of many differences potentially relevant to an individual's ability to perform a particular job. Hence, an individual might qualify for SSDI under the SSA's administrative rules and yet, due to special individual circumstances, remain capable of "perform[ing] the essential functions" of her job.

Further, the SSA sometimes grants SSDI benefits to individuals who not only can work, but are working. For example, to facilitate a disabled person's reentry into the workforce, the SSA authorizes a 9-month trial-work period during which SSDI recipients may receive full benefits. See 42 U.S.C. §§ 422(c), 423(e)(1); 20 CFR § 404.1592 (1998). Improvement in a totally disabled person's physical condition, while permitting that person to work, will not necessarily or immediately lead the SSA to terminate SSDI benefits. And the nature of an individual's disability may change over time, so that a statement about that disability at the time of an individual's application for SSDI benefits may not reflect an individual's capacities at the time of the relevant employment decision.

Finally, if an individual has merely applied for, but has not been awarded, SSDI benefits, any inconsistency in the theory of the claims is of the sort normally tolerated by our legal system. Our ordinary Rules recognize that a person may not be sure in advance upon which legal theory she will succeed, and so permit parties to "set forth two or more statements of a claim or defense alternately or hypothetically," and to "state as many separate claims or defenses as the party has regardless of consistency." Fed. Rule Civ. Proc. 8(e)(2). We do not see why the law in respect to the assertion of SSDI and ADA claims should differ.

In light of these examples, we would not apply a special legal presumption permitting someone who has applied for, or received, SSDI benefits to bring an ADA suit only in "some limited and highly unusual set of circumstances."

Nonetheless, in some cases an earlier SSDI claim may turn out genuinely to conflict with an ADA claim. . . . An ADA plaintiff bears the burden of proving that she is a "qualified individual with a disability"—that is, a person "who, with or without reasonable accommodation, can perform the essential functions" of her job. 42 U.S.C. § 12111(8). And a plaintiff's sworn assertion in an application for disability benefits that she is, for example, "unable to work" will appear to negate an essential element of her ADA case—at least if she does not offer a sufficient explanation. For that reason, we hold that an ADA plaintiff cannot simply ignore the apparent contradiction that arises out of the earlier SSDI total disability claim. Rather, she must proffer a sufficient explanation.

The lower courts, in somewhat comparable circumstances, have found a similar need for explanation. They have held with virtual unanimity that a party cannot create a genuine issue of fact sufficient to survive summary judgment simply by contradicting his or her own previous sworn statement (by, say, filing a later affidavit that flatly contradicts that party's earlier sworn deposition) without explaining the contradiction or attempting to resolve the disparity. Although these cases for the most part involve purely factual contradictions (as to which we do not necessarily endorse these cases, but leave the law as we found it), we believe that a similar insistence upon explanation is warranted here, where the conflict involves a legal conclusion. When faced with a plaintiff's previous sworn statement asserting "total disability" or the like, the court should require an explanation of any apparent inconsistency with the necessary elements of an ADA claim. To defeat summary judgment, that explanation must be sufficient to warrant a reasonable juror's concluding that, assuming the truth of, or the plaintiff's good-faith belief in, the earlier statement, the plaintiff could nonetheless "perform the essential functions" of her job, with or without "reasonable accommodation."

III

In her brief in this Court, Cleveland explains the discrepancy between her SSDI statements that she was "totally disabled" and her ADA claim that she could "perform the essential functions" of her job. The first statements, she says, "were made in a forum which does not consider the effect that reasonable workplace accommodations would have on the ability to work." Moreover, she claims the SSDI statements were "accurate statements" if examined "in the time period in which they were made." The parties should have the opportunity in the trial court to present, or to contest, these explanations, in sworn form where appropriate. Accordingly, we vacate the judgment of the Court of Appeals and remand the case for further proceedings consistent with this opinion.

NOTES AND QUESTIONS

1.   *Timing.* Does the *Cleveland* decision mean that an applicant for disability benefits who is not yet receiving benefits will have an easier time explaining statements made on the application than someone who is actually receiving benefits? If so, what is the logic of this distinction?

2.   *Explanation.* What type of explanation could an ADA plaintiff provide if her application for disability benefits stated that she was "totally disabled?" What if, instead, the application stated that "there is no way I can work at my old job or any other job?"

3.   *Counseling the client.* If you were representing an individual who is considering both applying for disability benefits and asserting an ADA claim, what would you counsel the individual to say or not say in applying for disability benefits?

4.   *Working and benefits.* If Cleveland were successful in returning to work as a result of her ADA claim, could she continue to receive SSDI benefits? The answer is eventually in the negative. Although an SSDI benefit recipient is entitled to a nine-month trial work period during which she would remain eligible for disability benefits, that eligibility is suspended if she is able to work beyond the nine-month period. 20 C.F.R. § 404.1596(b)(1)(ii).

C. REASONABLE ACCOMMODATION MANDATE

1. STATUTORY LANGUAGE AND EEOC REGULATIONS

Section 12112(5)(5) of the ADA provides that the term "discrimination" includes:

(A) Not making reasonable accommodations to the known physical or mental limitations of an otherwise qualified individual with a disability who is an applicant or employee, unless such covered entity can demonstrate that the accommodation would impose an undue hardship on the operation of the business of such covered entity; or

(B) Denying employment opportunities to a job applicant or employee who is an otherwise qualified individual with a disability, if such denial is based on the need of such covered entity to make reasonable accommodation to the physical or mental impairments of the employee or applicant.

Section 12111(9) states that the term "reasonable accommodation" may include:

(A) making existing facilities used by employees readily accessible to and usable by individuals with disabilities; and

(B) job restructuring, part-time, or modified work schedules, reassignment to a vacant position, acquisition or modification of equipment or devices, appropriate adjustment or modification of examinations, training materials, or policies, the provision of qualified readers or interpreters, and other similar accommodations for individuals with disabilities.

Regulations adopted by the EEOC, 29 C.F.R. § 1630.2(o)(1), provide a further gloss on the reasonable accommodation concept, stating that the term reasonable accommodation includes:

(i)   Modifications or adjustments to a job application process that enable a qualified applicant with a disability to be considered for the position such qualified applicant desires; or

(ii) Modifications or adjustments to the work environment, or to the manner or circumstances under which the position held or desired is customarily performed, that enable a qualified individual with a disability to perform the essential functions of that position; or

(iii) Modifications or adjustments that enable a covered entity's employee with a disability to enjoy equal benefits and privileges of employment as are enjoyed by its other similarly situated employees without disabilities.

2.   GENERAL CONCEPT

VANDE ZANDE V. STATE OF WISCONSIN DEPARTMENT OF ADMINISTRATION
44 F.3d 538 (7th Cir. 1995)

POSNER, CHIEF JUDGE.

In 1990, Congress passed the Americans with Disabilities Act, 42 U.S.C. §§ 12101 *et seq.* The stated purpose is "to provide a clear and comprehensive national mandate for the elimination of discrimination against individuals with disabilities," said by Congress to be 43 million in number and growing. §§ 12101(a), (b)(1). "Disability" is broadly defined. It includes not only "a physical or mental impairment that substantially limits one or more of the major life activities of [the disabled] individual," but also the state of "being regarded as having such an impairment." §§ 12102(2)(A), (C). The latter definition, although at first glance peculiar, actually makes a better fit with the elaborate preamble to the Act, in which people who have physical or mental impairments are compared to victims of racial and other invidious discrimination. Many such impairments are not in fact disabling but are believed to be so, and the people having them may be denied employment or otherwise shunned as a consequence. Such people, objectively capable of performing as well as the unimpaired, are analogous to capable workers discriminated against because of their skin color or some other vocationally irrelevant characteristic.

The more problematic case is that of an individual who has a vocationally relevant disability—an impairment such as blindness or paralysis that limits a major human capability, such as seeing or walking. In the common case in which such an impairment interferes with the individual's ability to perform up to the standards of the workplace, or increases the cost of employing him, hiring and firing decisions based on the impairment are not "discriminatory" in a sense closely analogous to employment discrimination on racial grounds. The draftsmen of the Act knew this. But they were unwilling to confine the concept of disability discrimination to cases in which the disability is irrelevant to the performance of the disabled person's job. Instead, they defined "discrimination" to include an employer's "not making reasonable accommodations to the known physical or mental limitations of an otherwise qualified individual with a disability who is an applicant or employee, unless . . . [the employer] can demonstrate that the accommodation would impose an undue hardship on the operation of the . . . [employer's] business." § 12112(b)(5)(A).

The term "reasonable accommodations" is not a legal novelty, even if we ignore its use (arguably with a different meaning, however,) in the provision of Title VII forbidding religious discrimination. It is one of a number of provisions in the employment subchapter that were borrowed from regulations issued by the Equal Employment Opportunity Commission in implementation of the Rehabilitation Act of 1973. See 29 C.F.R. § 1613.704. Indeed, to a great extent the employment provisions of the new Act merely generalize to the economy as a whole the duties, including that of reasonable accommodation, that the regulations under the Rehabilitation Act imposed on federal agencies and federal contractors. We can therefore look to the decisions interpreting those regulations for clues to the meaning of the same terms in the new law.

It is plain enough what "accommodation" means. The employer must be willing to consider making changes in its ordinary work rules, facilities, terms, and conditions in order to enable a disabled individual to work. The difficult term is "reasonable." The plaintiff in our case, a paraplegic, argues in effect that the term just means apt or efficacious. An accommodation is reasonable, she believes, when it is tailored to the particular individual's disability. A ramp or lift is thus a reasonable accommodation for a person who like this plaintiff is confined to a wheelchair. Considerations of cost do not enter into the term as the plaintiff would have us construe it. Cost is, she argues, the domain of "undue hardship" (another term borrowed from the regulations under the Rehabilitation Act)—a safe harbor for an employer that can show that it would go broke or suffer other excruciating financial distress were it compelled to make a reasonable accommodation in the sense of one effective in enabling the disabled person to overcome the vocational effects of the disability.

These are questionable interpretations both of "reasonable" and of "undue hardship." To "accommodate" a disability is to make some change that will enable the disabled person to work. An unrelated, inefficacious change would not be an accommodation of the disability at all. So "reasonable" may be intended to qualify (in the sense of weaken) "accommodation," in just the same way that if one requires a "reasonable effort" of someone this means less than the maximum possible effort, or in law that the duty of "reasonable care," the cornerstone of the law of negligence, requires something less than the maximum possible care. It is understood in that law that in deciding what care is reasonable the court considers the cost of increased care. (This is explicit in Judge Learned Hand's famous formula for negligence. United States v. Carroll Towing Co., 159 F.2d 169, 173 (2d Cir.1947).) Similar reasoning could be used to flesh out the meaning of the word "reasonable" in the term "reasonable accommodations." It would not follow that the costs and benefits of altering a workplace to enable a disabled person to work would always have to be quantified, or even that an accommodation would have to be deemed unreasonable if the cost exceeded the benefit however slightly. But, at the very least, the cost could not be disproportionate to the benefit. Even if an employer is so large or wealthy—or, like the principal defendant in this case, is a state, which can raise taxes in order to finance any accommodations that it must make to disabled employees—that it may not be able to plead "undue *hardship*," it would not be required to expend enormous sums in order to bring about a trivial improvement in the life of a disabled employee. If the nation's employers have potentially unlimited financial obligations to 43 million disabled persons, the Americans with Disabilities Act will have imposed an indirect tax potentially greater than the national debt. We do not find an intention to bring about such a radical result in either the language of the Act or its history. The preamble actually "markets" the Act as a cost saver, pointing to "billions of dollars in unnecessary expenses resulting from dependency and nonproductivity." § 12101(a)(9). The savings will be illusory if employers are required to expend many more billions in accommodation than will be saved by enabling disabled people to work.

The concept of reasonable accommodation is at the heart of this case. The plaintiff sought a number of accommodations to her paraplegia that were turned down. The principal defendant as we have said is a state, which does not argue that the plaintiff's proposals were rejected because accepting them would have imposed undue hardship on the state or because they would not have done her any good. The district judge nevertheless granted summary judgment for the defendants on the ground that the evidence obtained in discovery, construed as favorably to the plaintiff as the record permitted, showed that they had gone as far to accommodate the plaintiff's demands as reasonableness, in a sense distinct from either aptness or hardship—a sense based, rather, on considerations of cost and proportionality—required. On this analysis, the function of the "undue hardship" safe harbor, like the "failing company" defense to antitrust liability, is to excuse compliance by a firm that is financially distressed, even though the cost of the accommodation to the firm might be less than the benefit to disabled employees.

This interpretation of "undue hardship" is not inevitable-in fact probably is incorrect. It is a defined term in the Americans with Disabilities Act, and the definition is "an action requiring significant difficulty or expense." 42 U.S.C. § 12111(10)(A). The financial condition of the employer is only one consideration in determining whether an accommodation otherwise reasonable would impose an undue hardship. See 42 U.S.C. §§ 12111(10)(B)(ii), (iii). The legislative history equates "undue hardship" to "unduly costly." S.Rep. No. 116, *supra*, at 35. These are terms of relation. We must ask, "undue" in relation to what? Presumably (given the statutory definition and the legislative history) in relation to the benefits of the accommodation to the disabled worker as well as to the employer's resources.

So it seems that costs enter at two points in the analysis of claims to an accommodation to a disability. The employee must show that the accommodation is reasonable in the sense both of efficacious and of proportional to costs. Even if this prima facie showing is made, the employer has an opportunity to prove that upon more careful consideration the costs are excessive in relation either to the benefits of the accommodation or to the employer's financial survival or health. In a classic negligence case, the idiosyncrasies of the particular employer are irrelevant. Having above-average costs, or being in a precarious financial situation, is not a defense to negligence. One interpretation of "undue hardship" is that it permits an employer to escape liability if he can carry the burden of proving that a disability accommodation reasonable for a normal employer would break him.

Lori Vande Zande, aged 35, is paralyzed from the waist down as a result of a tumor of the spinal cord. Her paralysis makes her prone to develop pressure ulcers, treatment of which often requires that she stay at home for several weeks. The defendants and the amici curiae argue that there is no duty of reasonable accommodation of pressure ulcers because they do not fit the statutory definition of a disability. Intermittent, episodic impairments are not disabilities, the standard example being a broken leg. But an intermittent impairment that is a characteristic manifestation of an admitted disability is, we believe, a part of the underlying disability and hence a condition that the employer must reasonably accommodate. . . . We hold that Vande Zande's pressure ulcers are a part of her disability, and therefore a part of what the State of Wisconsin had a duty to accommodate—reasonably.

Vande Zande worked for the housing division of the state's department of administration for three years, beginning in January 1990. The housing division supervises the state's public housing programs. Her job was that of a program assistant, and involved preparing public information materials, planning meetings, interpreting regulations, typing, mailing, filing, and copying. In short, her tasks were of a clerical, secretarial, and administrative-assistant character. In order to enable her to do this work, the defendants, as she acknowledges, "made numerous accommodations relating to the plaintiff's disability." As examples, in her words, "they paid the landlord to have bathrooms modified and to have a step ramped; they bought special adjustable furniture for the plaintiff; they ordered and paid for one-half of the cost of a cot that the plaintiff needed for daily personal care at work; they sometimes adjusted the plaintiff's schedule to perform backup telephone duties to accommodate the plaintiff's medical appointments; they made changes to the plans for a locker room in the new state office building; and they agreed to provide some of the specific accommodations the plaintiff requested in her October 5, 1992 Reasonable Accommodation Request."

But she complains that the defendants did not go far enough in two principal respects. One concerns a period of eight weeks when a bout of pressure ulcers forced her to stay home. She wanted to work full time at home and believed that she would be able to do so if the division would provide her with a desktop computer at home (though she already had a laptop). Her supervisor refused, and told her that he probably would have only 15 to 20 hours of work for her to do at home per week and that she would have to make up the difference between that and a full work week out of her sick leave or vacation leave. In the event, she was able to work all but 16.5 hours in the eight-week period. She took 16.5 hours of sick leave to make up the difference. As a result, she incurred no loss of income, but did lose sick leave that she could have carried forward indefinitely. She now works for another agency of the State of Wisconsin, but any unused sick leave in her employment by the housing division would have accompanied her to her new job. Restoration of the 16.5 hours of lost sick leave is one form of relief that she seeks in this suit.

She argues that a jury might have found that a reasonable accommodation required the housing division either to give her the desktop computer or to excuse her from having to dig into her sick leave to get paid for the hours in which, in the absence of the computer, she was unable to do her work at home. No jury, however, could in our view be permitted to stretch the concept of "reasonable accommodation" so far. Most jobs in organizations public or private involve team work under supervision rather than solitary unsupervised work, and team work under supervision generally cannot be performed at home without a substantial reduction in the quality of the employee's performance. This will no doubt change as communications technology advances, but is the situation today. Generally, therefore, an employer is not required to accommodate a disability by allowing the disabled worker to work, by himself, without supervision, at home. This is the majority view, illustrated by Tyndall v. National Education Centers, Inc., 31 F.3d 209, 213–14 (4th Cir.1994), and Law v. United States Postal Service, 852 F.2d 1278 (Fed.Cir.1988) (per curiam). The District of Columbia Circuit disagrees. Langon v. Dept. of Health & Human Services, 959 F.2d 1053, 1060–61 (D.C.Cir.1992); Carr v. Reno, 23 F.3d 525, 530 (D.C.Cir.1994). But we think the majority view is correct. An employer is not required to allow disabled workers to work at home, where their productivity inevitably would be greatly reduced. No doubt to this as to any generalization about so complex and varied an activity as employment there are exceptions, but it would take a very extraordinary case for the employee to be able to create a triable issue of the employer's failure to allow the employee to work at home.

And if the employer, because it is a government agency and therefore is not under intense competitive pressure to minimize its labor costs or maximize the value of its output, or for some other reason, bends over backwards to accommodate a disabled worker—goes further than the law requires—by allowing the worker to work at home, it must not be punished for its generosity by being deemed to have conceded the reasonableness of so far-reaching an accommodation. That would hurt rather than help disabled workers. Wisconsin's housing division was not required by the Americans with Disabilities Act to allow Vande Zande to work at home; even more clearly it was not required to install a computer in her home so that she could avoid using up 16.5 hours of sick leave. It is conjectural that she will ever need those 16.5 hours; the expected cost of the loss must, therefore, surely be slight. An accommodation that allows a disabled worker to work at home, at full pay, subject only to a slight loss of sick leave that may never be needed, hence never missed, is, we hold, reasonable as a matter of law. . . .

Her second complaint has to do with the kitchenettes in the housing division's building, which are for the use of employees during lunch and coffee breaks. Both the sink and the counter in each of the kitchenettes were 36 inches high, which is too high for a person in a wheelchair. The building was under construction, and the kitchenettes not yet built, when the plaintiff complained about this feature of the design. But the defendants refused to alter the design to lower the sink and counter to 34 inches, the height convenient for a person in a wheelchair. Construction of the building had begun before the effective date of the Americans with Disabilities Act, and Vande Zande does not argue that the failure to include 34-inch sinks and counters in the design of the building violated the Act. She could not argue that; the Act is not retroactive. But she argues that once she brought the problem to the attention of her supervisors, they were obliged to lower the sink and counter, at least on the floor on which her office was located but possibly on the other floors in the building as well, since she might be moved to another floor. All that the defendants were willing to do was to install a shelf 34 inches high in the kitchenette area on Vande Zande's floor. That took care of the counter problem. As for the sink, the defendants took the position that since the plumbing was already in place it would be too costly to lower the sink and that the plaintiff could use the bathroom sink, which is 34 inches high.

Apparently it would have cost only about $150 to lower the sink on Vande Zande's floor; to lower it on all the floors might have cost as much as $2,000, though possibly less. Given the proximity of the bathroom sink, Vande Zande can hardly complain that the inaccessibility of the kitchenette sink interfered with her ability to work or with her physical comfort. Her argument rather is that forcing her to use the bathroom sink for activities (such as washing out her coffee cup) for which the other employees could use the kitchenette sink stigmatized her as different and inferior; she seeks an award of compensatory damages for the resulting emotional distress. We may assume without having to decide that emotional as well as physical barriers to the integration of disabled persons into the workforce are relevant in determining the reasonableness of an accommodation. But we do not think an employer has a duty to expend even modest amounts of money to bring about an absolute identity in working conditions between disabled and nondisabled workers. The creation of such a duty would be the inevitable consequence of deeming a failure to achieve identical conditions "stigmatizing." That is merely an epithet. We conclude that access to a particular sink, when access to an equivalent sink, conveniently located, is provided, is not a legal duty of an employer. The duty of reasonable accommodation is satisfied when the employer does what is necessary to enable the disabled worker to work in reasonable comfort.

In addition to making these specific complaints of failure of reasonable accommodation, Vande Zande argues that the defendants displayed a "pattern of insensitivity or discrimination." She relies on a number of minor incidents, such as her supervisor's response, "Cut me some slack," to her complaint on the first day on which the housing division moved into the new building that the bathrooms lacked adequate supplies. He meant that it would take a few days to iron out the bugs inevitable in any major move. It was clearly a reasonable request in the circumstances; and given all the accommodations that Vande Zande acknowledges the defendants made to her disability, a "pattern of insensitivity or discrimination" is hard to discern. But the more fundamental point is that there is no separate offense under the Americans with Disabilities Act called engaging in a pattern of insensitivity or discrimination. The word "pattern" does not appear in the employment subchapter, and the Act is not modeled on RICO. As in other cases of discrimination, a plaintiff can ask the trier of fact to draw an inference of discrimination from a pattern of behavior when each individual act making up that pattern might have an innocent explanation. The whole can be greater than the sum of the parts. But in this case all we have in the way of a pattern is that the employer made a number of reasonable   and   some   more   than   reasonable—unnecessary— accommodations, and turned down only requests for unreasonable accommodations. From such a pattern no inference of unlawful discrimination can be drawn.

NOTES AND QUESTIONS

1.   *The role of costs.* Judge Posner takes the position that an accommodation is reasonable if it is both a) efficacious and b) reasonable in terms of a cost/benefit relationship. Some other circuit court decisions agree with this view. *See, e.g.,* Borkowski v. Valley Central School Dist., 63 F.3d 131 (2d Cir. 1995). The Second Circuit in *Borkowski* adopted a shifting burden of proof on the reasonable accommodation issue. The plaintiff initially bears a burden of production to identify a plausible accommodation, "the costs of which, facially do not clearly exceed the benefits." 63 F.3d at 139. The defendant is then charged with carrying the ultimate burden of persuasion on the issue of reasonableness, which, in effect, merges with the burden of showing that the proposed accommodation would impose an undue hardship. *Id.* at 138. The EEOC's *Enforcement Guidance on Reasonable Accommodation and Undue Hardship*, on the other hand, takes the position that a modification or adjustment satisfies the reasonable accommodation requirement if it is "effective." According to the EEOC, considerations of cost come into play only with respect to the undue hardship defense. Which of these approaches is preferable and why?

2.   *Understanding the sink issue.* The *Vande Zande* court ruled that the state of Wisconsin did not violate the ADA when it declined to lower the kitchenette sink. Was this because a) lowering the sink would not be a reasonable accommodation, b) requiring such an accommodation would impose an undue hardship, or c) is there some other explanation?

3.   *Cost considerations.* Judge Posner asserts that considerations of cost are relevant for both reasonable accommodation and undue hardship analysis. How, if at all, does the cost calculus differ in these two contexts?

4.   *Stigma.* Judge Posner's opinion concludes by emphasizing that "stigma" or "insensitivity" are not, in themselves, actionable offenses under the ADA. Do you agree with this conclusion or does it represent an able-bodied perspective?

3.   DEFINING "REASONABLE"

Courts and scholars have struggled to define the term "reasonable" in the context of "reasonable accommodations." What role does the word "reasonable" play? Does it only mean "effective"? Or is "reasonable" simply the flip side of "undue hardship"? In other words, should an accommodation be deemed reasonable unless it causes an undue hardship? Or does "reasonable" have an independent meaning? As will be discussed below, the Supreme Court in *U.S. Airways v. Barnett*, 535 U.S. 391 (2002), agreed with the court in *Vande Zande* and held that the word reasonable in "reasonable accommodation" means something more than merely "effective." The Court reasoned that the word "accommodation" assumes that the change or modification is "effective." If it were not effective, it would not "accommodate" the employee's disability. Beyond that (and stating that reasonableness is to be determined in the run of cases, while undue hardship depends upon case-specific circumstances), however, the Supreme Court's only opinion dealing with reasonable accommodations does not define the scope or meaning of "reasonable accommodation." Two scholars have attempted to fill that void.

a.   Excerpt from Mark Weber, *Unreasonable Accommodation and Due Hardship*, 62 FLA. L. REV. 1119 (2010)

In his article, Professor Mark Weber argued that the term "reasonable" does not have any independent meaning apart from being the flip side of the coin of "undue hardship." Weber relies on the statutory text, legislative history, agency interpretations, and historical context to support his analysis.

> The legislative sources make clear that reasonable accommodation and undue hardship are a single concept. The words form parts of a statutory sentence that links them together into the same statutory term. The duty to make reasonable accommodations exists up to the limit of undue hardship. At the point of undue hardship, the accommodation is no longer reasonable. It should be no surprise that the ADA merely gives examples of reasonable accommodation while providing a definition and relevant factors to consider in determining undue hardship. If undue hardship can be determined, there is no need

to define what reasonable accommodation is. It is everything that is not undue hardship. Undue hardship is the laboring phrase in the term, not reasonable accommodation. If "unreasonable accommodation" seems not to make sense, it is because reasonable accommodation lacks a meaning other than the absence of undue hardship. The terms should be read together, and the opposite of the one is the other. Hence the play on words to make the title of this article: There is no such thing as unreasonable accommodation or due hardship.

Id. at 1148.

b. **Excerpt from Nicole Porter, *Martinizing Title I of the Americans with Disabilities Act,* 47 GA. L. REV. 527 (2013)**

Professor Porter believes "that there is some limitation to an employer's obligation to provide a reasonable accommodation besides the undue hardship limit." She states:

[S]ome accommodations are "unreasonable" even though they do not cause an undue hardship to the employer. For instance, employers should not have to monitor their employees' medications or pay for their employees' hearing aids, nor should employers be required to bump current employees out of their jobs in order to accommodate disabled employees. These accommodations are all "unreasonable." [Thus,] I disagree with Weber that "reasonable" has no meaning independent of the undue hardship defense. . . .

Id. at 545–46. As Porter further explains:

Most accommodations affect either the employer or the co-employees of an employee with a disability, and sometimes the accommodations affect both. The ADA's reasonable accommodation provision explicitly deals only with financial burdens on employers. Yet courts frequently have held that some accommodations are unreasonable even when they impose only minimal or no financial burdens on the employer. To coherently address these reasonable accommodation issues, we must find a way to give meaning to the amorphous "reasonable" standard.

Id. at 558. In order to give meaning to this standard, Porter argues that the Supreme Court's Title III (the public accommodations title) opinion in *PGA Tour, Inc. v. Martin,* 532 U.S. 661 (2001), provides a useful analogy for "proposing a unified approach to the reasonable accommodation provision." In the *Martin* case, the Court held that professional golfer Casey Martin should be allowed to use a golf cart in violation of the PGA's rules because the use of the golf cart did not "fundamentally alter the nature of the golf tournaments." First, the Court held it did not fundamentally alter an essential aspect of the game of golf even at the highest levels of professional tournament play; and second, because of the severity of Martin's disability (where walking any distance was both very painful and very dangerous) the use of the golf cart did not give Martin an unfair competitive advantage. Porter, *supra* at 560–61 (discussing the *Martin* case).

Porter argues that the first prong of this test can be analogized to the employment situation in cases where an accommodation affects the employer, but not coworkers. We know that accommodations that are overly expensive do not have to be provided because of the undue hardship provision. But what about accommodations that burden the employer but not financially? Porter argues that those accommodations should be required unless they "fundamentally alter the nature of the employer-employee relationship." *Id.* at 562. In defining the nature of the employer-employee relationship, Porter states:

> [A]s long as the accommodation remedies a socially or structurally imposed barrier, employers should provide it. These accommodations are required because they remove barriers that the employer itself caused or is responsible for perpetuating. On the other hand, . . . many barriers are not created explicitly or implicitly by the employer, and requiring the removal of these barriers would fundamentally alter the nature of the employer-employee relationship.

Id. at 565. Under this test, then, an employer would not have to monitor an employee's medications as a reasonable accommodation because doing so clearly falls outside of the scope of the employer-employee relationship. *Id.* at 566.

With regard to accommodations that cost nothing but affect other employees, Porter uses the second prong of *Martin* (that the accommodation of the golf cart is reasonable because it does not give Martin an unfair competitive advantage) to argue that accommodations in the workplace should have to be given unless they afford the employee with the disability an unfair advantage in the workplace. *Id.* at 571. Porter argues that an accommodation does not give an employee with a disability an unfair competitive advantage if it merely allows the employee to remain employed—such an accommodation simply "evens the playing field." *Id.* at 574. For instance, having other employees perform some marginal tasks that the disabled employee cannot perform does not give the employee with a disability an unfair advantage over his coworkers—it merely allows him to remain employed. *Id.* at 575.

4.   REASSIGNMENT TO A VACANT POSITION

U.S. AIRWAYS, INC. V. BARNETT
535 U.S. 391, 122 S.Ct. 1516 (2002)

JUSTICE BREYER delivered the opinion of the Court.

The Americans with Disabilities Act of 1990 (ADA or Act), 42 U.S.C. § 12101 *et seq.*, prohibits an employer from discriminating against an "individual with a disability" who, with "reasonable accommodation," can perform the essential functions of the job. §§ 12112(a) and (b). This case, arising in the context of summary judgment, asks us how the Act resolves a potential conflict between: (1) the interests of a disabled worker who seeks assignment to a particular position as a "reasonable accommodation," and (2) the interests of other workers with superior rights to bid for the job under an employer's seniority system. In such a case, does the accommodation demand trump the seniority system?

In our view, the seniority system will prevail in the run of cases. As we interpret the statute, to show that a requested accommodation conflicts with the rules of a seniority system is ordinarily to show that the accommodation is not "reasonable." Hence such a showing will entitle an employer/defendant to summary judgment on the question—unless there is more. The plaintiff remains free to present evidence of special circumstances that make "reasonable" a seniority rule exception in the particular case. And such a showing will defeat the employer's demand for summary judgment.

I

In 1990, Robert Barnett, the plaintiff and respondent here, injured his back while working in a cargo-handling position at petitioner U.S. Airways, Inc. He invoked seniority rights and transferred to a less physically demanding mailroom position. Under U.S. Airways' seniority system, that position, like others, periodically became open to seniority-based employee bidding. In 1992, Barnett learned that at least two employees senior to him intended to bid for the mailroom job. He asked U.S. Airways to accommodate his disability-imposed limitations by making an exception that would allow him to remain in the mailroom. After permitting Barnett to continue his mailroom work for five months while it considered the matter, U.S. Airways eventually decided not to make an exception. And Barnett lost his job.

Barnett then brought this ADA suit claiming, among other things, that he was an "individual with a disability" capable of performing the essential functions of the mailroom job, that the mailroom job amounted to a "reasonable accommodation" of his disability, and that U.S. Airways, in refusing to assign him the job, unlawfully discriminated against him. U.S. Airways moved for summary judgment. It supported its motion with appropriate affidavits, contending that its "well-established" seniority system granted other employees the right to obtain the mailroom position.

The District Court found that the undisputed facts about seniority warranted summary judgment in U.S. Airways' favor. The Act says that an employer who fails to make "reasonable accommodations to the known physical or mental limitations of an [employee] with a disability" discriminates *"unless"* the employer "can demonstrate that the accommodation would impose an *undue hardship* on the operation of [its] business." 42 U.S.C. § 12112(b)(5)(A). The court said:

> "[T]he uncontroverted evidence shows that the USAir seniority system has been in place for 'decades' and governs over 14,000 USAir Agents. Moreover, seniority policies such as the one at issue in this case are common to the airline industry. Given this context, it seems clear that the USAir employees were justified in relying upon the policy. As such, any significant alteration of that policy would result in undue hardship to both the company and its non-disabled employees."

An en banc panel of the United States Court of Appeals for the Ninth Circuit reversed. It said that the presence of a seniority system is merely "a factor in the undue hardship analysis." And it held that "[a] case-by-case fact intensive analysis is required to determine whether any particular reassignment would constitute an undue hardship to the employer."

U.S. Airways petitioned for certiorari, asking us to decide whether

> the [ADA] requires an employer to reassign a disabled employee to a position as a 'reasonable accommodation' even though another employee is entitled to hold the position under the employer's bona fide and established seniority system.

The Circuits have reached different conclusions about the legal significance of a seniority system. We agreed to answer U.S. Airways' question.

II

In answering the question presented, we must consider the following statutory provisions. First, the ADA says that an employer may not "discriminate against a qualified individual with a disability." 42 U.S.C. § 12112(a). Second, the ADA says that a "qualified" individual includes "an individual with a disability who, *with* or without *reasonable accommodation,* can perform the essential functions of" the relevant "employment position." § 12111(8). Third, the ADA says that "discrimination" includes an employer's *"not making reasonable accommodations* to the known physical or mental limitations of an otherwise qualified . . . employee, *unless* [the employer] can demonstrate that the accommodation would impose an *undue hardship* on the operation of [its] business." § 12112(b)(5)(A). Fourth, the ADA says that the term

" 'reasonable accommodation' may include . . . reassignment to a vacant position." § 12111(9)(B).

The parties interpret this statutory language as applied to seniority systems in radically different ways. In U.S. Airways' view, the fact that an accommodation would violate the rules of a seniority system always shows that the accommodation is not a "reasonable" one. In Barnett's polar opposite view, a seniority system violation never shows that an accommodation sought is not a "reasonable" one. Barnett concedes that a violation of seniority rules might help to show that the accommodation will work "undue" employer "hardship," but that is a matter for an employer to demonstrate case by case. We shall initially consider the parties' main legal arguments in support of these conflicting positions.

A

U.S. Airways' claim that a seniority system virtually always trumps a conflicting accommodation demand rests primarily upon its view of how the Act treats workplace "preferences." Insofar as a requested accommodation violates a disability-neutral workplace rule, such as a seniority rule, it grants the employee with a disability treatment that other workers could not receive. Yet the Act, U.S. Airways says, seeks only "equal" treatment for those with disabilities. Hence it does not require the employer to grant a request that, in violating a disability-neutral rule, would provide a preference.

While linguistically logical, this argument fails to recognize what the Act specifies, namely, that preferences will sometimes prove necessary to achieve the Act's basic equal opportunity goal. The Act requires preferences in the form of "reasonable accommodations" that are needed for those with disabilities to obtain the *same* workplace opportunities that those without disabilities automatically enjoy. By definition any special "accommodation" requires the employer to treat an employee with a disability differently, *i.e.*, preferentially. And the fact that the difference in treatment violates an employer's disability-neutral rule cannot by itself place the accommodation beyond the Act's potential reach.

Were that not so, the "reasonable accommodation" provision could not accomplish its intended objective. Neutral office assignment rules would automatically prevent the accommodation of an employee whose disability-imposed limitations require him to work on the ground floor. Neutral "break-from-work" rules would automatically prevent the accommodation of an individual who needs additional breaks from work, perhaps to permit medical visits. Neutral furniture budget rules would automatically prevent the accommodation of an individual who needs a different kind of chair or desk. Many employers will have neutral rules governing the kinds of actions most needed to reasonably accommodate a worker with a disability. See 42 U.S.C. § 12111(9)(b) (setting forth examples such as "job restructuring," "part-time or modified work schedules," "acquisition or modification of equipment or devices," "and other similar accommodations"). Yet Congress, while providing such examples, said nothing suggesting that the presence of such neutral rules would create an automatic exemption. Nor have the lower courts made any such suggestion. *Cf.* Garcia-Ayala v. Lederle Parenterals, Inc., 212 F.3d 638, 648 (C.A.1 2000) (requiring leave beyond that allowed under the company's own leave policy); Hendricks-Robinson v. Excel Corp., 154 F.3d 685, 699 (C.A.7 1998) (requiring exception to employer's neutral "physical fitness" job requirement).

In sum, the nature of the "reasonable accommodation" requirement, the statutory examples, and the Act's silence about the exempting effect of neutral rules together convince us that the Act does not create any such automatic exemption. The simple fact that an accommodation would provide a "preference"—in the sense that it would permit the worker with a disability to violate a rule that others must obey—cannot, *in and of itself,* automatically show that the accommodation is not "reasonable." As a result, we reject the position taken by U.S. Airways and Justice SCALIA to the contrary.

U.S. Airways also points to the ADA provisions stating that a " 'reasonable accommodation' may include . . . reassignment to a *vacant* position." § 12111(9)(B). And it claims that the fact that an established seniority system would assign that position to another worker automatically and always means that the position is not a "vacant" one. Nothing in the Act, however, suggests that Congress intended the word "vacant" to have a specialized meaning. And in ordinary English, a seniority system can give employees seniority rights allowing them to bid for a "vacant" position. The position in this case was held, at the time of suit, by Barnett, not by some other worker; and that position, under the U.S. Airways seniority system, became an "open" one. Moreover, U.S. Airways has said that it "reserves the right to change any and all" portions of the seniority system at will. Consequently, we cannot agree with U.S. Airways about the position's vacancy; nor do we agree that the Act would automatically deny Barnett's accommodation request for that reason.

B

Barnett argues that the statutory words "reasonable accommodation" mean only "effective accommodation," authorizing a court to consider the requested accommodation's ability to meet an individual's disability-related needs, and nothing more. On this view, a seniority rule violation, having nothing to do with the accommodation's effectiveness, has nothing to do with its "reasonableness." It might, at most, help to prove an "undue hardship on the operation of the business." But, he adds, that is a matter that the statute requires the employer to demonstrate, case by case.

In support of this interpretation Barnett points to Equal Employment Opportunity Commission (EEOC) regulations stating that "reasonable accommodation means . . . [m]odifications or adjustments . . . that *enable* a qualified individual with a disability to perform the essential functions of [a] position." 29 CFR § 1630(*o*)(ii) (2001). See also S.Rep. No. 101–116, at 35 (discussing reasonable accommodations in terms of "effectiveness," while discussing costs in terms of "undue hardship"). Barnett adds that any other view would make the words "reasonable accommodation" and "undue hardship" virtual mirror images—creating redundancy in the statute. And he says that any such other view would create a practical burden of proof dilemma.

The practical burden of proof dilemma arises, Barnett argues, because the statute imposes the burden of demonstrating an "undue hardship" upon the employer, while the burden of proving "reasonable accommodation" remains with the plaintiff, here the employee. This allocation seems sensible in that an employer can more frequently and easily prove the presence of business hardship than an employee can prove its absence. But suppose that an employee must counter a claim of "seniority rule violation" in order to prove that an "accommodation" request is "reasonable." Would that not force the employee to prove what is in effect an absence, *i.e.*, an absence of hardship, despite the statute's insistence that the employer "demonstrate" hardship's presence?

These arguments do not persuade us that Barnett's legal interpretation of "reasonable" is correct. For one thing, in ordinary English the word "reasonable" does not mean "effective." It is the word "accommodation," not the word "reasonable," that conveys the need for effectiveness. An *ineffective* "modification" or "adjustment" will not *accommodate* a disabled individual's limitations. Nor does an ordinary English meaning of the term "reasonable accommodation" make of it a simple, redundant mirror image of the term "undue hardship." The statute refers to an "undue hardship on the operation of the business." 42 U.S.C. § 12112(b)(5)(A). Yet a demand for an effective accommodation could prove unreasonable because of its impact, not on business operations, but on fellow employees—say, because it will lead to dismissals, relocations, or modification of employee benefits to which an employer, looking at the matter from the perspective of the business itself, may be relatively indifferent.

Neither does the statute's primary purpose require Barnett's special reading. The statute seeks to diminish or to eliminate the stereotypical thought processes, the thoughtless actions, and the hostile reactions that far too often bar those with disabilities from participating fully in the Nation's life, including the workplace. See generally §§ 12101(a) and (b). These objectives demand unprejudiced thought and reasonable responsive reaction on the part of employers and fellow workers alike. They will sometimes require affirmative conduct to promote entry of disabled people into the work force. They do not, however, demand action beyond the realm of the reasonable.

Neither has Congress indicated in the statute, or elsewhere, that the word "reasonable" means no more than "effective." The EEOC regulations do say that reasonable accommodations "enable" a person with a disability to perform the essential functions of a task. But that phrasing simply emphasizes the statutory provision's basic objective. The regulations do not say that "enable" and "reasonable" mean the same thing. And as discussed below, no court of appeals has so read them.

Finally, an ordinary language interpretation of the word "reasonable" does not create the "burden of proof" dilemma to which Barnett points. Many of the lower courts, while rejecting both U.S. Airways' and Barnett's more absolute views, have reconciled the phrases "reasonable accommodation" and "undue hardship" in a practical way.

They have held that a plaintiff/employee (to defeat a defendant/employer's motion for summary judgment) need only show that an "accommodation" seems reasonable on its face, *i.e.,* ordinarily or in the run of cases.

Once the plaintiff has made this showing, the defendant/employer then must show special (typically case-specific) circumstances that demonstrate undue hardship in the particular circumstances. . . .

Not every court has used the same language, but their results are functionally similar. In our opinion, that practical view of the statute, applied consistently with ordinary summary judgment principles, avoids Barnett's burden of proof dilemma, while reconciling the two statutory phrases ("reasonable accommodation" and "undue hardship").

III

The question in the present case focuses on the relationship between seniority systems and the plaintiff's need to show that an "accommodation" seems reasonable on its face, *i.e.,* ordinarily or in the run of cases. We must assume that the plaintiff, an employee, is an "individual with a disability." He has requested assignment to a mailroom position as a "reasonable accommodation." We also assume that normally such a request would be reasonable within the meaning of the statute, were it not for one circumstance, namely, that the assignment would violate the rules of a seniority system. See § 12111(9) ("reasonable accommodation" may include "reassignment to a vacant position"). Does that circumstance mean that the proposed accommodation is not a "reasonable" one?

In our view, the answer to this question ordinarily is "yes." The statute does not require proof on a case-by-case basis that a seniority system should prevail. That is because it would not be reasonable in the run of cases that the assignment in question trump the rules of a seniority system. To the contrary, it will ordinarily be unreasonable for the assignment to prevail.

A

Several factors support our conclusion that a proposed accommodation will not be reasonable in the run of cases. Analogous case law supports this conclusion, for it has recognized the importance of seniority to employee-management relations. This Court has held that, in the context of a Title VII religious discrimination case, an employer need not adapt to an employee's special worship schedule as a "reasonable accommodation" where doing so would conflict with the seniority rights of other employees. *Trans World Airlines, Inc. v. Hardison,* 432 U.S. 63 (1977). The lower courts have unanimously found that collectively bargained seniority trumps the need for reasonable accommodation in the context of the linguistically similar Rehabilitation Act. And several Circuits, though differing in their reasoning, have reached a similar conclusion in the context of seniority and the ADA. All these cases discuss *collectively bargained* seniority systems, not systems (like the present system) which are unilaterally imposed by management. But the relevant seniority system advantages, and related difficulties that result from violations of seniority rules, are not limited to collectively bargained systems.

For one thing, the typical seniority system provides important employee benefits by creating, and fulfilling, employee expectations of fair, uniform treatment. These benefits include "job security and an opportunity for steady and predictable advancement based on objective standards."

Most important for present purposes, to require the typical employer to show more than the existence of a seniority system might well undermine the employees' expectations of consistent, uniform treatment— expectations upon which the seniority system's benefits depend. That is because such a rule would substitute a complex case-specific "accommodation" decision made by management for the more uniform, impersonal operation of seniority rules. Such management decisionmaking, with its inevitable discretionary elements, would involve a matter of the greatest importance to employees, namely, layoffs; it would take place outside, as well as inside, the confines of a court case; and it might well take place fairly often. Cf. ADA, 42 U.S.C. § 12101(a)(1) (estimating that some 43 million Americans suffer from physical or mental disabilities). We can find nothing in the statute that suggests Congress intended to undermine seniority systems in this way. And we consequently conclude that the employer's showing of violation of the rules of a seniority system is by itself ordinarily sufficient.

B

The plaintiff (here the employee) nonetheless remains free to show that special circumstances warrant a finding that, despite the presence of a seniority system (which the ADA may not trump in the run of cases), the requested "accommodation" is "reasonable" on the particular facts. That is because special circumstances might alter the important expectations described above. Cf. *Borkowski*, 63 F.3d, at 137 ("[A]n accommodation that imposed burdens that would be unreasonable for most members of an industry might nevertheless be required of an individual defendant in light of that employer's particular circumstances"). The plaintiff might show, for example, that the employer, having retained the right to change the seniority system unilaterally, exercises that right fairly frequently, reducing employee expectations that the system will be followed—to the point where one more departure, needed to accommodate an individual with a disability, will not likely make a difference. The plaintiff might show that the system already contains exceptions such that, in the circumstances, one further exception is unlikely to matter. We do not mean these examples to exhaust the kinds of showings that a plaintiff might make. But we do mean to say that the plaintiff must bear the burden of showing special circumstances that make an exception from the seniority system reasonable in the particular case. And to do so, the plaintiff must explain why, in the particular case, an exception to the employer's seniority policy can constitute a "reasonable accommodation" even though in the ordinary case it cannot.

IV

In its question presented, U.S. Airways asked us whether the ADA requires an employer to assign a disabled employee to a particular position even though another employee is entitled to that position under the employer's "established seniority system." We answer that *ordinarily* the ADA does not require that assignment. Hence, a showing that the assignment would violate the rules of a seniority system warrants summary judgment for the employer—unless there is more. The plaintiff must present evidence of that "more," namely, special circumstances surrounding the particular case that demonstrate the assignment is nonetheless reasonable.

Because the lower courts took a different view of the matter, and because neither party has had an opportunity to seek summary judgment in accordance with the principles we set forth here, we vacate the Court of Appeals' judgment and remand the case for further proceedings consistent with this opinion.

JUSTICE O'CONNOR, concurring.

I agree with portions of the opinion of the Court, but I find problematic the Court's test for determining whether the fact that a job reassignment violates a seniority system makes the reassignment an unreasonable accommodation under the Americans with Disabilities Act of 1990 (ADA or Act), 42 U.S.C. § 12101 *et seq.* Although a seniority system plays an important role in the workplace, for the reasons I explain below, I would prefer to say that the effect of a seniority system on the reasonableness of a reassignment as an accommodation for purposes of the ADA depends on whether the seniority system is legally enforceable. "Were it possible for me to adhere to [this belief] in my vote, and for the Court at the same time to [adopt a majority rule]," I would do so. "The Court, however, is divided in opinion," and if each Member voted consistently with his or her beliefs, we would not agree on a resolution of the question presented in this case. Yet "[s]talemate should not prevail," particularly in a case in which we are merely interpreting a statute. Accordingly, in order that the Court may adopt a rule, and because I believe the Court's rule will often lead to the same outcome as the one I would have adopted, I join the Court's opinion despite my concerns.

The ADA specifically lists "reassignment to a vacant position" as one example of a "reasonable accommodation." 42 U.S.C. § 12111(9)(B). In deciding whether an otherwise reasonable accommodation involving a reassignment is unreasonable because it would require an exception to a seniority system, I think the relevant issue is whether the seniority system prevents the position in question from being vacant. The word "vacant" means "not filled or occupied by an incumbent [or] possessor." Webster's Third New International Dictionary 2527 (1976). In the context of a workplace, a vacant position is a position in which no employee currently works and to which no individual has a legal entitlement. For example, in a workplace without a seniority system, when an employee ceases working for the employer, the employee's former position is vacant until a replacement is hired. Even if the replacement does not start work immediately, once the replacement enters into a contractual agreement with the employer, the position is no longer vacant because it has a "possessor." In contrast, when an employee ceases working in a workplace with a legally enforceable seniority system, the employee's former position does not become vacant if the seniority system entitles another employee to it. Instead, the employee entitled to the position under the seniority system immediately becomes the new "possessor" of that position. . . .

Given this understanding of when a position can properly be considered vacant, if a seniority system, in the absence of the ADA, would give someone other than the individual seeking the accommodation a legal entitlement or contractual right to the position to which reassignment is sought, the seniority system prevents the position from being vacant. If a position is not vacant, then reassignment to it is not a reasonable accommodation. . . .

Petitioner's Personnel Policy Guide for Agents, which contains its seniority policy, specifically states that it is "*not* intended to be a contract (express or implied) or otherwise to create legally enforceable obligations," and that petitioner "reserves the right to change any and all of the stated policies and procedures in [the] Guide at any time, without advanc[e] notice." Petitioner conceded at oral argument that its seniority policy does not give employees any legally enforceable rights. Because the policy did not give any other employee a right to the position respondent sought, the position could be said to have been vacant when it became open for bidding, making the requested accommodation reasonable.

In Part II of its opinion, the Court correctly explains that "a plaintiff/employee (to defeat a defendant/employer's motion for summary judgment) need only show that an 'accommodation' seems reasonable on its face, *i.e.,* ordinarily or in the run of cases." In other words, the plaintiff must show that the method of accommodation the employee seeks is reasonable in the run of cases. When the Court turns to applying its interpretation of the Act to seniority systems, however, it seems to blend the two inquiries by suggesting that the plaintiff should have the opportunity to prove that there are special circumstances in the context of that particular seniority system that would cause an exception to the system to be reasonable despite the fact that such exceptions are unreasonable in the run of cases.

Although I am troubled by the Court's reasoning, I believe the Court's approach for evaluating seniority systems will often lead to the same outcome as the test I would have adopted. Unenforceable seniority systems are likely to involve policies in which employers "retai[n] the right to change the seniority system," and will often "contai[n] exceptions." They will also often contain disclaimers that "reduc[e] employee expectations that the system will be followed." Thus, under the Court's test, disabled employees seeking accommodations that would require exceptions to unenforceable seniority systems may be able to show circumstances that make the accommodation "reasonable in the[ir] particular case." Because I think the Court's test will often lead to the correct outcome, and because I think it important that a majority of the Court agree on a rule when interpreting statutes, I join the Court's opinion.

JUSTICE SCALIA, with whom JUSTICE THOMAS joins, dissenting.

. . . The principal defect of today's opinion . . . goes well beyond the uncertainty it produces regarding the relationship between the ADA and the infinite variety of seniority systems. The conclusion that any seniority system can ever be overridden is merely one consequence of a mistaken interpretation of the ADA that makes all employment rules and practices— even those which (like a seniority system) pose no *distinctive* obstacle to the disabled—subject to suspension when that is (in a court's view) a "reasonable" means of enabling a disabled employee to keep his job. That is a far cry from what I believe the accommodation provision of the ADA requires: the suspension (within reason) of those employment rules and practices *that the employee's disability prevents him from observing.*

I

. . . These provisions order employers to modify or remove (within reason) policies and practices that burden a disabled person "because of [his] disability." In other words, the ADA eliminates workplace barriers only if a disability prevents an employee from overcoming them—those barriers that would not be barriers *but for* the employee's disability. These include, for example, work stations that cannot accept the employee's wheelchair, or an assembly-line practice that requires long periods of standing. But they do not include rules and practices that bear no more heavily upon the disabled employee than upon others—even though an exemption from such a rule or practice might in a sense "make up for" the employee's disability. It is not a required accommodation, for example, to pay a disabled employee more than others at his grade level—even if that increment is earmarked for massage or physical therapy that would enable the employee to work with as little physical discomfort as his co-workers. That would be "accommodating" the disabled employee, but it would not be "making . . . accommodatio[n] *to the known physical or mental limitations*" of the employee, § 12112(b)(5)(A), because it would not eliminate any workplace practice that constitutes an obstacle *because of* his disability.

. . . There is no reason why the phrase "reassignment to a vacant position" should be thought to have a uniquely different focus. It envisions elimination of the obstacle of the *current position* (which requires activity that the disabled employee cannot tolerate) when there is an alternate position freely available. If he is qualified for that position, and no one else is seeking it, or no one else who seeks it is better qualified, he *must* be given the position. But "reassignment to a vacant position" does *not* envision the elimination of obstacles to the employee's service in the new position that have nothing to do with his disability—for example, another employee's claim to that position under a seniority system, or another employee's superior qualifications.

Unsurprisingly, most Courts of Appeals addressing the issue have held or assumed that the ADA does not mandate exceptions to a "legitimate, nondiscriminatory policy" such as a seniority system or a consistent policy of assigning the most qualified person to a vacant position. . . .

Sadly, this analysis is lost on the Court, which mistakenly and inexplicably concludes that my position here is the same as that attributed to U.S. Airways. In rejecting the argument that the ADA creates no "automatic exemption" for neutral workplace rules such as "break-from-work" and furniture budget rules, the Court rejects an argument I have not made.

JUSTICE SOUTER, with whom JUSTICE GINSBURG joins, dissenting.

Nothing in the ADA insulates seniority rules from the "reasonable accommodation" requirement, in marked contrast to Title VII of the Civil Rights Act of 1964 and the Age Discrimination in Employment Act of 1967, each of which has an explicit protection for seniority. Because Congress modeled several of the ADA's provisions on Title VII, its failure to replicate Title VII's exemption for seniority systems leaves the statute ambiguous, albeit with more than a hint that seniority rules do not inevitably carry the day.

. . . The Committee Reports from both the House of Representatives and the Senate explain that seniority protections contained in a collective-bargaining agreement should not amount to more than "a factor" when it comes to deciding whether some accommodation at odds with the seniority rules is "reasonable" nevertheless. . . . The point in this case, however, is simply to recognize that if Congress considered that sort of agreement no more than a factor in the analysis, surely no greater weight was meant for a seniority scheme like the one before us, unilaterally imposed by the employer, and, unlike collective-bargaining agreements, not singled out for protection by any positive federal statute. . . .

Because a unilaterally imposed seniority system enjoys no special protection under the ADA, a consideration of facts peculiar to this very case is needed to gauge whether Barnett has carried the burden of showing his proposed accommodation to be a "reasonable" one despite the policy in force at U.S. Airways. The majority describes this as a burden to show the accommodation is "plausible" or "feasible," and I believe Barnett has met it.

He held the mailroom job for two years before learning that employees with greater seniority planned to bid for the position, given U.S. Airways's decision to declare the job "vacant." Thus, perhaps unlike ADA claimants who request accommodation through reassignment, Barnett was seeking not a change but a continuation of the status quo. All he asked was that U.S. Airways refrain from declaring the position "vacant"; he did not ask to bump any other employee and no one would have lost a job on his account. There was no evidence in the District Court of any unmanageable ripple effects from Barnett's request, or showing that he would have overstepped an inordinate number of seniority levels by remaining where he was. . . .

With U.S. Airways itself insisting that its seniority system was noncontractual and modifiable at will, there is no reason to think that Barnett's accommodation would have resulted in anything more than minimal disruption to U.S. Airways's operations, if that. Barnett has shown his requested accommodation to be "reasonable," and the burden ought to shift to U.S. Airways if it wishes to claim that, in spite of surface appearances, violation of the seniority scheme would have worked an undue hardship. I would therefore affirm the Ninth Circuit.

NOTES AND QUESTIONS

1. *The benefits of seniority.* The *Barnett* Court holds that the terms of a seniority system ordinarily will trump the ADA's reassignment requirement. What attributes of seniority systems support such an outcome?

2. *Preferential treatment.* U.S. Airways argued that the ADA should not require any accommodation that would result in preferential treatment for the disabled. Justice Scalia contended that the reasonable accommodation

requirement should extend only to the removal of disability-related obstacles. (What does that mean?) The majority opinion rejects both suggested limitations and states that an accommodation is not automatically unreasonable simply because it results in preferential treatment. Following *Barnett*, is there any limit on an employer's duty to provide a preferential accommodation for the disabled?

3. *Reasonable accommodation or undue hardship?* The *Barnett* majority focuses on whether the reassignment of Barnett is a reasonable accommodation rather than on whether the reassignment would impose an undue hardship. How does the majority justify this approach? And what is the practical impact?

4. *Justice O'Connor's proposed test.* How does Justice O'Connor's suggested test for resolving the seniority/reassignment tension differ from that adopted by the majority? How would that test, if adopted, have impacted the outcome of the *Barnett* case?

5. *Burden of proof.* The *Barnett* majority endorsed the "practical way" that most lower courts have allocated the burden of proof in ADA accommodation cases. Under that approach, the plaintiff bears the burden of proof to show that an accommodation is reasonable in the run of cases, which, if established, shifts the burden to the employer to "demonstrate undue hardship in the particular circumstances." Some lower courts, however, have adopted more nuanced burden of proof schemes. The Second Circuit, for example, has ruled that the plaintiff bears a burden of persuasion to show that a particular accommodation would be effective coupled with a burden of production to show that the costs of such an accommodation would not clearly exceed its benefits. If established, the employer then carries the burden of proof to show that the proposed accommodation is unreasonable which merges with the employer's burden of proof to show that the accommodation would impose an undue hardship. Borkowski v. Valley Central School Dist., 63 F.3d 131 (2d Cir. 1995).

6. *Seniority in collective bargaining agreements.* U.S. Airways' seniority system was unilaterally promulgated. Most seniority systems, however, are the product of collective bargaining. How would the *Barnett* analysis likely play out in the context of a seniority system established in a collective bargaining agreement?

7. *Did Congress endorse the result in* Barnett? When Congress amended the ADA in 2008, it did not amend the reasonable accommodation provision; thus, it left the *Barnett* decision intact. Do you think this means that Congress agreed with the result in *Barnett*?

The circuit courts of appeals are currently split with respect to another reassignment issue. The competing positions are illustrated in the following two case excerpts.

HUBER V. WAL-MART STORES, INC.

486 F.3d 480 (8th Cir. 2007), *cert. granted,* 552 U.S. 1074, 128 S.Ct. 742 (2007),
and cert. dismissed, 552 U.S. 1136, 128 S.Ct. 1116 (2008)

RILEY, CIRCUIT JUDGE.

We are faced with an unanswered question: whether an employer who has an established policy to fill vacant job positions with the most qualified applicant is required to reassign a qualified disabled employee to a vacant position, although the disabled employee is not the most qualified applicant for the position. Pam Huber (Huber) brought an action against Wal-Mart Stores, Inc. (Wal-Mart), claiming discrimination under the Americans with Disabilities Act of 1990 (ADA), 42 U.S.C. §§ 12101 to 12213, and the Arkansas Civil Rights Act of 1993 (ACRA). The parties filed cross-motions for summary judgment. The district court granted summary judgment in favor of Huber. Wal-Mart appeals. For the reasons stated below, we reverse.

* * *

Huber contends Wal-Mart, as a reasonable accommodation, should have automatically reassigned her to the vacant router position without requiring her to compete with other applicants for that position. Wal-Mart disagrees, citing its nondiscriminatory policy to hire the most qualified applicant. Wal-Mart argues that, under the ADA, Huber was not entitled to be reassigned automatically to the router position without first competing with other applicants. This is a question of first impression in our circuit. As the district court noted, other circuits differ with respect to the meaning of the reassignment language under the ADA.

The Tenth Circuit in Smith v. Midland Brake, Inc., 180 F.3d 1154, 1164–65 (10th Cir.1999) (en banc), stated:

> [I]f the reassignment language merely requires employers to consider on an equal basis with all other applicants an otherwise qualified existing employee with a disability for reassignment to a vacant position, that language would add nothing to the obligation not to discriminate, and would thereby be redundant. . . .

Thus, the reassignment obligation must mean something more than merely allowing a disabled person to compete equally with the rest of the world for a vacant position.

In the Tenth Circuit, reassignment under the ADA results in automatically awarding a position to a qualified disabled employee regardless whether other better qualified applicants are available, and despite an employer's policy to hire the best applicant.

On the other hand, the Seventh Circuit in EEOC v. Humiston-Keeling, Inc., 227 F.3d 1024, 1027–28 (7th Cir. 2000), explained:

The reassignment provision makes clear that the employer must also consider the feasibility of assigning the worker to a different job in which his disability will not be an impediment to full performance, and if the reassignment is feasible and does not require the employer to turn away a superior applicant, the reassignment is mandatory.

In the Seventh Circuit, ADA reassignment does not require an employer to reassign a qualified disabled employee to a job for which there is a more qualified applicant, if the employer has a policy to hire the most qualified applicant.

Wal-Mart urges this court to adopt the Seventh Circuit's approach and to conclude (1) Huber was not entitled, as a reasonable accommodation, to be reassigned automatically to the router position, and (2) the ADA only requires Wal-Mart to allow Huber to compete for the job, but does not require Wal-Mart to turn away a superior applicant. We find this approach persuasive and in accordance with the purposes of the ADA. As the Seventh Circuit noted in *Humiston-Keeling*:

> The contrary rule would convert a nondiscrimination statute into a mandatory preference statute, a result which would be both inconsistent with the nondiscriminatory aims of the ADA and an unreasonable imposition on the employers and coworkers of disabled employees. A policy of giving the job to the best applicant is legitimate and nondiscriminatory. Decisions on the merits are not discriminatory.

Id. at 1028. "[T]he [ADA] is not a mandatory preference act." *Id.*

We agree and conclude the ADA is not an affirmative action statute and does not require an employer to reassign a qualified disabled employee to a vacant position when such a reassignment would violate a legitimate nondiscriminatory policy of the employer to hire the most qualified candidate. This conclusion is bolstered by the Supreme Court's decision in *U.S. Airways, Inc. v. Barnett*, 535 U.S. 391, 406, 122 S.Ct. 1516 (2002), holding that an employer ordinarily is not required to give a disabled employee a higher seniority status to enable the disabled employee to retain his or her job when another qualified employee invokes an entitlement to that position conferred by the employer's seniority system. . . .

Thus, the ADA does not require Wal-Mart to turn away a superior applicant for the router position in order to give the position to Huber. To conclude otherwise is "affirmative action with a vengeance. That is giving a job to someone solely on the basis of his status as a member of a statutorily protected group." *Humiston-Keeling*, 227 F.3d at 1029.

EQUAL EMPLOYMENT OPPORTUNITY COMMISSION
V. UNITED AIRLINES, INC.
693 F.3d 760 (7th Cir. 2012)

CUDAHY, CIRCUIT JUDGE.

. . . The EEOC invites this court to overturn *Humiston-Keeling*, arguing that *Barnett* undercuts the reasoning of *Humiston-Keeling*. . . .

The EEOC points out that U.S. Airways relied heavily on *Humiston-Keeling* and, more importantly, that the *Barnett* Court flatly contradicted much of the language of *Humiston-Keeling*. U.S. Airways argued that it was not required to grant a requested accommodation that would violate a disability-neutral rule, using the argument from *Humiston-Keeling* that the ADA is "not a mandatory preference act" but only a "nondiscrimination statute." The *Barnett* Court rejected this anti-preference interpretation of the ADA, noting that this argument "fails to recognize what the Act specifies, namely, that preferences will sometimes prove necessary to achieve the Act's basic equal opportunity goal." 535 U.S. at 397, 122 S.Ct. 1516. Merely following a "neutral rule" did not allow U.S. Airways to claim an "automatic exemption" from the accommodation requirement of the Act. Instead, U.S. Airways prevailed because its situation satisfied a much narrower, fact-specific exception based on the hardship that could be imposed on an employer utilizing a seniority system.

The analysis of *Barnett's* impact on *Humiston-Keeling* is further complicated by the fact that we are not the first panel to consider this issue. This court considered *Barnett's* relationship to *Humiston-Keeling*, albeit in an abbreviated fashion and without the benefit of briefing, in *Mays v. Principi*, 301 F.3d 866 (7th Cir.2002). In *Mays*, this court relied on *Humiston-Keeling* in finding that an employer did not violate the duty of reasonable accommodation in the Rehabilitation Act of 1973, 29 U.S.C. § 701 *et seq.*, by giving an administrative nursing position to a better qualified applicant, rather than to a disabled employee needing reassignment. The *Mays* Court interpreted the recently handed down *Barnett* decision actually to bolster *Humiston-Keeling* by equating seniority systems with any other normal method of filling vacancies.

> [*Barnett*] holds that an employer is not required to give a disabled employee superseniority to enable him to retain his job when a more senior employee invokes an entitlement to it conferred by the employer's seniority system. If for "more senior" we read "better qualified," for "seniority system" we read "the employer's normal method of filling vacancies," and for "superseniority" we read "a break," *U.S. Airways* becomes our case.

The EEOC argues, and we agree, that the *Mays* Court incorrectly asserted that a best-qualified selection policy is essentially the same as a seniority system. In equating the two, the *Mays* Court so enlarged the narrow, fact-specific exception set out in *Barnett* as to swallow the rule. While employers may prefer to hire the best qualified applicant, the violation of a best-qualified selection policy does not involve the property-rights and administrative concerns (and resulting burdens) presented by the violation of a seniority policy. To strengthen this critique, the EEOC points out the relative rarity of seniority systems and the distinct challenges of mandating reassignment in a system where employees are already entitled to particular positions based on years of employment.

The Supreme Court has found that accommodation through appointment to a vacant position is reasonable. Absent a showing of undue hardship, an employer must implement such a reassignment policy. The *Mays* Court understandably erred in suggesting that deviation from a best-qualified selection policy always represented such a hardship.

In any event, the *Barnett* framework does not contain categorical exceptions. On remand, the district court must conduct the *Barnett* analysis. In this case, the district court must first consider (under *Barnett* step one) if mandatory reassignment is ordinarily, in the run of cases, a reasonable accommodation. Assuming that the district court finds that mandatory reassignment is ordinarily reasonable, the district must then determine (under *Barnett* step two) if there are fact-specific considerations particular to United's employment system that would create an undue hardship and render mandatory reassignment unreasonable.

For its part, United argues that this court should not abandon *Humiston-Keeling*, in part because the Eighth Circuit explicitly adopted the reasoning of *Humiston-Keeling* in *Huber v. Wal-Mart*, 486 F.3d 480, 483–84 (8th Cir.2007). The Eighth Circuit's wholesale adoption of *Humiston-Keeling* has little import. The opinion adopts *Humiston-Keeling* without analysis, much less an analysis of *Humiston-Keeling* in the context of *Barnett*. Two of our sister Circuits have already determined that the ADA requires employers to appoint disabled employees to vacant positions, provided that such accommodations would not create an undue hardship (or run afoul of a collective bargaining agreement): the Tenth in *Smith v. Midland Brake, Inc.*, 180 F.3d 1154 (10th Cir.1999) (en banc) and the D.C. in *Aka v. Washington Hospital Center*, 156 F.3d 1284 (D.C.Cir.1998) (en banc). We feel that in light of *Barnett*, we must adopt a similar approach.

NOTES AND QUESTIONS

1.   *Most persuasive position?* As between the *Huber* decision and the *EEOC* decision, which position do you find to be most persuasive and why?

2.   In addition to the cases above, the Eleventh Circuit Court of Appeals weighed in on this debate, holding that the ADA does not require reassignment over a more qualified coworker. *See* EEOC v. St. Joseph's Hosp., 842 F.3d 1333, 134–47 (11th Cir. 2016).

3. *Vacant position.* The reassignment accommodation is required only to a position that is "vacant." What is the appropriate temporal measure for determining the existence of a vacancy? Several courts have stated that "[t]he term 'vacant position' not only includes positions that are presently vacant, but also those that the employer reasonably anticipates will become vacant in a short period of time." Cravens v. BlueCross & Blue Shield of Kansas City, 214 F.3d 1011, 1019 n. 5 (8th Cir. 2000), quoting Monette v. Elec. Data Sys. Corp., 90 F.3d 1173, 1187 (6th Cir. 1996). How should this concept be applied in practice? Should a position be deemed vacant if it becomes open and available within a week after an employee with a disability requests reassignment? How about three weeks? Six weeks?

4. *Does reassignment equal affirmative action?* Is reassignment as a reasonable accommodation the equivalent of affirmative action? What differences might exist between reassignment and affirmative action? Even if reassignment involves some type of preferential treatment, are preferences more defensible in the context of disability discrimination than in the context of race discrimination?

5. ACCOMMODATING THE STRUCTURAL NORMS OF THE WORKPLACE

One of the accommodation issues that gets litigated the most is an employee's request for a change to the "structural norms" of the workplace. The structural norms of the workplace refer to employer policies relating to when and where work gets performed—shifts, schedules, hours, attendance policies, leaves of absence, and requests to work from home. The legal issues regarding these accommodation requests are important for a couple of reasons. First, at least one study indicates that a modified schedule is the most frequently requested accommodation by individuals with disabilities. *See, e.g.,* Lisa Schur, Lisa Nishii, Meera Adya, Douglas Kruse, Susanne M. Bruyere, & Peter Blanck, *Accommodating Employees with and Without Disabilities,* 53 HUMAN RESOURCES MANAGEMENT 593, 601 (2014). Second, courts vary widely in how they approach these accommodation requests.

Most courts agree that attendance is an essential function of most positions. *See, e.g.,* Samper v. Providence St. Vincent Medical Center, 675 F.3d 1233 (9th Cir. 2011) (holding that reliable attendance is an essential function of the job of a neo-natal nurse and allowing unlimited, unpredictable absences is not a reasonable accommodation). Issues arise regarding how many hours an employee is required to work, or whether the required start time an employee works can be modified, but generally speaking, an employee who cannot work is not going to be qualified to perform the essential functions of the job.

The question then becomes: is there an accommodation available that would allow the employee to achieve more reliable attendance? Two possible accommodations that employees often seek are: 1) a leave of absence in order to get the medical issues surrounding the employee's disability under control or 2) to allow the employee to work from home. Below are excerpts of two cases for each of these accommodation requests that will illustrate the varied approaches courts take on these issues.

a. Leaves of Absence

GARCÍA-AYALA V. LEDERLE PARENTERALS, INC.
212 F.3d 638 (1st Cir. 2000)

LYNCH, CIRCUIT JUDGE.

Zenaida García-Ayala appeals an order granting summary judgment for her former employer, Lederle Parenterals, Inc., in a suit that alleges wrongful termination and demands injunctive relief and compensatory and punitive damages under the Americans with Disabilities Act. The district court held that García was not a "qualified individual" under the Act because the accommodation she requested from her employer was not "reasonable." We reverse and direct entry of judgment for the plaintiff.

I.

The parties stipulated to the following facts. García worked for Lederle Parenterals, Inc. as a secretary from October 1983 to June 13, 1996, when her employment was terminated. Most recently, she was the only clerical employee in the company's Validation Department.

Lederle's disability benefits program provides that an employee may receive up to fourteen continuous weeks of salary continuation and then short-term disability benefits (STD) at sixty percent of full salary. Under the plan, an employee could be absent from work for a twenty-six week period, work another two weeks, and then be out for an additional twenty-six weeks for the same disability. During her employment at Lederle, García used the salary continuation and short-term disability benefits on fourteen separate occasions, in addition to her sick leave. Lederle had a policy of reserving a job for one year when employees had been out on STD. It applied that policy and terminated García's employment after her one-year reservation period ended.

Since 1986, García has been stricken with breast cancer and has undergone several rounds of surgery and chemotherapy. From March 15, 1987 to September 16, 1987, she was absent from work for 184 days as a result of a modified radical mastectomy. During this period, she received salary continuation benefits for fourteen weeks, and then short-term disability for the remainder. From September 1987 until 1993 she was back at work. Six years later, in August 1993, a biopsy revealed adenocarcinoma of the breast, infiltrating duct type, persistent, and, as a result, García was absent for 115 days. She then returned to work.

In December 1994, García was diagnosed with adenocarcinoma of the breast, metastatic. On March 17, 1995, she underwent surgery to remove a nodule in her neck. Before that surgery, García used up her sick leave and was absent from work for a total of eighty-eight and a half hours. Following surgery, she received short-term disability benefits for thirty-four consecutive days. In May, she took an additional forty-six hours of leave. From June 9 through 25, 1995, she received salary continuation benefits in relation to the medical condition.

Sometime after her surgery, García saw a television report on a bone marrow transplant procedure that offered a treatment for her cancer. She was interviewed by doctors in June 1995 and García informed Lederle in July that she needed to undergo this procedure, which was only available at a Chicago hospital. From August 7 through 20, 1995, she was absent due to chemotherapy (for which she took nineteen hours sick leave and short-term disability). From September 13 through 27, 1995, she was again absent due to treatment (eight hours sick leave/fifteen days of short-term disability). In October 1995, García took eleven and one-half hours of sick leave.

García was hospitalized for the bone marrow treatment on November 14, 1995. She received STD payments until March 19, 1996. As of that date, she started receiving long-term disability (LTD). Lederle did not consider her to be an employee once she was on LTD. On April 9, 1996, doctors certified to Lederle that García would be able to return to work on July 30, 1996.

On June 10, 1996, Lederle's Human Resources Director, Aida Margarita Rodríguez, called García at home and asked her to come to work to meet with her. García complied and Rodríguez notified her that the company deemed her disability to have begun in March 1995, that her one-year period for job reservation had elapsed in March 1996, and that her employment was terminated. García asked that her job be reserved until July 30th, when her doctors expected her to return to work, but to no avail. On June 13th, Lederle sent García a letter confirming her conversation with Rodríguez and denying her request for additional leave.

As it turned out, although García had requested an accommodation until July 30th, it was on August 22, 1996 that García's doctors released her for work, though they did not notify Lederle of this and García did not re-apply for employment.

García's essential job functions did not go unfilled. At least three different temporary employees provided by agencies performed García's tasks at Lederle during her medical leave and after her dismissal. Indeed, from June 13, 1996, to January 31, 1997, a period of over seven months from García's dismissal, the company chose to use temporary employees. The company says her position was never filled by a permanent employee. There was no evidence that the temporary employees cost Lederle any more than García would have or that their performance was in any way unsatisfactory.

II.

On May 16, 1997, García brought suit against Lederle . . . for alleged violations of the ADA . . . as a result of the termination of her employment following surgery for breast cancer. She seeks back pay, reinstatement (or "front pay"), injunctive relief from future discrimination, compensatory and punitive damages, and attorney's fees. On March 30, 1998, the parties submitted a stipulation of material facts together with a Motion Submitting Stipulation of Uncontested Material Facts and Legal Controversies. On September 28, 1998, the court granted Lederle's cross-motion for summary judgment, denied García's motion for summary judgment, . . . and dismissed the case. García appeals.

III.

[Part III of the opinion, which contains a lengthy discussion of the standard of review on appeal from summary judgment entered after cross motions, and based on a stipulated statement of facts, is omitted. Ultimately, the court reviews the determination of the district court for clear error.]

IV.

García claims that Lederle violated the ADA when the company fired her after she requested additional leave supplemental to her sick and disability leave. Section 102(a) of the ADA states: "No covered entity shall discriminate against a qualified individual with a disability because of the disability of such individual in regard to . . . discharge of employees. . . ." 42 U.S.C. § 12112(a). Lederle's primary defense at summary judgment was that García was not a qualified individual because the accommodation she sought was not reasonable.[7] Lederle offered no evidence or argument that the requested accommodation was an undue hardship. In fact, Lederle's appellate argument is inconsistent with its factual stipulation that García's position was terminated because her one-year period of leave had expired. That was the reason the company gave in its letter of termination to García. The company's apparent position that the ADA can never impose an obligation on a company to grant an accommodation beyond the leave allowed under the company's own leave policy is flatly wrong under our precedent. *See, e.g., Ralph v. Lucent Technologies, Inc.*, 135 F.3d 166, 171–72 (1st Cir.1998). The district court order ignored the position stated in the record by the company and went instead to the issue of the reasonableness of the accommodation.

To establish an ADA claim, a plaintiff must prove by a preponderance of the evidence: first, "that she was disabled within the meaning of the Act;

---

[7] Lederle's argument ignores our case law that "[a]lthough the qualification analysis could be understood to subsume the concept of reasonable accommodation, we think it analytically sounder to treat the two topics separately." *EEOC v. Amego, Inc.*, 110 F.3d 135, 141 (1st Cir.1997).

second, . . . that with or without reasonable accommodation she was a qualified individual able to perform the essential functions of the job; and third, . . . that the employer discharged her because of her disability." *Criado v. IBM Corp.,* 145 F.3d 437, 441 (1st Cir.1998). The parties focus on the second of these three elements. Both the EEOC and García argue that the district court erroneously shifted the burden as to this factor.

In order to be a "qualified individual" under the Act, the burden is on the employee to show: first, that she "possess[es] 'the requisite skill, experience, education and other job-related requirements' for the position, and second, [that she is] able to perform the essential functions of the position with or without reasonable accommodation." *Criado,* 145 F.3d at 443 (quoting 29 C.F.R. § 1630.2(m)); *see also* 42 U.S.C. § 12111(8). There is no question here as to the first of these two prerequisites. The court correctly stated that "it is [the] plaintiff's burden to prove that, at the time she sought to resume her job, she had the ability to perform the essential functions of secretary to the Validation Department." But the statute also places the burden on the defendant to show that an accommodation would be an undue hardship. *See* 42 U.S.C. § 12112(b)(5)(A) (stating that the term "discriminate" includes "not making reasonable accommodations to the known physical or mental limitations of an otherwise qualified individual with a disability who is an . . . employee, unless such covered entity can demonstrate that the accommodation would impose an undue hardship on the operation of the business of such covered identity").

The court also went on to say, "[o]f course, an essential function of any job is the ability to appear for work." *Id.* The court then held that García's request for additional leave (until July 30, 1996) "was not reasonable under the circumstances" because "defendants had no guarantee that the additional leave requested was for a definite period of time and '[n]othing in the text of the reasonable accommodation provision requires an employer to wait an indefinite period for an accommodation to achieve its intended effect.' " *Id.* at 315 (quoting *Myers v. Hose,* 50 F.3d 278, 283 (4th Cir.1995)). The court also found that, although "some situations might mandate unpaid leave of absence as an appropriate accommodation," a five-month job reservation, "in excess of established policy[,] place[s] the employer in an untenable business position." The district court, in our view, committed two types of errors.

A. *Individualized Assessment*

It appears from the court's statements that it was applying per se rules, and not giving the type of individual assessment of the facts that the Act and the case law requires. The Supreme Court has deemed "essential" individualized attention to disability claims. As we said in *Criado,* "[w]hether [a] leave request is reasonable turns on the facts of the case." *Criado,* 145 F.3d at 443; *see also Kennedy v. Dresser Rand Co.,* 193 F.3d 120, 122 (2d Cir.1999). It is simply not the case, under our precedent that an employee's request for an extended medical leave will necessarily mean, as the district court suggested, that the employee is unable to perform the essential functions of her job.

First, the court did not focus on the employer's statement that the reason that it terminated García was because her medical leave period, under company policy, had expired. The court essentially found that a requested accommodation of an extension of a leave on top of a medical leave of fifteen months was per se unreasonable. But reasonable accommodations may include "job restructuring, part-time or modified work schedules, . . . and other similar accommodations for individuals with disabilities." 42 U.S.C. § 12111(9)(B). This court and others have held that a medical leave of absence—García's proposed accommodation—is a reasonable accommodation under the Act in some circumstances. *See Criado,* 145 F.3d at 443–44; *Nunes v. Wal-Mart Stores, Inc.,* 164 F.3d 1243, 1247 (9th Cir.1999).

Our concern that the court applied per se rules—rather than an individualized assessment of the facts—is heightened by other statements. Here, the leave that García requested on June 10 was for less than two months. The district court viewed the request as being for five months, since Rodriguez had advised García, albeit in June, that a one-year period for job reservation had lapsed in March. Even if the request were for an additional five months of unpaid leave, we see no reason to adopt a rule on these facts that the additional medical leave sought would be per se an unreasonable accommodation. Well after her termination, as well as during her medical leave, Lederle filled García's secretarial position with individuals hired from temporary agencies. Lederle had no business need apparent from this record to replace García with an in-house hire, and hence would not have suffered had it waited for several more months until García's return. In *Ralph v. Lucent Technologies, Inc.,* 135 F.3d 166, 171–72 (1st Cir.1998), the court held that a four-week additional accommodation, beyond a fifty-two week leave period for mental breakdown, was reasonable for purpose of a preliminary injunction. The district court's statement that the employer was left in an "untenable business position" also reinforces the sense of the use of per se rules and the lack of focus on the facts of this case, given that the employer put on no evidence of undue hardship.

Similarly, the court viewed García's requested accommodation—additional leave time with a specific date for return—as a request that her job be held open indefinitely. Lederle had argued that since García's doctor could not give absolute assurances that she would be fit to return to work on July 30th, the request was per se for an indefinite leave and so was unreasonable. García specified, however, when she would return, and her doctor released her for return several weeks thereafter. There is no evidence that either July 30th or the August 22nd date of medical release, would have imposed any specific hardship on Lederle. Some employees, by the nature of their disability, are unable to provide an absolutely assured time for their return to employment, but that does not necessarily make a request for leave to a particular date indefinite. Each case must be scrutinized on its own facts. An unvarying requirement for definiteness again departs from the need for individual factual evaluation. Of course, that a leave is not indefinite does not make it reasonable. Even short leaves may inflict undue hardship in a given employment situation, and there may be requested leaves so lengthy or open-ended as to be an unreasonable accommodation in any situation.

B. *Reasonable Accommodation and Undue Hardship*

The parties requested that the court determine the issue of liability on the basis of the facts before it. While the burden of showing reasonable accommodation is on the plaintiff, this is a case in which the employer did not contest the reasonableness of the accommodation except to embrace a per se rule that any leave beyond its one-year reservation period was too long. The employer, Lederle, has the burden of proof on the issue of undue hardship, and it did not put on any evidence of undue hardship from García's proposed accommodation.

While on different facts, a request for an extended leave could indeed be too long to be a reasonable accommodation and no reasonable factfinder could conclude otherwise, that is not this case for a number of reasons. It does not appear that García expected to be paid for the additional weeks away from work beyond those allowed under the employer's disability benefits program and while her job functions were being performed by temporary help. There is no evidence that the temporary employees were paid more than García or were less effective at her job than she. Indeed, Lederle's continued use of temporary employees and Lederle's failure to replace García indicates the contrary. There was, therefore, no financial burden on the employer from paying an employee who was not performing. It is true that an employer usually needs to have the functions of a job filled, and the fact that essential functions have gone unfilled for a lengthy period could well warrant judgment for an employer. But here, the essential functions of the job were filled, to all indications satisfactorily, by temporary employees. The use of temporary employees is not, of course, always a satisfactory or even a possible solution. But here, there is no evidence that Lederle was under business pressure to fill the slot with another permanent employee (indeed, it never did). In other situations, temporary replacements may be unavailable or unsuited to the position; here, the available evidence is all to the contrary. In addition, as said, there is no evidence that the cost of the temporary help was greater than the cost of a permanent employee; one might suppose it was less. Thus, the requested accommodation of a few additional months of unsalaried leave, with the job functions being satisfactorily performed in the meantime, is reasonable.

The employer presented the court with no evidence of any hardship, much less undue hardship. On this record, we see no basis for the court to do other than enter judgment for García. . . . As it was the employer's burden to produce evidence of hardship, we hold that it must bear the responsibility for the absence of such evidence here.

We stress that the Act does not require employers to retain disabled employees who cannot perform the essential functions of their jobs without reasonable accommodation. Applying this rule to the prolonged disability leave situation is tricky, however. An absent employee obviously cannot himself or herself perform; still, the employer may in some instances, such as here, be able to get temporary help or find some other alternative that will enable it to proceed satisfactorily with its business uninterrupted while a disabled employee is recovering. In situations like that, retaining the ailing employee's slot while granting unsalaried leave may be a reasonable accommodation required by the ADA. If, however, allowing the sick employee to retain his or her job places the employer in a hardship situation where it cannot secure in some reasonable alternative way the services for which it hired the ailing employee, and yet is blocked from effecting a rehire, the ADA does not require the retention of the disabled person. Hence, where it is unrealistic to expect to obtain someone to perform those essential functions temporarily until the sick employee returns, the employer may be entitled to discharge the ill employee and hire someone else. . . .

Other factors to be considered as to whether requests for leaves of absence are unreasonable include, for example: where the employee gave no indication as to when she might be able to return to work, and, instead, she simply demanded that her job be held open indefinitely; where the employee's absences from work were "erratic" and "unexplained"; where, upon the employee's return to work, she would be unqualified; and where the employee was hired to complete a specific task. . . .

These are difficult, fact intensive, case-by-case analyses, ill-served by per se rules or stereotypes. We emphasize that the stipulated record here contains no evidence whatever of *any* form of hardship to Lederle as a result of the requested accommodation. Were this not so, we would feel obligated to return the case to a factfinder for further evaluation. But given the employer's failure to meet, even minimally, its burden of proof on the issue of hardship, we award judgment to García as a matter of law.

V.

We *reverse* the entry of judgment in favor of Lederle, direct entry of judgment on liability under the ADA for García, and *remand* the case for further proceedings in accordance with this opinion.

So ordered. Costs to appellant.

[Judge O'Toole's dissent is omitted.]

SEVERSON V. HEARTLAND WOODCRAFT, INC.

872 F.3d 476 (7th Cir. 2017)

SYKES, CIRCUIT JUDGE.

From 2006 to 2013, Raymond Severson worked for Heartland Woodcraft, Inc., a fabricator of retail display fixtures. The work was physically demanding. In early June 2013, Severson took a 12-week medical leave under the Family Medical Leave Act ("FMLA") to deal with serious back pain. On the last day of his leave, he underwent back surgery, which required that he remain off of work for another two or three months.

Severson asked Heartland to continue his medical leave, but by then he had exhausted his FMLA entitlement. The company denied his request and terminated his employment, but invited him to reapply when he was medically cleared to work. About three months later, Severson's doctor lifted all restrictions and cleared him to resume work, but Severson did not reapply. Instead he sued Heartland alleging that it had discriminated against him in violation of the Americans with Disabilities Act ("ADA" or "the Act") by failing to provide a reasonable accommodation—namely, a three-month leave of absence after his FMLA leave expired. The district court awarded summary judgment to Heartland and Severson appealed.

We affirm. The ADA is an antidiscrimination statute, not a medical-leave entitlement. The Act forbids discrimination against a "qualified individual on the basis of disability." *Id.* § 12112(a). A "qualified individual" with a disability is a person who, "with or without reasonable accommodation, can perform the essential functions of the employment position." *Id.* § 12111(8). So defined, the term "reasonable accommodation" is expressly limited to those measures that will enable the employee to work. An employee who needs long-term medical leave *cannot* work and thus is not a "qualified individual" under the ADA. *Byrne v. Avon Prods., Inc.*, 328 F.3d 379, 381 (7th Cir. 2003).

With support from the EEOC, Severson urges us to retreat from or curtail our decision in *Byrne*. We decline to do so. *Byrne* is sound and we reaffirm it: A multimonth leave of absence is beyond the scope of a reasonable accommodation under the ADA.

I.   Background

Severson has suffered from back pain since 2005. In 2010 he was diagnosed with back myelopathy caused by impaired functioning and degenerative changes in his back, neck, and spinal cord. Typically Severson's back condition did not hamper his ability to work. But at times he experienced severe flare-ups, making it hard (and sometimes impossible) for him to walk, bend, lift, sit, stand, move, and work.

Severson began working for Heartland in 2006. Over time he was promoted from supervisor to shop superintendent to operations manager. He performed poorly in this last position, so Heartland relieved him of his duties and moved him to a second-shift "lead" position. According to the job description, an employee in this position performs manual labor in the production area of the plant, operates and troubleshoots production machinery, performs minor repairs as necessary, maintains the building, and frequently lifts materials and product weighing 50 pounds or more. Heartland notified Severson of the demotion in a meeting on June 5, 2013. He accepted it but never worked in his new assignment.

Earlier that same day, Severson wrenched his back at home, aggravating his preexisting condition and leaving him demonstrably uncomfortable. He left work early due to the pain and later requested and received FMLA leave retroactive to June 5. Over the summer months, Severson submitted periodic notes from his doctor informing Heartland that he had multiple herniated and bulging discs in his lumbar spine and was unable to work until further notice. His doctor treated him with steroid injections, to little effect. During this time period, Doug Lawrence, Heartland's general manager, and Jennifer Schroeder, the human resources manager, remained in regular phone and email contact with Severson and approved his requests for continuation of his FMLA leave.

On August 13 Severson called Schroeder and told her that his condition had not improved and he would undergo disc decompression surgery on August 27. He explained that the typical recovery time for this surgery was at least two months. He requested an extension of his medical leave. But he had already exhausted his FMLA entitlement; the maximum 12-week leave would expire on August 27, his scheduled surgery date.

Schroeder did not talk with Severson again until August 26. In a phone call that day, she and Lawrence told Severson that his employment with Heartland would end when his FMLA leave expired on August 27. Schroeder invited him to reapply with the company when he recovered from surgery and was medically cleared to work.

Severson had back surgery as planned on August 27. On October 17 his doctor gave him partial clearance to return to work as long as he did not lift anything heavier than 20 pounds. On December 5 Severson's doctor removed the 20-pound lifting restriction and cleared him to return to work without limitation. Instead of reapplying to work for Heartland, Severson sued the company alleging that it discriminated against him in violation of the ADA by failing to accommodate his physical disability. He pointed to three accommodations that the company could have offered him but did not: (1) a two- or three-month leave of absence; (2) a transfer to a vacant job; or (3) a temporary light-duty position with no heavy lifting.

Heartland moved for summary judgment, arguing that Severson's proposed accommodations were not reasonable. The district judge agreed and entered judgment for Heartland. Severson appealed. The EEOC filed a brief as amicus curiae in support of reversal.

II. Discussion

We review a summary judgment de novo, viewing the evidentiary record in the light most favorable to Severson and drawing reasonable inferences in his favor. Summary judgment is warranted "if the movant shows that there is no genuine dispute as to any material fact and the movant is entitled to judgment as a matter of law." FED. R. CIV. P. 56(a).

The ADA makes it unlawful for an employer to discriminate against a "qualified individual on the basis of disability." § 12112(a). A "qualified individual" is "an individual who, with or without reasonable accommodation, can perform the essential functions of the employment position that such individual holds or desires." § 12111(8).

The parties agree that Severson had a disability. They also agree that frequently lifting 50 pounds or more is an essential function of the second-shift lead position at Heartland and that Severson was unable to perform this function at the time he was fired. As in many ADA cases, liability thus turns on the accommodation question: Did Heartland violate the ADA by failing to reasonably accommodate his disability?

Severson identifies three possible accommodations: (1) a multimonth leave of absence following the expiration of his FMLA leave; (2) reassignment to a vacant job; or (3) a temporary assignment to a light-duty position that did not require heavy lifting. The parties focus most of their attention on whether a long-term leave of absence is a reasonable accommodation within the meaning of the ADA. We do the same.

The ADA contains a definition of "reasonable accommodation," but it tells us only what the term *may* include:

> The term "reasonable accommodation" may include—
>
> (A) making existing facilities used by employees readily accessible to and usable by individuals with disabilities; and
>
> (B) job restructuring, part-time or modified work schedules, reassignment to a vacant position, acquisition or modification of equipment or devices, appropriate adjustment or modifications of examinations, training materials or policies, the provision of qualified readers or interpreters, and other similar accommodations for individuals with disabilities.

42 U.S.C. § 12111(9).

The use of the permissive phrase "may include"—rather than "must include" or "includes"—means that the concept of "reasonable accommodation" is flexible and the listed examples are illustrative. But the baseline requirement found in the definition of "qualified individual" is concrete: A "reasonable accommodation" is one that allows the disabled employee to "perform the essential functions of the employment position." § 12111(8). If the proposed accommodation does not make it possible for the employee to perform his job, then the employee is not a "qualified individual" as that term is defined in the ADA. The illustrative examples listed in § 12111(9) are all measures that facilitate work.

Putting these interlocking definitions together, a long-term leave of absence cannot be a reasonable accommodation. As we noted in *Byrne*, "[n]ot working is not a means to perform the job's essential functions." 328 F.3d at 381. Simply put, an extended leave of absence does not give a disabled individual the means to work; it excuses his not working. Accordingly, we held in *Byrne* that "[a]n inability to do the job's essential tasks means that one is not 'qualified'; it does not mean that the employer must excuse the inability." *Id.*

Byrne leaves open the possibility that a brief period of leave to deal with a medical condition could be a reasonable accommodation in some circumstances. 328 F.3d at 381. For example, we noted that "[t]ime off may be an apt accommodation for intermittent conditions. Someone with arthritis or lupus may be able to do a given job even if, for brief periods, the inflammation is so painful that the person must stay home." *Byrne*, 328 F.3d at 381. Intermittent time off or a short leave of absence—say, a couple of days or even a couple of weeks—may, in appropriate circumstances, be analogous to a part-time or modified work schedule, two of the examples listed in § 12111(9). But a medical leave spanning multiple months does not permit the employee to perform the essential functions of his job. To the contrary, the "[i]nability to work for a multi-month period removes a person from the class protected by the ADA." *Id.*

Long-term medical leave is the domain of the FMLA, which entitles covered employees "to a total of 12 work-weeks of leave during any 12-month period . . . [b]ecause of a serious health condition that makes the employee unable to perform the functions of the position of such employee." 29 U.S.C. § 2612(a)(1)(D). The FMLA protects up to 12 weeks of medical leave, recognizing that employees will sometimes be *unable* to perform their job duties due to a serious health condition. In contrast, "the ADA applies only to those who can do the job." *Byrne*, 328 F.3d at 381.

The EEOC argues that a long-term medical leave of absence should qualify as a reasonable accommodation when the leave is (1) of a definite, time-limited duration; (2) requested in advance; and (3) likely to enable the employee to perform the essential job functions when he returns. On this understanding, the duration of the leave is irrelevant as long as it is likely to enable the employee to do his job when he returns.

That reading of the statute equates "reasonable accommodation" with "effective accommodation," an interpretation that the Supreme Court has rejected:

> [I]n ordinary English the word "reasonable" does not mean "effective." It is the word "accommodation," not the word "reasonable," that conveys the need for effectiveness. An *ineffective* "modification" or "adjustment" will not *accommodate* a disabled individual's limitations. . . . Yet a demand for an effective accommodation could prove unreasonable. . . .

U.S. Airways, Inc. v. Barnett, 535 U.S. 391, 400, 122 S.Ct. 1516 (2002). In other words, effectiveness is a necessary but not sufficient condition for a reasonable accommodation under the ADA.

Perhaps the more salient point is that on the EEOC's interpretation, the length of the leave does not matter. If, as the EEOC argues, employees are entitled to extended time off as a reasonable accommodation, the ADA is transformed into a medical-leave statute—in effect, an open-ended extension of the FMLA. That's an untenable interpretation of the term "reasonable accommodation."

[The court holds that Severson's failure-to-accommodate claim regarding his other proposed accommodations must fail because (1) he did not identify any vacant positions available at the time of his termination; and (2) the employer is not obligated to create a temporary light-duty position.]

AFFIRMED.

NOTES AND QUESTIONS

1. *Opposite ends of the spectrum.* The *García-Ayala* and *Severson* cases represent opposite ends of the spectrum regarding how courts treat requests for leaves of absence. In *García-Ayala*, the court held that multi-month leaves can never be *per se* unreasonable. Instead, courts should always analyze whether the extended leave (even after 15 months of leave) would cause the employer an undue hardship. *Severson*, on the other hand, held that a two-to-three-month extension of leave after the employee's FMLA leave had expired was unreasonable. The difference appears to be how the courts define "qualified." The *Severson* court stated that a long-term leave never makes an employee "qualified" to perform the essential functions of the job. One commentator has a similar (but more nuanced) argument that employers are not obligated to accommodate employees who cannot work at the time the leave would begin. *See* Ryan H. Nelson, *Now and Again: Reappraising Disability Leave as an Accommodation*, ___ BYU L. REV. ___, *7 (forthcoming 2021).

The court in *García-Ayala*, on the other hand, stated:

> We stress that the Act does not require employers to retain disabled employees who cannot perform the essential functions of their jobs without reasonable accommodation. Applying this rule to the

prolonged disability leave situation is tricky, however. An absent employee obviously cannot himself or herself perform; still, the employer may in some instances, such as here, be able to get temporary help or find some other alternative that will enable it to proceed satisfactorily with its business uninterrupted while a disabled employee is recovering. In situations like that, retaining the ailing employee's slot while granting unsalaried leave may be a reasonable accommodation required by the ADA.

García-Ayala, 212 F.3d at 649–50. Which approach is better?

2. *Other courts' approaches.* The Tenth Circuit appears to be aligned with the approach taken by the Seventh Circuit in *Severson. See* Hwang v. Kansas State Univ., 753 F.3d 1159, 1161 (10th Cir. 2014) (holding in a Rehabilitation Act case that an extended leave of absence for an employee recovering from cancer is not required: "It perhaps goes without saying that an employee who isn't capable of working for so long isn't an employee capable of performing a job's essential functions—and that requiring an employer to keep a job open for so long doesn't qualify as a reasonable accommodation."). *See also* Robert v. Board of County Com'rs of Brown County, Kans., 691 F.3d 1211, 1218 (10th Cir. 2012) (holding in an ADA case that there is a durational limit on when a leave of absence can be reasonable; six months is the outer limit). Other courts similarly have held that leaves that do not enable the employee to be qualified in the near future are not reasonable. *See, e.g.,* Moss v. Harris County Constable Precinct One, 851 F.3d 413 (5th Cir. 2017) (holding that a leave of absence that would last until the plaintiff's planned retirement date is not a reasonable accommodation because it would not allow him to be qualified to perform the functions of his job); Scruggs v. Pulaski County, Ark., 817 F.3d 1087, 1093 (8th Cir. 2016) (holding that an extension of an FMLA leave is not a reasonable accommodation); Graves v. Finch Pruyn & Co., Inc., 353 F. App'x 558, 561 (2d Cir. 2009) (stating that even a two-week leave of absence is not reasonable because plaintiff made no showing that the leave would allow him to perform the essential functions of his job).

Other courts are more closely aligned with the approach taken in *García-Ayala. See, e.g.,* Nunes v. Wal-Mart Stores, Inc., 164 F.3d 1243, 1247 (9th Cir. 1999) (holding that an extended leave of absence can be a reasonable accommodation); Cehrs v. Northeast Ohio Alzheimer's Research Center, 155 F.3d 775, 782–83 (6th Cir. 1998) (holding that a leave of absence can be a reasonable accommodation and if the employer cannot prove that the leave would unduly burden it, there is no reason to deny the leave of absence); Miller v. Hersman, 759 F.Supp.2d 1, 15 (D.D.C. 2010) (holding that a six-month leave of absence was not unreasonable and would not have created an undue hardship for the employer). Even when a long-term leave might be considered reasonable, it is possible that the court will find that it created an undue hardship. *See, e.g.,* Winnie v. Infectious Disease Associates, P.A., 750 F. App'x 954, 962 (11th Cir. 2018) (holding that a four-month leave of absence would create an undue hardship for the employer because of the highly trained work the plaintiff performed and the fact that the employer was already understaffed).

It is interesting to note that the cases that have held that extended leaves of absence can be reasonable accommodations are generally older than the cases that seem to be putting limits on the leave of absence accommodation. In other words, there seems to be a trend in favor of not allowing leaves of absence as a reasonable accommodation. The Supreme Court has not weighed in on this debate, and in fact denied certiorari in the *Severson* case. 138 S.Ct. 1441 (2018). Perhaps relevant to how the Supreme Court might decide this issue if it eventually grants certiorari is that Justice Gorsuch was the author of the *Hwang* opinion, discussed above, when he was a judge on the Tenth Circuit. Recall that the *Hwang* case is aligned with the approach in *Severson* that long-term leaves do not have to be provided because they do not enable the employee to perform the functions of the job.

3. *EEOC Guidance on Leave.* The EEOC has issued enforcement guidance on the reasonable accommodation provision, which includes guidance on leaves of absence. EEOC, ENFORCEMENT GUIDANCE: REASONABLE ACCOMMODATION AND UNDUE HARDSHIP UNDER THE AMERICANS WITH DISABILITIES ACT (Oct. 2002), https://www.eeoc.gov/laws/guidance/enforce ment-guidance-reasonable-accommodation-and-undue-hardship-under-ada# leave. In the guidance, the EEOC states that permitting the use of leave is a form of reasonable accommodation when necessitated by an employee's disability, and employers must hold open the employee's position while on leave, unless doing so causes an undue hardship for the employer. *Id.* Furthermore, the EEOC states that an employer cannot apply a "no-fault" leave policy, under which employees are automatically terminated after they have been on leave for a certain period of time. *Id.* Even when an employee has exhausted all applicable leave under the FMLA, discussed below, the employer is required to grant additional leave under the ADA unless doing so would cause an undue hardship. *Id.*

4. *Indefinite leave.* In addition to the EEOC guidance discussed above, the EEOC issued a guidance in 2016 that specifically addresses indefinite leave. EEOC, EMPLOYER-PROVIDED LEAVE AND THE AMERICANS WITH DISABILITIES ACT (May 9, 2016), https://www.eeoc.gov/laws/guidance/ employer-provided-leave-and-americans-disabilities-act. In that guidance, the EEOC notes that some employees might not be able to provide a definite date of return, but rather, only an approximate date. In other cases, the projected dates of return might need to be modified in light of changed circumstances. According to the EEOC, these situations will not necessarily result in undue hardship, but instead must be evaluated on a case-by-case basis. As the EEOC elaborates, however, "indefinite leave—meaning that an employee cannot say whether or when she will be able to return to work at all—will constitute an undue hardship, and so does not have to be provided as a reasonable accommodation." *Id.* The EEOC seems to be distinguishing between an *uncertain* return date and indefinite leave. Other courts make this same distinction. For instance, the court in *García-Ayala* stated that even though

some employees are unable to provide an "absolutely assured time for their return to employment," this does not necessarily "make a request for leave to a particular date indefinite." *García-Ayala*, 212 F.3d at 648. *See also* Humphrey v. Memorial Hospitals Ass'n, 239 F.3d 1128, 1136 (9th Cir. 2001) (stating that the "ADA does not require an employee to show that a leave of absence is certain or even likely to be successful to prove that it is a reasonable accommodation"). Other courts are less nuanced and if the date of return is uncertain, the court will classify it as "indefinite" leave and hold that the leave was not required. *See, e.g.*, Kieffer v. CPR Restoration & Cleaning Services, LLC, 733 F. App'x 632, 637–38 (3d Cir. 2018) (holding that a request for open-ended leave with no end date is not a reasonable accommodation); Wood v. Green, 323 F.3d 1309, 1314 (11th Cir. 2003) (holding that the plaintiff's frequent and unpredictable need for leave from work due to cluster headaches is not reasonable because it was a request for an indefinite leave of absence); Myers v. Hose, 50 F.3d 278, 283 (4th Cir. 1995) (employer is not required to wait indefinitely for the plaintiff's medical conditions to be corrected). *See also* Stephen F. Befort, *The Most Difficult Reasonable Accommodation Issues: Reassignment and Leave of Absence*, 37 WAKE FOREST L. REV. 439 (2002).

5.   *Overlap with the Family and Medical Leave Act (FMLA).* The FMLA requires covered employers (those with 50 or more employees in a 75-mile radius) to provide twelve weeks of leave every twelve months to eligible employees for certain enumerated reasons, including an employee's own "serious health condition." 29 U.S.C. § 2612. Now that the ADA's coverage has been broadened through the ADA Amendments Act, it is likely that many "serious health conditions" under the FMLA will also be considered disabilities under the ADA, and more employers will be required to consider the obligations of both statutes when determining employees' rights to medical leave. The Department of Labor (rather than the EEOC) administers the FMLA. Nevertheless, the EEOC has published a Fact Sheet that discusses the overlap between the FMLA and the ADA. *See* EEOC FACT SHEET: THE FAMILY AND MEDICAL LEAVE ACT, THE AMERICANS WITH DISABILITIES ACT, AND TITLE VII OF THE CIVIL RIGHTS ACT OF 1964, www.eeoc.gov/policy/docs/fmlaada.html. For a good discussion of the differences between FMLA leave and leave under the ADA, see *Fleck v. Wilmac Corp.*, 2012 WL 1033472, at *11 (E.D. Pa. March 27, 2012).

b.   Working from Home

EQUAL EMPLOYMENT OPPORTUNITY COMMISSION
V. FORD MOTOR COMPANY
782 F.3d 753 (6th Cir. 2014) (en banc)

McKEAGUE, CIRCUIT JUDGE.

The Americans with Disabilities Act (ADA) requires employers to reasonably accommodate their disabled employees; it does not endow all disabled persons with a job—or job schedule—of their choosing. Jane Harris, a Ford Motor Company employee with irritable bowel syndrome, sought a job schedule of her choosing: to work from home on an as-needed basis, up to four days per week. Ford denied her request, deeming regular and predictable on-site attendance essential to Harris's highly interactive job. Ford's papers and practices—and Harris's three past telecommuting failures—backed up its business judgment.

Nevertheless, the federal Equal Employment Opportunity Commission (EEOC) sued Ford under the ADA. It alleged that Ford failed to reasonably accommodate Harris by denying her telecommuting request and retaliated against her for bringing the issue to the EEOC's attention. The district court granted summary judgment to Ford on both claims. We affirm.

I

The Ford Motor Company employs about 224,000 employees worldwide. True to its founder's vision, Ford uses its employees in assembly lines to perform independent yet interconnected tasks. Resale buyers of steel come early on the lines—before any assembling begins. They purchase raw steel from steel suppliers and then, as their name suggests, resell the steel to parts manufacturers known as "stampers." The stampers then supply the steel parts to the vehicle assemblers, who put together the vehicles.

As an intermediary between steel and parts suppliers, the resale buyer's job is highly interactive. Some of the interactions occur by email and telephone. But many require good, old-fashioned interpersonal skills. During core business hours, for example, resale buyers meet with suppliers at their sites and with Ford employees and stampers at Ford's site— meetings that Ford says are most effectively performed face to face. And Ford's practice aligns with its preaching: It requires resale buyers to work in the same building as stampers so they can meet on a moment's notice. This high level of interactivity and teamwork is why, in Ford's judgment, "a resale buyer's regular and predictable attendance in the workplace" is "essential to being a fully functioning member of the resale team."

A former Ford resale buyer with irritable bowel syndrome takes center stage in this case: Jane Harris. Her job performance was, on the whole, subpar. Early on in her six-plus year tenure, she won a few awards, and Ford recognized her for her "strong commodity knowledge" and "diligent[ ]" work effort. But over time, the awards and compliments morphed into low ratings and criticisms. . . . Ford said she lacked interpersonal skills, delivered work late, didn't show a concern for quality, and failed to properly communicate with the suppliers. She ranked in the bottom 10% of her peers.

In addition to performing poorly while at work, she repeatedly missed work entirely. In 2008, she missed an average of 1.5 work days per week; in 2009, she was absent *more* than she was present. And when she didn't miss work, she would often come in late and leave early. As her coworkers and supervisors put it, Harris worked on a "sporadic and unpredictable basis," and had "chronic attendance issues."

Harris's poor performance and high absenteeism harmed those around her. When she missed work, her teammates had to pick up the slack, including by taking on the functions that Harris could not perform at home. Her supervisors also had to assume her job responsibilities. Her absences caused the resale-buyer team "stress and frustration," further compounded Harris's mistakes, and frustrated suppliers.

Harris's irritable bowel syndrome of course contributed to the situation. It gave her uncontrollable diarrhea and fecal incontinence, sometimes so bad that "it" could "start[ ] pouring out of [her]" at work. She occasionally couldn't even make the one-hour drive to work without having an accident. The vicious cycle continued, as her symptoms increased her stress, and the increased stress worsened her symptoms—making her less likely to come to work.

Ford tried to help. Harris's first supervisor, Dawn Gontko, for example, adjusted Harris's schedule to help her establish regular and predictable attendance. Most significantly, Gontko allowed Harris two opportunities to "telecommute on an ad hoc basis" in an "Alternative Work Schedule." Under this schedule, Harris worked four 10-hour days (known as flex time) and could telecommute as needed on her work days. Each trial lasted one to two months. But neither succeeded: Despite the *ad hoc* telecommuting and flexible schedules, Harris "was unable to establish regular and consistent work hours" and failed "to perform the core objectives of the job."

Ford next tried its "Workplace Guidelines"—a reporting tool specially designed to help employees with attendance issues tied to illnesses. These also failed to improve Harris's attendance or illness. . . .

Undeterred by these three failed telecommuting attempts, Harris requested leave "to work up to four days per week from home." Gontko had told her, after all, that her job would be appropriate for telecommuting. Ford's telecommuting policy generally said the same thing. And several of her coworkers telecommuted. So why couldn't Harris?

Ford's practice and policy limited telecommuting for resale buyers. In practice, Ford's buyers telecommuted, at most, on *one* set day per week. That aligned with its policy, which makes clear that those jobs that require "face-to-face contact"—and those individuals who were not "strong performers" and who had poor time-management skills—were among those not "appropriate for telecommuting."

Before making a decision on the request, two of Ford's human-resources representatives and Gordon met with Harris. In the meeting, Gordon went through Harris's ten main job responsibilities and asked Harris to comment on how she could perform those tasks from home. Of the ten tasks, Harris admitted that she could not perform four of them from home, including meetings with suppliers, making price quotes to stampers, and attending some required internal meetings. Harris added, however, that she did not envision needing to stay home four days per week, only that she wanted the freedom of "*up to* 4 days." Harris's higher-ups told her that they would get back to her about her request.

Ford determined that Harris's proposed accommodation was unreasonable. Management met with Harris to inform her of the decision. Gordon again listed Harris's ten job responsibilities: four that could *not* be performed at home; four that could not *effectively* be performed from home; and two that were "not significant enough to support telecommut[ing]." Gordon explained the circumstances under which telecommuting *could* work: on a predictable schedule where the strong-performing employee agrees to come to the worksite as needed even on days set for telecommuting. Harris's coworkers who telecommuted fit that bill. But Harris didn't, and neither did her proposed schedule.

Even though Ford did not grant her requested telecommuting schedule, management told Harris that they could accommodate her in other ways, such as moving her closer to the restroom or looking for jobs better suited for telecommuting. Harris turned down each alternative accommodation. The second meeting ended as Ford informed Harris that it would "talk with her again if she identifie[d] another accommodation." Harris never did. Rather, she sent an email one week later claiming that the denial of her request violated the ADA. And she filed a charge of discrimination with the EEOC a day after that.

The rest of Harris's time at Ford did not go well. . . . [She was terminated] on September 10, 2009.

Almost two years later, on August 25, 2011, the EEOC sued Ford under the ADA. It alleged that Ford failed to reasonably accommodate Harris's disability (violating 42 U.S.C. § 12112(a), (b)(5)(A)) . . . . On June 29, 2012, Ford moved for summary judgment.

The district court granted Ford's motion on September 10, 2012. It concluded that "working from home up to four days per week is not [a] reasonable" accommodation under the ADA . . . . The EEOC appealed, and a divided panel of this court reversed on both claims.

We granted en banc review, thereby vacating the panel's decision. Giving fresh review to the district court's summary-judgment decision and drawing reasonable inferences in the EEOC's favor, we must determine whether there exists a "genuine dispute as to any material fact." . . . Fed. Rule Civ. Proc. 56(a). . . . Undertaking this analysis, we hold that there is no genuine dispute of material fact on this record: A reasonable jury could not return a verdict for the EEOC . . . .

II

Many disabled individuals require accommodations to perform their jobs. The ADA addresses this reality by requiring companies like Ford to make "reasonable accommodations to the known . . . limitations of an otherwise qualified individual with a disability" where such an accommodation does not cause the employer "undue hardship." 42 U.S.C. § 12112(b)(5). To comply with the ADA, then, Ford must "reasonabl[y] accommodat[e]" Harris (undisputedly a disabled individual for purposes of this appeal) if she is *"qualified."* §§ 12112(a), (b)(5); *see Smith v. Ameritech,* 129 F.3d 857, 866 (6th Cir.1997).

To be "qualified" under the ADA, Harris must be able to "perform the essential functions of [a resale buyer]" "with or without reasonable accommodation." 42 U.S.C. § 12111(8). A "reasonable accommodation" may include "job restructuring [and] part-time or modified work schedules." *Id.* at § 12111(9)(B). But it does *not* include removing an "essential function [ ]" from the position, for that is *per se* unreasonable. *Brickers v. Cleveland Bd. of Educ.,* 145 F.3d 846, 850 (6th Cir.1998). The district court held that Harris was *not* qualified because her excessive absences prevented her from performing the essential functions of a resale buyer. We agree.

A

Is regular and predictable on-site job attendance an essential function (and a prerequisite to perform other essential functions) of Harris's resale-buyer job? We hold that it is.

1

We do not write on a clean slate. Much ink has been spilled establishing a general rule that, with few exceptions, "an employee who does not come to work cannot perform any of his job functions, essential or otherwise." *EEOC v. Yellow Freight Sys., Inc.,* 253 F.3d 943, 948 (7th Cir.2001) (en banc). We will save the reader a skim by omitting a long string-cite of opinions that agree, but they do. Our Circuit has not bucked the trend. And for good reason: "most jobs require the kind of teamwork, personal interaction, and supervision that simply cannot be had in a home office situation." *Rauen v. U.S. Tobacco Mfg. L.P.,* 319 F.3d 891, 896 (7th Cir.2003).

That general rule—that regularly attending work on-site is essential to most jobs, especially the interactive ones—aligns with the text of the ADA. Essential functions generally are those that the employer's "judgment" and "written [job] description" prior to litigation deem essential. *See* 42 U.S.C. § 12111(8). And in most jobs, especially those involving teamwork and a high level of interaction, the employer will require regular and predictable on-site attendance from all employees (as evidenced by its words, policies, and practices).

The same goes for the EEOC's regulations. They define essential functions as those that are "fundamental" (as opposed to "marginal"), 29 C.F.R. § 1630.2(n)(1), so that a job is "fundamentally alter[ed]" if an essential function is removed. 29 C.F.R. § Pt. 1630(n), App. at 394. To guide the essential-function inquiry, the regulations speak in factors—seven of them. The first two restate the statutory considerations. 29 C.F.R. § 1630.2(n)(3)(i)–(ii). The remaining five add other considerations. 29 C.F.R. § 1630.2(n)(3)(iii)–(vii). In many jobs, especially the interactive ones, all seven point toward finding regular and predictable on-site attendance essential. Take the amount of time performing that function, for example, § 1630.2(n)(3)(iii): Most of one's *work* time is spent *at work,* and many interactive functions simply cannot be performed off site. Or take the consequences of failing to show up for work, § 1630.2(n)(3)(iv): They can be severe. Ditto for the terms of the collective bargaining agreement, § 1630.2(n)(3)(v): They certainly won't typically exempt regular attendance. Other employees' work practices are no different, § 1630.2(n)(3)(vi)–(vii): Other employees usually attend work at the worksite. And so on, such that most jobs would be *fundamentally altered* if regular and predictable on-site attendance is removed.

* * *

A sometimes-forgotten guide likewise supports the general rule: common sense. Non-lawyers would readily understand that regular on-site attendance is required for interactive jobs. Perhaps they would view it as "the basic, most fundamental" "activity" of their job. Webster's Third New International Dictionary 777, 920 (1986) (defining "essential" and "function"). But equipped with a 1400-or-so page record, standards of review, burdens of proof, and a seven-factor balancing test, the answer may seem more difficult. Better to follow the commonsense notion that non-judges (and, to be fair to judges, our sister circuits) hold: Regular, in-person attendance is an essential function—and a prerequisite to essential functions—of most jobs, especially the interactive ones. That's the same rule that case law from around the country, the statute's language, its regulations, and the EEOC's guidance all point toward. And it's the controlling one here.

2

That rule has straightforward application here: Regular and predictable on-site attendance was essential for Harris's position, and Harris's repeated absences made her unable to perform the essential functions of a resale buyer. The required teamwork, meetings with suppliers and stampers, and on-site "availability to participate in ... face-to-face interactions," all necessitate a resale buyer's regular and predictable attendance. For years Ford has required resale buyers to work in the same building as stampers, further evidencing its judgment that on-site attendance is essential. And the practice has been consistent with the policy: all other resale buyers regularly and predictably attend work on site. Indeed, even those who telecommute do so only one set day per week and agree in advance to come into work if needed. Sealing the deal are Harris's experiences and admissions. Her excessive absences caused her to make mistakes and caused strife in those around her. And she agreed that four of her ten primary duties could not be performed from home. On this record, the EEOC cannot show that regularly attending work was merely incidental to Harris's job; it was *essential* to her job.

It follows that Harris's up-to-four-days telecommuting proposal-which removed that essential function of her job—was unreasonable. The *employee* bears the burden of proposing an accommodation that will permit her to effectively perform the essential functions of her job. Harris proposed only one accommodation—one that would exempt her regular and predictable attendance from her resale-buyer job. In failure-to-accommodate claims where the employee requests an "accommodation that *exempts* her from an essential function," "the essential functions and reasonable accommodation analyses [ ] run together." *Samper*, 675 F.3d at 1240. One conclusion (the function is essential) leads to the other (the accommodation is not reasonable). That's this case. Harris's proposed accommodation was unreasonable.

* * *

B

The EEOC sees it differently. It argues that three sources—(1) Harris's own testimony, (2) other resale buyers' telecommuting practices, and (3) technology—create a genuine dispute of fact as to whether regular on-site attendance is essential. But none does.

(1) *Harris's testimony.* An employee's unsupported testimony that she could perform her job functions from home does not preclude summary judgment, for it does not create a genuine dispute of fact. Neither the statute nor regulations nor EEOC guidance instructs courts to credit the employee's opinion about what functions are essential. That's because we do not "allow employees to define the essential functions of their positions based solely on their personal viewpoint and experience." *Mason*, 357 F.3d at 1122. And for good reason: If we did, every failure-to-accommodate claim involving essential functions would go to trial because all employees who *request* their employer to exempt an essential function *think* they can work without that essential function.

* * *

(2) *Other employees' telecommuting schedules.* The evidence of other buyers' schedules likewise doesn't do the trick. Unlike an employee's own testimony, though, this consideration has support in the regulations, 29 C.F.R. § 1630.2(n)(3)(vii), and in our case law, *Rorrer v. City of Stow*, 743 F.3d 1025, 1042 (6th Cir.2014). And unlike an employee's own testimony,

it makes sense to look at this kind of evidence: It reflects the *employer's* judgment—which is not just what the employer says but also what the employer *does*. Picking up on this, the EEOC argues that because Ford allowed several other resale buyers to telecommute, working from the worksite must not have been essential.

On this record, we disagree. This argument might work if the other employees' schedules were materially similar (say, unpredictably telecommuting three days per week). But Harris's coworkers worked from home on materially *different* schedules: on one set day per week—no more, and sometimes less.... And critically, every telecommuter agreed in advance to come into work on their set telecommuting day if needed at the worksite.... The [alleged comparators] thus do not create a genuine issue of fact.

In addition to being legally and factually unsupported, the EEOC's view here would cause practical harm to private employers.... [I]f the EEOC's position carries the day, once an employer allows *one* person the ability to telecommute on a *limited* basis, it must allow *all* people with a disability the right to telecommute on an *unpredictable* basis up to 80% of the week (or else face trial). That's 180-degrees backward. It encourages—indeed, requires—employers to *shut down* predictable and limited telecommuting as an accommodation for *any* employee. A "good deed would effectively ratchet up liability," which "would undermine Congress' stated purpose of eradicating discrimination against disabled persons." *Ameritech,* 129 F.3d at 868. The practical effect? Companies would tighten telecommuting policies to avoid liability, and countless employees who benefit from currently generous telecommuting policies would suffer. A protective tool becomes a weapon if used unwisely; and telecommuting should not become a weapon.

(3) *Technology.* Despite its commonsense charm, the EEOC's appeal to technology ultimately fails to create a genuine fact issue. It is "self-evident," the EEOC declares without citation to the record or any case law, that "technology has advanced" enough for employees to perform "at least some essential job functions" at home. In the abstract, no doubt, this is precisely right. *E.g., Vande Zande v. Wis. Dep't of Admin.,* 44 F.3d 538, 544 (7th Cir.1995) (recognizing as much). But technology changing *in the abstract* is not technology changing *on this record.* Our review of a district court's summary-judgment ruling is confined to the record. And no record evidence—*none*—shows that a great technological shift has made this highly interactive job one that can be effectively performed at home. The proper case to credit advances in technology is one where the record *evinces* that advancement. There is no such evidence here.

* * *

C

* * *

To sum up, the EEOC must prove that Harris is a "qualified individual," which means she can perform the essential functions of a resale buyer with a reasonable accommodation. The record shows that Harris cannot regularly and predictably attend the workplace—an essential function, and a prerequisite to other essential functions—even with the past reasonable accommodations of telecommuting trials and specialized plans to improve her attendance. And Harris's proposed unpredictable, *ad hoc* telecommuting schedule was not reasonable because it would have removed at least one essential function from her job. Harris is unqualified as a matter of law, and the district court correctly granted summary judgment on this claim.

III

[The court's discussion of the plaintiff's ADA retaliation claim has been omitted.]

IV

Nearly thirty years later, it's worth repeating: To overcome a well-supported motion for summary judgment, the non-moving party "must do more than simply show that there is some metaphysical doubt as to the material facts." *Matsushita Elec. Indus. Co. v. Zenith Radio Corp.*, 475 U.S. 574, 586, 106 S.Ct. 1348 (1986). The EEOC has not done so here. We affirm.

[The dissent by Judge Moore has been omitted.]

MOSBY-MEACHEM V. MEMPHIS LIGHT, GAS & WATER DIVISION
883 F.3d 595 (6th Cir. 2018)

JULIA SMITH GIBBONS, CIRCUIT JUDGE.

Andrea Mosby-Meachem, an in-house attorney for Memphis Light, Gas & Water Division, was denied a request to work from home for ten weeks while she was on bedrest due to complications from pregnancy. Following trial, a jury found in favor of Mosby-Meachem on her claim for disability discrimination and awarded her compensatory damages. . . . MLG&W moved for judgment as a matter of law or, in the alternative, a new trial, asserting that the evidence produced at trial and binding Sixth Circuit precedent precluded any reasonable jury from determining that Mosby-Meachem was a qualified individual while on bedrest because in-person attendance was an essential function of her job. The district court denied the motion and MLG&W appealed both the denial of its motion . . . . Because Mosby-Meachem produced sufficient evidence at trial for a reasonable jury to conclude that in-person attendance was not an essential function of her job for the 10-week period in which she requested to telework and the Sixth Circuit precedent relied upon by MLG&W is materially distinguishable from the facts of this case, we affirm the orders of the district court.

I.

Andrea Mosby-Meachem has worked as an in-house attorney for Memphis Light, Gas & Water Division ("MLG&W") since 2005. Her position title at MLG&W was Attorney 3.[1] As an Attorney 3, Mosby-Meachem's work focused primarily on the areas of labor, employment, and workers' compensation. Mosby-Meachem, however, never participated in a trial during her eight years with MLG&W prior to the initiation of this litigation.

In 2008, Cheryl Patterson was hired as the vice president and general counsel for MLG&W, becoming Mosby-Meachem's supervisor. On March 14, 2011, Patterson sent an email to all lawyers in the legal department outlining her policy regarding the hours the attorneys spent in the office. In this email, she stated:

> Please be reminded that office hours for the Legal Department are 8:30 a.m.–5:00 p.m. Monday through Friday. All employees, including the lawyers, are expected to be at work and devoting their time and attention to Division business during those hours. As professionals, you are expected to set a good example for the support staff by being in the office on time and staying at work until the end of the day. If you anticipate arriving after 8:30 a.m.,

---

[1]   The Job Description for the Attorney 3 position lists "essential functions" as follows:

1.   Perform senior level legal assistance to prosecute and defend, in accordance with the Vice President & General Counsel, all suits by or against the Division; and provide analysis and counsel on legal, policy, compliance issues, and actual or anticipated lawsuits.

2.   Review and evaluate investigations; based on laws or facts, determine the method of investigation, its extent, legal sufficiency of evidence, applicable laws and the basis and method of settlement. If settlement is not indicated, determine method of defense at law or equity in the court.

3.   Perform legal research on pending cases and current problems.

4.   Render legal services and opinions of rights, obligations and privileges for Division employees as requested.

5.   Draft, negotiate and prepare contracts and other legal documents; review and approve proposed contracts and legal documents.

6.   Negotiate, in accordance with the Vice President & General Counsel, insurance representatives, lawyers, etc. regarding settlements.

7.   Interview and take depositions of witnesses; arrange for and conduct pre-trial conferences; and keep Division up to date on new/revised laws, compliance standards, and regulations.

8.   Represent the Division and try cases in court; and may act as agent of the Division in various transactions.

9.   Supervise, direct and train assigned employees such as: paralegals, medical services, support staff, and/or legal students.

10. Perform other duties as directed.

please contact the office to inform me of the situation. Likewise, if you have a meeting or hearing in the downtown area that ends before 5:00, you are expected to return to the office to complete the day's work.

However, MLG&W did not maintain a formal written telecommuting policy at that time, and in practice, employees often telecommuted. Indeed, on one occasion in 2012, Mosby-Meachem herself was permitted to work from home for two weeks while she was recovering from neck surgery, during which time she appears to have adequately performed her duties to the satisfaction of MLG&W.

On January 2, 2013, during her 23rd week of pregnancy, Mosby-Meachem's doctors discovered a problem requiring her hospitalization. Prior to this occasion, Mosby-Meachem had already experienced problematic pregnancies and had suffered three miscarriages. . . . Following surgery, Mosby-Meachem's doctors placed her on "modified bed rest" for approximately ten weeks, during which time she was restricted from engaging in prolonged standing or sitting and from lifting heavy objects. . . .

On January 7, 2013, Mosby-Meachem made an official accommodation request that she be permitted to work from a bed either within the hospital or within her home for ten weeks. . . . On January 15, 2013, MLG&W assembled an ADA Committee consisting of Eric Conway, Steve Day, and Rutha Griffin, who along with Vernica Davis and Patterson,[2] conducted a telephonic process meeting with Mosby-Meachem. During the process meeting, Mosby-Meachem was asked whether she could perform each of the essential functions of her job remotely, which she answered in the affirmative. Despite Mosby-Meachem's assurances, the ADA Committee denied Mosby-Meachem's accommodation request on January 18, and, in a letter dated January 30, 2013, explained that the denial was based on the determination that physical presence was an essential function of Mosby-Meachem's job, and teleworking created concerns about maintaining confidentiality. . . .

Mosby-Meachem first appealed the denial on February 2, 2013 via email. When that appeal was denied on February 19, she again appealed on February 21, which appears to have again been denied. Following her ten weeks of restriction, Mosby-Meachem returned to work on April 1, 2013, and she continued to work up until her baby was born on April 14, 2013. During the time between January 3 and her return to work on April 1, Mosby-Meachem initially received sick leave under the FMLA for four weeks and then subsequently received short-term disability for the remainder of the period.

---

[2] Conway is MLG&W's Human Resources Compliance Coordinator; Day is its Manager of Labor and Employee Relations; Griffin is its Manager of Employment Services; and Davis is its Medical Services Coordinator and nurse.

* * *

Mosby-Meachem filed suit in state court on December 30, 2013, and MLG&W removed the action to federal court on March 5, 2014. In Mosby-Meachem's amended complaint, she brought claims for pregnancy discrimination in violation of the Tennessee Human Rights Act and failure to accommodate and retaliation in violation of the Americans with Disabilities Act. MLG&W moved for summary judgment following discovery, but the district court denied the motion and the case proceeded to trial. MLG&W moved for judgment as a matter of law at the close of Mosby-Meachem's proof, and the district court took the matter under advisement. The jury returned a verdict for Mosby-Meachem on her claim of disability discrimination and awarded her $92,000.00 in compensatory damages. The jury returned a verdict for MLG&W on Mosby-Meachem's claims of pregnancy discrimination and retaliation.

On September 30, 2015, MLG&W renewed its motion for judgment as a matter of law or, in the alternative, for a new trial. . . . The district court denied MLG&W's renewed motion on March 29, 2017. . . . MLG&W subsequently appealed those decisions to this Court.

II.

Although this Court reviews the denial of a renewed motion for judgment as a matter of law de novo, it nevertheless must "apply the same deferential standard as the district court." *Arnold v. Wilder*, 657 F.3d 353, 363 (6th Cir. 2011).

The Federal Rules of Civil Procedure authorize courts to enter judgment as a matter of law against a plaintiff upon finding that "a reasonable jury would not have a legally sufficient evidentiary basis to find" in his or her favor. FED. R. CIV. P. 50. . . .

This Court "review[s] a denial of a motion for a new trial for an abuse of discretion. . . ." *Anchor v. O'Toole*, 94 F.3d 1014, 1021 (6th Cir. 1996). . . .

III.

MLG&W['s] . . . primary argument is that it was entitled to judgment as a matter of law because the jury did not have a legally sufficient basis to find that Mosby-Meachem could have effectively performed all the essential functions of her job with her requested 10-week teleworking accommodation. . . .

For the reasons addressed below, we find all of MLG&W's arguments unpersuasive and affirm the district court's orders.

A.

In order to establish a prima facie case of disability discrimination under the ADA for failure to accommodate, Mosby-Meachem must show that: "(1) she is disabled within the meaning of the Act; (2) she is otherwise qualified for the position, with or without reasonable accommodation; (3) her employer knew or had reason to know about her disability; (4) she requested an accommodation; and (5) the employer failed to provide the necessary accommodation." *Johnson v. Cleveland City Sch. Dist.*, 443 Fed.Appx. 974, 982–83 (6th Cir. 2011) (citing *DiCarlo v. Potter*, 358 F.3d 408, 419 (6th Cir. 2004)). "Once a plaintiff establishes a prima facie case, the burden shifts to the employer to demonstrate that any particular accommodation would impose an undue hardship on the employer." *Id.* at 983.

MLG&W contends that it is entitled to judgment as a matter of law because Mosby-Meachem's requested accommodation to telework was *"per se unreasonable"* as it removed several essential functions of her job that could only be performed in person; therefore, she failed to establish a prima facie case of discrimination. Specifically, MLG&W argues that Mosby-Meachem's own testimony, the written description of the Attorney 3 position, and testimony from former MLG&W employees conclusively established that physical presence was an essential function of her job. Therefore, this evidence, along with this Court's prior precedent *E.E.O.C. v. Ford Motor Co.*, which stated that "[r]egular, in-person attendance is an essential function—and a prerequisite to essential functions—of most jobs, especially the interactive ones," precludes a reasonable jury from finding that Mosby-Meachem was "otherwise qualified" from performing her job while she was on bedrest. 782 F.3d 753, 762–63 (6th Cir. 2015) (en banc). However, while MLG&W is correct that there is some evidence showing that in-person attendance was an essential function of Mosby-Meachem's job, Mosby-Meachem proffered other evidence at trial, including testimony from coworkers, from which a jury could reasonably conclude that she was otherwise qualified to perform her job from home for ten weeks without being physically present in the office.

To be "otherwise qualified" for the job, the employee bears the burden of showing she can perform the "essential functions" of the job, with or without accommodation. 42 U.S.C. § 12111(8). "A job function is essential if its removal would fundamentally alter the position." *Kiphart v. Saturn Corp.*, 251 F.3d 573, 584 (6th Cir. 2001).

Several pieces of evidence produced at trial do support a finding that in-person attendance was an essential function of Mosby-Meachem's job. This evidence includes the enumerated list of essential functions in the Attorney 3 job description and Mosby-Meachem's testimony under oath that the first nine of these functions were in fact essential—although she also testified that they could be performed remotely. 29 C.F.R. § 1630.2(n)(3)(ii) ("Evidence of whether a particular function is essential includes . . . [w]ritten job descriptions . . ."). Several of these functions, especially "7. Interview and take depositions of witnesses," "8. Represent [MLG&W] and try cases in court," and "9. Supervise, direct and train assigned employees" all appear to inherently require Mosby-Meachem's in-person participation. Additionally, two former Attorney 3s testified about the need to be physically present to perform the job, especially for "call-outs," when an emergency required a physical appearance. 29 C.F.R. § 1630.2(n)(3)(vi) ("Evidence of whether a particular function is essential includes . . . [t]he work experience of past incumbents in the job . . .").

Nevertheless, under the deference that this Court affords a jury verdict, Mosby-Meachem presented sufficient evidence supporting a finding that she could perform all the essential functions of her job remotely for ten weeks. For example, several MLG&W employees as well as outside counsel who worked with Mosby-Meachem testified that they felt she could perform all essential functions during the 10-week period working from home. *See* 29 C.F.R. § 1630.2(n)(3)(vii) ("Evidence of whether a particular function is essential includes . . . [t]he current work experience of incumbents in similar jobs . . ."). Conway testified that he "d[id]n't think it would be a problem" for Mosby-Meachem to work from home. Davis similarly testified that she thought Mosby-Meachem could effectively perform her work from home. Further, Imad Abdullah, an outside counsel with whom Mosby-Meachem worked closely, stated that he believed she could have worked effectively from home. And another outside attorney, Sean Hunt, also stated that he told Patterson that Mosby-Meachem could "take[ ] care of" her duties and that she "[could] do this from her home."

Mosby-Meachem also presented evidence that undermined the strength of MLG&W's evidence, including uncontested testimony that Mosby-Meachem had never "tr[ied] cases in court" or "t[aken] depositions of witnesses"—two functions listed in the Attorney 3 job description—during the entire eight years she had worked for MLG&W. 29 C.F.R. § 1630.2(n)(3)(iii) ("Evidence of whether a particular function is essential includes . . . [t]he amount of time spent on the job performing the function . . ."). The jury also heard evidence that the job description on which MLG&W relied was based on a 20-year-old questionnaire that did not reflect changes in the job that have resulted from technological advancements since that time, rather than a 2010 questionnaire Mosby-Meachem herself had completed prior to any of the events in this litigation. Given all the evidence presented by Mosby-Meachem that both undermined MLG&W's evidence and independently supported a finding that she could perform the essential functions of her job remotely for ten weeks, a rational jury could find that she was a qualified employee and that working remotely for ten weeks was a reasonable accommodation.

Further, this Court's opinions in *Ford* and the recent case *Williams v. AT&T Mobility Services LLC*, 847 F.3d 384 (6th Cir. 2017) do not preclude such a finding because both cases are materially distinguishable from the one presented here. In *Ford*, we granted summary judgment to the employer, finding that "regular and predictable attendance" at work on-

site was an essential function of the plaintiff's employment. 782 F.3d at
763. The plaintiff in *Ford*, however, had an extensive history of poor
performance and high absenteeism, some of which stemmed from her
Irritable Bowel Syndrome, requiring other employees to cover for her. *Id.*
at 758–59. Ford attempted to accommodate the plaintiff, but her poor
performance and absenteeism eventually led to her termination. *Id.* at
759–60. Here, unlike the plaintiff in *Ford*, Mosby-Meachem had performed
her duties remotely in the past without any attendance issues or decline in
work product. Further, Mosby-Meachem's requested accommodation—
teleworking for a limited 10-week period—was significantly different from
that of the plaintiff in *Ford*, who sought to work off-site up to four days a
week indefinitely and on an indeterminate schedule. *Id.* at 759.

Williams is similarly distinguishable. In that case, this Court held that
attendance was an essential job function for a call center employee. *See
Williams*, 847 F.3d at 392–93. But there, the plaintiff had to be physically
present at her work station and logged into the computer to receive
customer service calls; otherwise those calls would automatically be routed
to another employee. *Id.* at 387–88. . . . Unlike the plaintiff in *Williams*,
Mosby-Meachem's job was not tied to her office desk, and she had already
demonstrated her ability to work remotely without issue. Further, her
disability—and corresponding accommodation—was for a limited time
rather than an indefinite period. Therefore, the finding that the plaintiff in
Williams was not qualified to do her job was premised on facts that are
dramatically different from the ones in the present case.

. . . Accordingly, because the *Ford* and *Williams* cases leave open the
possibility of teleworking as a reasonable accommodation, particularly for
a finite period of time, a jury could have reasonably concluded from the
evidence presented at trial that Mosby-Meachem could perform all the
essential functions of her job remotely for ten weeks.

* * *

IV.

For the above reasons, we affirm the orders of the district court denying
MLG&W's motion for judgment as a matter of law . . . .

NOTES AND QUESTIONS

1. *Explaining the different results.* These two decisions are decided by
the same court only five years apart. And yet, *Ford* held that working from
home was not a reasonable accommodation for most jobs, whereas *Mosby-
Meachem* held that working from home was a reasonable accommodation for
an in-house lawyer. Is the *Mosby-Meachem* court not properly following Sixth
Circuit precedent (recall that *Ford* was an *en banc* decision) or can you
distinguish the facts of these two cases? And if so, what facts are most
significant? Or is it more likely that the procedural posture of the cases—where

Ford involved an appeal from a grant of summary judgment to the employer, and *Mosby-Meachem* involved an employer's appeal after a jury decided in the plaintiff's favor—influenced the results? Do you think both cases were correctly decided? Why or why not?

2. *General rule.* The general rule is that working from home is not a reasonable accommodation. Despite Judge Posner's prediction in *Vande Zande* (reproduced above, in Section C) that technological advances might make it easier for employees to work from home in the future, as the court in *Ford* mentioned, the majority rule has remained the same. To some extent, these cases turn on a common-sense inquiry of whether it is possible to perform the essential functions of the job at home. Thus, it is easy to see why some employees, such as food servers, retail clerks, hotel housekeepers, and factory-line workers, could not perform their jobs at home. Such positions require personal contact or presence, interaction with others, and products that are only available at the workplace. But in some cases, the courts do not analyze the issue in any depth and simply assert that working from home is not a reasonable accommodation. *See, e.g.*, Mobley v. Allstate Ins. Co., 531 F.3d 539, 547–48 (7th Cir. 2008) ("[A]s a general matter, working at home is not a reasonable accommodation.").

3. *Exceptions to the general rule.* As the *Mosby-Meachem* case demonstrates, despite the majority rule, some courts are willing to acknowledge that working from home can be a reasonable accommodation. *See, e.g.*, Humphrey v. Memorial Hospitals Association, 239 F.3d 1128 (9th Cir. 2001); Langon v. Dep't of Health & Human Servs., 959 F.2d 1053, 1060 (D.C. Cir. 1992) (stating that the plaintiff's working from home may have caused some difficulty but not necessarily an undue hardship). When it is logistically feasible for an employee to work from home, should an employer have to consider a work-from-home accommodation? What factors might make an employer conclude that working from home would be unreasonable?

4. *Will COVID-19 change the general rule?* The second edition of this book is being written during the COVID-19 pandemic. Starting in March 2020, state after state issued stay-at home (or shelter-in-place) orders of varying levels of restrictions when the pandemic caused by COVID-19 made working in close contact with others unsafe. Millions of jobs that were traditionally conducted in offices were transitioned (quite quickly, in many cases) to work-from-home positions. Although having daycares and K–12 schools simultaneously closed during the pandemic certainly impacted the productivity of those workers who are also parents of young children, most workers were able to transition successfully to working from home. Companies that once refused to let *any* employees work from home will now be faced with pretty good evidence that many jobs can successfully be performed from home. Going forward, once this pandemic is over, do you think companies will change their tune about work-from-home requests? And if not, will more employees with disabilities sue to try to enforce the right to obtain a work-from-home accommodation? Finally, do you think the experience with COVID-19 will change how courts address this accommodation request?

5. *Think about your future job as an attorney.* For many areas of the law that require researching and writing, or drafting documents, all that is needed is a computer and an internet connection. If an attorney knows that there is nothing on her schedule that requires an in-person appearance (meeting with clients, court hearings, etc.), do you see any reason why the attorney should not be allowed to work from home? For some jobs, one concern with an employee working from home is that it is impossible to keep tabs on the employee and to know that he is being productive. However, lawyers generally bill their time, so there is a built-in mechanism to make sure employees who are working from home are actually working. On the other hand, even if there are not any in-person meetings scheduled, law firm practice is unpredictable. If you were the managing partner of a firm, what would be your policy regarding attorneys working from home? Justify your response.

6. *Adverse employment action.* As noted earlier in this chapter, the ADA defines discrimination to include an employer's failure to provide a reasonable accommodation to an employee's known disability-related limitations. Courts disagree on whether an adverse employment action is a required element in failure-to-accommodate claims. *Compare* Fenny v. Dakota, Minnesota & Eastern Railroad, 327 F.3d 707, 716–18 (8th Cir. 2003) (requiring the showing of an adverse employment action), *with* Exby-Stolley v. Board of County Commissioners, 979 F.3d 784 (10th Cir. 2020) (en banc) (reversing an earlier panel opinion that had held that an adverse employment action was a necessary element in a failure-to-accommodate claim), *and* EEOC v. LHC Group, Inc, 773 F.3d 688, 703–04 (5th Cir. 2014), EEOC v. AutoZone, Inc., 630 F.3d 635, 638–39 (7th Cir. 2010) (not requiring the showing of an adverse employment action). *See also* Nicole Buonocore Porter, *Adverse Employment Actions in Failure to Accommodate Claims: Much Ado About Nothing*, NYU L. REV. ONLINE (2020) (arguing that the Tenth Circuit's panel opinion in *Exby-Stolley* reached the wrong result and that the court also confused the issue of adverse employment actions with other reasonable accommodation issues). The confusion over whether an adverse employment action is a required element of the prima facie case in a failure-to-accommodate claim sometimes arises because the accommodation is not one that is required to perform the essential functions of the job; but instead is requested to allow the employee to enjoy privileges of the workplace, such as an on-site cafeteria or on-site gym. The EEOC's position is that the ADA *does* require employers to provide accommodations so that employees with disabilities can enjoy "the benefits and privileges of employment" equal to those without disabilities, such as training programs, employee assistance programs, cafeterias, lounges, gymnasiums, and social functions. *See* EEOC Enforcement Guidance, Reasonable Accommodation and Undue Hardship Under the Americans with Disabilities Act (Oct. 17, 2002), https://www.eeoc.gov/policy/docs/accommodation.html#N_44_. For instance, if the employer refused to provide an accommodation that would make an on-site gym accessible for someone in a wheelchair, the employer might argue that the employee has not suffered an adverse employment action because they have only been denied the use of the optional on-site gym. But the issue *should* turn on whether the employer is required to

provide accommodations that are not necessary to perform the functions of the job but that would allow the employee to enjoy the privileges of employment. How should that debate be resolved?

c. Schedules and Shifts

Another often-litigated structural norm is an employee's schedule, which includes how many hours they work, which shift (day versus night, if the business operates 24/7), and the employee's start and end times. More often than not, courts hold that these schedules and shifts are essential functions of the job, and therefore do not have to be accommodated. Of course, there are exceptions, which are discussed below.

1. *Start time.* In *Holly v. Clairson Industries, LLC,* 492 F.3d 1247 (11th Cir. 2007), the plaintiff was a paraplegic who used a wheelchair, and was employed by Clairson as a mold polisher, where he worked for many years polishing molds after they came off the assembly line. He frequently clocked in one to two minutes late for work because obstacles blocked his path getting to the time clock. The employer excused these minor delays for years, allowing Holly to make up the time at the end of his shift, until the employer instituted a no-fault attendance policy, declaring that strict punctuality was an essential function of the job and every late arrival (even one second late) would accumulate points that would accrue towards termination. This eventually led to Holly's termination as he continued to have difficulty navigating the obstacles placed in the way of the time clock. The district court granted the employer's motion for summary judgment, agreeing with the employer that strict punctuality was an essential function of the job. The Eleventh Circuit disagreed. It stated that there was no evidence, other than the employer's assertion, that Holly's slight delays caused any problems with the production schedule. No one was standing idle while he finished his work and he made up the couple of minutes he was late. Accordingly, strict punctuality was not an essential function and the employer should have continued to accommodate his late arrivals by letting him make up the lost time at the end of his shift. Can you think of jobs where strict punctuality *would* be considered an essential function?

2. *Help with commuting vs. schedule change.* Should employers be required to provide accommodations that help an employee with a disability navigate traveling to and from work? At one end of the spectrum, consider an employee's request that the employer provide transportation from the employee's home to the workplace. To our knowledge, no court has ever required that type of accommodation. One reason for such a result is the application of the "job-related rule," which relieves employers of the obligation to provide accommodations that are personal in nature. This rule, endorsed by the EEOC and a number of courts, states that the ADA requires employers to provide only those accommodations that are "job-related" and not "personal items." SAMUEL R. BAGENSTOS, LAW AND THE CONTRADICTIONS OF THE DISABILITY RIGHTS MOVEMENT 69–70 (2009).

In some cases, however, courts will require employers to provide closer parking spaces or even pay for a parking spot. For instance, in *Lyons v. Legal Aid Society,* the plaintiff was an employee at the Legal Aid Office in Manhattan. She became disabled and could only walk using assistive devices. She asked her employer to pay for a parking space near her work and near the courts she often visited. She could not use public transportation because she could not stand for long periods or climb stairs. Without the accommodation, she was spending 15–26% of her net salary on parking. The court held that "there is nothing inherently unreasonable . . . in requiring an employer to furnish an otherwise qualified disabled employee with assistance related to her ability to get to work." Lyons v. Legal Aid Society, 68 F.3d 1512, 1513–17 (2d Cir. 1995).

In most cases, the employee is not asking for help in getting to work or even parking at work. Instead, the requested accommodation is a schedule change that is needed because of difficulties with commuting to work caused by the employee's disability. Whether or not these accommodations are required often has to do with whether the court frames the issue as helping the employee commute to work or simply a schedule change request. For instance, in *Regan v. Faurecia Automotive Seating, Inc.,* 679 F.3d 475 (6th Cir. 2012), the plaintiff had narcolepsy, which caused difficulty sleeping, fatigue, falling asleep easily, and possible driving accidents. The employer changed the start time of the plaintiff's department from 6:00 to 7:00 a.m., with a corresponding later end time from 3:00 to 4:00 p.m. Because plaintiff had recently moved to a home 79 miles from the workplace, the change in shift time made her commute substantially longer because traffic was heavier later in the morning and later in the afternoon. This created a problem for her because of her narcolepsy, which was made worse by spending more time in the car. Accordingly, she requested an accommodation to keep her old start and end times and when the employer refused, she resigned, citing to the hardship the shift change would create for her. The court affirmed the dismissal of her failure-to-accommodate claim, stating that the ADA does not require the employer to accommodate the plaintiff's request for a commute during more convenient hours. The court framed the request as the plaintiff asking for help with her commute, and thus, the accommodation was not required.

But if the accommodation is framed simply as a schedule-change request, the court might view it differently. In *Colwell v. Rite Aid Corp.,* 602 F.3d 495 (3d Cir. 2010), the plaintiff was a part-time cashier at a Rite Aid store where she alternated between the 9 a.m. to 2 p.m. shift and the 5 to 9 p.m. shift. After she became blind in her left eye, and it was dangerous to drive at night, she requested a waiver from having to work the evening shift to accommodate her inability to drive at night. The appellate court reversed the district court's grant of summary judgment to the employer, stating that the accommodation request should not be viewed as one of helping the plaintiff commute to work. Instead, the court stated that changing an employee's schedule in order to alleviate her disability-related difficulties in getting to work is the type of accommodation the ADA contemplates. The court noted that the plaintiff was not asking for help in the method or means of her commute. Scheduling of shifts is something that happens inside of the workplace and therefore falls within the ambit of the reasonable accommodation obligation. For a discussion of this dispute, see Stephen F. Befort, *Accommodating an Employee's Commute to Work Under the ADA: Reasonable, Preferential, or Both?*, 63 DRAKE L. REV. 749 (2015).

3. *Rotating shifts.* Many employers that operate 24/7 use rotating shifts, so that employees are not permanently assigned to either the day or night shift. However, rotating shifts can cause problems for certain individuals with disabilities, including those employees with diabetes, mental illness, and others. Accordingly, some employees request a straight shift as an accommodation. Most courts who have decided this issue have held that rotating shifts are an essential function of the job. Because employers are never required to eliminate essential functions of the job, there is no possible accommodation. *See, e.g.,* Kallail v. Alliant Energy Corporate Services, Inc., 691 F.3d 925, 927–28, 931 (8th Cir. 2012); Rehrs v. Iams Co., 486 F.3d 353 (8th Cir. 2007); Turco v. Hoechst Celanese Corp., 101 F.3d 1090 (5th Cir. 1996); Tucker v. Mo. Dept. of Soc. Servs., 2012 WL 6115604, at *1, 4, 6 (W.D. Mo. Dec. 10, 2012); Azzam v. Baptist Healthcare Affiliates, Inc., 855 F.Supp.2d 653, 655–56, 662 (W.D. Ky. 2012); Bogner v. Wackenhut Corp., 05–CV–6171, 2008 WL 84590 (W.D.N.Y. Jan. 7, 2008); Dicksey v. New Hanover Sheriff's Department, 522 F.Supp.2d 742, 744–45 (E.D. N.C. 2007).

Only a couple of courts have allowed an accommodation requesting a straight shift. *See, e.g.,* Maes v. City of Espanola, 29 Am. Disabilities Cas. (BNA) 216 (D.N.M. Jan. 13, 2014) (denying the employer's motion for summary judgment on the plaintiff's failure-to-accommodate claim when the employer denied her request for a straight day shift because the night shift exacerbated her insomnia, migraine headaches, and depression); Holt v. Olmsted Twp. Bd. of Trustees, 43 F.Supp.2d 812 (N.D. Ohio 1998) (holding that plaintiff's request for a permanent change to the day shift is a reasonable accommodation). Interestingly, the employers in both of these cases did not contest that the employee was qualified. In other words, instead of focusing on whether working a rotating shift was an essential function of the job, both courts focused their discussion on whether a straight shift was a reasonable accommodation. Not surprisingly, both courts held that the accommodation was reasonable. After all, modified schedules are listed in the statute as a possible accommodation. 42 U.S.C. § 12111(9). Once you eliminate the employer's argument that a rotating shift is an essential function, a request to be excused from the rotating shift schedule is likely a reasonable accommodation.

One interesting question about this issue is whether it makes sense to refer to the time you do the job as an essential *function* of the job. In the *Rehrs* case cited above, the plaintiff argued that: "essential functions are duties to be *performed* and a rotating shift is not *performed*." The court disagreed. Is there something illogical in stating that *when* work is to be performed should be treated the same as *what* work is to be performed? Scholars have criticized the courts that classify when and where work is performed as "essential job functions." *See, e.g.,* Michelle A. Travis, *Recapturing the Transformative Potential of Employment Discrimination Law*, 62 WASH. & LEE. L. REV. 3, 23–35 (2005) (criticizing the courts that label the policies regarding when and where work is to be performed as essential job functions).

6. ACCOMMODATION MANDATE: AFFIRMATIVE ACTION OR ANTI-DISCRIMINATION?

STEPHEN F. BEFORT, ACCOMMODATING AN EMPLOYEE'S COMMUTE TO WORK UNDER THE ADA: REASONABLE, PREFERENTIAL, OR BOTH?
63 DRAKE L. REV. 739 (2015)

The source of the preferential treatment debate lies in the different models embodied in the various federal antidiscrimination statutes. Both Title VII and the Age Discrimination in Employment Act (ADEA) prohibit employers from making adverse employment decisions "because of" a protected characteristic such as race, sex, or age. These statutes, however, do not impose any affirmative obligation on employers to assist employees in satisfactorily performing the essential functions of the job. While the ADA also bans discrimination "on the basis of disability," it goes beyond traditional antidiscrimination laws by requiring employers to make "reasonable accommodations" that take the form of favorable adjustments for the disabled.

The presence of the reasonable accommodation provision has led some commentators to characterize the ADA as imposing an affirmative action requirement. One article described the ADA as "one of the most radical affirmative action laws in recent U.S. history."[147]

Admittedly, the ADA compels employers to provide favorable workplace adjustments for individuals with disabilities regardless of whether those same adjustments are provided to others. The preferential nature of the reasonable accommodation obligation is discomforting to those who are accustomed to Title VII's nondiscrimination model.

---

[147] Sandra R. Levitsky, *Reasonably Accommodating Race: Lessons from the ADA for Race-Targeted Affirmative Action*, 18 LAW & INEQ. 85, 85 (2000).

As this Author previously countered:

> [S]ignificant differences distinguish affirmative action with respect to race and gender, on the one hand, from reasonable accommodation under the ADA, on the other. Conventional affirmative action programs consist of pre-designed policies by which employers seek to increase the proportion of a historically underrepresented minority group in its overall workforce. Employers typically establish target goals through a statistical comparison of their workforce with the relevant labor market. Once a plan is established, an employer implements the plan throughout its recruitment and hiring processes until the numerical goals for the underrepresented group are met. In contrast, reasonable accommodation under the ADA occurs on a much more individualized basis. The reasonable accommodation process occurs only after the employer and disabled employee have engaged in an interactive process designed to identify both the essential functions of the position and the special needs of the disabled person.
>
> Viewed in this light, reassignment under the ADA is much less pervasive than conventional affirmative action programs in several respects. First, the reassignment accommodation applies only to employees and not to applicants. Second, reassignment does not involve the setting of pre-determined numerical goals or quotas. Third, no other employee loses employment as a result of a job reassignment since such a transfer occurs only to an already vacant position. In short, reassignment operates only as a post-hire mechanism by which an employer may retain the services of a current employee with a disability, while affirmative action operates as a pre-hire formula that reserves employment opportunities for one group of applicants at the expense of another group of applicants.[150]

This comparison underscores the different antidiscrimination formulas embodied in Title VII and the ADA. Title VII utilizes an equal-treatment model of discrimination. By prohibiting discrimination "because of" certain listed characteristics such as an employee's race or gender, Title VII compels employers to make employment decisions without reference to those listed traits. Prohibited discrimination occurs whenever an employer decides not to hire someone because of a specific trait or favorably takes account of a person's race or gender in making an employment decision.

The ADA requires different treatment by compelling employers to provide reasonable accommodations to qualified individuals with disabilities.

---

[150] Stephen F. Befort, *Reasonable Accommodation and Reassignment Under the Americans with Disabilities Act: Answers, Questions, and Suggested Solutions After* US Airways, Inc. v. Barnett, 45 ARIZ. L. REV. 931, 968–69 (2003).

Under this model, an employer who merely refrains from treating employees with disabilities differently than other employees may be engaging in prohibited discrimination. The incorporation of the reasonable accommodation requirement in the ADA, accordingly, represents Congress's recognition that "in order to treat some persons equally, we must treat them differently."

This objective likely explains Congress's decision to adopt a different treatment model of discrimination in the ADA. While consideration of race or gender may be inappropriate because neither characteristic bears any inherent relationship to an individual's work-related abilities, consideration of disability may be required because the impairment is often directly related to the ability to perform the job. Reasonable accommodation therefore ensures that persons with disabilities are not deprived of job opportunities they otherwise might not have access to under a disability-blind statute. The bottom line is that preferential treatment is not inimical to the ADA's purpose but part and parcel of the statutory design and key to enabling those with disabilities to move into mainstream American life, including the workforce.

NOTES AND QUESTIONS

1.   Do you agree with Befort's dual conclusions that the reasonable accommodation mandate compels preferential treatment for the disabled but in a more limited fashion than traditional affirmative action? Or do you believe that one or more of these conclusions miss the mark?

2.   *Equal treatment/special treatment?* In terms of policy, would you support amending the ADA to provide for an equal treatment response to disability discrimination? Note that the ADA Amendments Act adopted an equal treatment model for individuals who are deemed disabled only under the regarded as prong of the disability definition. Under this approach, an employer may not discriminate against someone who is "regarded as" disabled, but need not provide a reasonable accommodation to assist that individual in performing the job in question. Is there something about this context that makes an equal treatment approach more appropriate? Or, put another way, is there something about this context that makes a special treatment model less appropriate?

7.   INTERACTIVE PROCESS

BARNETT V. U.S. AIR, INC.
228 F.3d 1105 (9th Cir. 2000)

BETTY B. FLETCHER, CIRCUIT JUDGE:

[Eds. Note: This is the earlier appellate court decision in the litigation resulting in the Supreme Court's *U.S. Airways, Inc. v. Barnett* decision reprinted above on page 131. The facts are the same as summarized in that opinion.]

Robert Barnett brought suit under the Americans with Disabilities Act (ADA) and he appeals the district court's dismissal on summary judgment of his claims. Barnett, who suffered a serious back injury while on the job, argues that U.S. Air discriminated against him by denying him accommodation, by failing to engage in the interactive process and by retaliating against him for filing charges with the Equal Employment Opportunity Commission (EEOC). This appeal raises several issues of first impression in this circuit, including the nature and scope of an employer's obligation to engage in the interactive process, whether reassignment is a reasonable accommodation in the context of a seniority system and the appropriate standard for evaluating retaliation claims under the ADA. We reverse the district court's grant of summary judgment in favor of U.S. Air on all claims except for the retaliation claim and we remand for trial.

* * *

Barnett asserts that U.S. Air failed to fulfill its obligation to engage in an interactive process to find a reasonable accommodation. The legislative history makes clear that employers are required to engage in an interactive process with employees in order to identify and implement appropriate reasonable accommodations. The Senate Report explained that: "A problem-solving approach should be used to identify the particular tasks or aspects of the work environment that limit performance and to identify possible accommodations . . . employers first will consult with and involve the individual with a disability in deciding on the appropriate accommodation."

The ADA authorizes the EEOC to issue regulations implementing the ADA. *See* 42 U.S.C. § 12116. The EEOC regulations outline the nature of the interactive process:

> To determine the appropriate reasonable accommodation it may be necessary for the [employer] to initiate an informal, interactive process with the qualified individual with a disability in need of the accommodation. This process should identify the precise limitations resulting from the disability and potential reasonable accommodations that could overcome those limitations.

29 C.F.R. § 1630.2(*o*)(3).

The phrase "may be necessary" is merely a recognition that in some circumstances the employer and employee can easily identify an appropriate reasonable accommodation. Any doubt that the EEOC views the interactive process as a mandatory obligation is resolved by the EEOC's interpretive guidance, which states that "the employer must make a reasonable effort to determine the appropriate accommodation. The appropriate reasonable accommodation is best determined through a flexible, interactive process that involves both the employer and the [employee] with a disability." 29 C.F.R. Pt. 1630, App. § 1630.9. The EEOC's Enforcement Guidance also specifies the nature of the interactive process: "The employer and the individual with a disability should engage in an informal process to clarify what the individual needs and identify the appropriate accommodation." *EEOC Enforcement Guidance: Reasonable Accommodation and Undue Hardship Under the Americans with Disabilities Act*, EEOC Compliance Manual (CCH), § 902, No. 915.002 (March 1, 1999), at 5440.

The interactive process is triggered either by a request for accommodation by a disabled employee or by the employer's recognition of the need for such an accommodation. An employee requesting a reasonable accommodation should inform the employer of the need for an adjustment due to a medical condition using " 'plain English' and need not mention the ADA or use the phrase 'reasonable accommodation.' " In some circumstances, according to the EEOC, the employee need not even request the accommodation: "An employer should initiate the reasonable accommodation interactive process without being asked if the employer: (1) knows that the employee has a disability, (2) knows, or has reason to know, that the employee is experiencing workplace problems because of the disability, and (3) knows, or has reason to know, that the disability prevents the employee from requesting a reasonable accommodation."

Almost all of the circuits to rule on the question have held that an employer has a mandatory obligation to engage in the interactive process and that this obligation is triggered either by the employee's request for accommodation or by the employer's recognition of the need for accommodation. . . .

U.S. Air argues that Barnett bears the burden of demonstrating the availability of a reasonable accommodation. To put the entire burden for finding a reasonable accommodation on the disabled employee or, effectively, to exempt the employer from the process of identifying reasonable accommodations, conflicts with the goals of the ADA. The interactive process is at the heart of the ADA's process and essential to accomplishing its goals. It is the primary vehicle for identifying and achieving effective adjustments which allow disabled employees to continue working without placing an "undue burden" on employers. Employees do not have at their disposal the extensive information concerning possible alternative positions or possible accommodations which employers have. Putting the entire burden on the employee to identify a reasonable accommodation risks shutting out many workers simply because they do not have the superior knowledge of the workplace that the employer has.

As the Third Circuit explained, since the regulations require the interactive process to identify appropriate accommodations, "it would make little sense to insist that the employee must have arrived at the end product of the interactive process before the employer has a duty to participate in that process." At the same time, the employee holds essential information for the assessment of the type of reasonable accommodation which would be most effective. While employers have superior knowledge regarding the range of possible positions and can more easily perform analyses regarding the "essential functions" of each, employees generally know more about their own capabilities and limitations. . . .

Therefore, we join explicitly with the vast majority of our sister circuits in holding that the interactive process is a mandatory rather than a permissive obligation on the part of employers under the ADA and that this obligation is triggered by an employee or an employee's representative giving notice of the employee's disability and the desire for accommodation. In circumstances in which an employee is unable to make such a request, if the company knows of the existence of the employee's disability, the employer must assist in initiating the interactive process.

We next turn to the requirements of the interactive process. Both the legislative history and the EEOC regulations detail the nature of the interaction required of employers and employees. . . .

The EEOC also outlines the four steps critical to the interactive process. Once a request for a reasonable accommodation has been made, the EEOC requires an employer to:

> (1) Analyze the particular job involved and determine its purpose and essential functions;

> (2) Consult with the individual with a disability to ascertain the precise job-related limitations imposed by the individual's disability and how those limitations could be overcome with a reasonable accommodation;

> (3) In consultation with the individual to be accommodated, identify potential accommodations and assess the effectiveness each would have in enabling the individual to perform the essential functions of the position and;

> (4) Consider the preference of the individual to be accommodated and select and implement the accommodation that is most appropriate for both the employee and the employer.

29 C.F.R. Pt. 1630, App. § 1630.9.

The interactive process requires communication and good-faith exploration of possible accommodations between employers and individual employees. The shared goal is to identify an accommodation that allows the employee to perform the job effectively. Both sides must communicate directly, exchange essential information and neither side can delay or obstruct the process. *See Smith v. Midland Brake, Inc.*, 180 F.3d 1154, 1172 (10th Cir.

1999) ("The interactive process includes good-faith communications between the employer and employee."); *Beck v. University of Wis. Bd. of Regents,* 75 F.3d 1130, 1135 (7th Cir.1996) ("A party that obstructs or delays the interactive process is not acting in good faith. A party that fails to communicate, by way of initiation or response, may also be acting in bad faith.").

In order to demonstrate good faith, employers can point to cooperative behavior which promotes the identification of an appropriate accommodation. Employers should "meet with the employee who requests an accommodation, request information about the condition and what limitations the employee has, ask the employee what he or she specifically wants, show some sign of having considered employee's request, and offer and discuss available alternatives when the request is too burdensome."

The interactive process requires that employers analyze job functions to establish the essential and nonessential job tasks. In order to identify the barriers to job performance, employers must consult and cooperate with disabled employees so that both parties discover the precise limitations and the types of accommodations which would be most effective. The evaluation of proposed accommodations requires further dialogue and an assessment of the effectiveness of each accommodation, in terms of enabling the employee to successfully perform the job. *See* 29 C.F.R. Pt. 1630, App. § 1630.9.

Once the employer and employee have identified and assessed the range of possible reasonable accommodations, the legislative history directs that "the expressed choice of the applicant shall be given primary consideration unless another effective accommodation exists that would provide a meaningful equal employment opportunity." S.Rep. No. 101–116, at 35. An appropriate reasonable accommodation must be effective, in enabling the employee to perform the duties of the position.

We next turn to the consequences for employers who fail to engage in the interactive process in good faith. The Seventh Circuit held that "courts should attempt to isolate the cause of the breakdown [in the interactive process] and then assign responsibility" so that "[l]iability for failure to provide reasonable accommodations ensues only where the employer bears responsibility for the breakdown."

Most circuits have held that liability ensues for failure to engage in the interactive process when a reasonable accommodation would otherwise have been possible. The range of possible reasonable accommodations, for purposes of establishing liability for failure to accommodate, can extend beyond those proposed:

> an employer who acts in bad faith in the interactive process will be liable if the jury can reasonably conclude that the employee would have been able to perform the job with accommodations. In

making that determination, the jury is entitled to bear in mind that had the employer participated in good faith, there may have been other, unmentioned possible accommodations.

A number of circuits have further held that an employer cannot prevail at summary judgment if there is a genuine dispute as to whether the employer engaged in the interactive process in good faith. *See Fjellestad v. Pizza Hut of America, Inc.*, 188 F.3d 944, 953 (8th Cir. 1999) ("we find that summary judgment is typically precluded when there is a genuine dispute as to whether the employer acted in good faith and engaged in the interactive process of seeking reasonable accommodations"); *Taylor*, 184 F.3d at 318 ("where there is a genuine dispute about whether the employer acted in good faith, summary judgment will typically be precluded"); *Baert v. Euclid Beverage, Ltd.*, 149 F.3d 626, 633–34 (7th Cir.1998) (refusing to grant an employer summary judgment because disputes of fact remained about which party caused the breakdown in the interactive process).

The interactive process is the key mechanism for facilitating the integration of disabled employees into the workplace. Employers who reject this core process must face liability when a reasonable accommodation would have been possible. Without the interactive process, many employees will be unable to identify effective reasonable accommodations. Without the possibility of liability for failure to engage in the interactive process, employers would have less incentive to engage in a cooperative dialogue and to explore fully the existence and feasibility of reasonable accommodations. The result would be less accommodation and more litigation, as lawsuits become the only alternative for disabled employees seeking accommodation. This is a long way from the framework of cooperative problem solving based on open and individualized exchange in the workplace that the ADA intended. Therefore, summary judgment is available only where there is no genuine dispute that the employer has engaged in the interactive process in good faith.

We hold that employers, who fail to engage in the interactive process in good faith, face liability for the remedies imposed by the statute if a reasonable accommodation would have been possible. We further hold that an employer cannot prevail at the summary judgment stage if there is a genuine dispute as to whether the employer engaged in good faith in the interactive process.

In this case, Barnett triggered the interactive process obligation by communicating to U.S. Air his desire for accommodation based on his disability. In fact, Barnett went even further and identified, in addition to assignment to the mail room, at least two different accommodations which might have allowed him to remain in the cargo facility. However, U.S. Air appears not to have seriously considered the suggestions.

U.S. Air rejected all three of Barnett's proposed reasonable accommodations and offered no practical alternatives. The special lifting equipment Barnett requested for the cargo position may well have been an adequate reasonable accommodation. Barnett researched mechanical lifting devices and proposed that U.S. Air purchase a low-tech device to assist him in the loading and unloading of cargo. U.S. Air's only offer was for a forklift to lift individual suitcases. Proposing the use of a forklift to lift an individual suitcase is like giving Barnett a shotgun to swat a fly or a Phillips head screwdriver for a flat screw. U.S. Air might as well have told Barnett to use a backhoe. That a tool performs a similar function doesn't make it a proper tool for a particular job. Barnett sought a mechanical accommodation to compensate for his disability; U.S. Air, in effect, ignored his request. Thus, U.S. Air's failure to engage in the interactive process foreclosed at least one potentially reasonable accommodation.

It is less clear whether Barnett's other suggestion of modifying the cargo position to require only desk work was a reasonable accommodation. Although U.S. Air argues that this accommodation would require the elimination of essential functions of the cargo job, it may only have required reassignment of functions among personnel. Although U.S. Air had performed a job analysis on the position in 1992, for purposes of workers' compensation, this analysis did not involve an assessment of the position's essential functions. The duties of the cargo position were divided between front office, warehouse and lifting cargo. Not all cargo agents lifted cargo on any given day and employees were apparently allowed to trade job duties and avoid lifting cargo. Yet, the title of the position is a general one of "cargo agent." Thus, there is a sufficient factual dispute to require further proceedings to evaluate whether this accommodation would have required any elimination of the essential functions of the position.

U.S. Air rejected each of Barnett's several proposed reasonable accommodations and merely offered that Barnett could apply for any position for which he was qualified given his restrictions and for which he had sufficient seniority. U.S. Air did not seek to have a dialogue with Barnett but instead rejected his proposed accommodations by letter. The time between Barnett's initial accommodation request and U.S. Air's rejection letter was nearly five months. This delay and U.S. Air's failure to communicate do not reflect good faith engagement in the interactive process on the part of U.S. Air. Nor is U.S. Air's offer to Barnett to bid on other jobs, a right he already had, a reasonable accommodation of a disabled employee. There is no evidence in the record that Barnett was qualified for any other position, without accommodation, in San Francisco or elsewhere in the U.S. Air system. This is not a case where it is obvious that no modification could enable the employee to perform the essential functions of a job or where the employee has caused the process to break down. Given U.S. Air's failure to engage in the interactive process, liability would be appropriate if a reasonable accommodation would otherwise have been possible. There remains conflicting evidence in the record as to whether a reasonable accommodation without undue hardship to the employer was possible. Thus, a triable issue of fact exists on this issue.

NOTES AND QUESTIONS

1. *No sequel.* Interestingly, the Supreme Court's subsequent opinion in the *Barnett* litigation does not address the interactive process issue.

2. *Silent statute.* The ADA statute says nothing about an interactive process. Do the regulations that establish such a process exceed statutory authority? Summarize the EEOC's argument in support of establishing the interactive process requirement.

3. *Failing to participate.* The *Barnett* court held that participation in the interactive process is mandatory, and that an employer cannot prevail at the summary judgment stage if there is a genuine fact dispute as to whether the employer engaged in the interactive process in good faith. Not all courts agree. The Eleventh Circuit, for example, has ruled that an employer is obligated to participate in the interactive process only if the plaintiff produces evidence that a reasonable accommodation is actually available. Willis v. Conopco, 108 F.3d 282, 285 (11th Cir. 1997). In addition, many circuits take the position that an employer is liable for failure to participate in the interactive process only when a reasonable accommodation would otherwise have been possible. *See* Smith v. Midland Brake, Inc., 180 F.3d 1154, 1174 (10th Cir. 1999); Bultemeyer v. Fort Wayne Community Schools, 100 F.3d 1281, 1285 (7th Cir. 1996). Which of these approaches is preferable from a policy standpoint? What is the appropriate outcome if the party who fails to participate in good faith in the interactive process is the employee?

4. *Reasonable accommodation.* Are either of Barnett's alternative proposed accommodations (i.e., a lifting device or an assignment to only non-lifting duties) likely to be found to be reasonable accommodations?

5. *Explicit request not necessary.* Generally, an employer's duty to provide a reasonable accommodation arises only after an employee affirmatively requests a reasonable accommodation. *See* 29 C.F.R. pt. 1630, App. § 1630.9. The Eighth Circuit, however, has held such a request may be implied by the circumstances even in the absence of an explicit request. In *Kowitz v. Trinity Health*, 839 F.3d 742 (8th Cir. 2016), the court found that an employee who informed her employer that she could not satisfy the requirement of basic life support certification until she had completed four months of physical therapy adequately communicated an implicit request for the employer to excuse the certification requirement for a four-month period. Cases often turn on whether the employee has said enough to trigger the employer's obligation to engage in the interactive process.

What is the employer's obligation in the following scenarios?

1. Supervisor sees an employee who was recently out of work for a serious back injury sitting down on the job (when he was supposed to be working). The supervisor asks him what's wrong and why he's

sitting. The employee answers: "My back was really acting up; I just needed to sit down for a minute."

2.   Employee says: "I need a couple of weeks off to handle a personal issue." The supervisor knows that the employee suffers from a chronic disease that occasionally flares up.

D. UNDUE HARDSHIP

Statutory Language

Under the ADA, discrimination includes: "not making reasonable accommodations to the known physical or mental limitations of an otherwise qualified individual with a disability who is an applicant or employee, unless such covered entity can demonstrate that the accommodation would impose an undue hardship on the operation of the business of such covered entity." 42 U.S.C. § 12112(b)(5)(A).

Undue hardship is defined as: "an action requiring significant difficulty or expense, when considered in light of the factors set forth in subparagraph (B)." 42 U.S.C. § 12111(10)(A).

Subsection (B) provides the factors to be considered:

In determining whether an accommodation would impose an undue hardship on a covered entity, factors to be considered include:

(i)   the nature and cost of the accommodation needed under this chapter;

(ii) the overall financial resources of the facility or facilities involved in the provision of the reasonable accommodation; the number of persons employed at such facility; the effect on expenses and resources, or the impact otherwise of such accommodation upon the operation of the facility;

(iii) the overall financial resources of the covered entity; the overall size of the business of a covered entity with respect to the number of its employees; the number, type, and location of its facilities; and

(iv) the type of operation or operations of the covered entity, including the composition, structure, and functions of the workforce of such entity; the geographic separateness, administrative, or fiscal relationship of the facility or facilities in question to the covered entity.

EEOC Guidance

The EEOC Guidance elaborates on the undue hardship analysis. The Guidance states, for example, that an accommodation could impose an undue hardship if it "would fundamentally alter the nature of the operation or business." EEOC, ENFORCEMENT GUIDANCE: REASONABLE ACCOMMODATION AND UNDUE HARDSHIP UNDER THE AMERICANS WITH DISABILITIES ACT, Undue Hardship Issues, (Oct. 17, 2002), https://www. eeoc.gov/laws/guidance/enforcement-guidance-reasonable-accommodation-and-undue-hardship-under-ada#undue.

However, the Guidance notes that an employer cannot claim undue hardship based on employees' or customers' fears or prejudices toward the individual with a disability. Significantly, "nor can undue hardship be based on the fact that provision of a reasonable accommodation might have a negative impact on the morale of other employees." But, according to the EEOC, employers might be able to establish undue hardship if the accommodation would be "unduly disruptive to other employees' ability to work." *Id.*

As is discussed in the notes after this next case, there is very little case law interpreting the undue hardship provision and it is very rare for the result of a case to turn on this issue. Below is one of the few cases that actually discusses the application of a cost-based undue hardship defense.

REYAZUDDIN V. MONTGOMERY COUNTY, MARYLAND
789 F.3d 407 (4th Cir. 2015)

DIAZ, CIRCUIT JUDGE:

Montgomery County, Maryland, opened a new, consolidated call center using software that was inaccessible to blind employees. The County did not transfer employee Yasmin Reyazuddin, who is blind, to the call center along with her sighted coworkers. The County also did not hire her for a vacant position there. Reyazuddin challenged the County's actions as violating Section 504 of the Rehabilitation Act of 1973, 29 U.S.C. § 794, or Title II of the Americans with Disabilities Act of 1990 (the "ADA"), 42 U.S.C. § 12131 *et seq.*

Section 504 forbids an employer from discriminating against an employee because of her disability. It also requires an employer to accommodate an employee with a disability who can perform the essential functions of a job with a reasonable accommodation. But an employer avoids liability if it can show that providing an accommodation would constitute an "undue hardship."

We find that genuine issues of material fact remain as to (1) whether Reyazuddin could perform the essential job functions of a call center employee; (2) whether the County reasonably accommodated her; and (3) if the County did not, whether its failure to do so may be excused because of undue hardship. Accordingly, we reverse the district court's order granting summary judgment to the County on Reyazuddin's Section 504 claims. However, we affirm the district court's order granting summary judgment to the County on Reyazuddin's Title II claim because public employees cannot use Title II to bring employment discrimination claims against their employers.

I.

A.

In early 2008, as part of its $80 million Technology Modernization Project, Montgomery County decided to consolidate its 1,500 telephone numbers for 38 offices and departments into one call center that residents could reach by dialing 311. The County's goals for its consolidated call center (dubbed MC311) were to achieve accountability, responsiveness, and efficiency.

In January 2009, the County decided to outfit MC311 with software called Siebel Public Sector 8.1.1, licensed from Oracle. This software met the County's goals, was compatible with other Oracle software already used by the County, and was cost-effective as a "commercial-off-the-shelf," as opposed to custom, product.

The Siebel software can be operated in two modes: high-interactivity or standard-interactivity. High-interactivity mode is not accessible [to blind employees] because it is written in Microsoft ActiveX, a technology that screen reader software cannot interpret. Screen reader software enables users who are blind to operate a computer through keyboard shortcuts, instead of mouse clicks, and by hearing synthesized speech or using a refreshable Braille display, in place of reading the screen. Standard-interactivity mode, however, is accessible because it is written in standard HTML and Javascript, which are compatible with screen reader software.

The County's license allows it to run the software in either mode. Moreover, it is technologically feasible for some employees to operate the software in high-interactivity mode while others work in standard-interactivity mode. Doing so does not impact overall employee productivity.

The County nonetheless chose to configure the software at MC311 in high-interactivity mode for all employees. In this mode, employees use three features—the CTI Toolbar, SmartScript, and Email Response—that are not available in standard-interactivity mode.

The CTI Toolbar integrates MC311's phone system and the Siebel software. Employees use the CTI Toolbar to make themselves available to take calls and to answer and transfer calls. SmartScript generates a pop-up window containing a script for employees to read to callers, a field for typing notes about the call, and a function to transfer emergency calls to 911. Employees then close SmartScript and the service request template pops up with fields automatically filled in with the information previously typed into SmartScript.

The service request form has a keyword search function that generates a list of articles to help employees answer the caller's question. Once employees have identified the best article, they click on the "attach solution" button to add it to the service request form. This in turn causes several fields in the form to populate automatically. These fields include the appropriate department; the County's "public answer," which is a "short, concise paragraph about how the [C]ounty handles" the caller's particular concern; and instructions for employees on how to handle the call.

The County first asked Oracle about MC311's accessibility in November 2009, more than eleven months after purchasing the license. Oracle told the County that the CTI Toolbar, SmartScript, and Email Response features of the Siebel software would not be accessible until mid-2010. Oracle also estimated that it would cost $200,000 to make the Siebel software accessible through standard-interactivity mode, without those three features.

Over the next sixteen months, the County received increasing estimates about the cost of accessibility from Opus Group, a subcontractor hired to configure and implement the Siebel software at MC311. The first estimate to make standard-interactivity mode available at MC311 was $222,075. A second option to give "back office" employees access to assigned service requests would cost $65,625. By April 2011, these estimates rose to $399,270 and $240,867, respectively. All the while, the CTI Toolbar, SmartScript, and Email Response features remained inaccessible.

B.

Since 2002, Yasmin Reyazuddin has worked in the County's Department of Health and Human Services, most recently as one of five Information and Referral Aides. In that role, she answered questions from County residents who called about the Department's services, referrals to County programs, and the status of applications for benefits. Reyazuddin, who is blind, performed her job using screen reader software. Reyazuddin also used a Braille embosser, which allowed her to print in Braille.

Reyazuddin first learned about the County's plans to create MC311 in May 2008 from her then-supervisor. Over the next sixteen months, Reyazuddin and the other Information and Referral Aides received updates on MC311's general progress. During this time, the County was determining how to staff MC311's forty-nine positions.

In October 2009, JoAnne Calderone, Manager for Planning, Accountability, and Customer Service in the Department of Health and Human Services, met with the five Information and Referral Aides and formally told them that their unit was transferring to MC311. The County planned to transfer Reyazuddin and one other aide on November 9, with the three remaining aides to follow two weeks later. The other four Information and Referral Aides are not blind.

Reyazuddin expressed concern about MC311's accessibility. She also told Calderone that she had scheduled leave from October 28 to November 28,

2009, for a trip to India. Calderone emailed this information to Leslie Hamm, then-Manager and now-Director of MC311, who responded that the County's Disability Program Manager, Ricky Wright, suggested that "the date of [Reyazuddin's] detail to MC311 be delayed indefinitely or at least until . . . she returns from pre-approved leave."

One aide transferred as scheduled on November 9. By the time Reyazuddin returned from her trip, the other three aides had also transferred to MC311. But Reyazuddin was not transferred and instead was told to return to her pre-vacation job site at the main administrative building for the Department of Health and Human Services. She continued to perform her duties by answering the Department information line until February 4, 2010, when the information line was switched off and calls were transferred to MC311. For one day, Reyazuddin had nothing to do. Then the County decided that MC311 would not handle Manna Food Center referrals, which allow eligible low-income individuals to receive food from a private, non-profit food bank. Reyazuddin was assigned this task, but it was not full-time work.

In March 2010, Reyazuddin was assigned to work in the Department's Aging and Disability Unit for Adult Services Intake. For the next six months, Reyazuddin's supervisors struggled to find work for her. They thought her work situation was temporary until she could be transferred to MC311. However, on October 1, 2010, Wright informed Reyazuddin that she would not be transferring to MC311 because it would be too expensive for the County to make the software accessible. Wright "recommend[ed] the reasonable accommodation of 'reassignment to a vacant position' (priority consideration) in accordance with" the County employees' collective bargaining agreement.

From 2010 to 2012, Reyazuddin had the same salary, grade, and benefits as she did before MC311's launch. But although her supervisors pieced together tasks for her to perform, she did not have full-time work.

In 2012, Reyazuddin and eight other applicants were interviewed for one of two vacancies at MC311. Reyazuddin was not one of the two top-scoring applicants who the interviewers recommended to fill the vacancies. Although not required to do so under County policy, Hamm ultimately hired the recommended applicants.

C.

Reyazuddin alleges that, in 2009, the County violated Section 504 of the Rehabilitation Act by (1) failing to accommodate her disability by making MC311's software accessible and (2) discriminating against her when it did not transfer her to MC311 along with her coworkers. Reyazuddin also alleges that, in 2012, the County violated Title II of the ADA by not hiring her to fill an MC311 vacancy.

Reyazuddin retained an expert, Temeko Richardson, to evaluate the cost of making MC311 accessible by developing a custom "widget" as a workaround for the CTI Toolbar. The custom solution would be compatible with screen reader software. Richardson had previously seen this alternative at work in other call centers. Her lowest cost estimate was $129,600.

The County had an expert, Brad Ulrich, review Richardson's report. Ulrich noted flaws in the report and estimated that the actual cost to implement the least expensive accessibility option suggested by Richardson would be $648,000.

To give these cost estimates some context, the County's total budget for fiscal year 2010 was $3.73 billion. MC311's budget for fiscal year 2011 was about $4 million. By late January 2011, the County had spent about $11.4 million on MC311. But the County estimates that MC311 has saved it $10.3 million in fiscal years 2010 and 2011.

Following a period of discovery, both parties moved for summary judgment. The district court granted the County's motion and denied Reyazuddin's. Regarding the failure-to-accommodate claim, the court found that a genuine issue existed "as to whether [Reyazuddin's] proposed accommodation permits her to perform the essential functions of the [MC311] job." But the court determined that the County reasonably accommodated Reyazuddin by providing her with comparable employment. The court also concluded that no genuine issue existed on the County's undue hardship defense and that the County prevailed on that defense as a matter of law.

* * *

Reyazuddin appealed.

II.

We review de novo a district court's summary judgment order. *D.L. ex rel. K.L. v. Balt. Bd. of Sch. Comm'rs*, 706 F.3d 256, 258 (4th Cir.2013). "Summary judgment is appropriate only where there is no genuine issue of material fact and the movant is entitled to judgment as a matter of law." *Id.* The pertinent inquiry is whether "there are any genuine factual issues that properly can be resolved only by a finder of fact because they may reasonably be resolved in favor of either party." *Anderson v. Liberty Lobby, Inc.*, 477 U.S. 242, 250, 106 S.Ct. 2505 (1986). The evidence must be viewed in the light most favorable to the non-moving party, with all reasonable inferences drawn in that party's favor. . . .

Section 504 of the Rehabilitation Act mandates that "[n]o otherwise qualified individual with a disability . . . shall, solely by reason of her or his disability, be excluded from the participation in, be denied the benefits of, or be subjected to discrimination under any program or activity receiving Federal financial assistance." 29 U.S.C.A. § 794(a). . . .

Employment discrimination claims brought under Section 504 are evaluated using the same standards as those "applied under [T]itle I of the Americans with Disabilities Act of 1990." *Id.* § 794(d). Of significance here, Title I prohibits employers from "discriminat[ing] against a qualified individual on the basis of disability" by "not making reasonable accommodations to the known physical or mental limitations of an otherwise qualified individual with a disability who is an applicant or employee, unless [a] covered entity can demonstrate that the accommodation would impose an undue hardship on the operation of the business of such covered entity." 42 U.S.C. § 12112(b)(5)(A) (2012). A "qualified individual" is "an individual who, with or without reasonable accommodation, can perform the essential functions of the employment position that such individual holds or desires." *Id.* § 12111(8).

We consider in turn Reyazuddin's Section 504 failure-to-accommodate . . . claim[ ].

A.

To establish a prima facie case on her failure-to-accommodate claim, Reyazuddin must show that (1) she qualifies as an "individual with a disability" as defined in 29 U.S.C.A. § 705(20); (2) the County had notice of her disability; (3) she could perform the essential functions of her job with a reasonable accommodation; and (4) the County refused to make any reasonable accommodation. 29 U.S.C.A. § 794(a); *Wilson v. Dollar Gen. Corp.,* 717 F.3d 337, 345 (4th Cir.2013).

Even if Reyazuddin establishes her prima facie case, the County avoids liability if it can show as a matter of law that the proposed accommodation "will cause 'undue hardship in the particular circumstances.' " *Halpern v. Wake Forest Univ. Health Scis.,* 669 F.3d 454, 464 (4th Cir.2012) (quoting *U. S. Airways v. Barnett,* 535 U.S. 391, 401–02, 122 S.Ct. 1516 (2002)). Courts have reconciled and kept distinct the "reasonable accommodation" and "undue hardship" requirements by holding that, at the summary judgment stage, the employee "need only show that an 'accommodation' seems reasonable on its face," and then the employer "must show special (typically case-specific) circumstances that demonstrate undue hardship." *Barnett,* 535 U.S. at 401–02, 122 S.Ct. 1516.

That Reyazuddin satisfied the first two elements is undisputed, but the parties disagree on the third and fourth elements and the County's undue hardship defense.

1.

On the third element, the parties dispute whether Reyazuddin's proposed accommodations are reasonable and what constitutes the essential job functions of an MC311 employee. Title I provides that a "reasonable accommodation" includes

(A) making existing facilities used by employees readily accessible to and usable by individuals with disabilities; and

(B) job restructuring, part-time or modified work schedules, reassignment to a vacant position, acquisition or modification of equipment or devices, appropriate adjustment or modifications of examinations, training materials or policies, the provision of qualified readers or interpreters, and other similar accommodations for individuals with disabilities.

42 U.S.C. § 12111(9).

To overcome a motion for summary judgment, Reyazuddin was required to "present evidence from which a jury may infer that the [proposed] accommodation is 'reasonable on its face, i.e., ordinarily or in the run of cases.'" *Halpern,* 669 F.3d at 464 (quoting *Barnett,* 535 U.S. at 401, 122 S.Ct. 1516). A reasonable accommodation is one that is feasible or plausible. *Barnett,* 535 U.S. at 402, 122 S.Ct. 1516.

To determine essential job functions, Title I requires that consideration "be given to the employer's judgment as to what functions of a job are essential, and if an employer has prepared a written description before advertising or interviewing applicants for the job, this description shall be considered evidence of the essential functions of the job." 42 U.S.C. § 12111(8).

We agree with the district court that a genuine issue of material fact exists on this element. Reyazuddin has suggested two accommodations that she says will allow her to perform the essential job functions of an MC311 employee: the County could (1) configure its Siebel software to run concurrently in the accessible standard-interactivity mode or (2) create a custom workaround "widget" for the CTI Toolbar.

Reyazuddin supported the reasonableness of these proposals through evidence from her expert, Temeko Richardson. Richardson worked with two call centers in California and Pennsylvania that were accessible by operating simultaneously in high-interactivity and standard-interactivity modes. She also worked with a third call center in Illinois where all employees, including one blind employee, operated in standard-interactivity mode. And a fourth call center client in Pennsylvania was accessible through a custom solution.

The County counters that its decision to configure the Siebel software in the inaccessible high-interactivity mode, with the CTI Toolbar in particular, "maximize[s call center employees'] efficiency and productivity ... while keeping the cost of delivering government services as low as possible." The record, however, is silent about the productivity of employees operating in standard-interactivity mode, and so the County is left to speculate that employees operating without the bells and whistles of the high-interactivity mode configuration must be less productive. Even if we were willing to credit that assumption, it does not necessarily follow that using the high-interactivity software configuration is an essential job function, particularly in light of Reyazuddin's evidence of other call centers functioning without it.

The County also argues that Reyazuddin's proposed accommodations would not allow her to perform the essential job function of reading maps and PDF documents, which are used to respond to MC311's most frequent call about the estimated arrival time for the next public bus. However, this contention is contrary to the deposition testimony of the County's Disability Program Manager, Ricky Wright, that Reyazuddin "certainly has the knowledge, skills and abilities" to perform the essential functions of the MC311 job. Moreover, when Reyazuddin applied for a vacancy at MC311 in 2012, she was interviewed after the Office of Human Resources determined that she met the minimum qualifications. In light of this evidence, we think that a genuine issue remains as to whether Reyazuddin could perform the essential job functions with a reasonable accommodation.

2.

Turning to the fourth element of the failure-to-accommodate claim, Reyazuddin argues that the district court erred by finding as a matter of law that the County provided a reasonable accommodation by reassigning her to "comparable employment." We agree that the district court improperly engaged in fact finding instead of viewing the evidence in the light most favorable to Reyazuddin.

An employer may reasonably accommodate an employee without providing the exact accommodation that the employee requested. Rather, the employer may provide an alternative reasonable accommodation. Title I provides "job restructuring" and "reassignment to a vacant position" as examples of reasonable accommodations. 42 U.S.C. § 12111(9). Nonetheless, "a reasonable accommodation should provide a meaningful equal employment opportunity. Meaningful equal employment opportunity means an opportunity to attain the same level of performance as is available to nondisabled employees having similar skills and abilities." H.R.Rep. No. 101–485, pt. 2, at 66 (1990), *reprinted in* 1990 U.S.C.C.A.N. 303, 349.

Here, although Reyazuddin maintained her salary, pay grade, and benefits, the County cobbled together an assortment of "make-work" tasks that did not amount to full-time employment. For example, an email from a County employee shortly before Reyazuddin was assigned to work in the Aging and Disability Unit expressed concern that her job responsibilities would be "make work" as opposed to "real, meaningful work." In a later email, JoAnne Calderone, Manager for Planning, Accountability, and

Customer Service in the Department of Health and Human Services, suggested a meeting to discuss how to provide Reyazuddin "with a full day of meaningful work." And a separate series of emails demonstrates a tug-of-war between Calderone and MC311 over Manna referrals, Reyazuddin's primary responsibility, with the work being transferred from MC311 to Reyazuddin, back to MC311, and then back to Reyazuddin despite a County employee's opinion that residents "would be served better" by having these referrals handled within MC311.

Moreover, in her supplemental affidavit, Reyazuddin stated that Manna referrals—her only "regular task[ ]"—had decreased and "could be done in about one hour per day." She also estimated that it "takes a maximum of four to five hours per day . . . to complete all of [her] work."

We hold that the record evidence creates a genuine issue of material fact as to whether the accommodation provided by the County was reasonable.

3.

As an alternative to finding that Reyazuddin did not establish a prima facie case, the district court held that the County prevailed on its undue hardship defense as a matter of law. We cannot agree.

An employer is not liable under Section 504 if it "can demonstrate that the accommodation would impose an undue hardship on the operation of [its] business." 42 U.S.C. § 12112(b)(5)(A). Title I defines "undue hardship" as "an action requiring significant difficulty or expense, when considered in light of the factors set forth in subparagraph (B)." *Id.* § 12111(10)(A). Subparagraph (B), in turn, provides a non-exhaustive list of relevant factors:

> (i)   the nature and cost of the accommodation needed under this chapter;
>
> (ii) the overall financial resources of the facility or facilities involved in the provision of the reasonable accommodation; the number of persons employed at such facility; the effect on expenses and resources, or the impact otherwise of such accommodation upon the operation of the facility;
>
> (iii) the overall financial resources of the covered entity; the overall size of the business of a covered entity with respect to the number of its employees; the number, type, and location of its facilities; and
>
> (iv) the type of operation or operations of the covered entity, including the composition, structure, and functions of the workforce of such entity; the geographic separateness, administrative, or fiscal relationship of the facility or facilities in question to the covered entity.

Id. § 12111(10)(B).

The district court gave two reasons for its conclusion that the County was entitled to summary judgment on its undue hardship defense. First, the court criticized the estimated cost of $129,000 proffered by Reyazuddin's expert as "unsupported" because "it [did] not take into account increased costs for maintenance and upkeep." Second, the court explained that, as a result of Reyazuddin's proposed accommodation, the employee-facing portion of MC311 "would be altered and would result in increased maintenance and more downtime, which could spill over into the customer service realm." We believe that the district court's analysis improperly weighed conflicting evidence, did not view the evidence in the light most favorable to Reyazuddin, and overemphasized one factor while overlooking the others.

"At the summary judgment stage the judge's function is not [her]self to weigh the evidence and determine the truth of the matter but to determine whether there is a genuine issue for trial." *Anderson,* 477 U.S. at 249, 106 S.Ct. 2505. By concluding that the lowest estimate of cost was "unsupported," the district court credited the County's expert, Brad Ulrich, and discredited Reyazuddin's expert, Temeko Richardson. At this point, however, it is undisputed that both Ulrich and Richardson qualify as experts. The evidence therefore sets up a battle of the experts, which should not be resolved at summary judgment.

In addition, the district court focused almost exclusively on the cost of the accommodations, without regard to the other statutory factors. For instance, the district court's analysis does not mention the number of employees at MC311 (forty-nine) or the considerable savings the County realized from creating a centralized call center ($10 million).

The district court also did not acknowledge the County's substantial personnel resources at MC311 during the configuration and implementation of the Siebel software. At the project's peak, four Opus Group consultants were working for the County on MC311; one consultant who worked 40 hours per week for the County and spent 80% of his time doing maintenance of the call center application testified that he was "not too busy"; the County paid Opus Group $5,000 per week; and the County had a Senior IT Specialist on staff who was certified as a Siebel consultant. Thus, the evidence is in dispute about the additional resources the County would have needed to configure, implement, and maintain the Siebel software in standard-interactivity mode or adopt another accessibility solution.

Aside from cost, the district court credited the County's arguments that the proposed accommodations could negatively affect the overall operation of MC311, result in increased system maintenance and downtime, and potentially "spill over" to impact the overall customer service experience. This analysis misapplies the summary judgment standard. The evidence should be viewed in the light most favorable to Reyazuddin as the non-moving party, not the County. Reyazuddin presented evidence of other call centers operating simultaneously in high-interactivity and standard-interactivity mode as well as her expert's opinion that the proposed solutions for accessibility would "allow a blind user to work at MC311 without altering the experience of sighted users." Moreover, speculation about spillover effects cannot aid the County in establishing its undue hardship defense as a matter of law.

The district court also relied on an irrelevant factor in assessing undue hardship—the County's budget for reasonable accommodations. Specifically, the court noted the County's "meager budget for reasonable accommodations: the first $500 is paid for by the employee's department. Whatever costs remain can be paid from a $15,000 line-item in the County's overall budget."

Allowing the County to prevail on its undue hardship defense based on its own budgeting decisions would effectively cede the legal determination on this issue to the employer that allegedly failed to accommodate an employee with a disability. Taken to its logical extreme, the employer could budget $0 for reasonable accommodations and thereby always avoid liability. The County's overall budget ($3.73 billion in fiscal year 2010) and MC311's operating budget (about $4 million) are relevant factors. *See* 42 U.S.C. § 12111(10)(B)(ii)–(iii). But the County's line-item budget for reasonable accommodations is not.

In effect, the district court reduced a multi-factor analysis to a single factor—cost—that the court believed was simply too much for the County to bear. But while cost is important, it cannot be viewed in isolation. Rather, it is the relative cost, along with other factors, that matters. In that regard, we think it particularly relevant that other call centers have been able to accommodate blind employees.

Because we find a genuine issue for trial on the third and fourth elements of Reyazuddin's prima facie case and the County's defense, we reverse the district court's order granting summary judgment to the County on Reyazuddin's failure-to-accommodate claim.

* * *

[The court's discussion of the plaintiff's disparate treatment claim and her claim regarding the failure to transfer her into the vacant position in 2012 has been omitted.]

IV.

For the reasons given, the district court's judgment is affirmed in part and reversed in part, and the case is remanded for further proceedings.

NOTES AND QUESTIONS

1. *Understanding* Reyazuddin. If you don't know much about computers and coding (we don't), the facts and analysis of the feasibility of making the software accessible for blind individuals is complicated. That is why the parties hired experts, so that the experts could estimate costs and explain how the software could be made accessible. The important points to take from this case are: (1) that for a large government employer, proving undue hardship based on the costs of an accommodation is difficult because the undue hardship analysis looks at resources in addition to the costs of an accommodation and large government employers have very significant resources; and (2) employers cannot assign a relatively small budget line for accommodations and hope to win on the undue hardship analysis. As the court stated in *Reyazuddin*, "Allowing the County to prevail on its undue hardship defense based on its own budgeting decisions would effectively cede the legal determination on this issue to the employer . . . . Taken to its logical extreme, the employer could budget $0 for reasonable accommodations and thereby always avoid liability." On the other hand, the types and costs of accommodations that might be needed in any given year are unpredictable. As discussed below, high-cost accommodations are rare, so it is not that unusual that the employer in this case budgeted a relatively small amount of money for accommodations ($15,000). How should employers prepare for this unknown and unpredictable expense?

2. *High-cost accommodations are rare.* Although the accommodation requested in *Reyazuddin* was relatively expensive (although how expensive is uncertain based on the widely disparate experts' estimates), most accommodations are very inexpensive. *See, e.g.,* Helen Schartz, Kevin M. Schartz, D.J. Hendricks and Peter Blanck, *Workplace Accommodations: Empirical Study of Current Employees*, 75 MISS. L.J. 917, 937–38 (2006). Although many employers allege undue hardship as a defense, the undue hardship defense is dispositive in very few cases. In fact, in Professor Porter's review of almost 2,000 cases that cite to the "undue hardship" statutory language, only 120 of them actually engaged in a significant discussion of the undue hardship defense. *See* Nicole Buonocore Porter, *A New Look at the ADA's Undue Hardship Defense*, 84 MO. L. REV. 121, 123 (2019). And of those 120 cases, only sixteen of them actually discussed costs and resources. *Id.* at 139–44. In that sense, the *Reyazuddin* case is an outlier.

3. *Other undue hardship cases.* Despite the fact that employers very rarely win on the undue hardship issue based on the high costs of the accommodation, Professor Porter's analysis indicates that they more often win when the accommodation request involves restructuring job tasks. *See id.* at 148–49. And employers are most successful when the accommodation requested was a modification to the "structural norms" of the workplace, such as leaves of absence or requests for reduced hours. *Id.* at 149–56. Why do you think that is? Why would courts be more willing to side with employers when the accommodation is not costly in any monetary sense but causes some disruption or inconvenience to the employer?

4.   *Reasonable accommodation vs. undue hardship.* One other trend noted in Professor Porter's undue hardship article is how often courts conflated the reasonable accommodation inquiry with the undue hardship inquiry. *See id.* at 157–64. In other words, instead of holding that an accommodation was unreasonable, courts often held that an accommodation would cause an undue hardship. As one example, it is a well-known rule of law that an employer does not have to create a new position as an accommodation for an individual with a disability—such an accommodation is never reasonable. But in some cases involving a request to create a new position, the court held that such an accommodation would cause an undue hardship instead of holding that the accommodation was unreasonable. *See, e.g.,* Lamb v. Qualex, Inc., 28 F.Supp. 2d 374, 378 (E.D. Va. 1998). The Supreme Court arguably cleared up the confusion between reasonable accommodations and the undue hardship defense in *U.S. Airways, Inc. v. Barnett,* 535 U.S. 391, 122 S.Ct. 1516 (2002), where the Court stated that there are some accommodations that are unreasonable even though they do not cause an undue hardship on the employer. Recall that the accommodation in that case, reassignment to a vacant position when there were other more senior employees who wanted the position, did not cause an undue hardship on the employer (and in fact would be costless) but the Court nevertheless held that it was unreasonable for the employer to assign the plaintiff over the more qualified employees. *Id.* at 401–02. Although *Lamb* (cited above) predated *Barnett* (thereby explaining the confusion), there are some cases that make this mistake even after *Barnett. See, e.g.,* Jernigan v. Bellsouth Telecommunications, LLC, 17 F.Supp.3d 1317 1320–24 (N.D. Ga. 2014) (conflating the reasonable accommodation analysis with the undue hardship analysis). Of course, as discussed *supra* section C.3, scholars also disagree about whether the reasonable accommodation inquiry and undue hardship analysis are separate inquiries or two sides of the same coin, so it is not surprising that courts are confused.

E. QUALIFICATION STANDARDS

Statutory Language

The ADA defines discrimination to include: "using qualification standards, employment tests or other selection criteria that screen out or tend to screen out an individual with a disability or a class of individuals with disabilities unless the standard, test or other selection criteria, as used by the covered entity, is shown to be job-related for the position in question and is consistent with business necessity." 42 U.S.C. § 12112(b)(6). The ADA also provides certain defenses to a claim of disability discrimination. One of the defenses states: "It may be a defense to a charge of discrimination under this chapter that an alleged application of qualification standards, tests, or selection criteria that screen out or tend to screen out or otherwise deny a job or benefit to an individual with a disability has been shown to be job-related and consistent with business necessity, and that such performance cannot be accomplished by reasonable accommodation, as required under this subchapter." 42 U.S.C.

§ 12113(a). Qualification standards might include a requirement that an individual shall not pose a direct threat to the health or safety of others. 42 U.S.C. § 12113(b). This "direct threat" provision is discussed separately below.

BATES v. UNITED PARCEL SERVICE, INC.

511 F.3d 974 (9th Cir. 2007) (en banc)

McKEOWN, CIRCUIT JUDGE.

This appeal under the Americans with Disabilities Act (ADA) requires us to consider the intersection of a safety-based qualification standard and the "business necessity" defense. United Parcel Service (UPS) imposes a Department of Transportation (DOT) hearing standard on all package-car drivers, even though the DOT standard is federally mandated only for higher-weight vehicles. A class of hearing-impaired UPS employees and applicants who cannot meet the DOT hearing requirement challenges UPS's policy under Title I of the ADA, 42 U.S.C. §§ 12101–12213. . . .

Bates accepts, as he must, that UPS may lawfully exclude individuals who fail the DOT test from positions that would require them to drive DOT-regulated vehicles, i.e., vehicles exceeding a gross vehicle weight rating (GVWR) of 10,000 pounds. *See Albertson's, Inc. v. Kirkingburg*, 527 U.S. 555, 570 (1999). Bates contends, however, that UPS may not lawfully exclude hearing-impaired individuals from consideration for positions that involve vehicles whose GVWR is less than 10,001 pounds.

After a bench trial on liability, the district court found UPS liable on all of Bates's claims, enjoined UPS from using the blanket qualification standard, and required individualized assessment of candidates for the package-car driver positions. The court founded its analysis on the pattern-or-practice burden-shifting framework of *International Brotherhood of Teamsters v. United States*, 431 U.S. 324 (1977) [a Title VII race discrimination case]. In determining whether UPS met its asserted "business necessity" defense, the district court looked to our earlier decision involving hearing-impaired UPS drivers, *Morton v. United Parcel Service, Inc.*, 272 F.3d 1249 (9th Cir. 2001). *Morton* imported into its ADA analysis concepts from both the traditional Title VII business necessity defense to disparate impact claims and the "bona fide occupational qualification" (BFOQ) standard from Title VII disparate treatment challenges to a proscribed classification.

We granted rehearing en banc to consider the contours of a claim that an employer's safety qualification standard discriminates against otherwise "qualified" persons with disabilities, *see* 42 U.S.C. § 12112(a), (b)(6), and the showing required of an employer to successfully assert the business necessity defense to use of such qualification under 42 U.S.C. § 12113(a). Because this case involves a facially discriminatory qualification standard, we conclude that the *Teamsters'* burden-shifting protocol is inapplicable. In addition, we over-rule *Morton* to the extent that it imposes a BFOQ standard under the ADA, as the plain language of the ADA does not support such a construction. Because the district court considered this case under the framework of *Teamsters* and *Morton,* we vacate and remand for further proceedings. * * *

UPS AND PACKAGE-CAR DRIVERS

UPS package-car drivers deliver and pick up packages for UPS in the familiar brown UPS trucks. UPS employs more than 320,000 employees in the United States, over 70,000 of whom are package-car drivers.

When an opening for a driving position becomes available, UPS contacts the individual in that UPS center with the highest seniority who has bid on such a position. If that person is not interested, UPS moves down the list in descending seniority order until it finds an interested employee. The applicant must satisfy several requirements, which vary from district to district, but generally include (1) having completed an application; (2) being at least twenty-one years of age; (3) possessing a valid driver's license; and (4) having a "clean" driving record. Once the seniority threshold and other prerequisites to employment are met, all applicants for a package-car driver position must pass both UPS's road test and the DOT physical examination required of drivers of commercial vehicles over 10,000 pounds. UPS has a policy of hiring only drivers who can satisfy DOT standards.

At issue in this appeal is the hearing standard that is part of the DOT physical. An individual satisfies the DOT hearing standard if he

> [f]irst perceives a forced whispered voice in the better ear at not less than 5 feet with or without the use of a hearing aid or, if tested by use of an audiometric device, does not have an average hearing loss in the better ear greater than 40 decibels at 500 Hz, 1,000 Hz, and 2,000 Hz with or without a hearing aid when the audiometric device is calibrated to American National Standard (formerly ASA Standard) Z24.5–1951.

49 C.F.R. § 391.41(b)(11). According to the district court, the forced-whispered standard requires that potential drivers not only hear the sounds made but understand the words spoken.

Unlike UPS, which requires drivers of all package cars to pass the DOT physical, the DOT imposes this standard only for those driving vehicles with a GVWR of at least 10,001 pounds. A "gross vehicle weight rating" is the actual weight of the vehicle plus any cargo capacity. As of October 2003, UPS's fleet contained 65,198 vehicles, of which 5,902 vehicles had a GVWR of less than 10,001 pounds. The GVWR of the lighter vehicles ranged from 7,160 to 9,318 pounds, with the majority of these vehicles weighing 8,600 pounds. By way of comparison, automobiles, which include passenger cars, sport utility vehicles, light trucks and minivans, average 3,240 pounds. . . .

A. INITIAL CONSIDERATIONS

The hearing standard at issue here is a *facially discriminatory* qualification standard because it focuses directly on an individual's disabling or potentially disabling condition. Instead of recognizing this posture, the district court analyzed the claim as a "pattern-or-practice" disparate treatment claim, applying the burden-shifting protocol set out in *Teamsters.*

A burden-shifting protocol is, however, unnecessary in this circumstance. The fact to be uncovered by such a protocol—whether the employer made an employment decision on a proscribed basis (here, disability in the form of hearing impairment)—is not in dispute. *See Monette v. Elec. Data Sys. Corp.,* 90 F.3d 1173, 1182–83 (6th Cir.1996) (noting that when a defendant admits to taking account of disability status, the burden-shifting framework sometimes applicable to disparate treatment claims is unnecessary).

In addition, whether Bates established a prima facie case of employment discrimination in the summary judgment "burden-shifting" sense is moot after trial. The relevant inquiry now is simply whether the evidence presented at trial supports a finding of liability.

B. APPLICABLE PROVISIONS OF THE ADA

The enforcement provision of Title I of the ADA, under which Bates brought suit, provides:

> No covered entity shall discriminate against a qualified individual with a disability because of the disability of such individual in regard to job application procedures, the hiring, advancement, or discharge of employees, employee compensation, job training, and other terms, conditions, and privileges of employment.

42 U.S.C. § 12112(a). Thus, under the ADA, an employee bears the ultimate burden of proving that he is (1) disabled under the Act, (2) a "qualified individual with a disability," and (3) discriminated against "because of" the disability.

There is no dispute that the class members, who are hearing impaired, are disabled. Instead, we focus on the two other key terms in the statute: "qualified individual" and "discriminate." To unpack the meaning of these terms, we look to the statute.

A "qualified individual" is "an individual with a disability who, *with or without reasonable accommodation,* can perform the *essential functions* of the employment position that such individual holds or desires." "Essential functions" are "fundamental job duties of the employment position . . . not includ[ing] the marginal functions of the position." "If a disabled person cannot perform a job's 'essential functions' (even with a reasonable accommodation), then the ADA's employment protections do not apply." "If, on the other hand, a person can perform a job's essential functions, and therefore is a qualified individual, then the ADA prohibits discrimination" with respect to the employment actions outlined in 42 U.S.C. § 12112(a).

Discrimination under the ADA includes the use of *"qualification standards, employment tests or other selection criteria that screen out or tend to screen out* an individual with a disability or a *class of individuals with disabilities* unless the standard, test or other selection criteria, as used by the covered entity, is shown to be job-related for the position in question and is consistent with business necessity." 42 U.S.C. § 12112(b)(6). The EEOC regulations define "qualifications standards" as "the personal and professional attributes including the skill, experience, education, physical, medical, safety and other requirements established by a covered entity as requirements which an individual must meet in order to be eligible for the position held or desired."

In a case involving the use of a qualification standard, the ADA provides employers with a "business necessity" defense:

It may be a defense to a charge of discrimination under this chapter that an *alleged application of qualification standards, tests, or selection criteria* that screen out or tend to screen out or otherwise deny a job or benefit to an individual with a disability has been shown to be *job-related and consistent with business necessity,* and such performance *cannot be accomplished by reasonable accommodation,* as required under this subchapter.

42 U.S.C. § 12113(a).

Where an across-the-board safety "qualification standard" is invoked, the question then becomes what proof is required with respect to being a "qualified individual," that is, one who can perform the job's essential functions. Before an employee can challenge an employer's qualification standard, however, an employee must first prove that he is a "qualified individual" within the meaning of the ADA, that is, one who can perform the job's essential functions with or without reasonable accommodation. Bates argues that he meets all of the essential functions of the package-car driver position, including being a "safe" driver. Although Bates acknowledges that class members do not meet the DOT hearing standard, he contends that hearing is not an essential function, and thus there are qualified individuals who meet UPS's other job requirements.

UPS, on the other hand, urges that class members are not qualified individuals because they cannot meet UPS's requirement that all drivers pass the DOT hearing standard, and thus cannot meet an essential function of the job—DOT certification to drive all commercial vehicles. UPS also argues that each class member is required to show not only that he is a "safe" driver in the sense that he has a "clean driving record," but also that he is a safe driver *despite being hearing impaired.*

We turn first to the qualified individual inquiry and then to the question of discrimination.

C. QUALIFIED INDIVIDUAL WITH A DISABILITY

As the plaintiff, Bates bears the burden to prove that he is "qualified." Qualification for a position is a two-step inquiry. The court first examines whether the individual satisfies the "requisite skill, experience, education and other job-related requirements" of the position. The court then considers whether the individual "can perform the essential functions of such position" with or without a reasonable accommodation.

1. JOB REQUISITES

The package-car driver job requires an applicant to meet UPS's threshold seniority requirements for the package-car driver position, complete an application, be at least twenty-one years of age, possess a valid driver's license, and have a clean driving record by UPS's local standards. The district court's finding that named plaintiff Oloyede and class member Elias Habib meet these prerequisites is not clearly erroneous.

2. ESSENTIAL FUNCTIONS

To prove that he is "qualified," the applicant also must show that he can perform the "essential functions" of the job. As noted earlier, a job's "essential functions" are "fundamental job duties of the employment position ... not includ[ing] the marginal functions of the position." "Essential functions" are not to be confused with "qualification standards," which an employer may establish for a certain position. Whereas "essential functions" are basic "duties," 29 C.F.R. § 1630.2(n)(1), "qualification standards" are "personal and professional attributes" that may include "physical, medical [and] safety" requirements. *Id.* § 1630.2(q). The difference is crucial.

The statute does not require that a person meet each of an employer's established "qualification standards," however, to show that he is "qualified." And, indeed, it would make little sense to require an ADA plaintiff to show that he meets a qualification standard that he undisputedly *cannot* meet because of his disability and that forms the very basis of his discrimination challenge.

Although the plaintiff bears the ultimate burden of persuading the fact finder that he can perform the job's essential functions, we agree with the Eighth Circuit's approach that "an employer who disputes the plaintiff's claim that he can perform the essential functions must put forth evidence establishing those functions." The genesis of this rule is the recognition that "much of the information which determines those essential functions lies uniquely with the employer." In addition, the ADA and implementing regulations direct fact finders to consider, among other things, "the employer's judgment as to what functions of a job are essential," job descriptions prepared before advertising or interviewing applicants, "[t]he amount of time spent on the job performing the function," "[t]he consequences of not requiring the [applicant or employee] to perform the function," and the work experience of current and former employees. Thus, to the extent that an employer challenges an ADA plaintiff's claim that he can perform the job's essential functions, we think it appropriate to place a burden of production on the employer to come forward with evidence of those essential functions.

At trial the parties agreed that two of the "essential functions" of the package-car driver position are (1) "the ability to communicate effectively" and (2) "the ability to drive safely." UPS urged that "the ability to drive DOT-regulated vehicles" was another essential function. The district court rejected that contention, finding that UPS permits other drivers who cannot drive all DOT-regulated vehicles to drive package cars. For example, UPS has protocols in place for driver applicants who cannot pass certain DOT certification requirements because of their vision impairments or insulin-dependent diabetes, but who can pass less stringent physical requirements. UPS has not shown that the district court's determination that DOT certification is not an essential job function was clearly erroneous.

Only the second essential function, "safe driving," is at issue in this appeal. UPS argues that "hearing" at a level sufficient to pass the DOT hearing standard is either a stand-alone essential job function or part and parcel of being a safe driver. This point illustrates the critical difference between a job's essential functions—"effective communication" or "safe driving"— versus a qualification standard based on "personal or professional attributes," such as hearing at a certain level. The question, then, is whether plaintiffs established that they meet the essential function of safe driving.

The district court found that Oloyede met UPS's threshold requirements of having no accidents or moving violations within the last year, no DUI within the last three years, and no more than three moving violations in the last three years. Habib also met the prerequisites to apply for the position: a valid driver's license, twenty-seven years of driving experience, and no evidence of even a minor traffic accident.

UPS urges that Oloyede and Habib are required to show not only that they are "safe" drivers in the sense that they have a "clean driving record," but also that they are safe drivers even though they are hearing impaired. The district court rejected that argument, stating that imposing this burden would require plaintiffs to disprove the employer's business necessity affirmative defense, i.e., that the employer is justified in imposing a qualification standard that facially screens out individuals with a specific disability.

Because UPS has linked hearing with safe driving, UPS bears the burden to prove that nexus as part of its defense to use of the hearing qualification standard. The employees, however, bear the ultimate burden to show that they are qualified to perform the essential function of safely driving a package car. In so doing, Oloyede and Habib need not disprove the validity of the hearing standard, but must demonstrate their safe driving ability vis-a-vis package cars. The inquiry is not whether Oloyede and Habib are capable of safely driving their personal cars, but rather whether they can drive the package cars at issue in this litigation. The district court did not make a finding with respect to plaintiffs' ability to drive package cars safely. Merely finding an absence of evidence with respect to driving a package car is insufficient. In short, Oloyede and Habib bear the burden of proving that they are qualified individuals with disabilities. They must show that they can perform the essential job function of safely driving package cars. Only if they meet this burden does the question become whether the qualification standard used by the employer satisfies the business necessity defense.

By requiring UPS to justify the hearing test under the business necessity defense, but also requiring plaintiffs to show that they can perform the essential functions of the job, we are not saying, nor does the ADA require, that employers must hire employees who cannot safely perform the job, particularly where safety itself is an essential function. Nor are we saying that an employer can never impose a safety standard that exceeds minimum requirements imposed by law. However, when an employer asserts a blanket safety-based qualification standard—beyond the essential job function—that is not mandated by law and that qualification standard screens out or tends to screen out an individual with a disability, the employer—not the employee—bears the burden of showing that the higher qualification standard is job-related and consistent with business necessity, and that performance cannot be achieved through reasonable accommodation. 42 U.S.C. § 12113(a).

This approach is parallel to the one adopted in a "direct threat" case under the ADA. 42 U.S.C. § 12113(b) ("The term 'qualification standards' may include a requirement that an individual shall not pose a direct threat to the health or safety of other individuals in the workplace."). Although the specifics of proof in direct threat and business necessity cases may vary, the frameworks are parallel. We emphasize that UPS is not required to meet the requirements of the direct threat defense, but rather that cases under that section of the ADA illuminate our analysis.

In *Branham*, the Seventh Circuit considered a qualification standard that disqualified an individual from being an IRS criminal investigator if the applicant had "[a]ny condition that would hinder full, efficient performance of the duties of the[ ] position[ ] or that would cause the individual to be a hazard to himself/herself or to others. . . ." Safety was an issue in *Branham,* as it is here. The parties did not dispute that an essential job requirement was the ability to function safely under the working conditions imposed on such employees.

The IRS claimed that the applicant's diabetes placed him at risk of "subtle and/or sudden incapacitation, which would place the applicant and others . . . at an extreme risk of safety that would be unacceptable." The IRS also argued that the applicant bore the burden of establishing as part of his prima facie case that he did *not* pose a direct threat to himself or others. In rejecting the IRS's position, the Seventh Circuit concluded that the applicant need only establish that he was "otherwise qualified" for the criminal investigator job by meeting the job's "essential functions." And, because the IRS's "safety" qualification standard regarding the medical condition incorporated the "direct threat" defense under the ADA, the employer bore the burden of proving that the employee was a direct threat. The employee did not have to *disprove* the claim that he was a direct threat as part of his prima facie case of discrimination.

The *Branham* approach works equally well in framing our analysis of UPS's hearing qualification standard. The employee does not bear the burden to invalidate the employer's safety-based qualification standard. Nor is the employee required to disprove UPS's contention that, in order to be safe, the driver must pass the DOT hearing standard—the very qualification standard disputed in this case.

Similar to the court in *Branham*, we conclude that an employee who shows that he meets the basic qualifications for the package-car driver position (seniority, twenty-one years of age, and holding a valid driver's license) and can drive a package car safely, including having a clean driving record and passing the driving test, is an otherwise qualified individual.

The last step of the "qualified individual" inquiry requires a plaintiff to show that he is qualified "with or without reasonable accommodation." If the plaintiff proves that he can perform the job's essential functions either without a reasonable accommodation or with such an accommodation, then he has met his burden to show he is qualified. Here, the district court did not explicitly discuss reasonable accommodation, although in finding that Oloyede and Habib met the job requisites and could perform the essential function of safe driving, it implicitly found that no accommodation was necessary to meet those baseline requirements for UPS package-car driver applicants.

Because the district court did not analyze whether Oloyede and Habib are "qualified individuals" capable of performing the "essential function" of safely driving a package car in the framework discussed above, nor did it directly undertake the "qualified individual" inquiry, we remand to the district court for the employees to prove that they are so qualified and for an analysis of reasonable accommodation. Thus, we vacate the district court's order denying UPS's motion for judgment. . . .

D. DISCRIMINATION BECAUSE OF DISABILITY

An employee bears the burden of proving that he was discriminated against "because of" a disability. 42 U.S.C. § 12112(a). The qualification standard at issue—the DOT hearing standard—is facially discriminatory and falls squarely within the ADA's definition of discrimination. 42 U.S.C. § 12112(b)(6) ("discrimination" includes using qualification standards, employment tests or other selection criteria that screen out or tend to screen out an individual with a disability or a class of individuals with disabilities).

The district court found, and UPS does not contest, that UPS applies a qualification standard that has the effect of discriminating on the basis of disability and/or screens out the class of employees who cannot pass the DOT hearing standard. Such discrimination violates the ADA *unless* UPS can prove a valid defense to its use of the DOT hearing standard. We therefore turn to UPS's defense that its reliance on the DOT hearing standard is justified under the business necessity defense.

E. EMPLOYER'S "BUSINESS NECESSITY" DEFENSE

Under the ADA, an employer may assert an affirmative defense to a claim that application of a qualification standard, test or selection criteria discriminates on the basis of disability. Although the shorthand reference is the "business necessity" defense, the defense also incorporates requirements of job-relatedness and reasonable accommodation.

We most recently addressed the ADA's business necessity defense in *Morton*, 272 F.3d 1249. There, we held that the ADA's version of the business necessity defense incorporates concepts from both the traditional Title VII business necessity defense to disparate impact claims and the BFOQ defense in Title VII and Age Discrimination in Employment Act (ADEA) disparate treatment challenges to a proscribed classification. Today, we revisit our conception of the business necessity defense under the ADA and overrule *Morton* to the extent that it conflicts with this opinion. Specifically, we reject *Morton*'s adaptation of the Title VII and ADEA BFOQ safety standard requirement in the ADA context.

We look first and foremost to the text of the ADA:

> It may be a defense to a charge of discrimination under this chapter that an *alleged application of qualification standards, tests, or selection criteria* that screen out or tend to screen out or otherwise deny a job or benefit to an individual with a disability has been shown to be *job-related and consistent with business necessity,* and such performance *cannot be accomplished by reasonable accommodation,* as required under this subchapter.

42 U.S.C. § 12113(a). To successfully assert the business necessity defense to an allegedly discriminatory application of a qualification standard, test or selection criteria, an employer bears the burden of showing that the qualification standard is (1) "job-related," (2) "consistent with business necessity," and (3) that "performance cannot be accomplished by reasonable accommodation."

To show "job-relatedness," an employer must demonstrate that the qualification standard fairly and accurately measures the individual's actual ability to perform the essential functions of the job. When every person excluded by the qualification standard is a member of a protected class—that is, disabled persons—an employer must demonstrate a predictive or significant correlation between the qualification and performance of the job's essential functions.

To show that the disputed qualification standard is "consistent with business necessity," the employer must show that it "substantially promote [s]" the business's needs. *Cripe*, 261 F.3d at 890. As we observed in *Cripe*: "The 'business necessity' standard is quite high, and is not to be confused with mere expediency." For a safety-based qualification standard, "[i]n evaluating whether the risks addressed by . . . [the] qualification standard constitute a business necessity, the court should take into account the magnitude of possible harm as well as the probability of occurrence." *EEOC v. Exxon Corp.*, 203 F.3d 871, 875 (5th Cir.2000) (noting that "[t]he acceptable probability of an incident will vary with the potential hazard posed by the particular position: a probability that might be tolerable in an ordinary job might be intolerable for a position involving atomic reactors, for example").

In rejecting UPS's business necessity defense to application of the DOT hearing standard to all package-car driving positions, the district court concluded that "UPS has demonstrated neither that all or substantially all deaf drivers pose a higher risk of accidents than non-deaf drivers nor that there are no practical criteria for determining which deaf drivers pose a heightened risk and which do not. Additionally, UPS has not demonstrated that it would be impossible to develop empirical evidence that would be sufficient to make either showing." This finding does not track the statutory elements of the business necessity defense. Because the district court understandably based its rationale on the then-extant *Morton* framework, we vacate the finding that UPS violated Bates's rights under the ADA, vacate the injunction, and remand for proceedings consistent with this opinion. We leave to the district court the determination whether additional evidence is appropriate in light of the significant change in the legal landscape of this case.

One further aspect of *Morton* bears noting here. As part of its business necessity analysis under *Morton,* the district court also rejected UPS's reliance on the DOT's hearing standard. The district court pointed to

Morton's statement that "the existence of the—by its own terms inapplicable—DOT standard cannot shoulder UPS's statutory burden" to show business necessity. *Morton*, 272 F.3d at 1264–65 (holding that the mere existence of government safety standard did not demonstrate UPS's business necessity defense and fact issues precluded summary judgment).

Here, UPS offered up the DOT standard as evidence that, for safety purposes, a certain level of hearing is necessary to drive non-DOT-regulated vehicles. According to UPS, there is complete congruity between the positions of driving a DOT-regulated package car (more than 10,000 pounds) and driving a vehicle that weighs a little less. UPS argued that package cars weighing almost five tons do not have operating characteristics similar to passenger cars and pose greater risks than do passenger cars.

To be sure, DOT's regulation does not apply to the category of vehicles at issue in this case. However, that circumstance does not mean that the standard has no relevance to the employer's safety argument. UPS is entitled to use as some evidence of its business necessity defense the fact that it relied on a government safety standard, even where the standard is not applicable to the category of conduct at issue. To the extent *Morton* suggests or is interpreted to the contrary, it is overruled. The parallel consideration applies to an employee; that is, an employee may offer as evidence challenging the validity or applicability of a safety standard the government's refusal to adopt such standard to govern the conduct at issue. *See, e.g.,* 53 Fed.Reg. 18042, 18044 (discussing DOT's rejection of UPS's attempt to apply DOT's physical requirements to trucks under 10,000 pounds because (1) smaller trucks and vans have "operating characteristics" more comparable to cars; and (2) smaller trucks and vans pose a lesser "safety risk" than large trucks).

Thus, while certainly not dispositive of UPS's showing of job-relatedness, business necessity or the reasonableness of potential accommodations, UPS's reliance on the government safety standard with respect to other vehicles in its fleet should be entitled to some consideration as a safety benchmark. Whether, as UPS puts it, "non-DOT package cars in the UPS fleet share significant risk characteristics with their slightly larger cousins" is a factual question of the congruity between vehicles and drivers in UPS's non-DOT fleet and those regulated by DOT.

NOTES AND QUESTIONS

1. *Qualification standards vs. qualified individual—burden of proof.* Although the concepts of "qualified individual" and "qualification standards" overlap, it is important to remember that there are differences. For one thing, the burden of proving "qualified individual" is on the plaintiff (although, as stated by the court in *Bates*, the burden of articulating the essential functions

is on the defendant), while the burden of proving that a qualification standard is job related and consistent with business necessity falls on the defendant.

2. *Essential functions.* Is the hearing standard required by the employer in *Bates* (even in cases when not mandated by the DOT regulations) an essential function of the job? The regulations implementing the ADA provide:

> "Essential functions" are not to be confused with "qualification standards," which an employer may establish for a certain position. Whereas "essential functions" are basic "duties," 29 C.F.R. § 1630.2(n)(1), "qualification standards" are "personal and professional attributes" that may include "physical, medical [and] safety" requirements. *Id.* § 1630.2(q).

Thus, the court holds that "hearing" is not an essential function, but safe driving is. On remand, the plaintiffs will have to prove that they meet the essential function of "safe driving" and the employer will have to prove that the hearing requirement is "job related" and "consistent with business necessity." How do you think this case should have been resolved on remand?

3. *Uncorrected vision.* As noted in Chapter 2, when Congress amended the ADA to state that the ameliorative effects of mitigating measures *except* ordinary eyeglasses or contacts are not to be considered in determining whether an individual has a disability, Congress also added a provision regarding tests related to uncorrected vision. 42 U.S.C. § 12113(c) ("Notwithstanding section 12102(4)(E)(ii) of this title, a covered entity shall not use qualification standards, employment tests, or other selection criteria based on an individual's uncorrected vision unless the standard, test, or other selection criteria, as used by the covered entity, is shown to be job-related for the position in question and consistent with business necessity."). As discussed in the *Sutton* case (Chapter 2), United Airlines had a policy that required pilots to have uncorrected vision of 20/100. Because the Court found that the plaintiffs were not disabled (based on the fact that, in their mitigated state, they were not substantially limited in the major life activity of seeing) United Airlines was never required to justify its requirement that mandated a certain level of *uncorrected* vision. After the ADAAA, United Airlines would be required to prove that an uncorrected vision standard is "job related" and "consistent with business necessity." Do you think the airline would be successful in making this argument? Why might United Airlines care about uncorrected vision if the pilots' vision is completely correctable?

F. DIRECT THREAT

Statutory Language and EEOC Regulation

Section 12111(3) of the ADA defines "direct threat" as follows:

> The term "direct threat" means a significant risk to the health or safety of others that cannot be eliminated by reasonable accommodation.

Section 12113(b) states:

(b) Qualification standards

The term "qualification standards" may include a requirement
that an individual shall not pose a direct threat to the health or
safety of other individuals in the workplace.

EEOC regulation 29 CFR § 1630.2(r) states:

Direct threat means a significant risk of substantial harm to the
health or safety of the individual or others that cannot be
eliminated or reduced by reasonable accommodation. . . .

BRAGDON V. ABBOTT
524 U.S. 624, 118 S.Ct. 2196 (1998)

JUSTICE KENNEDY delivered the opinion of the Court.

[Eds. Note: The facts of this case are summarized in the opinion reprinted
in Chapter 2. In terms of procedural posture, both the district court and
the court of appeals ruled for the plaintiff, finding that she was disabled
and that treating her in the defendant's office would not have posed a direct
threat. The district court based its direct threat ruling on the affidavits
submitted by Dr. Marianos, Director of the Division of Oral Health of the
Centers for Disease Control and Prevention (CDC). The court of appeals
declined to rely on the Marianos affidavits, but reached the same result by
relying on the 1993 CDC Dentistry Guidelines and on a 1991 policy adopted
by the American Dental Association.]

* * *

The petition for certiorari presented three other questions for review. The
questions stated:

"3. When deciding under title III of the ADA whether a private
health care provider must perform invasive procedures on an
infectious patient in his office, should courts defer to the health
care provider's professional judgment, as long as it is reasonable
in light of then-current medical knowledge?

* * *

The question is phrased in an awkward way, for it conflates two separate
inquiries. In asking whether it is appropriate to defer to petitioner's
judgment, it assumes that petitioner's assessment of the objective facts was
reasonable. The central premise of the question and the assumption on
which it is based merit separate consideration.

Again, we begin with the statute. Notwithstanding the protection given
respondent by the ADA's definition of disability, petitioner could have
refused to treat her if her infectious condition "pose[d] a direct threat to the

health or safety of others." 42 U.S.C. § 12182(b)(3). The ADA defines a direct threat to be "a significant risk to the health or safety of others that cannot be eliminated by a modification of policies, practices, or procedures or by the provision of auxiliary aids or services." *Ibid.* Parallel provisions appear in the employment provisions of Title I. §§ 12111(3), 12113(b).

The ADA's direct threat provision stems from the recognition in *School Bd. of Nassau Cty. v. Arline,* 480 U.S. 273, 287, 107 S.Ct. 1123, 1130–1131 (1987), of the importance of prohibiting discrimination against individuals with disabilities while protecting others from significant health and safety risks, resulting, for instance, from a contagious disease. In *Arline,* the Court reconciled these objectives by construing the Rehabilitation Act not to require the hiring of a person who posed "a significant risk of communicating an infectious disease to others." Congress amended the Rehabilitation Act and the Fair Housing Act to incorporate the language. It later relied on the same language in enacting the ADA. See 28 CFR pt. 36, App. B, p. 626 (1997) (ADA's direct threat provision codifies *Arline*). Because few, if any, activities in life are risk free, *Arline* and the ADA do not ask whether a risk exists, but whether it is significant.

The existence, or nonexistence, of a significant risk must be determined from the standpoint of the person who refuses the treatment or accommodation, and the risk assessment must be based on medical or other objective evidence. *Arline, supra,* at 288, 107 S.Ct., at 1131. As a health care professional, petitioner had the duty to assess the risk of infection based on the objective, scientific information available to him and others in his profession. His belief that a significant risk existed, even if maintained in good faith, would not relieve him from liability. To use the words of the question presented, petitioner receives no special deference simply because he is a health care professional. It is true that *Arline* reserved "the question whether courts should also defer to the reasonable medical judgments of private physicians on which an employer has relied." At most, this statement reserved the possibility that employers could consult with individual physicians as objective third-party experts. It did not suggest that an individual physician's state of mind could excuse discrimination without regard to the objective reasonableness of his actions.

Our conclusion that courts should assess the objective reasonableness of the views of health care professionals without deferring to their individual judgments does not answer the implicit assumption in the question presented, whether petitioner's actions were reasonable in light of the available medical evidence. In assessing the reasonableness of petitioner's actions, the views of public health authorities, such as the U.S. Public Health Service, CDC, and the National Institutes of Health, are of special weight and authority. *Arline, supra,* at 288, 107 S.Ct., at 1130–1131. The views of these organizations are not conclusive, however. A health care professional who disagrees with the prevailing medical consensus may refute it by citing a credible scientific basis for deviating from the accepted norm.

We have reviewed so much of the record as necessary to illustrate the application of the rule to the facts of this case. For the most part, the Court of Appeals followed the proper standard in evaluating petitioner's position and conducted a thorough review of the evidence. Its rejection of the District Court's reliance on the Marianos affidavits was a correct application of the principle that petitioner's actions must be evaluated in light of the available, objective evidence. The record did not show that CDC had published the conclusion set out in the affidavits at the time petitioner refused to treat respondent.

A further illustration of a correct application of the objective standard is the Court of Appeals' refusal to give weight to petitioner's offer to treat respondent in a hospital. Petitioner testified that he believed hospitals had safety measures, such as air filtration, ultraviolet lights, and respirators, which would reduce the risk of HIV transmission. Petitioner made no showing, however, that any area hospital had these safeguards or even that he had hospital privileges. His expert also admitted the lack of any scientific basis for the conclusion that these measures would lower the risk of transmission. Petitioner failed to present any objective, medical evidence showing that treating respondent in a hospital would be safer or more efficient in preventing HIV transmission than treatment in a well-equipped dental office.

We are concerned, however, that the Court of Appeals might have placed mistaken reliance upon two other sources. In ruling no triable issue of fact existed on this point, the Court of Appeals relied on the 1993 CDC Dentistry Guidelines and the 1991 American Dental Association Policy on HIV. This evidence is not definitive. As noted earlier, the CDC Guidelines recommended certain universal precautions which, in CDC's view, "should reduce the risk of disease transmission in the dental environment." The Court of Appeals determined that, "[w]hile the guidelines do not state explicitly that no further risk-reduction measures are desirable or that routine dental care for HIV-positive individuals is safe, those two conclusions seem to be implicit in the guidelines' detailed delineation of procedures for office treatment of HIV-positive patients." In our view, the Guidelines do not necessarily contain implicit assumptions conclusive of the point to be decided. The Guidelines set out CDC's recommendation that the universal precautions are the best way to combat the risk of HIV transmission. They do not assess the level of risk.

Nor can we be certain, on this record, whether the 1991 American Dental Association Policy on HIV carries the weight the Court of Appeals attributed to it. The Policy does provide some evidence of the medical community's objective assessment of the risks posed by treating people infected with HIV in dental offices. It indicates:

> Current scientific and epidemiologic evidence indicates that there
> is little risk of transmission of infectious diseases through dental
> treatment if recommended infection control procedures are
> routinely followed. Patients with HIV infection may be safely
> treated in private dental offices when appropriate infection
> control procedures are employed. Such infection control
> procedures provide protection both for patients and dental
> personnel.

We note, however, that the Association is a professional organization,
which, although a respected source of information on the dental profession,
is not a public health authority. It is not clear the extent to which the Policy
was based on the Association's assessment of dentists' ethical and
professional duties in addition to its scientific assessment of the risk to
which the ADA refers. Efforts to clarify dentists' ethical obligations and to
encourage dentists to treat patients with HIV infection with compassion
may be commendable, but the question under the statute is one of
statistical likelihood, not professional responsibility. Without more
information on the manner in which the American Dental Association
formulated this Policy, we are unable to determine the Policy's value in
evaluating whether petitioner's assessment of the risks was reasonable as
a matter of law.

The court considered materials submitted by both parties on the cross-
motions for summary judgment. The petitioner was required to establish
that there existed a genuine issue of material fact. . . .

We acknowledge the presence of other evidence in the record before the
Court of Appeals which, subject to further arguments and examination,
might support affirmance of the trial court's ruling. For instance, the record
contains substantial testimony from numerous health experts indicating
that it is safe to treat patients infected with HIV in dental offices. We are
unable to determine the import of this evidence, however. The record does
not disclose whether the expert testimony submitted by respondent turned
on evidence available in September 1994.

There are reasons to doubt whether petitioner advanced evidence sufficient
to raise a triable issue of fact on the significance of the risk. Petitioner
relied on two principal points: First, he asserted that the use of high-speed
drills and surface cooling with water created a risk of airborne HIV
transmission. The study on which petitioner relied was inconclusive,
however, determining only that "[f]urther work is required to determine
whether such a risk exists." Petitioner's expert witness conceded,
moreover, that no evidence suggested the spray could transmit HIV. His
opinion on airborne risk was based on the absence of contrary evidence, not
on positive data. Scientific evidence and expert testimony must have a
traceable, analytical basis in objective fact before it may be considered on
summary judgment.

Second, petitioner argues that, as of September 1994, CDC had identified seven dental workers with possible occupational transmission of HIV. These dental workers were exposed to HIV in the course of their employment, but CDC could not determine whether HIV infection had resulted from this exposure. It is now known that CDC could not ascertain how the seven dental workers contracted the disease because they did not present themselves for HIV testing at an appropriate time after this occupational exposure. It is not clear on this record, however, whether this information was available to petitioner in September 1994. If not, the seven cases might have provided some, albeit not necessarily sufficient, support for petitioner's position. Standing alone, we doubt it would meet the objective, scientific basis for finding a significant risk to the petitioner.

Our evaluation of the evidence is constrained by the fact that on these and other points we have not had briefs and arguments directed to the entire record. In accepting the case for review, we declined to grant certiorari on question five, which asked whether petitioner raised a genuine issue of fact for trial. As a result, the briefs and arguments presented to us did not concentrate on the question of sufficiency in light all of the submissions in the summary judgment proceeding. "When attention has been focused on other issues, or when the court from which a case comes has expressed no views on a controlling question, it may be appropriate to remand the case rather than deal with the merits of that question in this Court." *Dandridge v. Williams*, 397 U.S. 471, 476, n. 6, 90 S.Ct. 1153, 1157, n. 6 (1970). This consideration carries particular force where, as here, full briefing directed at the issue would help place a complex factual record in proper perspective. Resolution of the issue will be of importance to health care workers not just for the result but also for the precision and comprehensiveness of the reasons given for the decision.

We conclude the proper course is to give the Court of Appeals the opportunity to determine whether our analysis of some of the studies cited by the parties would change its conclusion that petitioner presented neither objective evidence nor a triable issue of fact on the question of risk. In remanding the case, we do not foreclose the possibility that the Court of Appeals may reach the same conclusion it did earlier. A remand will permit a full exploration of the issue through the adversary process.

CHIEF JUSTICE REHNQUIST, with whom JUSTICE SCALIA, JUSTICE THOMAS and JUSTICE O'CONNOR join as to Part II, concurring in the judgment in part and dissenting in part.

II

While the Court concludes to the contrary as to the "disability" issue, it then quite correctly recognizes that petitioner could nonetheless have refused to treat respondent if her condition posed a "direct threat." The Court of Appeals affirmed the judgment of the District Court granting summary judgment to respondent on this issue. The Court vacates this portion of the Court of Appeals' decision, and remands the case to the lower court, presumably so that it may "determine whether our analysis of some of the studies cited by the parties would change its conclusion that petitioner presented neither objective evidence nor a triable issue of fact on the question of risk." I agree that the judgment should be vacated, although I am not sure I understand the Court's cryptic direction to the lower court.

"[D]irect threat" is defined as a "significant risk to the health or safety of others that cannot be eliminated by a modification of policies, practices, or procedures or by the provision of auxiliary aids or services." § 12182(b)(3). This statutory definition of a direct threat consists of two parts. First, a court must ask whether treating the infected patient *without precautionary techniques* would pose a "significant risk to the health or safety of others." Whether a particular risk is significant depends on:

> "(a) the nature of the risk (how the disease is transmitted), (b) the duration of the risk (how long is the carrier infectious), (c) the severity of the risk (what is the potential harm to third parties) and (d) the probabilities the disease will be transmitted and will cause varying degrees of harm." *School Bd. of Nassau Cty. v. Arline*, 480 U.S. 273, 288, 107 S.Ct. 1123, 1131 (1987).

Even if a significant risk exists, a health practitioner will still be required to treat the infected patient if "a modification of policies, practices, or procedures" (in this case, universal precautions) will "eliminat[e]" the risk. § 12182(b)(3).

I agree with the Court that "[t]he existence, or nonexistence, of a significant risk must be determined from the standpoint of the person who refuses the treatment or accommodation," as of the time that the decision refusing treatment is made. I disagree with the Court, however, that "[i]n assessing the reasonableness of petitioner's actions, the views of public health authorities . . . are of special weight and authority." Those views are, of course, entitled to a presumption of validity when the actions of those authorities themselves are challenged in court, and even in disputes between private parties where Congress has committed that dispute to adjudication by a public health authority. But in litigation between private parties originating in the federal courts, I am aware of no provision of law or judicial practice that would require or permit courts to give some scientific views more credence than others simply because they have been endorsed by a politically appointed public health authority (such as the Surgeon General). In litigation of this latter sort, which is what we face here, the credentials of the scientists employed by the public health authority, and the soundness of their studies, must stand on their own. The Court cites no authority for its limitation upon the courts' truth-finding function, except the statement in *School Bd. of Nassau Cty. v. Arline*, 480 U.S., at 288, 107 S.Ct., at 1131, that in making findings regarding the risk of contagion under the Rehabilitation Act, "courts normally should defer to the reasonable medical judgments of public health officials." But there is appended to that dictum the following footnote, which makes it very clear that the Court was urging respect for *medical* judgment, and not necessarily respect for "official" medical judgment over "private" medical judgment: "This case does not present, and we do not address, the question whether courts should also defer to the reasonable medical judgments of private physicians on which an employer has relied."

Applying these principles here, it is clear to me that petitioner has presented more than enough evidence to avoid summary judgment on the "direct threat" question. In June 1994, the Centers for Disease Control and Prevention published a study identifying seven instances of possible transmission of HIV from patients to dental workers. While it is not entirely certain whether these dental workers contracted HIV during the course of providing dental treatment, the potential that the disease was transmitted during the course of dental treatment is relevant evidence. One need only demonstrate "risk," not certainty of infection. See *Arline, supra,* at 288, 107 S.Ct., at 1131 (" '[T]he probabilities the disease will be transmitted' " is a factor in assessing risk). Given the "severity of the risk" involved here, *i.e.,* near certain death, and the fact that no public health authority had outlined a protocol for *eliminating* this risk in the context of routine dental treatment, it seems likely that petitioner can establish that it was objectively reasonable for him to conclude that treating respondent in his office posed a "direct threat" to his safety.

In addition, petitioner offered evidence of 42 documented incidents of occupational transmission of HIV to health-care workers other than dental professionals. The Court of Appeals dismissed this evidence as irrelevant because these health professionals were not dentists. But the fact that the health care workers were not dentists is no more valid a basis for distinguishing these transmissions of HIV than the fact that the health care workers did not practice in Maine. At a minimum, petitioner's evidence was sufficient to create a triable issue on this question, and summary judgment was accordingly not appropriate.

HUTTON V. ELF ATOCHEM NORTH AMERICA, INC.
273 F.3d 884 (9th Cir. 2001)

TASHIMA, CIRCUIT JUDGE:

Plaintiff-Appellant Norman Hutton ("Hutton") sued his former employer, Defendant-Appellee Elf Atochem North America, Inc. ("Elf"), for disability discrimination under Title I of the Americans with Disabilities Act of 1990 ("ADA") and Oregon's disability discrimination law in state court. The case was removed to federal district court on the basis of diversity jurisdiction, where the parties consented to having the case heard by a magistrate judge under 28 U.S.C. § 636(c)(1). The district court granted Elf's motion for summary judgment, concluding that Hutton had not established that he was a qualified individual under the relevant statutes. Hutton timely filed this appeal, arguing that the existence of genuine issues of material fact regarding his ability to perform the essential functions of his job precluded summary judgment. We have jurisdiction under 28 U.S.C. §§ 636(c)(3) & 1291, and we affirm.

I.   Factual Background

Elf operates a 55-acre facility in Portland, Oregon, where it manufactures chlorine and related chemical products. The plant operates on a 24-hour-per-day basis. Hutton began working for Elf in 1986 and, in 1989, became a chlorine finishing operator, a position that he held until 1998. Elf hired Hutton with the knowledge that he had been diagnosed as a Type I diabetic.

As a chlorine finishing operator, Hutton worked a rotating shift, which meant that he was required to work seven consecutive graveyard shifts, seven consecutive swing shifts, and six consecutive day shifts, with time off between each rotation. In his position, Hutton was responsible for operating the equipment that produced, stored, and transferred liquid chlorine. The chlorine was initially pumped into the chlorine finishing department in gas form, and it was Hutton's job to operate the refrigeration unit that chilled the gas, transforming it into liquid chlorine. Once the chlorine was liquified, Hutton was responsible for transferring it into storage tanks and monitoring their capacity through a variety of gauges and instruments. As chlorine accumulated in the storage tanks, Hutton was required to transfer the liquid chlorine to waiting rail cars. To do this, it was necessary for Hutton to set the brakes on the rail cars, weigh the cars, connect hoses from the storage tank units to the rail cars, perform safety checks, open the appropriate valves, and pump the chlorine. Once the cars were filled, Hutton had to shut off the pump, close the valves, and empty the lines between the storage tanks and rail cars. There was an alarm that sounded when a rail car was almost full.

During his tenure at Elf, Hutton experienced a number of diabetic episodes. On May 17, 1989, Hutton went into insulin shock while he was pumping chlorine from the storage tanks, causing him to have difficulty communicating with his co-workers. An ambulance was called and Hutton was treated with intravenous glucose. On July 26, 1989, Hutton experienced another diabetic episode while loading a barge. After this incident, the foreman of the finishing department spoke with Hutton and asked him to commit to taking better care of himself and eating properly. Hutton again experienced a diabetic episode on August 15, 1989, as he was hurrying to fill rail cars with chlorine. On this occasion, too, an ambulance was called and Hutton was given oral glucose.

On February 9, 1992, as Hutton was talking with his replacement at the end of his shift, he had a seizure and lost consciousness. An ambulance was called and, this time, Hutton was taken to the hospital. After examining

Hutton, Dr. Richard Bills advised him to check his blood sugar before each meal and approximately two hours after receiving insulin, and to keep a record of his insulin injections and chem strip measurements.

Following this incident, in a letter dated February 25, 1992, Elf's management notified Hutton that he would be required to meet specified conditions in order to continue his employment. In particular, the letter required that Hutton remain under the supervision of Dr. Bills; provide evidence of a medical examination and laboratory blood assessment to Elf on a periodic basis; maintain a daily log related to diet, insulin intake, and certain other activities; monitor blood sugar levels and regulate insulin intake in accordance with Dr. Bills' recommendations; and submit to company requests for chem strip blood sugar tests. Hutton signed the letter, which concluded by stating that the "[f]ailure to abide by any of the above conditions, or another incident of insulin reaction or diabetic loss of function," would leave Elf with no alternative but to terminate Hutton's employment immediately. Although Hutton subsequently maintained the required daily logs, he did not always do so consistently and was not asked to produce the information.

In accordance with the company's policy of medically certifying employees, like Hutton, who were provided with respirators to protect them from chlorine gas, Elf retained Legacy Occupational Medical Clinic to conduct annual physical examinations. Under this program, Dr. John Reichle, an occupational physician, performed medical examinations of Hutton from 1993 to 1998. Each of these examinations indicated that Hutton had elevated glucose levels. During the period from 1992 to 1996, Hutton experienced at least two additional diabetic episodes, outside work, during which he lost consciousness.

On February 10, 1998, Hutton was examined by Dr. Merrill Ahrens, his primary care physician. Dr. Ahrens' notes stated that it "sounds like [Hutton] practices very loose control" and that his "[r]otating shift is a major complicating factor." Dr. Reichle's annual examination on May 26, 1998, indicated that Hutton had elevated glucose levels and high blood pressure. Since Hutton had refused to submit to a blood test, Dr. Reichle requested that Hutton obtain one from his primary physician and deferred his determination of Hutton's fitness for his position pending receipt of the blood work analysis.

In a letter to Hutton dated June 24, 1998, Larry Hellie ("Hellie"), Elf's Regional Human Resources Manager, indicated that no blood work had yet been done and stated that Hutton's completion of the annual medical examination was a condition of his employment. The letter further reiterated Hutton's commitment to adhere to the written conditions of employment signed in February 1992, and stated that "[i]f the required blood work is not completed, and the results and analysis received by Legacy Occupational Medical Clinic before close of business on Wednesday

July 1, 1998, you will be place [sic] on a leave-of-absence pending discharge." In a letter dated July 1, 1998 and addressed "To Whom It May Concern," Dr. Ahrens stated that he last examined Hutton on March 17, 1998, and that "[h]is most recent laboratory test showed a fructosamine of 302 which indicates fairly good control of his diabetes." The letter concluded by stating that "[Hutton] tells me he needs a letter stating that his diabetes is adequately controlled to continue working and this is true." Despite this letter, Dr. Reichle refused to recommend that Hutton was fit for his position.

On July 2, 1998, Hutton experienced an insulin reaction while working the day shift. Hutton felt the episode coming on and went to get some food to counter the reaction, when an alarm sounded. Hutton returned to his office area, corrected the alarm, and then experienced a several-minute period in which he felt light-headed and could not communicate.

On July 8, 1998, Hutton received a letter from Hellie stating that he was being suspended. The letter stated in relevant part:

> Your medical suspension is based on three separate issues. First, you have not provided medical information regarding blood glucose stability from your personal physician as directed in the June 24, 1998 memorandum. Second, you failed to maintain your blood glucose within appropriate levels which caused an insulin reaction on Thursday, July 2, 1998, when you stated your blood glucose had dropped to 36, borderline for severe hypoglycemia. . . . Third, you are in violation of the Last Chance Agreement signed on February 25, 1992.

The letter further required that Hutton "provide appropriate and complete medical documentation to Dr. John Reichle . . . of [his] blood glucose stability," including "a medical history and narrative report" and a "record of capillary glucose readings." The letter also directed Hutton to submit to a "fitness for duty examination at Legacy Occupational Medical Clinic." It concluded by informing Hutton that failure "to complete the above listed medical conditions before October 6, 1998" would result in termination "effective October 7, 1998."

Following Hutton's suspension, Jim O'Connor, an attorney working for Hutton's union, wrote a letter to Dr. Ahrens asking him to provide Dr. Reichle documentation regarding Hutton's blood glucose stability. On September 2, 1998, Dr. Ahrens wrote a letter "To Whom It May Concern," in which he opined that, "[g]iven his medical history and current level of control, [Hutton] is at lower than average risk of low blood sugar reactions." Dr. Ahrens recommended that Hutton "simply needs to continue a standard dietary regimen and regular blood sugar monitoring and he can return to work."

* * *

In a letter to Hellie dated September 4, 1998, Dr. Reichle stated that a review of the medical records provided by Dr. Ahrens raised "several points of concern." In particular, Dr. Reichle indicated that Hutton's diabetes was "relatively unstable" and pointed out that Dr. Ahrens "states that it is entirely unrealistic to expect Mr. Hutton not to continue to have recurrent hypoglycemic events." Dr. Reichle also noted that Hutton was "developing diminishing awareness of his hypoglycemic symptoms" and that the records reflected "areas of poor self-management of his condition." Based on these issues, Dr. Reichle refused to recommend reinstatement of Hutton to his position as chlorine finishing operator, noting that "[a]s an unsupervised operator, he would be at serious risk of death and would be placing the surrounding community at risk of a catastrophic event."

* * *

Dr. Reichle and Dr. Ahrens decided to have Hutton's condition reviewed by a neutral third-party physician in accordance with the collective bargaining agreement applicable to Hutton's position. Dr. James Prihoda, a diabetes specialist, was selected. Dr. Prihoda was provided with copies of Hutton's medical records and was asked to consider Hutton's ability to either return to his job or to work as a relief operator. Dr. Prihoda examined Hutton on January 29, 1999, and February 5, 1999. On February 5, 1999, in a letter to Hellie, Dr. Prihoda stated that Hutton's control of his diabetes had "improved to fair" and that he had "not shown increased episodes of hypoglycemia." Dr. Prihoda concluded that "[t]here are some things that may improve [Hutton's] control overall and decrease his chance for low blood sugars but it is not possible to say that he will have no further hypoglycemic episodes or no periods of altered mentation. He is though clearly not disabled by his diabetes and should be able to be a productive worker."

. . . In his letter, Dr. Prihoda also made the following observations:

> E. As far as restricting from shift work, I can't make a final determination on this. I can't state he will not have hypoglycemic episodes but with the description of his job and potential for chlorine leaks, the risk of any hypoglycemic episode is small but if the right events were to come together, the result could be catastrophic. I think this ends up being a company decision as to whether with minimizing the risk for hypoglycemia with the above recommendations, they would consider his risk of employment acceptable.

* * *

On the basis of this information, Dr. Reichle issued his "fitness for duty evaluation" to Hellie on February 25, 1999. In this letter, Dr. Reichle stated that he would not recommend that Hutton be required to work overtime or rotating shifts due to the increased risk of hypoglycemia that such a schedule would cause. Dr. Reichle also found that "[i]f Mr. Hutton is engaged in crucial tasks that potentially could result in injury to himself or a catastrophic event, he should be under the observation of someone at all times." In addition, Dr. Reichle suggested that the use of a respirator by Hutton would "significantly increase" his risk of hypoglycemia. He concluded by asserting that "[i]t seems very clear . . . that the position of third relief operator is not suitable for Mr. Hutton at this time" and recommended that Hutton be placed in the company storeroom.

* * *

In a letter dated March 22, 1999, Hellie advised Hutton that Elf had "completed a thorough and comprehensive review of the medical reports" from Dr. Ahrens, Dr. Prihoda, and Dr. Reichle. Hellie stated that the reports were "very consistent" and "were used as our guide" in considering "which available vacant positions [Hutton] might be assigned to as an accommodation." In light of the review, Hellie informed Hutton that "there is no current vacant plant position where your medical restrictions and conditions can be accommodated. However, should such a position become available, we will immediately consider you for it." Since that time, eight positions have become available at Elf in the production department, none of which the company has determined is appropriate for Hutton.

* * *

III. Discussion

Hutton argues that the district court's ruling on Elf's motion for summary judgment was erroneous in light of the factual disputes regarding whether his termination violated the ADA. The ADA provides that "[n]o covered entity shall discriminate against a qualified individual with a disability because of the disability." 42 U.S.C. § 12112(a) (1995). To prevail on an ADA claim of unlawful discharge, the plaintiff must establish a prima facie case by showing that: (1) he is a disabled person within the meaning of the statute; (2) he is a qualified individual with a disability; and (3) he suffered an adverse employment action because of his disability.

The ADA defines "qualified individual with a disability" as "an individual with a disability who, with or without reasonable accommodation, can perform the essential functions of the employment position that such individual holds or desires." 42 U.S.C. § 12111(8). This definition "includes individuals who could perform the essential functions of a reassignment position, with or without reasonable accommodation, even if they cannot perform the essential functions of the current position."

The district court found that Hutton was unable to establish the second prong of the prima facie case because he could not show that he was a "qualified person with a disability" under the ADA. In particular, the district court held that Hutton had not produced evidence to demonstrate that he was able, with or without an accommodation, to perform the essential functions of the chlorine finishing operator position. As part of this analysis, the court determined that Hutton's diabetes created a risk of significant harm to himself and others, thereby disqualifying him from the position. Hutton contends that the existence of factual disputes should have precluded summary judgment on both the essential functions and direct-threat questions. Because we conclude that summary judgment was properly granted based on the existence of a direct threat, we do not reach the issue of whether Hutton could perform the essential functions of the job.

The "direct threat" defense to a charge of employment discrimination is set forth in the "Defenses" section of the ADA:

It may be a defense to a charge of discrimination under this chapter that an alleged application of qualification standards, tests, or selection criteria that screen out or tend to screen out or otherwise deny a job or benefit to an individual with a disability has been shown to be job-related and consistent with business necessity, and such performance cannot be accomplished by reasonable accommodation, as required under this subchapter.

42 U.S.C. § 12113(a) (1995). The ADA defines "qualification standards" as including "a requirement that an individual shall not pose a direct threat to the health or safety of other individuals in the workplace." Id. § 12113(b). In regulations interpreting the direct threat provision, the Equal Employment Opportunity Commission ("EEOC") provides the following guidance:

Direct Threat means a significant risk of substantial harm to the health or safety of the individual or others that cannot be eliminated or reduced by reasonable accommodation. The determination that an individual poses a "direct threat" shall be based on an individualized assessment of the individual's present ability to safely perform the essential functions of the job. This assessment shall be based on a reasonable medical judgment that relies on the most current medical knowledge and/or on the best available objective evidence. In determining whether an individual would pose a direct threat, the factors to be considered include:

(1) The duration of the risk;

(2) The nature and severity of the potential harm;

(3) The likelihood that the potential harm will occur; and

(4) The imminence of the potential harm.

29 C.F.R. § 1630.2(r) (2000). Because it is an affirmative defense, the employer bears the burden of proving that an employee constitutes a direct threat. *Nunes v. Wal-Mart Stores, Inc.*, 164 F.3d 1243, 1247 (9th Cir.1999).

Here, there is no dispute that Hutton's continuing employment poses some potential harm to others. The parties do disagree, however, as to whether the harm is of sufficient magnitude and likelihood to disqualify Hutton from the chlorine finishing operator position.

Hutton argues that, although a risk of harm exists, it is too remote to warrant disqualification. He cites Dr. Prihoda's assessment that his risk of any hypoglycemic episode is "small" and notes that, during his lengthy tenure at Elf, he lost consciousness only once. Hutton also points to the existence of an elaborate safety system that he claims would mitigate any harm should he experience a debilitating diabetic episode on the job. For instance, he suggests that the potential for harm during the refrigeration process is small, because there are cell operators who monitor the flow of the gas and are able to detect and adjust any irregularities in the gas pressure. In addition, he asserts that the size of the storage tanks is such that the finishing operators would have to ignore their responsibilities for three full shifts in order for the tanks to approach maximum capacity. Furthermore, Hutton contends that the structural characteristics of the liquid chlorine transfer equipment—which include a safety device that releases pressure in the event of a buildup, a chlorine sensor and automatic closing system, and a warning alarm—minimize serious risk.

Even were we to agree with Hutton, however, that the likelihood of an accident is small, we conclude that the severity and scale of the potential harm to others presented by Hutton's employment nevertheless pose a significant risk under the direct-threat analysis. *See Donahue v. Consol. Rail Corp.*, 224 F.3d 226, 231 (3d Cir.2000) (stating that "[i]f the threatened harm is grievous . . . even a small risk may be 'significant' "). Indeed, the reports of Dr. Reichle and Dr. Prihoda refer to the "catastrophic" nature of the risk of chlorine spillage created by Hutton's diabetes. Hutton himself conceded that, if he were unconscious, chlorine could spill from the rail cars, convert to gas, and cause severe—potentially fatal—harm to other workers and persons near the facility. Moreover, Hutton's treating physicians agreed that the rotating shifts and prolonged hours required by the chlorine finishing operator position made it difficult for him adequately to monitor his diabetes. None of the examining or consulting physicians could rule out the occurrence of a hypoglycemic event that would affect Hutton's ability to remain conscious, alert, and communicative, especially in light of Hutton's somewhat erratic medical history. Further, during swing and graveyard shifts, a chlorine finishing operator is required to work essentially alone.

Our conclusion regarding the existence of a direct threat is supported by *Turco v. Hoechst Celanese Corp.*, 101 F.3d 1090 (5th Cir.1996) (per curiam), which held, on facts similar to those in this case, that a chemical process operator who was diabetic was unqualified for his position under the ADA due to the safety risks he imposed on himself and others. Specifically, the court in *Turco* found that the plaintiff was a "walking time bomb" since "[a]ny diabetic episode or loss of concentration occurring while operating . . . machinery or chemicals had the potential to harm . . . others." *Id.* We see no distinction between *Turco* and this case, where it is not disputed that a significant physical or mental lapse by Hutton as a result of a diabetic episode could result in substantial harm to his co-workers and others.[6]

In sum, an individualized assessment of each factor in the EEOC's four-factor test supports the conclusion that Hutton would pose a direct threat: (1) The duration of the risk would exist for as long as Hutton held the chlorine finishing operator's job; (2) The nature and severity of the potential harm is catastrophic—many lives could be lost; (3) Although the likelihood that the potential harm will occur is small, whether and when it will occur cannot be predicted; and (4) The imminence of the potential harm is, as explained, unknown because of the unpredictability of Hutton's condition. *See* 29 C.F.R. § 1630.2(r) (2000). Consequently, we conclude that there is no genuine dispute of material fact regarding whether Hutton's diabetic condition posed a direct threat to the health and safety of other individuals in the workplace.

IV. Conclusion

For the foregoing reasons, we conclude that the district court properly granted summary judgment to Elf on the ground that Hutton was not a qualified person under the ADA. The judgment of the district court is therefore

AFFIRMED.

NOTES AND QUESTIONS

1.   *Subjective vs. objective inquiry.* According to the *Bragdon* Court, does the determination of whether a direct threat exists entail a subjective or objective inquiry? Or elements of each?

2.   *Role of public health authorities.* The majority in *Bragdon* states that the views of public health authorities are entitled to special weight in assessing the existence of a direct threat. Chief Justice Rehnquist disagrees. Who has the better of this debate and why?

3.   *Patients vs. healthcare workers. Bragdon* suggests that patients with HIV usually will not pose a direct threat to health care providers. The Eleventh Circuit, on the other hand, has suggested that a healthcare worker with HIV who performs exposure-prone duties usually will pose a direct threat to patients. *Waddell v. Valley Forge Dental Associates,* Inc, 276 F.3d 1275 (11th Cir. 2001). Why the difference in outcomes? Is this appropriate?

4.   As the *Hutton* case illustrates, the issues of qualified status and direct threat may overlap in certain circumstances. In *Hutton*, the district court ruled for the employer on the grounds that the plaintiff was not a

qualified person with a disability. On appeal, the Ninth Circuit affirmed, but on the grounds that the plaintiff posed a direct threat of harm. Which issue would employers generally prefer to be the focus of judicial attention and why? And which issue is the most appropriate for resolving this case and why?

5. *CDC guidelines regarding HIV.* The Center for Disease Control adopted guidelines in 1991 for healthcare workers. Since the risk of HIV transmission for most healthcare workers is low, the CDC does not recommend individual testing, but advises that workers follow universal precautions. For those healthcare workers who are engaged in exposure-prone procedures, the CDC recommends that such workers should self-monitor their health status and, if HIV positive, discontinue those duties until they consult with a panel of experts.

6. *Risk to self.* Section 12111(3) of the ADA defines "direct threat" as a significant risk to the health or safety of "others." The EEOC's regulations in 29 CFR § 1630.2(r), however, extend the direct threat concept to include risks posed to the health or safety "of the individual or others," and the Supreme Court upheld the regulation in *Chevron U.S.A., Inc. v. Echazabal*, 536 U.S. 73, 122 S.Ct. 2045 (2002). What policy considerations favor extending the direct threat concept to include risks directed at oneself? What policy considerations disfavor this broader coverage?

7. *Burden of proof.* Which party should bear the burden of proof to show the existence of a direct threat? Some courts have placed the burden on the employee as part of the qualified analysis, while others have placed the burden on the employer as an affirmative defense. The Tenth Circuit has adopted a middle approach that places the burden on an employee whose essential job duties implicate safety, but otherwise places the burden on the employer. McKenzie v. Benton, 388 F.3d 1342 (10th Cir. 2004). Which approach do you prefer and why?

8. *Dueling defenses.* In some cases, when an employer imposes a standard that is safety-related, there might be confusion regarding which defense the employer must prove. For instance, in *EEOC v. Exxon Corp.*, 203 F.3d 871 (5th Cir. 2000), the court had to decide whether the employer had to justify its substance abuse policy (which permanently precluded an employee who had undergone treatment for substance abuse from certain safety-sensitive positions) based on the "business necessity" standard (discussed in *Bates*) or on the arguably more difficult "direct threat" standard. The EEOC, relying on its interpretive guidance, argued that when an employer's safety requirement screens out or tends to screen out an individual with a disability, an employer must demonstrate that the requirement is justified using the direct threat standard. The court disagreed, explaining that the difference between the two standards is that the business necessity standard applies to across-the board rules, while the direct threat defense addresses a standard imposed on a particular individual. Thus, relying on the statutory language and the legislative history, the court held that an employer need not proceed under the direct threat provision in cases where an employer has developed a standard applicable to all employees of a given class; instead, the employer

must defend the standard as a business necessity. The direct threat defense, in contrast, applies to cases in which an employer responds to an individual employee's supposed risk that is not addressed by an existing qualification standard.

For a comparison of the direct threat and business necessity defenses, see Stephen F. Befort, *Direct Threat and Business Necessity: Understanding and Untangling Two ADA Defenses*, 39 BERKELEY J. EMP. & LAB. L. 377 (2018). With regard to the type of issue posed by the *Exxon* case, Professor Befort offers the following suggested framework for analysis:

> An employer generally should have the right to establish qualification standards that have a sufficient business necessity nexus to safety and job performance. But, if such a policy either directly or indirectly tends to screen out individuals with a substance addiction, the employer should be required to give the individual an opportunity for an individualized assessment. Analogizing to the EEOC's guidance regarding past criminal records, factors that might be relevant to an individualized assessment in the context of substance addiction are the nature of the job in question, the length of the individual's period of sobriety, and the steps taken by the individual to deter recidivism. Ultimately, an employer should consider this additional individualized information when determining whether the exclusion is job-related and consistent with business necessity.

Id. at 413. Do you agree with this suggested mode of analysis? Why or why not?

CHAPTER 4

EMPLOYMENT DISCRIMINATION: CONTEXTUAL APPLICATIONS

■ ■ ■

A. ILLEGAL DRUG AND ALCOHOL USE

Section 12114 of the ADA provides as follows:

(a) Qualified individual with a disability

For purposes of this subchapter, a qualified individual with a disability shall not include any employee or applicant who is currently engaging in the illegal use of drugs, when the covered entity acts on the basis of such use.

(b) Rules of construction

Nothing in subsection (a) of this section shall be construed to exclude as a qualified individual with a disability an individual who

> (1) has successfully completed a supervised drug rehabilitation program and is no longer engaging in the illegal use of drugs, or has otherwise been rehabilitated successfully and is no longer engaging in such use;
>
> (2) is participating in a supervised rehabilitation program and is no longer engaging in such use; or
>
> (3) is erroneously regarded as engaging in such use, but is not engaging in such use;
>
> except that it shall not be a violation of this chapter for a covered entity to adopt or administer reasonable policies or procedures, including but not limited to drug testing, designed to ensure that an individual described in paragraph (1) or (2) is no longer engaging in the illegal use of drugs.

(c) Authority of covered entity

A covered entity

> (1) may prohibit the illegal use of drugs and the use of alcohol at the workplace by all employees;

(2) may require that employees shall not be under the influence of alcohol or be engaging in the illegal use of drugs at the workplace

(3) may require that employees behave in conformance with the requirements established under the Drug-Free Workplace Act of 1988;

(4) may hold an employee who engages in the illegal use of drugs or who is an alcoholic to the same qualification standards for employment or job performance and behavior that such entity holds other employees, even if any unsatisfactory performance or behavior is related to the drug use or alcoholism of such employee. . . .

(d) Drug testing

(1) In general

For purposes of this subchapter, a test to determine the illegal use of drugs shall not be considered a medical examination.

(2) Construction

Nothing in this subchapter shall be construed to encourage, prohibit, restrict, or authorize the conducting of drug testing for the illegal use of drugs by job applicants or employees or making employment decisions based on such test results.

ZENOR V. EL PASO HEALTHCARE SYSTEM
176 F.3d 847 (5th Cir. 1999)

GARWOOD, CIRCUIT JUDGE:

Plaintiff-appellant Tom Zenor (Zenor) appeals the district court's grant of judgment as a matter of law in favor of his former employer, Vista Hills Medical Center, now defendant-appellee El Paso Healthcare Ltd., d/b/a/ Columbia Medical Center-East (Columbia). We affirm.

Facts and Proceedings Below

In 1991, Columbia hired Zenor to work as a pharmacist in the pharmacy at its Columbia Medical Center-East hospital. When Zenor began his employment, he received an employment manual expressing the at-will nature of his employment and disclaiming any contractual obligations between the employer and employee. Zenor also received a copy of Vista Hill's then-existing drug and alcohol policy. In 1993, Zenor received a copy of Columbia's Drug-Free/Alcohol-Free Workplace Policy (the Policy), which was in effect at all times relevant to this case.

In 1993, Zenor became addicted to cocaine. Between 1993 and 1995, Zenor injected himself with cocaine as many as four to five times a week. He also smoked marijuana on three or four occasions and more frequently used tranquilizers to offset the cocaine's effects. Despite his drug use, Zenor remained a generally adequate employee and usually received favorable employment evaluations. However, his evaluation for the year ended July 8, 1994, discussed with Zenor in October 1994, was not favorable, his performance was rated "below average," and he was placed in a probationary status for two months with the admonishment that discharge was possible if insufficient improvement were noted. Zenor successfully completed the probationary status. The record does not show any subsequent annual evaluation. Zenor testified he never used drugs at work, nor came to work under the influence of drugs. Columbia was unaware of Zenor's addiction until August 15, 1995.

Zenor had been working the night shift at the pharmacy. When Zenor left work on August 15, 1995, at approximately 8:30 a.m., he injected himself with cocaine. As Zenor prepared to return to work that night, he became dizzy and had difficulty walking. Suspecting that he was still impaired from the morning's cocaine injection, Zenor called the pharmacy director, Joe Quintana (Quintana), and stated that he could not report to work because he was under the influence of cocaine. During the conversation, Quintana asked whether Zenor would take advantage of Columbia's Employee Assistance Program, "ACCESS." Zenor replied that he would. Quintana then stated that he was on vacation, and instructed Zenor to contact Quintana's supervisor, Paschall Ike (Ike).

Zenor spoke to Ike, who was also on vacation and told Zenor to call his (Zenor's) own doctor. Zenor then called his personal physician, who arranged for Zenor to receive emergency treatment that evening. Zenor stayed overnight at R.E. Thomason General Hospital. The next morning, Zenor was transferred to the El Paso Alcohol and Drug Abuse Service Detox Center, where he remained hospitalized for nine days.

On August 23, while still at the Detox Center, Zenor became concerned about losing his job. Zenor and one of his Detox Center counselors, Pete McMillian (McMillian), contacted Yolanda Mendoza (Mendoza), Columbia's Human Resources Director. This was the first time Zenor had contacted Columbia since his conversation with Ike eight days earlier. Nobody at Columbia knew where Zenor had been since the night of August 15.

Zenor told Mendoza that he wished to enter a rehabilitation program and asked her whether his job would be secure until he returned. Although the evidence is disputed, there is evidence that Mendoza assured Zenor that his job would be secure until he completed the program. Mendoza then told McMillan that Zenor was eligible for a twelve-week leave of absence under the Family Medical Leave Act (FMLA), 29 U.S.C. § 2601 et. seq. Later that afternoon, McMillian retrieved from Mendoza the paperwork necessary for Zenor to take FMLA leave. Zenor completed the paperwork. The next day, August 24, Zenor checked into an independent residential rehabilitation facility, Landmark Adult Intensive Residential Services Center (Landmark). Landmark was not owned or operated by Columbia and was not part of its ACCESS program.

After consulting with Columbia's lawyers, Mendoza and Quintana decided to terminate Zenor's employment. On September 20, 1995, Mendoza, Quintana, and ACCESS director Joe Provencio had a meeting with Zenor, his Landmark counselor, and Landmark's Director of Adult Treatment Services Dorrance Guy (Guy). Zenor was told that he would remain an employee of Columbia until his medical leave expired, and then he would be terminated.

Zenor protested that Columbia could not fire him because the Policy stated that employees who completed rehabilitation would be returned to work. Zenor also argued that he had been told if he "self-reported" his addiction he would not be fired. Mendoza explained that Columbia was concerned because pharmaceutical cocaine would be readily available to Zenor in the pharmacy, and therefore Columbia would not allow Zenor to return to work.

Zenor offered to transfer to a day shift where he could be monitored, or to a satellite pharmacy where pharmaceutical cocaine would not be available. Columbia rejected these suggestions. The next day Guy wrote a letter to Provencio calling Columbia's action unfair, and contrary to Guy's interpretation of the Policy. Columbia did not respond to the letter.

Zenor completed the residential portion of his treatment program and was released from Landmark on October 9, 1995. On October 18, Zenor met with Mendoza and again asked to keep his job. Mendoza told Zenor that his termination stood. Zenor then requested that Mendoza write an official letter regarding his termination, in order to assist Zenor in continuing his medical benefits.

Zenor later sued Columbia, alleging that he was fired in violation of the Americans with Disabilities Act (ADA). . . .

Following discovery, Columbia moved for summary judgment. The district court . . . denied summary judgment on the [disability discrimination claim]. The case proceeded to trial. . . . At the conclusion of Zenor's case-in-chief, Columbia moved for judgment as a matter of law. The district court granted Columbia judgment as a matter of law on Zenor's disability discrimination . . . [claim]. . . .

Discussion

I.   The ADA

The ADA, 42 U.S.C. § 12101 *et. seq.*, prohibits an employer from discriminating against a "qualified individual with a disability" on the basis of that disability. 42 U.S.C. § 12112(a). To establish a *prima facie* discrimination claim under the ADA, a plaintiff must prove: (1) that he has a disability; (2) that he was qualified for the job; (3) that he was subject to an adverse employment decision on account of his disability.

At the close of Zenor's case-in-chief, the district court found insufficient evidence to support the ADA claim and granted Columbia's motion for judgment as a matter of law. On appeal, the parties raise three separate questions with respect to the ADA claim: (1) whether Zenor was disqualified from the ADA's protection because he was a "current user" of illegal drugs at the relevant time, (2) whether Zenor was an otherwise qualified individual, and (3) whether Zenor established that he suffered from a disability. . . .

The district court correctly granted judgment in favor of Columbia. First, Zenor is excluded from the definition of "qualified individual" under the ADA because he was a current user of illegal drugs. Similarly, due to Zenor's cocaine use, he was not otherwise qualified for the job of a pharmacist. Alternatively, regardless of whether Zenor was a current user of illegal drugs, Zenor failed to prove that he was disabled within the meaning of the statute.

The first issue is whether Zenor was "currently engaging in the illegal use of drugs" at the time the adverse employment action was taken. 42 U.S.C. § 12114 specifically exempts current illegal drug users from the definition of qualified individuals. *See* 42 U.S.C. § 12114(a) ("For purposes of this title, the term 'qualified individual with a disability' shall not include any employee or applicant who is currently engaging in the illegal use of drugs, when the covered entity acts on the basis of such use."). In other words, federal law does not proscribe an employer's firing someone who currently uses illegal drugs, regardless of whether or not that drug use could otherwise be considered a disability. The issue in this case, therefore, is whether Zenor was a "current" drug user within the meaning of the statute.

As a threshold matter, this Court must determine the proper time at which to evaluate whether Zenor was "currently engaging in the illegal use of drugs." Zenor urges this Court to look to the date his employment status officially ended: November 24, 1995. The Second Circuit adopted this approach in *Teahan v. Metro-North Commuter R.R. Co.*, 951 F.2d 511 (2d Cir. 1991). Teahan was an alcoholic who had missed an extensive amount of work due to his alcoholism. On December 28, 1987, Metro-North wrote a letter informing Teahan that his employment was terminated. That same day, before receiving the termination letter, Teahan voluntarily entered a rehabilitation program. While Teahan was in the rehabilitation program, Metro-North initiated procedures to fire Teahan pursuant to its collective bargaining agreement with the International Brotherhood of Electrical Workers (IBEW). However, the disciplinary procedures were not complete on January 28, 1988, when Teahan completed the rehabilitation program. Pursuant to its agreement with IBEW, therefore, Metro-North permitted Teahan to return to work temporarily. Metro-North finally terminated Teahan on April 11, 1989.

Teahan sued Metro-North, alleging that his dismissal violated the Rehabilitation Act. Teahan alleged that his absenteeism was caused solely by his alcoholism; since the Second Circuit considered alcoholism a handicap under the Rehabilitation Act, Teahan alleged that Metro-North fired him solely by reason of his handicap. Like the current ADA, the Rehabilitation Act did not protect "an alcoholic whose current use of alcohol prevents such individual from performing the duties of the job in question." The case therefore turned on whether Teahan was a current abuser of alcohol at the relevant time.

Metro-North asked the court to consider Teahan's status as a current alcohol abuser on December 28, 1987, at which time Metro-North began procedures to fire Teahan, although it was legally unable to do so until April 11, 1989. The Second Circuit disagreed, and decided instead to focus on the date on which Teahan was actually fired. The court reasoned that the word "current" within the statute prohibited an employer from firing an employee based on past substance abuse problems that the employee had overcome. That court feared that Metro-North's theory would create a loophole which would expose recovering substance abusers to retroactive punishment. Therefore, the court looked to the April 11, 1989, actual termination date to determine whether the drug use was current.

This Court has already, at least implicitly, rejected the Second Circuit's approach. *See McDaniel v. Mississippi Baptist Medical Center*, 877 F.Supp. 321 (S.D.Miss.1995) (interpreting current user provision under the ADA), *aff'd* 74 F.3d 1238 (5th Cir.1995). McDaniel was a recovered substance abuser who worked as an adolescent marketing representative for a substance abuse recovery program. On or around September 2, 1992, McDaniel voluntarily entered a rehabilitation program after suffering a relapse. On September 1, the day before McDaniel entered the program, McDaniel's employer notified him that he would not return to his current position but might be transferred within the company. The employer subsequently fired McDaniel on September 20, 1992.

McDaniel argued that he was not a current drug user on September 20, the date he was fired, and therefore he was protected by the ADA. The court disagreed, finding that the relevant adverse employment action was conveyed to McDaniel on September 1, before he entered the rehabilitation program. At that time, McDaniel was a current user of illegal drugs.

Similarly, the relevant adverse employment action in this case occurred on September 20, 1995, when Quintana and Mendoza informed Zenor that he would be terminated upon the expiration of his medical leave. We do not share the Second Circuit's fear that considering the notification date, rather than the actual termination date, creates a loophole by which employers can punish recovered addicts. There is nothing to suggest that Columbia was in any way punishing Zenor. Instead, Columbia was carrying out its rational and legally sound decision not to employ illegal cocaine users in its hospital pharmacy.

Looking to the notification of termination date provides a fair remedy both to the employer and employee. Otherwise, in this case, Columbia would effectively be penalized for allowing Zenor to take a medical leave of absence rather than terminating him right away. Such a ruling would encourage employers in Columbia's position to hasten effectuation of employment decisions, which could have adverse effects for employees who would benefit from remaining in an employee status, such as by retaining employer-provided health and insurance benefits, during their recovery programs.

Zenor suggests that he did not know with certainty whether he would be fired on September 20. However, this argument is untenable. Columbia representatives undisputably told Zenor he was being terminated September 20. Indeed, Zenor's counsel argued such to the jury in his closing argument: "They came to the Landmark Center on September 20th of 1995, and they told him, Mr. Zenor, we know we've made some promises, but we're going to fire you anyway." Zenor admits in his testimony that at this September 20 meeting "they said they were planning to terminate me." Zenor's witness Guy, Landmark's director present at the meeting on Zenor's behalf, testified on direct examination that at the meeting Columbia's "Mrs. Mendoza repeated the fact that he [Zenor] would not be taken back on staff there upon completion of the program" and that he protested but the meeting "broke up with Tom [Zenor] was still not going back to Columbia." On cross-examination, Guy agreed "there was no doubt in your mind at the end of that meeting on September 20th, that Columbia intended to fire Mr. Zenor." Furthermore, Guy's letter dated September 21, written on Zenor's behalf and calling Columbia's action unfair, also reflects that Zenor understood that he was being fired.

Nonetheless, Zenor persists in disputing that he understood the meaning of those statements. Zenor testified that although he was told on September 20 that he would be fired, he retained "the impression" that he "might" get his job back because "she [Mendoza] didn't say it was written in stone at that point that I might be, you know. She didn't say, you definitely will not get your job back." Such speculation or confusion on Zenor's part was unreasonable and cannot be attributed to any action or inaction by Columbia. Finally, Zenor suggests that he was surprised and "emotionally destroyed" to receive his termination letter on November 24. This is likewise legally unavailing in light of the foregoing and the undisputed evidence that Mendoza wrote that letter at Zenor's request, in order to help Zenor continue his health care benefits.

Columbia decided to terminate Zenor on or before September 20, 1995, and that decision was adequately conveyed to Zenor on September 20, 1995. The relevant employment action for Zenor's ADA case thus occurred on September 20, 1995. Therefore, the question is whether Zenor, who had used cocaine on August 15, 1995, was currently engaging in the illegal use of drugs when Columbia informed him on September 20, 1995, of its decision to terminate him. We conclude, as a matter of law, that he was.

Under the ADA, "currently" means that the drug use was sufficiently recent to justify the employer's reasonable belief that the drug abuse remained an ongoing problem. *See* 143 Cong. Rec. H 103–01 (1997). Thus, the characterization of "currently engaging in the illegal use of drugs" is properly applied to persons who have used illegal drugs in the weeks and months preceding a negative employment action.

In *McDaniel*, the district court held that an individual who had used drugs six weeks prior to being notified of his termination was not protected by the ADA. The Fourth and Ninth Circuits have similarly concluded that persons who had used illegal drugs in the weeks and months prior to being fired from their jobs were current drug users for purposes of the ADA. *See Shafer v. Preston Memorial Hospital Corp.*, 107 F.3d 274, 278 (4th Cir.1997); *Collings [v. Longview Fibre Co.]*, 63 F.3d [828,] 833 [(9th Cir. 1995)]. "Therefore, the fact that the employees may have been drug-free on the day of their discharge is not dispositive." *Id.*

In *Shafer*, the Fourth Circuit interpreted the phrase "currently engaging in the illegal use of drugs" to encompass a woman who had used illegal drugs approximately three weeks before she was fired from her job, and had in the interim enrolled in a rehabilitation program. The plaintiff in that case argued that the term current should mean, "at the precise time," or "at the exact moment." The Fourth Circuit rejected that interpretation. The term "currently," when modifying the phrase "engaging in the illegal use of drugs" should be construed in its broader sense, "mean[ing] a periodic or ongoing activity in which a person engages (even if doing something else at the precise moment) that has not yet permanently ended." Indeed, "the ordinary or natural meaning of the phrase 'currently using drugs' does not require that a drug user have a heroin syringe in his arm or a marijuana bong to his mouth at the exact moment contemplated." Thus, the plaintiff who had engaged in illegal drug use three weeks before her termination was currently engaging in illegal drug use at the time she was fired.

These holdings reflect Congress's unambiguous intent that "[t]he [current user] provision is not intended to be limited to persons who use drugs on the day of, or within a matter of days *or weeks* before, the employment action in question." H.R.Rep. No. 101–596, at 64 (1990), U.S. Code Cong. & Admin. News at 565, 573. *See also* 143 Cong. Rec. H 103–01 (1997) ("Current illegal use of drugs means illegal use of drugs that occurred recently enough to justify a reasonable belief that a person's drug use is current or that continuing use is a real and ongoing problem.").

The EEOC Compliance Manual on Title I of the ADA also supports this interpretation.

> 'Current' drug use means that the illegal use of drugs occurred recently enough to justify an employer's reasonable belief that involvement with drugs is an on-going problem. It is *not limited to* the day of use, or *recent weeks* or days, in terms of an employment action. It is determined on a case-by-case basis.

Additionally, the Second Circuit has suggested several factors which courts should examine to determine whether a person is a current substance abuser, including "the level of responsibility entrusted to the employee; the employer's applicable job and performance requirements; the level of competence ordinarily required to adequately perform the task in question; and the employee's past performance record." Rather than focusing solely on the timing of the employee's drug use, courts should consider whether an employer could reasonably conclude that the employee's substance abuse prohibited the employee from performing the essential job duties.

Zenor admits to having used cocaine as much as five times a week for approximately two years and to having been addicted. On September 20, 1995, Zenor had refrained from using cocaine for only five weeks, all while having been hospitalized or in a residential program. Such a short period of abstinence, particularly following such a severe drug problem, does not remove from the employer's mind a reasonable belief that the drug use remains a problem. Zenor's position as a pharmacist required a great deal of care and skill, and Zenor admits that any mistakes could gravely injure Columbia's patients. Moreover, Columbia presented substantial testimony about the extremely high relapse rate of cocaine addiction. Zenor's own counselors, while supportive and speaking highly of Zenor's progress, could not say with any real assurance that Zenor wouldn't relapse. Finally, Columbia presented substantial evidence regarding the on-going nature of cocaine-addiction recovery. The fact that Zenor completed the residential portion of his treatment was only the first step in a long-term recovery program. Based on these factors, Columbia was justified in believing that the risk of harm from a potential relapse was significant, and that Zenor's drug abuse remained an ongoing threat.

Nonetheless, Zenor argues that because he voluntarily enrolled in a rehabilitation program, he is entitled to protection under the ADA's "safe harbor" provision for drug users. The safe harbor provides an exception to

EMPLOYMENT DISCRIMINATION:
246   **CONTEXTUAL APPLICATIONS**   **CH. 4**

the current user exclusion of 42 U.S.C. § 12114(a) for individuals who are rehabilitated and no longer using drugs. *See* 42 U.S.C. § 12114(b):

> (b) Rules of construction. Nothing in subsection (a) shall be construed to exclude as a qualified individual with a disability an individual who—
>
>> (1) has successfully completed a supervised drug rehabilitation program and is no longer engaging in the illegal use of drugs, or has otherwise been rehabilitated successfully and is no longer engaging in such use; [or]
>>
>> (2) is participating in a supervised rehabilitation program and is no longer engaging in such use. . . .

However, the mere fact that an employee has entered a rehabilitation program does not automatically bring that employee within the safe harbor's protection. Instead, the House Report explains that the safe harbor provision applies only to individuals who have been drug-free for a significant period of time.

Zenor argues that he should be protected by the safe harbor provision because he "self-reported" his addiction and voluntarily entered the rehabilitation program. At least one court has distinguished employees who voluntarily seek help for their addictions from those employees who are caught by employers using drugs. *See Grimes v. U.S. Postal Serv.*, 872 F.Supp. 668, 675 (W.D.Mo.1994) (denying federal employee's Rehabilitation Act claim after employee was caught selling marijuana and noting that the Act "is designed to protect a drug addict who voluntarily identifies his problem, seeks assistance, and stops using illegal drugs.").

However, other courts have rejected the proposition that a "chemically dependent person . . . who is currently engaging in illegal drug use[ ] can escape termination by enrolling himself in a drug treatment program before he is caught by the employer.". These holdings better align with Congress' explicit statement that a plaintiff may not evade termination merely by entering into a rehabilitation program, without first showing a significant period of recovery. Thus, to the extent that Zenor's claim of "selfreporting" is genuine, it does not propel Zenor into the safe harbor's protection simply because he had entered a rehabilitation program before the adverse employment action was taken.

For similar reasons, Columbia was free to find that Zenor was not a "qualified individual" even in the absence of the statutory exclusion for illegal drug users. A qualified individual under the ADA must be able to perform essential job requirements. *See* 42 U.S.C. § 12111. The ADA directs courts to consider employers' definitions of essential job requirements. *See* 42 U.S.C. § 12111(8). Columbia reasonably may have felt that having a pharmacist who had recently been treated for cocaine addiction undermined the integrity of its hospital pharmacy operation.

Columbia was also entitled to consider the relapse rate for cocaine addiction in determining that Zenor was not qualified to work as a pharmacist. As noted, cocaine addiction has a very high relapse rate, and the risk of harm from a potential relapse was great.

Finally, this evidence should be viewed in light of what was known to Columbia on the date it fired Zenor. *See Teahan,* 951 F.2d at 521 (holding that inquiry into whether employee is otherwise qualified is "forward-looking"). Thus, the fact that Zenor has not thereafter relapsed does not affect the reasonableness of Columbia's decision on September 20, 1995. . . .

RAYTHEON CO. V. HERNANDEZ
540 U.S. 44, 124 S.Ct. 513 (2003)

JUSTICE THOMAS delivered the opinion of the Court.

The Americans with Disabilities Act of 1990 makes it unlawful for an employer, with respect to hiring, to "discriminate against a qualified individual with a disability because of the disability of such individual." § 12112(a). We are asked to decide in this case whether the ADA confers preferential rehire rights on disabled employees lawfully terminated for violating workplace conduct rules. The United States Court of Appeals for the Ninth Circuit held that an employer's unwritten policy not to rehire employees who left the company for violating personal conduct rules contravenes the ADA, at least as applied to employees who were lawfully forced to resign for illegal drug use but have since been rehabilitated. Because the Ninth Circuit improperly applied a disparate-impact analysis in a disparate-treatment case in order to reach this holding, we vacate its judgment and remand the case for further proceedings consistent with this opinion. We do not, however, reach the question on which we granted certiorari.

I

Respondent, Joel Hernandez, worked for Hughes Missile Systems for 25 years. On July 11, 1991, respondent's appearance and behavior at work suggested that he might be under the influence of drugs or alcohol. Pursuant to company policy, respondent took a drug test, which came back positive for cocaine. Respondent subsequently admitted that he had been up late drinking beer and using cocaine the night before the test. Because respondent's behavior violated petitioner's workplace conduct rules, respondent was forced to resign. Respondent's "Employee Separation Summary" indicated as the reason for separation: "discharge for personal conduct (quit in lieu of discharge)."

More than two years later, on January 24, 1994, respondent applied to be rehired by petitioner. Respondent stated on his application that he had previously been employed by petitioner. He also attached two reference letters to the application, one from his pastor, stating that respondent was a "faithful and active member" of the church, and the other from an Alcoholics Anonymous counselor, stating that respondent attends Alcoholics Anonymous meetings regularly and is in recovery.

Joanne Bockmiller, an employee in the company's Labor Relations Department, reviewed respondent's application. Bockmiller testified in her deposition that since respondent's application disclosed his prior employment with the company, she pulled his personnel file and reviewed his employee separation summary. She then rejected respondent's application. Bockmiller insisted that the company had a policy against rehiring employees who were terminated for workplace misconduct. Thus, when she reviewed the employment separation summary and found that respondent had been discharged for violating workplace conduct rules, she rejected respondent's application. She testified, in particular, that she did not know that respondent was a former drug addict when she made the employment decision and did not see anything that would constitute a "record of" addiction.

Respondent subsequently filed a charge with the Equal Employment Opportunity Commission (EEOC). Respondent's charge of discrimination indicated that petitioner did not give him a reason for his nonselection, but that respondent believed he had been discriminated against in violation of the ADA.

Petitioner responded to the charge by submitting a letter to the EEOC, in which George M. Medina, Sr., Manager of Diversity Development, wrote:

> The ADA specifically exempts from protection individuals currently engaging in the illegal use of drugs when the covered entity acts on the basis of that use. Contrary to Complainant's unfounded allegation, his non-selection for rehire is not based on any legitimate disability. Rather, Complainant's application was rejected based on his demonstrated drug use while previously employed and the complete lack of evidence indicating successful drug rehabilitation.

> The Company maintains it's [sic] right to deny re-employment to employees terminated for violation of Company rules and regulations. . . . Complainant has provided no evidence to alter the Company's position that Complainant's conduct while employed by [petitioner] makes him ineligible for rehire.

This response, together with evidence that the letters submitted with respondent's employment application may have alerted Bockmiller to the reason for respondent's prior termination, led the EEOC to conclude that petitioner may have "rejected [respondent's] application based on his record of past alcohol and drug use." The EEOC thus found that there was "reasonable cause to believe that [respondent] was denied hire to the position of Product Test Specialist because of his disability." The EEOC issued a right-to-sue letter, and respondent subsequently filed this action alleging a violation of the ADA.

Respondent proceeded through discovery on the theory that the company rejected his application because of his record of drug addiction and/or because he was regarded as being a drug addict. In response to petitioner's motion for summary judgment, respondent for the first time argued in the alternative that if the company really did apply a neutral no-rehire policy in his case, petitioner still violated the ADA because such a policy has a disparate impact. The District Court granted petitioner's motion for summary judgment with respect to respondent's disparate-treatment claim. However, the District Court refused to consider respondent's disparate-impact claim because respondent had failed to plead or raise the theory in a timely manner.

The Court of Appeals agreed with the District Court that respondent had failed timely to raise his disparate-impact claim. In addressing respondent's disparate-treatment claim, the Court of Appeals proceeded under the familiar burden-shifting approach first adopted by this Court in *McDonnell Douglas Corp. v. Green,* 411 U.S. 792, 93 S.Ct. 1817 (1973). First, the Ninth Circuit found that with respect to respondent's prima facie case of discrimination, there were genuine issues of material fact regarding whether respondent was qualified for the position for which he sought to be rehired, and whether the reason for petitioner's refusal to rehire him was his past record of drug addiction. The Court of Appeals thus held that with respect to respondent's prima facie case of discrimination, respondent had proffered sufficient evidence to preclude a grant of summary judgment. Because petitioner does not challenge this aspect of the Ninth Circuit's decision, we do not address it here.

The Court of Appeals then moved to the next step of *McDonnell Douglas,* where the burden shifts to the defendant to provide a legitimate, nondiscriminatory reason for its employment action. Here, petitioner contends that Bockmiller applied the neutral policy against rehiring employees previously terminated for violating workplace conduct rules and that this neutral company policy constituted a legitimate and nondiscriminatory reason for its decision not to rehire respondent. The Court of Appeals, although admitting that petitioner's no-rehire rule was lawful on its face, held the policy to be unlawful "as applied to former drug addicts whose only work-related offense was testing positive because of their addiction." The Court of Appeals concluded that petitioner's application of a neutral no-rehire policy was not a legitimate, nondiscriminatory reason for rejecting respondent's application:

> Maintaining a blanket policy against rehire of *all* former employees who violated company policy not only screens out persons with a record of addiction who have been successfully

rehabilitated, but may well result, as [petitioner] contends it did here, in the staff member who makes the employment decision remaining unaware of the 'disability' and thus of the fact that she is committing an unlawful act. . . . Additionally, we hold that a policy that serves to bar the reemployment of a drug addict despite his successful rehabilitation violates the ADA.

In other words, while ostensibly evaluating whether petitioner had proffered a legitimate, nondiscriminatory reason for failing to rehire respondent sufficient to rebut respondent's prima facie showing of disparate treatment, the Court of Appeals held that a neutral no-rehire policy could never suffice in a case where the employee was terminated for illegal drug use, because such a policy has a disparate impact on recovering drug addicts. In so holding, the Court of Appeals erred by conflating the analytical framework for disparate-impact and disparate-treatment claims. Had the Court of Appeals correctly applied the disparate-treatment framework, it would have been obliged to conclude that a neutral no-rehire policy is, by definition, a legitimate, nondiscriminatory reason under the ADA. And thus the only remaining question would be whether respondent could produce sufficient evidence from which a jury could conclude that "petitioner's stated reason for respondent's rejection was in fact pretext."

II

This Court has consistently recognized a distinction between claims of discrimination based on disparate treatment and claims of discrimination based on disparate impact. The Court has said that " '[d]isparate treatment' . . . is the most easily understood type of discrimination. The employer simply treats some people less favorably than others because of their race, color, religion, sex, or [other protected characteristic]." Liability in a disparate-treatment case "depends on whether the protected trait . . . actually motivated the employer's decision." By contrast, disparate-impact claims "involve employment practices that are facially neutral in their treatment of different groups but that in fact fall more harshly on one group than another and cannot be justified by business necessity." Under a disparate-impact theory of discrimination, "a facially neutral employment practice may be deemed [illegally discriminatory] without evidence of the employer's subjective intent to discriminate that is required in a 'disparate-treatment' case."

Both disparate-treatment and disparate-impact claims are cognizable under the ADA. Because "the factual issues, and therefore the character of the evidence presented, differ when the plaintiff claims that a facially neutral employment policy has a discriminatory impact on protected classes," courts must be careful to distinguish between these theories. Here, respondent did not timely pursue a disparate-impact claim. Rather, the District Court concluded, and the Court of Appeals agreed, that respondent's case was limited to a disparate-treatment theory, that the company refused to rehire respondent because it regarded respondent as being disabled and/or because of respondent's record of a disability.

Petitioner's proffer of its neutral no-rehire policy plainly satisfied its obligation under *McDonnell Douglas* to provide a legitimate, nondiscriminatory reason for refusing to rehire respondent. Thus, the only relevant question before the Court of Appeals, after petitioner presented a neutral explanation for its decision not to rehire respondent, was whether there was sufficient evidence from which a jury could conclude that petitioner did make its employment decision based on respondent's status as disabled despite petitioner's proffered explanation. Instead, the Court of Appeals concluded that, as a matter of law, a neutral no-rehire policy was not a legitimate, nondiscriminatory reason sufficient to defeat a prima facie case of discrimination. The Court of Appeals did not even attempt, in the remainder of its opinion, to treat this claim as one involving only disparate treatment. Instead, the Court of Appeals observed that petitioner's policy "screens out persons with a record of addiction," and further noted that the company had not raised a business necessity defense, factors that pertain to disparate-impact claims but not disparate-treatment claims. By improperly focusing on these factors, the Court of Appeals ignored the fact that petitioner's no-rehire policy is a quintessential legitimate, nondiscriminatory reason for refusing to rehire an employee who was terminated for violating workplace conduct rules. If petitioner did indeed apply a neutral, generally applicable no-rehire policy in rejecting respondent's application, petitioner's decision not to rehire respondent can, in no way, be said to have been motivated by respondent's disability.

The Court of Appeals rejected petitioner's legitimate, nondiscriminatory reason for refusing to rehire respondent because it "serves to bar the re-employment of a drug addict despite his successful rehabilitation." We hold that such an analysis is inapplicable to a disparate-treatment claim. Once respondent had made a prima facie showing of discrimination, the next question for the Court of Appeals was whether petitioner offered a legitimate, nondiscriminatory reason for its actions so as to demonstrate that its actions were not motivated by respondent's disability. To the extent that the Court of Appeals strayed from this task by considering not only discriminatory intent but also discriminatory impact, we vacate its judgment and remand the case for further proceedings consistent with this opinion.

NOTES AND QUESTIONS

1. *After the ADAAA.* Are all individuals who were once addicted to either illegal drugs or alcohol now protected as individuals with a disability following the enactment of the ADA Amendments Act? How would you characterize their claim for disability status?

2.   *Policy perspective.* Make a list of the competing policy arguments for the positions asserted by Zenor and by El Paso Healthcare System. Which set of policy considerations do you find most persuasive? How long do you think that an employee like Zenor has to be drug free before he can claim the protection of Section 12114(b)'s safe harbor provision?

3.   *Rum vs. coke.* Would it have made any difference if Zenor had been abusing alcohol rather than cocaine?

4.   *Disparate impact in* Hernandez. Could Hernandez have succeeded on a timely disparate impact claim if he could show that the no-rehire rule has the effect of disproportionately disqualifying individuals with a record of addiction? Should the potential for relapse be a valid defense?

5.   *Drug tests.* May an employer require a recovering drug addict employee to undergo a weekly drug test if it does not do so for other employees? *See* ADA § 12114(d).

6.   *Other testing statutes.* Although the ADA does not prohibit testing for illegal drugs, employers should be mindful that other statutes may limit the lawful circumstances of drug testing. In this regard, approximately ten states have enacted legislation regulating the permissibility and consequences of drug testing. Minnesota, for example, has adopted a Drug and Alcohol Testing in the Workplace statute, Minn. Stat. §§ 181.950–957, which, among other things, permits employers to conduct random testing only for safety-sensitive employees and authorizes termination upon the occurrence of a first positive confirmatory test only if the employee has declined to participate in a rehabilitation program.

7.   *Marijuana use.* Joseph Casias suffers from inoperable sinus and brain cancer. His doctor has recently prescribed medical marijuana to treat pain that other drugs cannot alleviate. He only uses the marijuana at home and has never come to work under the influence of the drug. After a workplace accident, Casias is given a drug test that detects his marijuana use, and he is fired. Does the test or his discharge violate the ADA? *See* Casias v. Wal-Mart Stores, Inc., 695 F.3d 428 (6th Cir. 2012) (holding that since the ADA defines "illegal drug use" by reference to federal law, and federal law does not authorize the plaintiffs' medical marijuana use, plaintiff's medical marijuana use is not protected by the ADA; however, the ADA would prohibit discrimination against the plaintiff aimed at the plaintiff's underlying medical condition). *But see* Noffsinger v. SSC Niantic Operating Co., 273 F.Supp.3d 326, 337–38 (D. Conn. 2017) (ADA does not preempt Connecticut's Palliative Use of Marijuana Act (PUMA), which prohibits employers from firing or refusing to hire someone who uses marijuana for medical purposes).

As described by one student commentator, thirty-four jurisdictions have legalized medical marijuana, but these states have taken a variety of approaches regarding how the legalized medical marijuana intersects with anti-discrimination statutes, such as the ADA. *See* Stephen M. Scannell, *Medical Marijuana and the ADA: Following the Path Blazed by State Courts to Extend Protection*, 12 ST. LOUIS U. J. HEALTH L. & POL'Y 391, 403 (2019). Of those thirty-four jurisdictions, Nevada is the sole one that explicitly requires an employer to attempt to make a reasonable accommodation of medical marijuana use for employees who are legally using the medical marijuana. *Id.* Twelve jurisdictions are "silent as to accommodations but do allow employers to prohibit the use of marijuana in the workplace and/or allow employers to prohibit employees [from] being under the influence at work." *Id.* at 404. The other twenty states explicitly do not require an employer to accommodate an employee's medical marijuana use, in large part based on the reasoning that marijuana is still unlawful under federal law. *Id.* at 405–06. As of the beginning of 2020, a smaller cohort of 11 states have legalized the recreational use of marijuana. For further commentary on the issue, see Stephanie Speirs, *Will the Smoke Blow Over? Employers' Concerns as States Expand Protections for Medical Marijuana Users?*, 36 HOFSTRA LAB. & EMP. L.J. 481 (2019); Russell Rendall, *Medical Marijuana and the ADA: Removing Barriers to Employment for Disabled Individuals,* 22 HEALTH MATRIX 315 (2012); Stacy A. Hickox, *Clearing the Smoke on Medical Marijuana Users in the Workplace*, 29 QUINNIPIAC L. REV. 1001 (2011).

B. MENTAL IMPAIRMENTS

DOYAL V. OKLAHOMA HEART, INC.
213 F.3d 492 (10th Cir. 2000)

ALARCÓN, CIRCUIT JUDGE.

Carol Doyal ("Doyal") appeals from the order granting summary judgment in favor of her former employer, Oklahoma Heart, Inc. ("Oklahoma Heart"). Doyal alleged that Oklahoma Heart terminated her employment as an administrator at Oklahoma Heart in violation of the Americans with Disabilities Act ("ADA"). Because Doyal failed to introduce evidence sufficient to support a reasonable conclusion that she was substantially limited in a major life activity or was regarded as such by Oklahoma Heart, we affirm.

I

Oklahoma Heart is a cardiology practice group. Doyal began working as an administrator at Oklahoma Heart in April 1992. The company grew and, over time, Doyal's responsibilities grew as well. In January 1995, Oklahoma Heart began moving its billing and accounting functions in house. At that time, Doyal was serving as the business office manager for Oklahoma Heart. The conversion to the new billing and accounting computer system was to be completed by April 1995. The conversion was stressful for the affected Oklahoma Heart employees, including Doyal.

In early 1995, Doyal began to experience "significant feelings of helplessness, anxiety, excessive stress and lack of motivation" as well as "difficulty thinking clearly, concentrating, learning, remembering, and interacting with others." She felt disinterested in work, life, eating, and caring for herself. She experienced insomnia, often sleeping only one to three hours a night. She also began to experience panic attacks. In March 1995, she experienced a "mental breakdown" at work, during which she cried and told her supervisor, Steven Struttman, how stressed and overworked she felt. Struttman told her to take a week off.

During Doyal's week off, she saw Dr. Katherine Klassen, a psychiatrist, who diagnosed her with "Major Depression, moderate, with anxiety attacks." Dr. Klassen prescribed an anti-depressant medication. Doyal testified during her deposition that the medication "helped tremendously." Dr. Klassen also recommended that she work with her employer to arrange for a "reduced stress/work load." Upon her return to work after her week off, Doyal asked Oklahoma Heart to give her a new position. She transferred to the position of human resources director. The change in her responsibilities was accompanied by a reduction in her pay.

In her new position, Doyal continued to have problems with her memory and concentration, forgetting the names and qualifications of candidates for jobs. She also threw away medical records on one occasion, believing that she had been given permission to do so by one of the doctors at Oklahoma Heart. In late April 1995, Doyal was briefly hospitalized for what her psychiatrist concluded was a stress-related illness. On May 16, 1995, Oklahoma Heart terminated her employment. Struttman provided Doyal with a letter listing the reasons for her discharge. The letter cited her inability to make decisions and her lapses of memory, judgment, and confidentiality.

II

* * *

In Doyal's brief to this court, she asserts that her depression limited her ability to perform the following life activities: learning, sleeping, thinking, and interacting with others. . . .

A. *Learning*

In her opposition to the motion for summary judgment, Doyal failed to present evidence of any specific instances where she had difficulty in learning. . . .

Forgetfulness is an exceedingly common human frailty. Many of us tend to forget names. This is particularly so where we briefly meet a lot of different people, as Doyal did in her role as human resources director for Oklahoma Heart. Without more, the fact that Doyal tended to forget the names of candidates for employment and other unspecified things is insufficient evidence to support a reasonable inference that she was significantly restricted in her ability to learn.

Doyal asserts for the first time before this court that she was unable to learn the new computer system. Doyal did not offer any evidence in her opposition to the motion for summary judgment regarding her inability to learn the new computer system, the efforts she undertook to learn it, or how her efforts to master the system compared with those of other employees. Indeed, Struttman and Dr. Wayne Leimbach testified during their depositions that the transition to the new computer system was difficult for all involved, not just for Doyal.

Because Doyal introduced no evidence suggesting she experienced greater difficulty than anybody else learning the new computer system or any other new material, she has failed to demonstrate that she was significantly restricted in learning. . . .

III

Doyal contends that, even if she was not actually disabled, she was perceived by Oklahoma Heart as being disabled as that term is defined in the ADA. . . .

The evidence introduced supports the conclusion that Oklahoma Heart's management perceived Doyal as being unmotivated, forgetful, and irremediably unhappy in her job. The evidence in this record does not, however, support the conclusion that management misperceived Doyal as being substantially limited in a major life activity, as [then] required under *Sutton*.

RANDAL I. GOLDSTEIN, MENTAL ILLNESS IN THE WORKPLACE AFTER *SUTTON V. UNITED AIRLINES*
86 CORNELL L. REV. 927 (2001)

The difficulties facing mentally ill individuals who assert ADA claims grow from longstanding societal misconceptions and the inherent inconsistencies between the ADA and the nature of mental illness itself. An underlying presumption of the ADA is the belief that disabled individuals can "do the job." In many respects, however, it appears Congress did not apply this presumption to the mentally ill. . . .

A physically disabled individual's impairments are both visible and involuntary—most people suspect that a wheelchair-bound person would prefer to walk. In this regard, the ADA identified physically impaired individuals and encouraged them to function "normally," providing them with the necessary accommodations. Concurrently, Congress attempted to dissolve preconceptions and reinforce notions that the physically disabled should be admired for perseverance

On the other hand, mental illness is often perceived as voluntary—mere laziness or irrationality—and, moreover, is not readily apparent. When an employee is unproductive, we assume she lacks a solid work ethic. Because we do not detect that she suffers from major depression—she does not look disabled—we reinforce this notion of voluntarism. In addition, since we have comparatively little information on psychological phenomena, society is generally suspicious of those affected by mental illness.

As such, many employers and courts believe that individuals who do not have severe mental disorders abuse the law—that people with minor emotional problems conjure up vague claims of stress disorders and threaten employers with ADA litigation in order to gain "concessions." In this view, only two types of mental impairment exist: total debilitation and mere phobia.

One explanation for the judiciary's distrust is that a mentally ill individual or his counsel often cannot precisely describe the individual's impairment or, in particular, how he is limited by the impairment. . . .

ADA claimants are faced with a catch-22 relating to the dual requirements of disabled status and qualification for the position. As stated above, "a qualified individual with a disability" is "an individual with a disability who, with or without reasonable accommodation, can perform the essential functions of the employment position that such individual holds or desires." Thus, the individual must initially demonstrate that her impairment substantially limits a major life activity. Then, she must establish that she is "otherwise qualified"—that she can perform the job's essential functions. Yet, the "otherwise qualified" criterion produces a trap for claimants: an individual must demonstrate that her impairment rises to the level of "substantially limiting" while simultaneously proving that this limitation does not prevent her from executing the essential functions of the position. This catch-22 is particularly troublesome in mental illness cases.

Individuals with mental illnesses face two common problems at work: (1) they have attendance difficulties, many of which result from the psychotropic drugs they use to treat their illnesses; and (2) they have trouble handling stress, a problem which often manifests itself in concentration lapses, interpersonal problems, and general misconduct.

As a result of these common problems, plaintiffs' cases are routinely dismissed as a matter of law, with courts declaring the mentally ill individual "not otherwise qualified." In doing so, courts proclaim that predictable attendance and handling stress without violating conduct standards are essential functions of every job.

NOTES AND QUESTIONS

1.   *After the ADAAA.* Would Doyal be considered an individual with a disability following the enactment of the ADA Amendments Act? How would you characterize her claim that she is disabled?

2.   *Analyzing* Doyal. The *Doyal* decision is illustrative of many decisions involving mental impairments. Does Doyal lose because of the weakness of her case or because of the court's perception of her claims? If Doyal had been found

to be disabled, is it likely that she would have passed muster under the "qualified" prong of analysis?

3.   *Mental vs. physical impairments.* An empirical study funded by the National Institute of Mental Health compared mental impairment with physical impairment ADA cases over a nine-year span. The study found that individuals with mental impairments experienced favorable outcomes in 25% fewer cases than their physically impaired counterparts. Jeffrey Swanson, et al., *Justice Disparities: Does the ADA Enforcement System Treat People with Psychiatric Disabilities Fairly?* 66 MD. L. REV. 94 (2006). Why do you think courts tend to be less receptive to mental impairment claims than they are to physical impairment claims?

C. ASSOCIATIONAL DISCRIMINATION

DEN HARTOG V. WASATCH ACADEMY
129 F.3d 1076 (10th Cir. 1997)

EBEL, CIRCUIT JUDGE.

Plaintiff-Appellant Howard Den Hartog ("Den Hartog") was discharged by defendant-appellee Wasatch Academy ("Wasatch"), a boarding school where Den Hartog had been teaching and working for over twenty-five years. He was discharged because his adult son Nathaniel, who suffers from bipolar affective disorder, attacked and threatened several members of the Wasatch community, including threats to the headmaster's two children, over a one-year period. Den Hartog sued Wasatch and its headmaster, alleging violation of the Americans with Disabilities Act ("ADA") and breach of contract. The district court granted the defendants' motion for summary judgment on the ADA claim, but allowed the breach of contract claim to proceed. After the district court denied Den Hartog's motion in limine to suppress certain evidence, a jury rendered a verdict in favor of the defendants on the contract claim. Den Hartog now appeals both the district court's grant of summary judgment on the ADA claim and its denial of his motion in limine.

We hold that the ADA allows an employer to discipline or discharge a non-disabled employee whose disabled relative or associate, because of such relative or associate's disability, poses a direct threat to the employer's workplace. Because there is no genuine dispute of fact on this record that Den Hartog's son, Nathaniel, posed such a threat to the workplace at Wasatch, we conclude that the discharge of Den Hartog did not violate the ADA. Accordingly, we affirm.

BACKGROUND

Defendant Wasatch is a private boarding school for students in the ninth through twelfth grades, located in Mt. Pleasant, Utah. In recent years, its student body has numbered approximately 160 students, and it has employed about 45 full-time staff and faculty members. Mt. Pleasant is a small town, consisting of less than 2 ½ square miles and approximately 2,000 residents. Co-defendant Joseph Loftin ("Loftin") has served as headmaster for Wasatch from 1988 to the present. During the times at issue, Loftin lived on campus with his wife and three children.

Except for two years during which he taught elsewhere, plaintiff Howard Den Hartog was employed by Wasatch Academy from 1964 until July 1994, pursuant to a series of one-year contracts. During that period, Den Hartog worked as a teacher, in the buildings and grounds department, and as a school historian. In accordance with Wasatch's general policy requiring full-time faculty to live on campus, Den Hartog lived on the Wasatch campus with his wife and four children every year that he taught there.

Den Hartog's youngest child, Nathaniel Den Hartog ("Nathaniel"), was born in December 1971. Nathaniel lived with his parents until he graduated from Wasatch in June 1990. During the 1990–91 school year, Nathaniel went away to college. However, Nathaniel did not return to college the next year, but instead lived on the Wasatch campus with his parents.

In July 1992, Den Hartog took Nathaniel to Dr. John Merriweather, a psychologist in private practice in Mt. Pleasant. Dr. Merriweather tentatively diagnosed Nathaniel as having "bipolar affective disorder" (formerly called "manic depressive psychosis"), and recommended that Nathaniel be hospitalized and treated. Accordingly, Nathaniel was admitted to the Western Institute of Neuropsychiatry in Salt Lake City on July 20, 1992, where Dr. Merriweather's diagnosis was confirmed and Nathaniel was treated with lithium. Nathaniel was discharged on July 30, 1992, and returned to his parents' home on the Wasatch campus. At that time, Loftin was aware of Nathaniel's diagnosis and at some point became aware of Nathaniel's lithium treatment. Upon Nathaniel's return, Loftin hired him to do part-time work on campus including yard work, painting, and assisting in the day care center.

Around November, 1992, Nathaniel moved to California. However, after two months there, he stopped taking his lithium and as a result suffered a manic episode. In January, 1993, the police found Nathaniel selling his possessions in a grocery store parking lot. Following that incident, his mother flew to California and brought him back to Wasatch, where Loftin once again hired him to do part-time work on campus.

During early 1993, when Nathaniel was twenty-one years old, he developed "close ties" with Loftin's sixteen-year-old son Travis. On March 12, 1993, Nathaniel took Travis to Provo, Utah, without the Loftins' knowledge, and attempted to have Travis admitted to Charter Canyon Hospital, a psychiatric hospital there. When a hospital employee called Joseph Loftin, Loftin went to Provo to pick up Travis. Before Loftin arrived, Nathaniel left the hospital without Travis.

Two days later, Nathaniel telephoned the Loftin home several times, looking for Travis. Nathaniel told Loftin that he would slit his own wrists if Loftin did not put Travis on the phone. Loftin, in response, called both the police and Nathaniel's counselor Brian Whipple. That same evening, Nathaniel visited his treating psychiatrist, Dr. J. Bruce Harless, to discuss these phone calls. At this visit, Nathaniel told Dr. Harless that he really had no intention of harming himself, but was merely attempting to coerce the Loftins into disclosing Travis's location.

On March 18, 1993, the Loftins found a number of messages from Nathaniel on their answering machine. In one of these messages, while speaking in a tone of voice which scared Loftin and which Dr. Harless "readily perceived as being threatening," Nathaniel stated that the Loftins should keep a very close eye out on their four-year-old daughter, Allison. In another message, Nathaniel said that he had drained quarts of blood from his body recently, and offered to show this blood to Loftin to prove he was "serious."

After listening to the recorded messages, Loftin called the police, who listened to the messages and told Loftin to take the threats seriously. The police also called Dr. Harless. Nathaniel's parents were then contacted. Although the Den Hartogs agreed to take Nathaniel to a hospital, they were unable to coax or coerce Nathaniel out of their house. Consequently, they called the police, who transported Nathaniel to the Utah Valley Regional Medical Center, where Nathaniel was temporarily admitted. The next day, at the request of Dr. Harless, Loftin applied for Nathaniel to be involuntarily committed to an institution.

On March 31, 1993, a Utah state judge determined that Nathaniel posed "an immediate danger of physical injury" to himself or others, and ordered his commitment to the custody of the Utah State Division of Mental Health for six months.

The next day, April 1, 1993, Den Hartog and his wife Esther met with Loftin and others to discuss the situation. The Den Hartogs recorded the meeting. At the meeting, Loftin repeatedly told the Den Hartogs that he did not want Nathaniel on campus because of his threatening behavior. Loftin also said that if Nathaniel's condition resulted in the Den Hartogs being unable to live at Wasatch, then Den Hartog might be terminated. Esther Den Hartog responded that "if we lived here [on campus] and we were having a Christmas celebration with our family we would not say, Nathaniel, you cannot come home because Joe Loftin says you cannot be here." Den Hartog did not object to this statement.

On April 16, 1993, the Wasatch Board of Trustees met and voted unanimously to:

endorse the action of the Headmaster, President of the Board, and the Executive Committee in this matter: essentially

1.   Restraining order on Nathaniel Den Hartog

2.   Apartment in [Salt Lake City] for Esther and Nathaniel for an undetermined period

3.   If necessary, pay out their contract if they must leave the community.

Pursuant to this vote, Wasatch rented an apartment in Salt Lake City for Nathaniel and his mother to live in after Nathaniel was released. Two Wasatch Trustees visited the Den Hartogs in their home the next day, to inform them of the Board's decision. No restraining order was ever obtained against Nathaniel.

Despite having been remanded to state custody for six months on March 31, Nathaniel was released from the Utah Valley Regional Medical Center on April 19, 1993. Within a week of his release, Nathaniel visited Mt. Pleasant, where he came onto the Wasatch campus. Several Wasatch Trustees received calls from staff and faculty who were concerned about Nathaniel's presence. Loftin became concerned that as long as Den Hartog worked and lived on campus Nathaniel would continue visiting. As a result, on May 14, 1993, Wasatch assigned Den Hartog to spend the 1993–94 school year writing a school history from Wasatch's development office in Salt Lake City. Den Hartog was to receive his full salary plus a living allowance to pay for a home, utilities, and food.

In August, 1993, Nathaniel enrolled in Snow College and moved to Ephraim, Utah, twenty miles from Mt. Pleasant. Den Hartog provided Nathaniel with a car and placed no restrictions on where Nathaniel could go. On one occasion Nathaniel drove to the Wasatch campus to attend a basketball game which his father was attending. Then, on Christmas Eve, 1993, and on another occasion the following week, Nathaniel went to the Loftin home in an attempt to see Travis Loftin. By that time, Nathaniel had dropped out of Snow College.

On January 24, 1994, Nathaniel and an accomplice battered Byron Bond, a former schoolmate of Nathaniel's, in Bond's home in Mt. Pleasant. Bond sustained several broken ribs and was treated in the hospital. After Bond was released from the hospital, he informed Loftin of the battery and warned him that during the attack Nathaniel had stated that he planned to "get" Loftin next. Nathaniel was arrested for aggravated assault, booked into Sanpete County Jail, and then sent to the Utah State Hospital in Provo for a competency evaluation.

In February, 1994, while Nathaniel was hospitalized, Loftin decided not to renew Den Hartog's contract for the next year. On March 4, 1994, Loftin met with Den Hartog and told him that his contract would not be renewed because the school historian position, which Den Hartog then held, was being eliminated. Although Loftin told Den Hartog that the reason for non-renewal was the elimination of his position, Loftin testified in his deposition that absent Nathaniel's behavior Den Hartog "[v]ery possibly" would still be employed by Wasatch. . . .

On May 16, 1994, after being found competent to stand trial, Nathaniel was discharged from the Utah State Hospital. He eventually pled guilty to assault and was sentenced to one year of probation. Loftin was unsuccessful in having Nathaniel prohibited from going on the Wasatch Academy campus as a condition of his probation. From his May 16, 1994 release through August, 1995, Nathaniel lived with his parents in Salt Lake City.

On November 10, 1994, Den Hartog sued Wasatch and Loftin in federal district court, alleging violations of Title I of the Americans with Disabilities Act ("ADA"), 42 U.S.C. §§ 12101–12117, and breach of contract under Utah law. In their answer, the defendants raised as affirmative defenses that they had properly terminated Den Hartog's employment because he and/or Nathaniel were "direct threats" under ADA Section 12113(b), and that Den Hartog's claims stemming from his transfer to Salt Lake City were time-barred under 42 U.S.C. § 12117.

Den Hartog then filed a motion for partial summary judgment to strike the defendants' affirmative defenses concerning any "direct threat," and a motion in limine to exclude Nathaniel's medical records; evidence of his behavior and his mental commitment hearing; police records and reports concerning his actions; and the expert testimony of Dr. Lincoln Clark regarding Nathaniel's behavior and mental state. Wasatch and Loftin, in turn, moved for summary judgment on both the ADA and contract claims.

The district court granted summary judgment in favor of Wasatch and Loftin on the ADA claim, and correspondingly denied Den Hartog's motion for partial summary judgment on that claim as moot. . . .

Den Hartog now appeals: (1) the district court's grant of summary judgment in favor of Wasatch and Loftin on the ADA claim. . . .

DISCUSSION

I. *BIPOLAR DISORDER AS A DISABILITY UNDER THE ADA*

As a threshold matter, we must consider whether "bipolar affective disorder" is a disability under the ADA, as was assumed without discussion by the district court. . . . Applying the statutory definition and the EEOC's guidance, every appellate court which has considered the question has held or assumed that "bipolar disorder" is a mental disability covered under the ADA, at least if it is sufficiently severe, as was the case here. We agree. We therefore proceed to analyze Den Hartog's claims under the framework of the ADA.

II. *THE ASSOCIATION PROVISION OF THE ADA*

A. *General Discussion*

As the district court noted, "Den Hartog's ADA claim is unique in that it is based on the rather new and undeveloped 'association discrimination' provision of the ADA." Title I of the ADA, which governs employment relationships, generally provides that "[n]o covered entity shall discriminate against a qualified individual with a disability because of the disability of such individual in regard to . . . discharge of employees . . . and other terms, conditions, and privileges of employment. 42 U.S.C. 12112(a). This provision, standing alone, would provide no protection to Den Hartog, who does not suffer from any disability.

Section 102(b)(4) of the ADA, however, defines "discriminate" to include "excluding or otherwise denying equal jobs or benefits to a qualified individual *because of the known disability of an individual with whom the qualified individual is known to have a relationship or association.*" 42 U.S.C. § 12112(b)(4) (the "association provision"). A family relationship is the paradigmatic example of a "relationship" under the association provision of the ADA. 29 C.F.R. § 1630.8.

The association provision has been the subject of very little litigation, and none in this court prior to the present case. It was apparently inspired in part by testimony before House and Senate Subcommittees pertaining to a woman who was fired from her long-held job because her employer found out that the woman's son, who had become ill with AIDS, had moved into her house so she could care for him.

By the time the ADA was enacted, two separate House Committees had reported favorably on the bill (H.R.2273), and had issued Committee Reports describing certain intended applications (and unintended misapplications) of the association provision. The House Committee on Education and Labor posed the following pair of hypotheticals to illustrate the association provision's parameters:

> [A]ssume, for example that an applicant applies for a job and discloses to the employer that his or her spouse has a disability. The employer believes the applicant is qualified for the job. The employer, however, assuming without foundation that the applicant will have to miss work or frequently leave work early or both, in order to care for his or her spouse, declines to hire the individual for such reasons. Such a refusal is prohibited by this subparagraph.

> In contrast, assume that the employer hires the applicant. If he or she violates a neutral employer policy concerning attendance or tardiness, he or she may be dismissed even if the reason for the absence or tardiness is to care for the spouse. The employer need not provide any accommodation to the nondisabled employee. The

individuals covered under this section are any individuals who are discriminated against because of their known association with an individual with a disability.

H.R.Rep. No. 101–485, pt. 2, at 61–62 (1990), *reprinted in* 1990 U.S.C.C.A.N. 303, 343–44.

The House Judiciary Committee sought to clarify the "intent" element which a plaintiff must prove to prevail on a claim brought under the association provision. As that Committee explained:

This provision applies only when the employer knows of the association with the other person and knows of that other person's disability. The burden of proof is on the individual claiming discrimination to prove that the discrimination was motivated by that individual's relationship or association with a person with a disability.

For example, it would be discriminatory for an employer to discriminate against a qualified employee who did volunteer work for people with AIDS, if the employer knew of the employee's relationship or association with the people with AIDS, and if the employment action was motivated by that relationship or association.

Similarly, it would be illegal for an employer to discriminate against a qualified employee because that employee had a family member or a friend who had a disability, if the employer knew about the relationship or association, knew that the friend or family member has a disability, and acted on that basis. Thus, if an employee had a spouse with a disability, and the employer took an adverse action against the employee based on the spouse's disability, this would then constitute discrimination.

This section would not apply if the employer did not know of the relationship or association, or if the employer did not know of the disability of the other person. Thus, if an employer fired an employee, and did not know of a relationship or association of the employee with a person with a disability, the employee could not claim discrimination under this section.

H.R.Rep. No. 101–485, pt. 3, at 38–39 (1990), *reprinted in* 1990 U.S.C.C.A.N. 445, 461–62.

In a floor debate held subsequent to the publication of these two reports, Congressman Bartlett, a sponsor of the bill, sought to answer what he characterized as some "frequent questions raised by business persons" about the ADA. One such question was the following: "If an able-bodied employee who is about to be terminated for cause, claims a relationship with a disabled individual, can he or she claim discrimination by association and be protected by the ADA?" Congressman Bartlett answered that "[g]iven the hypothetical posed, the terminating employee would have to prove that the employer knew of the association and was terminating the employee because of that association, and not because he or she was otherwise [un]qualified."

The few appellate cases that have been decided under the association provision have involved situations squarely anticipated by the 101st Congress. In *Tyndall v. National Educ. Ctrs., Inc.,* 31 F.3d 209 (4th Cir.1994), for example, an employee was terminated because she missed work repeatedly and extensively primarily to care for her disabled son. The terminated employee sued, alleging association discrimination. Consistent with the legislative intent expressed in the House Education and Labor Committee Report, however, the court rejected the plaintiff's claim.

In other cases, employees with disabled relatives who were terminated for poor job performance sued under the association provision, but presented no evidence linking their terminations in any way with the fact that they had disabled associates. In these cases, consistent with Congressman Bartlett's statements at floor debate, the employers have prevailed.

In the present case, Wasatch does not claim that Den Hartog's performance as a schoolteacher was in any way deficient, except inasmuch as his presence on the campus may have attracted Nathaniel to the campus. Thus, the primary question presented in the present case—whether the association provision of the ADA protects a qualified employee from adverse employment action based on his disabled associate's misconduct, where the associate's misconduct does not impair the employee's job performance—is different from those presented in *Tyndall, Rogers,* and *Ennis.* This question also appears not to have been confronted by the authors of the above-quoted House Reports, nor to have been addressed during Congressional floor debate on the ADA.

B. *Reasonable Accommodation*

Although no court has yet addressed the issue, it appears from the language and legislative history of the ADA, and also from the EEOC's "interpretive guidance" thereto, that the protection afforded to non-disabled employees who have an association with a disabled person differs in one significant respect from that afforded to disabled employees. This difference is the application of the ADA's "reasonable accommodation" requirements. . . .

The ADA states that no covered employer "shall discriminate against a qualified individual with a disability because of the disability of such individual. . . ." 42 U.S.C. § 12112(a). In the context of this general prohibition, the word "discriminate" is a term of art which includes "not making reasonable accommodations." *See* 42 U.S.C. 12112(b)(5). By the plain terms of § 12112(b)(5), however, the ADA does not require an employer to make any "reasonable accommodation" to the disabilities of relatives or associates of an employee who is not himself disabled.

Specifically, 42 U.S.C. 12112(b)(5)(A) defines the term "discriminate" to include "not making reasonable accommodations to the known physical or mental limitations of an otherwise qualified individual with a disability *who is an applicant or employee,* . . . ." Further, 42 U.S.C. § 12112(b)(5)(B) defines "discriminate" to include "denying employment opportunities to *a job applicant or employee* who is an otherwise qualified individual with a disability, if such denial is based on the need of such covered entity to make reasonable accommodation to the physical or mental impairments *of the employee or applicant.*" Thus, the plain language of both these provisions— the only two provisions requiring "reasonable accommodation" in Title I of the ADA—suggests that only job applicants or employees, but not their relatives or associates, need be reasonably accommodated.

We are confident that the lack of any reference to the associates or relatives of the employee or applicant in Section 12112(b)(5)'s articulation of the ADA's "reasonable accommodation" requirement is not due to any inadvertent omission. In its Report, the House Education and Labor Committee clearly expressed its intention that under the association provision, "[t]he employer need not provide any accommodation to the nondisabled employee." H.R.Rep. No. 101–485, pt. 2, at 61–62 (1990), *reprinted in* 1990 U.S.C.C.A.N. 303, 344.

Our conclusion in this regard has also been reached by the EEOC, which, pursuant to 42 U.S.C. § 12116, has issued regulations and Interpretive Guidance on the ADA. The Interpretive Guidance notes that where an associate or relative of the employee is disabled, but the employee himself is not disabled:

> an employer need not provide the applicant or employee without a disability with a reasonable accommodation because that duty only applies to qualified applicants or employees with disabilities. Thus, for example, an employee would not be entitled to a modified work schedule as an accommodation to enable the employee to care for a spouse with a disability.

29 C.F.R. Pt. 1630.8 app. at 349. Thus, Wasatch was not required under the ADA to provide Den Hartog with any "reasonable accommodation" of *Nathaniel's* disability.

C. *Prima Facie Case*

In order to determine whether Den Hartog has presented evidence sufficient to permit a jury to find that he was fired because of his son's disability, we must address how such a claim might be proven. In cases involving general discrimination claims brought under ADA § 102(a), 42 U.S.C. § 12112(a), this court has adopted the "burden shifting" scheme of *McDonnell Douglas Corp. v. Green,* 411 U.S. 792, 802, 93 S.Ct. 1817, 1824

(1973). All parties to the present case agree that the *McDonnell Douglas* framework should similarly be applied to claims of "association discrimination" brought under ADA § 102(b)(4). We agree.

Although they agree that *McDonnell Douglas* applies, the parties suggest different formulations of the elements constituting a *prima facie* case of "association discrimination" under the ADA. Taking into account the suggestions of both parties and the case law decided under the ADA's generic provisions, we hold that in order to establish a *prima facie* case of "association discrimination" under ADA § 102(b)(4), 42 U.S.C. § 12112(b)(4), a plaintiff must demonstrate the following:

> (1) the plaintiff was "qualified" for the job at the time of the adverse employment action;

> (2) the plaintiff was subjected to adverse employment action;

> (3) the plaintiff was known by his employer at the time to have a relative or associate with a disability;

> (4) the adverse employment action occurred under circumstances raising a reasonable inference that the disability of the relative or associate was a determining factor in the employer's decision.

If the plaintiff in an ADA "association discrimination" case can establish these four elements, then the burden shifts to the defendant to proffer a legitimate, nondiscriminatory reason for the adverse employment action. Once such a reason is proffered, the burden shifts back to the plaintiff to show that the employer's stated reason is pretextual.

In the present case, as Den Hartog notes, the court did not articulate these (or any other) elements of a *McDonnell Douglas prima facie* case. Nonetheless, we do not agree with Den Hartog that the district court's failure to state these elements formally means that Den Hartog was denied the benefit of the *McDonnell Douglas* framework. Rather, it appears that the court simply presumed that Den Hartog *made* his *prima facie* case, and thus proceeded to consider whether the defendants' proffered non-discriminatory reason for terminating Den Hartog—concerns about the "direct threat" posed by Nathaniel's crimes and threats—was pretextual. The fact that the district court resolved this subsequent question in favor of the defendants does not render harmful to Den Hartog any error that the court may have committed in failing to set forth and apply the elements of the *prima facie* case.

III. *DISABILITY-CAUSED MISCONDUCT UNDER THE ADA*

Both the district court and the appellees on appeal have attempted to draw a bright line between discrimination based on a disability (which they concede is generally prohibited by the ADA) and discrimination based on *misconduct* by the disabled person (which they agree is not prohibited by the ADA). In evaluating that proffered dichotomy, we look to the general provisions of the ADA. However, in looking to the general provisions of the ADA for guidance in this case where the misconduct comes not from the employee but rather from an associated person, we must keep in mind that 1) summary judgment in this case could not be predicated upon misconduct by Den Hartog and 2) Wasatch had no duty to reasonably accommodate Nathaniel's disability.

The text of the ADA makes only one specific reference to "disability-caused misconduct," where an employer is authorized to disregard the fact that the misconduct or prior performance may be caused by a disability and where the employer can hold the disabled person to exactly the same conduct as a non-disabled person. It provides that an employer:

> may hold an employee who engages in the illegal use of drugs or who is an alcoholic to the same qualification standards for employment or job performance and behavior that such entity holds other employees, even if any unsatisfactory performance or behavior is related to the alcoholism or drug use of such employee.

42 U.S.C. § 12114(c)(4); *see also* 42 U.S.C. § 12114(a) (providing that the term "qualified individual with a disability" under the ADA shall not include illegal drug users when the covered entity acts on that basis).

Den Hartog claims that because Congress only expressly permitted employers to hold illegal drug users and alcoholics to the same objective standards of conduct as other employees even though their disability *causes* misconduct or poor performance, Congress implicitly did not intend to extend the same employer prerogative to employees with *other* disabilities. He thus claims that the district court erred by importing the "disability v. disability-caused misconduct" dichotomy into a case in which neither drugs nor alcohol were involved. We agree.

As a general rule, an employer may *not* hold a disabled employee to precisely the same standards of conduct as a non-disabled employee unless such standards are job-related and consistent with business necessity. *See, e.g., EEOC Enforcement Guidance: Psychiatric Disabilities and the Americans with Disabilities Act*, 2 EEOC Compl. Man. (BNA) (stating by way of example that an employer must make some reasonable exception to a general policy requiring employees to be neat and courteous in order to accommodate a mentally disabled employee whose disability led to a deterioration of neatness and courtesy where neatness and courtesy are not essential to that employee's job because it does not involve interaction with customers or co-workers).

Pursuant to 42 U.S.C. § 12114(c)(4), employers need not make any reasonable accommodations for employees who are illegal drug users and alcoholics. However, that is in marked contrast to all other disabilities, where the ADA does require that the employer extend reasonable accommodations. Thus, the disability v. disability-caused conduct dichotomy seems to be unique to alcoholism and drugs.

Further, any such sharp dichotomy would make no sense when considering other provisions of the ADA. For example, an employer need not make any accommodation that would constitute an "undue hardship." In addition, an employer may take action against an employee who poses a "direct threat" to the health or safety of other individuals in the workplace. 42 U.S.C. § 12113(b). The availability of these affirmative defenses establishes that there are certain levels of disability-caused conduct that need not be tolerated or accommodated by employers. However, the necessary corollary is that there must be certain levels of disability-caused conduct that have to be tolerated or accommodated. Thus, appellees' effort to put all disability-caused conduct beyond the pale of ADA protection cannot be correct.

Mental illness is manifested by abnormal behavior, and is in fact normally diagnosed on the basis of abnormal behavior. *See Diagnostic and Statistical Manual of Mental Disorders* 350 (4th ed.1994) (stating that bipolar disorder may be diagnosed "by the occurrence of one or more Manic Episodes or Mixed Episodes"). To permit employers carte blanche to terminate employees with mental disabilities on the basis of any abnormal behavior would largely nullify the ADA's protection of the mentally disabled.

The district court misinterpreted the holdings of our sister circuits when it stated that "the majority of Circuit Courts of Appeal interpreting [42 U.S.C. § 12112(a)—the basic ADA provision prohibiting discrimination because of disability] have concluded that the 'because of the disability' language requires some discrimination caused by the disability itself and not on misconduct which may be caused by the disability." In fact, all three cases cited by the district court in direct support of this proposition involved either illegal drug using or alcoholic employees, expressly unprotected under 42 U.S.C. § 12114(c)(4).

One case cited in indirect support of the district court's proposition, *Siefken v. Village of Arlington Heights,* 65 F.3d 664 (7th Cir.1995), did involve a (physically) disabled plaintiff who was neither an illegal drug user nor an alcoholic. In *Siefken,* a diabetic police officer was terminated after he "erratically drove his squad car at high speed through residential areas some forty miles outside his jurisdiction," while suffering a severe diabetic reaction. The district court thus correctly characterized *Siefken* as a case involving a plaintiff terminated on account of "disability-caused misconduct," in which summary judgment in favor of the defendant was affirmed. The *Siefken* court, however, rested its holding primarily on the issue of causation. Rather than holding that "disability-caused misconduct" is never protected under the ADA, the court simply found that the plaintiff's diabetes was *not* the proximate cause of his misconduct, but rather was only a "but-for" cause. It found that the plaintiff's failure to monitor his condition—such failure being within his control and not caused by his disability—was the proximate cause. However, it did not adopt the proposition that "disability-caused misconduct" would never receive protection under the ADA if the conduct was proximately caused by the disability. Other cases and authorities cited by appellant are similarly inapposite.

We therefore disagree with the district court's conclusion that the ADA's general anti-discrimination provision, 42 U.S.C. § 12112(a), contemplates a stark dichotomy between "disability" and "disability-caused misconduct." Rather, the language of the ADA, its statutory structure, and the pertinent case law, suggest that an employer should normally consider whether a mentally disabled employee's purported misconduct could be remedied through a reasonable accommodation. If so, then the employer should attempt the accommodation. If not, the employer may discipline the disabled employee only if one of the affirmative defenses articulated in 42 U.S.C. §§ 12113, 12114 applies. Otherwise, the employer must tolerate eccentric or unusual conduct caused by the employee's mental disability, so long as the employee can satisfactorily perform the essential functions of his job.

We thus proceed to determine whether any such affirmative defenses apply to the present case.

IV. *"DIRECT THREAT" DEFENSE*

A. *Factual Record of Direct Threat by Den Hartog and Nathaniel*

The "direct threat" defense is codified at 42 U.S.C. §§ 12111(3), 12113(b). Under the ADA, the term "direct threat" means "a significant risk to the health or safety of others that cannot be eliminated by reasonable accommodation." 42 U.S.C. § 12111(3). Without running afoul of the ADA, an employer may define as a qualification for any job that "an individual shall not pose a direct threat to the health or safety of [the individual himself or] other individuals in the workplace." 42 U.S.C. § 12113(b); *see also* 29 C.F.R. § 1630.15(b)(2) (including "the individual" himself in the definition).

The C.F.R. provides several criteria for determining whether an individual poses a "direct threat." These factors include:

(1)   The duration of the risk;

(2)   The nature and severity of the potential harm;

(3)   The likelihood that the potential harm will occur; and

(4)   The imminence of the potential harm.

29 C.F.R. § 1630.2(r). These factors are to be evaluated "based on an individualized assessment of the individual's present ability to safely perform the essential functions of the job." Further, they are to be evaluated "based on a reasonable medical judgment that relies on the most current medical knowledge and/or on the best available objective evidence."

Because the district court granted summary judgment on the ground that the ADA never protects an employee from being terminated on the basis of his or any of his relatives' or associates' "disability-caused misconduct," it never ruled on the defendants' affirmative defenses that both Den Hartog and Nathaniel were "direct threats." These defenses were fully briefed and argued, however, before both the district court and this court. Because of our disagreement with the district court's resolution of the "disability-caused misconduct" issue, we must now address the application of the "direct threat" defense.

In the present case, Wasatch and Loftin have alleged that both Den Hartog and Nathaniel were "direct threats" under 42 U.S.C. §§ 12111(3), 12113(b). In particular, they have alleged that Nathaniel was a "direct threat" in the literal sense, while Den Hartog was a direct threat "insofar as he was unwilling to cooperate in keeping his son Nathaniel off campus and away from Mt. Pleasant."

Den Hartog disputes, as a factual matter, that he was a "direct threat" under the ADA. In addition, Den Hartog argues that the "direct threat" defense is only applicable to employees who constitute a direct threat and it does not, as a matter of law, apply to associates or relatives of an employee who may constitute a direct threat. Further, Den Hartog says there is no evidence of an individualized assessment based on valid medical analysis or objective evidence that Nathaniel posed a direct threat. We consider these arguments in turn.

First, Den Hartog argues that he himself was not a "direct threat" to Wasatch. In support of this assertion, Den Hartog notes that both Wasatch headmaster Loftin and Wasatch Trustee Park Loughlin testified that they did not consider Den Hartog to pose a direct threat to others at Wasatch. Wasatch and Loftin seek to minimize the significance of this testimony by asserting that Den Hartog was a "direct threat" to Wasatch "insofar as he was unwilling to cooperate in keeping his son Nathaniel off campus and away from Mt. Pleasant," even though he posed no risk in his personal capacity to the safety of members of the Wasatch community.

Given the presence in the record of Loftin and Loughlin's testimony stating that Den Hartog did not pose a direct threat to Wasatch, Den Hartog has created at least a genuine issue of material fact as to whether he did pose such a threat. Indeed, the gravamen of the defendants' argument on this issue seems to accuse Den Hartog of being an "indirect threat," rather than a "direct threat." Thus, the defendants are not entitled to summary judgment on the ground that Den Hartog posed a direct threat to Wasatch.

Alternatively, the defendants seek summary judgment on the ground that Nathaniel posed a "direct threat" to Wasatch or Loftin. Den Hartog responds, as a threshold matter, that the evidence in the record supporting the defendants' claim does not meet the evidentiary level established by 29 C.F.R. § 1630.2(r). Den Hartog predicates this response solely on Loftin's failure to obtain medical evidence prior to deciding that Nathaniel's presence on the Wasatch campus posed a risk to the safety of the members of the Wasatch community. Den Hartog's argument lacks merit.

As Den Hartog correctly asserts, the determination that an individual poses a "direct threat" should be based on an "individualized assessment" that relies on "the most current medical knowledge *and/or* on the best available objective evidence." However, 29 C.F.R. § 1630.2(r) does not require an independent medical examination when the available objective evidence is clear. It uses the conjunctive "and/or" between medical knowledge and objective evidence. Loftin's determination that Nathaniel posed a direct threat to the Wasatch community was based on the undisputed objective facts that Nathaniel repeatedly issued direct threats to members of the Wasatch community—including Loftin's own four-year-old daughter—and demonstrated his propensity to carry them out, including breaking the ribs of one of his former schoolmates and engaging in other violent behavior. The threat Nathaniel posed to the security of the Wasatch community objectively appeared to Wasatch and Loftin to be grave in nature, likely to result in harm severe in magnitude, and both imminent and ongoing in duration, thereby satisfying all the factors under 29 C.F.R. § 1630.2(r). Wasatch and Loftin came to these eminently reasonable conclusions based on their "individualized assessment" of Nathaniel, rather than upon any predetermined or unfounded general stereotypes about people with bipolar affective disorder.

We hold on this record that there is no genuine issue of material fact as to whether Nathaniel posed a significant risk to the safety of members of the Wasatch community.

B. *Does the "Direct Threat" Defense Apply to Associates or Relatives?*

The legal issue remaining is whether the ADA permits an employer to discipline or discharge a non-disabled employee whose disabled relative or associate, because of his or her disability, poses a direct threat to the employer's workplace. This issue appears to be one of first impression.

As Den Hartog notes, the language of the ADA might be read to suggest that the "direct threat" affirmative defense applies only where the *employee* poses the direct threat to the workplace, because the defense arises in the context of elaborating upon the permissible "qualification standards" for a job. *See* 42 U.S.C. § 12113(b). Job qualifications are expressed in 42 U.S.C. § 12113(a), which clearly refers to employees or job applicants. Job qualifications obviously do not apply directly to associates or relatives of an employee because they are not the ones being employed. However, although the pertinent EEOC regulations and interpretive guidance discuss the "direct threat" defense in terms of a threat to individuals in the workplace, they do not *require* that the threat come only from the employee, as opposed to the associate or relative of the employee.

Although the language of 42 U.S.C. §§ 12111(3), 12113(b) does not expressly cover the present situation, it would be odd that the ADA would permit an employer to take steps to protect its workplace from "direct threats" posed by mentally disabled *employees*, and also from "direct threats" posed by mentally disabled *customers*, but not allow the employer to protect its workplace from "direct threats" posed by mentally disabled *associates or relatives* of non-disabled employees. Because of the apparent oddness of a statutory scheme which would provide an employer with no recourse against "direct threats" posed by this one small group of individuals, but does provide recourse in all other "direct threat" situations, we feel compelled to search for evidence that Congress intended such a result before holding that result to obtain.

In its Committee Report on the ADA, the House Judiciary Committee expressed its intention that the "direct threat" standard should codify the standard applied under the Rehabilitation Act by the Supreme Court in *School Bd. Of Nassau County v. Arline*, 480 U.S. 273 (1987). In *Arline,* the Court remanded for further findings of the contagiousness of a schoolteacher who had contracted tuberculosis to determine whether she posed a significant risk of communicating her disease to others in the workplace and whether reasonable accommodation could eliminate that risk. Although the schoolteacher there was an employee, the thrust of the case was not whether the threat came from an employee or a relative or associate of an employee, but rather whether the employer was acting upon actual objective evidence of a threat, or upon stereotypical assumptions of the threat.

> [A]n employer may not assume that a person with a mental disability . . . poses a direct threat to others. This would be an assumption based on fear and stereotype. The purpose of creating the "direct threat" standard is to eliminate exclusions which are not based on objective evidence about the individual involved. Thus, in the case of a person with mental illness there must be objective evidence from the person's behavior that the person has a recent history of committing overt acts or making threats which caused harm or which directly threatened harm.

Elsewhere in the Report, the Committee also expressed its intention that the "direct threat" defense should extend to permit an entity to deny a disabled individual from participating in or benefiting from the goods, services, facilities, privileges, advantages and accommodations of the entity, where the disabled individual poses a direct threat to the health or safety of others. The Committee intended that "[t]his provision [be] identical to one added in the employment section," and advised that "the discussion of this issue there applies here as well."

The legislative history of the association provision, discussed Part IIA, *supra*, does not discuss any affirmative defenses to claims brought under that provision. In our view, this lack of discussion is most likely due to the Committee's presumption that the affirmative defenses available to employers defending association discrimination claims—including the "direct threat" defense—would be identical to those available in other ADA contexts. This presumption would logically follow from the association provision's location in the ADA, as part of the statutory definition of "discriminate," which appears in the basic anti-discrimination provisions of 42 U.S.C. § 12112(a).

Our conclusion in this regard is bolstered by the fact that the association provision does not require any "reasonable accommodation," *see* Part IIB, *supra*, and therefore provides *less* protection against discrimination to employees than does the ADA's basic provision, 42 U.S.C. § 12112(a). We see nothing in the legislative history indicating that Congress intended to provide *less* protection to non-disabled employees with disabled relatives or associates than to disabled employees and job applicants with respect to ADA's central "reasonable accommodation" requirement, yet simultaneously to provide, *sub silentio, more* protection to non-disabled employees whose disabled relatives or associates posed direct threats to the employees' workplace than to disabled employees and job applicants who posed identical direct threats to the same workplace. We think it far more likely that Congress assumed that 42 U.S.C. § 12113(b)'s "direct threat" defense would apply to cases where the direct threat came from relatives or associates of the employee as well as to those cases where the direct threat came from the employee himself or herself.

. . . [W]e think that the language of the association provision of the ADA reflects the dimensions of the particular problem that came to the attention of the legislature and that provision invites "the conclusion that the legislative policy is equally applicable to other situations in which the mischief is identical." Because the legislative policy underlying the availability of the "direct threat" defense under the primary provisions of the ADA is equally applicable to the association provision, we hold that the ADA permits an employer to discipline or discharge a non-disabled employee whose disabled relative or associate, because of his or her disability, poses a direct threat to the employer's workplace.

Accordingly, the district court's grant of summary judgment in favor of the defendants with respect to Den Hartog's ADA claim is affirmed.

DEWITT V. PROCTOR HOSPITAL

517 F.3d 944 (7th Cir. 2008)

EVANS, CIRCUIT JUDGE.

After she was fired from her job as a registered nurse at Proctor Hospital, 47-year-old Phillis Dewitt sued, alleging "association discrimination" under the Americans with Disabilities Act (ADA) as well as age and gender discrimination. The district court entered summary judgment in favor of Proctor. The court also denied Dewitt's motion for leave to amend her complaint to add a claim of ERISA retaliation. Today we resolve Dewitt's appeal from those decisions.

In September 2001, Proctor, a hospital in Peoria, Illinois, hired Dewitt to work as a nurse on an "as-needed" basis. Proctor apparently liked how Dewitt did her job because the following month she was promoted to the permanent position of second-shift clinical manager. In that role, Dewitt supervised nurses and other Proctor staff members.

Three years into the job, Dewitt switched to the first-shift clinical manager slot. In the summer of 2005, she switched to a part-time schedule, sharing the responsibilities of second-shift clinical manager with a coworker.

Dewitt, it appears (for we must assume the facts to be as she presents them at this stage of the proceedings), was a valuable employee. In her last evaluation, her supervisor, Mary Jane Davis, described her as an "outstanding clinical manager [who] consistently goes the extra mile." But things were not quite as rosy as they appeared.

Dewitt and her husband, Anthony, were covered under Proctor's health insurance plan. Throughout Dewitt's tenure at Proctor, Anthony suffered from prostate cancer and received expensive medical care. His covered medical expenses were paid by Proctor, which was partially self-insured. It paid for members' covered medical costs up to $250,000 per year. Anything above this "stop-loss" figure was covered by a policy issued by the Standard Security Life Insurance Company of New York.

Dewitt was able to maintain health insurance coverage for herself and Anthony even during her short part-time stint, since Proctor credited Dewitt with "hospital approved absence" (unpaid time), allowing her to reach the minimum number of hours necessary to qualify for benefits.

Since Proctor was self-insured, it took a keen interest in the medical claims submitted by its employees. Each quarter, in fact, Progressive Benefits Services, the administrator of Proctor's medical plan, prepared a "stop-loss report" for Linda K. Buck, Proctor's vice-president of human resources. The report identified all employees whose recent medical claims exceeded $25,000.

The stop-loss reports highlighted Dewitt's expenses. Although Dewitt was not listed on reports for 2001 and 2002 (indicating that her family's medical expenses, particularly those of her husband, were less than $25,000), during the next three years Anthony underwent costly medical procedures. In 2003, the Dewitts' medical claims for Anthony were $71,684. In 2004, the figure jumped to $177,826. In the first eight months of 2005, the expenses were $67,281.50.

In September 2004, Davis confronted Dewitt about Anthony's high medical claims. Specifically, she asked what treatment Anthony was receiving, and Dewitt responded that he was undergoing chemotherapy and radiation. Davis asked Dewitt if she had considered hospice care for her husband; Dewitt responded that Anthony's doctor considered less expensive hospice care placement to be premature. Davis explained that a committee was reviewing Anthony's medical expenses, which she described as unusually high.

In February 2005, Davis again pulled Dewitt aside to ask about Anthony's treatment. Dewitt informed her that Anthony's situation had not changed.

In May 2005, Davis organized a meeting for Proctor's clinical managers. She informed the employees that Proctor faced financial troubles, which, according to Davis, required a "creative" effort to cut costs.

Proctor fired Dewitt on August 3, 2005, and designated her as "ineligible to be rehired in the future." Proctor provided no explanation for its "ineligible for rehire" decision. Dewitt's medical benefits with Proctor continued through the end of August. After that, Dewitt paid for COBRA coverage (which she was able to get for a maximum of 18 months) for herself and her husband. But 18 months, as it turned out, wasn't necessary as Anthony, a year and a week after Dewitt was fired, gave up his fight with cancer. He died on August 9, 2006.

* * *

Now we come to Dewitt's best claim as she invokes the infrequently litigated "association discrimination" section of the ADA. Under 42 U.S.C. § 12112(b)(4), an employer is prohibited from discriminating against an employee as a result of "the known disability of an individual with whom [the employee] is known to have a relationship or association." Specifically, she alleges that Proctor fired her to avoid having to continue to pay for the substantial medical costs that were being incurred by her husband under Proctor's self-insured health insurance plan.

In our seminal case on this issue, *Larimer v. International Business Machines Corp.*, 370 F.3d 698, 700 (7th Cir.2004), we outlined three categories into which "association discrimination" plaintiffs generally fall. We called them (1) expense; (2) disability by association; and (3) distraction. In the "expense" scenario, we noted that an employee, fired because her spouse has a disability that is costly to the employer (i.e., he is covered by the company's health plan) is within the intended scope of the "associational discrimination" section of the ADA.

The *McDonnell Douglas* test is not easily adaptable to claims under the section of the ADA that permits causes of action for association discrimination. It's a bit like a mean stepsister trying to push her big foot into one of Cinderella's tiny glass slippers. In *Larimer,* we struggled with the task of reformulating the *McDonnell Douglas* test, suggesting that a similar effort in *Den Hartog v. Wasatch Academy,* 129 F.3d 1076 (10th Cir.1997), while close to the mark, could be tweaked and improved. And so we suggested that a plaintiff, without direct evidence of discrimination, could prove her case by establishing that: (1) she was qualified for the job at the time of the adverse employment action; (2) she was subjected to an adverse employment action; (3) she was known by her employer at the time to have a relative or associate with a disability; and (4) her case falls into one of the three relevant categories of expense, distraction, or association.

While all this may be well and good, we think Dewitt's case, in the final analysis, does not have to be considered in light of the tweaked *McDonnell Douglas* test because she has fairly persuasive circumstantial evidence suggesting that her case is best viewed as one relying on direct evidence. And so, we think, a jury should consider her claim.

The uncontroverted evidence suggests that Proctor, which faced financial trouble, was very concerned about cutting costs. Because Proctor's unusually high "stop-loss" coverage didn't kick in until claims exceeded $250,000, it personally felt the heavy bite of Dewitt's expenses. Proctor wasn't discreet about its concerns: in the May 2005 meeting, Davis informed Proctor's clinical managers that the hospital would have to be "creative" in cutting costs.

That the powers-that-be at Proctor were interested specifically in the high cost of Anthony's medical treatment is obvious. Davis, Dewitt's supervisor (and the person who ultimately fired her), pulled Dewitt aside twice in five months to inquire about Anthony's condition. These conversations indicate that Davis was very interested in limiting Anthony's claims. During their first chat, Davis informed Dewitt that a Proctor committee was reviewing Anthony's unusually high medical expenses. She also asked Dewitt whether Anthony's doctor had considered hospice placement—a far cheaper "alternative" to the costly chemotherapy and radiation Anthony was receiving.

Finally, the timing of Dewitt's termination suggests that the financial albatross of Anthony's continued cancer treatment was an important factor in Proctor's decision. Dewitt was fired in August 2005—five months after her last chat with Davis and three months after Proctor warned employees about impending "creative" cost-cutting measures. One could reasonably infer that Dewitt was terminated after Proctor conducted its latest periodic analysis of medical claim "outliers" and, this time around, decided that its "wait and see" strategy with the Dewitts was costing the hospital tens of thousands of dollars every year. A reasonable juror could conclude that

Proctor, which faced a financial struggle of indeterminate length, was concerned that Anthony—a multi-year cancer veteran—might linger on indefinitely. This later fact distinguishes Dewitt's case from the situation in *Larimer* where the fired employee's twin daughters were "healthy and normal" and thus no longer disabled when the employment termination decision was made.

Proctor makes several arguments, none of which we find persuasive. It contends that its decision to terminate Dewitt could not have been based on the high cost of Anthony's cancer treatment because the medical expenses of other female employees exceeded those of Dewitt. Specifically, Proctor points to evidence that in 2003, 2004, and 2005, Dewitt's claims were exceeded by those of one or two other employees. It is unclear, however, whether these employees (or other plan members), like Anthony, had conditions that Proctor feared would require prolonged, expensive medical treatment which could potentially continue far into the future. Thus, without a comparison of employees' cumulative medical expenses and treatment predictions, this argument has little appeal on the basis of this record at the summary judgment stage of the case.

In support of its claim that it never sought to restrict the Dewitts' access to health insurance, Proctor points to its decision to help Dewitt maintain her coverage when she switched to a part-time schedule in the summer of 2005. According to Dewitt, however, her switch to a part-time schedule was contingent on Proctor continuing her medical benefits. Since we must interpret the facts in Dewitt's favor, we therefore assume that Proctor was well-aware that regardless of how it responded to her request to maintain her health coverage, Dewitt would not have relinquished her benefits voluntarily.

Finally, Proctor argues that firing Dewitt would not have accomplished the goal Dewitt attributes to it—freeing itself of Anthony's steep medical bills—since Dewitt was eligible for post-termination COBRA insurance. This argument, however, leaves out an important piece of the puzzle. Even if Proctor shared some financial responsibility for the continuation of benefits, it would nonetheless save money by terminating Dewitt, since it feared that Anthony's expensive treatment might continue indefinitely and the COBRA coverage would expire after 18 months.

Because Dewitt has established that direct evidence of "association discrimination" may have motivated Proctor in its decision to fire her, a jury should be allowed to consider her claim.

* * *

POSNER, CIRCUIT JUDGE, concurring.

I agree with the decision and with most of Judge Evans's characteristically lucid majority opinion. I write separately to raise two questions that seem to me to be worth flagging although they do not have to be answered to decide the case—the alternative ways of establishing a prima facie case of discrimination and their suitability to the discrimination charged in this case—and a third question—the difference between discrimination on grounds of expense and discrimination on grounds forbidden by federal law—regarding which the discussion in the majority opinion seems to me incomplete and potentially misleading.

* * *

Some people do feel distaste for associating with a disabled person. But the employer (and employees whose prejudices the employer might share or condone) are not being asked in an "association" case to associate with a disabled person. He is not another employee, but a stranger to the workplace with whom one of the employees happens to have a relationship. Prejudice against an employee who merely has a relationship with a disabled person doubtless exists; as we pointed out in *Larimer v. International Business Machines Corp.*, 370 F.3d at 699–700, an employer might worry that the plaintiff would be distracted from his work by the disability of the person with whom he had a relationship, or might think the disease creating the disability catching (perhaps the person is the plaintiff's husband and has AIDS). But that is a sufficiently rare occurrence to require the plaintiff to go beyond a bobtailed *McDonnell Douglas* test and show, as the court in *Den Hartog v. Wasatch Academy*, 129 F.3d 1076, 1085, put it, that "the adverse employment action occurred under circumstances raising a reasonable inference that the disability of the relative or associate was a determining factor in the employer's decision." Otherwise the number of spurious suits would soar. An employee who, perhaps fearing the axe, wanted to prepare a discrimination case would have only to talk up at work his relationship to a disabled person; such relationships are not uncommon.

An employer's most likely concern about an employee who has a disabled relative, especially a spouse or child, is that the relative's medical expenses may be covered by the employer's employee health plan. There is a positive correlation between being disabled and having abnormally high medical expenses, just as there is a positive correlation between the age of an employee and his salary because most employees receive regular raises as long as they perform satisfactorily. Suppose a company encounters rough waters and decides to retrench by firing its most expensive employees. They are likely to be older on average than the employees who are retained, but as we said many years ago, and the Supreme Court confirmed in *Hazen Paper Co. v. Biggins*, 507 U.S. 604, 611–12, 113 S.Ct. 1701 (1993), "nothing in the Age Discrimination in Employment Act forbids an employer to vary employee benefits according to the cost to the employer; and if, because older workers cost more, the result of the employer's economizing efforts is disadvantageous to older workers, that is simply how the cookie crumbles."

Now it is true, as we know from the discussion in the *Larimer* case of the "expense" form of association discrimination, that an employer who discriminates against an employee because of the latter's association with a disabled person is liable even if the motivation is purely monetary. But if the disability plays no role in the employer's decision—if he would discriminate against any employee whose spouse or dependent ran up a big medical bill—then there is no *disability* discrimination. It's as if the defendant had simply placed a cap on the medical expenses, for whatever cause incurred, that it would reimburse an employee for. This appears to be such a case. So far as the record reveals, the defendant fired the plaintiff not because her husband was disabled but because his medical expenses— which might not have been any lower had they been due to a condition that did not meet the statutory definition of a disability—were costing the defendant an amount of money that it was unwilling to spend. All the evidence recited in the majority opinion concerns costs ("cutting costs," "high cost of Anthony's medical treatment," "financial albatross," etc.) that a person who had a nondisabling medical condition could equally incur.

If cost was indeed, as appears to be the case, the defendant's only motive for the action complained of, the defendant was not guilty of disability discrimination. But it has never made this argument, and so reversal is proper. Since, however, a defendant does not have to file a motion for summary judgment at all, and if he does file one doesn't have to include all his arguments in it, the defendant will be able to argue the cost point on remand unless the district judge finds that it has been forfeited by being withheld for so long. The majority opinion in this court need not be an obstacle to the defendant's making the argument. In not remarking the distinction between disability discrimination and expense discrimination, the opinion merely accepts the parties' framing of the issues.

NOTES AND QUESTIONS

1. *Reasonable accommodations.* Both the EEOC's Interpretive Guidance and *Den Hartog* state that an employer need not provide a reasonable accommodation for an individual who is covered by the associational discrimination provision. Is the no accommodation rule a good or bad result from a policy perspective?

2. *Misconduct.* The Tenth Circuit Court of Appeals in *Den Hartog* rejected a strict dichotomy between "disability" and disability-related misconduct. According to the court, how does disability-related misconduct in this context generally differ from that committed by individuals using illegal drugs or alcohol? Is that an appropriate distinction?

3. *Three categories of associational discrimination.* The Seventh Circuit in *Dewitt* identified three principal categories of associational discrimination: expense, disability by association, and distraction. The *Dewitt* case is an example of the expense category. What would be examples of the other two categories? Should the associational discrimination provision be limited to

these three categories? Can you think of a scenario that should be covered that does not fall within one of these three categories?

4. *Judge Posner's concurrence.* Judge Posner, in his concurrence in *Dewitt*, suggests that an employer's adverse action based solely on a desire to avoid high health care costs is not discriminatory. Do you agree?

D. MEDICAL EXAMINATIONS AND INQUIRIES

ADA Section 12112 provides as follows:

(d) Medical examinations and inquiries

    (1) In general

    The prohibition against discrimination as referred in subsection (a) of this section shall include medical examinations and inquiries.

    (2) Preemployment

        (A) Prohibited examination or inquiry

        Except as provided in paragraph (3), a covered entity shall not conduct a medical examination or make inquiries of a job applicant as to whether such applicant is an individual with a disability or as to the nature or severity of such disability

        (B) Acceptable inquiry

        A covered entity may make preemployment inquiries into the ability of an applicant to perform job-related functions.

    (3) Employment entrance examination

    A covered entity may require a medical examination after an offer of employment has been made to a job applicant, and may condition an offer of employment on the results of such examination, if

        (A) All entering employees are subjected to such an examination regardless of disability;

        (B) Information obtained regarding the medical condition or history of the applicant is collected and maintained on separate forms and in separate medical files and is treated as a confidential medical record, except that

            (i) Supervisors and managers may be informed regarding necessary restrictions on the work or duties of the employee and necessary accommodations;

       (ii) First aid and safety personnel may be informed, when appropriate, if the disability might require emergency treatment; and

       (iii) Government officials investigating compliance with this chapter shall be provided relevant information on request; and

    (C) The results of such examination are used only in accordance with this subchapter.

  (4) Examination and inquiry

    (A) Prohibited examinations and inquiries

    A covered entity shall not require a medical examination and shall not make inquiries of an employee as to whether such employee is an individual with a disability or as to the nature or severity of the disability, unless such examination or inquiry is shown to be job-related and consistent with business necessity.

    (B) Acceptable examinations and inquiries

    A covered entity may conduct voluntary medical examinations, including voluntary medical histories, which are part of an employee health program available to employees at that work site. A covered entity may make inquiries into the ability of an employee to perform job-related work functions.

    (C) Requirement

    Information obtained under subparagraph (B) regarding the medical condition or history of any employee are subject to the requirements of subparagraphs (B) and (C) of paragraph (3).

ADA Section 12112(d) essentially divides medical examinations and inquiries into three temporal categories. In the first category, the pre-offer stage, employers may not ask about the existence, nature or severity of a disabling condition or require an applicant to undergo a medical examination prior to the making of a conditional job offer. The EEOC's Enforcement Guidance on Pre-Employment Inquiries takes this ban a step further by prohibiting employers from asking any "disability-related" questions which are defined as inquiries likely to elicit information about a disability.

At the second, or post-offer stage, an employer may inquire about disability status even if not related to the job. Similarly, an employer may require a medical examination without any limit as to scope after making an offer of employment that is conditional on the satisfactory outcome of the examination if it is required of all new hires within the same job category. An employer, however, may not rescind a job offer because of the results of such inquiries or examination unless the disqualifying criterion is job-related and consistent with business necessity.

The third stage contemplated by the ADA occurs during the period of an individual's current employment. At this stage, the ADA permits disability-related inquiries and medical examinations only if such inquiries and examinations are job-related and consistent with business necessity.

LEONEL V. AMERICAN AIRLINES, INC.
400 F.3d 702 (9th Cir. 2005)

FISHER, CIRCUIT JUDGE:

Appellants Walber Leonel, Richard Branton and Vincent Fusco, who all have the human immunodeficiency virus ("HIV"), applied for flight attendant positions with American Airlines ("American"). Although they went through the application process at different times, the process was essentially the same for all of them. American interviewed them at its Dallas, Texas, headquarters and then issued them conditional offers of employment, contingent upon passing both background checks and medical examinations. Rather than wait for the background checks, American immediately sent the appellants to its on-site medical department for medical examinations, where they were required to fill out medical history questionnaires and give blood samples. None of them disclosed his HIV-positive status or related medications. Thereafter, alerted by the appellants' blood test results, American discovered their HIV-positive status and rescinded their job offers, citing their failure to disclose information during their medical examinations.

The appellants, all California residents, now challenge American's medical inquiries and examinations as prohibited by the Americans with Disabilities Act ("ADA"), 42 U.S.C. § 12101 et seq. (1999), and California's Fair Employment and Housing Act ("FEHA"), Cal. Gov't Code § 12900 et seq. (1999). They argue that American could not require them to disclose their personal medical information so early in the application process— before the company had completed its background checks such that the medical examination would be the only remaining contingency—and thus their nondisclosures could not be used to disqualify them. They further contend that American violated their rights to privacy under the California Constitution by conducting complete blood count tests ("CBC"s) on their blood samples without notifying them or obtaining their consent.

I.

Leonel, Branton and Fusco all participated in American's standard application process for flight attendant positions. They first responded to questions in telephone surveys and then provided more extensive information about their language abilities, previous employment and educational backgrounds in written applications. Based on these initial screening forms, American selected the appellants to fly to the company's headquarters in Dallas, Texas, for in-person interviews.

Leonel, Branton and Fusco flew to Dallas at American's expense on March 25, 1998, June 25, 1998 and May 27, 1999, respectively. There, they participated first in group interviews, and then, having been chosen to progress in the application process, in individual interviews. Immediately after these interviews, members of the American Airlines Flight Attendant Recruitment Team extended the appellants conditional offers of employment. Written letters that accompanied the oral offers read:

> At this point in our recruiting process, I am pleased to make you a conditional offer of employment as a flight attendant with American Airlines. It is important, however, that you fully understand the conditions of this offer as they are detailed below. . . . Our offer is contingent upon your successful completion of a drug test, a medical examination, and a satisfactory background check. . . .

After making the offers, American Airlines representatives directed the appellants to go immediately to the company's medical department for medical examinations.

There, the appellants were instructed to fill out series of forms. One, a "Notice and Acknowledgment of Drug Test," informed them that they would be asked to provide a urine specimen which would be tested for certain specified drugs, and solicited their written consent for the testing. This form also required them to list all medications they were taking at the time. None of the appellants listed the medications he was taking for HIV.

American also required the appellants to complete medical history forms that asked whether they had any of 56 listed medical conditions, including "blood disorder" (on Branton's and Leonel's forms) and "blood disorder or HIV/[AIDS]" (on Fusco's form). Here, too, none of the appellants disclosed his HIV-positive status. Fusco, who participated in the application process approximately 14 months after Branton and 11 months after Leonel, also had to sign an "Applicant Non-Disclosure Notice," which advised that during the examination he would be asked detailed and personal questions about his medical history and that it was important to disclose all conditions fully because of American's public safety responsibilities. After completing the forms, the appellants met with nurses to discuss their medical histories. Again they said nothing about their HIV-positive status or relevant medications despite questions asking for that kind of information.

At some point during the appellants' medical examinations, nurses drew blood samples. Unlike the urinalysis procedure, American did not provide notice or obtain written consent for its blood tests. Nor did any of the company's representatives disclose that a complete blood count would be run on the blood samples. When Fusco explicitly asked what his blood would be tested for, a nurse replied simply, "anemia."

A few days after the appellants' medical examinations, American's medical department ran CBC tests on their blood samples and discovered that they had elevated "mean corpuscular volumes" ("MCV"s). According to American's medical expert, Dr. McKenas, elevated MCV levels result from (1) alcoholism (approximately 26% of cases); (2) medications for HIV, seizure disorders, chemotherapy or transplants (approximately 38% of cases) and (3) sickle cell disease, bone marrow disorder, folate deficiency or liver disorder (approximately 36% of cases). The appellants' expert, Dr. Shelley Gordon, testified that approximately 99% of individuals with HIV have elevated MCV levels. As nothing in any of the appellants' medical histories indicated cause for an elevated MCV level, American wrote the appellants and requested explanations for the results. All of the appellants, acting through their personal physicians, then disclosed their HIV-positive status and medications.

After learning that the appellants had HIV, American's medical department sent forms to the company's recruiting department stating, as final dispositions, that the appellants "[did] not meet AA medical guidelines." The forms also specified the ground on which the appellants had failed to meet the medical guidelines as "nondisclosure." The recruiting department then wrote the appellants and rescinded their conditional offers of employment. The rescission letters stated:

> You received an offer of employment . . . conditioned upon your clearing our medical process and background check. Unfortunately, I have been informed by our Medical Department that you failed to be candid or provide full and correct information. Consequently, I am withdrawing our conditional offer of employment due to your inability to fulfill all conditions. . . .

> Because American Airlines strictly adheres to the requirements of the [ADA], I have not been informed of your particular situation. American Airlines will consider for employment any qualified individual if they can safely perform the essential functions of the job. . . . However, the Company will not tolerate willful omissions of fact on its employment applications. . . .

Upon learning that their offers had been rescinded, the appellants brought individual suits against American. Fusco and Branton originally filed their respective claims in the California courts; American removed those cases to the United States District Court for the Northern District of California based on diversity jurisdiction. Leonel brought suit in the district court in the first instance. The district court dismissed Leonel's direct claims that the examinations violated FEHA and the ADA in June 2001. It then consolidated the appellants' cases and, in April 2003, granted summary judgment for American on all claims. . . .

III.

The federal Americans with Disabilities Act and California's Fair Employment and Housing Act prohibit employers from refusing to hire job applicants whose disabilities would not prevent them from "perform[ing] the essential functions of the job with reasonable accommodation." To this end, the ADA and FEHA not only bar intentional discrimination, they also regulate the *sequence* of employers' hiring processes. Both statutes prohibit medical examinations and inquiries until *after* the employer has made a "real" job offer to an applicant. *See* 42 U.S.C. § 12112(d); Cal. Gov't Code § 12940(d). "A job offer is real if the employer has evaluated all relevant non-medical information which it reasonably could have obtained and analyzed prior to giving the offer." Equal Employment Opportunity Commission, ADA Enforcement Guidance: Preemployment Disability-Related Questions and Medical Examinations, 17 (1995) ("EEOC's ADA Enforcement Guidance"). To issue a "real" offer under the ADA and FEHA, therefore, an employer must have either completed all non-medical components of its application process or be able to demonstrate that it could not reasonably have done so before issuing the offer.

> The ADA recognizes that employers may need to conduct medical examinations to determine if an applicant can perform certain jobs effectively and safely. The ADA requires only that such examinations be conducted as a separate, second step of the selection process, after an individual has met all other job pre-requisites.

Equal Employment Opportunity Commission, Technical Assistance Manual on the Employment Provisions of the ADA, VI-4 (1992) ("EEOC's Technical Assistance Manual").

This two-step requirement serves in part to enable applicants to determine whether they were "rejected because of disability, or because of insufficient skills or experience or a bad report from a reference." EEOC's ADA Enforcement Guidance, 1. When employers rescind offers made conditional on both non-medical and medical contingencies, applicants cannot easily discern or challenge the grounds for rescission. When medical considerations are isolated, however, applicants know when they have been denied employment on medical grounds and can challenge an allegedly unlawful denial.

The two-step structure also protects applicants who wish to keep their personal medical information private. Many hidden medical conditions, like HIV, make individuals vulnerable to discrimination once revealed. The ADA and FEHA allow applicants to keep these conditions private until the last stage of the hiring process. Applicants may then choose whether or not to disclose their medical information once they have been assured that as long as they can perform the job's essential tasks, they will be hired.

American's offers to the appellants here were by their terms contingent not just on the appellants successfully completing the medical component of the hiring process but also on the completion of a critical *non-medical* component: undergoing background checks, including employment verification and criminal history checks. Other courts have found offers not real, and medical examinations thus unlawfully premature, when an offer remained contingent upon a polygraph test, personal interview and background investigation. Here, it is undisputed that American's offers were subject to both medical and non-medical conditions when they were made to the appellants and the appellants were required to undergo immediate medical examinations. Thus the offers were not real, the medical examination process was premature and American cannot penalize the appellants for failing to disclose their HIV-positive status- unless the company can establish that it could not reasonably have completed the background checks before subjecting the appellants to medical examinations and questioning. It has not done so.

As justification for accelerating the medical examinations, American's Manager of Flight Service Procedures, Julie Bourk-Suchman, explained that the company found it important to minimize the length of time that elapsed during the hiring process in order to compete for applicants. But competition in hiring is not in itself a reason to contravene the ADA's and FEHA's mandates to defer the medical component of the hiring process until the non-medical component is completed. The appellants' expert, Craig Pratt, a management consultant, testified that it is "the accepted practice for employers to complete such [background] checks *prior to* conducting a preemployment medical examination of the job applicant." American has not established that there are no reasonable alternatives that would address its asserted need for expedited hiring of flight attendants that would avoid jumping medical exams ahead of background checks. For instance, it has not shown why it could not expeditiously have issued two rounds of conditional offers—the first, after the interviews, informing applicants that they had reached the final stages of the application process and would be hired absent problems with their background checks or medical examinations; and the second, after completion of the background checks, ensuring employment if the applicant passed the medical examination.

American also suggests that it conducted the medical examinations before completing the background checks for the convenience of the applicants. As Bourk-Suchman put it, "[i]t's not a business reason. It just has to do with the applicants and trying to have it be convenient for them." Not only does this testimony undercut American's meeting-competition rationale, applicants' supposed convenience does not justify reordering the hiring process in a manner contrary to that set out by the ADA and FEHA. Congress and the California legislature both have determined that job applicants should not be required to undergo medical examinations before they hold real offers of employment. American—even if well-intentioned— cannot avoid that mandate simply because it believes doing so will be more convenient for its applicants.

In short, at the summary judgment stage, American has failed to show that it could not reasonably have completed the background checks and so notified the appellants before initiating the medical examination process. It might, for example, have performed the background checks before the appellants arrived in Dallas, kept them in Dallas longer, flown them to Dallas twice, performed the medical examinations at satellite sites or relied on the appellants' private doctors, as it did for explanation of the CBC results. American may be able to prove that alternatives such as these were not feasible and that it could not reasonably have implemented the sequence prescribed by the ADA and FEHA, but on this record it has not. Without such proof, American cannot require applicants to disclose personal medical information—and penalize them for not doing so—before it assures them that they have successfully passed through all non-medical stages of the hiring process.

American argues in the alternative that even if the offers were not real, the company did not violate the ADA or FEHA because it *evaluated* the appellants' non-medical information before it considered their medical information. Bourk-Suchman asserted that American's recruiting department actually performed the background check for each appellant before receiving the medical department's disposition of "[d]oes not meet AA guidelines." As we have explained, however, the statutes regulate the sequence in which employers collect information, not the order in which they evaluate it.

The words of the ADA and FEHA plainly address when employers can make medical inquiries or conduct medical examinations. *See* 42 U.S.C. § 12112(d)(3) ("A covered entity may require a medical examination after an offer of employment has been made . . . and prior to the commencement of the employment duties."). As the EEOC has stated explicitly, "[a]n employer may not ask disability-related questions or require a medical examination, *even if* the employer intends to shield itself from the answers to the questions or the results of the examination until the post-offer stage." EEOC's ADA Enforcement Guidance, 2.

The focus on the collection rather than the evaluation of medical information is important to the statutes' purposes. Both the ADA and FEHA deliberately allow job applicants to shield their private medical information until they know that, absent an inability to meet the medical requirements, they will be hired, and that if they are not hired, the true reason for the employer's decision will be transparent. American's attempt to focus on the evaluation rather than the collection of medical information squares with neither the text nor the purposes of the statutes. Whether or not it looked at the medical information it obtained from the appellants, American was not entitled to get the information at all until it had completed the background checks, unless it can demonstrate it could not reasonably have done so before initiating the medical examination process. As to that question, we hold that there are material issues of fact that require reversal of summary judgment on the appellants' claims that American's hiring process violated the ADA and FEHA.

OWUSU-ANSAH V. COCA-COLA CO.
715 F.3d 1306 (11th Cir. 2013)

JORDAN, CIRCUIT JUDGE:

On the recommendation of an independent psychologist, Coca-Cola placed Franklin Owusu-Ansah, one of its employees, on paid leave and required him to undergo a psychiatric/psychological fitness-for-duty evaluation. After he was cleared to return to work, Mr. Owusu-Ansah sued Coca-Cola, alleging that the evaluation violated 42 U.S.C. § 12112(d)(4)(A), a provision of the Americans with Disabilities Act. The district court granted Coca-Cola's motion for summary judgment, concluding that the evaluation was both job-related and consistent with business necessity, and therefore permissible under the ADA.

Mr. Owusu-Ansah now appeals. Following review of the record, and with the benefit of oral argument, we affirm.

* * *

II

Mr. Owusu-Ansah began working for Coca-Cola in 1999 as a customer service representative at a call center in Dunwoody, Georgia. Coca-Cola promoted Mr. Owusu-Ansah three times, eventually elevating him to the position of quality assurance specialist in 2005. In that position, Mr. Owusu-Ansah—who monitored the performance of frontline call center associates—worked from home but was still required to report to the call center for certain meetings.

One such meeting occurred on December 14, 2007, when Mr. Owusu-Ansah met with his manager, Tanika Cabral, for a routine one-on-one. Prior to the meeting, Mr. Owusu-Ansah completed a questionnaire, the answers to which would then be discussed with Ms. Cabral. Under a section entitled "Barriers to success & proposed resolutions," Mr. Owusu-Ansah wrote "Candid discussion about work environment." He also wrote a similar response to a question which asked, "What steps have you taken to move closer to your career goals?"

During his meeting with Ms. Cabral, Mr. Owusu-Ansah articulated several incidents of alleged mistreatment by his managers and co-workers at Coca-Cola over the course of his employment. Mr. Owusu-Ansah said that from 2000 to 2009, certain managers and employees had discriminated against him or harassed him because he was from Ghana. Prior to his meeting with Ms. Cabral, Mr. Owusu-Ansah had never complained to Coca-Cola about any such treatment. Ms. Cabral observed that Mr. Owusu-Ansah became agitated during the meeting, banged his hand on the table where they sat, and said that someone was "going to pay for this."

After the meeting, Ms. Cabral went to her own supervisor, Cassandra Cliette, and described Mr. Owusu-Ansah's conduct to her. Ms. Cabral and Ms. Cliette then contacted Melissa Welsh, Coca-Cola's senior human resources manager. Ms. Cabral explained to Ms. Welsh what had occurred during the meeting, including Mr. Owusu-Ansah banging his fist on the table and saying someone was "going to pay for this." Upon hearing Ms. Cabral's account, Ms. Welsh became concerned "because it sounded as though a threat had been made against an employee, or employees of the company."

Ms. Welsh told Leslie Davis, one of Coca-Cola's security managers, about the situation and asked what should be done. Ms. Davis, in turn, suggested they contact Dr. Marcus McElhaney, Ph.D., an independent consulting psychologist who specialized in crisis management and threat assessment.

On December 19, 2007, Ms. Welsh met with Mr. Owusu-Ansah and asked him to discuss in detail the concerns he had previously expressed to Ms. Cabral. Mr. Owusu-Ansah declined to do so. Ms. Welsh then asked Mr. Owusu-Ansah if he would be willing to speak to a consultant Coca-Cola used to resolve workplace issues. Mr. Owusu-Ansah agreed, and was introduced to Dr. McElhaney, who interviewed him right away at the Dunwoody call center.

In a private conversation with Dr. McElhaney, Mr. Owusu-Ansah discussed his concerns and described the alleged instances of discrimination. After this meeting, Dr. McElhaney expressed concern to Coca-Cola over the emotional and psychological stability of Mr. Owusu-Ansah, noting that there was a "strong possibility that he was delusional." Dr. McElhaney concluded that Mr. Owusu-Ansah was a "very stressed and agitated individual," and recommended that he be placed on paid leave to allow for further evaluation. Coca-Cola followed Dr. McElhaney's recommendation and placed Mr. Owusu-Ansah on paid leave effective December 19, 2007.

Following this initial meeting, Dr. McElhaney continued his assessment of Mr. Owusu-Ansah by phone and email. At Dr. McElhaney's suggestion, Mr. Owusu-Ansah agreed to visit a psychiatrist, Dr. Christopher Riddell, on January 14, 2008. At this session, however, Mr. Owusu-Ansah declined to answer questions regarding his employment and workplace issues. He also refused to sign a release allowing Dr. Riddell to discuss his impressions with Dr. McElhaney. As a result, Dr. McElhaney was unable to complete his evaluation.

On January 22, 2008, Dr. McElhaney informed Ms. Welsh in writing that he remained "concern[ed] about Mr. Owusu-Ansah's apparent level of emotional distress and also about his ability to perceive events accurately." Dr. McElhaney recommended that Mr. Owusu-Ansah undergo a psychiatric/psychological fitness-for-duty evaluation "to rule out the possibility of a mental condition that could interfere with his ability to successfully and safely carry out his job duties."

A week later, Ms. Welsh sent a letter to Mr. Owusu-Ansah informing him that, as a condition to his continued employment with Coca-Cola, he was to "complete an evaluation to identify whether there were any issues that could represent a risk to the safety of others in the workplace." Failure to do so, explained Ms. Welsh, would subject Mr. Owusu-Ansah to immediate termination. Mr. Owusu-Ansah received the letter on February 1, 2008.

Mr. Owusu-Ansah returned for another session with Dr. Riddell—the evaluation complained of in this case—on February 20, 2008. As part of the psychiatric evaluation, Dr. Riddell recommended that Mr. Owusu-Ansah undergo a personality test, the Minnesota Multiphasic Personality Inventory, before being cleared for work. When Mr. Owusu-Ansah failed to attend a scheduled appointment to take the MMPI, Coca-Cola sent a letter advising him that he was not in compliance with the conditions outlined in the prior correspondence. Coca-Cola also informed Mr. Owusu-Ansah that he would be placed on unpaid leave on March 16, 2008, and warned him that continued noncompliance with the evaluation process would be considered a voluntary resignation.

Mr. Owusu-Ansah took the MMPI on March 20, 2008. After reviewing the results of the MMPI, which indicated that Mr. Owusu-Ansah's profile was "within normal limits," Dr. McElhaney cleared Mr. Owusu-Ansah for return to work. On April 22, 2008, Mr. Owusu-Ansah returned to work with Coca-Cola.

III

The ADA, in § 12112(d)(4)(A), provides that

> [a] covered entity shall not require a medical examination and shall not make inquiries of an employee as to whether such employee is an individual with a disability or as to the nature or severity of the disability, unless such examination or inquiry is shown to be job-related and consistent with business necessity.

Mr. Owusu-Ansah argues that, contrary to what the district court concluded, Coca-Cola violated § 12112(d)(4)(A) by requiring him to undergo the fitness-for-duty evaluation. Coca-Cola, not surprisingly, disagrees.

A

We have not yet ruled on whether an employee claiming protection under § 12112(d)(4)(A) of the ADA must prove that he is disabled. Today we conclude, as have other circuits, that § 12112(d)(4)(A) protects employees who are not disabled.

Unlike other provisions of the ADA, § 12112(d)(4)(A) does not refer to a "qualified individual"—a person who "can perform the essential functions of the job" he or she holds or desires "with or without reasonable accommodation," 42 U.S.C. § 12111(8)—but rather to an "employee." We agree with the Tenth Circuit that "[i]t makes little sense to require an employee to demonstrate that he has a disability to prevent his employer from inquiring as to whether he has a disability." Our ruling, moreover, is consistent with our interpretation of 42 U.S.C. § 12112(d)(2) (prohibiting a medical examination to determine "whether [a job] applicant is an individual with a disability or as to the nature or severity of such disability," except in limited situations), as not limiting coverage to those with disabilities.

Nevertheless, as explained below, the evaluation conducted at the behest of Coca-Cola was both "job-related and consistent with business necessity." It was therefore valid under § 12112(d)(4)(A).

B

The phrase "job-related and consistent with business necessity" appears not only in § 12112(d)(4)(A) of the ADA, but in §§ 12112(b)(6), 12113(a), and 12113(c) as well. We have said that "job-relatedness is used in analyzing the questions or subject matter contained in a test or criteria used by an employer" as a basis for an employment decision, while "[b]usiness necessity, in context, is larger in scope and analyzes whether there is a business reason that makes necessary the use by an employer of a test or criteria" for such a decision. Because "[a] term appearing in several places in a statutory text is generally read the same way each time it appears."

In *Watson v. City of Miami Beach*, 177 F.3d 932, 935 (11th Cir. 1999), we held that in "any case where a police department reasonably perceives an officer to be even mildly paranoid, hostile, or oppositional, a fitness for duty examination is job related and consistent with business necessity." We explained that "the ADA does not, indeed cannot, require a police department to forgo a fitness for duty examination to wait until a perceived threat becomes real or questionable behavior results in injuries." Although Mr. Owusu-Ansah was not employed as a police officer engaged in dangerous work, *Watson* provides some guidance for us. Given the information it had about Mr. Owusu-Ansah at the time, Coca-Cola did not violate § 12112(d)(4)(A) by requiring him to undergo a psychiatric/psychological fitness-for-duty evaluation. The evaluation, in our view, was "job-related and consistent with business necessity."

The evaluation was "job-related" because an "employee's ability to handle reasonably necessary stress and work reasonably well with others are essential functions of any position." Ms. Cabral reported that Mr. Owusu-Ansah—in the course of complaining about discrimination and harassment—banged his fist on the table and said in a raised voice that someone was "going to pay for this." When he was deposed, Mr. Owusu-Ansah denied having behaved that way during his meeting with Ms. Cabral, and he now points out that there were no prior incidents showing that he had a propensity for workplace violence. That, however, is not dispositive. Although Coca-Cola apparently never asked Mr. Owusu-Ansah for his version of what happened at the meeting, it did not rely solely on Ms. Cabral's account in ordering the evaluation. Coca-Cola knew that Mr. Owusu-Ansah had refused to speak to Ms. Welsh and Dr. Riddell about his workplace problems. In addition, Dr. McElhaney—the consulting psychologist—expressed "significant concerns" to Coca-Cola about Mr. Owusu-Ansah's emotional and psychological stability, and recommended a psychiatric/psychological fitness-for-duty evaluation.

On this record, we conclude that Coca-Cola had a reasonable, objective concern about Mr. Owusu-Ansah's mental state, which affected job performance and potentially threatened the safety of its other employees. Though Mr. Owusu-Ansah worked from home, he had access to and was required to attend meetings at the Dunwoody call center.

For basically the same reasons, the evaluation was also "consistent with business necessity." Though it may not be one of the traditional canons of statutory construction, common sense is not irrelevant in construing statutes, and in our view an employer can lawfully require a psychiatric/psychological fitness-for-duty evaluation under § 12112(d)(4)(A) if it has information suggesting that an employee is unstable and may pose a danger to others. ("[B]usiness necessities may include ensuring that the workplace is safe and secure.").

C

In challenging the district court's grant of summary judgment, Mr. Owusu-Ansah relies on enforcement guidance issued by the EEOC with respect to when § 12112(d)(4)(A) permits medical examinations. This EEOC guidance, in relevant part, provides that a "medical examination of an employee may be 'job-related and consistent with business necessity' when an employer has a reasonable belief, based on objective evidence, that (1) an employee's ability to perform essential job functions will be impaired by a medical condition; or (2) an employee will pose a direct threat due to a medical condition."

An agency guidance document is entitled to respect only to the extent that it has the "power to persuade." To the extent that it says that objective evidence is needed, we find the EEOC enforcement guidance persuasive, but that does not mean reversal is in order. As explained earlier, Coca-Cola had Ms. Cabral's account of Mr. Owusu-Ansah's conduct and statements at the meeting; it knew that Mr. Owusu-Ansah had declined to discuss his workplace concerns with Ms. Welsh and Dr. Riddell; and it received the observations and recommendations of Dr. McElhaney, the consulting psychologist who had met with Mr. Owusu-Ansah. Coca-Cola therefore had sufficient objective evidence that Mr. Owusu-Ansah had a potentially dangerous mental condition.

Insofar as Mr. Owusu-Ansah contends that Coca-Cola also needed evidence that he was a "direct threat," a term defined by the ADA as "a significant risk to the health or safety of others that cannot be eliminated by reasonable accommodation," *see* 42 U.S.C. § 12111(3), we disagree. Significantly, ¶ 5 of the EEOC's enforcement guidance is worded disjunctively, so that a "direct threat" is required only if the employer does not have objective evidence that a medical condition will impair an employee's ability to perform an essential job function. Here, as we have explained, Coca-Cola had objective evidence—e.g., the concerns of Ms. Cabral and the observations and recommendations of Dr. McElhaney— that Mr. Owusu-Ansah was under emotional distress and was exhibiting signs of mental instability. And, as we have said before, "an employee's ability to handle reasonably necessary stress and work reasonably well with others are essential functions of any position. Absence of such skills prevents the employee from being 'otherwise qualified.'"

IV

The district court's grant of summary judgment in favor of Coca-Cola is affirmed.

NOTES AND QUESTIONS

1.   *Why is asking illegal?* Title VII and the Age Discrimination in Employment Act only prohibit the discriminatory *use* of information obtained from applicants, but the ADA goes further and bans both the asking of disability-related questions and the discriminatory use of such information. As a matter of policy, why should the mere asking of a question, without more, be illegal?

2.   *What can an employer ask?* An interviewer sees a job applicant limp slightly upon arriving for an in-person interview for a job that requires moderate lifting and walking. Is it permissible for the interviewer to ask, "what is wrong with your leg?" What alternative questions might you suggest? May the interviewer require the applicant to demonstrate her ability to walk across a large room while carrying a twenty-pound weight? Would your answer be any different if the company nurse took the applicant's blood pressure following the demonstration?

3.   *What did the employer do wrong in* Leonel? Why does the court reject the employer's defense that it evaluated the non-medical information prior to evaluating the medical examination results? If the employer in *Leonel* violated

the ADA by requiring the untimely medical examination, what remedy should the court award to the plaintiffs?

4. *Protecting individuals who are NOT disabled.* An individual generally must be "disabled" in order to assert a claim under the ADA. But, the court in *Owusu-Ansah* adopts the position that an employee need not be disabled to have standing to challenge impermissible questions and examinations. What arguments support this conclusion?

5. *"Job-related" and "business necessity."* Are "job-relatedness" and "business necessity" the same or different concepts? How does the court in *Owusu-Ansah* distinguish the two concepts? And, on what basis did the court conclude that the employer had made an adequate showing under the job-relatedness, business necessity standard?

6. *Psychological and personality testing.* The Seventh Circuit has ruled that the Minnesota Multiphasic Inventory test, a psychological screening test, is a "medical examination" because the test is designed to reveal mental illnesses and hurts the employment prospects of individuals with mental disabilities. Karraker v. Rent-A-Center, Inc., 411 F.3d 831 (7th Cir. 2005). On the other hand, personality tests that measure only non-impairment traits such as honesty, tastes, and habits are unlikely to be considered "medical examinations."

7. *Doctor's notes.* A circuit split exists as to the validity of attendance policies that require an employee to submit a doctor's note explaining the reason for an employee's absence from work and the medical nature of the underlying condition. The Second Circuit has ruled that such a policy impermissibly elicits disability-related information concerning an actual or perceived impairment. Conroy v. New York Department of Correctional Services, 333 F.3d 88 (2d Cir. 2003). In contrast, the Sixth Circuit found that such a policy was not disability-related since most of the submitted responses would not reveal the existence of a disabling condition. Lee v. City of Columbus, 636 F.3d 245 (6th Cir. 2011). Which do you think is the better view? How do you think the expansion of the disability definition in the ADA Amendments Act affects this analysis?

8. *Paying for medical examination.* The Ninth Circuit has ruled that while it is permissible for an employer to impose the cost of a required medical examination on prospective employees as a matter of policy, an employer violates the ADA if it requires only applicants with actual or perceived disabilities to pay for the cost of such examinations. *See* BNSF Ry Co. v. EEOC, 902 F.3d 916 (9th Cir. 2018). Do you agree with this distinction? Why or why not?

9. *Wellness plans.* Many employers have adopted "wellness plans" that provide incentives to employees to engage in healthy behaviors, including fitness programs and regular medical checkups. The EEOC promulgated regulations in 2016 that took the position that employee wellness program incentives, whether in the form of a reward or penalty, were considered voluntary under the ADA, as long as the incentive did not exceed 30% of the

cost of self-only coverage. 29 C.F.R. Pt. 1630, App., § 1630.14(d)(3) (effective July 17, 2016). However, the United States District Court for the District of Columbia found that the EEOC had failed to provide an adequate explanation to construe the term "voluntary" as it did. AARP v. United States Equal Employment Opportunity Commission, 267 F. Supp. 3d 14, 38 (D.D.C. 2017), *on reconsideration*, 292 F. Supp. 3d 238 (D.D.C. 2017). As a result, the court vacated the portions of the regulations defining "voluntary," but stayed the effective date of the vacatur order until January 1, 2019. In December 2018, the EEOC rescinded the regulations. Removal of Final ADA Wellness Rule Vacated by Court, 83 Fed. Reg. 65296 (Dec. 20, 2018).

10. *GINA.* The Genetic Information Nondiscrimination Act (GINA) prohibits employers from requesting or disclosing genetic information and from using genetic information in making employment decisions. 42 U.S.C. § 2000ff et seq. Covered "genetic information" includes an individual's genetic test results, the genetic test results of family members, and the collection of information about the manifestation of disease or disorder among family members. Accordingly, an employer's use of a checklist to ascertain diseases or disorders experienced by an applicant's family members would violate GINA.

The COVID-19 Pandemic

The World Health Organization declared the coronavirus disease (COVID-19) to be a pandemic on March 11, 2020. The EEOC subsequently released guidance documents concerning the enforcement of anti-discrimination laws in the wake of the COVID-19 pandemic. The documents adopted the position that unless a disability constitutes a "direct threat," an employer cannot exclude an employee from the workplace or otherwise subject an employee to adverse actions. EEOC, *EEOC Continues to Serve the Public During COVID-19 Crisis* (2020), https://www.eeoc.gov/newsroom/eeoc-continues-serve-public-during-covid-19-crisis. Based on guidance from the CDC, the EEOC determined that COVID-19 does constitute a "direct threat," but advised that the ADA does not allow an employer to exclude an employee or take any other adverse action solely because the employee has a disability that the CDC identifies as potentially placing him at higher risk for severe illness if he gets COVID-19. Exclusion and other adverse action are only permissible absent reasonable accommodations. EEOC, *Pandemic Preparedness in the Workplace and the Americans with Disabilities Act* (March 21, 2020), https://www.eeoc.gov/laws/guidance/pandemic-preparedness-workplace-and-americans-disabilities-act.

A.   Screening Applicants

The guidance documents allow employers to screen all applicants for COVID-19 symptoms after a conditional job offer is made so long as it does so for all entering employees in the same type of job. An employer may delay or withdraw a job offer if an applicant tests positive for COVID-19 or exhibits associated symptoms, but not because an individual is pregnant or 65 or older, even though they might be at a higher risk due to the virus. EEOC, *EEOC Continues to Serve the Public During COVID-19 Crisis* (2020), https://www.eeoc.gov/newsroom/eeoc-continues-serve-public-during-covid-19-crisis.

B. Current employees: medical exams and disability-related inquiries

If an employee calls in sick during the pandemic, the guidance documents permit employers to inquire whether the employee is exhibiting symptoms of COVID-19. If an employee is exhibiting symptoms consistent with those identified by the CDC or other public health officials, employers may administer "reliable" tests for detecting COVID-19 and require those employees to stay home without violating the ADA. EEOC, *What You Should Know About COVID-19 and the ADA, the Rehabilitation Act, and Other EEO Laws* (June 17, 2020), https://www.eeoc.gov/wysk/what-you-should-know-about-covid-19-and-ada-rehabilitation-act-and-other-eeo-laws. While taking an employee's temperature does constitute a medical examination for ADA purposes, employers are permitted to measure their employee's temperatures and keep a log of those results in existing medical files. If an employee tests positive for COVID-19, the employer may disclose the employee's name to a public health official. *Id.*

The guidance documents also permit employers to require doctors' notes and similar assurances that an employee is fit to return to work. However, the documents clarify that antibody tests seeking to determine the existence of a past infection of the virus are not sufficiently job related and may not be required under the ADA. *Id.*

C. Reasonable Accommodations

The guidance documents note that pre-existing conditions render some individuals more susceptible to COVID-19, and those individuals may request reasonable accommodations to eliminate exposure risks absent undue hardship to the employer. However, employees are not entitled to accommodations solely by virtue of having family members who are especially susceptible to the virus. Low cost accommodations include one-way aisles, using plexiglass, tables, or other barriers, and modifying work schedules. Employers may require employees to wear masks or other personal protective equipment and to follow infection control practices such as hand washing. If an accommodation is necessary for an individual to follow these practices (for example, modified masks for employees who lip read), it should be made as long as there is no undue hardship on the employer. *Id.*

E. SPECIAL ISSUES

The vast majority of ADA Title I lawsuits allege claims of disparate treatment resulting in an adverse employment action. But three other types of claims also are possible. One of these is explicitly established by statute, while the other two are judicially recognized by analogy to Title VII.

1. RETALIATION

ADA Section 12203(a) expressly prohibits retaliatory acts:

> No person shall discriminate against any individual because such individual has opposed any act or practice made unlawful by this chapter or because such individual made a charge, testified, assisted, or participated in any manner in an investigation, proceeding, or hearing under this chapter.

The basic elements of a retaliation claim are established if a plaintiff can show: 1) that she engaged in protected activity (i.e., oppose or participate), 2) that she suffered a materially adverse action, and 3) the existence of a causal connection between the protected activity and the adverse action. Proctor v. UPS, 502 F.3d 1200, 1208 (10th Cir. 2007).

Regulations promulgated by the Department of Justice provide illustrations of four types of prohibited retaliatory conduct:

(1) Coercing an individual to deny or limit the benefits, services, or advantages to which he or she is entitled under the Act of this part;

(2) Threatening, intimidating, or interfering with an individual with a disability who is seeking to obtain or use the goods, services, facilities, privileges, advantages, or accommodations of a public accommodation;

(3) Intimidating or threatening any person because that person is assisting or encouraging and individual or group entitled to claim the rights granted or protected by the Act or this part to exercise those rights; or

(4) Retaliating against any person because that person has participated in any investigation or action to enforce the Act or this part.

28 C.F.R. § 36.206(c).

The ADA's requirement of an adverse employment action is substantially similar to the Title VII provision as construed by the Supreme Court in *Burlington Northern & Santa Fe Railroad v. White*, 548 U.S. 53, 126 S.Ct. 2405 (2006). In that case, the Court found Title VII's provision to prohibit discrimination even beyond a change in the terms and conditions of employment. *Burlington Northern* requires proof that the challenged retaliatory conduct is materially adverse and "well might have dissuaded a reasonable worker from making or supporting a charge of discrimination." Courts have adopted this standard with respect to ADA retaliation claims. *See, e.g.*, Reinhardt v. Albuquerque Pub. Sch. Bd. of Educ., 595 F.3d 1126, 1131–35 (10th Cir. 2010).

As for the applicable causation standard in ADA retaliation cases, courts generally follow Supreme Court cases interpreting other anti-discrimination statutes. In *Gross v. FBL Financial Services, Inc.*, 557 U.S. 167, 176–77, 129 S.Ct. 2350–51 (2009), the Supreme Court held that, based on the Age Discrimination in Employment Act's (ADEA) language, age must be the "but for" cause of a materially adverse employment action and not simply a motivating factor. Several years later in *University of Texas Southwestern Medical Center v. Nassar*, 570 U.S. 338, 133 S.Ct. 2517, 2521 (2013), the Court extended *Gross*' rationale to Title VII retaliation claims stating that "[g]iven the lack of any meaningful textual difference between [the ADEA and Title VII's anti-retaliation provision], the proper conclusion is that Title VII retaliation claims require proof that the desire to retaliate was the but-for cause of the challenged employment action."

Federal courts have adopted this "but-for" causation standard for ADA retaliation claims using a similar analysis. One court asserted that "[g]iven the similar use of the 'because of' language in both Title VII's anti-retaliation provision and ADA's anti-retaliation provision as well as the Ninth Circuit's application of the Title VII framework for ADA retaliation claims, this [c]ourt sees no logical reason why Title VII retaliation claims are subject to but-for causation while ADA retaliation claims may still be brought using the lesser motivating factor causation standard." Gallagher v. San Diego Unified Port Dist., 14 F. Supp. 3d 1380, 1386 (S.D. Cal. 2014).

While retaliation claims are highly fact-based and context-dependent, courts generally adhere to the position that temporal proximity alone is insufficient to establish a causal connection to materially adverse employment actions. *See, e.g.*, Staley v. Gruenberg, 575 Fed. Appx. 153, 156 (4th Cir. 2014).

A notable distinction between ADA retaliation claims and other retaliation claims is in the "protected activity" element of the claim. In addition to complaints to supervisors or human resources personnel about perceived unlawful treatment under the ADA, most courts hold that requesting an accommodation under the ADA is protected activity for a retaliation claim. One of the first appellate courts to discuss this issue was the First Circuit in *Soileau v. Guilford of Maine, Inc.*, 105 F.3d 12 (1st Cir. 1997), where the court stated:

> It is questionable whether Soileau fits within the literal language
> of the statute: he filed no charge, nor participated in any
> investigation. Moreover, he did not literally oppose any act or

> practice, but simply requested an accommodation, which was given. It would seem anomalous, however, to think Congress intended no retaliation protection for employees who request a reasonable accommodation unless they also file a formal charge. This would leave employees unprotected if an employer granted the accommodation and shortly thereafter terminated the employee in retaliation.

Id. at 16. Most courts have followed suit. *See* Nicole Buonocore Porter, *Disabling ADA Retaliation Claims*, 19 NEV. L. J. 823, 829–30 (2019). This broadened definition of protected activity means that some ADA retaliation claims will succeed even if the underlying discrimination claim fails and even when there is not "protected activity" as it is defined in the other anti-discrimination statutes. For instance, in *Cloe v. City of Indianapolis*, 712 F.3d 1171 (7th Cir. 2013), the plaintiff was diagnosed with multiple sclerosis and requested and received time off for medical appointments. Her supervisor expressed anger about the accommodation and terminated her one week later. *Id.* at 1173–75. Even though she did not engage in traditional protected activity (she did not complain internally and did not file a charge with the EEOC), her claim succeeded because she was retaliated against for requesting the accommodation of time off for the medical appointments. *Id.* at 1180–81.

Despite this broadened definition of protected activity under the ADA, Professor Porter's study of all ADA retaliation claims after the ADAAA went into effect demonstrates that these claims are hard to win for plaintiffs. In fact, employers' dispositive motions (either motions to dismiss or motions for summary judgment) were granted in almost 75% of the cases in Professor Porter's dataset. *See* Porter, *supra* at 837. Part of the explanation for this low rate of plaintiff success may be the courts' use of the "reasonable belief rule." Under this rule, courts may dismiss a plaintiff's claim on the grounds that the employee could not have had a reasonable belief that the accommodation being requested was reasonable or required. *See* Porter, *supra* at 829–31.

2. DISPARATE IMPACT

The Supreme Court has recognized that disparate-impact claims are cognizable under the ADA. Raytheon Co. v. Hernandez, 540 U.S. 44, 52, 124 S.Ct. 513 (2003). These claims "involve employment practices that are facially neutral in their treatment of different groups but that in fact fall more harshly on one group than another and cannot be justified by business necessity." *Id.* 540 U.S. at 52. Lower courts have ruled similarly. *See, e.g.,* Corbin v. Town of Palm Beach, 996 F.Supp.2d 1275 (S.D. Fla 2014); Kintz v. United Parcel Service, Inc., 766 F.Supp.2d 1245 (M.D. Ala. 2011).

Nonetheless, disparate impact claims under Title I are seldom successful. Three reasons likely account for this result.

First, the individualized analysis required for Title I claims makes courts hesitant to certify claims as class actions. As one court has stated:

> The variance in the named plaintiffs' personal characteristics, coupled with the individualized, case-by-case analysis required by the ADA, renders the proposed representatives in this action unable to establish the necessary elements of the claims of the class in the course of establishing their own. Furthermore, the highly personal nature of each representative's disability also subjects their claims to unique defenses under the ADA which are significant enough to destroy typicality.

Lintemuth v. Saturn Corp., 1994 WL 760811 at *4 (M.D. Tenn.).

Second, it is often difficult for Title I plaintiffs to produce the requisite evidence establishing the existence of a policy's disproportionate impact. For example, the Ninth Circuit has held that a "one-strike" policy that disqualified applicants who tested positive for drug or alcohol use during a pre-employment screening process did not have a disparate impact on recovering drug addicts. Lopez v. Pac. Mar. Ass'n, 657 F.3d 762, 766 (9th Cir. 2011). Lopez first applied to be a longshoreman in 1997 and was disqualified from consideration after he tested positive for marijuana. He then reapplied in 2004 after recovering from his drug addiction and was rejected a second time because of Pacific's one-strike rule. Lopez alleged that Pacific's one-strike rule had a disparate impact on recovered drug addicts by disqualifying applicants who previously tested positive for drug use. The court, however, found that Lopez failed to produce evidence that the policy resulted in fewer recovered addicts in Pacific's workforce, as compared to the number of qualified recovered drug addicts in the relevant labor market. Lopez attempted to prove the existence of a disproportionate impact by comparing Pacific's hiring rate of the population of longshoreman applicants (48%) to the selection rate of recovered drug addicts who previously failed Pacific's pre-employment screening process (0%). But that effort failed because Lopez could not produce any evidence of the number of recovered drug addicts employed by Pacific or in the relevant labor market. The court recognized the difficulty plaintiffs have in producing such evidence, but concluded that plaintiffs must produce some evidence that tends to show a policy excludes a protected group disproportionately in order to establish disparate impact liability.

Finally, employees covered by the ADA have an often more convenient alternative. Rather than challenge an employer policy on disparate impact grounds, a disabled employee can request an individual variation of or exemption from a policy through the reasonable accommodation process. *But see* Michelle A. Travis, *Lashing Back at the Backlash: How the Americans with Disabilities Act Benefits Americans Without Disabilities,*

76 TENN. L. REV. 311, 354–56 (2009) (suggesting that many failure to accommodate claims could be recast as disparate impact claims, thereby potentially enabling more systemic workplace changes).

3. HARASSMENT

A number of courts have recognized a cause of action for disability-based harassment. *See, e.g.*, Fox v. General Motors, 247 F.3d 169 (4th Cir. 2001); Flowers v. Southern Regional Physician Services, 247 F.3d 229 (5th Cir. 2001). These courts have authorized such a claim by analogy to Title VII case law. Both Title VII and the ADA ban discrimination with respect to "terms, conditions, and privileges of employment." 42 U.S.C. § 2000e–2(a) (Title VII); 42 U.S.C. § 12112 (a) (ADA). Since the Supreme Court has found an actionable discrimination claim with respect to sexually harassing conduct that alters an employee's terms, conditions or privileges of employment, *Meritor Savings Bank, FSB v. Vinson*, 477 U.S. 57 (1986), both the *Fox* and *Flowers* decisions concluded that a similar claim should flow from disability-based harassment that has the same impact. *See Fox*, 247 F.3d at 175–76, *Flowers*, 247 F.3d at 233–34. Indeed, the *Flowers* court stated, "we conclude that the language of Title VII and the ADA dictates a consistent reading of the two statutes." 247 F.3d at 233. The Second and Eighth Circuits also have expressly recognized that hostile work environment claims may be brought under the ADA. *See* Fox v. Costco Wholesale Corp., 918 F.3d 65, 73–75 (2d Cir. 2019); Shaver v. Indep. Stave Co., 350 F,3d 716, 719–20 (8th Cir. 2003).

Also consistent with Title VII jurisprudence, courts have limited actionable harassment under the ADA to conduct "that is sufficiently severe or pervasive as to alter the conditions of employment." Silk v. City of Chicago, 194 F.3d 788, 804 (7th Cir. 1999). This high bar has frequently been invoked by courts concluding that the conduct in question, while perhaps insensitive, nonetheless falls short of being actionable. *See, e.g.*, Mannie v. Potter, 394 F.3d 977 (7th Cir. 2005); Walton v. Mental Health Ass'n., 168 F.3d 661 (8th Cir. 1999).

In his book, DISABILITY HARASSMENT (2007), Mark Weber argues that the ADA contains a separate provision that should be read as an independent basis for challenging harassing behavior. ADA Section 12203(b) states:

> It shall be unlawful to coerce, intimidate, threaten, or interfere with any individual in the exercise or enjoyment of, or on account of his or her having exercised or enjoyed, or on account of his or her having aided or encouraged any other individual in the exercise or enjoyment of, any right granted or protected by this chapter.

Because Section 12203(b) is unique to the ADA and not borrowed from Title VII, Weber maintains that the rights afforded by this provision should not be read as limited by the "severe or pervasive" requirement. *Id.* at 43–47.

F. FAMILY AND MEDICAL LEAVE ACT

In the world of employment law practice, ADA issues frequently overlap with issues arising under the Family and Medical Leave Act (FMLA). Both statutes provide a basis by which an employee may obtain a leave of absence for health-related reasons, although the grounds for such a leave differ significantly under the two statutes. Because of this overlap, we include a brief introduction to the FMLA in this section.

The Family and Medical Leave Act, 29 U.S.C.A. § 2601–54 (FMLA), provides that covered employees may take up to twelve weeks of unpaid leave per year for the following purposes:

> (1)   the birth of a child;

> (2)   the adoption or placement for foster care of a child;

> (3)   to care for the employee's spouse, son, daughter or parent who has a serious health condition;

> (4)   *for an employee's own serious health condition which makes the employee unable to perform the functions of his or her job;*

> (5)   for the occurrence of a qualifying exigency arising out of the fact that an employee's spouse, son, daughter, or parent is on or has been notified of impending call to active duty in the Armed Forces in support of a contingency operation; or

> (6)   to care for the employee's spouse, son, daughter, parent, or next of kin who is a covered service member (for a total of 26 work weeks during a 12-month period).

29 U.S.C. § 2612 (emphasis added).

Department of Labor regulations define a "serious health condition" as an illness, injury, impairment, or physical or mental condition that involves:

> (1)   Any period of incapacity or treatment in connection with or consequent to inpatient care (i.e., an overnight stay) in a hospital, hospice, or residential medical care facility;

> (2)   Any period of incapacity requiring absence from work, school, or other regular daily activities, of more than three calendar days, that also involves continuing treatment by (or under the supervision of) a health care provider; or

(3) Continuing treatment by (or under the supervision of) a health care provider for a chronic or long-term health condition that is incurable or so serious that, if not treated, would likely result in a period of incapacity of more than three calendar days; or for prenatal care.

29 C.F.R. § 825.114.

To be eligible for FMLA leave, an employee must (1) have been employed by the current employer for at least twelve months, (2) worked at least 1,250 hours during the twelve-month period immediately preceding the beginning of the leave, and (3) be employed at a worksite where fifty or more employees are employed within 75 miles of that work site. 29 U.S.C. § 2611; 29 C.F.R. § 825.110–11. Covered employers are broadly defined to include any person engaged in any industry or activity affecting commerce that employs fifty or more employees for each working day during each of twenty or more calendar work weeks in the current or preceding calendar year. 29 U.S.C. § 2611; 29 C.F.R. §§ 825.104–05.

In cases of leave to care for an ill family member or because of an employee's own serious health condition, leave may be taken on an intermittent basis or on a reduced leave schedule when medically necessary. In this case, an employer may require an employee to transfer temporarily to an alternative position that better accommodates recurring periods of leave so long as the employer provides equivalent pay and benefits. 29 U.S.C. § 2612(b)(1), (2); 29 C.F.R. §§ 825.203–05.

Employees are required to provide 30 days advanced notice of the need for leave that is foreseeable. In cases where the need for leave is unforeseeable, an employee is obligated to provide notice as soon as practicable under the circumstances. 29 U.S.C. § 2612(e); 29 C.F.R. § 825.302–03. An employee must provide an employer with sufficient information to give reasonable notice of a leave request, but is not required to invoke the FMLA expressly. The regulations require an employer to designate whether the requested leave is for an FMLA-qualifying reason within five business days. 29 C.F.R. § 825.300(d).

An employer may require that an employee provide a medical certificate from a health care provider to support a request for leave based upon the employee's own serious health condition or that of the employee's family member for whom care is provided. 29 U.S.C. § 2613; 29 C.F.R. §§ 825.305–06. If an employee fails to provide requested medical certification within the time established by an employer, which may not be less than fifteen calendar days, an employer may treat the leave as non-qualifying under the FMLA. 29 C.F.R. § 825.311(b). An employer normally may request recertification no more than every 30 days and then only in conjunction with an absence. 29 C.F.R. § 825.308(a).

The FMLA does not require a covered employer to provide paid leave. However, an employee may elect, or an employer may require, substitution of accrued paid vacation leave, personal leave, or family leave to care for a family member who has a serious medical condition. In the case of the employee's own serious medical condition, the employee also may elect, or the employer may require, use of the employee's accrued paid sick or medical leave. 29 U.S.C. § 2612(d)(2). If an employer contributes to a group health plan on the employee's behalf, it must continue to do so while the employee is on FMLA leave at the same level that it would have if the employee was not on leave. 29 U.S.C. § 2614(c)(1).

An employer must reinstate an employee who has taken FMLA leave to the position held before taking the leave or to a position with equivalent benefits, pay and other terms and conditions of employment. 29 U.S.C. § 2614(a)(1). Certain limited exceptions apply to this reinstatement requirement. First, an employer may deny reinstatement to an employee who is laid off or terminated for a reason unrelated to the taking of FMLA leave. The appellate courts are split as to which party bears the burden of persuasion under such circumstances. Second, an employer may decline to reinstate an employee who fraudulently obtains FMLA leave. Finally, once an employee takes leave beyond that protected by the FMLA, the employer is relieved of its reinstatement obligation.

An employee who believes that their FMLA rights have been violated may file a private lawsuit against their employer or file a complaint with any local office of the Wage and Hour Division of the Department of Labor. The Secretary of Labor may investigate and attempt to resolve complaints of FMLA violations or bring a civil action against the employer to recover damages to be paid to the employee. 29 U.S.C. § 2617(b).

Employees may bring two categories of lawsuits against the employer for violation of the FMLA: interference claims and retaliation claims. Interference claims, such as those challenging a denial of leave or reinstatement, do not require a showing of discriminatory intent. In contrast, a plaintiff is required to show a discriminatory motive in order to establish a claim for retaliation.

The statute of limitations on FMLA claims is two years following the date of the last event constituting the alleged violation. However, in cases of a willful violation the limitations period increases to three years. 29 U.S.C. § 2617(c). Remedies under the FMLA include actual damages, interest, liquidated damages equal to the amount of actual damages plus interest, and equitable relief. The court also may award reasonable attorney fees, expert witness fees, and other costs. 29 U.S.C. § 2617; 29 C.F.R. § 825.400.

The two cases below discuss two issues commonly addressed in FMLA litigation. The *Caldwell* decision discusses when an employee or an employee's family member has a serious health condition as defined by the

FMLA. In *Diaz*, the court analyzes and distinguishes the proof requirements applicable to interference and retaliation or discrimination claims.

CALDWELL V. HOLLAND OF TEXAS, INC.

208 F.3d 671 (8th Cir. 2000)

BRIGHT, CIRCUIT JUDGE.

Juanita Caldwell ("Caldwell") appeals the district court's grant of summary judgment to her former employer, Holland of Texas, Inc. ("Holland"), on her claim that Holland terminated her employment in violation of the Family and Medical Leave Act ("FMLA"), 29 U.S.C. §§ 2611–2612. The district court determined as a legal matter that Caldwell's son did not suffer a "serious health condition" under the FMLA, and therefore, the FMLA does not give her any benefits. We determine that Caldwell's evidence showing that her three-year-old son sustained a sudden onset of an ear infection— a condition that required immediate attention by a physician, a series of antibiotic treatments, and surgery—is sufficient to present a fact question regarding whether Caldwell's son's illness and disability qualifies as a "serious health condition" entitling the employee to FMLA leave. Accordingly, we reverse and remand.

I.   BACKGROUND

Caldwell is a single mother, working to support herself and her three-year-old son, Kejuan. Before she was summarily fired, Caldwell worked for Holland, which owns and operates several Kentucky Fried Chicken restaurants in Texarkana, Arkansas. Caldwell worked for Holland for three years, and during that time, she developed an excellent record working at the Kentucky Fried Chicken on Hickory Street.

On Saturday, June 7, 1997, Kejuan awoke with a high fever, pain in his ears, and congestion. Caldwell promptly notified Assistant Manager Loyce, prior to the start of her morning shift, that she would be absent because Kejuan required immediate medical attention. Loyce gave Caldwell permission to miss her shift. That morning, a doctor at an emergency clinic diagnosed Kejuan as having an acute ear infection. During this visit, the doctor prescribed a ten-day course of antibiotics and a two-day decongestant for Kejuan. At the same time, the treating physician informed Caldwell that her son's condition probably would require surgery if her son was to avoid permanent hearing loss, and he recommended that Caldwell schedule a follow-up examination with her son's regular pediatrician, Dr. Mark Wright.

Later that Saturday night, upon the request of an assistant manager, Caldwell worked an evening shift at one of Holland's other restaurant locations. While Caldwell was working, her elderly mother cared for her son and administered his medications. Caldwell did not have any shifts on

Sunday. When Caldwell returned to her regular work on Monday morning, June 9, 1997, Mark Monholland, a manager at the Hickory Street restaurant, abruptly fired Caldwell without discussing her absence of June 7, 1997.

The supplemental affidavit of Ms. Caldwell, Kejuan's mother, asserts that Kejuan suffered "incapacity" for more than three consecutive days following his trip to the clinic and recites that Kejuan did not participate in his "normal activities," remained inside the house, and was kept in bed as much as possible. He remained under the care of either his mother or grandmother who administered prescribed medications during "this entire time." During a follow-up visit on July 1, 1997, Dr. Wright prescribed a second ten-day course of antibiotics for Kejuan in an attempt to treat his "persistent ear infection." On July 17, 1997, Kejuan had surgery to remove his adenoids and tonsils and to place tubes in his ears. Following surgery, Kejuan received another course of antibiotics and orders to remain in bed for one week. His mother and grandmother kept him inside following the operation and restricted him from engaging in normal activities.

Caldwell sued and argued that her termination violated the FMLA. On Holland's motion for summary judgment, the district court dismissed the suit because it concluded that, although the Act generally protects employees when their immediate family members have a "serious health condition," Kejuan's condition did not qualify. Caldwell appeals. We reverse and remand.

II. DISCUSSION

The FMLA allows eligible employees to take up to a total of twelve workweeks of leave per year for, among other things, "serious health conditions" that afflict their immediate family members. *See* 29 U.S.C. § 2612(a)(1)(C) ("to care for the spouse, or son, daughter, or parent, of the employee . . . [who] has a serious health condition"). The employee must show that her family member suffered a serious health condition and that her absence was attributable to the family member's serious health condition.

A "serious health condition" occurs, under the regulations, when the family member suffers an "illness, injury, impairment, or physical or mental condition" that requires "inpatient care" or "continuing treatment" by a health care provider. *See* 29 C.F.R. § 825.114(a). Here, the parties agree that Kejuan never received inpatient care. The pertinent issue is whether Kejuan received continuing treatment. A family member receives continuing treatment if the person experiences "[a] period of *incapacity* . . . of more than three consecutive calendar days" and then receives subsequent treatment, or experiences further incapacity relating to, the same condition. 29 C.F.R. § 825.114(a)(2)(i). The subsequent treatment must include, either "[t]reatment two or more times by a health care provider . . . ," or "[t]reatment by a health care provider on at least one occasion which results in a regimen of continuing treatment under the supervision of the health care provider." 29 C.F.R. § 825.114(a)(2)(i)(A)–(B).

The applicability of the FMLA, here, turns on whether Caldwell can prove a two-pronged inquiry: first, she must show that Kejuan suffered "a period of incapacity of more than three consecutive calendar days"; second, she must show that Kejuan subsequently received continued, supervised treatment relating to the same condition. The district court found, when applying the regulations, that Caldwell "has not provided any proof whatsoever of Kejuan's incapacity for the three days following his June 7 examination." Therefore, the district court determined that Caldwell failed to raise a material issue of fact regarding the first prong of her case, namely that Kejuan was not incapacitated for three consecutive days following Caldwell's absence from work on June 7, 1997. Caldwell argues that this finding was error, and we agree. Caldwell has presented sufficient evidence to raise a question of fact as to whether Kejuan's ear infection incapacitated him for more than three days and whether Kejuan then received subsequent treatment for his condition.

In assessing the first prong of Caldwell's case, we note at the outset that the question of what constitutes incapacity of a three-year-old raises an issue not directly addressed by the regulations. The regulations state that incapacity may be determined based on an individual's "inability to work, attend school or perform other regular daily activities due to the serious health condition, treatment therefor, or recovery therefrom." *See* 29 C.F.R. § 825.114(a)(2)(i). Because most three-year-old children do not work or attend school, the standard offered by the regulations is an insufficient guide. The fact finder must determine whether the child's illness demonstrably affected his normal activity. In making this determination, the fact finder may consider a variety of factors, including but not limited to: whether the child participated in his daily routines or was particularly difficult to care for during that period, and whether a daycare facility would have allowed a child with Kejuan's illness to attend its sessions.

Caldwell avers that Kejuan's ear infection, which was severe enough to warrant emergency treatment, required constant care for a period of more than three days. She states in her supplemental affidavit that Kejuan was incapacitated beginning Saturday, June 7, 1997, for more than three consecutive days. She further states:

> He [Kejuan] remained inside the house and was kept in bed as much as possible. He did not participate in any of his normal activities. He was under the constant care of me (his mother) and his grandmother, and both the prescribed medications and a fever reducer were administered to him during this entire time.

In addition to Caldwell's affidavit, the medical records show that Kejuan's ear infection was a continuing, persistent condition that could only be treated by surgery. Kejuan's period of incapacity, therefore, may be measured over the entire time during which he was suffering from this illness and being treated for it. We note that Kejuan was treated for his condition for ten days following his first visit to the emergency clinic. The medical records state that the condition did not improve, and as a result, Dr. Wright, his regular physician, prescribed another ten-day course of antibiotics. Despite the two medical treatments, Kejuan's condition continued to persist until Dr. Trone, a surgical specialist, performed surgery to remove his tonsils and adenoids on July 17, 1997. This entire period, from June 7–July 17, 1997, may constitute Kejuan's period of incapacity if his illness and these various treatments disrupted his basic daily routines, and if, as the record suggests, his ongoing treatment was not successfully alleviating his condition of disability.

Alternatively, the ten-day period beginning on June 7, 1997 could constitute Kejuan's period of incapacity. As we have noted, his mother's supplemental affidavit refers to constant care and administration of prescribed medications during "this entire time." The affidavit also refers to the doctor's report which stated that on July 1 Kejuan's condition "was not greatly improved." All of this evidence indicates a continuing period of incapacity which may have lasted for ten days.

Even if Kejuan did not sustain "incapacity" under the regulations *prior* to his surgery, the record clearly shows that the inflammation and infection in his ears resulted in a period of incapacity that lasted more than three days once he had the tonsillectomy and adenoidectomy. His mother's affidavit states:

> [T]he doctor stated that [after the operation] Kejuan was to be kept in bed for one (1) week. Kejuan stayed in bed two or three days but was kept inside the house and did not participate in his normal activities for a week following his surgery. During this period of time, he was prescribed his third round of antibiotics.

This surgery was the necessary and only treatment for Kejuan's condition. Although Kejuan's condition did not require immediate surgery, after the first round of antibiotics, the doctors determined that the condition could be cured only by surgical operation.

Both the First and the Seventh Circuits have recognized that medical diseases do not afflict people in methodical and predictable ways: certain serious diseases can elude diagnosis, change in severity, and have cumulative effects on the body over time. *See, e.g., Hodgens v. General Dynamics Corp.*, 144 F.3d 151, 163 (1st Cir.1998); *Price v. City of Fort Wayne*, 117 F.3d 1022, 1024–25 (7th Cir.1997). These unpredictable characteristics of illness can result in an individual's inability to care for himself and perform his daily tasks, after experiencing a series of less debilitating symptoms. In *Hodgens*, the First Circuit recognized the possibility of FMLA coverage for "intermittent leave":

> [O]ne reason for taking "intermittent leave" under the FMLA would be to visit the doctor for purposes of diagnosis and treatment, even if the employee does not take leave for the periods in between such visits. It would seem that Congress intended to include visits to a doctor when the employee has symptoms that are eventually diagnosed as constituting a serious health condition, even if, at the time of the initial medical appointments, the illness has not yet been diagnosed nor its degree of seriousness determined. . . . Thus, as long as Hodgens satisfied, at some point in time, the "more than three consecutive days" requirement for establishing a serious health condition, his intermittent absences for less than four days . . . were protected under the FMLA if they were necessary "to determine if a serious health condition exists," . . . or to treat such a condition. This is true even if the intermittent absences occurred before the consecutive absences.

Hodgens, 144 F.3d at 163. This passage reflects the importance of looking at the disease's effects on the body over the entire period of illness. The Seventh Circuit has even recognized that multiple illnesses, when temporally linked, can result in a serious health condition protected by the FMLA. *See Price*, 117 F.3d at 1025 ("how can one's ability to perform at work be seriously impaired by a single serious illness but not by multiple illnesses having a serious impact? The answer, of course, is that it cannot; the disability is related to the cumulative impacts of illness on one's body and mind.").

FMLA's purpose is to help working men and women balance the conflicting demands of work and personal life. The law requires courts to consider the seriousness of the afflicted individual's condition because the law was designed to prevent individuals like Juanita Caldwell from having to choose between their livelihood and treatment for their own or their family members' serious health conditions. Upon examining the seriousness of Kejuan's ear infection, which required surgery to prevent deafness, we hold that there is at least a question of fact as to whether Kejuan's condition was "serious" under the regulations.

On the second prong of the threshold inquiry, we believe that Caldwell has generated a genuine issue of fact regarding whether Kejuan received "subsequent treatment." By regulation, a plaintiff will show subsequent treatment if the patient merely undergoes "[t]reatment two or more times by a health care provider . . . " or "[t]reatment by a health care provider on at least one occasion which results in a regimen of continuing treatment under the supervision of the health care provider." 29 C.F.R. § 825.114(a)(2)(i)(A)–(B). Here, after the first ten-day antibiotic treatment, Kejuan was treated by Dr. Wright and later by Dr. Trone in surgery. After visits to both Dr. Wright and Dr. Trone, Kejuan received antibiotic treatments. Furthermore, the record shows at least two post-operative medical visits to monitor Kejuan's condition. Caldwell has presented sufficient evidence of subsequent treatment to defeat summary judgment on this second prong.

An employer does not avoid liability by discharging an employee who takes leave in order to seek treatment for a condition that is later held to be covered by the FMLA. The employer who precipitously fires an employee, when the latter claims the benefits of leave under FMLA, bears the risk that the health condition in question later develops into a serious health condition within the meaning of 29 C.F.R. § 825.114(a).

In our view, a fact finder could determine that Kejuan suffered a serious health condition: his infection caused an acute phase, followed by a course of continuing treatment and disability, requiring further treatment and eventual surgery. While the record does not clearly delineate the nature of the incapacity at all times during this extensive period, the evidence does support a fact finding of incapacity extending more than three consecutive calendar days starting on June 7, 1997.

III. CONCLUSION

For the reasons stated above, the district court erred in granting a summary judgment of dismissal. Accordingly, we reverse and remand for further proceedings.

HANSEN, CIRCUIT JUDGE, dissenting.

The district court correctly concluded that Kejuan did not have a "serious health condition" as defined by the Family and Medical Leave Act (FMLA). In this case involving continuing treatment by a health care provider, rather than inpatient care, Kejuan's ear infection would qualify as a "serious health condition" only if it resulted in "[a] period of incapacity . . . of more than three consecutive calendar days, *and* any subsequent treatment or period of incapacity relating to the same condition. . . ." 29 C.F.R. § 825.114(a)(2)(i). In order to qualify as continuing treatment, the regulations specifically require an incapacity of more than three consecutive calendar days at the onset of the condition plus subsequent treatment or incapacity.

The record does not support Ms. Caldwell's contention that Kejuan was incapacitated for more than three consecutive days at the time of the onset of the condition. Ms. Caldwell's complaint listed no periods of incapacity. Ms. Caldwell's sworn response to interrogatory number 4, which asked her to list the dates of incapacitation, stated, "June 7, 8, and 9." Ms. Caldwell's brief in response to Holland's motion for summary judgment stated that Kejuan was incapacitated the week following his July 17 surgery. Likewise, Ms. Caldwell's statement of facts stated he was incapacitated the week following his July 17 surgery. Also, Ms. Caldwell's affidavit alleged Kejuan was incapacitated the week following his surgery. Ms. Caldwell's response to Holland's reply to her response to its motion for summary judgment listed no periods of incapacity. Consequently, the district court noted in its March 18, 1999, order that Ms. Caldwell "provided no evidence that her son was incapacitated for more than three consecutive days during the time period of the June 7 absence as required by the regulations." The district court ordered Ms. Caldwell "to supplement [her] response to [Holland's] motion for summary judgment with any evidence regarding the incapacity of [Kejuan] immediately following his June 7 examination." It was not until Ms. Caldwell filed her supplemental affidavit in response to the district court's order that she, for the first time, alleged that her son was "incapacitated beginning Saturday, June 7, 1997, for more than three (3) consecutive days." Prior to this supplemental affidavit, Ms. Caldwell had alleged that Kejuan was incapacitated only on June 7, 8, and 9, and during the one-week period following his surgery on July 17. Ms. Caldwell made no attempt to amend her sworn answer to interrogatory number 4.

At oral argument, I asked counsel for Ms. Caldwell about the dates of Kejuan's incapacity. The following exchange occurred:

> Judge Hansen: In your response to interrogatory number 4, which is in the appendix at page 27, you state that this boy was incapacitated on June 7, 8, and 9, but in the supplemental affidavit from your client she states that he was incapacitated beginning on June 7 for more than three days, that's appendix at 89, how do you explain that inconsistency?

> Counsel: I guess I should have said at least three days, that's what I was saying, it's at least three days, 7, 8, and 9.

> Judge Hansen: Is that what the rule is, at least three days?

> Counsel: I think the rule is more than three days, in any event he was incapacitated. Let me move on.

. . . Clearly, the statement by counsel for Ms. Caldwell was an acknowledgment that the assertion in the supplemental affidavit was incorrect and that it should have stated "at least three days." Counsel's last statement was not an attempt to show conformity with the regulations, as [the majority] suggests. Counsel's last statement before changing the subject away from the dates of incapacity was an acknowledgment that "at least three days" of incapacity does not meet the FMLA requirement of more than three days of incapacity. Additionally, my interpretation of counsel's concession at oral argument is consistent with the record. Nowhere in the record did Ms. Caldwell ever allege more than three days of incapacity during the time period of the June 7 absence until she was ordered by the district court to offer such evidence. If anything is inconsistent with or in the record, it is Ms. Caldwell's supplemental affidavit. Kejuan's ear infection did not, according to counsel's own concession, incapacitate him for more than three days at the onset of the condition on June 7. The supplemental affidavit in response to Holland's motion for summary judgment, as qualified by counsel at argument, does not present evidence sufficient to show a *genuine* dispute of material fact such that a reasonable jury could return a verdict in favor of Ms. Caldwell.

An affidavit submitted in response to a motion for summary judgment which contradicts earlier sworn testimony without explanation of the difference does not create a genuine issue of material fact. Here, Ms. Caldwell's supplemental affidavit asserts for the first time that her son was incapacitated for more than three days following the onset of his condition. This statement directly contradicts the sworn interrogatory response that Kejuan was incapacitated only on June 7, 8, and 9. . . .

The court would like to add together Kejuan's incapacity on June 7, 8, and 9, along with his one-week period of incapacity following his July 17 surgery to remove his adenoids and tonsils and to place tubes in his ears, in order to meet the "more than three consecutive calendar days" requirement. Such an interpretation is inconsistent with the language of the regulation. Section 825.114(a)(2)(i) requires a period of more than three days incapacity *and* subsequent treatment or incapacity. As the court's opinion explains, the applicability of the FMLA relies on a two-pronged inquiry. First, Kejuan must have been incapacitated for a period of "more than three consecutive calendar days;" second, Kejuan must have been subsequently treated or incapacitated. Although Kejuan's one-week recovery from his July 17 surgery met the second-prong "subsequent treatment or period of incapacity relating to the same condition" requirement of § 825.114(a)(2)(i), Kejuan's initial condition did not meet the first-prong requirement of a period "of more than three consecutive calendar" days of incapacity.

The court relies on *Hodgens v. General Dynamics Corp.*, 144 F.3d 151 (1st Cir.1998), to support its contention that the time period following Kejuan's surgery on July 17 meets the first prong requirement of more than three days of incapacity. However, *Hodgens* is distinguishable. In *Hodgens,* the plaintiff suffered from atrial fibrillation, a serious and potentially life-threatening heart condition. Unfortunately, the doctor was unable to initially diagnose his condition. The plaintiff's first visit to the doctor was on August 4, 1993, but he was not correctly diagnosed until September 21, 1993. During that time period, the plaintiff had numerous doctor's appointments and medical tests to evaluate his condition. Once the plaintiff was correctly diagnosed, the doctor excused the plaintiff from work during the period of September 22 to September 27, 1993. The First Circuit determined that the four-consecutive-day period of September 22 to September 27 met the three-day requirement of § 825.114(a)(2). Thus, the First Circuit concluded that even the plaintiff's intermittent absences before the diagnosis were protected under the FMLA if the absences "were necessary to determine if a serious health condition exist[ed] or to treat such a condition." However, only the absences that were actually necessary for the plaintiff to attend medical appointments related to his atrial fibrillation were protected under the FMLA. ("[A]part from the period from September 22–27, while [the plaintiff's] medical condition clearly did require him to be absent from work . . . for his medical visits, it did not require the vast majority of his absences during August and September.").

Assuming *Hodgens* is a correct interpretation of the FMLA regulations pertaining to intermittent leave, its conclusion is not applicable to this case. The doctor for Ms. Caldwell's son did not have any difficulty in correctly diagnosing Kejuan's condition. At the initial June 7 visit, the doctor informed Ms. Caldwell that Kejuan suffered from an acute ear infection and that he would probably require surgery to avoid hearing loss. Although Kejuan's condition may have become a serious health condition at the time of his surgery, Kejuan did not suffer from a serious health condition at the time of his initial doctor's appointment. "[T]he FMLA and its implementing regulations defining 'serious health condition' are not concerned with the potential dangers of an illness but only with the present state of that illness."

In contrast, the plaintiff in *Hodgens* suffered from a serious condition at the time of his initial doctor's appointment, even though the doctor did not know exactly what that condition was. The doctor did, however, recognize that the plaintiff might be suffering from a serious condition, and therefore, the doctor ordered the plaintiff to undergo a series of tests. *Hodgens,* 144 F.3d at 157. In fact, the doctor initially suspected that the plaintiff might be suffering from angina, "which could be extremely serious or even fatal." The doctor testified that it was reasonable for the plaintiff to stay home from work until he got the results of his stress test. This situation is completely different from Ms. Caldwell's situation as evidenced by the fact that the doctor correctly diagnosed Kejuan's condition, did not order any tests, recommended surgery in the future to correct the problem, and did not suggest that Kejuan should stay in bed or not participate in his normal activities. Certainly there is a distinction between an undiagnosed, potentially life-threatening heart condition and a properly diagnosed and promptly treated ear infection.

Unlike the First Circuit, this court today has greatly expanded the definition of incapacity to include periods of time when a patient is taking antibiotics or if the illness disrupts basic daily routines. The court suggests that Kejuan may have been incapacitated for at least the ten-day period following the onset of the illness during which time Kejuan was taking antibiotics and that he may have been incapacitated for the entire period from June 7 to July 17, an assertion never made even by Ms. Caldwell. The court has supplanted the express guidance provided by the FMLA regulations with its own view of what constitutes an incapacity. *See* 29 C.F.R. § 825.114(a)(2)(i) (Incapacity is an "inability to work, attend school or perform other regular daily activities."). In this respect, I reject the court's suggestion that "incapacity" under the FMLA may be defined by the sniffle standards imposed by a local daycare center.

The legislative history of the FMLA indicates that Congress intended the FMLA to apply only to serious health conditions. Congress did not include those "minor illnesses which last only a few days and surgical procedures which typically do not require hospitalization and require only a brief recovery period." Kejuan's ear infection, up until the point of his surgery, was a minor illness as shown by his not more than three days of incapacity, his improvement on the onset day which allowed his mother to work on the evening of onset (June 7) and to return to work on June 9, the lack of any restrictions placed on him by his doctor, the length of time between his June 7 initial doctor visit and his next follow-up visit on July 1, and the scheduling of his surgery nearly six weeks after the onset of his illness. Ms. Caldwell's one-day absence from work on June 7 to take her son to the doctor is not the type of absence that Congress enacted the FMLA to cover. Congress expected absences for these types of minor illnesses to be covered under an employer's sick leave policy.

Consequently, I would affirm the judgment of the district court because Kejuan did not have a "serious health condition" as defined by the FMLA and its regulations.

DIAZ V. FORT WAYNE FOUNDRY CORP.
131 F.3d 711 (7th Cir. 1997)

EASTERBROOK, CIRCUIT JUDGE.

Alfredo Diaz took a month's leave from his job under the Family and Medical Leave Act of 1993 when his physician certified that he had bronchitis. Fort Wayne Foundry, the employer, told Diaz to return to work on April 30, 1995. Diaz did not come back but called on May 1 to inform the Foundry that he was receiving medical treatment in Mexico, and that the Foundry would hear from his new physician by May 5. On May 8 the Foundry received a note from a Dr. Llamas asserting that Diaz suffered from irritable bowel syndrome, hiatal hernia, gastroesophageal reflux, and a duodenal peptic ulcer, requiring a month and a half of rest. These conditions are unrelated to bronchitis, raising suspicions at the Foundry. But instead of invoking its option under 29 U.S.C. § 2613(c) to require a second opinion, the firm sent Diaz a letter postponing his return until May 18 (52 days from the start of his leave).

Diaz did not return to work after May 18 or explain his absence. On May 30 the Foundry received a fax from Dr. Llamas, who asserted that Diaz needed yet another month to recuperate. To resolve the conflict between Diaz's two physicians, and to learn when it could expect him back at work, the Foundry directed Diaz to report for a physical examination on June 8. This instruction was sent by certified mail to his home address, and the receipt was signed "Alfredo D.". But Diaz neither appeared for the medical examination nor asked the Foundry to set a more convenient schedule. Diaz was fired on June 15 for failing to work despite the end of his leave. This at last persuaded Diaz to communicate with the Foundry: with this lawsuit under the FMLA.

The district court granted summary judgment to the Foundry after stepping through a series of questions inspired by *McDonnell Douglas Corp. v. Green*, 411 U.S. 792, 800–06, 93 S.Ct. 1817, 1823–26 (1973): first the employee must establish a *prima facie* case; if this has been done, the employer must articulate a lawful explanation for its conduct; then the burden shifts back to the employee to prove that the statute has been violated. Although the Supreme Court developed this burden-shifting approach as a filter, to concentrate judicial attention on (and limit the burdens of discovery to) the cases with the greatest prospects of success, it has not succeeded at that task even within its original domain. District courts regularly treat the *prima facie* case as a throwaway—holding discovery before deciding whether the plaintiff has satisfied the initial burden, then assuming its existence on the way to resolving the suit on other grounds. That is how the district judge proceeded in Diaz's case, which implies that it is best to take Occam's Razor and slice off unnecessary steps and proceed directly to the question whether the evidence would permit a rational trier of fact to conclude that the statute has been violated. Eventually the burden-shifting framework disappears anyway. If a trial is held, the whole apparatus drops out (although lawyers and judges sometimes forget this, leading to error).

Although a burden-shifting approach can be useful in discrimination cases as a heuristic, claims under the FMLA do not depend on discrimination. The question in a discrimination case is whether the employer treated one employee worse than another on account of something (race, religion, sex, age, etc.) that a statute makes irrelevant. A firm may treat all employees equally poorly without discriminating. A statute such as the FMLA, however, creates substantive rights. A firm *must* honor statutory entitlements; when one employee sues, the firm may not defend by saying that it treated all employees identically. The FMLA requires an employer to accommodate rather than ignore particular circumstances. In this respect the FMLA is like the National Labor Relations Act, the Fair Labor Standards Act, and the Employee Retirement and Income Security Act, all implemented without using the *McDonnell Douglas* approach. Applying rules designed for anti-discrimination laws to statutes creating substantive entitlements is apt to confuse, even if the adaptation is cleverly done. The district court's approach shows what can go wrong. The judge stated the inquiry this way:

> Under the burden shifting approach, Diaz must initially establish
> a *prima facie* case of discrimination by showing: (1) he was

protected under the FMLA; (2) he suffered an adverse employment action; and (3) he was treated less favorably than employees who did not avail themselves of the act or that the adverse decision was a result of his invocation of the act. If Diaz is successful in establishing a *prima facie* case, "the burden of production then shifts to the Foundry to show a legitimate nondiscriminatory reason for the challenged employment action...." If the Foundry produces a legitimate, non-discriminatory reason, the burden shifts back to Diaz to prove by a preponderance of the evidence that the reasons offered by the Foundry are a pretext for discrimination.

This is not a sound extension of *McDonnell Douglas*. Under the FMLA an employee need *not* show that other employees were treated less favorably. The question is not how the Foundry treats others, but whether it respected each employee's entitlements. This is the big difference between anti-discrimination statutes and laws such as the FMLA that set substantive floors. The FMLA does have an anti-discrimination component: "It shall be unlawful for any employer to discharge or in any other manner discriminate against any individual for opposing any practice made unlawful by this subchapter." 29 U.S.C. § 2615(a)(2). But Diaz does not say that he is a victim of discrimination in this sense. The second problem in the district court's summary is the statement that at the third stage the employee must "prove by a preponderance of the evidence that the reasons offered by the [employer] are a pretext for discrimination." This is inconsistent with *St. Mary's Honor Center v. Hicks*, 509 U.S. 502, 113 S.Ct. 2742 (1993), which held that the employee's burden is to prove a violation of the statute; proof of "pretext" may have evidentiary value but is neither necessary nor sufficient.

Our research has not turned up any appellate decision applying the *McDonnell Douglas* framework to substantive claims under the FMLA. At least one court of appeals has used a derivative burden-shifting approach for claims based on the anti-retaliation provision of the FMLA, see *Morgan v. Hilti, Inc.*, 108 F.3d 1319 (10th Cir.1997), and we reserve judgment on this possibility. (It is not clear what a burden-shifting approach could add, but at least it would not misdirect attention, as it does for substantive claims.) Although several district judges have used a variant of *McDonnell Douglas* for substantive FMLA cases, we disapprove their conclusions. We shall continue to resolve suits under the FMLA in the same direct way we did in *Price v. Ft. Wayne*, 117 F.3d 1022 (7th Cir.1997): by asking whether the plaintiff has established, by a preponderance of the evidence, that he is entitled to the benefit he claims. Disagreement with the district court's framework does not imply disagreement with its judgment, however.

An employee who meets the tenure and hours requirements of 29 U.S.C. § 2611(2)(A), as Diaz does, is entitled to as many as 12 weeks of unpaid leave over the course of 12 months "[b]ecause of a serious health condition that makes the employee unable to perform the functions of the position of such employee." 29 U.S.C. § 2612(a)(1)(D). To establish the existence of such a condition an employee must submit medical certification. 29 U.S.C. § 2613(a). An employer that doubts the sufficiency or veracity of the certification may require another opinion, § 2613(c):

> (1) In any case in which the employer has reason to doubt the validity of the certification provided under subsection (a) for leave under subparagraph (C) or (D) of section 2612(a)(1) of this title, the employer may require, at the expense of the employer, that the eligible employee obtain the opinion of a second health care provider designated or approved by the employer concerning any information certified under subsection (b) of this section for such leave. (2) A health care provider designated or approved under paragraph (1) shall not be employed on a regular basis by the employer.

Fort Wayne Foundry exercised its option under § 2613(c), designating a physician that it did not employ on a regular basis (avoiding the ground on which the employer tripped in *Price*). See also 29 C.F.R. § 825.307(A)(2). Diaz does not deny that the disparity between the medical opinions rendered by his two physicians gave the Foundry "reason to doubt the validity of the certification". Yet he did not appear for the medical examination. An employee who fails to cooperate with the second-opinion process under § 2613(c) loses the benefit of leave under § 2612(a)(1)(C) or (D). After missing the appointment set for June 8, Diaz was AWOL and could not invoke the FMLA to avoid discharge.

As Diaz sees things, he did not have to appear on June 8 (or ever) because the Foundry sent the notice to Indiana rather than Mexico. Notice sent to his home was the same as no notice, he insists, because the Foundry knew that he was not there. The Foundry responds, without contradiction, that it sent the letter to Diaz's last address of record because this is what its collective bargaining agreement requires, and that the signature "Alfredo D." implied that he had returned from Mexico. Federal labor law requires employers to adhere to collective bargaining agreements; nothing in the FMLA entitles employees to variance from neutral rules about ways and means of giving notice. If Diaz wanted to ensure that he received communications from the Foundry, he had to do one (or both) of two things: (i) tell the people receiving mail (and signing his name) in his absence to open the mail and call him with news (or forward the letters); or (ii) give his employer an address where he could be reached. Diaz asserts that occasionally he called a security guard at the plant to reveal his continuing interest in employment, but the collective bargaining agreement and the firm's work rules require notice to the personnel department, not the security department. What matters for current purposes is that the FMLA does not tell employers how to send notices. A firm safely may use the method prescribed by collective bargaining agreements or some other source of rules. Doubtless the FMLA implies a duty to set a *reasonable* time for the medical examination; the Foundry would have had to allow Diaz a few days to return from Mexico, but he did not ask for more time. As far as the FMLA is concerned, his leave was over. So is this case.

NOTES AND QUESTIONS

1.   *Understanding "serious health conditions."* The *Caldwell* decision illustrates the difficulty of applying the three-plus days standard for determining the existence of a serious health condition. The majority opinion offers three possible bases for finding a fact question as to coverage: a) perhaps Kejuan was incapacitated for the entire June 7 to July 17 period; b) perhaps the ten days of incapacity following the July surgery can be causally linked to the June 7–9 absences; and c) the intermittent absences in June were necessary to determine if a subsequent serious health condition existed. The dissent, in contrast, finds no evidence to show more than three days of consecutive absences beginning on June 7. Which of these positions strikes you as the most plausible?

2.   Why does the Seventh Circuit Court of Appeals in *Diaz* reject application of the *McDonnell Douglas* framework to FMLA interference claims? What evidentiary standard does the court instead adopt? Do you agree with this approach? Should the *McDonnell Douglas* framework apply to FMLA retaliation claims?

3.   *Understanding* Diaz. At the time that Fort Wayne Foundry terminated Diaz, he had not yet exhausted his twelve-week FMLA leave entitlement. Diaz also informed a security guard working for the employer of his continuing interest in working for the foundry. And, the employer sent notice of the scheduled second-opinion physical examination to Diaz's Indiana residence even though it knew that Diaz was in Mexico. Under these circumstances, why did the court uphold the termination?

4.   *Incapacity.* A serious health condition requires a period of "incapacity," which the regulations define as the "inability to work, attend school or perform other regular daily activities." 29 C.F.R. § 825.114(a)(2). The severity of an employee's underlying medical condition may not always provide much guidance as to the existence of a sufficient period of incapacity. *Compare* Thorson v. Gemini, Inc., 205 F.3d 370 (8th Cir. 2000) (upset stomach and minor ulcer may result in a serious health condition), Manuel v. Westlake Polymers Corp., 66 F.3d 758 (5th Cir. 1995) (ingrown toenail may result in a serious health condition), *with* Dalton v. ManorCare of W. Des Moines, 782 F.3d 955 (8th Cir. 2015) (early stage kidney disease is not a serious health condition), Oswalt v. Sara Lee Corp., 74 F.3d 91 (5th Cir. 1996) (food poisoning is not a serious health condition). *See also* Price v. City of Fort Wayne, 117 F.3d 1022 (7th Cir. 1997) (finding that several minor health problems, none of which

alone constitutes a serious health condition, may, when taken together, rise to the level of a serious health condition).

5.   *Providing care.* An employee's absence for providing care to a family member is protected under the FMLA only if the employee actually was providing "care" during the period of absence. *Compare* Ballard v. Chicago Park District, 741 F.3d 838 (7th Cir. 2014) (finding that the employee cared for her terminally ill mother when she provided assistance during a trip to Las Vegas funded by the Fairygodmother Foundation), *with* Tellis v. Alaska Airlines, Inc., 414 F.3d 1045 (9th Cir. 2005) (finding that the employee's regular telephone calls to his pregnant wife while he was driving on a cross-country trip to bring her a more reliable car did not constitute care for FMLA purposes).

6.   *Designating leave.* The U.S. Supreme Court in *Ragsdale v. Wolverine World Wide, Inc.*, 535 U.S. 81, 122 S.Ct. 1155 (2002) held that a Department of Labor regulation providing that leave taken by an employee does not count against an employee's FMLA entitlement if the employer does not timely designate the leave as FMLA-qualifying was contrary to the FMLA and beyond the authority of the Secretary of Labor to adopt. The Court noted that the regulation punished employers for failing to provide timely designation notice without requiring the employee to show any evidence of resulting harm. Following *Ragsdale*, since an employee still may be able to make out a violation if it can show that the employer's failure to provide notice results in tangible harm, the best practice for a doubting employer is to provisionally designate the leave as FMLA-qualifying and then remove the designation if the medical certification process establishes that the leave does not qualify for FMLA coverage.

7.   *Denying reinstatement.* As noted above, an employer may deny reinstatement to an employee who is laid off or terminated for a reason unrelated to the taking of FMLA leave. The appellate courts are split as to which party bears the burden of persuasion under such circumstances. *Compare* O'Connor v. PCA Family Health Plan, Inc., 200 F.3d 1349, 1354 (11th Cir. 2000) (referencing 29 C.F.R. § 825.216(d), which states "[a]n employer would have the burden of proving that an employee would have been laid off during the FMLA leave period and, therefore, would not be entitled to restoration"), *with* Rice v. Sunrise Express, Inc., 209 F.3d 1008, 1018 (7th Cir. 2000) (holding that the employee bears the burden of persuasion to show that the termination was in retaliation for taking FMLA leave).

8.   *FMLA/ADA/workers' compensation triad.* An employer may offer a light duty assignment to facilitate an employee's return from workers' compensation leave. How does such an offer impact FMLA and ADA rights? Three points are clear: a) an employee with FMLA coverage may lawfully decline light duty until the FMLA leave period is exhausted; b) an employee covered by the ADA who declines light duty may forfeit the right to another accommodation if the light duty offer is itself a reasonable accommodation; and c) in either event, such a refusal will terminate the employee's right to continued workers' compensation benefits.

9.   *Eleventh Amendment immunity.* The Eleventh Amendment to the U.S. Constitution bars suits for damages against states in federal court unless Congress has unequivocally expressed its intent to permit such suits and acts pursuant to a valid grant of constitutional authority. Applying this principle, the Supreme Court has held that the Eleventh Amendment does not bar suits alleging a state employer's failure to comply with the family care provisions of the FMLA. Nevada Dept. of Human Resources v. Hibbs, 538 U.S. 721, 123 S.Ct. 1972 (2003). In contrast, the Supreme Court has held that state employees may not bring federal court suits for damages against a state employer with respect to the self-care provision of the FMLA. Coleman v. Court of Appeals of Maryland, 566 U.S. 30, 132 S.Ct. 1327 (2012).

10.   *State paid leave laws.* As of 2020, eight states—California, Connecticut, Massachusetts, New Jersey, New York, Oregon, Rhode Island, and Washington—plus the District of Columbia and numerous cities have enacted family and medical leave laws that provide for time off work with pay. The paid leave periods run from a low of four weeks per year in Rhode Island to twelve weeks in Washington. Some states such as California, fund the pay solely out of employee payroll contributions, while others, such as New York, provide for joint employer and employee contributions. *See* National Partnership for Women & Families, *State Paid Family and Medical Leave Insurance Laws* www.nationalpartnership.org/our-work/resources/economic-justice/paid-leave/state-paid-family-leave-laws.pdf.

Interplay with ADA

ADA and FMLA claims often arise in the same case. It is important to be aware that an employee may be covered by both statutes, and, as a general rule, "an employer must . . . provide leave under whichever statutory provision provides the greater rights to employees." 29 CFR § 825.702(a).

The ADA and FMLA, however, differ in a number of significant respects:

- First, the concept of a serious health condition is broader than that of a disability. An individual with a relatively minor ailment that lasts four or five days, such as the flu, may be entitled to leave under the FMLA even though such an illness most likely would not be considered an impairment that substantially limits a major life activity under the ADA (although this is a closer question after the ADA Amendments Act).

- Second, while the ADA is an anti-discriminatory statute, the FMLA, as explained in *Diaz*, is primarily an entitlement statue. Accordingly, an employee with a serious health condition is *entitled* to take protected leave regardless of whether the employer treats similarly situated co-employees in the same manner.

- Third, FMLA provides leave rights for a time certain, while the ADA provides leave rights for an uncertain duration. At the end of twelve weeks, an employee's right to FMLA leave ceases. In contrast, the length of an employee's leave right under the ADA is frequently difficult to predict; depending on the extent to which time off constitutes a reasonable accommodation or imposes an undue hardship in the particular context. Notably, employers have no undue hardship safety valve available by which to truncate FMLA leave taken under burdensome circumstances.

It is important to consider both statutes in response to leave requests. Human resource managers generally favor a sequential analysis. They first determine if the employee is entitled to leave under the FMLA. If so, the employer must grant up to twelve weeks of leave within a year. After that period runs, the FMLA entitlement ceases, but the employer may have a duty to grant extended leave under the ADA if the employee's condition qualifies as a disability, and if additional leave would be a reasonable accommodation and not impose an undue hardship. Even though the analysis is sequential, most HR managers designate the entire leave period as ADA-qualifying.

G. PROCEDURES AND REMEDIES

The ADA expressly incorporates Title VII's enforcement procedures and remedies as its own. ADA Section 12117 states:

The powers, remedies, and procedures set forth in sections 2000e–4, 2000e–5, 2000e–6, 2000e–8, and 2000e–9 of this title shall be the powers, remedies, and procedures this subchapter provides to the Commission, to the Attorney General, or to any person alleging discrimination on the basis of disability in violation of any provision of this chapter, or regulations promulgated under section 12116 of this title, concerning employment.

As explained below, Title VII provides for enforcement through a unique blend of administrative and litigation-based mechanisms.

1. JURISDICTION

The ADA applies to all employers having 15 or more employees other than the federal government and its subdivisions. 42 U.S.C. § 12111(5). The Supreme Court has adopted a "payroll method" for counting employees for coverage purposes, by which an employer is deemed to have all employees with which it has an employment relationship on the day in question, regardless of the number of employees that actually worked or were compensated on a given day. Walters v. Metropolitan Educational Enterprises, Inc., 519 U.S. 202, 117 S.Ct. 660 (1997).

The Rehabilitation Act applies to the federal government, employers having federal government contracts in excess of $10,000, and recipients of federal financial assistance. 29 U.S.C. §§ 791, 793(a), 794. Section 791(g) of the Rehabilitation Act states that the standards used to determine the existence of employment discrimination under the Rehabilitation Act "shall be the standards applied under Title I of the ADA."

The ADA applies only to "employees" and not independent contractors. 42 U.S.C. § 12111(4). The Supreme Court has held that the common law definition of the master-servant relationship, which emphasizes the degree of a master's control over a servant, should be used to determine the existence of "employee" status. Clackamas Gastroenterology Associates, P.C., 538 U.S. 440, 123 S.Ct. 1673 (2003).

2. AGENCY ENFORCEMENT

The ADA, like Title VII, is administered by the Equal Employment Opportunity Commission ("EEOC"), an agency of the federal government. The EEOC is composed of five members appointed by the President. In addition to processing claims of discrimination, the EEOC is empowered to adopt regulations implementing ADA Title I.

The administrative enforcement process is initiated by the filing of a charge with the EEOC. Title VII states that "charges shall be in writing under oath or affirmation and shall contain such information and be in such form as the Commission requires." EEOC regulations provide that a valid charge is a written document "sufficiently precise to identify the parties and to describe generally the action or practice complained of." 29 C.F.R. § 1601.12(b).

A charge must be filed within 180 days of the alleged unlawful employment practice, but that deadline is expanded to 300 days in states which have a fair employment practice law and an enforcement mechanism recognized by the EEOC (known as "deferral" jurisdictions). 42 U.S.C. § 2000e–5(c). In deferral jurisdictions, the charge must initially be filed with the state or local agency, and that agency has exclusive jurisdiction over the charge for the first 60 days. If the charge is not resolved within that time period, the individual may file a charge with the EEOC. The individual must file the charge with the EEOC within 30 days of notice that the deferral agency has terminated its proceedings or no later than 300 days following the alleged discriminatory act, whichever event is earlier in time.

Once the charge is before the EEOC, the agency has exclusive jurisdiction for 180 days. Title VII provides that "notice of the charge (including date, place and circumstances of the alleged unlawful employment practice) shall be served upon the person against whom such charge is made within ten days [after filing.]" 42 U.S.C. § 2000e–5(e)(1). The EEOC is directed to investigate the charge in order to determine whether there is reasonable cause to believe that the charge is accurate. If reasonable cause is found to exist, the Commission is to "endeavor to eliminate such alleged unlawful employment practice by informal methods of conference, conciliation, and persuasion." 42 U.S.C. § 2000e–5(b). If no reasonable cause is found, the statute directs the agency to dismiss the charge, inform the parties, and notify the charging party of its right to bring a private suit.

The EEOC also has the right to seek enforcement of a charge by filing suit at any time after 30 days following the filing of the charge. 42 U.S.C. § 2000e–6(f)(1). The Supreme Court has ruled that the EEOC may not initiate suit until it has first attempted to remedy the alleged discrimination through conciliation. Mach Mining, LLC v. E.E.O.C., 565 U.S. 480, 135 S.Ct. 1645 (2015).

Once the 180 days of exclusive jurisdiction comes to an end, the EEOC must relinquish jurisdiction and provide the charging party with a "right to sue" letter.

3.   PRIVATE LITIGATION ENFORCEMENT

Once a charging party has received a "right to sue" letter from the EEOC, the employee has a 90-day window to commence a private lawsuit. A charging party may not initiate a private lawsuit with respect to any charge that has not been administratively exhausted before the EEOC. Lyons v. England, 307 F.3d 1092 (9th Cir. 2002). Courts have held, however, that litigants can pursue claims that were not filed as separate charges if those claims are "like or reasonably related to" an alleged unlawful employment practice that was properly exhausted. Anderson v. Block, 807 F.2d 145, 148 (8th Cir. 1986). The circuit courts currently are split on the issue of whether a plaintiff who has filed a timely charge of discrimination may pursue a post-filing claim of retaliation without also filing a charge with respect to the alleged retaliatory act. *Compare* Richter v. Advance Auto Parts, Inc., 686 F.3d 847 (8th Cir. 2012) (holding that a retaliation claim may not be asserted without a separate filing), *with* Jones v. Calvert Group, Ltd., 551 F.3d 297 (4th Cir. 2009) (holding that a post-filing retaliation claim is like or reasonably related to a filed charge of discrimination).

The Civil Rights Act of 1991 amended Title VII to provide that an individual seeking compensatory or punitive damages in a disparate treatment case is entitled to a jury trial. 42 U.S.C. § 1981a(c). Other cases, including claims of disparate impact, are tried to the court.

4.   REMEDIES

Remedies under Title VII and the ADA include back pay, reinstatement, attorneys' fees, interest, and other equitable relief. 42 U.S.C. § 2000e–5(g)(k). While reinstatement is a favored remedy that should be granted in the ordinary course, a court may award front pay in lieu of reinstatement when the latter remedy is not feasible. *See* Gunter v. Bemis Co., 906 F.3d 484 (6th Cir. 2018).

The Civil Rights Act of 1991 expanded the remedies available under Title VII in cases of intentional discrimination to include compensatory and punitive damages. 42 U.S.C. § 1981a. Compensatory damages are damages for future economic losses, emotional pain and suffering, inconvenience, mental anguish, loss of enjoyment of life, and other nonpecuniary losses. Punitive damages may be awarded when the claimant demonstrates that illegal action was taken with "malice or reckless indifference to" the individual's federally protected rights. The Supreme Court has held that punitive damages must be based on conscious wrongdoing, and rest on a finding of "malice or reckless indifference" linked to the employer's state of mind, rather than whether the discrimination itself is egregious or outrageous in nature. Kolstad v. American Dental Ass'n, 527 U.S. 526, 119 S.Ct. 2118 (1999).

The 1991 amendments establish caps on the amount of compensatory and punitive damages that a court may award based upon the size of the employing entity. For each complaining party, the sum of compensatory and punitive damages awarded is limited to $50,000 for any employer with 15–100 employees; $100,000 for employers with 101–200 employees; $200,000 for employers with 201–500 employees; and $300,000 for employers with more than 500 employees. 42 U.S.C. § 1981a(b)(3). The Supreme Court has ruled that front pay is not an element of compensatory damages under the Civil Rights Act and therefore is not subject to the statutory caps. Pollard v. E.I. DuPont De Nemours & Co., 532 U.S. 279, 122 S.Ct. 754 (2002).

The Civil Rights Act of 1991 also adopted a limitation on when damages can be awarded based upon an employer's failure to provide a reasonable accommodation under Title I of the ADA. The amendment provides that damages may not be awarded

> . . . where the covered entity demonstrates good faith efforts, in consultation with the person with the disability . . . to identify and make a reasonable accommodation that would provide such individual with an equally effective opportunity and would not cause an undue hardship on the operation of the business.

42 U.S.C. § 1981a(a)(3).

While the damage provisions of the Civil Rights Act of 1991 apply to Section 501 of the Rehabilitation Act (providing for affirmative action plans for federal agencies), they do not apply to Section 504. Thus, a successful claimant under Section 504 can recover compensatory damages that are not subject to the Act's damage caps. Punitive damages, however, are not available under Section 504. Barnes v. Gorman, 536 U.S. 181, 122 S.Ct. 2097 (2002).

NOTES AND QUESTIONS

1. *Statutes of limitations.* Most common law employment claims have a statute of limitations of two years or more. What policies are served by the shorter limitations period for employment discrimination claims?

2. *Exhaustion of remedies.* The requirement of administrative exhaustion prior to suit adds time and red tape to the enforcement process. What policies support the exhaustion requirement?

3. *Arbitration.* Arbitration is a possible alternative to court-based litigation for employment discrimination claims. The Supreme Court has issued a series of rulings that generally make individual arbitration agreements enforceable. In *Gilmer v. Interstate/Johnson Lane Corp.,* 500 U.S. 20, 111 S.Ct. 1647 (1991), the Court held that an employee's agreement to submit all disputes to arbitration was valid so long as it waived only resort to a judicial forum, but not the substantive rights conferred by federal antidiscrimination statutes. A decade later, the Court held that the Federal Arbitration Act's exclusion of coverage with respect to contracts for workers engaged in interstate commerce precluded the enforcement of arbitration agreements only for those employees engaged in the actual movement of goods across state lines. Circuit City Stores, Inc. v. Adams, 532 U.S. 105, 121 S.Ct. 1302 (2001). More recently, the Court has upheld the validity of arbitration agreements that contain class action waivers. AT&T Mobility LLC v. Concepcion, 563 U.S. 333, 131 S.Ct. 1740 (2011). In spite of these rulings, Senator Al Franken (D-Minn.) has introduced legislation that would make pre-dispute arbitration agreements unenforceable in the context of employment and consumer disputes. What are the pros and cons of such a proposal?

The Supreme Court has ruled that an arbitration agreement between an employer and an employee does not bind the EEOC in its enforcement of federal anti-discrimination laws. EEOC v. Waffle House, Inc., 534 U.S. 279, 122 S.Ct. 754 (2002). Thus, even in the presence of an otherwise valid arbitration clause, the EEOC may initiate enforcement action in a judicial forum and seek victim-specific relief.

H. IS THE ADA WORKING?

SHARONA HOFFMAN, SETTLING THE MATTER: DOES TITLE I OF THE ADA WORK?

59 ALA. L. REV. 305 (2007–2008)

* * *

Another arena in which Title I of the ADA has failed to produce an improvement for individuals with disabilities is entry into the workforce and employment rates. According to a 1999 Census Bureau Current Population Survey, 34% "of men and 33% of women with work disabilities were employed [that year], compared to 95% of men and 82% of women without work disabilities." According to a 2000 Harris Survey, only 32% of adults with disabilities between the ages of eighteen and sixty-four stated that they were employed, while 81% of people without disabilities in the same age group had employment.

Experts who have studied employment statistics have also concluded that employment rates for those with disabilities declined in the 1990s after enactment of the ADA.[149] According to one source, from 1989 to 2000 the employment rate for men with disabilities fell by 22%, while that of men without disabilities diminished by only 1%. During the same time, the employment rates of women with disabilities fell by 1%, while that of women without disabilities grew[150]. . . .

The reasons for this decline have puzzled many scholars, and several potential explanations for it have been developed. First, it is possible that the vagueness of the term "disability" makes it difficult to elicit accurate responses through a survey instrument. . . .

A second explanation could be that the ADA's reasonable accommodation requirement has made employers even more reluctant to hire individuals with disabilities than they were before the statute's enactment. Employers, fearing that they will have to absorb high costs of accommodations if they employ individuals with disabilities, might prefer to reject their applications, thereby avoiding the accommodation question. Employers might calculate that the risk of litigation over an adverse hiring decision is minimal because discrimination is very difficult to prove with respect to subjective hiring decisions. The employer can often argue convincingly that the candidate was not sufficiently impressive during her interview or that it seemed as though the applicant's personality was not a good fit for the job, and the unsuccessful candidate will not have a performance record at the company to prove her competence.

It is also possible that lingering stereotypes and biases contribute to the exclusion of individuals with disabilities from the workplace. . . .

These data suggest that employers often bar employment to people with disabilities because they believe them to be unqualified or too inexperienced for the job, and these beliefs might be erroneous in more than a few cases. Thus, low employment rates for people with disabilities may be partly attributable to employers' tendency to deny serious consideration to some applicants with disabilities because of perceived educational, training, or prior work history deficiencies, or, more bluntly, because of biased attitudes towards people with disabilities. . . .

---

[149] *See, e.g.,* DAVID C. STAPLETON ET AL., HAS THE EMPLOYMENT RATE OF PEOPLE WITH DISABILITIES DECLINED? 1 (December 2004), *available at* http://digitalcommons.ilr.cornell.edu/edicollect/92.

[150] *Id.*

The most compelling explanation, however, might relate to the lack of universal health care coverage in this country. Ironically, employment can adversely affect the ability of individuals with disabilities to obtain adequate health care coverage because it renders them ineligible to receive Social Security Disability Benefits. . . .

The picture painted by data other than judicial outcomes and employment rate statistics is much brighter for individuals with disabilities. For those individuals with disabilities who are members of the workforce, the post ADA workplace appears to offer a more comfortable and hospitable environment. . . .

EEOC merit resolution rates for ADA cases (22.1% in 2005 and 23.4% in 2006) are well within the range of merit resolutions for charges brought under the other statutes enforced by the EEOC. . . .

Most significantly, reports concerning reasonable accommodations provided by employers outside of the litigation or administrative enforcement context reveal that many employers are generous in providing accommodations without any prompting by external parties.

NOTES AND QUESTIONS

1. *Applicants vs. current employees.* Why might an employer treat disabled individuals who are currently employed more favorably than disabled applicants?

2. *Enhancing Title I.* Overall, do you think Title I of the ADA has been more helpful or harmful for individuals with disabilities? How could Title I be modified to better serve disabled applicants and employees without unduly burdening employers?

CHAPTER 5

GOVERNMENT SERVICES:
TITLE II OF THE ADA

■ ■ ■

A. BACKGROUND AND STATUTORY LANGUAGE

Title II of the ADA prohibits discrimination by state and local governmental entities. Title II consists of two main sections. Part A has a general focus that sets out the definitions and general prohibition against discrimination. Part B focuses more narrowly, containing specific rules applicable to public transportation entities.

Part A initially provides two foundational definitions. First, Section 12131(1) defines a covered "public entity" as

(A) any State or local government;

(B) any department, agency, special purpose district, or other instrumentality of a State or States or local government; and

(C) the National Railroad Passenger Corporation, and any commuter authority (as defined in Section 24102(4) of Title 49).

Second, Section 12131(2) defines a "qualified individual with a disability" to mean

an individual with a disability who, with or without reasonable modifications to rules, policies, or practices, the removal of architectural, communication, or transportation barriers, or the provision of auxiliary aids and services, meets the essential eligibility requirements for receipt of services or participation in programs or activities provided by a public entity.

Part A then broadly bans discrimination in the following provision:

Subject to the provisions of this subchapter, no qualified individual with a disability shall, by reason of such disability, be excluded from participation in or be denied the benefits of the services, programs, or activities of a public entity, or be subjected to discrimination by any such entity.

42 U.S.C. § 12132. Part A authorizes the Attorney General to promulgate implementing regulations.

Title II does not apply to the federal government, which instead is subject to the anti-discrimination provisions of the Rehabilitation Act. However, Title II and Section 504 of the Rehabilitation Act are intertwined in several respects. First, the two statutes apply to many of the same entities. Since most state and local government units receive federal financial assistance, they are covered by Section 504 as well as Title II. Second, Part A's anti-discrimination language closely tracks that of Section 504. Third, the regulations implementing Part A are patterned after and interpreted consistently with the regulations implementing Section 504. *See* 42 U.S.C. § 12134(b). Finally, Part A provides that the remedies, procedures, and rights applicable to Section 504 shall also apply in enforcing Part A. 42 U.S.C. § 12133.

Part B of Title II addresses the matter of disability discrimination in public transportation. The statute provides considerable detail about the compliance requirements for public entities that provide transportation services. The statute vests regulatory authority over part B with the Secretary of Transportation. 42 U.S.C. § 12149. Because Part B is far narrower than Part A, most of this chapter will focus on Part A.

B. COVERAGE

PENNSYLVANIA DEPARTMENT OF CORRECTIONS V. YESKEY
524 U.S. 206, 118 S.Ct. 1952 (1998)

JUSTICE SCALIA delivered the opinion of the Court.

The question before us is whether Title II of the Americans with Disabilities Act of 1990 (ADA), 104 Stat. 337, 42 U.S.C. § 12131 et seq., which prohibits a "public entity" from discriminating against a "qualified individual with a disability" on account of that individual's disability, see § 12132, covers inmates in state prisons. Respondent Ronald Yeskey was such an inmate, sentenced in May 1994 to serve 18 to 36 months in a Pennsylvania correctional facility. The sentencing court recommended that he be placed in Pennsylvania's Motivational Boot Camp for first-time offenders, the successful completion of which would have led to his release on parole in just six months. Because of his medical history of hypertension, however, he was refused admission. He filed this suit against petitioners, the Commonwealth of Pennsylvania's Department of Corrections and several department officials, alleging that his exclusion from the Boot Camp violated the ADA. The District Court dismissed for failure to state a claim, Fed. Rule Civ. Proc. 12(b)(6), holding the ADA inapplicable to inmates in state prisons; the Third Circuit reversed.

Petitioners argue that state prisoners are not covered by the ADA for the same reason we held in Gregory v. Ashcroft, 501 U.S. 452, 111 S.Ct. 2395

(1991), that state judges were not covered by the Age Discrimination in Employment Act of 1967 (ADEA), 29 U.S.C. § 621 et seq. Gregory relied on the canon of construction that absent an "unmistakably clear" expression of intent to "alter the usual constitutional balance between the States and the Federal Government," we will interpret a statute to preserve rather than destroy the States' "substantial sovereign powers." It may well be that exercising ultimate control over the management of state prisons, like establishing the qualifications of state government officials, is a traditional and essential state function subject to the plain-statement rule of Gregory. "One of the primary functions of government," we have said, "is the preservation of societal order through enforcement of the criminal law, and the maintenance of penal institutions is an essential part of that task." "It is difficult to imagine an activity in which a State has a stronger interest."

Assuming, without deciding, that the plain-statement rule does govern application of the ADA to the administration of state prisons, we think the requirement of the rule is amply met: the statute's language unmistakably includes State prisons and prisoners within its coverage. The situation here is not comparable to that in Gregory. There, although the ADEA plainly covered state employees, it contained an exception for " 'appointee[s] on the policymaking level' " which made it impossible for us to "conclude that the statute plainly cover[ed] appointed state judges." Here, the ADA plainly covers state institutions *without* any exception that could cast the coverage of prisons into doubt. Title II of the ADA provides:

> "Subject to the provisions of this subchapter, no qualified individual with a disability shall, by reason of such disability, be excluded from participation in or be denied the benefits of the services, programs, or activities of a public entity, or be subjected to discrimination by any such entity." 42 U.S.C. § 12132.

State prisons fall squarely within the statutory definition of "public entity," which includes "any department, agency, special purpose district, or other instrumentality of a State or States or local government." § 12131(1)(B).

Petitioners contend that the phrase "benefits of the services, programs, or activities of a public entity," § 12132, creates an ambiguity, because state prisons do not provide prisoners with "benefits" of "programs, services, or activities" as those terms are ordinarily understood. We disagree. Modern prisons provide inmates with many recreational "activities," medical "services," and educational and vocational "programs," all of which at least theoretically "benefit" the prisoners (and any of which disabled prisoners could be "excluded from participation in"). Indeed, the statute establishing the Motivational Boot Camp at issue in this very case refers to it as a "program." The text of the ADA provides no basis for distinguishing these programs, services, and activities from those provided by public entities that are not prisons.

We also disagree with petitioners' contention that the term "qualified individual with a disability" is ambiguous insofar as concerns its application to state prisoners. The statute defines the term to include anyone with a disability

> "who, with or without reasonable modifications to rules, policies, or practices, the removal of architectural, communication, or transportation barriers, or the provision of auxiliary aids and services, meets the essential eligibility requirements for the receipt of services or the participation in programs or activities provided by a public entity." 42 U.S.C. § 12131(2).

Petitioners argue that the words "eligibility" and "participation" imply voluntariness on the part of an applicant who seeks a benefit from the State, and thus do not connote prisoners who are being held against their will. This is wrong on two counts: First, because the words do not connote voluntariness. See, *e.g.*, Webster's New International Dictionary 831 (2d ed. 1949) ("eligible": "Fitted or qualified to be chosen or elected; legally or morally suitable; as, an *eligible* candidate"); *id.*, at 1782 ("participate": "To have a share in common with others; to partake; share, as in a debate"). While "eligible" individuals "participate" voluntarily in many programs, services, and activities, there are others for which they are "eligible" in which "participation" is mandatory. A drug addict convicted of drug possession, for example, might, as part of his sentence, be required to "participate" in a drug treatment program for which only addicts are "eligible." And secondly, even if the words did connote voluntariness, it would still not be true that all prison "services," "programs," and "activities" are excluded from the ADA because participation in them is not voluntary. The prison law library, for example, is a service (and the use of it an activity), which prisoners are free to take or leave.

Finally, petitioners point out that the statute's statement of findings and purpose, 42 U.S.C. § 12101, does not mention prisons and prisoners. That is perhaps questionable, since the provision's reference to discrimination "in such critical areas as . . . institutionalization," § 12101(a)(3), can be thought to include penal institutions. But assuming it to be true, and assuming further that it proves, as petitioners contend, that Congress did not "envisio[n] that the ADA would be applied to state prisoners," in the context of an unambiguous statutory text that is irrelevant. As we have said before, the fact that a statute can be " 'applied in situations not expressly anticipated by Congress does not demonstrate ambiguity. It demonstrates breadth.' "

* * *

Because the plain text of Title II of the ADA unambiguously extends to state prison inmates, the judgment of the Court of Appeals is affirmed.

NOTES AND QUESTIONS

1. *Broad coverage.* The *Yeskey* decision adopted a broad view of Title II coverage. According to *Yeskey*, Title II encompasses all services, programs, and activities of a public entity regardless of whether individual participation in those activities is voluntary or involuntary. Several other cases involving prisons have similarly adopted a broad range of coverage. *See, e.g.*, Furgess v. Pennsylvania Dep't of Corrections, 933 F.3d 285 (3d Cir. 2019) (ruling that state prison violated Title II by failing to provide inmate with an accessible shower facility); Pierce v. District of Columbia. 128 F.Supp. 3d 250 (D.D.C. 2015) (ruling that prison denied meaningful access to services by failing to provide deaf inmate with a sign language interpreter).

2. *Title II and prisons.* In a pre-*Yeskey* decision, Judge Posner expressed the following concern about applying Title II to prisons:

> It is very far from clear that prisoners should be considered "qualified individual[s]" within the meaning of the Act. Could Congress really have intended disabled prisoners to be mainstreamed into an already highly restricted prison society? There are formidable practical objections to burdening prisons with having to comply with the onerous requirements of the Act, especially when we reflect in that alcoholism and other forms of addiction are disabilities within the meaning of the Act and afflict substantial portions of the prison population.

Bryant v. Madigan, 84 F.3d 246, 248 (7th Cir. 1996). Following *Yeskey*, what services, programs and activities must prisons now provide to inmates with disabilities? Is the practical impact of *Yeskey* likely to be burdensome and onerous?

3. *Quasi-public entities.* Coverage issues arise with respect to quasi-public entities created by public-private partnerships such as charter schools and detention centers operated by private companies. The Department of Justice has indicated that the following four factors should be considered in determining whether such an entity is subject to Title II:

(1) Whether the entity is operated with public funds;

(2) Whether the entity's employees are considered government employees;

(3) Whether the entity receives significant assistance from the government by provision of property or equipment; and

(4) Whether the entity is governed by an independent board selected by members of a private organization or a board elected by the voters or appointed by elected officials.

Letter from John L. Wodatch, Chief, Public Access Section, U.S. Dep't of Justice, to C. Todd Jones, Assistant Counsel for Indus. Rehab & ADA Issues, Nat'l Ass'n of Rehab. Facilities (Jan. 1993).

4.   *Proceedings seeking to terminate parental rights.* A number of courts have held that Title II does not apply to state-court proceedings seeking to terminate parental rights. The Rhode Island Supreme Court explained the logic of this position in *In re Kayla N.*, 900 A.2d 1202, 1208 (R.I. 2006), stating that such "proceedings are held for the benefit of the child, not the parent. Therefore, the ADA is inapplicable when used as a defense by the parents in [those] proceedings." Some other courts, however, have suggested that Title II may be asserted as an affirmative defense in such a proceeding. *See* In re T.M., 715 N.W.2d 771 (Iowa Ct. App, 2006); In re C.M., 996 S.W.2d 269 (Tex. App. 1999). The concern here is that courts may more readily terminate the rights of disabled parents, particularly those with mental impairments, as compared to nondisabled parents. *See* Susan Kerr, *The Application of the Americans with Disabilities Act to the Termination of the Parental Rights of Individuals with Mental Disabilities*, 16 J. CONTEMP. HEALTH L. & POL'Y 387 (2000). Should Title II apply in this context? If so, what should be the extent of the state court's obligation?

In 2015, the Department of Justice and Department of Health and Human Services weighed in with an investigatory letter taking the position that Title II applies to proceedings to terminate parental rights. According to the letter, the position that Title II does not apply to such proceedings cannot be squared with the *Yeskey* decision. *See* U.S. Dep't of Justice & U.S. Dep't of Health and Human Services, *Investigation of the Massachusetts Dep't of Children and Families,* DJ No. 204–36–216 and HHS No. 14–182176 (29 Jan. 2015), https:// perma.cc/UD7J-D5Y8). The letter, while persuasive, is not binding on the courts. *See* Nicole Buonocore Porter, *Mothers with Disabilities*, 33 BERKELEY J. GENDER L. & JUST. 75, 102–03 (2018).

5.   *Title II and arrests.* Does Title II apply to conduct occurring during arrests carried out by police officers? Two types of claims are possible in this context. First, an individual with a disability may have a claim for wrongful arrest if the police erroneously perceive lawful conduct associated with the disability to be illegal activity. Second, an individual with a disability may have a discrimination claim if he or she suffers harm as the result of police failing to reasonably accommodate the individual's disability during the course of an arrest. A circuit split currently exists on this coverage issue. Most circuit courts have ruled that Title II does apply to arrests. *See, e.g.*, Bircoll v. Miami-Dade County, 480 F.3d 1072 (11th Cir. 2007); Gohier v. Enright, 186 F.3d 1216 (10th Cir. 1999). In contrast, the Fifth Circuit has held that Title II is inapplicable to arrests due to the exigent circumstances that police officers frequently face in carrying out arrests. *See* Hainze v. Richards, 207 F.3d 796 (5th Cir. 2000). Under the majority approach, the impact of exigent circumstances goes to the reasonableness of possible accommodations rather than to the coverage issue. *See* Shanna Rifkin, *Safeguarding the ADA's Antidiscrimination Mandate: Subjecting Arrests to Title II Coverage*, 66 DUKE L.J. 913 (2017); Carly A. Myers, *Police Violence Against People With Mental Disabilities: The Immutable Duty Under the ADA to Reasonable Accommodate During Arrest*, 70 VAND. L. REV. 1393 (2017).

REYAZUDDIN V. MONTGOMERY COUNTY, MARYLAND
789 F.3d 407 (4th Cir. 2015)

DIAZ, CIRCUIT JUDGE:

Montgomery County, Maryland, opened a new, consolidated call center using software that was inaccessible to blind employees. The County did not transfer employee Yasmin Reyazuddin, who is blind, to the call center along with her sighted coworkers. The County also did not hire her for a vacant position there. Reyazuddin challenged the County's actions as violating Section 504 of the Rehabilitation Act of 1973, 29 U.S.C.A. § 794 (West 2014), or Title II of the Americans with Disabilities Act of 1990 (the "ADA"), 42 U.S.C. § 12131 *et seq.* (2012)

Section 504 forbids an employer from discriminating against an employee because of her disability. It also requires an employer to accommodate an employee with a disability who can perform the essential functions of a job with a reasonable accommodation. But an employer avoids liability if it can show that providing an accommodation would constitute an "undue hardship."

We find that genuine issues of material fact remain as to (1) whether Reyazuddin could perform the essential job functions of a call center employee; (2) whether the County reasonably accommodated her; and (3) if the County did not, whether its failure to do so may be excused because of undue hardship. Accordingly, we reverse the district court's order granting summary judgment to the County on Reyazuddin's Section 504 claims. However, we affirm the district court's order granting summary judgment to the County on Reyazuddin's Title II claim because public employees cannot use Title II to bring employment discrimination claims against their employers.

[The facts of this case are set out in Chapter 3 of this casebook and will not be repeated here.]

* * *

III.

Reyazuddin's final claim is that the County violated Title II of the ADA by not hiring her to fill a vacancy at MC311. Title II prohibits discrimination against "qualified individual[s] with a disability" in the delivery of "services, programs, or activities of a public entity." 42 U.S.C. § 12132. The district court assumed without deciding that Title II applies to public employment discrimination claims based on two of our previous cases that similarly assumed without analysis that Title II could be used in this context. *Reyazuddin,* 7 F.Supp.3d at 556 (citing *Rogers v. Dep't of Health & Envtl. Control,* 174 F.3d 431, 432–33 (4th Cir. 1999), and *Doe,* 50 F.3d at 1264–65).

Our sister circuits have divided on this issue. *See Bd. of Trustees of the Univ. of Ala. v. Garrett,* 531 U.S. 356, 360 n. 1, 121 S.Ct. 955, 148 L.Ed.2d 866 (2001) (acknowledging but not resolving the split). The Second, Seventh, Ninth, and Tenth Circuits have held that litigants asserting public employment discrimination claims against their state and local government employers cannot rely on Title II. *Brumfield v. City of Chicago,* 735 F.3d 619, 626 (7th Cir.2013); *Mary Jo C. v. N.Y. State & Local Ret. Sys.,* 707 F.3d 144, 171 (2d Cir.2013); *Elwell v. Okla. ex rel. Bd. of Regents of the Univ. of Okla.,* 693 F.3d 1303, 1313 (10th Cir.2012); *Zimmerman v. Or. Dep't of Justice,* 170 F.3d 1169, 1178 (9th Cir.1999). In addition, the Third and Sixth Circuits "have expressed the view that Title I is the exclusive province of employment discrimination within the ADA." *Elwell,* 693 F.3d at 1314 (citing *Menkowitz v. Pottstown Mem'l Med. Ctr.,* 154 F.3d 113, 118–19 (3d Cir.1998), and *Parker v. Metro. Life Ins. Co.,* 121 F.3d 1006, 1014 (6th Cir.1997)). Only the Eleventh Circuit has reached a contrary conclusion. *Bledsoe v. Palm Beach Cnty. Soil & Water Conservation Dist.,* 133 F.3d 816, 820 (11th Cir.1998).

We join the majority view. The Second, Seventh, Ninth, and Tenth Circuits' thorough analysis of the ADA's text and structure, both of which support the more limited reading of Title II's scope, is persuasive. *See Brumfield,* 735 F.3d at 624–29; *Mary Jo C.,* 707 F.3d at 168–72; *Elwell,* 693 F.3d at 1306–14; *Zimmerman,* 170 F.3d at 1172–79. As these courts have explained, the phrase "services, programs, or activities" in Title II most naturally refers to an entity's outputs provided to the public rather than its inputs, such as employees. *Brumfield,* 735 F.3d at 627; *Mary Jo C.,* 707 F.3d at 167–68; *Elwell,* 693 F.3d at 1306; *Zimmerman,* 170 F.3d at 1174. And unlike Section 504 of the Rehabilitation Act, which extends to employment discrimination claims by broadly defining "program or activity" to mean "all of the operations" of a state or local government, Title II does not provide a special definition for "services, programs, or activities." *Compare* 29 U.S.C.A. § 794(b)(1)(A) *with* 42 U.S.C. § 12131.

Title II does, however, define "qualified individual" to mean "an individual with a disability who, with or without reasonable modifications . . . meets the essential eligibility requirements for the receipt of services or the participation in programs or activities provided by a public entity." 42 U.S.C. § 12131(2). In contrast, a "qualified individual" under Title I is "an individual who, with or without reasonable accommodation, can perform the essential functions of the employment position." *Id.* § 12111(8). Interpreting Title II not to cover employment thus gives effect to Congress's decision to define the term of art "qualified individual" differently in Title I and Title II.

In terms of structure, courts in the majority have noted that Congress divided the ADA's prohibitions on discrimination against individuals with disabilities into three parts, each with its own heading: Title I for employment, Title II for public services, and Title III for public accommodations. *Mary Jo C.,* 707 F.3d at 169; *Elwell,* 693 F.3d at 1309; *Zimmerman,* 170 F.3d at 1176. To read Title II to cover employment would "diminish[ ], duplicate [ ], even render[ ] superfluous" Title I. *Elwell,* 693 F.3d at 1309. That Title I and Title II should encompass distinct spheres is further supported by Congress's decision to delegate authority to promulgate regulations to the Equal Employment Opportunity Commission under Title I, but to the Attorney General under Title II. *Mary Jo C.,* 707 F.3d at 169–70 (comparing 42 U.S.C. § 12116 with § 12134(a)); *Elwell,* 693 F.3d at 1309 (same); *Zimmerman,* 170 F.3d at 1178 (same).

Lastly, Congress expressly cross-referenced Title I, but not Title II, when mandating the standards that apply to employment discrimination claims brought under Section 504 of the Rehabilitation Act. 29 U.S.C.A. § 794(d). This provides strong evidence of Congress's view that Title I, but not Title II, covers employment. *Elwell,* 693 F.3d at 1312; *Zimmerman,* 170 F.3d at 1178.

Based on the text and structure of Title II and the ADA, we agree with the majority of circuits to have considered the question that Title II unambiguously does not provide a vehicle for public employment discrimination claims. The Eleventh Circuit in *Bledsoe* reached the opposite view after a cursory recitation of part of Title II's text, no analysis of the ADA's structure, and heavy reliance on legislative history and the Attorney General's regulations. 133 F.3d at 820–23. However, our conclusion that Title II is unambiguous means that we do not reach legislative history or regulations. *Dep't of Housing & Urban Dev. v. Rucker,* 535 U.S. 125, 132, 122 S.Ct. 1230, 152 L.Ed.2d 258 (2002) ("[R]eference to legislative history is inappropriate when the text of the statute is unambiguous."); *Chevron, U.S.A., Inc. v. Natural Res. Def. Council, Inc.,* 467 U.S. 837, 842–43, 104 S.Ct. 2778, 81 L.Ed.2d 694 (1984) ("If the intent of Congress is clear, that is the end of the matter; for the court, as well as the agency, must give effect to the unambiguously expressed intent of Congress.").

Our previous cases do not compel a different result. In *Rogers,* we did not reach the appellee's alternative argument that the appellant could not use Title II to bring his discrimination claim against his state employer. Instead, we affirmed dismissal for failure to state a claim based on the appellee's primary argument that "the ADA does not require [a state] to provide the same level of benefits for mental and physical disabilities in its long-term disability plan for state employees." *Rogers,* 174 F.3d at 436. For purposes of that case, we implicitly assumed, but did not decide, that Title II covered employee benefits. And in *Doe,* the appellant advanced his claim against his state employer under both Section 504 of the Rehabilitation Act and Title II of the ADA. 50 F.3d at 1262. Thus, we had no occasion to decide whether the appellant could have used Title II alone. Here, in contrast,

Reyazuddin alleges that the County's 2012 conduct violated only Title II and not the Rehabilitation Act.

Because we hold that public employment discrimination claims may not be brought under Title II, we affirm the district court's summary judgment order on Reyazuddin's Title II claim.

NOTES AND QUESTIONS

1. Why might a disabled employee or applicant prefer to use Title II rather than Title I to assert an employment claim? We can think of two potential advantages. First, Title II does not require a plaintiff to first exhaust administrative remedies. Second, the Supreme Court has ruled that the Eleventh Amendment bars Title I suits against states in federal court, but that issue is not yet resolved in the Title II context. Can you think of any other possible reasons?

2. *The public employment coverage debate.* As *Reyazuddin* summarizes, the courts are split as to whether an employment claim may be asserted via Title II. Which side of the debate has the better of this argument and why? Do you buy the court's distinction between "outputs" and "inputs?" Does the fact that the DOJ regulations implementing Title II (28 C.F.R. § 35.140) recognize that employment claims may be brought under Title II deserve any deference?

3. *Eleventh Amendment immunity.* Even if a plaintiff could maintain a suit for employment discrimination under Title II, the question remains whether a suit for money damages may nonetheless be barred by the Eleventh Amendment to the U.S. Constitution. In general, the Eleventh Amendment prohibits suits for damages against states in federal court unless Congress has unequivocally abrogated such immunity pursuant to a valid grant of constitutional authority. In *Board of Trustees of the University of Alabama v. Garrett*, 531 U.S. 356, 121 S.Ct. 955 (2001), the Supreme Court held that the Eleventh Amendment bars suits for money damages under Title I against states in federal court. In contrast, the Supreme Court ruled in *Tennessee v. Lane*, 541 U.S. 509, 124 S.Ct. 1978 (2004), that the Eleventh Amendment does not preclude a federal suit under Title II against a state concerning a disabled employee's access to the courts. A still unanswered question is whether the Eleventh Amendment bars suits against a state involving other Title II issues, such as access to governmental services or activities.

C. ACCESS/CONTENT DISTINCTION

ALEXANDER V. CHOATE
469 U.S. 287, 105 S.Ct. 712 (1985)

JUSTICE MARSHALL delivered the opinion of the Court.

In 1980, Tennessee proposed reducing the number of annual days of inpatient hospital care covered by its state Medicaid program. The question presented is whether the effect upon the handicapped that this reduction will have is cognizable under § 504 of the Rehabilitation Act of 1973 or its implementing regulations. We hold that it is not.

I

Faced in 1980–1981 with projected state Medicaid costs of $42 million more than the State's Medicaid budget of $388 million, the directors of the Tennessee Medicaid program decided to institute a variety of cost-saving measures. Among these changes was a reduction from 20 to 14 in the number of inpatient hospital days per fiscal year that Tennessee Medicaid would pay hospitals on behalf of a Medicaid recipient. Before the new measures took effect, respondents, Tennessee Medicaid recipients, brought a class action for declaratory and injunctive relief in which they alleged, *inter alia,* that the proposed 14-day limitation on inpatient coverage would have a discriminatory effect on the handicapped. Statistical evidence, which petitioners do not dispute, indicated that in the 1979–1980 fiscal year, 27.4% of all handicapped users of hospital services who received Medicaid required more than 14 days of care, while only 7.8% of nonhandicapped users required more than 14 days of inpatient care.

Based on this evidence, respondents asserted that the reduction would violate § 504 of the Rehabilitation Act of 1973, as amended, 29 U.S.C. § 794, and its implementing regulations. Section 504 provides:

> "No otherwise qualified handicapped individual . . . shall, solely by reason of his handicap, be excluded from the participation in, be denied the benefits of, or be subjected to discrimination under any program or activity receiving Federal financial assistance. . . ." 29 U.S.C. § 794.

Respondents' position was twofold. First, they argued that the change from 20 to 14 days of coverage would have a disproportionate effect on the handicapped and hence was discriminatory. The second, and major, thrust of respondents' attack was directed at the use of *any* annual limitation on the number of inpatient days covered, for respondents acknowledged that, given the special needs of the handicapped for medical care, any such limitation was likely to disadvantage the handicapped disproportionately. Respondents noted, however, that federal law does not require States to impose any annual durational limitation on inpatient coverage, and that the Medicaid programs of only 10 States impose such restrictions. Respondents therefore suggested that Tennessee follow these other States and do away with any limitation on the number of annual inpatient days covered. Instead, argued respondents, the State could limit the number of days of hospital coverage on a per-stay basis, with the number of covered days to vary depending on the recipient's illness (for example, fixing the number of days covered for an appendectomy); the period to be covered for each illness could then be set at a level that would keep Tennessee's Medicaid program as a whole within its budget. The State's refusal to adopt this plan was said to result in the imposition of gratuitous costs on the handicapped and thus to constitute discrimination under § 504.

A divided panel of the Court of Appeals for the Sixth Circuit held that respondents had indeed established a prima facie case of a § 504 violation. *Jennings v. Alexander,* 715 F.2d 1036 (1983). The majority apparently concluded that any action by a federal grantee that disparately affects the handicapped states a cause of action under § 504 and its implementing regulations. Because both the 14-day rule and any annual limitation on inpatient coverage disparately affected the handicapped, the panel found that a prima facie case had been made out, and the case was remanded to give Tennessee an opportunity for rebuttal. According to the panel majority, the State on remand could either demonstrate the unavailability of alternative plans that would achieve the State's legitimate cost-saving goals with a less disproportionate impact on the handicapped, or the State could offer "a substantial justification for the adoption of the plan with the greater discriminatory impact." We granted certiorari to consider whether the type of impact at issue in this case is cognizable under § 504 or its implementing regulations, and we now reverse.

II

The first question the parties urge on the Court is whether proof of discriminatory animus is always required to establish a violation of § 504 and its implementing regulations, or whether federal law also reaches action by a recipient of federal funding that discriminates against the handicapped by effect rather than by design. The State of Tennessee argues that § 504 reaches only purposeful discrimination against the handicapped. . . .

Discrimination against the handicapped was perceived by Congress to be most often the product, not of invidious animus, but rather of thoughtlessness and indifference—of benign neglect. . . . Federal agencies and commentators on the plight of the handicapped similarly have found that discrimination against the handicapped is primarily the result of apathetic attitudes rather than affirmative animus.

In addition, much of the conduct that Congress sought to alter in passing the Rehabilitation Act would be difficult if not impossible to reach were the Act construed to proscribe only conduct fueled by a discriminatory intent. For example, elimination of architectural barriers was one of the central aims of the Act, yet such barriers were clearly not erected with the aim or intent of excluding the handicapped. Similarly, Senator Williams, the chairman of the Labor and Public Welfare Committee that reported out § 504, asserted that the handicapped were the victims of "[d]iscrimination in access to public transportation" and "[d]iscrimination because they do not have the simplest forms of special educational and rehabilitation services they need. . . ." And Senator Humphrey, again in introducing the proposal that later became § 504, listed, among the instances of discrimination that the section would prohibit, the use of "transportation and architectural barriers," the "discriminatory effect of job qualification . . . procedures," and the denial of "special educational assistance" for handicapped children. These statements would ring hollow if the resulting legislation could not rectify the harms resulting from action that discriminated by effect as well as by design.

At the same time, the position urged by respondents—that we interpret § 504 to reach all action disparately affecting the handicapped—is also troubling. Because the handicapped typically are not similarly situated to the nonhandicapped, respondents' position would in essence require each recipient of federal funds first to evaluate the effect on the handicapped of every proposed action that might touch the interests of the handicapped, and then to consider alternatives for achieving the same objectives with less severe disadvantage to the handicapped. The formalization and policing of this process could lead to a wholly unwieldy administrative and adjudicative burden. Had Congress intended § 504 to be a National Environmental Policy Act for the handicapped, requiring the preparation of "Handicapped Impact Statements" before any action was taken by a grantee that affected the handicapped, we would expect some indication of that purpose in the statute or its legislative history. Yet there is nothing to suggest that such was Congress' purpose. Thus, just as there is reason to question whether Congress intended § 504 to reach only intentional discrimination, there is similarly reason to question whether Congress intended § 504 to embrace all claims of disparate-impact discrimination.

Any interpretation of § 504 must therefore be responsive to two powerful but countervailing considerations—the need to give effect to the statutory objectives and the desire to keep § 504 within manageable bounds. Given the legitimacy of both of these goals and the tension between them, we decline the parties' invitation to decide today that one of these goals so overshadows the other as to eclipse it. While we reject the boundless notion that all disparate-impact showings constitute prima facie cases under § 504, we assume without deciding that § 504 reaches at least some conduct that has an unjustifiable disparate impact upon the handicapped. On that assumption, we must then determine whether the disparate effect of which respondents complain is the sort of disparate impact that federal law might recognize.

III

To determine which disparate impacts § 504 might make actionable, the proper starting point is *Southeastern Community College v. Davis,* 442 U.S. 397, 99 S.Ct. 2361 (1979), our major previous attempt to define the scope of § 504. *Davis* involved a plaintiff with a major hearing disability who sought admission to a college to be trained as a registered nurse, but who would not be capable of safely performing as a registered nurse even with full-time personal supervision. We stated that, under some circumstances, a "refusal to modify an existing program might become unreasonable and discriminatory. Identification of those instances where a refusal to accommodate the needs of a disabled person amounts to discrimination against the handicapped [is] an important responsibility of HEW." We held that the college was not required to admit Davis because it appeared unlikely that she could benefit from any modifications that the relevant HEW regulations required, and because the further modifications Davis sought—full-time, personal supervision whenever she attended patients and elimination of all clinical courses—would have compromised the essential nature of the college's nursing program. Such a "fundamental alteration in the nature of a program" was far more than the reasonable modifications the statute or regulations required. *Davis* thus struck a balance between the statutory rights of the handicapped to be integrated into society and the legitimate interests of federal grantees in preserving the integrity of their programs: while a grantee need not be required to make "fundamental" or "substantial" modifications to accommodate the handicapped, it may be required to make "reasonable" ones.

The balance struck in *Davis* requires that an otherwise qualified handicapped individual must be provided with meaningful access to the benefit that the grantee offers. The benefit itself, of course, cannot be defined in a way that effectively denies otherwise qualified handicapped individuals the meaningful access to which they are entitled; to assure meaningful access, reasonable accommodations in the grantee's program or benefit may have to be made. In this case, respondents argue that the 14-day rule, or any annual durational limitation, denies meaningful access to Medicaid services in Tennessee. We examine each of these arguments in turn.

A

The 14-day limitation will not deny respondents meaningful access to Tennessee Medicaid services or exclude them from those services. The new limitation does not invoke criteria that have a particular exclusionary effect on the handicapped; the reduction, neutral on its face, does not distinguish between those whose coverage will be reduced and those whose coverage will not on the basis of any test, judgment, or trait that the handicapped as a class are less capable of meeting or less likely of having. Moreover, it cannot be argued that "meaningful access" to state Medicaid services will be denied by the 14-day limitation on inpatient coverage; nothing in the record suggests that the handicapped in Tennessee will be unable to benefit meaningfully from the coverage they will receive under the 14-day rule. The reduction in inpatient coverage will leave both handicapped and nonhandicapped Medicaid users with identical and effective hospital services fully available for their use, with both classes of users subject to the same durational limitation. The 14-day limitation, therefore, does not exclude the handicapped from or deny them the benefits of the 14 days of care the State has chosen to provide.

To the extent respondents further suggest that their greater need for prolonged inpatient care means that, to provide meaningful access to Medicaid services, Tennessee must single out the handicapped for *more* than 14 days of coverage, the suggestion is simply unsound. At base, such a suggestion must rest on the notion that the benefit provided through state Medicaid programs is the amorphous objective of "adequate health care." But Medicaid programs do not guarantee that each recipient will receive that level of health care precisely tailored to his or her particular needs. Instead, the benefit provided through Medicaid is a particular package of health care services, such as 14 days of inpatient coverage. That package of services has the general aim of assuring that individuals will receive necessary medical care, but the benefit provided remains the individual services offered—not "adequate health care."

The federal Medicaid Act makes this point clear. The Act gives the States substantial discretion to choose the proper mix of amount, scope, and duration limitations on coverage, as long as care and services are provided in "the best interests of the recipients." 42 U.S.C. § 1396a(a)(19). The District Court found that the 14-day limitation would fully serve 95% of even handicapped individuals eligible for Tennessee Medicaid, and both lower courts concluded that Tennessee's proposed Medicaid plan would meet the "best interests" standard. That unchallenged conclusion indicates that Tennessee is free, as a matter of the Medicaid Act, to choose to define the benefit it will be providing as 14 days of inpatient coverage.

Section 504 does not require the State to alter this definition of the benefit being offered simply to meet the reality that the handicapped have greater medical needs. To conclude otherwise would be to find that the Rehabilitation Act requires States to view certain illnesses, *i.e.,* those particularly affecting the handicapped, as more important than others and more worthy of cure through government subsidization. Nothing in the legislative history of the Act supports such a conclusion. Section 504 seeks to assure evenhanded treatment and the opportunity for handicapped individuals to participate in and benefit from programs receiving federal assistance. The Act does not, however, guarantee the handicapped equal results from the provision of state Medicaid, even assuming some measure of equality of health could be constructed.

Regulations promulgated by the Department of Health and Human Services (HHS) pursuant to the Act further support this conclusion. These regulations state that recipients of federal funds who provide health services cannot "provide a qualified handicapped person with benefits or services that are not as effective (as defined in § 84.4(b)) as the benefits or services provided to others." 45 CFR § 84.52(a)(3) (1984). The regulations also prohibit a recipient of federal funding from adopting "criteria or methods of administration that have the purpose or effect of defeating or substantially impairing accomplishment of the objectives of the recipient's program with respect to the handicapped." 45 CFR § 84.4(b)(4)(ii).

While these regulations, read in isolation, could be taken to suggest that a state Medicaid program must make the handicapped as healthy as the nonhandicapped, other regulations reveal that HHS does not contemplate imposing such a requirement. Title 45 CFR § 84.4(b)(2), referred to in the regulations quoted above, makes clear that

> "[f]or purposes of this part, aids, benefits, and services, to be equally effective, are not required to produce the identical result or level of achievement for handicapped and nonhandicapped persons, but must afford handicapped persons equal opportunity to obtain the same result, to gain the same benefit, or to reach the same level of achievement. . . ."

This regulation, while indicating that adjustments to existing programs are contemplated, also makes clear that Tennessee is not required to assure that its handicapped Medicaid users will be as healthy as its nonhandicapped users. Thus, to the extent respondents are seeking a distinct durational limitation for the handicapped, Tennessee is entitled to respond by asserting that the relevant benefit is 14 days of coverage. Because the handicapped have meaningful and equal access to that benefit, Tennessee is not obligated to reinstate its 20-day rule or to provide the handicapped with more than 14 days of inpatient coverage.

B

We turn next to respondents' alternative contention, a contention directed not at the 14-day rule itself but rather at Tennessee's Medicaid *plan* as a whole. Respondents argue that the inclusion of any annual durational limitation on inpatient coverage in a state Medicaid plan violates § 504. The thrust of this challenge is that all annual durational limitations discriminate against the handicapped because (1) the effect of such limitations falls most heavily on the handicapped and because (2) this harm could be avoided by the choice of other Medicaid plans that would meet the State's budgetary constraints without disproportionately disadvantaging the handicapped. Viewed in this light, Tennessee's current plan is said to inflict a gratuitous harm on the handicapped that denies them meaningful access to Medicaid services.

Whatever the merits of this conception of meaningful access, it is clear that § 504 does not require the changes respondents seek. In enacting the Rehabilitation Act and in subsequent amendments, Congress did focus on several substantive areas—employment, education, and the elimination of physical barriers to access—in which it considered the societal and personal costs of refusals to provide meaningful access to the handicapped to be particularly high. But nothing in the pre- or post-1973 legislative discussion of § 504 suggests that Congress desired to make major inroads on the States' longstanding discretion to choose the proper mix of amount, scope, and duration limitations on services covered by state Medicaid. And, more generally, we have already stated that § 504 does not impose a general NEPA-like requirement on federal grantees.

The costs of such a requirement would be far from minimal, and thus Tennessee's refusal to pursue this course does not, as respondents suggest, inflict a "gratuitous" harm on the handicapped. On the contrary, to require that the sort of broad-based distributive decision at issue in this case always be made in the way most favorable, or least disadvantageous, to the handicapped, even when the same benefit is meaningfully and equally offered to them, would be to impose a virtually unworkable requirement on state Medicaid administrators. Before taking any across-the-board action affecting Medicaid recipients, an analysis of the effect of the proposed change on the handicapped would have to be prepared. Presumably, that analysis would have to be further broken down by class of handicap—the change at issue here, for example, might be significantly less harmful to the blind, who use inpatient services only minimally, than to other subclasses of handicapped Medicaid recipients; the State would then have to balance the harms and benefits to various groups to determine, on balance, the extent to which the action disparately impacts the handicapped. In addition, respondents offer no reason that similar treatment would not have to be accorded other groups protected by statute or regulation from disparate-impact discrimination.

It should be obvious that administrative costs of implementing such a regime would be well beyond the accommodations that are required under *Davis*. As a result, Tennessee need not redefine its Medicaid program to eliminate durational limitations on inpatient coverage, even if in doing so the State could achieve its immediate fiscal objectives in a way less harmful to the handicapped.

IV

The 14-day rule challenged in this case is neutral on its face, is not alleged to rest on a discriminatory motive, and does not deny the handicapped access to or exclude them from the particular package of Medicaid services Tennessee has chosen to provide. The State has made the same benefit— 14 days of coverage—equally accessible to both handicapped and nonhandicapped persons, and the State is not required to assure the handicapped "adequate health care" by providing them with more coverage than the nonhandicapped. In addition, the State is not obligated to modify its Medicaid program by abandoning reliance on annual durational limitations on inpatient coverage. Assuming, then, that § 504 or its implementing regulations reach some claims of disparate-impact discrimination, the effect of Tennessee's reduction in annual inpatient coverage is not among them. For that reason, the Court of Appeals erred in holding that respondents had established a prima facie violation of § 504. The judgment below is accordingly reversed.

NOTES AND QUESTIONS

1. *What disparate impact claims remain?* The Court in *Alexander* suggests that some disparate impact claims are cognizable under Section 504 of the Rehabilitation Act while others, including the claims at issue, are not. Is there a principled way to predict what types of disparate impact claims may be asserted and what types may not?

2. *Access/content distinction.* Justice Marshall states that Section 504 requires "that an otherwise qualified handicapped individual must be provided with meaningful access to the benefit that the grantee offers." But, Justice Marshall goes on to state that Section 504 "does not require the State to alter this definition of the benefit being offered simply to meet the reality that the handicapped have greater medical needs." In essence, the Court is holding that while a public entity must make government benefits accessible to individuals with disabilities, it does not need to alter the substantive mix of those benefits to reflect the needs or desires of disabled individuals. What is the logic of this access/content distinction and do you agree with it? Is discrimination under Title I limited solely to actions that deny access to employment? If not, why is discrimination in government benefits treated differently than discrimination in employment?

3. *Benefit levels.* The *Alexander* Court concluded that the fundamental benefit provided by the State of Tennessee is 14 days of inpatient health care coverage as opposed to an adequate level of health care coverage. Is that an appropriate way to define the benefit at issue? What impact does this characterization have on the analysis of the case? Do you agree that it would be "unworkable" to require a change in benefit levels that disproportionately disadvantage disabled recipients?

4. *Rationing health care.* The coronavirus pandemic led to concerns about the possible need to ration medical care. That potential prompted the question of whether it would violate the ADA for a public hospital to provide emergency care—such as ventilators—more readily to otherwise healthy patients as compared to individuals with disabilities who may have a shorter life expectancy. Professor Samuel Bagenstos, citing the *Alexander* decision, argues that the denial of scarce medical treatment to individuals with pre-existing disabilities violates the ADA, at least where the disability bears no relation to the type of medical treatment being denied. Samuel R. Bagenstos, *Who Gets the Ventilator? Disability Discrimination in COVID-19 Medical-Rationing Protocols*, 130 YALE L.J. FORUM 1 (2020). In contrast, Professor Govind Persad maintains that the ADA permits triage and rationing approaches that use medical evidence to pursue the goal of saving more lives, even when those approaches assign lower priority to patients with certain disabilities. Govind Persad, *Disability Law and the Case for Evidence-Based Triage*, 130 YALE L.J. FORUM 26 (2020). Which position seems most persuasive?

As a matter of policy, what is the best way to allocate scarce medical resources during the time of a health-related emergency?

D. INTEGRATION

OLMSTEAD V. L.C. EX REL. ZIMRING
527 U.S. 581, 119 S.Ct. 2176 (1999)

JUSTICE GINSBURG announced the judgment of the Court and delivered the opinion of the Court with respect to Parts I, II, and III-A, and an opinion with respect to Part III-B, in which JUSTICE O'CONNOR, JUSTICE SOUTER, and JUSTICE BREYER join.

This case concerns the proper construction of the anti-discrimination provision contained in the public services portion (Title II) of the Americans with Disabilities Act of 1990 (ADA), 42 U.S.C. § 12132. Specifically, we confront the question whether the proscription of discrimination may require placement of persons with mental disabilities in community settings rather than in institutions. The answer, we hold, is a qualified yes. Such action is in order when the State's treatment professionals have determined that community placement is appropriate, the transfer from institutional care to a less restrictive setting is not opposed by the affected individual, and the placement can be reasonably accommodated, taking into account the resources available to the State and the needs of others with mental disabilities. In so ruling, we affirm the decision of the Eleventh Circuit in substantial part. We remand the case, however, for further consideration of the appropriate relief, given the range of facilities the State maintains for the care and treatment of persons with diverse mental disabilities, and its obligation to administer services with an even hand.

I

... Mindful that it is a statute we are construing, we set out first the legislative and regulatory prescriptions on which the case turns.

In the opening provisions of the ADA, Congress stated findings applicable to the statute in all its parts. Most relevant to this case, Congress determined that

> (2) historically, society has tended to isolate and segregate individuals with disabilities, and, despite some improvements, such forms of discrimination against individuals with disabilities continue to be a serious and pervasive social problem;

> (3) discrimination against individuals with disabilities persists in such critical areas as ... institutionalization ... ;

> . . . .

(5) individuals with disabilities continually encounter various forms of discrimination, including outright intentional exclusion, ... failure to make modifications to existing facilities and practices, ... [and] segregation. ... 42 U.S.C. §§ 12101(a)(2), (3), (5).

Congress then set forth prohibitions against discrimination in employment (Title I, §§ 12111–12117), public services furnished by governmental entities (Title II, §§ 12131–12165), and public accommodations provided by private entities (Title III, §§ 12181–12189). The statute as a whole is intended "to provide a clear and comprehensive national mandate for the elimination of discrimination against individuals with disabilities." § 12101(b)(1).

This case concerns Title II, the public services portion of the ADA. The provision of Title II centrally at issue reads:

> Subject to the provisions of this subchapter, no qualified individual with a disability shall, by reason of such disability, be excluded from participation in or be denied the benefits of the services, programs, or activities of a public entity, or be subjected to discrimination by any such entity.

42 U.S.C. § 12132. Title II's definition section states that "public entity" includes "any State or local government," and "any department, agency, [or] special purpose district." §§ 12131(1)(A), (B). The same section defines "qualified individual with a disability" as

> an individual with a disability who, with or without reasonable modifications to rules, policies, or practices, the removal of architectural, communication, or transportation barriers, or the provision of auxiliary aids and services, meets the essential eligibility requirements for the receipt of services or the participation in programs or activities provided by a public entity.

§ 12131(2). ...

Congress instructed the Attorney General to issue regulations implementing provisions of Title II, including § 12132's discrimination proscription. The Attorney General's regulations, Congress further directed, "shall be consistent with this chapter and with the coordination regulations ... applicable to recipients of Federal financial assistance under [§ 504 of the Rehabilitation Act], as set forth in 42 U.S.C. § 12134(b). One of the § 504 regulations requires recipients of federal funds to "administer programs and activities in the most integrated setting appropriate to the needs of qualified handicapped persons." 28 CFR § 41.51(d).

As Congress instructed, the Attorney General issued Title II regulations, see 28 CFR pt. 35, including one modeled on the § 504 regulation just quoted; called the "integration regulation," it reads:

> A public entity shall administer services, programs, and activities in the most integrated setting appropriate to the needs of qualified individuals with disabilities.

28 CFR § 35.130(d). The preamble to the Attorney General's Title II regulations defines "the most integrated setting appropriate to the needs of qualified individuals with disabilities" to mean "a setting that enables individuals with disabilities to interact with non-disabled persons to the fullest extent possible." 28 CFR pt. 35, App. A, p. 450. Another regulation requires public entities to "make reasonable modifications" to avoid "discrimination on the basis of disability," unless those modifications would entail a "fundamenta[l] alter[ation]"; called here the "reasonable-modifications regulation," it provides:

> A public entity shall make reasonable modifications in policies, practices, or procedures when the modifications are necessary to avoid discrimination on the basis of disability, unless the public entity can demonstrate that making the modifications would fundamentally alter the nature of the service, program, or activity.

28 CFR § 35.130(b)(7). We recite these regulations with the caveat that we do not here determine their validity. . . .

II

With the key legislative provisions in full view, we summarize the facts underlying this dispute. Respondents L.C. and E.W. are mentally retarded women; L.C. has also been diagnosed with schizophrenia, and E.W. with a personality disorder. Both women have a history of treatment in institutional settings. In May 1992, L.C. was voluntarily admitted to Georgia Regional Hospital at Atlanta (GRH), where she was confined for treatment in a psychiatric unit. By May 1993, her psychiatric condition had stabilized, and L.C.'s treatment team at GRH agreed that her needs could be met appropriately in one of the community-based programs the State supported. Despite this evaluation, L.C. remained institutionalized until February 1996, when the State placed her in a community-based treatment program.

E.W. was voluntarily admitted to GRH in February 1995; like L.C., E.W. was confined for treatment in a psychiatric unit. In March 1995, GRH sought to discharge E.W. to a homeless shelter, but abandoned that plan after her attorney filed an administrative complaint. By 1996, E.W.'s treating psychiatrist concluded that she could be treated appropriately in a community-based setting. She nonetheless remained institutionalized until a few months after the District Court issued its judgment in this case in 1997.

In May 1995, when she was still institutionalized at GRH, L.C. filed suit in the United States District Court for the Northern District of Georgia, challenging her continued confinement in a segregated environment. L.C. alleged that the State's failure to place her in a community-based program, once her treating professionals determined that such placement was appropriate, violated, *inter alia*, Title II of the ADA. L.C.'s pleading requested, among other things, that the State place her in a community care residential program, and that she receive treatment with the ultimate goal of integrating her into the mainstream of society. E.W. intervened in the action, stating an identical claim.

The District Court granted partial summary judgment in favor of L.C. and E.W. The court held that the State's failure to place L.C. and E.W. in an appropriate community-based treatment program violated Title II of the ADA. In so ruling, the court rejected the State's argument that inadequate funding, not discrimination against L.C. and E.W. "by reason of" their disabilities, accounted for their retention at GRH. Under Title II, the court concluded, "unnecessary institutional segregation of the disabled constitutes discrimination *per se,* which cannot be justified by a lack of funding."

In addition to contending that L.C. and E.W. had not shown discrimination "by reason of [their] disabilit[ies]," the State resisted court intervention on the ground that requiring immediate transfers in cases of this order would "fundamentally alter" the State's activity. The State reasserted that it was already using all available funds to provide services to other persons with disabilities. Rejecting the State's "fundamental alteration" defense, the court observed that existing state programs provided community-based treatment of the kind for which L.C. and E.W. qualified, and that the State could "provide services to plaintiffs in the community at considerably *less* cost than is required to maintain them in an institution."

The Court of Appeals for the Eleventh Circuit affirmed the judgment of the District Court, but remanded for reassessment of the State's cost-based defense. As the appeals court read the statute and regulations: When "a disabled individual's treating professionals find that a community-based placement is appropriate for that individual, the ADA imposes a duty to provide treatment in a community setting—the most integrated setting appropriate to that patient's needs"; "[w]here there is no such finding [by the treating professionals], nothing in the ADA requires the deinstitutionalization of th[e] patient."

The Court of Appeals recognized that the State's duty to provide integrated services "is not absolute"; under the Attorney General's Title II regulation, "reasonable modifications" were required of the State, but fundamental alterations were not demanded. The appeals court thought it clear, however, that "Congress wanted to permit a cost defense only in the most limited of circumstances." In conclusion, the court stated that a cost justification would fail "[u]nless the State can prove that requiring it to [expend additional funds in order to provide L.C. and E.W. with integrated services] would be so unreasonable given the demands of the State's mental health budget that it would fundamentally alter the service [the State] provides." Because it appeared that the District Court had entirely ruled out a "lack of funding" justification, the appeals court remanded, repeating that the District Court should consider, among other things, "whether the additional expenditures necessary to treat L.C. and E.W. in community-based care would be unreasonable given the demands of the State's mental health budget."

We granted certiorari in view of the importance of the question presented to the States and affected individuals.

III

Endeavoring to carry out Congress' instruction to issue regulations implementing Title II, the Attorney General, in the integration and reasonable-modifications regulations, made two key determinations. The first concerned the scope of the ADA's discrimination proscription, 42 U.S.C. § 12132; the second concerned the obligation of the States to counter discrimination. As to the first, the Attorney General concluded that unjustified placement or retention of persons in institutions, severely limiting their exposure to the outside community, constitutes a form of discrimination based on disability prohibited by Title II. See 28 CFR § 35.130(d). Regarding the States' obligation to avoid unjustified isolation of individuals with disabilities, the Attorney General provided that States could resist modifications that "would fundamentally alter the nature of the service, program, or activity." 28 CFR § 35.130(b)(7).

The Court of Appeals essentially upheld the Attorney General's construction of the ADA. . . .

We affirm the Court of Appeals' decision in substantial part. Unjustified isolation, we hold, is properly regarded as discrimination based on disability. But we recognize, as well, the States' need to maintain a range of facilities for the care and treatment of persons with diverse mental disabilities, and the States' obligation to administer services with an even hand. Accordingly, we further hold that the Court of Appeals' remand instruction was unduly restrictive. In evaluating a State's fundamental-alteration defense, the District Court must consider, in view of the resources available to the State, not only the cost of providing community-based care to the litigants, but also the range of services the State provides others with mental disabilities, and the State's obligation to mete out those services equitably.

A

We examine first whether, as the Eleventh Circuit held, undue institutionalization qualifies as discrimination "by reason of . . . disability." The Department of Justice has consistently advocated that it does. Because the Department is the agency directed by Congress to issue regulations implementing Title II, its views warrant respect. We need not inquire whether the degree of deference described in *Chevron U.S.A. Inc. v. Natural Resources Defense Council, Inc.*, 467 U.S. 837, 844, 104 S.Ct. 2778 (1984), is in order; "[i]t is enough to observe that the well-reasoned views of the agencies implementing a statute 'constitute a body of experience and informed judgment to which courts and litigants may properly resort for guidance.' " *Bragdon v. Abbott*, 524 U.S. 624, 642, 118 S.Ct. 2196 (1998) (quoting *Skidmore v. Swift & Co.*, 323 U.S. 134, 139–140, 65 S.Ct. 161 (1944)).

The State argues that L.C. and E.W. encountered no discrimination "by reason of" their disabilities because they were not denied community placement on account of those disabilities. Nor were they subjected to "discrimination," the State contends, because " 'discrimination' necessarily requires uneven treatment of similarly situated individuals," and L.C. and E.W. had identified no comparison class, *i.e.*, no similarly situated individuals given preferential treatment. We are satisfied that Congress had a more comprehensive view of the concept of discrimination advanced in the ADA. . . .

Recognition that unjustified institutional isolation of persons with disabilities is a form of discrimination reflects two evident judgments. First, institutional placement of persons who can handle and benefit from community settings perpetuates unwarranted assumptions that persons so isolated are incapable or unworthy of participating in community life. Second, confinement in an institution severely diminishes the everyday life activities of individuals, including family relations, social contacts, work options, economic independence, educational advancement, and cultural enrichment. Dissimilar treatment correspondingly exists in this key respect: In order to receive needed medical services, persons with mental disabilities must, because of those disabilities, relinquish participation in community life they could enjoy given reasonable accommodations, while persons without mental disabilities can receive the medical services they need without similar sacrifice.

The State urges that, whatever Congress may have stated as its findings in the ADA, the Medicaid statute "reflected a congressional policy preference for treatment in the institution over treatment in the community." The State correctly used the past tense. Since 1981, Medicaid has provided funding for state-run home and community-based care through a waiver program. Indeed, the United States points out that the Department of Health and Human Services (HHS) "has a policy of encouraging States to take advantage of the waiver program, and often approves more waiver slots than a State ultimately uses."

We emphasize that nothing in the ADA or its implementing regulations condones termination of institutional settings for persons unable to handle or benefit from community settings. Title II provides only that "qualified individual[s] with a disability" may not "be subjected to discrimination." 42 U.S.C. § 12132. "Qualified individuals," the ADA further explains, are persons with disabilities who, "with or without reasonable modifications to rules, policies, or practices, . . . mee[t] the essential eligibility requirements for the receipt of services or the participation in programs or activities provided by a public entity." § 12131(2).

Consistent with these provisions, the State generally may rely on the reasonable assessments of its own professionals in determining whether an individual "meets the essential eligibility requirements" for habilitation in a community-based program. Absent such qualification, it would be inappropriate to remove a patient from the more restrictive setting. Nor is there any federal requirement that community-based treatment be imposed on patients who do not desire it. In this case, however, there is no genuine dispute concerning the status of L.C. and E.W. as individuals "qualified" for noninstitutional care: The State's own professionals determined that community-based treatment would be appropriate for L.C. and E.W., and neither woman opposed such treatment.

B

The State's responsibility, once it provides community-based treatment to qualified persons with disabilities, is not boundless. The reasonable-modifications regulation speaks of "reasonable modifications" to avoid discrimination, and allows States to resist modifications that entail a "fundamenta[l] alter[ation]" of the States' services and programs. 28 CFR § 35.130(b)(7). The Court of Appeals construed this regulation to permit a cost-based defense "only in the most limited of circumstances," and remanded to the District Court to consider, among other things, "whether the additional expenditures necessary to treat L.C. and E.W. in community-based care would be unreasonable given the demands of the State's mental health budget."

The Court of Appeals' construction of the reasonable-modifications regulation is unacceptable for it would leave the State virtually defenseless once it is shown that the plaintiff is qualified for the service or program she seeks. If the expense entailed in placing one or two people in a community-based treatment program is properly measured for reasonableness against the State's entire mental health budget, it is unlikely that a State, relying on the fundamental-alteration defense, could ever prevail. Sensibly construed, the fundamental-alteration component of the reasonable-modifications regulation would allow the State to show that, in the allocation of available resources, immediate relief for the plaintiffs would be inequitable, given the responsibility the State has undertaken for the care and treatment of a large and diverse population of persons with mental disabilities.

When it granted summary judgment for plaintiffs in this case, the District Court compared the cost of caring for the plaintiffs in a community-based setting with the cost of caring for them in an institution. That simple comparison showed that community placements cost less than institutional confinements. As the United States recognizes, however, a comparison so simple overlooks costs the State cannot avoid; most notably, a "State . . . may experience increased overall expenses by funding community placements without being able to take advantage of the savings associated with the closure of institutions."

As already observed, the ADA is not reasonably read to impel States to phase out institutions, placing patients in need of close care at risk. Nor is it the ADA's mission to drive States to move institutionalized patients into an inappropriate setting, such as a homeless shelter, a placement the State proposed, then retracted, for E.W. Some individuals, like L.C. and E.W. in prior years, may need institutional care from time to time "to stabilize acute psychiatric symptoms." For other individuals, no placement outside the institution may ever be appropriate.

To maintain a range of facilities and to administer services with an even hand, the State must have more leeway than the courts below understood the fundamental-alteration defense to allow. If, for example, the State were to demonstrate that it had a comprehensive, effectively working plan for placing qualified persons with mental disabilities in less restrictive settings, and a waiting list that moved at a reasonable pace not controlled by the State's endeavors to keep its institutions fully populated, the reasonable-modifications standard would be met. In such circumstances, a court would have no warrant effectively to order displacement of persons at the top of the community-based treatment waiting list by individuals lower down who commenced civil actions.

For the reasons stated, we conclude that, under Title II of the ADA, States are required to provide community-based treatment for persons with mental disabilities when the State's treatment professionals determine that such placement is appropriate, the affected persons do not oppose such treatment, and the placement can be reasonably accommodated, taking into account the resources available to the State and the needs of others with mental disabilities. The judgment of the Eleventh Circuit is therefore affirmed in part and vacated in part, and the case is remanded for further proceedings.

JUSTICE KENNEDY, with whom JUSTICE BREYER joins as to Part I, concurring in the judgment.

I

Despite remarkable advances and achievements by medical science, and agreement among many professionals that even severe mental illness is often treatable, the extent of public resources to devote to this cause remains controversial. Knowledgeable professionals tell us that our society, and the governments which reflect its attitudes and preferences, have yet to grasp the potential for treating mental disorders, especially severe mental illness. As a result, necessary resources for the endeavor often are not forthcoming. During the course of a year, about 5.6 million Americans will suffer from severe mental illness. Some 2.2 million of these persons receive no treatment. Millions of other Americans suffer from mental disabilities of less serious degree, such as mild depression. These facts are part of the background against which this case arises. In addition, of course, persons with mental disabilities have been subject to historic mistreatment, indifference, and hostility.

Despite these obstacles, the States have acknowledged that the care of the mentally disabled is their special obligation. They operate and support facilities and programs, sometimes elaborate ones, to provide care. It is a continuing challenge, though, to provide the care in an effective and humane way, particularly because societal attitudes and the responses of public authorities have changed from time to time. . . .

It must be remembered that for the person with severe mental illness who has no treatment the most dreaded of confinements can be the imprisonment inflicted by his own mind, which shuts reality out and subjects him to the torment of voices and images beyond our own powers to describe.

It would be unreasonable, it would be a tragic event, then, were the Americans with Disabilities Act of 1990 (ADA) to be interpreted so that States had some incentive, for fear of litigation, to drive those in need of medical care and treatment out of appropriate care and into settings with too little assistance and supervision. The opinion of a responsible treating physician in determining the appropriate conditions for treatment ought to be given the greatest of deference. It is a common phenomenon that a patient functions well with medication, yet, because of the mental illness itself, lacks the discipline or capacity to follow the regime the medication requires. This is illustrative of the factors a responsible physician will consider in recommending the appropriate setting or facility for treatment. Justice Ginsburg's opinion takes account of this background. It is careful, and quite correct, to say that it is not "the ADA's mission to drive States to move institutionalized patients into an inappropriate setting, such as a homeless shelter. . . ."

In light of these concerns, if the principle of liability announced by the Court is not applied with caution and circumspection, States may be pressured into attempting compliance on the cheap, placing marginal patients into integrated settings devoid of the services and attention necessary for their condition. This danger is in addition to the federalism costs inherent in referring state decisions regarding the administration of treatment programs and the allocation of resources to the reviewing authority of the federal courts. It is of central importance, then, that courts apply today's decision with great deference to the medical decisions of the responsible, treating physicians and, as the Court makes clear, with appropriate deference to the program funding decisions of state policymakers.

II

With these reservations made explicit, in my view we must remand the case for a determination of the questions the Court poses and for a determination whether respondents can show a violation of 42 U.S.C. § 12132's ban on discrimination based on the summary judgment materials on file or any further pleadings and materials properly allowed.

At the outset it should be noted there is no allegation that Georgia officials acted on the basis of animus or unfair stereotypes regarding the disabled. Underlying much discrimination law is the notion that animus can lead to false and unjustified stereotypes, and vice versa. Of course, the line between animus and stereotype is often indistinct, and it is not always necessary to distinguish between them. Section 12132 can be understood to deem as irrational, and so to prohibit, distinctions by which a class of disabled persons, or some within that class, are, by reason of their disability and without adequate justification, exposed by a state entity to more onerous treatment than a comparison group in the provision of services or the administration of existing programs, or indeed entirely excluded from state programs or facilities. Discrimination under this statute might in principle be shown in the case before us, though further proceedings should be required.

Putting aside issues of animus or unfair stereotype, I agree with Justice Thomas that on the ordinary interpretation and meaning of the term, one who alleges discrimination must show that she "received differential treatment vis-à-vis members of a different group on the basis of a statutorily described characteristic." In my view, however, discrimination so defined might be shown here. Although the Court seems to reject Justice Thomas' definition of discrimination, it asserts that unnecessary institutional care does lead to "[d]issimilar treatment." According to the Court, "[i]n order to receive needed medical services, persons with mental disabilities must, because of those disabilities, relinquish participation in community life they could enjoy given reasonable accommodations, while persons without mental disabilities can receive the medical services they need without similar sacrifice." . . .

The possibility therefore remains that, on the facts of this case, respondents would be able to support a claim under § 12132 by showing that they have been subject to discrimination by Georgia officials on the basis of their disability. This inquiry would not be simple. Comparisons of different medical conditions and the corresponding treatment regimens might be difficult, as would be assessments of the degree of integration of various settings in which medical treatment is offered. For example, the evidence might show that, apart from services for the mentally disabled, medical treatment is rarely offered in a community setting but also is rarely offered in facilities comparable to state mental hospitals. Determining the relevance of that type of evidence would require considerable judgment and analysis. However, as petitioners observe, "[i]n this case, no class of similarly situated individuals was even identified, let alone shown to be given preferential treatment." Without additional information regarding the details of state-provided medical services in Georgia, we cannot address the issue in the way the statute demands. As a consequence, the judgment of the courts below, granting partial summary judgment to respondents, ought not to be sustained. In addition, as Justice Ginsburg's opinion is careful to note, it was error in the earlier proceedings to restrict the relevance and force of the State's evidence regarding the comparative costs of treatment. The State is entitled to wide discretion in adopting its own systems of cost analysis, and, if it chooses, to allocate health care resources based on fixed and overhead costs for whole institutions and programs. We must be cautious when we seek to infer specific rules limiting States' choices when Congress has used only general language in the controlling statute.

I would remand the case to the Court of Appeals or the District Court for it to determine in the first instance whether a statutory violation is sufficiently alleged and supported in respondents' summary judgment materials and, if not, whether they should be given leave to replead and to introduce evidence and argument along the lines suggested above.

For these reasons, I concur in the judgment of the Court.

JUSTICE THOMAS, with whom THE CHIEF JUSTICE and JUSTICE SCALIA join, dissenting.

... The majority concludes that petitioners "discriminated" against respondents—as a matter of law—by continuing to treat them in an institutional setting after they became eligible for community placement. I disagree. Temporary exclusion from community placement does not amount to "discrimination" in the traditional sense of the word, nor have respondents shown that petitioners "discriminated" against them "by reason of" their disabilities.

Until today, this Court has never endorsed an interpretation of the term "discrimination" that encompassed disparate treatment among members of the *same* protected class. Discrimination, as typically understood, requires a showing that a claimant received differential treatment vis-à-vis members of a different group on the basis of a statutorily described characteristic. This interpretation comports with dictionary definitions of the term discrimination, which means to "distinguish," to "differentiate," or to make a "distinction in favor of or against, a person or thing based on the group, class, or category to which that person or thing belongs rather than on individual merit."

Our decisions construing various statutory prohibitions against "discrimination" have not wavered from this path. The best place to begin is with Title VII of the Civil Rights Act of 1964, the paradigmatic anti-discrimination law. Title VII makes it "an unlawful employment practice for an employer . . . to *discriminate* against any individual with respect to his compensation, terms, conditions, or privileges of employment, because of such individual's race, color, religion, sex, or national origin." 42 U.S.C. § 2000e–2(a)(1). We have explained that this language is designed "to achieve equality of employment opportunities and remove barriers that have operated in the past to favor an identifiable group of white employees over other employees."

Under Title VII, a finding of discrimination requires a comparison of otherwise similarly situated persons who are in different groups by reason of certain characteristics provided by statute. For this reason, we have described as "nonsensical" the comparison of the racial composition of different classes of job categories in determining whether there existed disparate impact discrimination with respect to a particular job category. . . .

Despite this traditional understanding, the majority derives a more "comprehensive" definition of "discrimination," as that term is used in Title II of the ADA, one that includes "institutional isolation of persons with disabilities." It chiefly relies on certain congressional findings contained within the ADA. To be sure, those findings appear to equate institutional isolation with segregation, and thereby discrimination. The congressional findings, however, are written in general, hortatory terms and provide little guidance to the interpretation of the specific language of § 12132. In my view, the vague congressional findings upon which the majority relies simply do not suffice to show that Congress sought to overturn a well-established understanding of a statutory term (here, "discrimination"). Moreover, the majority fails to explain why terms in the findings should be given a medical content, pertaining to the place where a mentally retarded person is treated. When read in context, the findings instead suggest that terms such as "segregation" were used in a more general sense, pertaining to matters such as access to employment, facilities, and transportation. Absent a clear directive to the contrary, we must read "discrimination" in light of the common understanding of the term. We cannot expand the meaning of the term "discrimination" in order to invalidate policies we may find unfortunate.

Elsewhere in the ADA, Congress chose to alter the traditional definition of discrimination. Title I of the ADA, § 12112(b)(1), defines discrimination to include "limiting, segregating, or classifying a job applicant or employee in a way that adversely affects the opportunities or status of such applicant or employee." Notably, however, Congress did not provide that this definition of discrimination, unlike other aspects of the ADA, applies to Title II. Ordinary canons of construction require that we respect the limited applicability of this definition of "discrimination" and not import it into other parts of the law where Congress did not see fit. The majority's definition of discrimination—although not specifically delineated—substantially imports the definition of Title I into Title II by necessarily assuming that it is sufficient to focus exclusively on members of one particular group. Under this view, discrimination occurs when some members of a protected group are treated differently from other members of that same group. As the preceding discussion emphasizes, absent a special definition supplied by Congress, this conclusion is a remarkable and novel proposition that finds no support in our decisions in analogous areas. For example, the majority's conclusion that petitioners "discriminated" against respondents is the equivalent to finding discrimination under Title VII where a black employee with deficient management skills is denied in-house training by his employer (allegedly because of lack of funding) because other similarly situated black employees are given the in-house training. Such a claim would fly in the face of our prior case law, which requires more than the assertion that a person belongs to a protected group and did not receive some benefit.

At bottom, the type of claim approved of by the majority does not concern a prohibition against certain conduct (the traditional understanding of discrimination), but rather concerns imposition of a standard of care. As such, the majority can offer no principle limiting this new species of "discrimination" claim apart from an affirmative defense because it looks merely to an individual in isolation, without comparing him to otherwise similarly situated persons, and determines that discrimination occurs merely because that individual does not receive the treatment he wishes to receive. By adopting such a broad view of discrimination, the majority drains the term of any meaning other than as a proxy for decisions disapproved of by this Court.

Further, I fear that the majority's approach imposes significant federalism costs, directing States how to make decisions about their delivery of public services. We previously have recognized that constitutional principles of federalism erect limits on the Federal Government's ability to direct state officers or to interfere with the functions of state governments. We have suggested that these principles specifically apply to whether States are required to provide a certain level of benefits to individuals with disabilities. As noted in *Alexander v. Choate,* 469 U.S. 287, 105 S.Ct. 712 (1985), in rejecting a similar theory under § 504 of the Rehabilitation Act:

"[N]othing . . . suggests that Congress desired to make major inroads on the States' longstanding discretion to choose the proper mix of amount, scope, and duration limitations on services. . . ." The majority's affirmative defense will likely come as cold comfort to the States that will now be forced to defend themselves in federal court every time resources prevent the immediate placement of a qualified individual. In keeping with our traditional deference in this area, the appropriate course would be to respect the States' historical role as the dominant authority responsible for providing services to individuals with disabilities. . . .

For the foregoing reasons, I respectfully dissent.

NOTES AND QUESTIONS

1.   Why does Justice Ginsburg find that undue institutionalism is a form of discrimination? Do you agree?

2.   *Is* Olmstead *consistent with* Alexander? In his dissent in *Olmstead*, Justice Thomas contends that the majority opinion goes beyond the normal understanding of discrimination to impose a standard of care. According to Justice Thomas, actionable discrimination ordinarily results from the differential treatment of members of a protected class when compared to individuals outside of that class. But here, the majority opinion finds discrimination even though the complained of isolation only results in differential treatment in comparison to other disabled individuals. How does Justice Ginsburg respond to this argument?

3.   *Cost defense.* How would you summarize the scope of the cost defense adopted by the plurality opinion? Does this provide a sufficiently predictable standard?

4.   Olmstead *reinterpreted.* In *Brown v. District of Columbia*, 928 F.3d 1070 (D.C. Cir. 2019), individuals with disabilities who received Medicare-funded long-term care services filed suit claiming that they were unnecessarily segregated in nursing facilities and not receiving transition services for community-based care. The district court granted the defendant's motion for summary judgment on the grounds that the plaintiffs had failed to identify a "concrete, systematic deficiency" in transition services. The D. C. Circuit Court of Appeals reversed, holding that once plaintiffs showed that the defendant's treatment professionals had determined that community placement was appropriate, the defendant bore the burden of persuasion to prove that the requested accommodation would require an unreasonable transfer of state resources away from other disabled individuals. Is this ruling consistent with *Olmstead*? Why or why not?

5.   *De-institutionalization.* The *Olmstead* decision has spurred efforts to de-institutionalize the treatment of disabled individuals. More than 200 *Olmstead* suits had been filed against state governments, and 36 states have adopted *Olmstead* plans promoting greater community-based integration. But the process has not been a smooth one, and community-based alternatives

remain underfunded in many states. *See* Brittany S. Mitchell, *Expanding the Integration Mandate to Employment: The Push to Apply the Principles of the ADA and the Olmstead Decision to Disability Employment Services*, 30 ABA J. LAB. & EMP. L. 155, 159 (2014).

E. CIVIC PARTICIPATION

GALLOWAY V. SUPERIOR COURT
816 F.Supp. 12 (D.D.C. 1993)

JOYCE HENS GREEN, DISTRICT JUDGE.

> Individuals with disabilities . . . have been faced with restrictions and limitations, subjected to a history of purposeful unequal treatment, . . . based on characteristics that are beyond the control of such individuals and resulting from stereotypic assumptions not truly indicative of the individual ability of such individuals to participate in, and contribute to, society.

42 U.S.C. § 12101(a)(7).

Declaring that he has been the subject of precisely this type of discrimination, plaintiff Donald Galloway ("plaintiff" or "Galloway") initiated this action, alleging that defendants' policy and practice of refusing to permit persons who are blind to serve on juries of the Superior Court of the District of Columbia ("Superior Court") violates the Rehabilitation Act of 1973 ("Rehabilitation Act"), *as amended,* 29 U.S.C. § 794, regulations implementing that law, and the Civil Rights Act of 1871, 42 U.S.C. § 1983. Plaintiff subsequently filed a second amended complaint, which added a cause of action alleging a violation of Title II of the Americans with Disabilities Act

Presently pending are cross-motions for summary judgment, in which plaintiff seeks, *inter alia,* declaratory and injunctive relief. Specifically, Galloway asks that the Court declare the policy of excluding blind jurors from Superior Court juries discriminatory, and accordingly enjoin defendants from barring blind persons from participating in the jury pool. Defendant, on the other hand, continues to maintain that blind persons cannot be deemed "qualified" to perform the essential functions of a juror. After consideration of all of the pleadings and for the reasons stated below, plaintiff's motion is granted, and defendants' motion is denied.

BACKGROUND

Plaintiff Galloway is a United States citizen, who lives in and is registered to vote in the District of Columbia. He is also blind and has been blind since the age of sixteen. Presently, he is employed as a Special Assistant and Manager by the District of Columbia Department of Housing and Community Development. Prior to attaining his current position, Galloway received both a Bachelors of Arts degree in sociology and a Masters of Arts in social work. After completing his education, he held a variety of research and supervisory positions in both the private and public sectors. For instance, early in his career, Galloway worked for the University of California, assisting the establishment of a prepaid health care program and health care centers. Later, Galloway served for three years as the Director of the Peace Corps for Jamaica, and then became assistant to the Deputy Director of the Peace Corps. In his current position with the District of Columbia government, as well as in his past positions, Galloway has had "to evaluate facts and people and to weigh evidence and make judgments based on this information."

Like many registered voters in the District of Columbia, Galloway received a notice from the Superior Court indicating that he had been selected for jury duty. Accordingly, accompanied by his guide dog, he duly reported to Superior Court at 8:00 a.m. on the specified date, March 1, 1991. Although he attempted to register for the jury pool, Galloway was informed by Superior Court personnel that he was barred from serving as a juror because he is blind—the official policy of the Superior Court excludes all blind persons from jury service.

DISCUSSION

After careful consideration of the statutes invoked and the pleadings submitted, it is clear that defendants have violated the Rehabilitation Act, the ADA, and the Civil Rights Act of 1871 by implementing a policy that categorically excludes blind individuals from jury service.

A. *The Rehabilitation Act*

Section 504 of the Rehabilitation Act provides that:

> No otherwise qualified individual with handicaps in the United States, . . . shall, solely by reason of her or his handicap, be excluded from the participation in, be denied the benefits of, or be subjected to discrimination under any program or activity receiving Federal financial assistance.

29 U.S.C. § 794(a). "[T]he basic purpose of § 504 . . . is to ensure that handicapped individuals are not denied jobs or other benefits because of the prejudiced attitudes or ignorance of others." School Bd. of Nassau County, Florida v. Arline, 480 U.S. 273, 284, 107 S.Ct. 1123, 1129 (1987). Accordingly, "mere possession of a handicap is not a permissible ground for assuming an inability to function in a particular context." Southeastern Community College v. Davis, 442 U.S. 397, 405, 99 S.Ct. 2361, 2366 (1979). In promulgating the Rehabilitation Act, Congress was concerned not only with "archaic attitudes" held by the general populace, but also with archaic laws.

It is readily apparent that the Superior Court jury system falls within the purview of Section 504 of the Rehabilitation Act. First, the Act defines "program" as "all of the operations of . . . a department, agency, special purpose district, or other instrumentality of a State or of a local government." 29 U.S.C. § 794(b)(1)(A). In addition, the Superior Court receives "Federal financial assistance" in the form of grants from the United States Department of Justice. Nor is there any question that a blind person is a "handicapped individual" within the meaning of the Act.

Accordingly, the sole remaining issue is whether Galloway or any blind person is "otherwise qualified" to sit on a jury. Defendant bases its policy of excluding blind persons from jury service on the assertion that no blind person is ever "qualified" to serve as a juror because he or she is not able to assess adequately the veracity or credibility of witnesses or to view physical evidence and thus cannot participate in the fair administration of justice. Defendants' position is not only profoundly troubling, but clearly violates the Rehabilitation Act.

Without doubt, there exists "the tendency on the part of officialdom to overgeneralize about the handicapped." The policy at issue here is an excellent example of this penchant for overgeneralization. It is furthermore the reason why a court "must look behind the qualifications [invoked by defendants]. To do otherwise reduces the term 'otherwise qualified' and any arbitrary set of requirements to a tautology." Thus, two questions exist: What are the essential attributes of performing jury duty, and can Galloway or other blind persons meet these requirements?

Defendants' policy is based on the assumption that visual observation is an essential function or attribute of a juror's duties. In reaching this conclusion however, defendants failed to examine any studies or review any literature on the ability of blind individuals to serve on juries or the ability of these individuals to assess credibility. Even now, defendants only conclusorily contend that plaintiff "is not capable of performing all of the essential aspects of jury service." However, plaintiff has offered uncontradicted testimony that blind individuals, like sighted jurors, weigh the content of the testimony given and examine speech patterns, intonation, and syntax in assessing credibility. Thus, "[t]he nervous tic or darting glance, the uneasy shifting or revealing gesture is almost always accompanied by auditory correlates[, including *inter alia,*] clearing the throat, pausing to swallow, voice quavering or inaudibility due to stress or looking downward and permits a blind juror to make credibility assessments just as the juror's sighted counterparts do.

Interestingly, at least ten states—Oklahoma, California, Virginia, Oregon, Texas, South Carolina, Washington, Massachusetts, Wisconsin, and New York—have enacted statutes that forbid the exclusion of blind persons from jury pools solely because of their disability. Similarly, the United States District Court for the District of Columbia allows blind persons to serve as jurors, if they so elect. In many of these jurisdictions, visual impairment is not a *per se* disqualification, but may result in the exclusion of a blind individual from the jury pool if the case involves a significant amount of physical evidence or if the right to a fair trial is otherwise threatened by that juror's service.

Similarly, in the United States, there are several active judges who are blind. Indeed, it is highly persuasive that Judge David Norman, a blind person, served as a judge on the Superior Court of the District of Columbia and presided over numerous trials where he was the sole trier of fact and had to assess the credibility of the witnesses before him and evaluate the documentation and physical evidence. Defendants have never claimed that "those trials were invalid because [Judge Norman] was blind." It is thus illogical to suggest that *all* blind persons are unqualified to sit on a jury when a blind judge in the same Superior Court successfully fulfilled those very duties a blind juror would have to discharge. No distinction can be drawn between a blind judge's ability to make factual findings and the abilities of a blind juror.

In addition, the Superior Court admits persons who are deaf to jury panels and has never suggested that simply because they cannot hear, they cannot serve. In fact, the Superior Court accommodates those individuals by providing sign language interpreters. Yet, a deaf juror cannot hear a witness' words and cannot make credibility determinations based on inflection and intonation of voice, but still is able to make the requisite credibility determinations. Defendants obviously recognize deaf individuals' qualifications to serve on a Superior Court jury since no policy excluding deaf jurors exists. Applying the same logic to a blind individual demonstrates that although a blind juror cannot rely on sight, the individual can certainly hear the witness testify, hear the quaver in a voice, listen to the witness clear his or her throat, or analyze the pause between question and answer, then add these sensory impressions to the words spoken and assess the witness' credibility. Defendants' policy toward deaf jurors evidences a lack of prejudice towards those with hearing impairments and demonstrates their ability to look behind archaic stereotypes thrust upon disabled persons; it is thus difficult to fathom why the policy differs toward blind jurors.

Moreover, even if the individual does not initially appear to be "otherwise qualified," it must still be determined whether reasonable accommodation would make the individual otherwise qualified. In the instant case, no accommodation was offered to Galloway or to any other blind person. According to Galloway he was turned away after being expressly informed that blind jurors could not be accommodated. Plaintiff has established that, in many instances, accommodation could indeed result in an "otherwise qualified" individual. As noted above, sign language interpreters are provided to deaf individuals serving on Superior Court juries. A similar service could be employed for blind jurors.[11] With this type of "reasonable accommodation," a blind juror such as plaintiff should be able to serve satisfactorily in most cases.

In addition to the evidence presented showing that visual observation is not necessarily an essential function of a juror, Galloway introduced substantial evidence to support his individual qualifications to serve competently on a jury. Plaintiff's educational and employment history underscores the fact that he can, and does, make credibility determinations daily. Galloway has served in a number of executive positions in the private sector, the federal government, and the state government and is presently responsibly employed by the District of Columbia, one of the defendants herein. In these capacities, Galloway has been called upon to evaluate facts, weigh evidence, and make judgments. He assesses credibility by listening carefully to the content and consistency of a person's speech and pays particular attention to auditory clues: the rhythm of a person's breathing and the sounds of a person moving, for example.

Yet, just as no *per se* rule of exclusion should be employed against blind persons who wish to serve as jurors, no *per se* rule of inclusion should apply either. Plaintiff has never argued that he should be permitted to participate in every trial. Rather, he has consistently conceded that there may be cases in which it would be inappropriate for a blind person to serve as a juror—cases in which there is a substantial amount of documentary evidence, for example—and that the decision as to whether he should be empaneled in any particular case should be left to the Judge, the attorneys, and the *voir dire* process. In many cases, a blind juror can certainly provide competent jury service.

B. *The Americans with Disabilities Act*

It is equally obvious that the Superior Court jury system falls within the parameters of the ADA.

The Superior Court and the District of Columbia are public entities within the meaning of the Act; "public entity" is defined as "any State or local government" or "any department, agency, special purpose district, or other instrumentality of a State or States or local government." § 12131(1). It is

---

[11] An organization called "Metropolitan Washington Ear, Inc." employs "audio describers"— individuals, trained to describe physical movements, dress, and physical settings for the blind. This or a similar service could be utilized in the Superior Court or the attorneys could be reminded to take special care in questioning witnesses to ensure accurate and complete descriptions of exhibits or diagrams. Moreover, if necessary, documentary evidence could be read to a blind juror by a sighted person and physical evidence could be described. In fact, the Library of Congress utilizes a device called a Kurzweil Reading Machine, which translates printed material into audio. Nevertheless, these suggestions are just that, suggestions—because no accommodation was offered to Galloway, the Court takes no position on the reasonableness of any particular accommodation other than to note that solutions are as limitless as a willing imagination can conceive.

also evident that pursuant to the terms of the ADA, a blind person is an "individual with a disability."

Here, too, the question under the ADA turns on an individual's qualification to sit on a jury. And once again, defendants' policy that all blind persons cannot not serve on any Superior Court jury is unavailing. For substantially the same reasons as earlier set forth, the Court finds that blindness alone, does not disqualify an individual from serving on many juries. Moreover, with reasonable accommodation, the number of cases for which a blind person could be chosen increases even further. Consequently, the policy of categorical exclusion of all blind persons from Superior Court juries violates the ADA. . . .

CONCLUSION

As the Supreme Court noted in *Powers v. Ohio:*

> Jury service preserves the democratic element of the law, as it guards the rights of the parties and insures continued acceptance of the laws by all the people. . . . It "affords ordinary citizens a valuable opportunity to participate in a process of government, an experience fostering, one hopes, a respect for the law." . . . Indeed, with the exception of voting, for most citizens the honor and privilege of jury duty is their most significant opportunity to participate in the democratic process.

Thus, "the honor and privilege of jury duty" may not be abridged simply because an individual is blind. The Rehabilitation Act and the ADA were enacted to prevent old-fashioned and unfounded prejudices against disabled persons from interfering with those individuals' rights to enjoy the same privileges and duties afforded to all United States citizens.

The policies of the Superior Court of the District of Columbia are inherently self-contradictory. They allow a deaf person to serve as a juror and provide accommodation to those deaf individuals who need it. At the same time, they categorically exclude blind persons without even considering or offering accommodation. Defendants' rationale for this distinction is irrational and cannot withstand scrutiny.

Accordingly, it is hereby ORDERED that plaintiff's motion for summary judgment is granted.

NOTES AND QUESTIONS

1. *Blind vs. deaf.* Do you think *Galloway* would have been decided differently if the court had a practice of excluding both blind and deaf individuals from jury service? Are both similarly situated in terms of their relative capabilities as potential jurors?

2. *Automatic exclusion upon request.* What if an individual seeks to be excused from jury service on the grounds that she is blind? Should this request automatically be granted? Or automatically be denied?

3. *Targeted exclusion.* The *Galloway* court indicated that a blind individual may be ineligible to serve as a juror in some type of cases, such as those involving a substantial amount of documentary evidence. How should this determination be made and by whom?

F. ZONING

WISCONSIN COMMUNITY SERVICES, INC. v. CITY OF MILWAUKEE
465 F.3d 737 (7th Cir. 2006)

RIPPLE, CIRCUIT JUDGE.

Wisconsin Community Services ("WCS"), a provider of treatment to mentally ill patients, brought this action under Title II of the Americans with Disabilities Act ("ADA"), 42 U.S.C. §§ 12131–12134, and section 504 of the Rehabilitation Act of 1973, *id.* § 794. The WCS sought an injunction ordering the City of Milwaukee ("the City") to issue a zoning permit that would allow it to move its mental health clinic to an area of Milwaukee, Wisconsin, where health clinics are permitted only on a case-by-case basis. The district court granted partial summary judgment to WCS, concluding that the ADA and the Rehabilitation Act obligated the City to accommodate the disabilities of WCS' patients by allowing WCS to move to its desired location. For the reasons set forth in this opinion, we reverse the judgment of the district court and remand for proceedings consistent with this opinion.

I
BACKGROUND

A. Wisconsin Community Services

WCS is a private, non-profit organization that provides a variety of inpatient and outpatient services to individuals afflicted with severe mental illnesses. WCS provides patients, who cannot live alone without substantial assistance, with psychiatric treatment, counseling, medication monitoring, transportation and help in finding housing and employment. A number of WCS' patients have a history of substance abuse, and a majority have had previous run-ins with the criminal justice system; WCS often accepts patient referrals from court-related agencies such as the United States Probation Service. Although WCS staff sometimes will treat patients in their homes, most of WCS' services are administered in a 7,500 square-foot mental health clinic located at 2023 West Wisconsin Avenue in the City of Milwaukee. Originally, WCS shared this facility with other non-profit organizations, but, as its clientele grew, WCS expanded to occupy the entire building. In 1994, at the time of this initial expansion, WCS employed twenty full-time employees and served 250 patients.

By 1998, the staff at WCS' 2023 West Wisconsin Avenue facility had grown to approximately forty full-time employees serving approximately 400 patients. This increase in clients, services and personnel had caused a shortage in space available for employee parking, client treatment, group therapy sessions and other services. Faced with the shortage, WCS at first considered remodeling, but finally concluded that such a project would be too costly and would interfere with client care. WCS then began searching for a new building. Despite having a limited budget, WCS needed a facility that was located in a safe neighborhood and had adequate floor space, parking and access to public transit. After searching for three years, WCS was able to find two buildings that met its criteria. Neither property, unfortunately, was located in a neighborhood zoned for health clinics. Both were in areas where health clinics are permitted only as "special uses" that require issuance of a permit by the Milwaukee zoning authorities.

WCS previously had received this type of special use permit for some of its other facilities. It therefore made an offer of purchase for one of the properties, contingent on obtaining the necessary special use permit from the Milwaukee zoning board. The seller of this property, concerned about this contingency, declined to accept the offer. WCS then abandoned its efforts to purchase that property and instead made a similar contingent offer on the other identified property. This facility was an 81,000 square-foot building located about one mile from its current facility at 3716 West Wisconsin Avenue. The larger facility is located in an area zoned as a "local business district." According to the City Code's "use table," health care clinics, except for nursing homes, are deemed "special uses" for this zone. Incidentally, the same zone allows foster homes, shelter care facilities, community living arrangements and animal hospitals either as "permitted" or "limited" (no special approval required) uses. The seller accepted WCS' offer.

B. The First Proceeding Before the Board of Zoning Appeals

Milwaukee's City Code defines "special use" as "[a] use which is generally acceptable in a particular zoning district but which, because of its characteristics and the characteristics of the zoning district in which it would be located, requires review on a case by case basis to determine whether it should be permitted, conditionally permitted, or denied." Milwaukee, Wis.Code § 295–7–166. Special use designations are instruments of municipal planning that allow city officials to retain review power over land uses that, although presumptively allowed, may pose special problems or hazards to a neighborhood.

In Milwaukee, an applicant for a special use permit must present its plans to the Department of City Development ("the DCD"), where they are reviewed by a plan examiner. If the DCD denies the special use application, the applicant may appeal the decision to the Milwaukee Board of Zoning Appeals ("BOZA"), where the application is reviewed, a public hearing is held and evidence is heard. Consistent with this procedure, WCS submitted a plan to DCD, outlining its intent to relocate the mental health clinic and several of its administrative offices to the new building. The plan stated that WCS would occupy 32,000 out of the 81,000 square feet of space in the building. An additional 12,000 square feet, according to the plan, would be occupied by two existing tenants, a Walgreens pharmacy and an office of the Social Security Administration. The remaining 37,000 square feet, the plan stated, would be rented out for use as office space or for other commercial purposes.

Under Wisconsin law, in deciding whether to issue a special use permit, the City's zoning officials are guided by four statutory considerations: (1) protection of public health, safety and welfare; (2) protection of the use, value and enjoyment of other property in the neighborhood; (3) traffic and pedestrian safety; and (4) consistency with the City's comprehensive plan. After reviewing WCS' plan, DCD concluded that these criteria had not been met. Specifically, DCD expressed concern over the second factor, protection of neighboring property value. It stated that use of the property as a mental health clinic would jeopardize the commercial revitalization that the neighborhood currently was undergoing. WCS, availing itself of its right to administrative review, then appealed the DCD's decision to Milwaukee's BOZA.

On March 22, 2001, BOZA held a hearing on WCS' appeal. At the outset, WCS argued that, even if its proposal did not meet the special-use criteria, the ADA required BOZA to modify these criteria so that WCS would have the same opportunity to obtain a permit as would a clinic serving non-disabled individuals. BOZA denied this request because it did not believe that it had the authority to deviate from the City's zoning code. Indeed, BOZA prohibited WCS from introducing evidence on the issue. Confined to making its case under the unmodified special use considerations, WCS presented evidence in an effort to refute the perception that the mental health clinic posed a safety threat and would discourage businesses from locating in the neighborhood. This evidence included testimony from a security official who told BOZA that, based on his own investigation, WCS' patients had not been the source of any safety problems in WCS' current neighborhood. WCS also presented letters from its current neighbors to the same effect. Finally, WCS submitted evidence of an award it had received from the National Institute of Justice for exemplary care of previously institutionalized individuals with mental health needs.

BOZA then heard testimony in opposition to the permit. An attorney representing several area businesses testified that opening a mental health clinic that serves a large number of young, unemployed males with histories of mental illness and illegal behavior substantially increases the chance of crime and anti-social behavior in the neighborhood. In a similar vein, a nearby high school voiced its fear that WCS' clients would be riding public transit alongside its "young and vulnerable" students. Additionally, a neighborhood organization encouraged residents to object to WCS' request; it circulated leaflets that argued that the clustering of WCS' clientele "in one location on a daily basis raises a serious risk for the health and well being of people living and working in surrounding neighborhoods."

On May 9, 2001, BOZA voted unanimously to deny WCS' application for a special use permit. The accompanying written decision said only that the proposed use was inconsistent with the considerations set forth in the zoning code. However, several board members orally announced the reasoning behind their decision. One member noted that the "overwhelming" opposition from neighborhood residents convinced him that the WCS clinic would have "a damaging effect upon neighboring business." Another member stated that WCS' clientele, with its large number of convicted criminals, raised "red flags" for local residents. These board members did not think that BOZA had the duty to question the "perceptions" of local residents regarding the possible dangers presented by WCS' patients.

C. The First Federal Court Proceeding

[WCS sued in federal district court alleging] that BOZA had violated the ADA and the Rehabilitation Act by failing to make reasonable modifications to its methods for determining whether to issue a special use permit. . . .

The district court held that BOZA had violated the federal disability laws when it failed even to consider making a reasonable modification to its policies to accommodate WCS' request. . . . The court directed that BOZA hear evidence on WCS' accommodation claim and determine: (1) whether WCS' patients are "disabled"; (2) whether the requested accommodation is "reasonable" and "necessary"; and (3) whether the requested relief would work a "fundamental change" to the services being rendered.

D. The Second Proceeding Before the Board of Zoning Appeals

On September 12, 2002, BOZA reconvened a public hearing. . . .

Jill Fuller, WCS' clinic administrator, was the first to testify. She described the state of overcrowding at WCS' current facility and the effect that these conditions were having on WCS' patients. Individuals with severe mental disabilities, Fuller explained, are particularly sensitive to external stimuli and often have poor socials skills. Overcrowding in the common area of WCS' facility—a room described by another WCS administrator as noisy, smoky and packed—created an extremely stressful environment for these patients and caused their symptoms to become more acute. Additionally, Fuller testified that overcrowding compromised the privacy of one-on-one therapy sessions, which represent a primary component of WCS' treatment.

WCS then presented testimony from its executive director, Stephen Swigart. He described the search process under-taken by WCS to find a new facility that, in addition to being of adequate size, would satisfy the clinic's need for a central location, access to public transit, a serviceable floor plan, low renovation costs and a safe neighborhood. Swigart testified that, after being denied the special use permit, WCS had worked with city planners to locate a suitably zoned property, but that its efforts had been unsuccessful. Any potential alternatives, Swigart explained, were either unavailable or too costly.

Finally, WCS presented expert testimony from Dr. Nancy Frank, the Chair and Associate Dean of the Department of Architecture and Urban Planning at the University of Wisconsin-Milwaukee. She opined that locating the mental health clinic at WCS' desired location, 3716 West Wisconsin Avenue, would have a positive rather than an adverse effect on the surrounding neighborhood. Pointing out that a properly zoned health clinic already was located directly across the street from the proposed site, Frank noted that WCS' clinic would be a consistent addition to the neighborhood and encourage commercial uses of a similar nature. In addition, Frank testified that the building at 3716 West Wisconsin Avenue had been mostly vacant for some time. According to Frank, the goal of city planners seeking to revitalize a commercial area should be to fill vacant space as quickly as possible. Frank predicted that relocating WCS and all of its employees to the area would attract businesses such as "restaurants, dry cleaners [and] coffee shops" eager to serve the new influx of professionals. Frank further stated that "[i]t's actually a strategy in urban redevelopment to try to get a good non-profit anchor in an area first because they're often less dependant [sic] on having an area that already has a lot of consumer demand, and you can then build on that employee base." When asked about safety concerns, Frank stated that four of the six parole offices in the City of Milwaukee were located in areas zoned for business use. Frank saw no reason why WCS' clinic would present any more of a safety risk than these offices.

BOZA then heard testimony from Michael Murphy, an alderman representing the area in which WCS was seeking to relocate its clinic. Steadfastly opposed to WCS' plans, Alderman Murphy stated that "WCS' thrust to rip an 81,000 square foot building out of the heart of this emerging business district could be fatal to this area." When pressed on whether the new clinic conceivably could bring economic benefits to the neighborhood, Alderman Murphy conceded that the influx of professionals potentially could draw new businesses. He stated, nevertheless, that he objected to the plan because it meant that WCS, as a non-profit, would not pay tax on the space used for its clinic and operations; Alderman Murphy preferred a taxpaying commercial tenant in the space. Notably, the only submission on whether WCS' patients were a safety risk to the community were affidavits from business owners near the proposed site. None of these opinions, however, was supported by actual evidence.

On December 22, 2002, BOZA issued a written decision denying the special use permit to WCS. It concluded that WCS' claim for an accommodation under the disabilities laws failed because such an accommodation was neither reasonable nor necessary. . . .

E.   The Second Federal Court Proceeding

[WCS challenged BOZA's action in a second federal court proceeding, and the court concluded that BOZA's denial violated the ADA and the Rehabilitation Act.]

II

DISCUSSION

The legal question before us is whether, and to what extent, a city must modify its zoning standards to prevent them from discriminating against the disabled. The statutes relevant to answering that question are three separate but interrelated federal laws that protect persons with disabilities from discrimination. . . .

3.   Title II of the Americans with Disabilities Act

. . . This case concerns Title II, commonly referred to as the public services portion of the ADA. Title II provides that "no qualified individual with a disability shall, by reason of such disability, be excluded from participation in or be denied the benefits of the services, programs, or activities of a public entity." 42 U.S.C. § 12132.

As courts have held, municipal zoning qualifies as a public "program" or "service," as those terms are employed in the ADA, and the enforcement of those rules is an "activity" of a local government. . . .

Unlike Title I and Title III, Title II of the ADA does not contain a specific accommodation requirement. Instead, the Attorney General, at the instruction of Congress, has issued an implementing regulation that outlines the duty of a public entity to accommodate reasonably the needs of the disabled. The Title II regulation reads:

> A public entity shall make reasonable modifications in policies, practices, or procedures when the modifications are necessary to avoid discrimination on the basis of disability, unless the public entity can demonstrate that making the modifications would fundamentally alter the nature of the service, program, or activity.

28 C.F.R. § 35.130(b)(7). . . .

B.

[W]e must decide whether, and to what extent, the Rehabilitation Act and Title II require the City to modify its zoning practices in order to accommodate the needs of the disabled individuals served by WCS.

WCS submits that the City must waive application of its normal special-use criteria for WCS because it has shown that granting the permit will ameliorate overcrowding, a condition that particularly affects its disabled clients. Before accepting this position, however, we must ask whether WCS has satisfied the "necessity" element contained in the Rehabilitation Act as interpreted by *Alexander v. Choate,* 469 U.S. 287, 105 S.Ct. 712 (1985) and in the Title II regulation, *see* 28 C.F.R. § 35.130(b)(7). WCS contends that the necessity element is satisfied simply when a modification *helps* the disabled, regardless of whether it is *necessary* to alleviate discrimination. Implicit in this position is that the federal accommodation obligation reaches not only rules that create barriers "on the basis of" a person's disability, but also rules that are not disability-based and create obstacles to persons because of some factor unrelated to disability.

[W]ith respect to the Rehabilitation Act, *Choate* held that a modification is "necessary" only when it allows the disabled to obtain benefits that they ordinarily could not have by reason of their disabilities, and not because of some quality that they share with the public generally. The inquiry is the same under the ADA regulation, which asks whether a modification is "necessary to avoid discrimination on the basis of disability." 28 C.F.R. § 35.130(b)(7). Framed by our cases as a causation inquiry, the element is satisfied only when the plaintiff shows that, "but for" his disability, he would have been able to access the services or benefits desired.

On the present record, WCS' inability to meet the City's special use criteria appears due not to its client's disabilities but to its plan to open a non-profit health clinic in a location where the City desired a commercial, taxpaying tenant instead. As far as this record indicates, the City would have rejected similar proposals from non-profit health clinics serving the non-disabled. WCS contends that Title II's accommodation requirement calls, in such a situation, for " 'preferential' treatment and 'is not limited only to lowering barriers created by the disability itself.' " WCS' view, however, is inconsistent with the "necessity" element as it has been defined under the Rehabilitation Act, the FHAA and Title II of the ADA. On this record, because the mental illness of WCS' patients is not the cause-in-fact of WCS' inability to obtain a suitable facility, the program that it seeks modified does not hurt persons with disabilities *"by reason of their handicap."*

WCS responds that the Supreme Court's decision in U.S. Airways, Inc. v. Barnett, 535 U.S. 391, 122 S.Ct. 1516 (2001), has overruled the principle, central to previous Title II accommodation decisions, that the proposed modification must be necessary to avoid discrimination on the basis of a disability. In *Barnett,* a case decided under Title I of the ADA, a U.S.

Airways baggage handler injured his back and requested transfer to a mailroom position that recently had become available. U.S. Airways refused because, under its seniority policy, the company was required to award the position to a more senior employee. Recognizing that U.S. Airways' seniority policy must yield, under certain circumstances, to the needs created by the plaintiff's disability, the Supreme Court held that the plaintiff should be permitted to rebut the presumption that his requested modification to the neutral seniority policy was unreasonable.

According to WCS' characterization, in *Barnett,* the seniority policy treated the disabled and non-disabled alike, and it was a non-disability characteristic (seniority) that denied Barnett the job. WCS sees no distinction between *Barnett* and the present case: Just as the plaintiff in *Barnett* was ineligible for the mail room position because of his seniority rather than his disability, WCS was ineligible for a special use permit because it was a non-profit health clinic, not because its clients were disabled. Because the Supreme Court allowed *Barnett's* claim to go forward, albeit with a heightened burden of persuasion, WCS submits that it has satisfied the necessity element of its accommodation claim.

We cannot accept this argument. *Barnett* and the present case simply deal with different analytical problems. Fairly read, *Barnett* did not deal with the issue of necessity-causality, which was addressed in the cases we discussed earlier. Rather, it dealt with the second question that courts must confront in Title II accommodation cases: whether the accommodation was reasonable. Yet, this element cannot be reached until it has been determined that an accommodation is necessary because a person's disability is the cause for his being denied the service or benefit. As we explained earlier, to satisfy Title II's necessity element, a plaintiff must show that, "but for" its disability, it would have received the ultimate benefit being sought—which, in WCS' case, is a larger facility. The same is true under the Rehabilitation Act. If the City's zoning rules are to be compared to the seniority policy in *Barnett,* WCS must demonstrate that, *because* of its clients' disabilities, it cannot relocate to a suitable site. Only then will the unmodified policy hurt the disabled *on account of* their disability. Only then will the modification be "necessary to avoid discrimination on the basis of disability."

The district court assumed that the proposed modification could be deemed "necessary" even if the disabilities suffered by WCS' patients were not the cause-in-fact of its inability to find a larger building. The district court failed to apply a "but for" causation standard in determining the necessity element of WCS' accommodation claim. Choosing this course was error in light of the prevailing standards under our case law. We therefore must remand to the district court so that it may afford the parties the opportunity to develop the question of whether WCS has been prevented, *because of its clients' disabilities,* from locating a satisfactory new facility.

* * *

NEW DIRECTIONS TREATMENT SERVICES
V. CITY OF READING
490 F.3d 293 (3d Cir. 2007)

SMITH, CIRCUIT JUDGE.

This case presents the familiar conflict between the legal principle of non-discrimination and the political principle of not-in-my-backyard. New Directions Treatment Services, a reputable and longstanding provider of methadone treatment, sought to locate a new facility in the City of Reading. A Pennsylvania statute that facially singles out methadone clinics gave the City of Reading the opportunity to vote to deny the permit. The City of Reading availed itself of that opportunity.

New Directions and individual methadone patients brought suit on constitutional and federal statutory grounds, raising both facial and as applied challenges to the statute. The City of Reading successfully moved for summary judgment against all of plaintiffs' claims. New Directions and the individual plaintiffs' appeal is before us.

I.   Summary of facts and procedural history

New Directions Treatment Services ("NDTS") operates several methadone clinics throughout Pennsylvania, including one in West Reading. NDTS provides methadone maintenance for adults who have been addicted to heroin for at least a year. NDTS's Executive Director, Glen Cooper, contacted the City of Reading ("the City") to discuss opening an additional treatment center, as their West Reading facility had developed a waiting list for treatment. NDTS met with City officials on January 24, 2001, to discuss potential sites within the City. NDTS met with the City Council two months later to continue the discussion. Although NDTS had not yet obtained an operating permit from the City, NDTS signed a ten-year lease on a property located at 700 Lancaster Avenue. NDTS then submitted a zoning permit application.

The Lancaster Avenue property is located on a commercial highway that is interspersed with 40–75 private residences. The Berks Counseling Center previously occupied the site, providing treatment to patients with mental health problems and drug addictions. It did not provide methadone treatment. NDTS intended to serve "a couple hundred or so" methadone patients at the new facility. NDTS proposed a 4,000 square foot addition to the property to accommodate this increased usage. NDTS planned to operate the new facility from 5:30 a.m. to 6:00 p.m. on weekdays, as well as more limited hours on weekends.

In 1999, Pennsylvania adopted a zoning statute regulating locations of methadone treatment facilities. The statute provides that "a methadone treatment facility shall not be established or operated within 500 feet of an existing school, public playground, public park, residential housing area, child-care facility, church, meetinghouse or other actual place of regularly stated religious worship established prior to the proposed methadone treatment facility," unless, "by majority vote, the governing body for the municipality in which the proposed methadone treatment facility is to be located votes in favor of the issuance of an occupancy permit." The Lancaster Avenue property falls within the ambit of the statute. When NDTS inquired about sites not covered by the statute, a City zoning official referred them to three sites, including a cemetery and a heavy industrial area, all of which NDTS considered unsuitable.

[After two public hearings where] NDTS acknowledged that it had experienced some loitering and littering at its West Reading facility . . . , the City voted against NDTS's application.

NDTS and several individual plaintiffs proceeding in pseudonym filed suit in the United States District Court for the Eastern District of Pennsylvania on March 25, 2004. . . . NDTS alleged that the statute, both facially and as applied, violates § 504 of the Rehabilitation Act. 29 U.S.C. § 794, [as well as] Title II of the Americans with Disabilities Act ("ADA"). 42 U.S.C. § 12132. . . .

The City moved for summary judgment. NDTS filed a cross-motion for partial summary judgment on their claims against the validity of the statute. The District Court granted the City's motion in its entirety and denied NDTS's cross-motion on August 22, 2005. NDTS timely appealed.

II. Discussion

. . . Section 12132 of Title II of the ADA provides that "[s]ubject to the provisions of this subchapter, no qualified individual with a disability shall, by reason of such disability, be excluded from participation in or be denied the benefits of the services, programs, or activities of a public entity, or be subjected to discrimination by any such entity." 42 U.S.C. § 12132. This statement constitutes a general prohibition against discrimination by public entities, regardless of activity. Bay Area Addiction Research and Treatment, Inc. v. City of Antioch, 179 F.3d 725, 730–31 (9th Cir.1999) (striking down a ban on methadone clinics within 500 feet of a residential area). Section 504 of the Rehabilitation Act similarly provides that "[n]o otherwise qualified individual with a disability . . . shall, solely by reason of her or his disability, be excluded from the participation in, be denied the benefits of, or be subjected to discrimination under any program or activity receiving Federal financial assistance." 29 U.S.C. § 794(a). We have noted that "[a]s the ADA simply expands the Rehabilitation Act's prohibitions against discrimination into the private sector, Congress has directed that the two acts' judicial and agency standards be harmonized" and we will accordingly analyze the two provisions together.

The Sixth and Ninth Circuits have considered the issue of whether a municipal ordinance prohibiting methadone clinics within 500 feet of a residential area violated the general proscription contained in the ADA and Rehabilitation Act. Both Courts concluded that the ordinances were "facially discriminatory laws" and therefore "present[ed] per se violations of § 12132."

The Ninth Circuit confronted many of the issues presented in this case when the Bay Area Addiction Research and Treatment, Inc. ("BAART") and California Detoxification Programs, Inc. ("CDP") tried to relocate their methadone clinic to the City of Antioch, California. BAART had been operating a methadone clinic near the courthouse in Pittsburg, California for 13 years. BAART and CDP received notice from Antioch that the proposed location could be used for a methadone clinic under Antioch's zoning plan. However, the Antioch City Council enacted an urgency ordinance banning methadone clinics within 500 feet of residential areas, thereby barring use of the proposed site. BAART and other plaintiffs alleged that Antioch had violated both Title II of the ADA and § 504 of the Rehabilitation Act. The District Court denied Bay Area's motion for a preliminary injunction enjoining the ordinance. BAART appealed.

[T]he Ninth Circuit analyzed whether the District Court had abused its discretion by denying the preliminary injunction in part because BAART did not have a likelihood of success on the merits. The Ninth Circuit held that the District Court had abused its discretion by applying an erroneous legal standard and remanded the case. The Ninth Circuit first held that the District Court erred by applying the "reasonable modification" test to a facially discriminatory law. U.S. Department of Justice regulations require that would-be plaintiffs request reasonable modifications to avoid discrimination unless the modification would fundamentally alter the program, activity, ordinance, or statute. 28 C.F.R. § 35.130(b)(7). However, where the "statute discriminates against qualified individuals on its face rather than in its application," the applicable regulation interpreting Title II, which only requires "reasonable" accommodation, makes little sense. The only way to alter a facially discriminatory ordinance is to remove the discriminating language. The Antioch ordinance could only have been "rendered facially neutral by expanding the class of entities that may not operate within 500 feet of a residential neighborhood to include all clinics at which medical services are provided, or by striking the reference to methadone clinics entirely," and, "[e]ither modification would fundamentally alter the zoning ordinance, the former by expanding the covered establishments dramatically, and the latter by rendering the ordinance a nullity." Therefore, the reasonable modifications test could not apply to a facially discriminatory ordinance.

The Ninth Circuit noted that this determination does not end the inquiry, however, as both statutes withhold protection from any "individual who poses a significant risk to the health or safety of others that cannot be ameliorated by means of a reasonable modification." The Supreme Court developed the significant risk test in *School Board of Nassau County v. Arline,* a case involving a teacher who alleged a violation of § 504 of the Rehabilitation Act after she was discharged because she had an active case of tuberculosis. 480 U.S. 273, 276, 107 S.Ct. 1123 (1987). The Supreme Court held that "[a] person who poses a significant risk of communicating an infectious disease to others in the workplace will not be otherwise qualified for his or her job if reasonable accommodation will not eliminate that risk."

Although the Ninth Circuit disclaimed any conclusion about the outcome of this inquiry or the ultimate merits of the claim, it repeatedly emphasized that *Arline* was designed to "ensure that decisions are not made on the basis of 'the prejudiced attitudes or the ignorance of others,' " and that "[t]his is particularly important because, as with individuals with contagious diseases, '[f]ew aspects of a handicap give rise to the same level of public fear and misapprehension,' as the challenges facing recovering drug addicts." The Ninth Circuit held that, in order for a methadone clinic to fail the significant risk test, it must present "severe and likely harms to the community that are directly associated with the operation of the methadone clinic." Such alleged harms must be supported by evidence and "may include a reasonable likelihood of a significant increase in crime." The Ninth Circuit noted that courts should be mindful of the ADA and Rehabilitation Act's goals of eliminating discrimination against individuals with disabilities and protecting those individuals "from deprivations based on prejudice, stereotypes, or unfounded fear." Therefore, "it is not enough that individuals pose a hypothetical or presumed risk"—the evidence must reflect a risk that is significant and harm that is serious.

Three years later, the Sixth Circuit invoked *Bay Area* and reached a similar result in MX Group v. City of Covington. 293 F.3d 326, 344–45 (6th Cir.2002). . . .

Although *Bay Area* and *MX Group* dealt with outright bans, we believe that the reasoning of those cases is equally applicable here. The Pennsylvania statute imposes a ban on the establishment of methadone clinics within 500 feet of many structures, including schools, churches, and residential housing developments. The Pennsylvania law differs from those in *Bay Area* and *MX Group* in that the "the governing body for the municipality in which the proposed methadone treatment facility is to be located" can waive the ban if, and only if, it approves the issuance of a permit by majority vote. However, this ability of municipalities to waive the statutory ban in no way alters the fact that [the statute] facially singles out methadone clinics, and thereby methadone patients, for different treatment, thereby rendering the statute facially discriminatory.

We agree with the Sixth and Ninth Circuits that a law that singles out methadone clinics for different zoning procedures is facially discriminatory under the ADA and the Rehabilitation Act. We also agree that it is inappropriate to apply the "reasonable modification" test to facially discriminatory laws. The only way to modify a facially discriminatory statute is to remove the discriminatory language. However, amending [the statute] to remove the facial discrimination against methadone clinics would "fundamentally alter" the statute.

Having concluded that [the statute] is facially discriminatory and that the reasonable modification test does not apply, we proceed to inquire whether NDTS's clients pose a significant risk. . . .

The Supreme Court emphasized in *Bragdon v. Abbott* that the significant risk test requires a rigorous objective inquiry. 524 U.S. 624, 626, 118 S.Ct. 2196 (1998). In *Bragdon*, a dentist refused to fill a cavity for an asymptomatic AIDS patient. The Court held that:

> The existence, or nonexistence, of a significant risk must be determined from the standpoint of the person who refuses the treatment or accommodation, and the risk of assessment must be based on medical or other objective evidence. . . . As a health care professional, petitioner had the duty to assess the risk of infection based on the objective, scientific information available to him and others in his profession. His belief that a significant risk existed, even if maintained in good faith, would not relieve him of liability.

Accordingly, we cannot base our decision on the subjective judgments of the people purportedly at risk, the Reading residents, City Council, or even Pennsylvania citizens, but must look to objective evidence in the record of any dangers posed by methadone clinics and patients. The purported risk must be substantial, not speculative or remote.

The record contains ample evidence that NDTS's clients, and methadone patients as a class, do not pose a significant risk. Neither the City nor its amicus, the Commonwealth, have offered any evidence to the contrary. The City refers to the deposition of Glen Cooper, the Executive Director of NDTS, in which he estimated that 20 to 30 percent of the clinic's patients would test positive for illegal drugs. However, NDTS also submitted the results of drug screens at its West Reading and Bethlehem clinics showing that only patients enrolled for less than six months test positive at the 30 percent rate, whereas less than six percent of patients enrolled for more than six months test positive for illegal drugs.

More importantly, the record demonstrates no link between methadone clinics and increased crime. Cooper testified that there had been no criminal incidents at NDTS's West Reading facility. The Commonwealth offered no evidence to support its contrary assertion that there is a "frequent association" between methadone clinics and criminal activity. In depositions, City Council members expressed concerns about heavy traffic, loitering, noise pollution, littering, double parking, and jaywalking. However, the City offered no evidence to support an association between these concerns and methadone clinics. Even if such connections existed, we are skeptical that they would qualify as the substantial harms contemplated by the *Arline* and *Bragdon* Courts.

The brief legislative history of [the statute] provides no further evidence that methadone patients pose a significant risk. Representative Platts, the bill's principal sponsor, stated that the legislation would protect "children from the high crime rates associated with heroin addicts," that, "[o]n average heroin addicts before treatment commit a crime on average 200 days of the year," and that "[e]ven after 6 months of methadone treatment, they still average once a month committing a crime." Representative Platts offered no source for this statistic. We find it difficult to place much weight on this unsupported statistic given Cooper's unrebutted testimony that other NDTS facilities had experienced no criminal incidents and the extremely positive reports of the National Institute on Drug Abuse and the Office of National Drug Control Policy. In addition, the statement of Representative Serafini betrays the generalized prejudice and fear warned against by the *Arline* Court:

> It is unfortunate that we have to have methadone treatment facilities at all, but to locate them in areas that are residential or close to where young people might congregate or the community might meet and gather is a definite mistake, and these facilities, in my opinion, do not benefit anyone but the heroin addict, and they should be located either in a community that welcomes this kind of facility or out in an area away from people who have kept themselves clean and free of drugs and should not be confronted by this kind of a pollution in their community.

* * *

We have no doubt that some methadone patients are inclined to criminal or otherwise dangerous behavior. However, in the words of the *Arline* Court:

> The fact that *some* persons who have contagious diseases may pose a serious health threat to others under certain circumstances does not justify excluding from the coverage of the Act *all* persons with actual or perceived contagious diseases. Such exclusion would mean that those accused of being contagious would never have the opportunity to have their condition evaluated in light of medical evidence and a determination made as to whether they were "otherwise qualified." Rather, they would be vulnerable to

discrimination on the basis of mythology—precisely the type of injury Congress sought to prevent.

480 U.S. at 285, 107 S.Ct. 1123.

We will reverse the order of the District Court and remand with instructions that it grant NDTS's motion for partial summary judgment because [the statute] facially violates the ADA and the Rehabilitation Act.

NOTES AND QUESTIONS

1. *Disability-related exclusion.* The Seventh Circuit in *WCS* states that Title II and the Rehabilitation Act require a modification in practices only if an individual establishes that access to the benefit or service in question is precluded because of his or her disability. Where does this requirement come from? And what impact did this requirement have on the outcome of the *WCS* case? As a factual matter, do you think that causation was established in this case?

2. *Distinguishing* Barnett. In *U.S. Airways v. Barnett*, the majority opinion rejected Justice Scalia's assertion that Title I of the ADA only requires employers to provide reasonable accommodations to disability-related obstacles. In that case, the plaintiff was denied a transfer to a mailroom position, not because of his disability, but because of his lack of seniority. Although the plaintiff ultimately did not prevail in *Barnett*, the majority opinion explained that "an employer's disability-neutral rule cannot by itself place the accommodation beyond the Act's potential reach." 535 U.S. at 397. Are you convinced by the Seventh Circuit's attempt to distinguish *Barnett*? If not, is there a good policy reason to require a showing of disability-related causation under Title II when such is not required under Title I?

3. *Alteration of zoning policies.* Given the Seventh Circuit's analysis in *WCS*, when, if at all, must a city alter its zoning policies as a reasonable modification for the disabled? Or does *WCS* stand for the proposition that Title II only bars intentional discrimination in zoning policies?

4. *Reasonable modification requirement.* The Third Circuit in *New Directions* strikes down a zoning policy that is facially discriminatory. Why does the Third Circuit state that "it is inappropriate to apply the 'reasonable modification' test to facially discriminatory laws?" Taking *WCS* and *New Directions* together, what remains of the reasonable modification requirement under Title II?

5. *Direct threat.* The Third Circuit concluded that the Pennsylvania zoning statute was not justified as a means to avoid a "direct threat" of harm to the public. Unlike Title I, Title II does not expressly codify a "direct threat" defense. The DOJ regulations, however, do recognize the direct threat concept as applicable under Title II. *See* 28 C.F.R. §§ 35.104, 35.130(h). Should the direct threat defense apply in the Title II context? And, does the *Arline* and *Bragdon* articulation of that defense set an appropriate standard for Title II analysis? Are there other alternatives that the court should have considered?

6. *Difference in tone.* Although the outcomes in the *WCS* and *New Directions* decisions are not necessarily inconsistent, the two opinions are markedly different in tone. Where the Seventh Circuit sees a requested zoning variance as asking for "preferential" treatment, the Third Circuit sees the denial of such a variance as based on "generalized prejudice and fear." Do you think that the outcomes of either of these cases would have been different if they had been decided by the other court?

G. ACCESSIBILITY

BARDON V. CITY OF SACRAMENTO
292 F.3d 1073 (9th Cir. 2002)

TASHIMA, CIRCUIT JUDGE.

We must decide whether public sidewalks in the City of Sacramento are a service, program, or activity of the City within the meaning of Title II of the Americans with Disabilities Act ("ADA"), 42 U.S.C. § 12132, or § 504 of the Rehabilitation Act, 29 U.S.C. § 794. We hold that they are and, accordingly, that the sidewalks are subject to program accessibility regulations promulgated in furtherance of these statutes. We therefore reverse the order of the district court and remand for further proceedings.

BACKGROUND

Appellants, various individuals with mobility and/or vision disabilities, commenced this class action against the City of Sacramento. Appellants alleged that the City violated the ADA and the Rehabilitation Act by failing to install curb ramps in newly-constructed or altered sidewalks and by failing to maintain existing sidewalks so as to ensure accessibility by persons with disabilities. The parties stipulated to the entry of an injunction regarding the curb ramps; however, they did not reach agreement on the City's obligation to remove other barriers to sidewalk accessibility, such as benches, sign posts, or wires.

The district court . . . held that the public sidewalks in Sacramento are not a service, program, or activity of the City and, accordingly, are not subject to the program access requirements of either the ADA or the Rehabilitation Act. . . .

DISCUSSION

Title II of the ADA provides that "no qualified individual with a disability shall, by reason of such disability, be excluded from participation in or be denied the benefits of the services, programs, or activities of a public entity, or be subjected to discrimination by any such entity." 42 U.S.C. § 12132. Similarly, § 504 of the Rehabilitation Act provides that "[n]o otherwise qualified individual with a disability . . . shall, solely by reason of her or his disability, be excluded from the participation in, be denied the benefits of, or be subjected to discrimination under any program or activity receiving Federal financial assistance." 29 U.S.C. § 794(a). One form of prohibited discrimination is the exclusion from a public entity's services, programs, or activities because of the inaccessibility of the entity's facility—thus, the program accessibility regulations at issue here.

The access requirements are set forth in 28 C.F.R. §§ 35.149–35.151. Section 35.150 requires a public entity to "operate each service, program, or activity so that the service, program, or activity, when viewed in its entirety, is readily accessible to and usable by individuals with disabilities." 28 C.F.R. § 35.150(a). The public entity is required to develop a transition plan for making structural changes to facilities in order to make its programs accessible. Id. at § 35.150(d)(1). The regulation also requires the transition plan to include a schedule for providing curb ramps to make pedestrian walkways accessible. Id. at § 35.150(d)(2). Section 35.151 similarly requires newly-constructed or altered roads and walkways to contain curb ramps at intersections. 28 C.F.R. § 35.151(e).

The district court's order was based on its conclusion that sidewalks are not a service, program, or activity of the City. Rather than determining whether each function of a city can be characterized as a service, program, or activity for purposes of Title II, however, we have construed "the ADA's broad language [as] bring[ing] within its scope 'anything a public entity does.'" Attempting to distinguish which public functions are services, programs, or activities, and which are not, would disintegrate into needless "hair-splitting arguments." The focus of the inquiry, therefore, is not so much on whether a particular public function can technically be characterized as a service, program, or activity, but whether it is "'a normal function of a governmental entity.'" Thus, we have held that medical licensing is a service, program, or activity for purposes of Title II, as is zoning, and parole hearings.

In keeping with our precedent, maintaining public sidewalks is a normal function of a city and "without a doubt something that the [City] 'does.'" Maintaining their accessibility for individuals with disabilities therefore falls within the scope of Title II.

This broad construction of the phrase, "services, programs, or activities," is supported by the plain language of the Rehabilitation Act because, although the ADA does not define "services, programs, or activities," the Rehabilitation Act defines "program or activity" as "all of the operations of" a qualifying local government. 29 U.S.C. § 794(b)(1)(A). The legislative history of the ADA similarly supports construing the language generously, providing that Title II "essentially simply extends the anti-discrimination prohibition embodied in section 504 [of the Rehabilitation Act] to *all actions of state and local governments*." In fact, the ADA must be construed "broadly in order to effectively implement the ADA's fundamental purpose of 'provid[ing] a clear and comprehensive national mandate for the elimination of discrimination against individuals with disabilities.' "

Requiring the City to maintain its sidewalks so that they are accessible to individuals with disabilities is consistent with the tenor of § 35.150, which requires the provision of curb ramps, "giving priority to walkways serving" government offices, "transportation, places of public accommodation, and employers," but then "followed by walkways serving other areas." 28 C.F.R. § 35.150(d)(2). Section 35.150's requirement of curb ramps in all pedestrian walkways reveals a general concern for the accessibility of public sidewalks, as well as a recognition that sidewalks fall within the ADA's coverage, and would be meaningless if the sidewalks between the curb ramps were inaccessible.

Moreover, the conclusion that sidewalks are subject to the accessibility regulations is the position taken by the Department of Justice ("DOJ"), the agency responsible for issuing the regulations. An agency's interpretation of its own regulation is entitled to deference when the language of the regulation is ambiguous and the interpretation is not plainly erroneous or inconsistent with the regulation. The regulation is ambiguous because, while it does not specifically address the accessibility of sidewalks, it does address curb ramps. The curb ramps, however, could not be covered unless the sidewalks themselves are covered. The DOJ's interpretation of its own regulation, that sidewalks are encompassed by the regulation, is not plainly erroneous or inconsistent with the regulation. We therefore defer to the interpretation of the DOJ under *Auer*.

CONCLUSION

Title II's prohibition of discrimination in the provision of public services applies to the maintenance of public sidewalks, which is a normal function of a municipal entity. The legislative history of Title II indicates that all activities of local governments are subject to this prohibition of discrimination. This conclusion is also supported by the language of § 35.150, which requires the provision of curb ramps in order for sidewalks to be accessible to individuals with disabilities. The order of the district court accordingly is reversed and the case remanded for further proceedings.

NOTES AND QUESTIONS

1. *Broad coverage. Bardon* demonstrates the broad coverage of Title II. According to the regulations, Title II applies to all governmental "facilities" which are defined to mean "all or any portion of buildings, structures, sites, complexes, equipment, rolling stock or other conveyances, roads, walks, passageways, parking lots, or other real or personal property." 28 C.F.R. § 35.104. Can you think of a governmental activity or physical structure that is not covered by Title II?

2.   *Facility access.* What is the facility access responsibility of governmental entities? The regulations state that governmental entities may not exclude disabled individuals from participation in services, programs, or activities by virtue of facilities that are "inaccessible to or unusable by" such individuals. 28 C.F.R. § 35.149. The regulations establish a sliding scale of responsibilities depending upon whether a facility is new, altered, or existing:

a.   *New facilities.* Governmental entities must design and construct new facilities so that they are "readily accessible and usable by individuals with disabilities." 28 C.F.R. § 35.151(a).

b.   *Altered facilities.* If a governmental entity alters an existing facility, the portion that is altered must be made "readily accessible to and usable by individuals with disabilities" to the "maximum extent feasible." 28 C.F.R. § 35.151(b).

c.   *Existing facilities.* Governmental entities are required to make existing facilities accessible and usable unless they can demonstrate that such action "would result in a fundamental alteration in the nature of a service, program, or activity or in undue financial and administrative burdens." 28 C.F.R. § 35.150(a).

3.   *Alterations.* Assume that a public library renovates a second story storage room that is currently accessible only by a staircase to serve as a new computer and internet access room for patrons. Must the library also install an elevator to enable wheelchair access to the second floor as part of the renovation? What if the second-story room, instead, already served as a computer room, but the library replaces the old computers and adds high speed internet access? *See* 28 C.F.R. § 35.151(b).

4.   In *Kinney v. Yerusalim*, 9 F.3d 1067 (3d Cir. 1993), the Third Circuit considered whether the resurfacing of a city street constituted an "alteration." The court stated that "an 'alteration' within the meaning of the regulations is a change that affects the usability of the facility involved." The Third Circuit held that, because the resurfacing affected the street's usability, the resurfacing constituted an alteration, which triggered the city's responsibility to install curb cuts in order to enable access to the "maximum extent feasible."

5.   *Beyond wheelchairs.* Title II regulations are particularly focused on requiring access to individuals who use wheelchairs. What are the access requirements for other types of disabilities? Does a public library have an obligation to provide books in braille for the blind, oversized chairs for the obese, or handrails for individuals with cerebral palsy?

6.   *Alternative means of access.* In situations where making an existing facility accessible would be unduly burdensome, the regulations state that a public entity "shall take any other action that would not result in such . . . burdens but would nevertheless ensure that individuals with disabilities receive the benefits or services provided by the public entity." If installing an elevator in an existing library building would be unduly burdensome, what alternative actions should the library consider?

NATIONAL FEDERATION OF THE BLIND V. LAMONE
813 F.3d 494 (4th Cir. 2016)

FLOYD, CIRCUIT JUDGE:

Maryland allows any voter to vote via absentee ballot. A voter may obtain a blank hardcopy absentee ballot by mail, fax, or by downloading and printing one from a website. The hardcopy ballot must be marked by hand, signed, and returned via mail or hand-delivery to the voter's local election board.

The National Federation of the Blind and individual disabled Maryland voters sued state election officials under Title II of the Americans with Disabilities Act ("ADA") and Section 504 of the Rehabilitation Act. Plaintiffs allege that marking a hardcopy ballot by hand without assistance is impossible for voters with various disabilities, and that they have therefore been denied meaningful access to absentee voting. After a bench trial, the district court found that Maryland's program, as then structured, did not comport with ADA and Rehabilitation Act requirements. The district court further found that plaintiffs' proposed remedy—the use of an "online ballot marking tool" that would enable disabled voters to mark their ballots electronically—was a reasonable modification that did not fundamentally alter Maryland's absentee voting program. Defendant election officials now appeal all these aspects of the district court's decision. For the reasons below, we affirm.

I.

A.

Elections in the State of Maryland are overseen by the State Board of Elections ("Board"). Md.Code Ann., Elec. Law §§ 2–101 to 102 ("Elec. Law"). The Board is comprised of five members. The Board appoints a State Administrator of Elections who is designated as "the chief State election official" and tasked with administering Maryland's election apparatus.

Maryland provides its voters with a number of different means to vote. Maryland has nearly 2,000 polling places at which a voter may cast a ballot on Election Day. The overwhelming majority of these polling places are accessible to physically disabled voters and are staffed with election judges trained in serving voters with disabilities. The polling place voting machines have a number of accessibility features designed to assist disabled voters in casting their ballots. Maryland's voting machines allow voters to magnify the font of the ballot, to alter the color contrast, and to position the interface screen such that voters can sit down while casting their ballots. The voting machines can also be programmed for nonvisual access by means of an audio ballot; when using the audio features a voter receives a headset and numeric keypad to navigate the ballot choices. Voters who desire assistance in marking their ballots may be assisted by an individual of their choosing or by an election judge (in the presence of an election judge of another political party). The voting machines are not compatible with some common personal accessibility devices such as refreshable Braille displays.

Maryland also allows voters to vote in person for an eight-day period before Election Day at sixty-four early voting polling stations. All of these early voting polling places are physically accessible.

Finally, any Maryland voter may vote by absentee ballot. A voter can obtain a ballot by mail, fax, or electronically by downloading a ballot from a website. A voter who electronically downloads an absentee ballot must print out the ballot in hardcopy, mark their choices by hand, and then sign and return the hardcopy ballot to their local board of elections. An absentee voter may designate an agent to pick up and deliver a ballot. Absentee voters may also have an individual of their choice assist them in hand marking the ballot.

B.

Historically, as noted, an absentee voter who obtained an absentee ballot electronically needed to print out the blank ballot and mark their choices by hand on the printed hardcopy ballot. For several years, Maryland has been developing a piece of software referred to as an "online ballot marking tool." The tool can be used by absentee voters who choose to obtain their absentee ballots electronically; the tool enables voters to mark their choices electronically and then print out a completed ballot. When the ballot is printed, the voter's selections appear on a number of pages followed by a separate signature page. The voter must still sign the signature page and return the entire hardcopy ballot to the local board of elections. Only printed and signed ballots received by a local board of elections are counted in determining the result of an election.

Maryland's Board developed the online ballot marking tool over a number of years, including with the participation of plaintiff National Federation of the Blind. The Board has solicited feedback and implemented a number of usability and accessibility enhancements for disabled voters. The tool is not compatible with all computer browsers or operating systems, but does function properly with a variety of reasonably up-to-date products. Importantly for individuals with certain disabilities, the ability to use the tool on their own computers may enable them to use the personal assistive devices that they ordinarily use to interface with the computer, such as a refreshable Braille display, to mark their ballot choices.

C.

An early, non-accessible version of the online ballot marking tool was available to absentee voters during Maryland's 2012 primary elections. Following the primary elections, a question arose as to whether the tool needed to be officially certified pursuant to Maryland Election Law Section 9–102, which requires certification of any "voting system" prior to use. The

Maryland Attorney General provided an opinion that the tool did not meet the statutory definition of a "voting system" and did not require certification. However, apparently due to lingering concerns over the status of the online ballot marking tool, the Board only made the tool available to certain overseas and military absentee voters for the 2012 general election. Use of the tool in the 2012 primary and general elections was apparently uneventful.

The Maryland General Assembly subsequently clarified the status of the tool. In 2013, the General Assembly passed the "Improving Access to Voting Act," 2013 Md. Laws Ch. 157, which, among other things, explicitly required the Board to certify any online ballot marking tool prior to use by voters. *See id.* (codified at Certification requires a supermajority: at least four of the five members of the Board must vote in favor of certification.

The Board continued to make improvements to the version of the tool that had been used in the 2012 election cycle. In particular, the Board implemented certain changes to make the tool more accessible to voters with disabilities. Additionally, in accordance with the 2013 Improving Access to Voting Act, the Board hired an independent consultant, Unatek Inc. ("Unatek"), to perform security testing on the tool. Unatek produced a report in December 2013 concluding that use of the tool was secure.

In February 2014, the Board met and discussed the online ballot marking tool. The Board reviewed the December 2013 Unatek report and interviewed the report's author. Some Board members continued to express concerns about the security of the tool, and the Board did not hold a certification vote.

The Board subsequently hired a second independent consultant, Mainstay Enterprises, Inc. ("Mainstay"), to audit the Unatek security report. The Mainstay audit concluded that Unatek's security assessment had followed industry best practices. The Board also received and reviewed public comments and had Board staff obtain information on the use of similar ballot marking tools in other states.

The certification issue was again discussed at the Board's April 2014 meeting. At the meeting, Mainstay briefed the Board on the results of its audit. Some Board members continued to express concerns about certification and the Board did not take a certification vote.

D.

On May 19, 2014, plaintiffs sued Linda Lamone, Maryland's State Administrator of Elections, and the five Board members, all in their official capacities. At the heart of plaintiffs' suit are claims that Maryland's absentee voting process violates the ADA and the Rehabilitation Act. Plaintiffs sought both a declaratory judgment to that effect as well as an injunction requiring state election officials to make the online ballot marking tool available for use starting with the 2014 general election. The district court subsequently scheduled a bench trial to begin on August 13, 2014. The schedule would provide defendants with sufficient time to implement the tool before the 2014 general election in the event that plaintiffs prevailed.

While the suit was pending, the Board held a specially-scheduled meeting on July 10, 2014, with one Board member absent. The four Board members in attendance voted 3 to 1 to certify the online ballot marking tool. The vote did not satisfy the statutory supermajority requirement and the tool was not certified.

The district court held a three-day bench trial beginning on August 13, 2014. The district court heard testimony on: the difficulties disabled voters have experienced while voting; the Board's development of the online ballot marking tool and the Board's deliberation over certification; the accessibility of the tool for disabled voters; and the security risks posed by the tool.

The district court found that "the evidence demonstrated specific difficulties that some disabled voters have experienced while voting," and that "under the current absentee ballot voting program, individuals with disabilities such as those of the Plaintiffs cannot vote privately and independently." The district court credited the results of a University of Baltimore usability study that concluded the tool was "highly accessible for disabled voters," though the district court acknowledged that two individuals testified that they had difficulty accessing and using the tool during a public demonstration period. The district court found the tool "compatible with reasonably up-to-date computer and screen access software," "designed in accordance with the Web Content Accessibility Guidelines," and "compatible with refreshable Braille displays." The district court did find that there were still "challenges to private and independent voting by absentee ballot for disabled voters even when using the tool," including that "disabled voters may need assistance in signing their ballots before submission." "However, the testimony at trial also indicated that, because the signature sheet prints on a separate page, the risk of disclosure of a disabled voter's selections was minimalized and, in any event, was significantly less than that afforded under the current paper absentee ballot system. . . ."

With respect to the security risks posed by the online ballot marking tool, the district court credited expert testimony that the tool "exhibited software independence, meaning a change to the voting software used for an election cannot cause an undetectable change to the outcome of an election" and that "there were no additional risks that did not exist in other methods already available to Maryland voters." The district court found that the tool was "not without some security risks" including that "malware could enable [a] third party to observe a voter's selections" and that "a voter's selections could be captured if a third party infiltrated the Board's server during the time a voter's selections and/or the printable ballot were being transmitted." Additionally, "[t]here was no evidence at trial that the online ballot marking tool had been tested against intentional attempts to infiltrate or hack into the Board's server or the tool."

The district court further found that "it is clear that most voters may mark their absentee ballots without assistance" and that plaintiffs "should be afforded the same opportunity, but the State's current voting program does not allow for it." Based on the facts found at trial, the district court concluded that plaintiffs had established that they had been denied meaningful access to absentee voting in Maryland in violation of Title II of the ADA and Section 504 of the Rehabilitation Act. The district court entered a declaratory judgment for plaintiffs to this effect. The district court further concluded that plaintiffs' proposed remedy, access to the online ballot marking tool, was a reasonable modification that did not fundamentally alter Maryland's voting program. Consistent with these conclusions, the district court entered a permanent injunction prohibiting defendants from violating plaintiffs' rights under the ADA and the Rehabilitation Act and requiring defendants to make the online ballot marking tool available to plaintiffs for the 2014 general election. This appeal followed.

II.

* * *

Defendants' appeal principally focuses on the district court's three core legal conclusions: (1) that plaintiffs have been denied meaningful access to absentee voting in violation of the ADA and the Rehabilitation Act; (2) that the online ballot marking tool constitutes a reasonable remedial modification; and (3) that requiring defendants to allow use of the tool does not fundamentally alter Maryland's voting program. We address each of these issues in turn.

III.

Title II of the ADA provides that "no qualified individual with a disability shall, by reason of such disability, be excluded from participation in or be denied the benefits of the services, programs, or activities of a public entity, or be subjected to discrimination by any such entity." 42 U.S.C. § 12132. To make out a violation of Title II, plaintiffs must show: (1) they have a disability; (2) they are otherwise qualified to receive the benefits of a public service, program, or activity; and (3) they were denied the benefits of such service, program, or activity, or otherwise discriminated against, on the basis of their disability. *Constantine v. Rectors & Visitors of George Mason Univ.*, 411 F.3d 474, 498 (4th Cir.2005).

Only the third of these elements—whether plaintiffs were denied the benefits of a public service, program, or activity on the basis of their disability—is at issue here. Much of the dispute revolves around the proper way to define the scope of the relevant public service or program at issue. Plaintiffs argue that the appropriate analytic scope is Maryland's absentee voting program. Defendants urge analysis of Maryland's voting program in its entirety, encompassing the various voting alternatives—including in-person voting—available to Maryland voters. Defendants argue that even if absentee voting is not fully accessible, the full accessibility of Maryland's in-person polling places provides disabled voters with meaningful access to voting. As explained below, we conclude that defendants' proposed focus is overbroad and would undermine the purpose of the ADA and its implementing regulations.

A.

Defendants' argument for holistic consideration of Maryland's voting program is in some immediate tension with the text of the ADA. Title II states that a disabled individual may not be "excluded from participation in or be denied the benefits of the services, programs, or activities of a public entity, or be subjected to discrimination by any such entity." 42 U.S.C. § 12132. Defendants' proposed focus on voting in its entirety effectively reads out much of this language, suggesting that Title II prohibits only complete exclusion from participation in broadly-defined public programs. However, Title II is disjunctive. By its own terms it is not limited only to public "programs"; it applies to "services, programs, *or* activities." *Id.* (emphasis added). Title II does not only prohibit "exclusion from participation" in a public program; it also separately prohibits "den[ying] the benefits" of that program. *Id.* And in addition to those prohibitions, Title II separately generally prohibits "discrimination by any [public] entity." *Id.* Although the bare language of Title II does not definitively resolve the question of appropriate scope, it does suggest to us that some granularity in analytic focus is necessary.

The Supreme Court has cautioned against defining the scope of a public benefit so as to avoid questions of discriminatory effects. In *Alexander v. Choate,* 469 U.S. 287, 301, 105 S.Ct. 712 (1985), a Rehabilitation Act case, a unanimous Court counseled that in assessing whether a disabled individual had been provided with meaningful access to a benefit, "[t]he benefit itself, of course, cannot be defined in a way that effectively denies otherwise qualified handicapped individuals the meaningful access to which they are entitled." The logic of *Alexander* further suggests that we should proceed cautiously to avoid defining a public program so generally that we overlook real difficulties in accessing government services.

Also significant for our analysis of the proper scope of review here is the fact that Maryland allows *any* voter to vote by absentee ballot. Elec. Law §§ 9–301, 9–304. Absentee ballots are not provided only to a limited set of voters with a demonstrated need to vote absentee; they are instead provided to the entire Maryland electorate at the option of each individual voter. On the whole, then, we think it is far more natural to view absentee voting—rather than the entire voting program—as the appropriate object of scrutiny for compliance with the ADA and the Rehabilitation Act.

Defendants' remaining arguments against this straightforward conclusion are unpersuasive. Defendants cite an ADA-implementing regulation, 28 C.F.R. § 35.150(a), which they assert requires a reviewing court to view Maryland's voting program "in its entirety." However, the cited regulation expressly pertains to "existing facilities." *See id.* On its face, this regulation simply provides that a public entity does not have to make each of its facilities accessible as long as individuals with disabilities have access to that entity's offered public services. This regulation is targeted principally at physical accessibility and allows a public entity to provide accessibility alternatives that would not require large-scale architectural modifications of existing facilities.

Other ADA-implementing regulations, however, are applicable here and conflict with defendants' proposed focus on the entirety of Maryland's voting program. As one example, 28 C.F.R. § 35.130 ("General prohibitions against discrimination") directly implements the general antidiscrimination mandate of Title II. Subsection (b)(7) of the regulation requires public entities to make certain reasonable modifications in "policies, practices, or procedures when the modifications are necessary to avoid discrimination on the basis of disability"; this regulation clearly contemplates a focus on accessibility at a more granular level than entire government programs—the level of "policies, practices, and procedures." *Id.*

* * *

B.

Having determined that Maryland's absentee voting program is the appropriate subject of our ADA analysis, we must determine whether absentee voting is accessible to disabled individuals as required by statute and implementing regulations. As the Supreme Court has explained:

> Congress enacted the ADA in 1990 to remedy widespread discrimination against disabled individuals. In studying the need for such legislation, Congress found that "historically, society has tended to isolate and segregate individuals with disabilities, and, despite some improvements, such forms of discrimination against individuals with disabilities continue to be a serious and pervasive social problem."

PGA Tour, Inc. v. Martin, 532 U.S. 661, 674–75, 121 S.Ct. 1879 (2001) (quoting 42 U.S.C. § 12101(a)(2)). Congress explicitly found that discrimination was not limited to "outright intentional exclusion," but was also to be found in "the 'failure to make modifications to existing facilities and practices.'" After thorough investigation and debate, Congress concluded that there was a "compelling need" for a "clear and comprehensive national mandate" to both eliminate discrimination *and* to integrate disabled individuals into the social mainstream of American life. "In the ADA, Congress provided that broad mandate." *Id.*

Congress has explicitly directed the Attorney General to promulgate regulations implementing Title II's non-discrimination mandate. 42 U.S.C. § 12134. Pursuant to this directive, the Department of Justice ("DoJ") promulgated a number of regulations, including 28 C.F.R. § 35.130. That regulation provides:

> A public entity, in providing any aid, benefit, or service, may not . . . [a]fford a qualified individual with a disability an opportunity to participate in or benefit from the aid, benefit, or service that is not equal to that afforded others . . . [or] [p]rovide a qualified individual with a disability with an aid, benefit, or service that is not as effective in affording equal opportunity to obtain the same result.

28 C.F.R. § 35.130(b)(1)(ii)–(iii). We have recognized that "[t]he department's regulations are the agency's interpretation of the statute, and they are therefore given 'controlling weight' unless they conflict with other departmental regulations or the ADA itself." *Seremeth*, 673 F.3d at 338 (citing *Stinson v. United States*, 508 U.S. 36, 113 S.Ct. 1913 (1993), and *Chevron, U.S.A., Inc. v. Nat. Res. Def. Council, Inc.*, 467 U.S. 837, 844, 104 S.Ct. 2778 (1984)).

We have little trouble concluding from the record before us that Maryland's absentee voting program does not provide disabled individuals an "opportunity to participate . . . equal to that afforded others." *See* 28 C.F.R. § 35.130(b)(1)(ii). The district court found that "it is clear that most voters may mark their absentee ballots without assistance." This finding is not clearly erroneous. The district court further found that Maryland's current absentee voting program does not allow disabled individuals such as plaintiffs to mark their ballots without assistance. *Id.* This finding is also not clearly erroneous. This sharp disparity makes obvious that defendants have provided "an aid, benefit, or service [to disabled individuals] that is not as effective in affording equal opportunity to obtain the same result, to gain the same benefit, or to reach the same level of achievement as that provided to others." *See* 28 C.F.R. § 35.130(b)(1)(iii). The ADA requires more.

Defendants do not seriously challenge the district court's factual findings concerning plaintiffs' current inability to vote without assistance. Instead, defendants argue that plaintiffs have not been denied meaningful access to absentee voting because disabled individuals such as plaintiffs have no right to vote without assistance. This argument simply misapprehends the nature of plaintiffs' claims.

This case does not turn on whether there is a standalone right to vote privately and independently without assistance. Plaintiffs' argument is that defendants have provided such a benefit to non-disabled voters while denying that same benefit to plaintiffs on the basis of their disability. This is precisely the sort of harm the ADA seeks to prevent. * * *

Voting is a quintessential public activity. In enacting the ADA, Congress explicitly found that " 'individuals with disabilities ... have been ... relegated to a position of political powerlessness in our society, based on characteristics that are beyond the control of such individuals.' " *Tennessee v. Lane,* 541 U.S. 509, 516, 124 S.Ct. 1978 (2004) (quoting 42 U.S.C. § 12101(a)(7)). Ensuring that disabled individuals are afforded an opportunity to participate in voting that is equal to that afforded others, 28 C.F.R. § 35.130, helps ensure that those individuals are never relegated to a position of political powerlessness. We affirm the district court's conclusion that by effectively requiring disabled individuals to rely on the assistance of others to vote absentee, defendants have not provided plaintiffs with meaningful access to Maryland's absentee voting program.

IV.

Determining that plaintiffs have been denied meaningful access to absentee voting does not end our analysis. Not all public services, programs, or activities can be made meaningfully accessible to all citizens, or at least they cannot be made so without a prohibitive cost or unreasonable effort on the part of the public entity. For this reason, to prevail on their ADA claim, plaintiffs must propose a reasonable modification to the challenged public program that will allow them the meaningful access they seek. *See, e.g., Halpern v. Wake Forest Univ. Health Scis.,* 669 F.3d 454, 464 (4th Cir.2012) (noting that federal law mandates that federal grantees and public accommodations make "reasonable" modifications to accommodate persons with disabilities).

DoJ regulations implementing the ADA explain that "[a] public entity shall make reasonable modifications in policies, practices, or procedures when the modifications are necessary to avoid discrimination on the basis of disability." 28 C.F.R. § 35.130(b)(7). A modification is reasonable if it is "reasonable on its face" or used "ordinarily or in the run of cases" and will not cause "undue hardship." Determination of the reasonableness of a proposed modification is generally fact-specific.

The district court here found that plaintiffs' proposed modification—the online ballot marking tool—was both reasonably secure and reasonably accessible to disabled voters. Reviewing the record as a whole, these findings do not appear clearly erroneous and we see no need to disturb them. Further, although not determinative by itself, the fact that a version of the tool was voluntarily implemented by defendants in the 2012 elections—"without any apparent incident,"—speaks to the reasonableness of using the tool. Additionally, because the tool has already been developed, there does not appear to be any substantial cost or implementation burden that would need to be borne by Maryland to make the tool available for use. On the facts before us, we conclude that plaintiffs' proposed use of the online ballot marking tool is a reasonable modification to Maryland's absentee voting policies and procedures.

V.

Defendants correctly argue that even a reasonable modification to Maryland's absentee voting program need not be made if that modification would "fundamentally alter" the program. *See* 28 C.F.R. § 35.130(b)(7); *Halpern,* 669 F.3d at 464. Defendants bear the burden of proving that the requested modification would be a fundamental alteration to the program. *See* 28 C.F.R. § 35.130(b)(7). After considering defendants' arguments and reviewing the record as a whole, we conclude that they have not met this burden.

Defendants' principal argument is that certification of voting systems, including certification of the online ballot marking tool under Election Law Section 9–308.1, is fundamental to Maryland's voting program. They argue from this that requiring them to make the online ballot marking tool available for plaintiffs' use, where that tool has not yet received the statutorily-required supermajority vote, works a fundamental alteration to Maryland's voting program. Therefore, defendants argue, the district court abused its discretion in enjoining them to make the tool available to plaintiffs. We disagree.

As an initial matter, the strong form of defendants' argument—that the mere fact of a state statutory requirement insulates public entities from making otherwise reasonable modifications to prevent disability discrimination—cannot be correct. The Constitution's Supremacy Clause establishes that valid federal legislation can pre-empt state laws. *Oneok, Inc. v. Learjet, Inc.,* ___ U.S. ___, 135 S.Ct. 1591, 1595 (2015) (citing U.S. Const. Art. VI, cl. 2). The Supreme Court has held that the ADA's Title II, at least in certain circumstances, represents a valid exercise of 14th Amendment powers, *Lane,* 541 U.S. at 533–34, 124 S.Ct. 1978, and as such it trumps state regulations that conflict with its requirements. As the Sixth Circuit has put it, "[r]equiring public entities to make changes to rules, policies, practices, or services is exactly what the ADA does."

However, we also think that the converse proposition cannot be correct either. Certain requirements of state law could in fact be fundamental to a public program in a way that might resist reasonable modifications otherwise necessary to bring that program into compliance with the ADA. Defendants here urge that Maryland's statutory certification requirement is just such an example: certification, they argue, goes to the very heart of the voting program by ensuring the integrity of the voting process as a whole. Public confidence in elections is undoubtedly an important governmental concern. But on the record before us defendants simply have not established their premise, that is, that use of the online ballot marking tool degrades the integrity of Maryland's voting processes.

Put another way, defendants are merging Maryland's *procedural* certification requirement with substantive concerns about whether the tool should be certified. The mere fact that a procedural requirement has not been met does not necessarily mean that the underlying substantive purpose of that requirement has not been met. The underlying question is fact-specific.

Here, the district court found, after a three-day bench trial, that the tool is reasonably secure, safeguards disabled voters' privacy, and (in earlier versions at least) has been used in actual elections without apparent incident. We do not think these findings are clearly erroneous and defendants have not provided any substantial reasons that they should be called into question. On the record as a whole, we do not conclude that use of the online ballot marking tool is so at odds with the purposes of certification that its use would be unreasonable. We agree with the district court that defendants have not met their burden to show that plaintiffs' proposed modification—use of the online ballot marking tool—would fundamentally alter Maryland's voting program.

VI.

We recognize that some of the standard analytic language used in evaluating ADA claims—"failure to make reasonable accommodations"; "denial of meaningful access"—carries with it certain negative connotations. We would be remiss in not highlighting that the record is devoid of any evidence that the defendants acted with discriminatory animus in implementing Maryland's absentee voting program. Indeed, we recognize that Maryland's decision to provide "no excuse" absentee voting to all its citizens provides a benefit that is far from universal across the United States.

However, the ADA and the Rehabilitation Act do more than simply provide a remedy for intentional discrimination. They reflect broad legislative consensus that making the promises of the Constitution a reality for individuals with disabilities may require even well-intentioned public entities to make certain reasonable accommodations. Our conclusions here are not driven by concern that defendants are manipulating the election apparatus intentionally to discriminate against individuals with disabilities; our conclusions simply flow from the basic promise of equality in public services that animates the ADA.

For the foregoing reasons, we affirm.

NOTES AND QUESTIONS

1. *The analytical framework.* The *National Federation of the Blind* decision illustrates the three-step analytical framework applicable to Title II

accessibility claims. The steps are: 1) does the action complained of deny meaningful access to governmental service, programs, or activities, 2) does the governmental agency have available a reasonable modification of practices that would enable access to the program in question, and 3) would such a modification fundamentally alter the program offered by the governmental agency? A plaintiff makes out a violation of Title II if a court answers the first two questions in the affirmative and the third question in the negative.

2. *The appropriate focus.* The parties disagreed as how to characterize the program or activity to which the plaintiffs were arguably being denied access. The plaintiffs argued that the proper focus should be on the accessibility of voting by absentee ballot, while the defendants argued that the appropriate focus should be on the ability of plaintiffs to vote in general. Do you agree with the court's conclusion deciding this issue in the plaintiffs' favor? Why or why not? More generally, what is the practical significance of the focus debate?

3. *Fundamental alteration.* Maryland state law provides that the State Board of Elections must certify any online ballot marking tool before it can be used by voters in an election. Since the board in *National Federation of the Blind* had not certified the use of such a tool, why doesn't a modification that requires its use in contravention of statute constitute a "fundamental alteration" in the state's program?

4. *No intentional discrimination.* The court in *National Federation of the Blind* states that a violation of Title II may be found even in the absence of a showing of intentional discrimination against the disabled? Why is that so?

5. *Fashioning remedies.* Courts not infrequently fashion more participatory orders in attempting to remedy Title II violations. In *Disabled in Action v. Board of Elections in City of New York*, 752 F.3d 189 (2d Cir. 2014), for example, the court found that the City of New York violated Title II by failing to provide individuals with disabilities with meaningful access to various polling locations. But rather than order a specific remedy, the court set up a process to afford the defendant Board of Elections with "an opportunity to propose ways to remedy statutory deficiencies." The court also appointed a magistrate to oversee the remedial implementation process, a practice that is common in many Title II cases. Why might courts be more likely to adopt such measures in Title II cases as compared to Title I cases?

H. LICENSING RULES

APPLICANTS V. TEXAS STATE BOARD OF LAW EXAMINERS
1994 WL 923404 (W.D. Tex. 1994)

SPARKS, DISTRICT JUDGE.

The plaintiffs, individually and on behalf of those similarly situated, allege that the Texas Board of Law Examiners' inquiries and investigation into the mental health history of applicants seeking to practice law in the State of Texas violate the Americans with Disabilities Act (ADA), 42 U.S.C. §§ 12101–12213. The defendants are the Texas Board of Law Examiners and Rachel Martin, its executive director, collectively referred to as the defendants or the Board.

The plaintiffs, three law students who wish to be admitted to the Texas Bar, specifically challenge Section 82.027(b)(2) of the Texas Government Code requiring applicants to verify they are not mentally ill, the Texas Rules of Court governing admission that require applicants to execute an authorization for release of psychiatric records, and the Board's inquiries concerning treatment or hospitalization for mental illness in the preceding ten years and the follow-up investigations and hearings. The plaintiffs contend the statute, rules, inquiries, and investigations violate the ADA's prohibitions of discrimination against individuals on the basis of mental disability, a history of mental disability, or perceived mental disability. For these alleged violations, the plaintiffs seek injunctive and declaratory relief.

This cause was tried before the Court, without a jury, on July 7, 1994. For the reasons set forth below, the Court finds the Board's narrowly focused inquiries and investigation into the mental fitness of applicants to the Texas Bar who have been diagnosed or treated for bipolar disorder, schizophrenia, paranoia, or any other psychotic disorder do not violate the ADA.

I.   FINDINGS OF FACT

Pursuant to Texas Government Code, the Texas Supreme Court adopted the Texas Rules of Court that "govern the administration of the [Board's] functions relating to the licensing of lawyers." The Texas Government Code further requires each person intending to apply for admission to the Texas Bar to file with the Board a declaration of intention to study law and, before taking the bar examination, an application for examination.

The Board is charged with assessing each applicant's moral character and fitness to practice law based on its investigation of the character and fitness of applicants. The Board, in fulfilling its statutory duties, must recommend denial of a license if the Board finds "a clear and rational connection between the applicant's present mental or emotional condition and the likelihood that the applicant will not discharge properly the applicant's responsibilities to a client, a court, or the legal profession if the applicant is licensed to practice law."

The Board's investigation is limited to areas "clearly related to the applicant's moral character and present fitness to practice law." The rules promulgated by the Texas Supreme Court that govern admission to the Texas Bar define fitness as "the assessment of mental and emotional health as it affects the competence of a prospective lawyer." The fitness requirement is designed to exclude from the practice of law in Texas those persons having a mental or emotional condition that "would prevent the person from carrying out duties to clients, courts, or the profession." The fitness requirement is limited to present fitness; "prior mental or emotional illness or conditions are relevant only so far as they indicate the existence of a present lack of fitness."

Persons intending to seek admission to the Texas Bar usually file their declarations during the first year of law school. The rules require each applicant filing a declaration to provide extensive information about his or her background, including a history of mental illness. The Rules also provide that the Board may require the applicant to execute a consent form authorizing the release of records to the Board.

The questions formulated by the Board to seek information about an applicant's mental health history have been substantially revised since 1992 in efforts to comply with the ADA. Question 11, the question the Board used in the declaration before April 1992, asked whether the applicant had been treated for any mental, emotional, or nervous condition in the past ten years and if the condition had resulted in either voluntary or involuntary admission to a hospital or institution. Between April 1992 and July 1993, the Board used a version of question 11 that narrowed the focus to mental illness as defined by the Texas Health and Safety Code. The current version of question 11 further narrows the inquiry to the diagnosis of certain specified mental illnesses that may bear on an applicant's present fitness to practice law.[6]

Dr. Richard Coons, one of the experts who testified on the Board's behalf and who is educated as a lawyer, medical doctor, and psychiatrist, was a consultant to the Board in the Board's formulation of the current version of question 11. An affirmative answer to any part of question 11 triggers a requirement that the applicant provide a detailed description of the diagnosis or treatment and identify and provide the address of each individual that has treated the applicant. The current declaration also includes a general authorization and release for records that each applicant must sign. The current authorization limits the release of mental health records to only those pertaining to diagnosis of the conditions specified in question 11.

---

[6]   The current version of question 11 asks:

a) Within the last ten years, have you been diagnosed with or have you been treated [for] bi-polar disorder, schizophrenia, paranoia, or any other psychotic disorder?

b) Have you, since attaining the age of eighteen or within the last ten years, whichever period is shorter, been admitted to a hospital or other facility for the treatment of bi-polar disorder, schizophrenia, paranoia, or any other psychotic disorder?

If you answered "YES" to any part of this question, please provide details on a *Supplemental Form*, including date(s) of diagnosis or treatment, a description of the course of treatment, and a description of your present condition. Include the name, current mailing address, and telephone number of each person who treated you, as well as each facility where you received treatment, and the reason for treatment.

As part of the investigation process, each applicant must identify employers or clients and provide character references. The Board then sends forms to the identified references requesting information about the applicant. The current form sent to individuals listed in the declaration by the applicant as character references, employers, or former clients includes a question regarding the reference's knowledge about whether the applicant has been diagnosed or treated in the past ten years for bipolar disorder, schizophrenia, paranoia, or any psychotic disorder.

In addition to the declaration, each person wishing to take the Bar exam must file an application not later than 180 days before the examination. By law, the application is to consist of a verified affidavit that requires, among other statements, an assertion that the applicant is not mentally ill. This statutory requirement is implemented in the Board's current application by requiring each applicant to sign a verified affidavit stating, among other things, that the applicant has not been diagnosed, treated, or hospitalized since the filing of the declaration for bipolar disorder, schizophrenia, or any psychotic disorder.

Bipolar disorder, schizophrenia, paranoia, and psychotic disorders are serious mental illnesses that may affect a person's ability to practice law. People suffering from these illnesses may suffer debilitating symptoms that inhibit their ability to function normally. The fact that a person may have experienced an episode of one of these mental illnesses in the past but is not currently experiencing symptoms does not mean that the person will not experience another episode in the future or that the person is currently fit to practice law. Indeed, a person suffering from one of these illnesses may have extended periods between episodes, possibly as much as ten years for bipolar disorder or schizophrenia. Although a past diagnosis of the mental illness will not necessarily predict the applicant's future behavior, the mental health history is important to provide the Board with information regarding the applicant's insight into his or her illness and degree of cooperation in controlling it through counseling and medication. In summary, inquiry into past diagnosis and treatment of the severe mental illnesses is necessary to provide the Board with the best information available with which to assess the functional capacity of the individual.

The plaintiffs are law students in ABA-approved law schools. Applicant A, a first-year law student, was hospitalized in the past five years in a psychiatric facility for the treatment of depression with psychotic features and currently takes anti-depressant medication. Applicant A has not filed a declaration, pending resolution of this lawsuit. Under the current question, applicant A would be required to answer "yes."

Applicant B, a first-year law student, received out-patient mental health services in the past ten years for the treatment of a depressive disorder and is currently involved in group therapy. Applicant B filed a declaration on

November 15, 1993, in which Applicant B, who has not been treated for the mental illnesses specified in the current version of question 11, answered the question "no."

Applicant C, a second-year law student, received out-patient mental health services in the past ten years for the treatment of a depressive disorder, currently takes anti-depressant and anti-anxiety medications, and receives therapy. Applicant C completed the declaration before the Board's 1993 amendments to the questions concerning mental health treatment, answering "yes" to the preceding question used from April 92 to July 93. Applicant C has not been treated or hospitalized for bipolar disorder, schizophrenia, paranoia, or any other psychotic condition in the past ten years and, therefore, would answer the current question 11 "no."

None of the plaintiffs have a history of criminal activity, financial irresponsibility, or academic discipline. At this time, none of the applicants have filed the application to take the Bar exam.

Before the current wording of question 11, if an applicant answered any part of the question affirmatively, the staff technician screening the file generally would order the treatment records. In many cases, the technician would then forward the file and records to the director of fitness and character, Jack Marshall, or his assistant. If after his review, Marshall was concerned about the mental health history of the person, he would place the person's name on the "Potentials Hearing Report" and discuss the file with Board's executive director or a staff attorney. Thus, following the conclusion of the investigation of the applicant, one of three things occurred: 1) the person's technician certified the person's present fitness; 2) if the person's name had been placed on the "Potential Hearings List," Marshall, following discussion with the executive director or staff attorney, would instruct the technician to certify the person's present fitness; or 3) Marshall, in consultation with the executive director or a staff attorney, made a preliminary determination that the applicant did not possess the present fitness to practice law, necessitating consideration of the matter by the actual Board. . . .

Because of the narrowed focus of the current question 11, the Board's current policy is that Marshall will review all affirmative responses to the mental health question. Marshall will determine, based on the information provided in the declaration, whether direct inquiries for additional information to mental health professionals who have treated the applicant are necessary. If Marshall deems it necessary to receive additional information, he, in consultation with the executive director and a staff attorney, will review the response. If they are not convinced the person's mental health problem is completely under control, Marshall will request complete records of treatment and send the applicant to an expert chosen by the Board for evaluation. If the expert recommends that the Board continue to investigate the person and if after that continued investigation a determination is made that the person may pose potential harm to clients, the person will be sent a preliminary determination of lack of present fitness and notice of a right to a hearing before the Board.

The Board has received only one affirmative response to the current mental health question. In that case, Marshall has requested a summary of treatment from the treating professional.

As a result of this litigation, Marshall researched the issue of the number of applicants whose files raised mental health concerns. Since August 1987, the earliest "Potential Hearings Report" Marshall could find, thirty cases involved mental health issues. Of the thirty cases, nineteen raised serious mental health concerns. In thirteen of the cases, the information provided by the applicant was the only source of mental health information. Twenty-one of the cases were set for hearing, and in ten cases, the Board required a psychiatric evaluation or psychiatric review of the record following the hearing.

Of the nineteen cases involving serious mental health concerns, one remains under investigation and two were cleared either by the staff following a review of recent psychological evaluations. The sixteen remaining cases were set for hearing with the following dispositions: one was denied admission to the Bar on mental health grounds; one was denied but not on mental health grounds; seven were approved by the Board; two had hearings set but not held, and the applicants have taken no further action; one applicant's file was terminated for failure to execute a release for mental health records; one was approved by the Board with the caveat that a mental health update may be required upon filing of the application; one file was terminated for failure to complete a Board-required examination; one was approved for a temporary license that included a condition requiring mental health counseling; and one has been required to submit to a post-hearing psychological evaluation, the results of which are pending.

Eight of these cases resulted in either denial or inconclusive results. In five of the eight cases, the Board would have been unaware of mental health concerns absent the applicant's disclosure. In the three remaining cases in this group, mental health concerns were developed as a result of the applicant's disclosure and information received from other sources.

CONCLUSIONS OF LAW

. . . The prohibition against discrimination extends to "qualified individual [s] with a disability." A person is a "qualified individual with a disability" in the context of licensing or certification if the person can meet the essential eligibility requirements for receiving a license or certification. The regulations prohibit the imposition of eligibility criteria that "screen out or tend to screen out" a disabled individual from "fully and equally enjoying any service, program, or activity, *unless such criteria can be shown to be necessary for the provision of the service, program, or activity being offered.* § 35.130(b)(8). When, as in this case, questions of public safety are involved, the determination of whether an applicant meets "essential eligibility requirements" involves consideration of whether the individual with a disability poses a direct threat to the health and safety of others. 28 C.F.R. pt. 35, app. A, at 448. However, a determination that a person poses such a threat may not be based on generalizations or stereotypes about the effects of a particular disability but must be based on

> an individualized assessment, based on reasonable judgment that relies on current medical evidence or on the best available objective evidence, to determine: the nature, duration, and severity of the risk; the probability that the potential injury will actually occur; and whether reasonable modifications of policies, practices, or procedures will mitigate the risk.

The plaintiffs argue that all of the mental health questions the Board has used, including the present narrow inquiry, inquire into an individual's status as mentally ill rather than focusing on behaviors that would affect the individual's ability to practice law. They contend such inquiry is not necessary, the standard required by the ADA to justify the application of criteria that "screen out or tend to screen out," because the same information can be ascertained through other sources and means. In support of their position, the plaintiffs direct the Court's attention to recent court orders holding that mental health questions asked on other states' licensing applications violate the ADA. *See Medical Soc'y v. Jacobs,* No. 93–3670 (U.S.D.C.N.J. Oct. 5, 1993) (question whether physicians seeking renewal of licenses had ever suffered or been treated for mental illness violated ADA); *In re Applications of Plano and Underwood,* No. BAR–93–21 (Me. Dec. 7, 1993) (questions regarding whether applicants had ever been diagnosed with "an emotional, nervous or mental disorder" and whether they had received treatment of the disorder in the past ten years were invalid under ADA).

The plaintiffs suggest that applicants to the Board have already been extensively screened by virtue of successfully completing college and achieving admission to law school. Further, any aberrant behavior that might bear on their present mental fitness would be apparent from a criminal, educational, or employment history. The plaintiffs presented evidence that, in fact, the current question was imperfect in that some who suffer from the specified mental illnesses may be missed by [the] current question because they have not sought diagnosis or treatment. The plaintiffs suggest reliance on other facets of the investigatory process applied to all applicants or a series of question aimed at behavior would comply with the ADA and would be just as effective as the process the Board currently employs. Alternatively, the plaintiffs suggest asking applicants to voluntarily disclose if they suffer from any mental illness that could affect their ability to perform the functions essential to being a lawyer.

The ADA prohibits the use of licensing procedures that "screen out or tend to screen out" individuals defined as disabled under the ADA unless the screening criteria are *necessary* to the service being offered. The defendant's expert testified that a direct mental health inquiry like the current question 11 is necessary in the licensing process to get a full understanding of the functional capacity of the applicant's mental fitness. The defendant's expert further testified that the inquiry should go back a minimum of five years and optimally ten years because of the chronic nature of the severe mental illnesses specified in the current question 11, which often have an onset during adolescence. Although relying on past behavior in other areas may reveal behavior relevant to mental fitness, the evidence reflected that in the majority of cases already reviewed by the Board, this was not the case. Further, self-disclosure-type questions suffer, possibly to a greater degree, from some of the same defects the plaintiffs criticize in the current question—those who answer untruthfully or who do not recognize or understand the nature and extent of their illness will not be identified.

The plaintiffs further contend that because only one person has been denied admission to the bar since 1986 based on mental health concerns, the question serves no useful purpose. The Court finds this contention also to be without merit. The plaintiffs' argument ignores the fact that other applicants subjected to investigation as a result of an affirmative answer to question 11 have not pursued the process, have had their files terminated for failure to comply with requirements, and have received temporary licenses contingent upon continued counseling. Further, for those applicants answering the mental health question affirmatively, the Board engages in an individualized, case-by-case investigation. In fact, the evidence reflects that many of the applicants answering the mental health question affirmatively are ultimately cleared by the Board and certified to have the present fitness to practice law. This highlights the Board's efforts to avoid improper generalization or stereotyping of mentally disabled individuals, as defined by the ADA, and to apply objective criteria on an individualized basis to determine if an applicant poses a threat to the public if licensed. The Court, therefore, finds the Board discharges its duty in a responsible manner while making every effort not to discriminate against those who have suffered a mental illness but have the present fitness to practice law.

The inquiries courts in other states have held prohibited by the ADA were virtually identical to the previous broad-based forms of question 11 used by the Board that intruded into an applicant's mental health history without focusing on only those mental illnesses that pose a potential threat to the applicant's present fitness to practice law. The Court concurs that such a broad-based inquiry violates the ADA.

As stated above, however, the ADA does not preclude a licensing body from any inquiry and investigation related to mental illness, instead allowing for such inquiry and investigation when they are necessary to protect the integrity of the service provided and the public. The Court recognizes that no perfect question can be formulated that will ensure all individuals suffering mental illnesses affecting their fitness to practice will be detected. As the plaintiff's expert testified, some may defer treatment to avoid having to answer affirmatively and others may not recognize that they suffer from a mental illness, thereby precluding diagnosis or treatment. However, reliance on "behaviors" occurring in other facets of an individual's life as triggers to indicate a mental illness affecting present fitness may be present is a much more inexact and potentially unreliable method of ascertaining mental fitness.

The plaintiffs, seeking to vindicate the rights of the mentally disabled, fail to account for the awesome responsibility with which the Board is charged. The Board has a duty not to just the applicants, but also to the Bar and the citizens of Texas to make every effort to ensure that those individuals licensed to practice in Texas have the good moral character and present fitness to practice law and will not present a potential danger to the individuals they will represent. The Board has a limited opportunity to accomplish this task—the time of the filing of the declaration and application. The Board, therefore, must make every effort to investigate each applicant as thoroughly as possible and as efficiently as possible during this limited time.

Although a negative light is often cast upon the legal profession in the information that the general public receives and hears, in reality, lawyers serve the important role in our society of assisting people in the management of the most important of their affairs. Therefore, as a practical concern, the Board must evaluate each applicant's ability in light of the important responsibilities lawyers assume. Lawyers counsel individuals contemplating everything from divorce, bankruptcy, and the disposal of assets to the institutionalization of a loved one. Is it necessary that the Board inquire whether an applicant has been diagnosed or treated for bipolar disorder, schizophrenia, paranoia, or other psychosis before licensing the individual to assume these responsibilities? Before licensing the individual to write wills, manage trusts set up for minors and disabled individuals, or draft contracts affecting parties' rights and finances? Before licensing the individual to represent a parent in a proceeding to determine if the parent will maintain or lose custody of a child? Before licensing the individual to represent a[n] individual charged with a crime who faces loss of liberty or even life? In each of these proceedings, the lawyer must be prepared to offer competent legal advice and representation despite the stress of understanding the responsibility the lawyer has assumed while balancing other clients' interests and time demands. The rigorous application procedure, including investigating whether an applicant has been diagnosed or treated for certain serious mental illnesses, is indeed necessary to ensure that Texas' lawyers are capable, morally and mentally, to provide these important services. . . .

III. CONCLUSION

The purpose of the ADA is to protect disabled individuals from discrimination and to promote integration of disabled individuals into the mainstream of society. It is ludicrous, however, to propose that this purpose can only be accomplished by prohibiting a state from directly investigating and assessing an applicant's emotional and mental fitness to determine if the applicant has sufficient competence to discharge the responsibilities of a lawyer before the state warrants by licensing to the citizens that the individual has the mental and emotional fitness to fulfill a lawyer's legal, ethical, and moral responsibilities. The Board would be derelict in its duty if it did not investigate the mental health of prospective lawyers. It has made every effort to do so in the least intrusive, least discriminatory manner possible, focusing on only those serious mental illnesses that experts have indicated are likely to affect present fitness to practice law. It has limited the inquiry to a specified time frame, primarily spanning late adolescence and adult life. Although affirmative answers do trigger investigation that applicants answering negatively do not have to undergo, the affirmative answer does not result in an immediate denial of a license to practice law. The ensuing investigation serves two purposes: protection of the Bar and public as well as an opportunity for the applicant to indicate present fitness. Therefore, the Court finds, by a preponderance of the evidence that the Board's use of the current question 11, a narrowly focused question, and the subsequent investigation based on an affirmative response to the question are necessary to ensure the integrity of the Board's licensing procedure, as well as to provide a practical means of striking an appropriate balance between important societal goals. The Board's process furthers the goal of the ADA to integrate those defined as mentally disabled into society while ensuring that individuals licensed to practice law in Texas are capable of practicing law in a competent and ethical manner.

U.S. DEPARTMENT OF JUSTICE, CIVIL RIGHTS DIVISION, RE: THE UNITED STATES' INVESTIGATION OF THE LOUISIANA ATTORNEY LICENSURE SYSTEM PURSUANT TO THE AMERICANS WITH DISABILITIES ACT

February 5, 2014
(DJ No. 204–32M–60, 204–32–88, 204–32–89)

THE HONORABLE CHIEF JUSTICE JOHNSON, MS. SCHELL, and MR. PLATTSMIER:

We write concerning the Civil Rights Division's investigation of Louisiana's attorney licensure system pursuant to Title II of the Americans with Disabilities Act ("ADA"), 42 U.S.C. § 12132 *et seq.*

The United States recognizes and respects the great responsibility placed on the Louisiana Supreme Court to safeguard the administration of justice by ensuring that all attorneys licensed in the State of Louisiana are competent to practice law and worthy of the trust and confidence clients place in their attorneys. The Court can, should, and does fulfill this important responsibility by asking questions related to the conduct of applicants. These questions enable the Court and the Admissions Committee to assess effectively and fully the applicant's fitness to practice law, and the Court can appropriately take responses to them into account in its licensing decisions. In contrast, however, questions based on an applicant's *status* as a person with a mental health diagnosis do not serve the Court's worthy goal of identifying unfit applicants, are in fact counterproductive to ensuring that attorneys are fit to practice, and violate the standards of applicable civil rights laws.

III. FACTUAL BACKGROUND

B. Character Report Required by Admissions Committee

. . . The Admissions Committee requires each applicant—including all prospective applicants enrolled in law schools in Louisiana—to request that the National Conference of Bar Examiners ("NCBE") prepare a character report. . . . To request an NCBE character report, the applicant must establish a character and fitness electronic account with NCBE and answer 28 questions, including questions about previous disbarment or disciplinary measures; revocation of other professional licenses; accusations of fraud, forgery, or malpractice; arrests and convictions; bankruptcy; and loan defaults. The applicant is required to sign releases allowing third parties to disclose information to NCBE for the purposes of its investigation. NCBE reviews the applicant's responses, conducts an investigation, and submits a report of findings to the Admissions Committee.

The Request for Preparation of a Character Report that the Admissions Committee requires each applicant to complete includes the following questions:

25. Within the past five years, have you been diagnosed with or have you been treated for bipolar disorder, schizophrenia, paranoia, or any other psychotic disorder?

26A. Do you currently have any condition or impairment (including, but not limited to, substance abuse, alcohol abuse, or a mental, emotional, or nervous disorder or condition) which in any way currently affects, or if untreated could affect, your ability to practice law in a competent and professional manner?

26B. If your answer to Question 26(A) is yes, are the limitations caused by your mental health condition ... reduced or ameliorated because you receive ongoing treatment (with or without medication) or because you participate in a monitoring program?

27. Within the past five years, have you ever raised the issue of consumption of drugs or alcohol or the issue of a mental, emotional, nervous, or behavioral disorder or condition as a defense, mitigation, or explanation for your actions in the course of any administrative or judicial proceeding or investigation; any inquiry or other proceeding; or any proposed termination by an educational institution, employer, government agency, professional organization, or licensing authority?

Applicants who respond affirmatively to Questions 25 or Question 26 must complete a form authorizing each of their treatment providers "to provide information, without limitation, relating to mental illness . . . , including copies of records, concerning advice, care, or treatment provided. . . ." . . .

Applicants who respond affirmatively to Question 27 are asked to "furnish a thorough explanation," but are not required to provide forms authorizing their treatment professionals to provide information regarding their mental health disability, nor are they required to complete a form describing their condition and treatment or monitoring program. . . .

C. Supplemental Character and Fitness Investigations by the Admissions Committee

The Admissions Committee frequently conducts further investigations when the NCBE has reported that an applicant has disclosed a mental health diagnosis or treatment in response to Question 25. According to spreadsheet data provided to us by the Admissions Committee, 53 of 68 applicants who responded affirmatively to Question 25 between August 1, 2008 and December 11, 2012 whose character and fitness investigations were completed, were required to provide detailed medical information related to their condition, to submit to an Independent Medical Examination ("IME"), or to do both. Of these, at least 46 were required to provide medical records related to treatment for their diagnosis for the past five years and any hospitalization records from the past ten years. In several instances, the only justification given by the Admissions Committee to the applicant for its decision to conduct further investigation was the applicant's diagnosis, rather than any problematic conduct by the applicant. The Department has obtained five letters from applicants in which the Admissions Committee stated that further inquiry is necessary "given the nature of [the applicant's] diagnosis." For example, the Admissions Committee notified one applicant, referred to herein as TQ, that:

> Review of your NCBE Character and Fitness Report and/or other information obtained by the Committee reveals your diagnosis of Bi-Polar Disorder. Given the nature of the diagnosis, the Committee has determined that further inquiry will be necessary in order to make an appropriate assessment regarding your fitness to practice.

The documentation requested by the Admissions Committee can contain information of an extremely personal nature which is irrelevant to the applicant's ability to practice law. For example, the Admissions Committee reviewed TQ's psychiatrist's treatment notes, which describe each therapy session since she began treatment. These notes include details of intimate information discussed in therapy, such as her upbringing, relationships with members of her family, sexual history, body image, and romantic relationships. Applicants are reminded that failure to comply with the request for information and medical documentation will be considered a lack of cooperation that could prevent the applicant from being certified for admission (*i.e.*, that the Admissions Committee could recommend that the Supreme Court deny the application for admission to the bar).

In numerous cases, the Admissions Committee forwards the applicant's medical records to its consulting psychiatrist, who reviews them to determine if more information is necessary. At least 29 applicants who have completed character and fitness reviews since 2008 and responded affirmatively to Question 25 had their medical records forwarded to the consulting psychiatrist. Admissions Committee Q25 Spreadsheet. In many instances, the Admissions Committee has subsequently recommended evaluations by independent psychiatrists or psychologists, and in some cases has recommended that an individual be examined by several different professionals. Applicants have been required to pay the costs of these IMEs. For example, applicant JA was charged $562.50 for such an evaluation and applicant ME was charged approximately $800.

D. Conditional Admission Recommendations by the Admissions Committee

According to the Louisiana Supreme Court Rules, conditional admission is warranted only when an applicant's record shows *conduct* that may otherwise warrant denial. For non-disabled individuals, conditional admission is often imposed upon those who have engaged in conduct such as defaulting on financial obligations, engaging in criminal activity, displaying a lack of candor (often on a law school or bar application), or having disciplinary complaints as a licensed attorney in another jurisdiction.

The Admissions Committee has recommended conditional admission where there is no evidence of conduct that may otherwise warrant denial. For instance, an Admissions Committee attorney proposed to members reviewing TQ's application that she be recommended for "conditional admission with standard 5 yr consent agreement." The only "factors [sic] for consideration" listed to support this recommendation was that TQ had been "diagnosed with bipolar disorder." The Admissions Committee made this recommendation even though TQ's treating psychiatrist told the Admissions Committee that TQ has "adhered to the prescribed treatment regimen and kept careful track of her mood" and "has at no time since I have known her been a danger to herself or others." Significantly, the Admissions Committee's own consulting psychiatrist stated that "all psychiatric problems appear to be well-managed and stable at this time."
. . .

Even when applicants have demonstrated their ability to practice law successfully in other jurisdictions without oversight, the Admissions Committee has recommended that they be conditionally admitted based on their mental health diagnoses. . . .

By contrast, others who have engaged in substantial misconduct relevant to their practice of law—and some who have even committed felonies—have been admitted to the Louisiana bar without *any* condition or oversight whatsoever. . . .

The consent agreements entered into by JA, LD, JH, LH, TB, TQ, and ME contain virtually identical conditions. Typically, applicants with mental health diagnoses who are conditionally admitted must:

- Enter into, and comply with, probation agreements with the Office of Disciplinary Counsel ("ODC") who will assign them to practice monitors or probation monitors.

- Consult with their treating health care providers not less than every three months;

- Authorize their treating health care providers to submit substantive reports to the ODC every three months;

- Have their treating health care providers inform ODC of prescribed medications and notify ODC of any changes in medication;

- Inform ODC of changes in doctors and therapists;

- Agree to personally appear at their own expense before psychiatrists or health care professionals designated by ODC for an assessment of their recovery and medical status; and

- Grant ODC "full and unfettered access to any and all information contained in files kept by any health care professional regarding [their] diagnosis, treatment, and recovery" and execute medical authorizations required to facilitate full disclosure.

If applicants fail to comply with any condition of the agreement, their licenses may be revoked.

IV. STATUTORY AND REGULATORY BACKGROUND

Pursuant to a Congressional directive, 42 U.S.C. § 12134(a), the Department has issued several regulatory provisions that govern the Court's policies and practices for attorney licensure. A public entity may not "directly or through contractual or other arrangements, utilize criteria or methods of administration [t]hat have the effect of subjecting qualified individuals with disabilities to discrimination on the basis of disability." 28 C.F.R. § 35.130(b)(3)(i). Specifically, a public entity may not "administer a licensing or certification program in a manner that subjects qualified individuals with disabilities to discrimination on the basis of a disability." Id. § 35.130(b)(6). Further, a public entity may not impose or apply "eligibility criteria that screen out or tend to screen out an individual with a disability or any class of individuals with disabilities from fully and equally enjoying any service, program, or activity, unless such criteria can be shown to be necessary" for the provision of the service, program, or activity. Id. § 35.130(b)(8). Policies that "unnecessarily impose requirements or burdens on individuals with disabilities that are not placed on others" are also prohibited. 28 C.F.R. pt. 35, app. B at 673. Legitimate safety requirements necessary for the safe operation of an entity's programs, services, and activities must be "based on actual risks, not on mere speculation, stereotypes, or generalizations about individuals with disabilities." 28 C.F.R. § 35.130(h).

V. FINDINGS

We conclude that the Court's process for evaluating applicants to the Louisiana bar who have mental health diagnoses discriminates against qualified individuals with disabilities in violation of the ADA. 42 U.S.C. § 12132. The Admissions Committee's requirement that applicants for admission to the Louisiana bar answer Questions 25–27 of the NCBE Request for Preparation of a Character Report (hereinafter "the Questions") violates the ADA because these questions are eligibility criteria that screen out or tend to screen out individuals with disabilities based on stereotypes and assumptions about their disabilities and are not necessary to assess the applicants' fitness to practice law. Other forms of discrimination flow from the Admissions Committee's use of these discriminatory eligibility criteria, including 1) imposing additional burdens on applicants with disabilities in the form of expansive and intrusive requests for medical records; 2) making admissions recommendations that are based on the mere existence of a mental health disability rather than on conduct; 3) placing burdensome conditions upon applicants' legal licenses because of mental health diagnosis or treatment; 4) imposing additional financial burdens on applicants and attorneys with disabilities; and 5) failing to protect the confidentiality of the medical information of applicants with disabilities.

A.   The Questions Violate Title II of the ADA

1.   The Questions Are Eligibility Criteria that Tend to Screen Out Persons with Disabilities and Subject Them to Additional Burdens

Requiring applicants for admission to the Louisiana bar to state whether they have been diagnosed with or treated for bipolar disorder, schizophrenia, paranoia, or any other psychotic disorder (Question 25), and to provide additional information if they have, utilizes an eligibility criterion that tends to screen out individuals with disabilities and subjects them to additional burdens. *See, e.g., Clark v. Virginia Bd. of Bar Examiners*, 880 F. Supp. 430, 442–43 (E.D. Va. 1995) (finding that questions requiring individuals with mental disabilities to subject themselves to further inquiry and scrutiny discriminate against those with mental disabilities); *Medical Society of New Jersey v. Jacobs*, 1993 WL 413016 at *7 (D. N.J. 1993) (refusing to allow questions that substitute an inquiry into the status of disabled applicants for an inquiry into the applicants' behavior and place a burden of additional investigations on applicants who answer in the affirmative).

Inquiring about applicants' medical conditions substitutes inappropriate questions about an applicant's status as a person with a disability for legitimate questions about an applicant's conduct. The applicant's diagnosis and treatment history, by virtue of their mere existence, are presumed by these questions to be appropriate bases for further investigation. The Admissions Committee's inquiry, and the actions that flow from inappropriate disability status-based inquiries, are therefore based on "mere speculation, stereotypes, or generalizations about individuals with disabilities." *See* 28 C.F.R. § 35.130(h); 42 U.S.C. § 12101(a)(7) (criticizing unequal treatment "resulting from stereotypic assumptions not truly indicative of the individual ability [of people with disabilities] to participate in, and contribute to, society").

2.   The Questions Are Not Necessary to Determine Whether Applicants Are Fit to Practice Law.

       a.   The Questions Are Unnecessary Because Questions Related to Applicants' Conduct Are Sufficient, and Most Effective, to Evaluate Fitness.

The Admissions Committee can achieve its objective of identifying applicants who are not fit to practice law without utilizing questions that focus on an applicant's status as a person with a mental health disability. Questions designed to disclose the applicant's prior misconduct would serve the legitimate purposes of identifying those who are unfit to practice law or are unworthy of public trust, and would do so in a non-discriminatory manner.

The Request for Preparation of a Character Report that the Admissions Committee currently uses already asks a multitude of questions that will allow the Admissions Committee to evaluate applicants' record of conduct. . . .

Conduct-based questions are most effective in assessing whether applicants are fit to practice law. Based on testimony from experts for both the applicants and the licensing entity that "past behavior is the best predictor of present and future mental fitness," a federal court in Virginia found that the mental health inquiry at issue was not necessary. *Clark v. Virginia Bd. of Bar Examiners*, 880 F. Supp. 430, 446 (E.D. Va. 1995).

       b.   The Questions Are Unnecessary Because They Do Not Effectively Identify Unfit Applicants.

. . . The Questions also are not necessary to determine whether applicants will be able to fulfill their professional responsibilities as attorneys because a history of mental health diagnosis or treatment does not provide an accurate basis for predicting future misconduct. *See* Am. Bar Ass'n Comm'n on Mental and Physical Disability Law, *Recommendation to the House of Delegates*, 22 MENTAL & PHYSICAL DISABILITY L. REP. 266, 267 (Feb. 1998) ("Research in the health field and clinical experience demonstrate that neither diagnosis nor the fact of having undergone treatment support any inferences about a person's ability to carry out professional responsibilities or to act with integrity, competence, or honor."); Jon Bauer, *The Character of the Questions and the Fitness of the Process: Mental Health, Bar Admissions and the Americans with Disabilities Act*, 49 UCLA L. REV. 93, 141 (2001) ("there is simply no empirical evidence that applicants' mental health histories are significantly predictive of future misconduct or malpractice as an attorney").

Courts in Rhode Island and Virginia have agreed that licensing questions related to mental health status or treatment are not necessary because they have little or no predictive value. *Clark*, 880 F. Supp. at 446 (finding that questions were unnecessary where "the Board presented no evidence of correlation between obtaining mental counseling and employment dysfunction."); *In re: Petition & Questionnaire for Admission to Rhode Island Bar*, 683 A.2d 1333, 1336 (R.I. 1996) (noting that "[r]esearch has failed to establish that a history of previous psychiatric treatment can be correlated with an individual's capacity to function effectively in the workplace"). . . .

> c.   The Questions Are Unnecessary Because They Are Counterproductive to the Court's Interests.

The Questions are likely to deter applicants from seeking counseling and treatment for mental health concerns, which fails to serve the Court's interest in ensuring the fitness of licensed attorneys. . . .

In *Clark v. Virginia Board of Bar Examiners*, a law school dean and a law school professor both testified that, in their experience, mental health questions deter law students from seeking treatment. The *Clark* court relied on its finding that the licensing question "deters the counseling and treatment from which [persons with disabilities] could benefit" and "has strong negative stigmatic and deterrent effects upon applicants" in finding that the question was unnecessary. As the *Clark* court observed:

> [B]road mental health questions may inhibit the treatment of applicants who do seek counseling. Faced with the knowledge that one's treating physician may be required to disclose diagnosis and treatment information, an applicant may be less than totally candid with their therapist. Without full disclosure of a patient's condition, physicians are restricted in their ability to accurately diagnose and treat the patient. Thus, it is possible that open-ended mental health inquiries may prevent the very treatment which, if given, would help control the applicant's condition and make the practice of law possible.

Questions that dissuade applicants from seeking needed mental health treatment fail to serve the Court's interest in ensuring that licensed attorneys are fit to practice. Rather than improving the quality, dependability, and trustworthiness of attorneys, the Admissions Committee's inquiries may have the perverse effect of deterring those who could benefit from treatment from obtaining it while penalizing those who will be better able to successfully practice law and pose less of a risk to clients because they have acted responsibly and taken steps to manage their condition.

B. Other Processes Flowing from the Admissions Committee's Use of the Questions Also Discriminate on the Basis of Disability.

Many of the actions that the Admissions Committee and ODC take as a result of an applicant's affirmative response to the Questions are also discriminatory. Specifically, we find that the Admissions Committee and

ODC violate the ADA when they subject individuals who disclose certain disabilities in response to the Questions to additional burdens in the form of 1) supplemental investigations and requests for medical records based on the applicant's diagnosis; 2) conditional admissions decisions that are improperly rooted in mental health diagnosis or treatment; 3) onerous conditions of admission; 4) additional costs as part of the application process and for monitoring; and 5) exposure of personal medical information to public scrutiny. . . .

CIVIL RIGHTS TRUSTEES, NEWS RELEASE: DEPARTMENT OF JUSTICE REACHES AGREEMENT WITH THE LOUISIANA SUPREME COURT TO PROTECT BAR CANDIDATES WITH DISABILITIES

August 15, 2014
DOJ 14–860, 2014 WL 3974361

The Justice Department announced today that it had entered into a settlement agreement with the Louisiana Supreme Court that will resolve the department's investigation of the court's policies, practices and procedures for evaluating bar applicants with mental health disabilities. The department's investigation found that during the Louisiana bar admission process licensing entities based recommendations about bar admissions on mental health diagnosis and treatment rather than conduct that would warrant denial of admission to the bar. . . .

Under the agreement, the court will, among other actions:

- Revise its character and fitness screening questions so that they focus on applicants' conduct or behavior, and ask about an applicant's condition or impairment only when it currently affects the applicant's ability to practice law in a competent, ethical and professional manner or is disclosed to explain conduct that may otherwise warrant denial of admission;

- Refrain from imposing unnecessary burdens on applicants with mental health disabilities by placing onerous disability-related conditions on their admission, invading their privacy, or violating their confidentiality;

- Re-evaluate prior and pending applications of applicants who disclosed mental health disabilities under the revised, non-discriminatory procedures set forth in the agreement; and

- Pay $200,000 to compensate a number of affected bar applicants and attorneys.

NOTES AND QUESTIONS

1. *Scope of inquiry.* The *Applicants v. Texas State Board of Law Examiners* court suggests that the older version of question 11 which inquired

about any mental, emotional, or nervous condition likely would have violated Title II, but not the newer version which limits inquiries to bipolar disorder, schizophrenia, paranoia, and other psychotic disorders. What is the court's rationale for this distinction? Do you agree?

2.   *Diagnosis vs. conduct.* The Department of Justice letter contends that questions about mental health diagnosis or treatment do "not provide an accurate basis for predicting future misconduct." The court in *Applicants*, in contrast, expressed the belief that such information has predictive value for future conduct and that reliance only on behaviors is "potentially unreliable." Who has the better of this argument? What role do you think the passage of time between 1994 and 2014 and the evolution of views concerning mental impairments played in the difference between these opinions?

3.   *Disincentive to seek treatment.* The Department of Justice letter expresses the concern that asking questions about mental health history will provide an incentive for individuals with mental impairments to hide information and to avoid treatment. How significant do you think this concern plays out in practical terms?

I.   A NOTE ON ENFORCEMENT AND REMEDIES

1.   STATUTORY SYNCHRONICITY

ADA Title II and Section 504 of the Rehabilitation Act have matching remedies and enforcement mechanisms. ADA Section 12133 provides that:

> The remedies, procedures and rights set forth in section 794a of title 29 [Section 505] shall be the remedies, procedures, and rights this subchapter provides to any person alleging discrimination on the basis of disability in violation of section 12132 of this title [ADA Title II].

This statutory cross-referencing is extended a step further by Section 505 which states that the remedies, procedures and rights of that statute shall be the same as those set forth in Title VI of the Civil Rights Act of 1964 which prohibits racial discrimination in federally funded programs and activities. Interestingly, since Title VI does not specify available remedies, the courts have spent considerable efforts in attempting to determine the remedies that should be available under these three statutes.

2.   ENFORCEMENT PROCEDURES

Two options exist for the enforcement of Title II rights. First, a claimant may proceed administratively. Pursuant to the DOJ regulations, a complaint must be filed within 180 days of the alleged discriminatory act with the appropriate federal agency. 28 C.F.R. § 35.170. The appropriate federal agency is any agency designated in 28 C.F.R. § 35.170, any agency that provides funding to the public entity in question, or the Department of Justice. The agency receiving the complaint is charged with investigating the claim of discrimination and attempting to negotiate a voluntary settlement agreement with the public entity. 28 C.F.R. § 35.172. If a settlement is not reached, the designated agency is to refer the matter to the Attorney General for litigation.

The second option is a private suit. Unlike Title I, an individual need not exhaust administrative remedies before initiating a private enforcement action in federal court. *See, e.g.,* Bogovich v. Sandoval, 189 F.3d 999 (9th Cir. 1999).

3. REMEDIES

As one court has stated, plaintiffs in Section 504 cases are entitled to the "full spectrum of legal and equitable remedies needed to redress their injuries." Matthews v. Jefferson, 29 F.Supp.2d 525, 535 (W.D. Ark. 1998) (quoting Gorman v. Bartch, 152 F.3d 907, 908 (8th Cir. 1998)). Accordingly, courts have recognized that ADA Title II and Section 504 plaintiffs may recover compensatory damages, including damages for economic losses, emotional distress, and pain and suffering. *See, e.g.,* Niece v. Fitzner, 922 F.Supp. 1208, 1219 (E.D. Mich. 1996).

In spite of this broad principle, the courts have recognized two significant limitations on damages claims under Title II and Section 504. First, the unanimous view of the circuit courts is that compensatory damages are not available under Title II or Section 504 absent a showing of discriminatory intent. *See, e.g.,* Ferguson v. City of Phoenix, 157 F.3d 668 (9th Cir. 1998). Some courts have used a "deliberate indifference" standard to determine if the requisite intent has been established. Under this approach, a discriminatory intent may be inferred in situations in which a governmental entity knows that harm to a federally protected right is substantially likely, but takes no action to prevent that likelihood from occurring. *See, e.g.,* Duvall v. County of Kitsap, 260 F.3d 1124, 1139 (9th Cir. 2001).

Second, the Supreme Court has held that a court may not award punitive damages in Title II and Section 504 cases. Barnes v. Gorman, 536 U.S. 181, 122 S.Ct. 2097 (2002). The Court explained that Title VI is legislation in the nature of a contract since it was enacted pursuant to the Constitution's Spending Clause, and that punitive damages generally are not available for breach of contract. Having reached that conclusion with respect to Title VI actions, the Court went on to hold that punitive damages also are unavailable under Title II and Section 504.

CHAPTER 6

PUBLIC ACCOMMODATIONS: TITLE III OF THE ADA

■ ■ ■

A. STATUTORY PROVISIONS

Title III of the ADA prohibits discrimination against individuals with disabilities in places of public accommodation. Because Congress believed that integrating individuals with disabilities into all aspects of public life was important, the coverage of Title III is broad. Unlike Title I, which does not apply to small employers (those with fewer than 15 employees), Title III applies to *all* places of public accommodation. However, for buildings that were built before the effective date of the ADA, the statute only requires removal of architectural barriers to the extent such removal is "readily achievable," which means that many smaller businesses in older buildings are still not very accessible. Exacerbating the problem, damages are unavailable in Title III claims—plaintiffs can only seek injunctive relief. As you proceed through this chapter, ask yourself whether the compromise Congress struck (broad coverage in exchange for no damages) is working.

The primary prohibition section of Title III of the ADA states:

No individual shall be discriminated against on the basis of disability in the full and equal enjoyment of the goods, services, facilities, privileges, advantages, or accommodations of any place of public accommodation by any person who owns, leases (or leases to), or operates a place of public accommodation.

42 U.S.C. § 12182(a). The phrase "public accommodation" is defined by using a list of 12 extensive categories that provide specific examples of places of public accommodation. They are:

(A) an inn, hotel, motel, or other place of lodging, except for an establishment located within a building that contains not more than five rooms for rent or hire and that is actually occupied by the proprietor of such establishment as the residence of such proprietor;

(B) a restaurant, bar, or other establishment serving food or drink;

(C) a motion picture house, theater, concert hall, stadium, or other place of exhibition or entertainment;

(D) an auditorium, convention center, lecture hall, or other place of public gathering;

(E) a bakery, grocery store, clothing store, hardware store, shopping center, or other sales or rental establishment;

(F) a laundromat, dry-cleaner, bank, barber shop, beauty shop, travel service, shoe repair service, funeral parlor, gas station, office of an accountant or lawyer, pharmacy, insurance office, professional office of a health care provider, hospital, or other service establishment;

(G) a terminal, depot, or other station used for specific public transportation;

(H) a museum, library, gallery, or other place of display or collection;

(I) a park, zoo, amusement park, or other place of recreation;

(J) a nursery, elementary, secondary, undergraduate, or postgraduate private school, or other place of education;

(K) a day care center, senior citizen center, homeless shelter, food bank, adoption agency, or other social service center establishment; and

(L) a gymnasium, health spa, bowling alley, golf course, or other place of exercise or recreation.

42 U.S.C. § 12181(7). Although this appears to be a fairly comprehensive list, coverage issues occasionally arise. These issues are addressed in and after the *PGA Tour, Inc. v. Martin* case, excerpted below, and the *Gil v. Winn Dixie Stores, Inc.* case, also excerpted below, regarding website accessibility.

Title III of the ADA defines discrimination to include:

(i) the imposition or application of eligibility criteria that screen out or tend to screen out an individual with a disability or any class of individuals with disabilities from fully and equally enjoying any goods, services, facilities, privileges, advantages, or accommodations, unless such criteria can be shown to be necessary for the provision of the goods, services, facilities, privileges, advantages, or accommodations being offered;

(ii) a failure to make reasonable modifications in policies, practices, or procedures, when such modifications are necessary to afford such goods, services, facilities, privileges, advantages, or accommodations to individuals with disabilities unless the entity can demonstrate that making such modifications would fundamentally alter the nature of such goods, services, facilities, privileges, advantages, or accommodations;

(iii) a failure to take such steps as may be necessary to ensure that no individual with a disability is excluded, denied services, segregated or otherwise treated differently than other individuals because of the absence of auxiliary aids and services, unless the entity can demonstrate that taking such steps would fundamentally alter the nature of the good, service, facility, privilege, advantage, or accommodation being offered or would result in an undue burden;

(iv) a failure to remove architectural barriers, and communication barriers that are structural in nature, in existing facilities, and transportation barriers in existing vehicles and rail passenger cars used by an establishment for transporting individuals (not including barriers that can only be removed through the retrofitting of vehicles or rail passenger cars by the installation of a hydraulic or other lift), where such removal is readily achievable; and

(v) where an entity can demonstrate that the removal of a barrier under clause (iv) is not readily achievable, a failure to make such goods, services, facilities, privileges, advantages, or accommodations available through alternative methods if such methods are readily achievable.

42 U.S.C. § 12182(b)(2)(A).

Cases brought under Title III most often involve the refusal to provide reasonable modifications to individuals with disabilities and the refusal to remove architectural or other barriers. Both issues are addressed in turn below.

B. REASONABLE MODIFICATIONS

PGA TOUR, INC. V. MARTIN
532 U.S. 661, 121 S.Ct. 1879 (2001)

JUSTICE STEVENS delivered the opinion of the Court.

This case raises two questions concerning the application of the Americans with Disabilities Act of 1990, 42 U.S.C. § 12101 *et seq.,* to a gifted athlete: first, whether the Act protects access to professional golf tournaments by a qualified entrant with a disability; and second, whether a disabled contestant may be denied the use of a golf cart because it would "fundamentally alter the nature" of the tournaments, § 12182(b)(2)(A)(ii), to allow him to ride when all other contestants must walk.

I

Petitioner PGA TOUR, Inc., a nonprofit entity formed in 1968, sponsors and cosponsors professional golf tournaments conducted on three annual tours. About 200 golfers participate in the PGA TOUR; about 170 in the NIKE TOUR; and about 100 in the SENIOR PGA TOUR. PGA TOUR and NIKE TOUR tournaments typically are 4-day events, played on courses leased and operated by petitioner. The entire field usually competes in two 18-hole rounds played on Thursday and Friday; those who survive the "cut" play on Saturday and Sunday and receive prize money in amounts determined by their aggregate scores for all four rounds. The revenues generated by television, admissions, concessions, and contributions from cosponsors amount to about $300 million a year, much of which is distributed in prize money.

There are various ways of gaining entry into particular tours. For example, a player who wins three NIKE TOUR events in the same year, or is among the top-15 money winners on that tour, earns the right to play in the PGA TOUR. Additionally, a golfer may obtain a spot in an official tournament through successfully competing in "open" qualifying rounds, which are conducted the week before each tournament. Most participants, however, earn playing privileges in the PGA TOUR or NIKE TOUR by way of a three-stage qualifying tournament known as the "Q-School."

Any member of the public may enter the Q-School by paying a $3,000 entry fee and submitting two letters of reference from, among others, PGA TOUR or NIKE TOUR members. The $3,000 entry fee covers the players' greens fees and the cost of golf carts, which are permitted during the first two stages, but which have been prohibited during the third stage since 1997. Each year, over a thousand contestants compete in the first stage, which consists of four 18-hole rounds at different locations. Approximately half of them make it to the second stage, which also includes 72 holes. Around 168 players survive the second stage and advance to the final one, where they compete over 108 holes. Of those finalists, about a fourth qualify for membership in the PGA TOUR, and the rest gain membership in the NIKE TOUR. The significance of making it into either tour is illuminated by the fact that there are about 25 million golfers in the country.

Three sets of rules govern competition in tour events. First, the "Rules of Golf," jointly written by the United States Golf Association (USGA) and the Royal and Ancient Golf Club of Scotland, apply to the game as it is played, not only by millions of amateurs on public courses and in private country clubs throughout the United States and worldwide, but also by the professionals in the tournaments conducted by petitioner, the USGA, the Ladies' Professional Golf Association, and the Senior Women's Golf Association. Those rules do not prohibit the use of golf carts at any time.

Second, the "Conditions of Competition and Local Rules," often described as the "hard card," apply specifically to petitioner's professional tours. The

SEC. B REASONABLE MODIFICATIONS 423

hard cards for the PGA TOUR and NIKE TOUR require players to walk the golf course during tournaments, but not during open qualifying rounds. On the SENIOR PGA TOUR, which is limited to golfers age 50 and older, the contestants may use golf carts. Most seniors, however, prefer to walk.

Third, "Notices to Competitors" are issued for particular tournaments and cover conditions for that specific event. Such a notice may, for example, explain how the Rules of Golf should be applied to a particular water hazard or manmade obstruction. It might also authorize the use of carts to speed up play when there is an unusual distance between one green and the next tee.

The basic Rules of Golf, the hard cards, and the weekly notices apply equally to all players in tour competitions. As one of petitioner's witnesses explained with reference to "the Masters Tournament, which is golf at its very highest level, . . . the key is to have everyone tee off on the first hole under exactly the same conditions and all of them be tested over that 72-hole event under the conditions that exist during those four days of the event."

II

Casey Martin is a talented golfer. As an amateur, he won 17 Oregon Golf Association junior events before he was 15, and won the state championship as a high school senior. He played on the Stanford University golf team that won the 1994 National Collegiate Athletic Association (NCAA) championship. As a professional, Martin qualified for the NIKE TOUR in 1998 and 1999, and based on his 1999 performance, qualified for the PGA TOUR in 2000. In the 1999 season, he entered 24 events, made the cut 13 times, and had 6 top-10 finishes, coming in second twice and third once.

Martin is also an individual with a disability as defined in the Americans with Disabilities Act of 1990 (ADA or Act). Since birth he has been afflicted with Klippel-Trenaunay-Weber Syndrome, a degenerative circulatory disorder that obstructs the flow of blood from his right leg back to his heart. The disease is progressive; it causes severe pain and has atrophied his right leg. During the latter part of his college career, because of the progress of the disease, Martin could no longer walk an 18-hole golf course.[8] Walking not only caused him pain, fatigue, and anxiety, but also created a significant risk of hemorrhaging, developing blood clots, and fracturing his tibia so badly that an amputation might be required. For these reasons, Stanford made written requests to the Pacific 10 Conference and the NCAA to waive for Martin their rules requiring players to walk and carry their own clubs. The requests were granted.[9]

---

[8] Before then, even when Martin was in extreme pain, and was offered a cart, he declined.

[9] When asked about the other teams' reaction to Martin's use of a cart, the Stanford coach testified:

When Martin turned pro and entered petitioner's Q-School, the hard card permitted him to use a cart during his successful progress through the first two stages. He made a request, supported by detailed medical records, for permission to use a golf cart during the third stage. Petitioner refused to review those records or to waive its walking rule for the third stage. Martin therefore filed this action. A preliminary injunction entered by the District Court made it possible for him to use a cart in the final stage of the Q-School and as a competitor in the NIKE TOUR and PGA TOUR. Although not bound by the injunction, and despite its support for petitioner's position in this litigation, the USGA voluntarily granted Martin a similar waiver in events that it sponsors, including the U.S. Open.

III

In the District Court, petitioner moved for summary judgment on the ground that it is exempt from coverage under Title III of the ADA as a "private clu[b] or establishmen[t]," or alternatively, that the play areas of its tour competitions do not constitute places of "public accommodation" within the scope of that Title. The Magistrate Judge concluded that petitioner should be viewed as a commercial enterprise operating in the entertainment industry for the economic benefit of its members rather than as a private club. Furthermore, after noting that the statutory definition of public accommodation included a "golf course," he rejected petitioner's argument that its competitions are only places of public accommodation in the areas open to spectators. The operator of a public accommodation could not, in his view, "create private enclaves within the facility . . . and thus relegate the ADA to hop-scotch areas." Accordingly, he denied petitioner's motion for summary judgment.

At trial, petitioner did not contest the conclusion that Martin has a disability covered by the ADA, or the fact "that his disability prevents him from walking the course during a round of golf." Rather, petitioner asserted that the condition of walking is a substantive rule of competition, and that waiving it as to any individual for any reason would fundamentally alter the nature of the competition. Petitioner's evidence included the testimony of a number of experts, among them some of the greatest golfers in history. Arnold Palmer, Jack Nicklaus, and Ken Venturi explained that fatigue can be a critical factor in a tournament, particularly on the last day when psychological pressure is at a maximum. Their testimony makes it clear that, in their view, permission to use a cart might well give some players a

---

"Q. Was there any complaint ever made to you by the coaches when he was allowed a cart that that gave a competitive advantage over the—

"A. Any complaints? No sir, there were exactly—exactly the opposite. Everybody recognized Casey for the person he was, and what he was doing with his life, and every coach, to my knowledge, and every player wanted Casey in the tournament and they welcomed him there.

"Q. Did anyone contend that that constituted an alteration of the competition to the extent that it didn't constitute the game to your level, the college level?

"A. Not at all, sir."

competitive advantage over other players who must walk. They did not, however, express any opinion on whether a cart would give Martin such an advantage.

Rejecting petitioner's argument that an individualized inquiry into the necessity of the walking rule in Martin's case would be inappropriate, the District Court stated that it had "the independent duty to inquire into the purpose of the rule at issue, and to ascertain whether there can be a reasonable modification made to accommodate plaintiff without frustrating the purpose of the rule" and thereby fundamentally altering the nature of petitioner's tournaments. The judge found that the purpose of the rule was to inject fatigue into the skill of shotmaking, but that the fatigue injected "by walking the course cannot be deemed significant under normal circumstances." Furthermore, Martin presented evidence, and the judge found, that even with the use of a cart, Martin must walk over a mile during an 18-hole round,[17] and that the fatigue he suffers from coping with his disability is "undeniably greater" than the fatigue his able-bodied competitors endure from walking the course. As the judge observed:

> [P]laintiff is in significant pain when he walks, and even when he is getting in and out of the cart. With each step, he is at risk of fracturing his tibia and hemorrhaging. The other golfers have to endure the psychological stress of competition as part of their fatigue; Martin has the same stress plus the added stress of pain and risk of serious injury. As he put it, he would gladly trade the cart for a good leg. To perceive that the cart puts him—with his condition—at a competitive advantage is a gross distortion of reality.

As a result, the judge concluded that it would "not fundamentally alter the nature of the PGA Tour's game to accommodate him with a cart." The judge accordingly entered a permanent injunction requiring petitioner to permit Martin to use a cart in tour and qualifying events.

[The Ninth Circuit affirmed.] . . .

The day after the Ninth Circuit ruled in Martin's favor, the Seventh Circuit came to a contrary conclusion in a case brought against the USGA by a disabled golfer who failed to qualify for "America's greatest—and most democratic—golf tournament, the United States Open." *Olinger v. United States Golf Assn.*, 205 F.3d 1001 (C.A.7 2000).[19]

. . . Although the Seventh Circuit merely assumed that the ADA applies to professional golf tournaments, and therefore did not disagree with the Ninth on the threshold coverage issue, our grant of certiorari, 530 U.S.

---

[17] In the first place, he does walk while on the course—even with a cart, he must move from cart to shot and back to the cart. In essence, he still must walk approximately 25% of the course. On a course roughly five miles in length, Martin will walk 1 ¼ miles.

[19] The golfer in the Seventh Circuit case, Ford Olinger, suffers from bilateral avascular necrosis, a degenerative condition that significantly hinders his ability to walk.

1306, 121 S.Ct. 30 (2000), encompasses that question as well as the conflict between those courts.

IV

* * *

It seems apparent, from both the general rule and the comprehensive definition of "public accommodation," that petitioner's golf tours and their qualifying rounds fit comfortably within the coverage of Title III, and Martin within its protection. The events occur on "golf course[s]," a type of place specifically identified by the Act as a public accommodation. § 12181(7)(L). In addition, at all relevant times, petitioner "leases" and "operates" golf courses to conduct its Q-School and tours. § 12182(a). As a lessor and operator of golf courses, then, petitioner must not discriminate against any "individual" in the "full and equal enjoyment of the goods, services, facilities, privileges, advantages, or accommodations" of those courses. Certainly, among the "privileges" offered by petitioner on the courses are those of competing in the Q-School and playing in the tours; indeed, the former is a privilege for which thousands of individuals from the general public pay, and the latter is one for which they vie. Martin, of course, is one of those individuals. It would therefore appear that Title III of the ADA, by its plain terms, prohibits petitioner from denying Martin equal access to its tours on the basis of his disability.

Petitioner argues otherwise. To be clear about its position, it does not assert (as it did in the District Court) that it is a private club altogether exempt from Title III's coverage. In fact, petitioner admits that its tournaments are conducted at places of public accommodation. Nor does petitioner contend (as it did in both the District Court and the Court of Appeals) that the competitors' area "behind the ropes" is not a public accommodation, notwithstanding the status of the rest of the golf course. Rather, petitioner reframes the coverage issue by arguing that the competing golfers are not members of the class protected by Title III of the ADA.

According to petitioner, Title III is concerned with discrimination against "clients and customers" seeking to obtain "goods and services" at places of public accommodation, whereas it is Title I that protects persons who work at such places. As the argument goes, petitioner operates not a "golf course" during its tournaments but a "place of exhibition or entertainment," 42 U.S.C. § 12181(7)(C), and a professional golfer such as Martin, like an actor in a theater production, is a provider rather than a consumer of the entertainment that petitioner sells to the public. Martin therefore cannot bring a claim under Title III because he is not one of the " '*clients or customers* of the covered public accommodation.' " Rather, Martin's claim of discrimination is "job-related" and could only be brought under Title I—but that Title does not apply because he is an independent contractor (as the District Court found) rather than an employee.

* * *

... [P]etitioner's argument falters even on its own terms. If Title III's protected class were limited to "clients or customers," it would be entirely appropriate to classify the golfers who pay petitioner $3,000 for the chance to compete in the Q-School and, if successful, in the subsequent tour events, as petitioner's clients or customers. In our view, petitioner's tournaments (whether situated at a "golf course" or at a "place of exhibition or entertainment") simultaneously offer at least two "privileges" to the public—that of watching the golf competition and that of competing in it. Although the latter is more difficult and more expensive to obtain than the former, it is nonetheless a privilege that petitioner makes available to members of the general public. In consideration of the entry fee, any golfer with the requisite letters of recommendation acquires the opportunity to qualify for and compete in petitioner's tours. Additionally, any golfer who succeeds in the open qualifying rounds for a tournament may play in the event. That petitioner identifies one set of clients or customers that it serves (spectators at tournaments) does not preclude it from having another set (players in tournaments) against whom it may not discriminate. It would be inconsistent with the literal text of the statute as well as its expansive purpose to read Title III's coverage, even given petitioner's suggested limitation, any less broadly.[33]

V

As we have noted, 42 U.S.C. § 12182(a) sets forth Title III's general rule prohibiting public accommodations from discriminating against individuals because of their disabilities. The question whether petitioner has violated that rule depends on a proper construction of the term "discrimination," which is defined by Title III to include

> "a failure to make reasonable modifications in policies, practices, or procedures, when such modifications are necessary to afford such goods, services, facilities, privileges, advantages, or accommodations to individuals with disabilities, *unless the entity can demonstrate that making such modifications would fundamentally alter the nature* of such goods, services, facilities, privileges, advantages, or accommodations." § 12182(b)(2)(A)(ii).

---

[33] Contrary to the dissent's suggestion, our view of the Q-School does not make "everyone who seeks a job" at a public accommodation, through "an open tryout" or otherwise, "a customer." Unlike those who successfully apply for a job at a place of public accommodation, or those who successfully bid for a contract, the golfers who qualify for petitioner's tours play at their own pleasure (perhaps, but not necessarily, for prize money), and although they commit to playing in at least 15 tournaments, they are not bound by any obligations typically associated with employment. Furthermore, unlike athletes in "other professional sports, such as baseball," in which players are employed by their clubs, the golfers on tour are not employed by petitioner or any related organizations. The record does not support the proposition that the purpose of the Q-School "is to hire," rather than to narrow the field of participants in the sporting events that petitioner sponsors at places of public accommodation.

Petitioner does not contest that a golf cart is a reasonable modification that is necessary if Martin is to play in its tournaments. Martin's claim thus differs from one that might be asserted by players with less serious afflictions that make walking the course uncomfortable or difficult, but not beyond their capacity. In such cases, an accommodation might be reasonable but not necessary. In this case, however, the narrow dispute is whether allowing Martin to use a golf cart, despite the walking requirement that applies to the PGA TOUR, the NIKE TOUR, and the third stage of the Q-School, is a modification that would "fundamentally alter the nature" of those events.

In theory, a modification of petitioner's golf tournaments might constitute a fundamental alteration in two different ways. It might alter such an essential aspect of the game of golf that it would be unacceptable even if it affected all competitors equally; changing the diameter of the hole from three to six inches might be such a modification. Alternatively, a less significant change that has only a peripheral impact on the game itself might nevertheless give a disabled player, in addition to access to the competition as required by Title III, an advantage over others and, for that reason, fundamentally alter the character of the competition. We are not persuaded that a waiver of the walking rule for Martin would work a fundamental alteration in either sense.

As an initial matter, we observe that the use of carts is not itself inconsistent with the fundamental character of the game of golf. From early on, the essence of the game has been shotmaking—using clubs to cause a ball to progress from the teeing ground to a hole some distance away with as few strokes as possible. That essential aspect of the game is still reflected in the very first of the Rules of Golf, which declares: "The Game of Golf consists in playing a ball from the *teeing ground* into the hole by a *stroke* or successive strokes in accordance with the rules." Over the years, there have been many changes in the players' equipment, in golf course design, in the Rules of Golf, and in the method of transporting clubs from hole to hole. Originally, so few clubs were used that each player could carry them without a bag. Then came golf bags, caddies, carts that were pulled by hand, and eventually motorized carts that carried players as well as clubs. "Golf carts started appearing with increasing regularity on American golf courses in the 1950's. Today they are everywhere. And they are encouraged. For one thing, they often speed up play, and for another, they are great revenue producers." There is nothing in the Rules of Golf that either forbids the use of carts or penalizes a player for using a cart. That set of rules, as we have observed, is widely accepted in both the amateur and professional golf world as the rules of the game. The walking rule that is contained in petitioner's hard cards, based on an optional condition buried in an appendix to the Rules of Golf, is not an essential attribute of the game itself.

Indeed, the walking rule is not an indispensable feature of tournament golf either. As already mentioned, petitioner permits golf carts to be used in the SENIOR PGA TOUR, the open qualifying events for petitioner's tournaments, the first two stages of the Q-School, and, until 1997, the third stage of the Q-School as well. Moreover, petitioner allows the use of carts during certain tournament rounds in both the PGA TOUR and the NIKE TOUR. In addition, although the USGA enforces a walking rule in most of the tournaments that it sponsors, it permits carts in the Senior Amateur and the Senior Women's Amateur championships.

Petitioner, however, distinguishes the game of golf as it is generally played from the game that it sponsors in the PGA TOUR, NIKE TOUR, and (at least recently) the last stage of the Q-School—golf at the "highest level." According to petitioner, "[t]he goal of the highest-level competitive athletics is to assess and compare the performance of different competitors, a task that is meaningful only if the competitors are subject to identical substantive rules." The waiver of any possibly "outcome-affecting" rule for a contestant would violate this principle and therefore, in petitioner's view, fundamentally alter the nature of the highest level athletic event. The walking rule is one such rule, petitioner submits, because its purpose is "to inject the element of fatigue into the skill of shot-making," and thus its effect may be the critical loss of a stroke. As a consequence, the reasonable modification Martin seeks would fundamentally alter the nature of petitioner's highest level tournaments even if he were the only person in the world who has both the talent to compete in those elite events and a disability sufficiently serious that he cannot do so without using a cart.

The force of petitioner's argument is, first of all, mitigated by the fact that golf is a game in which it is impossible to guarantee that all competitors will play under exactly the same conditions or that an individual's ability will be the sole determinant of the outcome. For example, changes in the weather may produce harder greens and more head winds for the tournament leader than for his closest pursuers. A lucky bounce may save a shot or two. Whether such happenstance events are more or less probable than the likelihood that a golfer afflicted with Klippel-Trenaunay-Weber Syndrome would one day qualify for the NIKE TOUR and PGA TOUR, they at least demonstrate that pure chance may have a greater impact on the outcome of elite golf tournaments than the fatigue resulting from the enforcement of the walking rule.

Further, the factual basis of petitioner's argument is undermined by the District Court's finding that the fatigue from walking during one of petitioner's 4-day tournaments cannot be deemed significant. The District Court credited the testimony of a professor in physiology and expert on fatigue, who calculated the calories expended in walking a golf course (about five miles) to be approximately 500 calories—" 'nutritionally . . . less than a Big Mac.' " What is more, that energy is expended over a 5-hour period, during which golfers have numerous intervals for rest and refreshment. In fact, the expert concluded, because golf is a low intensity activity, fatigue from the game is primarily a psychological phenomenon in which stress and motivation are the key ingredients. And even under conditions of severe heat and humidity, the critical factor in fatigue is fluid loss rather than exercise from walking.

Moreover, when given the option of using a cart, the majority of golfers in petitioner's tournaments have chosen to walk, often to relieve stress or for other strategic reasons. As NIKE TOUR member Eric Johnson testified, walking allows him to keep in rhythm, stay warmer when it is chilly, and develop a better sense of the elements and the course than riding a cart.

Even if we accept the factual predicate for petitioner's argument—that the walking rule is "outcome affecting" because fatigue may adversely affect performance—its legal position is fatally flawed. Petitioner's refusal to consider Martin's personal circumstances in deciding whether to accommodate his disability runs counter to the clear language and purpose of the ADA. As previously stated, the ADA was enacted to eliminate discrimination against "individuals" with disabilities, 42 U.S.C. § 12101(b)(1), and to that end Title III of the Act requires without exception that any "policies, practices, or procedures" of a public accommodation be reasonably modified for disabled "individuals" as necessary to afford access unless doing so would fundamentally alter what is offered, § 12182(b)(2)(A)(ii). To comply with this command, an individualized inquiry must be made to determine whether a specific modification for a particular person's disability would be reasonable under the circumstances as well as necessary for that person, and yet at the same time not work a fundamental alteration.

To be sure, the waiver of an essential rule of competition for anyone would fundamentally alter the nature of petitioner's tournaments. As we have demonstrated, however, the walking rule is at best peripheral to the nature of petitioner's athletic events, and thus it might be waived in individual cases without working a fundamental alteration. Therefore, petitioner's claim that all the substantive rules for its "highest-level" competitions are sacrosanct and cannot be modified under any circumstances is effectively a contention that it is exempt from Title III's reasonable modification requirement. But that provision carves out no exemption for elite athletics, and given Title III's coverage not only of places of "exhibition or entertainment" but also of "golf course[s]," its application to petitioner's tournaments cannot be said to be unintended or unexpected. Even if it were, "the fact that a statute can be applied in situations not expressly anticipated by Congress does not demonstrate ambiguity. It demonstrates breadth." *Pennsylvania Dept. of Corrections v. Yeskey*, 524 U.S., at 212, 118 S.Ct. 1952.[51]

Under the ADA's basic requirement that the need of a disabled person be evaluated on an individual basis, we have no doubt that allowing Martin to use a golf cart would not fundamentally alter the nature of petitioner's tournaments. As we have discussed, the purpose of the walking rule is to subject players to fatigue, which in turn may influence the outcome of tournaments. Even if the rule does serve that purpose, it is an uncontested finding of the District Court that Martin "easily endures greater fatigue even with a cart than his able-bodied competitors do by walking." The purpose of the walking rule is therefore not compromised in the slightest by allowing Martin to use a cart. A modification that provides an exception to a peripheral tournament rule without impairing its purpose cannot be said to "fundamentally alter" the tournament. What it can be said to do, on the other hand, is to allow Martin the chance to qualify for, and compete in, the athletic events petitioner offers to those members of the public who have the skill and desire to enter. That is exactly what the ADA requires. As a result, Martin's request for a waiver of the walking rule should have been granted.

* * *

The judgment of the Court of Appeals is affirmed.

It is so ordered.

JUSTICE SCALIA, with whom JUSTICE THOMAS joins, dissenting.

In my view today's opinion exercises a benevolent compassion that the law does not place it within our power to impose. The judgment distorts the text of Title III, the structure of the ADA, and common sense. I respectfully dissent.

I

The Court holds that a professional sport is a place of public accommodation and that respondent is a "custome[r]" of "competition" when he practices his profession. It finds that this strange conclusion is

---

[51] Hence, petitioner's questioning of the ability of courts to apply the reasonable modification requirement to athletic competition is a complaint more properly directed to Congress, which drafted the ADA's coverage broadly, than to us. Even more misguided is Justice SCALIA's suggestion that Congress did not place that inquiry into the hands of the courts at all. According to the dissent, the game of golf as sponsored by petitioner is, like all sports games, the sum of its "arbitrary rules," and no one, including courts, "can pronounce one or another of them to be 'nonessential' if the rulemaker (here the PGA TOUR) deems it to be essential." Whatever the merit of Justice SCALIA's postmodern view of "What Is [Sport]," it is clear that Congress did not enshrine it in Title III of the ADA. While Congress expressly exempted "private clubs or establishments" and "religious organizations or entities" from Title III's coverage, Congress made no such exception for athletic competitions, much less did it give sports organizations *carte blanche* authority to exempt themselves from the fundamental alteration inquiry by deeming any rule, no matter how peripheral to the competition, to be essential. In short, Justice SCALIA's reading of the statute renders the word "fundamentally" largely superfluous, because it treats the alteration of any rule governing an event at a public accommodation to be a fundamental alteration.

compelled by the "literal text" of Title III of the Americans with Disabilities Act of 1990 (ADA), 42 U.S.C. § 12101 *et seq.*, by the "expansive purpose" of the ADA, and by the fact that Title II of the Civil Rights Act of 1964 has been applied to an amusement park and public golf courses. I disagree.

The ADA has three separate titles: Title I covers employment discrimination, Title II covers discrimination by government entities, and Title III covers discrimination by places of public accommodation. Title II is irrelevant to this case. Title I protects only "employees" of employers who have 15 or more employees, §§ 12112(a), 12111(5)(A). It does not protect independent contractors. Respondent claimed employment discrimination under Title I, but the District Court found him to be an independent contractor rather than an employee.

Respondent also claimed protection under § 12182 of Title III. That section applies only to particular places and persons. The place must be a "place of public accommodation," and the person must be an "individual" seeking "enjoyment of the goods, services, facilities, privileges, advantages, or accommodations" of the covered place. § 12182(a). Of course a court indiscriminately invoking the "sweeping" and "expansive" purposes of the ADA could argue that when a place of public accommodation denied *any* "individual," on the basis of his disability, *anything* that might be called a "privileg[e]," the individual has a valid Title III claim. On such an interpretation, the employees and independent contractors of every place of public accommodation come within Title III: The employee enjoys the "privilege" of employment, the contractor the "privilege" of the contract.

* * *

The Court . . . pronounces respondent to be a "customer" of the PGA TOUR or of the golf courses on which it is played. That seems to me quite incredible. The PGA TOUR is a professional sporting event, staged for the entertainment of a live and TV audience, the receipts from whom (the TV audience's admission price is paid by advertisers) pay the expenses of the tour, including the cash prizes for the winning golfers. The professional golfers on the tour are no more "enjoying" (the statutory term) the entertainment that the tour provides, or the facilities of the golf courses on which it is held, than professional baseball players "enjoy" the baseball games in which they play or the facilities of Yankee Stadium. To be sure, professional ballplayers *participate* in the games, and *use* the ballfields, but no one in his right mind would think that they are *customers* of the American League or of Yankee Stadium. They are themselves the entertainment that the customers pay to watch. And professional golfers are no different. It makes not a bit of difference, insofar as their "customer" status is concerned, that the remuneration for their performance (unlike most of the remuneration for ballplayers) is not fixed but contingent—viz., the purses for the winners in the various events, and the compensation from product endorsements that consistent winners are assured. The compensation of *many* independent contractors is contingent upon their success—real estate brokers, for example, or insurance salesmen.

. . . Respondent did not seek to "exercise" or "recreate" at the PGA TOUR events; he sought to make money (which is why he is called a *professional* golfer). He was not a customer *buying* recreation or entertainment; he was a professional athlete *selling* it. . . .

The Court relies heavily upon the Q-School. It says that petitioner offers the golfing public the "privilege" of "competing in the Q-School and playing in the tours; indeed, the former is a privilege for which thousands of individuals from the general public pay, and the latter is one for which they vie." But the Q-School is no more a "privilege" offered for the general public's "enjoyment" than is the California Bar Exam. It is a competition for entry into the PGA TOUR—an open tryout, no different in principle from open casting for a movie or stage production, or walk-on tryouts for other professional sports, such as baseball. It may well be that some amateur golfers enjoy trying to make the grade, just as some amateur actors may enjoy auditions, and amateur baseball players may enjoy open tryouts (I hesitate to say that amateur lawyers may enjoy taking the California Bar Exam). But the purpose of holding those tryouts is not to provide entertainment; it is to hire. . . .

II

* * *

Since it has held (or assumed) professional golfers to be customers "enjoying" the "privilege" that consists of PGA TOUR golf; and since it inexplicably regards the rules of PGA TOUR golf as merely "policies, practices, or procedures" by which access to PGA TOUR golf is provided, the Court must then confront the question whether respondent's requested modification of the supposed policy, practice, or procedure of walking would "fundamentally alter the nature" of the PGA TOUR game, § 12182(b)(2)(A)(ii). The Court attacks this "fundamental alteration" analysis by asking two questions: first, whether the "essence" or an "essential aspect" of the sport of golf has been altered; and second, whether the change, even if not essential to the game, would give the disabled player an advantage over others and thereby "fundamentally alter the character of the competition." It answers no to both.

Before considering the Court's answer to the first question, it is worth pointing out that the assumption which underlies that question is false. Nowhere is it writ that PGA TOUR golf must be classic "essential" golf. Why cannot the PGA TOUR, if it wishes, promote a new game, with distinctive rules (much as the American League promotes a game of baseball in which the pitcher's turn at the plate can be taken by a "designated hitter")? If members of the public do not like the new rules—if they feel that these rules do not truly test the individual's skill at "real golf" (or the team's skill at "real baseball") they can withdraw their patronage. But the rules are the rules. They are (as in all games) entirely arbitrary, and there is no basis on which anyone—not even the Supreme Court of the United States—can pronounce one or another of them to be "nonessential" if the rulemaker (here the PGA TOUR) deems it to be essential.

If one assumes, however, that the PGA TOUR has some legal obligation to play classic, Platonic golf—and if one assumes the correctness of all the other wrong turns the Court has made to get to this point—then we Justices must confront what is indeed an awesome responsibility. It has been rendered the solemn duty of the Supreme Court of the United States, laid upon it by Congress in pursuance of the Federal Government's power "[t]o regulate Commerce with foreign Nations, and among the several States," U.S. Const., Art. I, § 8, cl. 3, to decide What Is Golf. I am sure that the Framers of the Constitution, aware of the 1457 edict of King James II of Scotland prohibiting golf because it interfered with the practice of archery, fully expected that sooner or later the paths of golf and government, the law and the links, would once again cross, and that the judges of this august Court would some day have to wrestle with that age-old jurisprudential question, for which their years of study in the law have so well prepared them: Is someone riding around a golf course from shot to shot *really* a golfer? The answer, we learn, is yes. The Court ultimately concludes, and it will henceforth be the Law of the Land, that walking is not a "fundamental" aspect of golf.

Either out of humility or out of self-respect (one or the other) the Court should decline to answer this incredibly difficult and incredibly silly question. To say that something is "essential" is ordinarily to say that it is necessary to the achievement of a certain object. But since it is the very nature of a game to have no object except amusement (that is what distinguishes games from productive activity), it is quite impossible to say that any of a game's arbitrary rules is "essential." Eighteen-hole golf courses, 10-foot-high basketball hoops, 90-foot baselines, 100-yard football fields—all are arbitrary and none is essential. The only support for any of them is tradition and (in more modern times) insistence by what has come to be regarded as the ruling body of the sport—both of which factors support the PGA TOUR's position in the present case. (Many, indeed, consider walking to be *the central feature* of the game of golf—hence Mark Twain's classic criticism of the sport: "a good walk spoiled.") I suppose there is some point at which the rules of a well-known game are changed to such a degree that no reasonable person would call it the same game. If the PGA TOUR competitors were required to dribble a large, inflated ball and put it through a round hoop, the game could no longer reasonably be called golf. But this criterion—destroying recognizability as the same generic game—is surely not the test of "essentialness" or "fundamentalness" that the Court applies, since it apparently thinks that merely changing the diameter of the *cup* might "fundamentally alter" the game of golf.

Having concluded that dispensing with the walking rule would not violate federal-Platonic "golf" (and, implicitly, that it is federal-Platonic golf, and no other, that the PGA TOUR can insist upon), the Court moves on to the second part of its test: the competitive effects of waiving this nonessential rule. In this part of its analysis, the Court first finds that the effects of the change are "mitigated" by the fact that in the game of golf weather, a "lucky bounce," and "pure chance" provide different conditions for each competitor and individual ability may not "be the sole determinant of the outcome." I guess that is why those who follow professional golfing consider Jack Nicklaus the *luckiest* golfer of all time, only to be challenged of late by the phenomenal *luck* of Tiger Woods. The Court's empiricism is unpersuasive. "Pure chance" is randomly distributed among the players, but allowing respondent to use a cart gives him a "lucky" break every time he plays. Pure chance also only matters at the margin—a stroke here or there; the cart substantially improves this respondent's competitive prospects beyond a couple of strokes. But even granting that there are significant nonhuman variables affecting competition, that fact does not justify adding another variable that always favors one player.

In an apparent effort to make its opinion as narrow as possible, the Court relies upon the District Court's finding that even with a cart, respondent will be at least as fatigued as everyone else. This, the Court says, *proves* that competition will not be affected. Far from thinking that reliance on this finding cabins the effect of today's opinion, I think it will prove to be its most expansive and destructive feature. Because step one of the Court's two-part inquiry into whether a requested change in a sport will "fundamentally alter [its] nature," § 12182(b)(2)(A)(ii), consists of an utterly unprincipled ontology of sports (pursuant to which the Court is not even sure whether golf's "essence" requires a 3-inch hole), there is every reason to think that in future cases involving requests for special treatment by would-be athletes the second step of the analysis will be determinative. In resolving that second step—determining whether waiver of the "nonessential" rule will have an impermissible "competitive effect"—by measuring the athletic capacity of the requesting individual, and asking whether the special dispensation would do no more than place him on a par (so to speak) with other competitors, the Court guarantees that future cases of this sort will have to be decided on the basis of individualized factual findings. Which means that future cases of this sort will be numerous, and a rich source of lucrative litigation. One can envision the parents of a Little League player with attention deficit disorder trying to convince a judge that their son's disability makes it at least 25% more difficult to hit a pitched ball. (If they are successful, the only thing that could prevent a court order giving the kid four strikes would be a judicial determination that, in baseball, three strikes are metaphysically necessary, which is quite absurd.)

* * *

My belief that today's judgment is clearly in error should not be mistaken for a belief that the PGA TOUR clearly *ought not* allow respondent to use a golf cart. *That* is a close question, on which even those who compete in the PGA TOUR are apparently divided; but it is a *different* question from the one before the Court. . . .

And it should not be assumed that today's decent, tolerant, and progressive judgment will, in the long run, accrue to the benefit of sports competitors with disabilities. Now that it is clear courts will review the rules of sports for "fundamentalness," organizations that value their autonomy have every incentive to defend vigorously the necessity of every regulation. They may still be second-guessed in the end as to the Platonic requirements of the sport, but they will *assuredly* lose if they have at all wavered in their enforcement. The lesson the PGA TOUR and other sports organizations should take from this case is to make sure that the same written rules are set forth for all levels of play, and never voluntarily to grant any modifications. The second lesson is to end open tryouts. I doubt that, in the long run, even disabled athletes will be well served by these incentives that the Court has created.

Complaints about this case are not "properly directed to Congress." They are properly directed to this Court's Kafkaesque determination that professional sports organizations, and the fields they rent for their exhibitions, are "places of public accommodation" to the competing athletes, and the athletes themselves "customers" of the organization that pays them; its Alice in Wonderland determination that there are such things as judicially determinable "essential" and "nonessential" rules of a made-up game; and its Animal Farm determination that fairness and the ADA mean that everyone gets to play by individualized rules which will assure that no one's lack of ability (or at least no one's lack of ability so pronounced that it amounts to a disability) will be a handicap. The year was 2001, and "everybody was finally equal." K. Vonnegut, Harrison Bergeron, in Animal Farm and Related Readings 129 (1997).

NOTES AND QUESTIONS

1.   *The coverage issue in* Martin. The majority in the *Martin* case holds that the PGA golf tournament is covered by Title III of the ADA, and that Casey Martin is protected by the Act as a "customer" because he had to pay $3,000 to get into the Q-School. The dissent argues that Martin is not a customer of the golf tournament; instead, he is the one providing the entertainment. And if he is working at the golf tournament, rather than enjoying it as a customer, he would not be covered by the ADA because he is not an employee covered by Title I; rather, he is an independent contractor. Which side has the better argument? Were you at all persuaded by the fact that, if Casey Martin and others like him (perhaps those auditioning for a theatre show, as the dissent mentions) were not covered by Title III, they would not be covered at all? In

other words, would it make sense if Congress deliberately left this gap in the statute's coverage?

2.   *Coverage of cruise ships.* One coverage issue that the Supreme Court had to decide is whether the ADA applies to foreign-flag cruise ships in United States waters. *See* Spector v. Norwegian Cruise Line Ltd., 545 U.S. 119, 125 S.Ct. 2169 (2005). Addressing a circuit split in the Courts of Appeals, a plurality of the Court held that the answer is "sometimes." The plurality began by explaining that a clear statement of congressional intent is necessary before a general statutory requirement can interfere with matters that concern a foreign-flag vessel's internal affairs and operations, as contrasted with statutory requirements that concern the security and well-being of United States citizens. In interpreting the requirements of Title III, the plurality stated that Title III's own limitations and qualifications (e.g., only "readily achievable" modifications are required) will generally prevent the statute from imposing requirements that would conflict with international obligations or threaten shipboard safety. And to the extent that Title III's requirements do not interfere with the internal affairs of foreign-flag cruise ships, the plurality reversed the "decision of the Court of Appeals for the Fifth Circuit that the ADA is altogether inapplicable to foreign vessels," and remanded for further proceedings. On June 23, 2013, the Architectural and Transportation Barriers Compliance Board proposed accessibility guidelines for the construction and alteration of passenger vessels covered by the ADA. The comment period was closed as of January 24, 2014. The U.S. Department of Transportation and the U.S. Department of Justice are required to issue accessibility standards consistent with the guidelines. However, as of this writing, regulations had not yet been issued.

3.   *The golf cart as a "necessary" modification.* In the *Martin* case, the parties agreed that Casey Martin *needed* the golf cart in order to be able to compete in the tournament. Without it, not only would walking the course have been physically exhausting (prohibitively so) but also very dangerous. But one can imagine other cases where the necessity of the accommodation is not as clear-cut. For instance, imagine that there is a talented golfer who had a knee injury, such that walking the course caused him pain, but did not cause him any danger. Is a waiver of the walking rule *necessary* in that case?

4.   *The necessity requirement.* Although most courts hold that a requested modification must be necessary under Title III, not all courts agree. For instance, in *Baughman v. Walt Disney World Company*, 685 F.3d 1131 (9th Cir. 2012), the plaintiff was requesting a waiver of Disneyland's policy prohibiting the use of a Segway, a two-wheeled mobility device operated while standing. The defendant argued that the use of the Segway was not technically necessary because the plaintiff could use a scooter or wheelchair for mobility. *Id.* at 1134. The Ninth Circuit disagreed, holding that modifications should be made that allow the disabled plaintiff to have "full and equal enjoyment" of the products or services offered by the place of public accommodation. As the court stated:

Read as Disney suggests, the ADA would require very few accommodations indeed. After all, a paraplegic *can* enter a courthouse by dragging himself up the steps . . . so lifts and reasonable accommodations would not be "necessary" under Disney's reading of the term. And no facility would be required to provide wheelchair-accessible doors or bathrooms, because disabled individuals could be carried in litters or on the backs of their friends. That's not the world we live in, and we are disappointed to see such a retrograde position taken by a company whose reputation is built on service to the public.

Id. at 1134–35. Can you reconcile this case with the discussion above in note 3? Would the Court in *Martin* have allowed the golf cart modification if it was not strictly necessary for Casey Martin? If not, is *Baughman* wrongly decided? Or is there something else going on that distinguishes these two cases?

5.   *The golf cart as a fundamental alteration.* The majority argues that there are two ways that the golf cart could constitute a fundamental alteration of the golf tournament. First, it might alter such an essential aspect of the game of golf that it would be unacceptable even if it affected all competitors equally. Second, a less significant change might nevertheless give a disabled player an unfair competitive advantage over others.

Do you agree with the majority that walking the course is not an "essential aspect" of the game of golf? What is the majority's best argument in favor of its conclusion that walking the course is not essential to the game of golf? Or do you think the dissent has the better argument that, because the rules of all games are arbitrary, it is impossible and silly for the court to determine which rules of the game are essential? If you think the dissent has the better argument, would the dissent think it was permissible for PGA Tours to have a rule that stated that only white people can compete in the golf tournament? If not, how would the dissent distinguish the two? Regardless of how you come out on the first question (whether or not the walking rule is essential) do you agree with the majority that the golf cart does not give Casey Martin an unfair competitive advantage? Can you explain the dissent's argument to the contrary?

6.   *Other cases involving athletics.* The dissent in the *Martin* case seemed to be worried that the majority's holding would mean that every disabled athlete would be able to litigate to obtain special rules that only applied to them, such as baseball players with ADD getting an extra strike before they're out. That concern does not seem to have been warranted. For instance, in *A.H. by Holzmueller v. Illinois High School Association*, 881 F.3d 587 (7th Cir. 2018), the court rejected the challenge of a disabled runner that wanted the Illinois High School Association to create a separate division with different time standards for para-ambulatory runners to qualify for sectional and state championship track and field meets. The court held that lowering the qualifying times would constitute a fundamental alteration of the meets. *Id.* at 595–96. The more common fact scenario for accommodation cases involving athletics is one where a student-athlete has a learning disability that

prevents them from graduating on time. Because most athletic associations have rules regarding how many semesters or years an athlete is eligible to play, the delay caused by the learning disability might mean that the student-athlete would not be eligible to play in his last year of high school or college. In those cases, courts often hold that waiving the time limitation on participating in sports is a reasonable modification. *See, e.g.,* Washington v. Indiana High School Athletic Association, 181 F.3d 840, 848 (7th Cir. 1999). This might seem unproblematic for college sports, but can you imagine the possible size and strength difference between a 14-year-old freshman in high school compared to a 19 or 20-year-old senior playing a high contact sport such as football? Would the waiver of the time limits be reasonable in such a circumstance?

AIKINS V. ST. HELENA HOSPITAL
843 F.Supp. 1329 (N.D. Cal. 1994)

FERN M. SMITH, DISTRICT JUDGE.

INTRODUCTION

Plaintiffs Elaine Aikins ("Mrs. Aikins") and California Association of the Deaf ("CAD") have brought suit against defendants St. Helena Hospital ("St. Helena," "the hospital") and Dr. James Lies ("Dr. Lies") under the Americans with Disabilities Act ("the ADA"), the Rehabilitation Act of 1973, and various California civil rights statutes. Both defendants have filed motions to dismiss or, in the alternative, for summary judgment. Defendants have also sought to have CAD dismissed from the lawsuit on the basis that CAD lacks standing.[*]

BACKGROUND

The events giving rise to this lawsuit occurred between October 30 and November 4, 1992. Mrs. Aikins is a deaf woman whose husband, Harvey Aikins, suffered a massive cardiac arrest at approximately 8:00 p.m. on October 30, 1992. Following Mr. Aikins's attack, Mrs. Aikins went to the home of some neighbors and had them call 911. According to Mrs. Aikins, the paramedics arrived at her home approximately four minutes after the call to 911, which defendants assert was approximately fifteen minutes after Mr. Aikins suffered the attack.[5] The paramedics then transported Mr. Aikins to St. Helena Hospital.

[* Eds. Note: Because the court holds that CAD lacks standing in this case, its claims will not be discussed in this excerpt of the opinion.]

[5] There is some conflict among the parties as to the timing of these events. Mrs. Aikins maintains that the paramedics arrived four minutes after the call and worked on Mr. Aikins for another fifteen minutes. Defendants initially thought that the paramedics arrived four minutes after the attack but assert that they later learned that they had not arrived until fifteen minutes after the attack. As Mrs. Aikins's claims relate not to the propriety of her husband's treatment but rather to the hospital's and Dr. Lies's ineffective communication with her, the difference in these time estimates is relevant only to the issue of the effectiveness of the communication between Mrs. Aikins and hospital officials.

Dr. Lies was working in St. Helena's emergency room when Mr. Aikins was brought in. Dr. Lies is an independent contractor on staff at the hospital. He exercises no authority over hospital policy. When the paramedics informed Dr. Lies that they had arrived within four minutes of Mr. Aikins's attack, Dr. Lies decided to perform an emergency angioplasty. He attempted to consult Mrs. Aikins and to obtain her consent, but Mrs. Aikins could not understand him and requested that interpreters be provided. A hospital operator with some knowledge of fingerspelling was summoned and attempted to fingerspell Dr. Lies's comments for Mrs. Aikins. The woman became frustrated, however, and gave up her efforts within a minute. Shortly thereafter, Mrs. Aikins's neighbors arrived and attempted to mediate between Dr. Lies and Mrs. Aikins. Dr. Lies asserts that the neighbors "were quite able to communicate with [Mrs. Aikins]" and relayed to her his opinion that, with immediate medical intervention, Dr. Lies might be able to save Mr. Aikins's life. Mrs. Aikins submits that the neighbors only passed her a terse note stating that Mr. Aikins may have had a massive cardiac arrest and that he was "brain dead."

Subsequently, Mrs. Aikins went to the hospital's administrative office and made further attempts to secure interpreter services. At approximately 9:00 p.m., she was approached by a member of the hospital staff who sought to obtain her signature on forms consenting to the emergency procedure. Although the forms say that "[y]our signature on this form indicates . . . (2) that the operation procedure set forth above has been adequately explained to you by your physician, (3) that you have had a chance to ask questions, [and] (4) that you have received all of the information you desire concerning the operation or procedure . . . ," Mrs. Aikins claims that she was told only that "Dr. Lies needed [her] signature to permit him to perform surgery to save [her] husband's life." Dr. Lies claims that, although he believed that it was unnecessary under the circumstances to obtain Mrs. Aikins's consent to the surgery, "given [her] disability, [he] wanted her to be involved."

Later that evening, Dr. Lies contacted Mrs. Aikins's daughter, Francine Stern, to request that she fly up to Calistoga from Los Angeles to help her mother. Ms. Stern, who was Mr. Aikins's stepdaughter, is a fluent signer. Ms. Stern told Dr. Lies that she would be unable to come up until November 2nd.

Mrs. Aikins went to her husband's room at approximately 12:30 on the night of the operation. She claims that the nurse on duty told her that Mr. Aikins would not survive without life support and that Mrs. Aikins then requested that life support be discontinued. She then went to the administrative office, accompanied by a deaf friend, to request interpreter services again. Both the office and another nurse whom Mrs. Aikins and her friend later encountered in Mr. Aikins's room allegedly told Mrs. Aikins that the hospital had no means of procuring interpreter services.

The following day, October 31, 1992, Mr. Aikins showed no neurologic improvement, prompting Dr. Lies to question Mrs. Aikins about the length of time between the heart attack and the arrival of the paramedics. Dr. Lies submits that it was during this questioning, seemingly conducted through Mrs. Aikins's in-laws, that he first learned that fifteen minutes, not four, had elapsed between Mr. Aikins's heart attack and the commencement of CPR. Based on this new information, Dr. Lies ordered an EEG. The EEG was performed on November 1, 1992, at 9:00 a.m. and revealed that Mr. Aikins had no brain activity.

On November 2nd, Mrs. Aikins's daughter arrived and participated in a meeting with Dr. Lies and Mrs. Aikins. Mrs. Aikins claims that this meeting was the first opportunity that she had to communicate directly with Dr. Lies and to receive complete answers to her questions. As a result of the meeting, Mrs. Aikins requested that her husband's life support be discontinued. Mr. Aikins died two days later.

Defendants have each filed motions to dismiss or, in the alternative, for summary judgment. Dr. Lies argues that he is not covered by the ADA; that the Rehabilitation Act is inapplicable; and that plaintiffs cannot recover against him on their state law causes of action. St. Helena argues that it complied with both the ADA and the Rehabilitation Act as a matter of law. Both defendants also submit that CAD is not a proper party to the action and that monetary relief is unavailable under the federal statutes.

DISCUSSION

I.   Plaintiffs' Standing to Seek Injunctive Relief

[Eds. Note: The court holds that both plaintiffs lack standing to seek injunctive relief under the ADA. However, with respect to Mrs. Aikins's ADA claim, the court gives her leave to amend her complaint to allege sufficient facts to establish her standing.]

* * *

II.   Plaintiffs' Claims under the Americans with Disabilities Act

Plaintiffs claim that defendants violated the Americans with Disabilities Act ("ADA") by denying Mrs. Aikins access to information in connection with the treatment of her husband. The ADA provides, in pertinent part: "No individual shall be discriminated against on the basis of disability in the full and equal enjoyment of the goods, services, facilities, privileges, advantages, or accommodations of any place of public accommodation by any person who owns, leases (or leases to), or operates a place of public accommodation." 42 U.S.C. § 12182(a).

A.   The ADA Does Not Apply to Dr. Lies

Dr. Lies contends that plaintiffs' claims against him under the ADA must fail because the Act does not apply to him in his capacity as an independent contractor with St. Helena. The regulations implementing the ADA alter the language of the statute slightly to read as follows: "No individual shall be discriminated against on the basis of disability . . . by any private entity who owns, leases (or leases to), or operates a place of public accommodation." 28 C.F.R. § 36.201(a). The preamble to the regulation notes that the change was designed to make clear that the regulation "places the ADA's nondiscrimination obligations on 'public accommodations' rather than on 'persons' or 'places of public accommodation.'" 36 C.F.R. App. B § 36.104.

The statute and the regulation both indicate that individuals may be liable under the ADA if they "own, lease[ ] (or lease[ ] to), or operate[ ]" a place of public accommodation. 42 U.S.C. § 12182(a); 28 C.F.R. § 35.201(a). The use of language relating to ownership or operation implies a requirement of control over the place providing services. Dr. Lies, however, is an independent contractor with St. Helena. He is not on the hospital's board of directors, and he has no authority to enact or amend hospital policy. Because he lacks the power to control hospital policy on the use of interpreters, this Court holds that Dr. Lies is not a proper defendant under the ADA.

Plaintiffs contend that this construction of the ADA undercuts the Act's purpose. Noting that the Act defines "public accommodation" to include the "professional office of a health care provider," 42 U.S.C. § 12181(7)(F), plaintiffs maintain that the Act would clearly cover Dr. Lies had he provided services to Mr. and Mrs. Aikins at his own office. They argue that he should not be able to escape liability under the ADA merely because in this case he provided services outside his office. "To hold otherwise," plaintiffs suggest, "would allow individuals to discriminate whenever they provide part of their services outside of their place of public accommodation while disallowing the very same type of discrimination for those services provided at the place of public accommodation."

Plaintiffs' policy argument does not warrant a departure from the statute's implicit requirement of ownership or control. The Court's construction of the Act is not at odds with the ADA's fundamental purpose of eliminating discrimination against individuals with disabilities, because it retains accountability for those in a position to ensure nondiscrimination.

B. St. Helena Has Not Shown That It Complied with the Act as a Matter of Law

St. Helena does not dispute that the ADA applies to it, *see* 42 U.S.C. § 12181(7)(F), but claims that it complied with the Act as a matter of law. Alternatively, St. Helena argues that compliance is excused, as it would impose an undue burden on the hospital. The regulations implementing the ADA provide that a "public accommodation shall furnish appropriate auxiliary aids and services where necessary to ensure effective communication with individuals with disabilities." 28 C.F.R. § 36.303(c).

This requirement is tempered by the general qualification that a public accommodation may treat disabled individuals in need of auxiliary aids and services differently from other individuals if "the public accommodation can demonstrate that [ensuring equality of treatment] would . . . result in an undue burden, i.e. significant difficulty or expense." § 36.303(a).

St. Helena bases its contention that it complied with the ADA as a matter of law on the following evidence and allegations: that its human resources department had in place a policy of providing interpreters to those in need of them; that the hospital posted signs notifying the public that information about T.D.D. services could be obtained by going to the switchboard; that the switchboard operator and the office of human resources maintained lists of interpreters; that Mr. Aikins's medical records contain a statement that "there were interpreters present at all times during the discussion with the patient and the family"; and that "the complaint is replete with descriptions of instances where information was exchanged between plaintiff Aikins and members of the St. Helena hospital staff." Defendant argues alternatively that provision of an interpreter on a twenty-four hour a day basis would impose an undue burden on the hospital.

The record does not reveal that St. Helena complied with the ADA as a matter of law. St. Helena has not demonstrated that it communicated effectively with plaintiff Aikins during her husband's stay in the hospital. Indeed, the hospital's allegations that communication was effective are undercut not only by plaintiff's own account of the episode but also by the fact that, for between twenty-four to thirty-six hours, Dr. Lies was under the concededly mistaken impression that Mr. Aikins had been without CPR for only four minutes following his heart attack, a critical fact. Furthermore, although the regulations provide that the hospital "shall furnish" appropriate auxiliary aids and services for non-hearing individuals, § 36.303(c), it appears that St. Helena relied almost exclusively on Mrs. Aikins to provide her own interpreters. There exists a genuine dispute as to the issue of St. Helena's compliance with the ADA.

Finally, the Court cannot say as a matter of law that provision of interpreters would have imposed an undue burden on the hospital. The regulations set out criteria for determining whether a proposed accommodation imposes an undue burden within the meaning of section 36.303(a). Section 36.104 provides, in pertinent part:

> In determining whether an action would result in an undue burden, factors to be considered include—(1) The nature and cost of the action needed under this part; (2) The overall financial resources of the site or sites involved in the action; the number of persons employed at the site; the effect on expenses and resources; legitimate safety requirements that are necessary for safe operation . . . ; or the impact otherwise of the action upon the

operation of the site; (3) The geographic separateness, and the administrative or fiscal relationship of the site or sites in question to any parent corporation or entity; (4) If applicable, the overall financial resources of any parent corporation or entity; the overall size of the parent corporation or entity with respect to the number of its employees; the number, type, and location of its facilities; and (5) If applicable, the type of operation or operations of any parent corporation or entity, including the composition, structure, and functions of the workforce of the parent corporation or entity.

§ 36.104.The question whether provision of interpreter services on some basis would pose an undue burden on St. Helena raises material issues of fact.

* * *

III. Plaintiffs' Claims under the Rehabilitation Act

* * *

B. Defendants Have Not Shown That They Complied with the Act as a Matter of Law

Defendants finally argue that they complied with the Rehabilitation Act as a matter of law. Defendant Lies argues that Mr. Aikins received precisely the same treatment that he would have received had Mrs. Aikins not been deaf. Defendant St. Helena maintains that it provided all that it was required to provide under the Act.

Both arguments are without merit. Even if Mr. Aikins received exactly the care that he would have received had Mrs. Aikins not been deaf, Dr. Lies misses the point. Mrs. Aikins's claims relate to her exclusion from meaningful participation in the decisions affecting her husband's treatment, not to the appropriateness of the treatment itself. As to the hospital's argument, the Court cannot infer from defendant's reference to its policies on interpreters and its own self-serving statements that it communicated effectively with plaintiff at all times that it complied with the Rehabilitation Act as a matter of law.

IV. Availability of Damages under the Federal Statutes

Defendants argue that Mrs. Aikins is not entitled to compensatory relief under either the ADA or the Rehabilitation Act. They are correct about the ADA. In cases involving claims under subchapter three of the ADA, the Act provides only for injunctive relief.... Plaintiffs appear to concede the unavailability of compensatory relief under the ADA in their opposition papers.

Because plaintiffs lack standing on the present record to assert claims for injunctive relief, the unavailability of damages under the ADA requires dismissal of all claims under the ADA. Such dismissal is without prejudice to plaintiffs' reinstating the ADA claims for injunctive relief upon a proper showing of standing.

As to Mrs. Aikins's claims under the Rehabilitation Act, the Ninth Circuit has held that damages are available for violations of the Act. Section 794a provides, in pertinent part: "The remedies, procedures, and rights set forth in title VI of the Civil Rights Act of 1964 shall be available to any person aggrieved by any act or failure to act by any recipient of Federal assistance . . . under section 794 of this title." 29 U.S.C. § 794a(a)(2). Exhaustion of administrative remedies is not a prerequisite to suit in the Ninth Circuit. The settled interpretation of section 794a in the Ninth Circuit is that money damages are available for violations of section 504 of the Rehabilitation Act, codified as section 794 of Title 29 of the United States Code. . . .

* * *

CONCLUSION

For the foregoing reasons, the Court hereby DISMISSES the following claims WITHOUT LEAVE TO AMEND: CAD's claims for damages; Mrs. Aikins's claims for damages under the ADA; [and] plaintiffs' claims against Dr. Lies under the ADA. . . .

Plaintiffs' remaining claims for injunctive relief are DISMISSED WITH LEAVE TO AMEND. . . .

Summary judgment is DENIED to both defendants on Mrs. Aikins's claims for damages under the Rehabilitation Act. . . .

NOTES AND QUESTIONS

1. *The personal side of* Aikins. Try to put yourself in Mrs. Aikins's shoes. Imagine how frightening it must have been to not be able to adequately communicate with the doctors about her husband's heart attack and then to find out that her husband had undergone a surgery that was completely unnecessary because he likely arrived at the hospital already brain dead. Short of having an interpreter available (which is arguably what should have occurred), could Mrs. Aikins or the hospital have done anything differently to avoid this situation? Is there any other method of communication that might have been effective? Assuming Mrs. Aikins could adequately type and read, what about typing messages back and forth on a computer screen? Do you think this method would result in effective communication?

2. *The ADA does not apply to Dr. Lies.* As the court discusses in *Aikins*, the ADA does not apply to Dr. Lies in his personal capacity because he is an independent contractor of the hospital and Title III of the ADA only applies to those who own, operate, or lease a place of public accommodation. Does the court's decision make sense to you? Or do you agree with Mrs. Aikins's argument that it does not make sense to not hold Dr. Lies liable when he is

working at the hospital but he would be liable if he were in his private practice office?

3. *Undue hardship.* The court states that there are genuine issues of fact regarding whether providing interpreter services would cause an undue hardship for the defendant. Imagine that you are in charge of complying with the ADA for the hospital. And imagine that the need for interpreter services at the hospital is completely unpredictable but that, on average, a sign language interpreter is requested about once per week. How would you structure the provision of sign language interpreters in a way that does not cause an undue hardship?

MATHEIS V. CSL PLASMA, INC.
936 F.3d 171 (3d Cir. 2019)

AMBRO, CIRCUIT JUDGE.

Congress, when it passed the Americans with Disabilities Act ("ADA"), found that "physical or mental disabilities in no way diminish a person's right to fully participate in all aspects of society, yet many people with physical or mental disabilities have been precluded from doing so because of discrimination." 42 U.S.C. § 12101(a)(1). The remedy for this finding was "to provide a clear and comprehensive national mandate for the elimination of discrimination against individuals with disabilities." 42 U.S.C. § 12101(b)(1). But is it discrimination for an establishment, in the name of safety, to bar everyone who uses a psychiatric service animal, including someone who safely participated more than four score times without assistance?

George Matheis, a retired police officer who has successfully managed a diagnosis of post-traumatic stress disorder ("PTSD"), routinely and safely donated plasma roughly 90 times in an 11-month period at CSL Plasma, Inc.'s plasma donation facility. CSL barred him from making further donations when he brought his new service dog, Odin, to the facility the next time. It reasoned that it has a policy to bar any individual who is prescribed daily more than two separate anxiety medications or who uses a service animal to manage anxiety. In its view, these people are categorically unsafe to donate plasma. The company required Matheis to provide a letter from his doctor stating he had no need for a service animal before it would screen him for further plasma donation. He sued, lost, and appeals to us.

We have two issues. We determine first whether plasma donation centers— facilities where members of the public have their plasma extracted in exchange for money—are subject to the ADA's prohibition on unreasonable discrimination. This turns on whether these facilities are "service establishments" under 42 U.S.C. § 12181(7)(F), which has produced a circuit split between the Tenth and Fifth Circuits. We conclude, like the

District Court here, that the Tenth Circuit got it right: the ADA applies to plasma donation centers.

So we next consider the question posed initially, whether CSL violated the ADA by imposing a blanket ban on prospective donors who use a psychiatric service animal. Here we part with the District Court. Public accommodations like CSL must permit disabled individuals to use service animals unless they can show a regulatory exception applies. CSL has failed to provide evidence to satisfy the relevant exception here—that any safety rule "be based on actual risks and not on mere speculation, stereotypes, or generalizations about individuals with disabilities." 28 C.F.R. § 36.301(B). Thus we reverse the grant of summary judgment and remand.

I.   Factual Background

CSL owns and operates a plasma donation facility in York, Pennsylvania. Its business is collecting human blood plasma from the public and selling it to third parties. It screens prospective donors for known health risks, extracts plasma from qualifying individuals, freezes it, and then ships it to manufacturing plants to be made into medicines. The donation process is intense; each session lasts as long as two hours, and donors, who give blood as often as twice a week, must each time pass an individualized screening process. This process includes a check of the donor's blood pressure and protein levels, along with questions to see how the donor is feeling and to check that he or she has not engaged in risky activities. CSL pays its donors as much as several hundred dollars a month for their plasma.

Matheis was involved in a deadly shooting incident while on duty as a SWAT officer with his police department in 2000. After that incident, he had problems socializing and was soon diagnosed with PTSD. His condition sometimes causes him to suffer panic attacks when exposed to crowded or confined spaces, altercations, or helicopter noise. He retired from the police force in 2007 to become a small business owner.

In 2016, Matheis decided to donate plasma to raise extra money. As noted, he did so approximately 90 times during that year at the CSL facility in York. These went off without a hitch, and CSL paid Matheis between $250–300 a month for his donations.

In October 2016, Matheis's eldest daughter enlisted in the Navy. Seeing the stress that her leaving caused her father, she bought him a dog, Odin, to help him cope with her absence. Odin was trained as a service dog for Matheis soon thereafter.

During Odin's initial training, Matheis brought him to CSL to introduce him to the facility. Immediately on entering the building, his phlebotomist (someone trained to draw blood from patients or donors) told him he could not have a dog on the premises. Matheis did not undergo CSL's individualized assessment to determine if he could safely donate that day;

instead his phlebotomist referred him to the CSL nurses' station. There he explained that Odin was a service animal that helped him manage his PTSD. The nurse referred him to a CSL manager, who explained that, under its policies, CSL permitted service animals for the blind but not for anxiety. Matheis again explained that Odin helped him manage his PTSD, a disability under the ADA. After a phone call, the manager told him he could not donate. Matheis offered to leave Odin in his car and donate without him. The manager rejected this, stating he could not donate until he brought back a letter from his healthcare provider saying he could safely donate without Odin. Matheis left CSL and has not returned to donate plasma since.

CSL's concern is not related to any health concerns that dogs like Odin pose; rather it has concluded that using a service animal for anxiety means that the donor's condition is too severe to undergo safely the donation process.

Matheis filed suit alleging discrimination for a failure to accommodate his condition. To establish his claim, he must show that (1) he is disabled, (2) CSL is a "public accommodation" under Title III of the ADA, and (3) it unlawfully discriminated against him on the basis of his disability by (a) failing to make a reasonable modification that was (b) necessary to accommodate his disability. *See PGA Tour, Inc. v. Martin*, 532 U.S. 661, 683 n.38, 121 S.Ct. 1879 (2001); *Berardelli v. Allied Servs. Inst. of Rehab. Med.*, 900 F.3d 104, 123 (3d Cir. 2018).

CSL does not dispute that Matheis is disabled or that Odin is a trained service animal. Thus this appeal hinges on the two issues noted above: whether the ADA applies to CSL; and, if so, whether its conduct was unlawful discrimination under the ADA. It moved for summary judgment contending that it was not subject to the ADA or, alternatively, that its policy—barring all individuals who use service animals for anxiety—was reasonable.

The District Court ruled that the ADA covered CSL, but that the company did not unlawfully discriminate because it had a legitimate, non-discriminatory reason for refusing to allow Matheis to donate plasma, a concern that he had severe anxiety. *Matheis v. CSL Plasma, Inc.*, 346 F. Supp. 3d 723, 734 (M.D. Pa. 2018). The Court buttressed what it recognized as a "necessary, yet counterintuitive," conclusion, *id.* at 735, by stressing CSL would let Matheis donate with Odin once he cleared it with a doctor. *Id.* at 737. But CSL's stance is that Matheis may not donate until he can safely donate *without* Odin.

Matheis appeals the ruling, while CSL cross-appeals contending it is not subject to the ADA at all. . . .

II. Jurisdiction and Standard of Review

The District Court had jurisdiction per 28 U.S.C. §§ 1331 and 1343(a)(4). Its grant of summary judgment was a final order, and so we have jurisdiction under 28 U.S.C. § 1291.

We review *de novo* a grant of summary judgment. We apply the same test the District Court would use. *Dwyer v. Cappell*, 762 F.3d 275, 279 (3d Cir. 2014). Under this test, reviewing the facts in the light most favorable to the non mover, we grant summary judgment "if the movant shows that there is no genuine dispute as to any material fact and the movant is entitled to judgment as a matter of law." Fed. R. Civ. P. 56(a).

III. Discussion

A. Does the ADA apply to plasma donation centers?

The ADA is divided into three titles of regulation—Title I (employers), Title II (governments), and Title III (public accommodations). Title III states that "[n]o individual shall be discriminated against on the basis of disability in the full and equal enjoyment of the goods, services, facilities, privileges, advantages, or accommodations of any place of public accommodation . . . ." 42 U.S.C. § 12182. It reflects the ADA's "comprehensive character," *Martin*, 532 U.S. at 675, 121 S.Ct. 1879, and defines "public accommodation" to include, in relevant part:

> a laundromat, dry-cleaner, bank, barber shop, beauty shop, travel service, shoe repair service, funeral parlor, gas station, office of an accountant or lawyer, pharmacy, insurance office, professional office of a health care provider, hospital, *or other service establishment*;

42 U.S.C. § 12181(7)(F) (emphasis added). Our focus narrows to whether a plasma donation facility is an "other service establishment."

This question has already produced a circuit split. In *Levorsen v. Octapharma Plasma, Inc.*, 828 F.3d 1227, 1229 (10th Cir. 2016), a divided panel held that plasma donation centers were subject to the ADA as service establishments. The Court relied on a broad, common definition of "service" and "establishment"—"conduct or performance that assists or benefits someone or something" and a "place of business," respectively. *Id.* at 1231. It reasoned that giving the term "service establishment" the ordinary meaning of its components yielded neither ambiguity nor an irrational result. Plasma donation centers "are 'place[s] of business.' . . . And they 'assist[ ] or benefit[ ]' those who wish to provide plasma for medical use— whether for altruistic reasons or for pecuniary gain—by supplying the trained personnel and medical equipment necessary to accomplish that goal." *Id.* at 1234.

The Fifth Circuit in *Silguero v. CSL Plasma, Inc.*, 907 F.3d 323 (5th Cir. 2018), viewed things differently. It made two base observations—the donor is not benefited by donating, and each of the listed service establishments provides services to the public in exchange for money. These features did not apply to plasma donation services. *Id.* at 329.

The dissent in *Levorsen* took a similar line. It followed *ejusdem generis*, a canon of statutory interpretation that interprets a last, general term by looking to the preceding examples. From these the dissenting judge proposed the following definition: a service establishment "offer[s] the public a 'service' (1) in the form of (a) expertise (e.g., barbers, beauticians. . ., and hospitals) or (b) specialized equipment (e.g., laundromats and gas stations), (2) for use in achieving some desired end, (3) in exchange for monetary compensation." *Levorsen*, 828 F.3d at 1235 (Holmes, J., dissenting). He concluded that plasma donation centers could not qualify as service establishments because donors do not pay money for the service and (confusingly) because the donation centers do not offer their services in order to benefit the public.

> [T]o the extent that plasma-donation centers provide services to the public—such as those services identified by Mr. Levorsen and the United States—they do not do so for the *public's* use in achieving a desired end; instead, they provide them for the *centers'* use in achieving a desired end. More specifically, plasma-donation centers provide the public with the expertise associated with blood [extraction] . . . so that the centers can sell the plasma to their customers in the pharmaceutical industry (i.e., the desired end)— not so that they can assist the public to achieve some desired end.

Id. at 1243 (emphases in original).

We align with the majority in the Tenth Circuit. First, at least here no support exists for the Fifth Circuit's statement that donors "do not benefit" from the act of donating. The record is unequivocal that Matheis and other donors receive money, a clear benefit, to donate plasma.

Second, Judge Holmes's attempt in his dissent to distinguish this benefit on the basis of the secondary profit motive of plasma facilities is unpersuasive. A bank, one of the listed examples in § 12181(7)(F), is an obvious example of a service establishment that uses the fruits of its public-facing services for subsequent profit. Not only does it provide the means and expertise to hold safely the public's money, it also may provide interest or other benefits (including cash or rewards) to convince customers to entrust them with their savings. That a bank subsequently invests, trades, or loans this money to third parties does not make it any less a service establishment with respect to the public.

Moreover, any emphasis on the direction of monetary compensation is, to us, unhelpful. Businesses that offer services to the public convey something of economic value in return for something else of economic value. The value received by the service provider and given by the customer is often money, but it need not be. Money is one proxy for economic value, and economic value is fungible.

The bank example shows we should not arbitrarily narrow the scope of "service establishments" to entities that receive compensation from customers in the form of money. Banks and their customers exchange sources of economic value that do not always fit into a simple "money for service" model. As noted, customers often receive money from banks for using the bank's service. Banks are hardly the only example of companies that pay the public to use their services. *Amicus* Plasma Protein Therapeutics Association conceded at oral argument that a pawnshop is a service establishment under Title III. It pays money in exchange for people's possessions. So too, as the District Court noted, is a recycling center a service establishment; it compensates consumers in exchange for their waste and has been held subject to the ADA. These examples underscore a simple fact: providing services means providing something of economic value to the public; it does not matter whether it is paid for with money or something else of value.

Hence we conclude that a plasma donation center is a service establishment under the ADA. It offers a service to the public, the extracting of plasma for money, with the plasma then used by the center in its business of supplying a vital product to healthcare providers. That both the center and members of the public derive economic value from the center's provision and public's use of a commercial service does not divorce the center from the other listed examples in § 12181(7)(F). Indeed this is an irreducible feature of a market system.

B. Did CSL discriminate against Matheis?

We next turn to whether CSL violated the ADA when it barred Matheis from donating plasma.

i. Legal standard

The statute requires that public accommodations not discriminate on the basis of disability. Discrimination includes:

> a failure to make *reasonable* modifications in policies, practices, or procedures, when such modifications are *necessary* to afford such goods, services, facilities, privileges, advantages, or accommodations to individuals with disabilities, unless the entity can demonstrate that making such modifications would *fundamentally alter the nature* of such goods, services, [etc.].

42 U.S.C. § 12182(b)(2)(A)(ii) (emphases added).

A company regulated under Title III may be held liable for failing to accommodate. This is "a standard that turn[s] on (1) whether the requested accommodation to the program was 'reasonable'; (2) whether it was necessary 'to assure meaningful access'; and (3) whether it would represent 'a fundamental alteration in the nature of [the] program.' " *Berardelli*, 900 F.3d at 115. The plaintiff bears the initial burden of establishing that the desired accommodation is reasonable and necessary, while the defendant bears the burden of showing that it would fundamentally alter the nature of the program. *Id.* at 124.

CSL does not contend that permitting Odin to accompany Matheis would fundamentally alter the nature of its service. Nor does it dispute Matheis's evidence showing that Odin is a necessary accommodation (indeed, CSL's policy assumes that Odin is a necessary accommodation and bars Matheis outright for it). The only question is whether his use of Odin is reasonable.

Title III entities are required by regulation to "modify policies, practices, or procedures to permit the use of a service animal by an individual with a disability." 28 C.F.R. § 36.302. In other words, use of a service animal by a disabled individual "is reasonable under the ADA as a matter of law" so long as no Department of Justice-promulgated regulation supersedes this general rule. *Berardelli*, 900 F.3d at 119 (vacating a jury verdict for a school district that denied one of its students with epilepsy use of her service dog).[2] The service-animal regulations satisfy Matheis's initial burden to show an accommodation is reasonable; CSL must establish that an exception to those regulations applies. *Id.* at 124.

This burden differs significantly from the test the District Court seems to have applied when it concluded CSL's denial was not based on a "discriminatory animus." It borrowed the employment discrimination framework from *McDonnell Douglas Corp. v. Green*, 411 U.S. 792, 93 S.Ct. 1817 (1973). That framework involves burden shifting: a plaintiff must establish a *prima facie* case of discrimination; when he does, the burden shifts to the employer to articulate some legitimate, nondiscriminatory reason for the adverse action against the employee. If the employer does so, the employee may attempt to show the reason is a pretext to hide discrimination.

Because a plaintiff need not show intentional discrimination to demonstrate a violation of Title III of the ADA, *Lentini v. Calif. Ctr. for the Arts, Escondido*, 370 F.3d 837, 846–47 (9th Cir. 2004), we reject using *McDonnell Douglas* in this context, and instead follow the *Berardelli* framework for ADA claims against a public accommodation. Thus we must determine whether CSL has established exceptions that permit a plasma donation center to deny a disabled individual's use of a service animal. If none apply, Matheis's use of Odin is a reasonable accommodation, and his claim succeeds.

---

[2] Though *Berardelli* involved the reasonableness of service animals under the Title II regulations (Part 35), the approach here is identical, as those animal service regulations use "materially identical language" as the regulations under the Title III regulations (Part 36). *Id.* at 118–19.

ii.   Regulatory exceptions

In *Berardelli* we concluded that a small group of regulatory exceptions, both within the animal service regulations and listed elsewhere in Part 35, formed the exclusive bases for a government entity to deny a service animal who is a necessary accommodation for a disabled person:

> [The regulations] specify the limited circumstances in which it would be unreasonable to require these actors to allow the use of service animals: if granting access would . . . pose a "direct threat" to the health or safety of others, *id.* §§ 35.139, 36.208, or if the animal is either "out of control" or "not housebroken,"[ ] *id.* §§ 35.136(b)(1)–(2), 36.302(c)(2)(i)–(ii) . . . . Subject to these exceptions, however, the regulations mandate that "[i]ndividuals with disabilities shall be permitted to be accompanied by their service animals in all areas of [a covered actor's facilities] where . . . program participants . . . are allowed to go." *Id.* § 36.302(c)(7); *see also id.* § 35.136(g).

Id. at 119.

As the citations to Part 36 indicate, identical regulations exist for Title III entities. None is relevant here. The closest fit is 28 C.F.R. § 36.208, which permits public accommodations to deny anyone who poses a "direct threat" to others. While CSL expresses concern that people like Matheis are a threat to staff and other donors, the "direct threat" exception requires "an individualized assessment" to determine "[t]he nature, duration, and severity of the risk; the probability that the potential injury will actually occur; and whether reasonable modifications of policies, practices, or procedures or the provision of auxiliary aids or services will mitigate the risk," 28 C.F.R. § 36.208, an assessment CSL did not perform.

That is not all that is relevant, however. The parties and the District Court each note the eligibility regulation for Title III public accommodations, 28 C.F.R. § 36.301, and it ultimately controls our inquiry. It states that "[a] public accommodation may impose legitimate safety requirements that are necessary for safe operation. Safety requirements must be based on actual risks and not on mere speculation, stereotypes, or generalizations about individuals with disabilities." 28 C.F.R. § 36.301(b). The parties agree CSL's policy deferring donors who use multiple anxiety medications or a service animal is a safety rule, so it must pass muster under § 36.301(b).

* * *

iii.   Is CSL's policy a valid safety rule?

Though CSL bears the burden to show its service animal policy is valid under § 36.301(b), the evidence it marshals on its behalf is unimpressive and not remotely adequate to confer summary judgment. It relies exclusively on a declaration from Dr. John Nelson, its divisional medical director, stating that "[d]onors with severe anxiety may be unable to follow directions, cause disturbances, impact the donation process . . .[,] putting staff at risk of getting stuck with the needle and other donors at risk of getting blood on them." It also states that "[i]t is my professional medical opinion that donors with severe anxiety present serious health and safety risks to themselves, medical staff, and other donors." The declaration's lone statement addressing the use of a service animal is that

> CSL's general policy is to defer a donor who requires more than two medications daily or a service animal for anxiety, until the need for medications or service animal decreases. . . . This policy is not directed to the use of a service dog, as CSL allows service dogs for vision-and hearing-impaired donors, but is based on the severity of the anxiety.

These statements don't get the job done. Indeed, they seem clearly speculative and to generalize widely about individuals who use psychiatric service animals, all of whom CSL apparently views as people with "severe anxiety." No medical justification or other scientific evidence undergirds CSL's implicit conclusion that all those persons have "severe anxiety" and will put staff, other donors, or themselves at risk when donating plasma. This conclusion is not even stated; Dr. Nelson does not connect the dots by attesting that using a service animal indicates "severe anxiety." This is clearly inadequate to show that CSL's policy is based on actual risk and not based on speculation, stereotypes, or generalizations.

* * *

IV. Conclusion

CSL is a public accommodation under Title III of the ADA, and so it applies to CSL's plasma donation center. Hence we affirm the District Court's ruling on this issue.

We reverse, however, its grant of summary judgment to CSL on whether it complied with the ADA. In doing so, we do not suggest that CSL would be wrong in the future to require a doctor's note stating Matheis may safely donate with Odin. Indeed, had CSL adopted such a stance from the start, we might agree with how the District Court ruled. But CSL concedes that it will only consider Matheis as a potential donor when he provides a doctor's note attesting he can safely donate *without* Odin. CSL's lone justification is its service animal policy, which it does not support with evidence showing that policy is based on actual risk and not speculation, generalizations, or stereotypes. Moreover, CSL fails to explain why Matheis, who has managed his PTSD for nearly two decades and safely donated plasma roughly 90 times, should only be considered safe to donate when he renounces the new service animal that helps him *better* manage his PTSD.

Thus we reverse and remand the District Court's grant of summary judgment in favor of CSL. On remand, the Court may determine whether to permit CSL to move for summary judgment on other grounds, to hold trial, or to conclude on the facts presented that CSL violated the ADA.

NOTES AND QUESTIONS

1.   *The coverage issue.* Were you surprised to see the coverage issue at play in this case? Unlike websites and insurance policies (both discussed in this chapter), plasma donation centers are actual physical structures open to the public. The court in *Matheis* holds that they fall into the category of public accommodations that includes: "a laundromat, dry-cleaner, bank, barber shop, travel service, shoe repair service, funeral parlor, gas station, office of an accountant or lawyer, pharmacy insurance office, professional office of a health care provider, hospital, or *other service establishment.*" 42 U.S.C. § 12181(7)(F). Perhaps surprisingly, there is a circuit split on this issue with the Fifth Circuit holding that because the donor is not benefiting by donating and the other establishments in this category provide services to the public in exchange for money, plasma donation centers do not fall under the coverage of Title III. *See* Silguero v. CSL Plasma, Inc., 907 F.3d 323, 329 (5th Cir. 2018). The court in *Matheis* points out that plasma donors *do* benefit from donating plasma—they are paid for it. *Matheis*, 936 F.3d at 177. And the court also notes that the fact that plasma donation centers do not receive money from the public does not mean they do not receive something of value. As a comparison, the court points to banks, who often pay customers in the form of interest or other rewards, as well as pawnshops who give money to customers in exchange for their used goods. *Id.* at 178. Was the court's analysis in *Matheis* straightforward to you or do you agree with the other side that there is something odd about classifying a plasma donation center as a service establishment?

2.   *Analyzing* Matheis. Once we get past the coverage issue, *Matheis* presents a straightforward application of two rules we've seen before in the Title I context. First, as the court noted, the district court was wrong to apply the *McDonnell Douglas* burden-shifting framework to Matheis's claim because that framework is designed to prove causation, which involves the intent to discriminate. But for a failure-to-accommodate claim under Title I or Title III—here, the failure to provide the plaintiff a reasonable modification by allowing in his service dog—intent to discriminate is not a necessary element. Second, as was discussed in the direct threat materials in Chapter 3, the plasma donation center cannot deny the plaintiff's admission with his service dog based on an alleged threat without undertaking an individualized analysis. The donation center had no evidence that Matheis's PTSD made it too dangerous for him to donate plasma, with or without his service dog.

3.   *Regulations regarding service animals.* The court in *Matheis* briefly discussed the Department of Justice's regulations regarding service animals. First, the regulations define service animal as any dog or miniature horse that is "individual trained to do work or perform tasks for the benefit of an individual with a disability. . . ." 28 C.F.R. § 36.104. The work performed by

the service animal must be directly related to the individual's disability, and may include tasks such as:

> assisting individuals who are blind . . . with navigation and other tasks, alerting individuals who are deaf . . . to the presence of people or sounds, providing non-violent protection or rescue work, pulling a wheelchair, assisting an individual during a seizure, alerting individuals to the presence of allergens, retrieving items . . ., providing physical support and assistance with balance and stability to individuals with mobility disabilities, and helping persons with psychiatric and neurological disability by preventing or interrupting impulsive or destructive behaviors.

Id. The regulations require public accommodations to modify their normal rules to allow the use of a service animal. The only exceptions are if the animal is out of control and the animal's handler does not take effective action to control it or if the animal is not housebroken. 28 C.F.R. § 36.302(c)(1)–(2). As for permissible inquiries to the disabled person seeking to enter the establishment with the service animal, only two questions can be asked: (1) if the animal is required because of a disability and (2) what work or task the animal has been trained to perform. The entity cannot ask about the person's disability, and cannot ask for documentation regarding the service animal or require the person to demonstrate the work or task that the animal has been trained to perform. *Id.* at § 36.302(c)(6).

Because documentation is not required, and because it is easy to purchase a service dog vest online, there have been many stories about individuals trying to enter places of public accommodation with "fake" service dogs. In fact, several states have prohibited falsely claiming pets as service animals so that they can be brought into places of public accommodation. *See* Adam Edelman, *Collared: New Laws Crack Down on Fake Service Dogs*, NBC NEWS (May 5, 2018), https://www.nbcnews.com/politics/politics-news/collared-new-laws-crack-down-fake-service-dogs-n871541. And yet, some pet owners are very emotionally attached to their pets and feel comforted by having their pets with them at all times. Should these pet owners have the same rights as those individuals who have valid service animals?

4.   *Only dogs or miniature horses.* The regulations regarding service animals make clear that only dogs and miniature horses can qualify as a service animal. That did not stop one pro se plaintiff from suing the City of Chicago because the City would not let the plaintiff bring his Guinea hog (named Chief Wiggum) with him to public places, including city beaches (where he was ejected after swimming with the hog in Lake Michigan) and other public parks. Mayle v. City of Chicago, 803 F.App'x 31 (7th Cir. 2020). Although this case was brought under Title II, as the court makes clear in footnote 2 in *Matheis*, the regulations regarding service animals are identical under Titles II and III. The City agreed with the plaintiff's assertion that the hog was necessary to alleviate his anxiety attacks and depression that are the result of his bipolar disorder. *Mayle*, 803 F.App'x at 32. But the court held that the regulations make clear that only dogs and miniature horses can be service

animals. 28 C.F.R. § 30.104 ("Other species of animals, whether wild or domestic, trained or untrained, are not service animals for the purposes of this definition."). The plaintiff also challenged the constitutionality of the regulation stating that it violates his right to equal protection. The court dismissed that claim, stating that the government only needs a rational basis for limiting service animals to dogs and miniature horses and the government has a legitimate interest in maintaining social order and public safety as well as giving the public predictability regarding what animals they might encounter in public places. *Mayle*, 803 F.App'x at 33. What do you think about the plaintiff's claim? Although dogs are very commonly used as service animals, once we move beyond dogs, who should get to decide whether other animals can be used as service animals? And what criteria should be used in making those decisions? In other words, why miniature horses and not Guinea hogs?

C. ACCESSIBILITY

Similar to the three levels of accessibility compliance under Title II (discussed in Section G of Chapter 5), public accommodations covered under Title III must comply with the accessibility rules based on when the entity was built or altered.

New buildings. As originally written, the ADA required public accommodations to design and construct new buildings to be readily accessible to and useable by individuals with disabilities. 42 U.S.C. 12183(a)(1). There are very lengthy and complicated guidelines that specify all aspects of the design of a new facility to make sure it is as fully accessible to individuals with disabilities as possible. These guidelines were modified in 2010, so that buildings that are built after March 15, 2012 must comply with these new guidelines. *See* https://www.ada.gov/regs2010/2010ADAStandards/2010ADAStandards.pdf.

Altered buildings. The ADA applies slightly less stringent requirements for buildings that were not built new after the ADA went into effect but that have been altered after that date. Thus, "with respect to a facility or part thereof that is altered . . . in a manner that affects or could affect the usability of the facility or part thereof, a failure to make alterations in such a manner that, to the maximum extent feasible, the altered portions of the facility are readily accessible to and usable by individuals with disabilities" violates the statute. 42 U.S.C. § 12183(a)(2). Not surprisingly, parties litigate over what constitutes an alteration sufficient to trigger the requirements of this section. Some examples of alterations include: "remodeling, renovation, rehabilitation, reconstruction, historic restoration, changes or rearrangement in structural parts or elements, and changes or rearrangement in the plan configuration of walls and full-height partitions." 28 C.F.R. § 36.402(b)(1). Changes that do not constitute an alteration might include normal maintenance, re-roofing, painting or wallpapering, asbestos removal, or changes to mechanical and electrical systems. 28 C.F.R. § 36.402(b)(2).

Existing buildings. For facilities that have not been built or altered after the ADA effective date, discrimination is defined to include: "(iv) a failure to remove architectural barriers, and communication barriers that are structural in nature, in existing facilities, . . . where such removal is *readily achievable.*" 42 U.S.C. § 12182(2)(A)(iv). This "readily achievable" standard is the subject of a great deal of litigation under Title III. Below is a case discussing how the standard operates in practice.

KENNEDY V. OMEGAGAS & OIL, LLC
748 F.App'x 886 (11th Cir. 2018)

PER CURIAM:

Plaintiff-Appellant Patricia Kennedy ("Plaintiff"), who is disabled, sued Defendant-Appellee Omega Gas & Oil, LLC ("Omega Gas" or "Defendant") to compel it to bring its premises at the gasoline service station and convenience store into compliance with Title III of the Americans with Disabilities Act, 42 U.S.C. §§ 12181–12189 ("ADA"). After a bench trial, the district court determined the majority of Plaintiff's complaint to be moot due to Defendant's remediation of the noncompliant structure or features and further held the alteration of the remaining barrier was not readily achievable. After reviewing the record and the parties' briefs, we affirm.

I.   BACKGROUND

Plaintiff Kennedy is mobility impaired and ambulates by wheelchair; she also struggles with the ability to grasp or turn objects with her hands. Omega Gas owns and operates a gas station and convenience store located at 1974 South Congress Avenue in West Palm Beach, Florida ("the Property"). Walid Alsheikh is the managing member of Omega Oil. Plaintiff visited Defendant's Property on January 14, 2017 and discovered several barriers that precluded her use of the Property and allegedly violated the ADA. Plaintiff documented evidence of the improperly marked and blocked handicapped parking space, including the placement of a dumpster and other barriers in the access aisle and faded blue paint to indicate the access aisle. She further noted unsecured floor mats at the entrance to the store and to the restroom. Due to the various barriers at the Property, Plaintiff was unable to enter the restroom but did observe several noncompliant features of the bathroom, including: the presence of a mop and bucket in the middle of the floor; a pedestal sink, which would prohibit her from utilizing the sink; sink and doorknob hardware in the shape of knobs, which require gripping and twisting to operate; missing or improperly placed grab bars near the toilet; a flush control on the incorrect side of the toilet; and a paper towel dispenser located too high to be reached.

Plaintiff retained an ADA inspector, who visited the property on March 20, 2017.

After filing her suit, Plaintiff revisited the Property on July 18, 2017 and again faced multiple barriers. While she did not attempt to access the bathroom on this visit, she noted that the handicap parking space was poorly marked by faded paint, that the access aisle was not clearly marked, and that furniture obstructed the access aisle to the space.

As the managing member of Omega Gas, Alsheihk operates the gas station and store on a day-to-day basis and has the authority to make and to enforce policies and procedures. Omega Gas acquired the Property in 2002 but did not know the age of the building. Alsheihk further stated that, prior to this suit, he had not made any improvements to the Property, with the exception of replacing existing fuel tanks. He believed, however, that the Property was in compliance with the ADA based on annual inspections by the State of Florida as part of the State's lottery licensing system and because he had never received any complaints. After receiving Plaintiff's complaint, Alsheikh used his background in civil engineering to remedy the noncompliant features of the Property. To do so, he obtained a copy of the ADA statute and performed some of the work himself or with the assistance of a handyman or plumber. Prior to the Plaintiff's inspector's visit, Alsheikh took the following action: removed the floor mats from inside the store and the bathroom; installed new grab bars in the bathroom to meet requirements for length and height; replaced the hardware on the bathroom door and the sink with lever handles; replaced the toilet with the flush located on the top of the toilet; installed a new paper towel dispenser at the correct height; replaced the sink and moved it to the correct height; replaced the sign for the bathroom and the handicap parking space to meet ADA requirements; and moved the handicap parking spot to a space not obstructed by the dumpster. Alsheikh's improvements to the Property were ongoing when it was inspected by Plaintiff's expert.

Plaintiff's expert inspector, Carlos Herrera, routinely conducts inspections to ensure ADA compliance. He holds a bachelor's degree in civil engineering, a Florida general contractor's license, and a certification for accessibility and plan review. During his March 20, 2017, inspection, Herrera noted several noncompliant features of the Property. He observed that it appeared that work was being done on the Property to make improvements, including the reassignment of the handicap parking space. At his visit, however, furniture was sitting in the handicap space. The signage was properly worded. In the bathroom, Herrera detailed the following problems with ADA compliance: the sign was improperly placed; the door did not have sufficient maneuvering clearance; the flush control was located on the top of the toilet rather than the open side of the toilet; the toilet was located at an improper distance from the wall; the sink was one inch too high from the floor; and the bathroom did not have the requisite sixty inches of maneuverable floor space. To obtain a compliant bathroom, the floor space would have to comply with either the circle or t-shape methods. The circle method requires a sixty inch radius in all directions, while the t-shape requires four feet of clear floor space in one direction and three feet of clear floor space in the other direction. In his report, Herrera estimated the noncompliant features could be remedied for approximately $7,075. This estimate included a projected cost of $4,650 to remedy the lack of maneuverable floor space in the bathroom by moving a bathroom wall approximately three inches to achieve sixty inches of maneuverable space. Herrera's estimate, however, did not factor in the actual mechanics of moving the restroom wall at the site; it reflects a cost analysis for a simple separating wall based on an average of other sites he had visited in his career rather than a specific estimate for the actual Property. In addition, Herrera testified his assessment did not consider whether moving the wall to add three inches of floor space was readily achievable.

After receiving Herrera's report during discovery, Alsheikh continued to make alterations to the Property to bring it into compliance with the ADA. He added two more handicap signs to the bathroom, placing one on the latch side as required by the ADA. He also removed the door closer, which obviated the need for twelve inches of maneuvering space. He removed the new toilet with the flush control on the top and bought and installed a second toilet with flush controls on the open side. The new toilet was installed so that the center was the proper distance from the wall. The sink was lowered one more inch to be compliant with ADA requirements. The noncompliant bathroom finishes that were replaced—the sink, toilet, hardware, and paper towel dispenser—were thrown away. At trial, Defendant presented photographic evidence that all items noted in Herrera's report were addressed and fixed to ADA standards, with the exception of moving the bathroom wall to obtain three more inches of maneuverable space. In addition, Alsheikh instituted a new policy requiring Omega Gas's employees and tenants to keep the handicap parking space and bathroom free from any obstacles or obstructions, such as furniture left near the dumpster or cleaning supplies left in the bathroom. All parties were instructed to remove any barriers or obstructions left by customers promptly.

Alsheikh testified that he contacted two contractors to provide estimates for renovating the bathroom to meet the requirements for maneuverable space. At trial, the contractors testified that they estimated the renovation would cost $80,000 or $85,950. Neither contractor was familiar with the t-shape method of ADA compliance, and both based their estimates off of the circle method, which required moving a wall. Both contractors recognized that the wall in question contained electrical, gas, and plumbing lines, and Alsheihk testified he would be required close the gas station and store during the renovation. One of the contracting companies also suggested retaining an engineer, at an additional cost, for the project.

II. PROCEDURAL HISTORY

After a bench trial, the district court issued its Memorandum Opinion finding that Plaintiff was not entitled to judgment in her favor. The district court found that Defendant had remedied all of Plaintiff's complaints, except for the maneuvering space in the bathroom, and that because the violations could not reasonably be expected to recur, they were moot. The district court further found Plaintiff failed to meet her burden to prove that the widening of the bathroom by moving the wall was readily achievable. After entry of this order and the final judgment, Plaintiff timely appealed.

III. ISSUES

1. Whether the district court erred in finding Plaintiff's claims, with the exception of the maneuverable floor space, were moot due to Defendant's remedial conduct.

2. Whether the district court erred in finding Plaintiff failed to meet her burden at trial that the widening of the bathroom was readily achievable.

* * *

V. ANALYSIS

We first address whether Defendant's remedial actions have mooted Plaintiff's claim and then turn to the question of whether Plaintiff carried her burden on the readily achievable analysis for the sole remaining barrier to ADA compliance.

A. Mootness

This court may only entertain "Cases and Controversies" pursuant to Article III of the United States Constitution. *See Sheely*, 505 F.3d at 1183. We have held "a case is moot when it no longer presents a live controversy with respect to which the court can give meaningful relief. If events that occur subsequent to the filing of a lawsuit . . . deprive the court of the ability to give the plaintiff . . . meaningful relief, then the case is moot and must be dismissed." *Id.* This doctrine, however, does not end our inquiry. An exception to the case at hand requires our attention: "The doctrine of *voluntary* cessation provides an important exception to the general rule that a case is mooted by the end of the offending behavior." *Id.* The Supreme Court has spoken to this issue:

> It is well settled that a defendant's voluntary cessation of a challenged practice does not deprive a federal court of its power to determine the legality of the practice. If it did, the courts would be compelled to leave the defendant free to return to his old ways. In accordance with this principle, the standard we have announced for determining whether a case has been mooted by

the defendant's voluntary conduct is *stringent*: A case *might* become moot if the subsequent events made it *absolutely clear* that the allegedly wrongful behavior *could not reasonably be expected to recur*.

Friends of the Earth, Inc. v. Laidlaw Envtl. Servs. (TOC), Inc., 528 U.S. 167, 189, 120 S.Ct. 693 (2000). The party asserting mootness carries the "formidable" and "heavy burden" of persuasion when asserting its conduct cannot reasonably be expected to recur. *Sheely*, 505 F.3d at 1184. In assessing this standard, this Court looks to the following factors:

> (1) whether the challenged conduct was isolated or unintentional, as opposed to a continuing and deliberate practice; (2) whether the defendant's cessation of the offending conduct was motivated by a genuine change of heart or timed to anticipate suit; and (3) whether, in ceasing the conduct, the defendant has acknowledged liability.

Id.

After reviewing the record, including photographic evidence and the bench trial transcript, we conclude Defendant remediated each of the ADA violations noted by Plaintiff and her expert, Herrera—with the exception of the maneuverable floor space in the bathroom—and thus rendered Plaintiff's complaint as to these noncompliant features moot. Defendant's testimony, through its managing partner Alsheikh, indicated that its ongoing violations of the ADA were unintentional and erroneously founded on the belief that its Property was not in violation. Alsheikh testified that the Property was inspected annually by the State for the purposes of its lottery licensure, and Omega Gas had never been informed of its noncompliance. Plaintiff did not put forth evidence of a malicious or reckless disregard for the ADA or for any disabled customers. In fact, the testimony indicated Omega Gas had never before received a complaint that its Property was noncompliant. Thus, the first factor weighs in favor of Defendant.

The second prong involves Defendant's motivation behind the remedial changes to its Property. As we have stated before, "we are more likely to find that cessation moots a case when cessation is motivated by a defendant's genuine change of heart rather than his desire to avoid liability." *Sheely*, 505 F.3d at 1186. The record clearly demonstrates Omega Gas immediately began correcting any barriers or noncompliant features of its Property upon service of Plaintiff's complaint. Alsheikh testified that he obtained a copy of the ADA statute to educate himself as to the requirements and personally performed or oversaw all of the remedial work to ensure it was done correctly. Plaintiff's expert stated he observed work in progress when he visited the Property for his inspection, and Plaintiff herself did not note any noncompliant features during her third visit to the Property in September 2017, two months before the bench trial. Further,

Defendant instituted new policies and procedures for its employees and tenants to follow regarding the monitoring of the handicap parking space and the proper storage of equipment to ensure movable barriers, such as the mop bucket or furniture, do not preclude access to or navigation around the Property. *Contra Sheely*, 505 F.3d at 1186 (noting that defendant's voluntary cessation occurred on the eve of trial after months of discovery and mediation).

As to the third element, we conclude the Defendant acknowledged liability by admitting that the Property was noncompliant and by actively working to correct the noncompliant features. Plaintiff's contention that Defendant never acknowledged liability is not supported by the record. We conclude each factor of the *Sheely* test weights in Defendant's favor.

Plaintiff further argues Defendant should be subject to an injunction ensuring compliance with the ADA because the changes made are not permanent in nature and thus can reasonably be expected to recur. We disagree. Defendant's changes are mostly structural, in that they concern fixed features of the Property such as the sink, toilet, and grab bars. Unlike in *Sheely*, which involved a discriminatory policy prohibiting the presence of service dogs at a radiology clinic, the changes here are more permanent in nature. Alsheikh testified that he disposed of the old, noncompliant fixtures, and we note it would be an unorthodox business practice to spend thousands of dollars on purchasing and installing new fixtures (e.g., the toilet, sink, paper towel dispenser, grab bars, signage, and hardware) simply to rip them out and replace them with new, noncompliant fixtures. Thus, we conclude Defendant has effectively remediated each of the ADA violations noted in Herrera's expert report, with the exception of the maneuverable floor space in the bathroom, and has thus deprived this court of jurisdiction under the mootness doctrine.

B. Readily Achievable

With regard to the lack of maneuverable space in the bathroom, Plaintiff contends Defendant failed to correct the issue, despite the fact that the bathroom wall could have been moved approximate three inches to achieve ADA compliance. Both parties agree that the Property constituted an "existing facility" rather than "new construction." As this court has previously determined, "[t]he ADA imposes different requirements on the owners and operators of facilities that existed prior to [the ADA's] enactment date [in 1993]." *Gathright-Dietrich v. Atlanta Landmarks, Inc.*, 452 F.3d 1269, 1273 (11th Cir 2006). In an existing facility, "the ADA states that discrimination includes a private entity's 'failure to remove architectural barriers . . . where such removal is readily achievable.' " *Id.* (quoting 42 U.S.C. § 12192(b)(2)(A)(iv)). "Readily achievable" is defined under the ADA as "easily accomplished and able to be carried out without much difficulty or expense." 42 U.S.C. § 12181(9). In establishing this standard, Congress included a list of factors to consider when evaluating whether the barrier removal is "readily achievable":

> (1) nature and cost of the action; (2) overall financial resources of the facility or facilities involved; (3) number of persons employed at such facility; (4) effect on expenses and resources; (5) impact of such action upon the operation of the facility; (6) overall financial resources of the covered entity; (7) overall size of the business of the covered entity; (8) the number, type, and location of its facilities; (9) type of operation or operations of the covered entity, including composition, structure, and functions of the workforce of such entity; and (10) geographic separateness, administrative or fiscal relationship of the facility of facilities in question to the covered entity.

Gathright-Dietrich, 452 F.3d at 1273 (citing 42 U.S.C. § 12181(9)). In this action, Plaintiff and Defendant disagree on the burden of production. Our case law, however, clearly speaks to this issue. In *Gathright-Dietrich*, this court adopted the approach set out by the Tenth Circuit in *Colorado Cross Disability Coalition v. Hermanson Family Ltd. Partnership*, 264 F.3d 999 (10th Cir. 2001). *See Gathright-Dietrich*, 452 F.3d at 1273. As we announced in that seminal decision:

> Under this approach [as established in *Colorado Cross*], the plaintiff has the initial burden of production to show (1) that an architectural barrier exists; and (2) that the proposed method of architectural barrier removal is "readily achievable," i.e., "easily accomplishable and able to be carried out without much difficulty or expense" under the particular circumstances of the case. If the plaintiff meets this burden, the defendant then bears the ultimate burden of persuasion that barrier removal is not "readily achievable."

Id. The plaintiff's initial burden is not light. Rather, "a plaintiff must present sufficient evidence so that a defendant can evaluate the proposed solution to a barrier, the difficulty of accomplishing it, the cost implementation, and the economic operation of the facility. Without evidence on these issues, a defendant cannot determine if it can meet is subsequent burden of persuasion." *Id.* at 1274.

The facts considered and analysis conducted by the *Gathright-Dietrich* court are illustrative to the facts presented in this case. In *Gathright-Dietrich*, disabled persons sought alterations to The Fox Theatre, a historic theater and event space in Atlanta, Georgia. The court concluded the plaintiffs "submitted three proposed options relating to wheelchair seating, but they failed to produce any reliable evidence that those proposals were 'readily achievable.'" *Id.* at 1274. Moreover, the proposed modifications "were non-specific, conceptual proposals that did not provide any detailed cost analysis," and the plaintiffs "failed to provide expert testimony to assure the feasibility of their proposed seating modifications and did not, in any meaningful way, address the engineering and structural concerns associated with their proposals[.]" *Id.* at 1274–75. Finally, the plaintiffs did not "produce a financial expert to link the estimated costs of their proposals with The Fox's ability to pay for them" and also "failed to take even the rudimentary steps of formulating what those estimated costs might be or providing any evidence of The Fox's financial position and ability to pay those costs." *Id.* at 1275. The court readily concluded the plaintiffs fundamentally failed to carry their initial burden that the proposed modifications were "readily achievable." *Id.*

The same can be said for this case. At trial, Plaintiff, through her expert, presented evidence that moving the bathroom wall to provide the required maneuverable space would cost an estimated $4,560. Herrera based this figure off of his past experience and the work he has performed as a contractor, and this estimate was described at trial as "a ballpark figure for moving a plumbing wall and a partition wall, new flooring, new ceiling, that is it." During his testimony, Herrera admitted that he did not conduct any analysis as to the structure of the building, including the presence of plumbing, electrical, and gas lines or the material of the wall. Further, Herrera admitted that his estimate was not specific to the Property but rather "an average based on other sites." He further stated he failed to conduct a "readily achievable" analysis in preparing his report. Furthermore, Plaintiff failed to present any evidence as to Defendant's ability to fund this remediation—much less the $80,000 plus estimates Alsheikh received from contractors he contacted—or the effects that construction would have on the business (i.e., requiring the business to cease operations while gas, electrical, and plumbing lines were moved). In short, Plaintiff failed to carry her burden of proof by failing to provide "sufficient evidence for [Defendant to] evaluate the proposed solution," by utilizing only a generalized, non-specific proposal, and by failing to provide any semblance of a cost analysis.

VI. CONCLUSION

For the foregoing reasons, we affirm the district court's judgment finding Plaintiff's claim for all the ADA violations—excepting the maneuverable floor space in the bathroom—to be moot and ruling that Plaintiff failed to carry her burden in proving that remediation of the bathroom floor space was "readily achievable."

AFFIRMED.

[Concurring opinion has been omitted.]

NOTES AND QUESTIONS

1. *Understanding mootness.* This is the first time we have come across the issue of mootness in this book. The reason for that is because of the

remedial scheme for Title III. As mentioned earlier, because Congress wanted Title III to be applied broadly (to *all* places of public accommodation, regardless of how small) the compromise struck was that there are no money damages available when a private plaintiff files suit under Title III. Instead, plaintiffs can only sue for injunctive relief (and attorney's fees, if the plaintiff is the prevailing party). The mootness issue arises when the defendant has already remedied all of plaintiff's alleged violations of the statute. If the defendant does so, the plaintiff's suit becomes "moot" because there is nothing left for the judge to do. There is no longer a "live controversy with respect to which the court can give meaningful relief." If the plaintiff could seek monetary damages, then the claim wouldn't be moot even if the defendant cured its violations of the ADA because the court could still award the plaintiff money damages. But because the plaintiff cannot seek money damages under Title III, and if the injunctive relief the plaintiff sought has already been accomplished, there is nothing for the court to award. The defendant in *Kennedy* had already remedied the structural features that plaintiff's complaint addressed, and seemed to do so in good faith; accordingly, the court held that the dispute was moot with respect to all of the alleged violations besides the maneuverable floor space in the bathroom (the one issue the defendant had not remedied).

More difficult mootness issues arise when the challenge is not to accessibility features as in this case, but rather to the defendant's failure to provide reasonable modifications, such as refusing to allow service animals or not providing a sign language interpreter in a hospital. In those cases, the plaintiff might be able to successfully argue that the violating behavior is likely to recur. As the court stated in this case, "A case *might* become moot if the subsequent events made it *absolutely clear* that the allegedly wrongful behavior *could not reasonably be expected to recur.*" *Kennedy*, 748 F. App'x at 891 (quoting Friends of the Earth, Inc. v. Laidlaw Envtl. Servs. (TOC), Inc., 528 U.S. 167, 189, 120 S.Ct. 693 (2000)). Analysis of this exception to the mootness rule entails three elements: (1) whether the challenged conduct was isolated or unintentional, as opposed to a continuing and deliberate practice; (2) whether the defendant's cessation of the offending conduct was motivated by a genuine change of heart or timed to anticipate suit; and (3) whether, in ceasing the conduct, the defendant has acknowledged liability. *Id.* Examples of a plaintiff's claim not being moot include the situation where the defendant alleges that it will cease the discriminatory practice (such as refusing service animals) on the eve of trial and perhaps without acknowledging any wrongdoing. In those situations, it is easy to see how the violating behavior is likely to recur.

2.   *Readily achievable.* The defendant in the *Kennedy* case was wise to make many of the changes that the plaintiff noted were in violation of the Title III because the defendant would very likely have lost in claiming they were not "readily achievable," which is defined as "easily accomplishable and able to be carried out without much difficult or expense." 42 U.S.C. § 12181(9). Modifications such as placing paper towel dispensers at the right height and changing the type of door handles would easily meet that standard. The one change the defendant objected to as not readily achievable was reconfiguring

the restroom so that it had more maneuverable floor space. This barrier as well as a request to ramp steps are probably the two most often litigated accessibility barriers. Although the DOJ regulations (provided below) mention both as barriers for which the removal of might be readily achievable, many defendants succeed in proving that the barrier removal is *not* readily achievable. As discussed in *Kennedy*, although it is the defendant's ultimate burden to prove that removing a barrier is not readily achievable, the court relies on a leading Tenth Circuit case that held that the plaintiff must initially "present evidence tending to show that the suggested method of barrier removal is readily achievable under the particular circumstances." *See* Colorado Cross Disability Coalition v. Hermanson Family Ltd. Partnership I, 264 F.3d 999, 1002 (10th Cir. 2001). As the court stated in *Kennedy*, the plaintiff's burden is not light. In *Colorado Cross*, the barrier at issue was steps providing access to a building that was historically significant. The plaintiff presented two expert witnesses—one that testified about the conceptual design of a ramp that would comport with the building's historic significance and gave a cost estimate and another that presented evidence about the defendant's ability to afford the ramp. *Id.* at 1007–08. Despite this, the court in *Colorado Cross* held that:

> While this is a close case, we conclude Plaintiff introduced evidence regarding only speculative concepts of ramp installation, rather than evidence that a specific design was readily achievable. . . . Plaintiff also failed to provide any precise cost estimates regarding the proposed modification. Perhaps most importantly, Plaintiff's expert testimony failed to demonstrate that under the particular circumstances installing a ramp would be readily achievable. Instead, [plaintiff's] expert provided speculative conceptual ideas, rather than a specific design which would be easily accomplishable and able to be carried out without much difficulty or expense. [Plaintiff's expert] acknowledged that his sketch was conceptual and that he did not intend the sketch to be a construction drawing.

Id. at 1009. Similarly, in the *Kennedy* case, the plaintiff's claim failed because her expert's testimony only provided a ball-park estimate of the cost of removing a wall to provide more maneuverable space in the bathroom. Should the burden placed on plaintiffs in these cases be this high? In other words, is it fair for the plaintiff to have the obligation of figuring out how the defendant's barriers (which arguably violate the ADA) should be removed? Why or why not?

Not all courts agree with the standard set by the Tenth Circuit in *Colorado Cross*. In *Molski v. Foley Estates Vineyard and Winery, LLC,* 531 F.3d 1043 (9th Cir. 2008), the court said that, at least with respect to barrier removal for historic facilities, the defendant should have the initial burden of production, not the plaintiff.

> By placing the burden of production on the defendant, we place the burden on the party with the best access to information regarding the historical significance of the building. The defendant sought the

historical designation in this case. Thus, the defendant possesses the best understanding of the circumstances under which that designation might be threatened. . . . As a result, the defendant is in a better position to introduce, as part of its affirmative defense, detailed evidence and expert testimony concerning whether the historic significance of a structure would be threatened or destroyed by the proposed barrier removal plan.

Id. at 1048. The court in *Molski* also stated: "We need not require an ADA plaintiff to undertake such heroic measures. Congress relies on private actors, i.e., disabled individuals, to enforce the ADA by filing lawsuits. Thus plaintiffs should not be deterred from filing meritorious claims by an inappropriate allocation of the burden of production." *Id.* at 1049. Does this court's analysis change your mind about which party should bear the initial burden of production in these cases?

3. *DOJ Regulations.* The regulations promulgated by the Department of Justice (DOJ) provide specific examples of removal of barriers that should be readily achievable:

1. Installing ramps;
2. Making curb cuts in sidewalks and entrances;
3. Repositioning shelves;
4. Rearranging tables, chairs, vending machines, display racks, and other furniture;
5. Repositioning telephones;
6. Adding raised markings on elevator control buttons;
7. Installing flashing alarm lights;
8. Widening doors;
9. Installing offset hinges to widen doorways;
10. Eliminating a turnstile or providing an alternative accessible path;
11. Installing accessible door hardware;
12. Installing grab bars in toilet stalls;
13. Rearranging toilet partitions to increase maneuvering space;
14. Insulating laboratory pipes under sinks to prevent burns;
15. Installing a raised toilet seat;
16. Installing a full-length bathroom mirror;
17. Repositioning the paper towel dispenser in a bathroom;
18. Creating designated accessible parking spaces;
19. Installing an accessible paper cup dispenser at an existing inaccessible water fountain;

20.   Removing high pile, low density carpeting; or

21.   Installing vehicle hand controls.

28 C.F.R. § 36.304(b). As was demonstrated in the *Kennedy* case, the expense of these items varies widely. Repositioning a paper towel dispenser is very cheap, but widening doors or installing ramps is likely to be much more expensive. Accordingly, the fact that a modification is mentioned in this DOJ regulation does not mean that a court will necessarily find removal of the barrier to be readily achievable. Courts decide these issues on a case-by-case basis. Because the statute cites to factors that should inform the readily achievable standard, *see* 42 U.S.C. § 12181(9) (quoted in *Kennedy*), the size and resources of the defendant is going to be pivotal in the determination of whether barrier removal is readily achievable.

4.   *An accessibility exercise.* The next time you are in a small, locally owned store or restaurant (i.e., not a national chain), try to imagine encountering the business as if you were using a wheelchair (assuming you do not already do so). Could you easily get from the parking lot to the front door? Is the front door flush with the sidewalk in front of it or is there a step (or steps) to enter the business? Would the front door be hard to open if you had limited upper body strength or mobility? Could the wheelchair fit through the door easily? Once inside, could you maneuver your wheelchair easily through the store or restaurant or are there tables, chairs, or racks or shelves with merchandise in the way? Visit the restroom. Could you get your wheelchair through the restroom door? Could you maneuver the wheelchair to and inside a bathroom stall? Are there grab bars inside of the bathroom stall? Would you be able to reach the sink? The soap dispenser? The paper towel dispenser? If there are pipes exposed under the sink, are they insulated? Do you know why this matters? Could you easily pull open the restroom door to get out? Most importantly, how did this exercise make you feel about accessibility barriers more generally?

GIL V. WINN DIXIE STORES, INC.

242 F.Supp.3d 1315 (S.D. Fla. 2017)

ROBERT N. SCOLA, JR., UNITED STATES DISTRICT JUDGE.

The Plaintiff, Juan Carlos Gil, sued Winn-Dixie Stores, Inc. ("Winn-Dixie") for injunctive relief under Title III of the Americans with Disabilities Act of 1990, 42 U.S.C. §§ 12181–12189 (the "ADA"). This matter is before the Court on Winn-Dixie's Motion for Judgment on the Pleadings. . . . For the following reasons, the Court . . . **denies** the Motion for Judgment on the Pleadings.

1.   Background

Plaintiff Gil is legally blind and suffers from a learning disability; "therefore [he] is substantially limited in performing one or more major life activities . . . ." In order to access and comprehend information on the internet, Mr. Gil must use screen reader software. Defendant Winn-Dixie is a grocery and pharmacy store chain. Winn-Dixie operates a website, www.winndixie.com, that allows consumers to locate physical Winn-Dixie store locations, fill and refill prescriptions for in-store pick-up or delivery, learn about Winn-Dixie brand items, access home-cooking recipes, and receive information about product recalls.

The Plaintiff alleges that when he attempted to access Winn-Dixie's website, the website did not integrate with his screen reader software, "nor was there any function within [the] website to permit access for [the] visually impaired through other means." The Plaintiff alleges that due to the website's inaccessibility, the Defendant has not provided full and equal enjoyment of the services, facilities, privileges, advantages and accommodations provided by and through its website. He also claims that, for individuals "who are limited in their ability to travel outside their home, the internet is one of the few available means of access to the goods and services in our society."

On July 12, 2016, the Plaintiff filed the instant lawsuit, claiming that Winn-Dixie's website is in violation of the ADA because it is inaccessible to the visually impaired. On October 24, 2016, the Defendant filed its Motion for Judgment on the Pleadings, asserting that websites are not places of public accommodation under the ADA, and thus its website could not have violated the ADA as a matter of law. . . .

* * *

3.   Analysis

* * *

Title III of the ADA prohibits the owner of a place of public accommodation from discriminating "on the basis of disability in the full and equal enjoyment of the goods, services, facilities, privileges, advantages, or accommodations of any place of public accommodation. . ." 42 U.S.C. § 12182(a). The ADA defines a public accommodation as a private entity whose operations affect commerce, and which falls within one of the following twelve categories:

A)   an inn, hotel, motel, or other place of lodging, except for an establishment located within a building that contains not more than five rooms for rent or hire and that is actually occupied by the proprietor of such establishment as the residence of such proprietor;

B)   a restaurant, bar, or other establishment serving food or drink;

C)   a motion picture house, theater, concert hall, stadium, or other place of exhibition or entertainment;

D) an auditorium, convention center, lecture hall, or other place of public gathering;

E) a bakery, grocery store, clothing store, hardware store, shopping center, or other sales or rental establishment;

F) a laundromat, dry-cleaner, bank, barber shop, beauty shop, travel service, shoe repair service, funeral parlor, gas station, office of an accountant or lawyer, pharmacy, insurance office, professional office of a health care provider, hospital, or other service establishment;

G) a terminal, depot, or other station used for specified public transportation;

H) a museum, library, gallery, or other place of public display or collection;

I) a park, zoo, amusement park, or other place of recreation;

J) a nursery, elementary, secondary, undergraduate, or postgraduate private school, or other place of education;

K) a day care center, senior citizen center, homeless shelter, food bank, adoption agency, or other social service center establishment; and

L) a gymnasium, health spa, bowling alley, golf course, or other place of exercise or recreation.

42 U.S.C. § 12181(7).

The Attorney General has promulgated regulations that further define a public accommodation as "a facility operated by a private entity, whose operations affect commerce and fall within at least one of [42 U.S.C. § 12181(7)'s twelve categories]." 28 C.F.R. § 36.104. The regulation defines "facility" as "all or any portion of buildings, structures, sites, complexes, equipment, rolling stock or other conveyances, roads, walks, passageways, parking lots, or other real or personal property, including the site where the building, property, structure, or equipment is located." *Id.*

Winn-Dixie admits that its physical grocery stores and pharmacies are places of public accommodation. However, Winn-Dixie disputes that its website qualifies as a public accommodation under the ADA. The Plaintiff asserts that Winn-Dixie's website is a public accommodation for two reasons. First, the Plaintiff asserts that Winn-Dixie's website is a public accommodation in and of itself because it allows customers to fill or re-fill prescriptions for in-store pick up or for delivery. Therefore, the Plaintiff asserts that this service makes Winn-Dixie's website a sales establishment, which is an enumerated public accommodation pursuant to the ADA. Second, the Plaintiff asserts that the website is "directly connected" to the physical stores and has a "true nexus" to Winn-Dixie's grocery and pharmacy stores. In furtherance of this assertion, the Plaintiff alleges that the website "augments" Winn-Dixie's physical store locations by assisting customers in finding physical store locations, educating the public as to the line of Winn-Dixie brand grocery items as well as other grocery items, and providing the public with the ability to fill and re-fill prescriptions from its pharmacy for in-store pick-up and delivery.

Courts are split on whether the ADA limits places of public accommodation to physical spaces. Courts in the First, Second, and Seventh Circuits have found that the ADA can apply to a website independent of any connection between the website and a physical place. *See, e.g., Morgan v. Joint Admin. Bd., Retirement Plan of the Pillsbury, Co., and others*, 268 F.3d 456, 459 (7th Cir. 2001) (stating that "An insurance company can no more refuse to sell a policy to a disabled person over the Internet than a furniture store can refuse to sell furniture to a disabled person who enters the store. . . The site of the sale is irrelevant to Congress's goal of granting the disabled equal access to sellers of goods and services."); *Nat'l Fed'n of the Blind v. Scribd Inc.*, 97 F.Supp.3d 565, 576 (D. Vt. 2015) (holding that Scribd's website, which allows consumers to access a digital library for a monthly fee, is a place of public accommodation even though it is not associated with any physical location); *Nat'l Ass'n of the Deaf v. Netflix, Inc.*, 869 F.Supp.2d 196, 200–02 (D. Mass. 2012) (concluding that Netflix's on-demand service website is a place of public accommodation even though its services are accessed exclusively in the home). Courts in these circuits have typically looked at Congress's intent that individuals with disabilities fully enjoy the goods, services, privileges and advantages available indiscriminately to other members of the public, and at the legislative history of the ADA, which indicates that Congress intended the ADA to adapt to changes in technology. *See, e.g., Scribd Inc.*, 97 F.Supp.3d at 574–76; *Netflix, Inc.*, 869 F.Supp.2d at 200–01.

On the other hand, courts in the Third, Sixth, and Ninth Circuits have concluded that places of public accommodation must be physical places, and that goods and services provided by a public accommodation must have a sufficient nexus to a physical place in order to be covered by the ADA. *See, e.g., Earll v. eBay, Inc.*, 599 Fed.Appx. 695, 696 (9th Cir. 2015) (the term "place of public accommodation" requires some connection between the good or service alleged to be discriminatory and a physical place); *Ford v. Schering-Plough Corp.*, 145 F.3d 601, 614 (3rd Cir. 1998) (finding that the term public accommodation does not refer to non-physical access); *Parker v. Metro. Life Ins. Co.*, 121 F.3d 1006, 1010–11 (6th Cir. 1997) (stating that a public accommodation is a physical place). Courts in these circuits have concluded that a public accommodation must be a physical place because the twelve enumerated categories of public accommodations in the statute are all physical places. *See, e.g., Weyer v. Twentieth Century Fox Film Corp.*, 198 F.3d 1104, 1114 (9th Cir. 2000); *Parker*, 121 F.3d at 1010–11; *Ford*, 145 F.3d at 612–13.

The Eleventh Circuit has not addressed whether websites are public accommodations for purposes of the ADA. However, the Eleventh Circuit's decision in *Rendon v. Valleycrest Prods., Inc.* offers some guidance. 294 F.3d 1279 (11th Cir. 2002). The *Rendon* Court noted that the plain language of Title III of the ADA covers both tangible, physical barriers that prevent a disabled person from accessing a public accommodation, as well as "intangible barriers, such as eligibility requirements and screening rules or discriminatory policies and procedures that restrict a disabled person's ability to enjoy the defendant entity's goods, services and privileges. . ." 294 F.3d at 1283. *Rendon* involved an automated telephone answering system used by the television show "Who Wants to Be a Millionaire" to select contestants to appear on the program. *Id.* at 1280. The *Rendon* Court held that the plaintiffs stated a valid claim under the ADA because the plaintiffs alleged that the inaccessibility of the automated system to persons with hearing and upper-body mobility impairments effectively denied them access to a privilege (competing in the television show) offered by a public accommodation (the television studio). *Id.* at 1284–86 (noting that the plaintiffs "seek the privilege of competing in a contest held in a concrete space. . .").

District courts within the Eleventh Circuit that have considered the question of whether websites are public accommodations have uniformly held that the ADA does not apply to a website that is wholly unconnected to a physical location. *Gomez v. Bang & Olufsen Am., Inc.*, No. 16–23801, at 8, 2017 WL 1957182 (S.D. Fla. Feb. 2, 2017) (Lenard, J.) (holding that a website that is wholly unconnected to a physical location is generally not a place of public accommodation under the ADA); *Access Now, Inc. v. Southwest Airlines, Co.*, 227 F.Supp.2d 1312, 1321 (S.D. Fla. 2002) (Seitz, J.) (dismissing complaint because the plaintiffs failed to establish a nexus between the defendant's website and a physical, concrete place of public accommodation); *Kidwell v. Florida Comm'n on Human Relations*, No. 16–403, 2017 WL 176897, at *4 (M.D. Fla. Jan. 17, 2017) (holding that a website is not a public accommodation under the ADA). However, district courts in the Eleventh Circuit have found that websites are subject to the ADA if a plaintiff can establish a nexus between the website and the physical premises of a public accommodation. *Gomez v. Bang & Olufsen Am., Inc.*, No. 16–23801 at 9 (citing *Rendon* for the proposition that if a plaintiff establishes some nexus between the website and the physical place of public accommodation, the plaintiff's ADA claim can survive a motion to dismiss); *Gomez v. J. Lindeberg USA, LLC*, No. 16–22966, at 2–3 (S.D. Fla. Oct. 17, 2016) (Williams, J.) (order granting default judgment in part) (finding that plaintiff stated a claim under the ADA by alleging that the inaccessibility of the defendant's website prevented him from purchasing the defendant's clothing online and searching for physical store locations); *Access Now*, 227 F.Supp.2d at 1320. Indeed, this concept has support in *Rendon*. There, the Eleventh Circuit noted that some courts require a nexus between the challenged service and the premises of the public accommodation, and that the plaintiffs in that matter demonstrated such a nexus. 294 F.3d at 1284 n.8.

Here, the Defendant asserts that the Plaintiff has not alleged an adequate nexus between its website and its physical grocery stores and pharmacies, reasoning that the Plaintiff does not assert that the inaccessibility of the website prevented him from visiting a Winn-Dixie store or pharmacy. The Defendant cites *Rendon* in support of this argument. However, the *Rendon* Court noted that the ADA bars "intangible barriers. . . that restrict a disabled person's ability to enjoy the defendant entity's goods, services and privileges. . ." 294 F.3d at 1283. In *Rendon*, the issue was not that the inaccessibility of the automated phone system prevented the plaintiffs from physically accessing the television studio, but rather that the inaccessibility of the phone system prevented the plaintiffs from accessing a privilege (the opportunity to be a contestant on the television show) afforded by the television studio.

In a case remarkably similar to this one, the Northern District of California denied the defendant's motion to dismiss a complaint alleging that Target Corp.'s ("Target") website failed to comply with the ADA. *Nat'l Fed'n of the Blind v. Target Corp.*, 452 F.Supp.2d 946, 949 (N.D. Cal. 2006). The plaintiff alleged that Target's website, which was inaccessible to blind individuals, allowed customers to perform functions related to Target stores, such as access information about store locations and hours, refill prescriptions, and order photo prints for pick-up at a store. *Id.* The *Target Corp.* court noted that in *Rendon*, even though the plaintiffs did not contest the actual physical barriers of the studio, the Eleventh Circuit found that the ADA was implicated because the plaintiffs were deprived of the opportunity to compete to be a contestant on the television show. *Id.* at 955 (citations omitted). The *Target Corp.* court further noted that the statutory language of the ADA "applies to the services *of* a place of public accommodation, not services *in* a place of public accommodation," and concluded that Target's website was "heavily integrated with the brick-and-mortar stores and operates in many ways as a gateway to the stores." *Target Corp.*, 452 F.Supp.2d at 953, 955.

In *Gomez v. J. Lindeberg, Inc.*, Judge Williams cited to *Target Corp.* in finding that a plaintiff stated a claim that the defendant's website violated the ADA because the plaintiff alleged that the website was inaccessible to blind individuals and allowed customers to purchase the defendant's clothing online and search for physical store locations. *Gomez v. J. Lindeberg, Inc.*, No. 16–22966 at 3. Similarly, here the Plaintiff has alleged that the inaccessibility of Winn-Dixie's website has denied blind individuals the ability to enjoy the services, privileges, and advantages of Winn-Dixie's stores. Specifically, the Plaintiff has alleged, among other things, that Winn-Dixie's website allows customers to locate physical

Winn-Dixie store locations and fill and refill prescriptions for in-store pick-up or delivery. Viewing the facts in the light most favorable to the Plaintiff, it appears that, just as in *Target Corp.*, Winn-Dixie's website is heavily integrated with, and in many ways operates as a gateway to, Winn-Dixie's physical store locations. The website's alleged inaccessibility therefore denies the Plaintiff equal access to the services, privileges, and advantages of Winn-Dixie's physical stores and pharmacies.

The Court finds that the Plaintiff has sufficiently alleged a nexus between Winn-Dixie's website and its physical stores such that the Defendant is not entitled to judgment as a matter of law. Therefore, the Court need not determine whether Winn-Dixie's website is a public accommodation in and of itself.

4. Conclusion

For the reasons set forth above, the Court **denies** . . . the Defendant's Motion for Judgment on the Pleadings.

NOTES AND QUESTIONS

1. *The result in* Gil *and the circuit split.* As you can see from this case, the law was slow to develop and is still in a state of flux regarding whether websites must be accessible to individuals with visual impairments. As some courts have emphasized, the statutory list of "places of public accommodation" are all physical locations, or "brick and mortar" buildings. Do you think this means that Congress had no intention to require websites to be accessible for blind individuals? Or perhaps, does it indicate that in 1990, Congress did not anticipate the prevalence of shopping online, or more generally, the ubiquitous nature of the Internet? The *Gil* case represents a middle ground, where places of public accommodation have to make their websites accessible for blind individuals as long as there is a nexus between the website and the physical facility. The more difficult issue is where the entity only operates online, which is discussed below.

2. *Internet only entities.* As the court notes in *Gil*, there are some courts that have been willing to apply Title III to an entity that exclusively operates online. *Gil*, 242 F.Supp.3d at 1319 (discussing Title III's applicability to Scribd, a company that provides consumers with access to a digital library for a fee, and to Netflix, even though neither has a physical location open to the public). As a policy matter, do you think that Title III *should* apply to businesses who operate exclusively online? Why or why not?

3. *The DOJ's failure to act and due process concerns.* In a 2019 Ninth Circuit case, *Robles v. Domino's Pizza, LLC*, 913 F.3d 898 (9th Cir. 2019), the defendant Domino's Pizza argued that imposing liability on it for failing to have an accessible website and mobile app violated its due process rights because the plaintiff sought to impose liability for Domino's failure to comply with the Web Content Accessibility Guidelines (WCAG) 2.0, which are "private industry standards for website accessibility developed by technology and

accessibility experts," *id.* at n.1, and because the DOJ has not issued regulations specifying technical standards for compliance so that Domino's did not have fair notice of what it specifically must do to make its website accessible. *Id.* at 907. The court rejected Domino's challenge, first noting that the plaintiff is not trying to impose liability on Domino's for failure to comply with WCAG 2.0. Instead, the plaintiff argued, and the Ninth Circuit agreed, that the "district court can order compliance with WCAG 2.0 as an equitable remedy" if it found that Domino's website and app violated the ADA. *Id.* The court also addressed Domino's argument regarding lack of due process based on the DOJ's failure to promulgate regulations addressing the technical standards for website accessibility. (The DOJ issued an Advanced Notice of Proposed Rule Making in 2010 but withdrew it in 2017.) The court in *Robles* held that even though Domino's wants specific guidelines for website accessibility, the "Constitution only requires that Domino's receives fair notice of its legal duties, not a blueprint for compliance with its statutory obligations." *Id.* at 908. Accordingly, the court held that "Domino's had received fair notice that its website and app must provide effective communication and facilitate 'full and equal enjoyment' of Domino's goods and services to its customers who are disabled." *Id.* What do you think about the DOJ's failure to issue regulations regarding website accessibility? If you owned a company that had not yet made its website accessible, would you be concerned about not knowing exactly what technical standard should apply? Does the DOJ's failure to act mean that most companies will choose to voluntarily adopt the WCAG 2.0 guidelines, even though they are private industry guidelines, and not necessarily required by the ADA? And if so, is that a problem?

D. EXAMINATIONS AND COURSES

1. STATUTORY PROVISIONS AND REGULATIONS

The ADA contains a separate provision relating to courses and examinations:

> Any person that offers examinations or courses related to applications, licensing, certification, or credentialing for secondary or post-secondary education, professional, or trade purposes shall offer such examinations or courses in a place and manner accessible to persons with disabilities or offer alternative accessible arrangements for such individuals.

42 U.S.C. § 12189.

The DOJ has promulgated regulations related to this section. In pertinent part, they provide:

> (b) Examinations.
>
> (1) Any private entity offering an examination covered by this section must assure that—

(i)   The examination is selected and administered so as to best ensure that, when the examination is administered to an individual with a disability that impairs sensory, manual, or speaking skills, the examination results accurately reflect the individual's aptitude or achievement level or whatever other factor the examination purports to measure, rather than reflecting the individual's impaired sensory, manual, or speaking skills (except where those skills are the factors that the examination purports to measure);

(ii) An examination that is designed for individuals with impaired sensory, manual, or speaking skills is offered at equally convenient locations, as often, and in as timely a manner as are other examinations; and

(iii) The examination is administered in facilities that are accessible to individuals with disabilities or alternative accessible arrangements are made.

* * *

(2)   Required modifications to an examination may include changes in the length of time permitted for completion of the examination and adaptation of the manner in which the examination is given.

(3)   A private entity offering an examination covered by this section shall provide appropriate auxiliary aids for persons with impaired sensory, manual, or speaking skills, unless that private entity can demonstrate that offering a particular auxiliary aid would fundamentally alter the measurement of the skills or knowledge the examination is intended to test or would result in an undue burden. Auxiliary aids and services required by this section may include taped examinations, interpreters or other effective methods of making orally delivered materials available to individuals with hearing impairments, Brailled or large print examinations and answer sheets or qualified readers for individuals with visual impairments or learning disabilities, transcribers for individuals with manual impairments, and other similar services and actions.

* * *

28 C.F.R. 36.309.

2. TESTING ACCOMMODATIONS

ENYART V. NATIONAL CONFERENCE OF BAR EXAMINERS, INC.

630 F.3d 1153 (9th Cir. 2011)

SILVERMAN, CIRCUIT JUDGE:

Stephanie Enyart, a legally blind law school graduate, sought to take the Multistate Professional Responsibility Exam and the Multistate Bar Exam using a computer equipped with assistive technology software known as JAWS and ZoomText. The State Bar of California had no problem with Enyart's request but the National Conference of Bar Examiners refused to grant this particular accommodation. Enyart sued NCBE under the Americans with Disabilities Act seeking injunctive relief. The district court issued preliminary injunctions requiring NCBE to allow Enyart to take the exams using the assistive software, and NCBE appealed. We hold that in granting the injunctions, the district court did not abuse its discretion. We affirm.

I. Background

Enyart suffers from Stargardt's Disease, a form of juvenile macular degeneration that causes her to experience a large blind spot in the center of her visual field and extreme sensitivity to light. Her disease has progressively worsened since she became legally blind at age fifteen. Enyart relies on assistive technology to read.

Enyart graduated from UCLA School of Law in 2009. Before she could be admitted to practice law in California, Enyart needed to pass two exams: the Multistate Professional Responsibility Exam, a 60-question, multiple-choice exam testing applicants' knowledge of the standards governing lawyers' professional conduct; and the California Bar Exam. The Bar Exam spans three days, on one of which the Multistate Bar Exam is administered. The MBE is a six-hour, 200-question, multiple-choice exam that tests applicants' knowledge of the law in a number of subject areas. NCBE develops both the MPRE and the MBE. NCBE contracts with another testing company, ACT, to administer the MPRE and licenses the MBE to the California Committee of Bar Examiners for use in the Bar Exam.

Enyart registered to take the March 2009 administration of the MPRE and wrote to ACT requesting a number of accommodations for her disability: extra time, a private room, hourly breaks, permission to bring and use her own lamp, digital clock, sunglasses, yoga mat, and migraine medication during the exam, and permission to take the exam on a laptop equipped with JAWS and ZoomText software. JAWS is an assistive screen-reader program that reads aloud text on a computer screen. ZoomText is a screen-magnification program that allows the user to adjust the font, size, and color of text and to control a high-visibility cursor.

ACT granted all of Enyart's requests with the exception of the computer equipped with JAWS and ZoomText. ACT explained that it was unable to offer this accommodation because NCBE would not make the MPRE available in electronic format. In lieu of Enyart's requested accommodation, ACT offered her a choice between a live reader or an audio CD of the exam, along with use of closed-circuit television for text magnification. Enyart sought reconsideration of ACT's denial of her request to use JAWS and ZoomText, asserting that the options offered would be ineffective because they would not allow her to synchronize the auditory and visual inputs. After ACT denied Enyart's request for reconsideration, Enyart cancelled her registration for the March 2009 MPRE.

In April 2009, Enyart applied to take the July 2009 California Bar Exam, requesting the same accommodations she asked for on the MPRE. The California Committee of Bar Examiners granted all of Enyart's requested accommodations with the exception of her request to take the MBE portion of the test using a computer equipped with ZoomText and JAWS. The Committee denied this request because NCBE would not provide the MBE in electronic format. Because of this denial, Enyart cancelled her registration for the July 2009 Bar Exam.

Enyart registered for the November 2009 MPRE and requested the same accommodations she previously sought for the March 2009 administration. NCBE again declined to allow Enyart to take the MPRE using a computer equipped with ZoomText and JAWS. Instead, they offered to provide a human reader, an audio CD of the test questions, a braille version of the test, and/or a CCTV with a hard-copy version in large font with white letters printed on a black background. Because of NCBE's denial of her request to use a computer with ZoomText and JAWS, Enyart cancelled her registration for the November 2009 MPRE.

After these repeated denials of her requests to take the MPRE and MBE using assistive technology software, Enyart filed this action against NCBE, ACT, and the State Bar of California, alleging violations of the ADA and the Unruh Act, California's civil rights law. Enyart sought declaratory and injunctive relief.

Enyart moved for a preliminary injunction, asking the district court to order NCBE to allow Enyart to use a computer equipped with ZoomText and JAWS on the February 2010 MBE and the March 2010 MPRE. After hearing oral argument, the court granted Enyart's motion, addressing the factors for deciding whether to issue a preliminary injunction in a well-reasoned order:

Because the accommodations provided by NCBE will not permit Enyart to take the exam without severe discomfort and disadvantage, she has demonstrated the test is not "accessible" to her, and that the accommodations [offered by NCBE] therefore are not "reasonable." Therefore, this Court concludes, based on the current record and moving papers, that it is more likely than not that Enyart will succeed on the merits at trial. . . .

NCBE spends a good portion of its brief disputing Enyart's factual claims that the accommodations offered by NCBE will not permit her to comfortably complete the exam. NCBE points out that in the past Enyart has "successfully utilized a number of different accommodations." She used readers and audiotapes during her undergraduate years at Stanford, and used CCTV while working as an administrative assistant before law school. Further, NCBE points out that Enyart used a reader to help her complete her LSAT prep program, and used audiotapes and the services of a human reader on her examinations.

These factual claims, however, are somewhat beside the point. First, Enyart avers that hers is a progressive condition, so there is no reason to believe an accommodation that may or may not have been sufficient during Enyart's undergraduate coursework would be sufficient. Second, none of those examinations compare to the bar exam, which is a multi-day, eight hour per day examination. Hence, an accommodation that might be sufficient for a law school examination is not necessarily sufficient for the bar exam. Third, the relevant question is not whether Enyart would be able, despite extreme discomfort and disability-related disadvantage, to pass the relevant exams. NCBE points to no authority to support the position that an accommodation which results in "eye fatigue, disorientation and nausea within five minutes, which become fully developed several minutes after that" is "reasonable."

* * *

The facts as outlined in the attachments to Plaintiff's motion therefore strongly suggest that the accommodations offered by NCBE would either result in extreme discomfort and nausea, or would not permit Enyart to sufficiently comprehend and retain the language used on the test. This would result in Enyart's disability severely limiting her performance on the exam, which is clearly forbidden both by the statute [42 U.S.C. § 12189] and the corresponding regulation [28 C.F.R. § 36.309].

NCBE's citation to other regulations and cases does not overcome this factual presentation. . . . [T]he examples [of auxiliary aids] offered in the regulation and the statute cannot be read as exclusive, nor do those examples support the conclusion that such accommodations are reasonable even where they do not permit effective communication. On the contrary, the statute and relevant regulations all emphasize access and effective communication. The statute itself illustrates that the central question is whether the disabled individual is able to employ an "effective method[ ] of making visually delivered materials available." The evidence submitted by Plaintiff strongly suggests that the *only* auxiliary aid that meets this criteria is a computer with JAWS and ZoomText. While NCBE may be successful at trial in establishing that this is not the case, the record presently before this Court more strongly supports the conclusion that only ZoomText and JAWS make the test "accessible" to Enyart. *See* 42 U.S.C. § 12189.

The district court required Enyart to post a $5,000 injunction bond. NCBE immediately appealed the preliminary injunction.

Meanwhile, while NCBE's appeal of the preliminary injunction was pending, Enyart learned that her score on the March 2010 MPRE was not high enough to allow her to qualify for admission to the California Bar. She moved for a second preliminary injunction, asking the court to order NCBE to provide her requested accommodations on the August 2010 MPRE and "any other administration to Ms. Enyart of the California Bar Exam, the Multistate Bar Exam ('MBE') and/or the MPRE." After filing her motion, Enyart learned that she did not pass the July 2009 Bar Exam. The district court granted a second preliminary injunction ordering NCBE to allow Enyart to take the July 2010 MBE and the August 2010 MPRE on a computer equipped with ZoomText and JAWS, stating:

> The relevant question here is whether the auxiliary aids offered by NCBE make the test's "visually delivered materials available" to Enyart. As this Court has previously concluded, they do not. . . . NCBE continues to argue that Enyart is not entitled to her preferred accommodations, and in so doing continues to miss the point. She does not argue that she simply "prefers" to use JAWS and ZoomText. On the contrary, she has presented evidence that the accommodations offered by NCBE do not permit her to fully understand the test material, and that some of the offered accommodations result in serious physical discomfort. CCTV makes her nauseous and results in eye strain, and the use of human readers is not suited to the kind of test where one must re-read both questions and answers, and continually shift back and forth between different passages of text. . . . Such accommodations do not make the test accessible to Enyart, and so do not satisfy the standard under the ADA.

The court required Enyart to post an additional $5,000 injunction bond. NCBE immediately appealed, and the appeal was consolidated with NCBE's appeal of the first preliminary injunction.

* * *

II. Discussion

A. Jurisdiction and Standard of Review

We have jurisdiction to review the district court's orders granting these preliminary injunctions pursuant to 28 U.S.C. § 1292(a)(1). Our review is for an abuse of discretion. . . .

B. Mootness

As an initial matter, we hold that even though the injunctions only related to the March and August 2010 MPRE exams and the February and July 2010 California Bar Exams, which have since come and gone, NCBE's appeals are not moot because the situation is capable of repetition, yet evading review. "The test for mootness of an appeal is whether the appellate court can give the appellant any effective relief in the event that it decides the matter on the merits in his favor. If it can grant such relief, the matter is not moot." *Garcia v. Lawn*, 805 F.2d 1400, 1402 (9th Cir.1986). An established exception to mootness applies where "(1) the challenged action is in its duration too short to be fully litigated prior to cessation or expiration; and (2) there is a reasonable expectation that the same complaining party will be subject to the same action again." *Fed. Election Comm'n v. Wis. Right to Life, Inc.*, 551 U.S. 449, 462, 127 S.Ct. 2652 (2007).

There is a reasonable expectation that NCBE will be subject to another preliminary injunction in this case. After failing to achieve a passing score on the February 2010 California Bar Exam, Enyart took the test again in July 2010. Now that she failed the July 2010 exam, it is reasonable to expect that she will sign up for a future administration and that she will seek another preliminary injunction. The situation is capable of repetition, satisfying the first prong of the capable-of-repetition-yet-evading-review exception to mootness.

These preliminary injunctions also evade review. On February 4, 2010, the district court issued the first preliminary injunction in this case, which required NCBE to allow Enyart to use JAWS and ZoomText for the February 2010 MBE and the March 2010 MPRE. Once Enyart took these two exams, the terms of the preliminary injunction were fully and irrevocably carried out. The second injunction issued June 22, 2010, and required NCBE to allow Enyart to use JAWS and ZoomText for the July 2010 MBE and the August 2010 MPRE. Again, once Enyart took these exams, the terms of the second preliminary injunction were fully and irrevocably carried out. Due to the limited duration of these injunctions—

little more than a month passed between the issuance of the injunctions and the final execution of their terms—NCBE could not practically obtain appellate review of the district court's orders until after the administration of the exams. Because the duration of these injunctions is too short to allow full litigation prior to their expiration, they meet the "evading review" prong of the capable-of-repetition-yet-evading-review exception to mootness.

C. Preliminary Injunctions

A plaintiff seeking a preliminary injunction must show that: (1) she is likely to succeed on the merits, (2) she is likely to suffer irreparable harm in the absence of preliminary relief, (3) the balance of equities tips in her favor, and (4) an injunction is in the public interest.

1. Likelihood of Success on the Merits

* * *

42 U.S.C. § 12189, which falls within Title III of the ADA, governs professional licensing examinations. This section requires entities that offer examinations "related to applications, licensing, certification, or credentialing for ... professional, or trade purposes" to "offer such examinations ... in a place and manner *accessible* to persons with disabilities or offer alternative accessible arrangements for such individuals." 42 U.S.C. § 12189. The purpose of this section is "to assure that persons with disabilities are not foreclosed from educational, professional, or trade opportunities because an examination or course is conducted in an inaccessible site or without an accommodation."

The Attorney General is charged with carrying out many of the provisions of the ADA and issuing such regulations as he deems necessary. Relevant here, the Attorney General is responsible for issuing regulations carrying out all non-transportation provisions of Title III, including issuing accessibility standards. 42 U.S.C. § 12186(b).

Pursuant to its authority to issue regulations carrying out the provisions of Title III, the Department of Justice has adopted a regulation interpreting § 12189. This regulation defines the obligations of testing entities:

> Any private entity offering an examination covered by this section must assure that ... [t]he examination is selected and administered so as to *best ensure* that, when the examination is administered to an individual with a disability that impairs sensory, manual, or speaking skills, the examination results accurately reflect the individual's aptitude or achievement level or whatever other factor the examination purports to measure, rather than reflecting the individual's impaired sensory, manual, or speaking skills . . .[.]

28 C.F.R. § 36.309(b)(1)(i). The regulation continues:

> A private entity offering an examination covered by this section shall provide appropriate auxiliary aids for persons with impaired sensory, manual, or speaking skills, unless that entity can demonstrate that offering a particular auxiliary aid would fundamentally alter the measurement of the skills or knowledge the examination is intended to test or would result in an undue burden.

Id. § 36.309(b)(3).

Enyart argues that DOJ's regulation requires NCBE to administer the MBE and MPRE "so as to best ensure" that her results on the tests accurately reflect her aptitude, rather than her disability. NCBE argues that the regulation is invalid and asks this court to apply a reasonableness standard in lieu of the regulation's "best ensure" standard. The district court declined to rule on the validity of 28 C.F.R. § 36.309, and instead held that "even assuming NCBE's more defendant-friendly standard applies," Enyart had demonstrated a likelihood of success on the merits.

We defer to an agency's interpretation of a statute it is charged with administering if the statute "is silent or ambiguous with respect to the specific issue" and the agency's interpretation is "based upon a permissible construction of the statute." *Contract Mgmt., Inc. v. Rumsfeld,* 434 F.3d 1145, 1146–47 (9th Cir.2006) (quoting *Chevron U.S.A. Inc. v. Natural Res. Def. Council, Inc.,* 467 U.S. 837, 842–43, 104 S.Ct. 2778 (1984)). We hold that 28 C.F.R. § 36.309 is entitled to *Chevron* deference.

Section 12189 requires entities like NCBE to offer licensing exams in a manner "accessible" to disabled people or to offer "alternative accessible arrangements." 42 U.S.C. § 12189. Congress's use of the phrases "accessible" and "alternative accessible arrangements" is ambiguous in the context of licensing exams. Nowhere in § 12189, in Title III more broadly, or in the entire ADA did Congress define these terms. The phrase "readily accessible" appears in Titles II and III, but only with respect to physical spaces, i.e., facilities, vehicles, and rail cars. The phrase is not defined; instead, the Act directs . . . the Attorney General to issue regulations establishing accessibility standards for new construction and alterations in public accommodations and commercial facilities, 42 U.S.C. § 12186(b). The text of these other ADA provisions does not resolve the ambiguity in § 12189's use of [the] term "accessible" because an examination is not equivalent to a physical space.

Because § 12189 is ambiguous with respect to its requirement that entities administer licensing exams in a manner "accessible" to individuals with disabilities, we defer to DOJ's interpretation of the statute so long as that interpretation is based upon a permissible construction of the statute. NCBE seeks to invalidate 28 C.F.R. § 36.309, arguing that the regulation imposes an obligation beyond the statutory mandate. Instead of the regulation's requirement that entities administer licensing exams in a manner "so as to best ensure" that the results reflect whatever skill or aptitude the exam purports to measure, NCBE argues that the ADA only requires such entities to provide "reasonable accommodations."

The "reasonable accommodation" standard advocated by NCBE originated in the Department of Health and Human Services' regulations implementing the Rehabilitation Act of 1973. *See* 45 C.F.R. 84.12(a). When Congress enacted the ADA, it incorporated 45 C.F.R. 84.12's "reasonable accommodation" standard into Title I, which applies in the employment context.

Notably, Congress did *not* incorporate 45 C.F.R. 84.12's "reasonable accommodation" standard into § 12189. Instead, § 12189 states that entities offering licensing exams "shall offer such examinations . . . in a place and manner accessible to persons with disabilities or offer alternative arrangements for such individuals." 42 U.S.C. § 12189. One reasonable reading of § 12189's requirement that entities make licensing exams "accessible" is that such entities must provide disabled people with an equal opportunity to demonstrate their knowledge or abilities to the same degree as nondisabled people taking the exam—in other words, the entities must administer the exam "so as to best ensure" that exam results accurately reflect aptitude rather than disabilities. DOJ's regulation is not based upon an impermissible construction of § 12189, so this court affords *Chevron* deference to 28 C.F.R. § 36.309 and applies the regulation's "best ensure" standard.

Applying 28 C.F.R. § 36.309's "best ensure" standard, we conclude that the district court did not abuse its discretion by holding that Enyart demonstrated a likelihood of success on the merits. The district court found that the accommodations offered by NCBE did not make the MBE and MPRE accessible to Enyart. This finding is supported by evidence that Enyart would suffer eye fatigue, disorientation, and nausea if she used a CCTV, so CCTV does not best ensure that the exams are accessible to her; that auditory input alone is insufficient to allow Enyart to effectively comprehend and retain the language used on the exam; and that, according to Enyart's ophthalmologist, the combination of ZoomText and JAWS is the only way she can fully comprehend the material she reads.

NCBE argues that because Enyart has taken other standardized tests using accommodations comparable to those offered by NCBE, the district court erred in finding that those accommodations did not make the MPRE and MBE accessible to her. In support of this argument, NCBE points out that Enyart took the SAT college admissions test using large-print exam booklets; that she used CCTV for her Advanced Placement tests; and that she relied on a human reader and scribe during the LSAT. Although Enyart's prior experiences with the accommodations offered by NCBE may be relevant to establishing whether those accommodations make the MPRE and MBE accessible, they are not conclusive, especially as to whether those accommodations best ensure that the exams are accessible. Enyart graduated from college more than a decade ago, and took the LSAT six years ago. Enyart's disability is a progressive one, and as the district court noted, an accommodation that may or may not have been sufficient years ago is not necessarily sufficient today. Moreover, assistive technology is not frozen in time: as technology advances, testing accommodations should advance as well.

NCBE also argues that because it offered to provide auxiliary aids expressly identified in the ADA, the regulations, a DOJ settlement agreement, and a Resolution of the National Federation of the Blind, courts should not require it do more. We do not find this argument persuasive. The issue in this case is not what might or might not accommodate other people with vision impairments, but what is necessary to make the MPRE and MBE accessible to Enyart given her specific impairment and the specific nature of these exams.

As NCBE concedes, the lists of auxiliary aids contained at 42 U.S.C. § 12103 and at 28 C.F.R. § 36.309 are not exhaustive. . . . To hold that, as a matter of law, an entity fulfills its obligation to administer an exam in an accessible manner so long as it offers some or all of the auxiliary aids enumerated in the statute or regulation would be inconsistent with Congressional intent:

> The Committee wishes to make it clear that technological advances can be expected to further enhance options for making meaningful and effective opportunities available to individuals with disabilities. Such advances may require public accommodations to provide auxiliary aids and services in the future which today they would not be required because they would be held to impose undue burdens on such entities. . . .

H.R. Rep. 101–485(II), at 108 (1990), *reprinted in* 1990 U.S.C.C.A.N. 303, 391.

* * *

Finally, NCBE makes much of a Resolution of the National Federation of the Blind from 2000 that called upon the American Council on Education to ensure that it administered the GED exam in "the four standard media routinely used by blind persons to access standardized tests: large print, Braille, tape, and live reader." This NFB Resolution appears to have been written to address a specific problem identified in the administration of the GED exam, namely the prohibition on the use of live readers. Moreover, the NFB has no power to define testing entities' obligations under the ADA. The fact that the NFB ten years ago urged the American Council on Education to allow test-takers to choose among large print, Braille, tape, and live reader accommodations does not lead to the conclusion that, as a matter of law, the accommodations offered by NCBE made the MBE and MPRE accessible to Enyart.

The sources described above—the lists of auxiliary aids contained in the statute and regulation, the AASSWB settlement agreement, and the NFB's Resolution—possibly support a conclusion that the accommodations offered by NCBE are sufficient to meet their obligations with respect to many blind people in many situations. As we have tried to make clear already, accommodations that make an exam accessible to many blind people may not make the exam accessible to Enyart, and our analysis depends on the individual circumstances of each case, requiring a "fact-specific, individualized analysis of the disabled individual's circumstances."

Enyart provided the district court with evidence that the accommodations offered by NCBE will put her at a disadvantage by making her nauseated or by preventing her from comprehending the test material. Enyart presented evidence that she used JAWS and ZoomText for all but one of her law school examinations; that a combination of JAWS and ZoomText is the only way she can effectively access the exam; and that use of a CCTV causes her to suffer nausea and eye fatigue. In a sworn statement, Enyart's ophthalmologist stated that the only way Enyart can fully comprehend the material she reads is if she is able to simultaneously listen to and see magnified test material, as JAWS and ZoomText allow.

The district court reviewed the evidence of Enyart's disability and her history of using auxiliary aids including JAWS and ZoomText, and concluded that "the accommodations offered by NCBE would either result in extreme discomfort and nausea, or would not permit Enyart to sufficiently comprehend and retain the language used on the text. This would result in Enyart's disability severely limiting her performance on the exam, which is clearly forbidden both by the statute and the corresponding regulation." The court compared Enyart's evidence to that offered by NCBE, and found that the balance "more strongly supports the conclusion that only ZoomText and JAWS make the text 'accessible' to Enyart." This is a logical conclusion, supported by the evidence, and therefore we conclude that the district court did not abuse its discretion in holding that Enyart demonstrated a likelihood of success on the merits.

[Eds. Note: The court also held that the other elements necessary for granting a preliminary injunction—that the plaintiff would suffer irreparable harm, that the balance of equities tips in her favor, and that the injunction is in the public's interest—were met.]

* * *

III. Conclusion

For the foregoing reasons, we affirm the district court's February 4, 2010 and June 22, 2010 orders issuing preliminary injunctions requiring NCBE to permit Enyart to take the MBE and MPRE using a laptop equipped with JAWS and ZoomText.

AFFIRMED.

NOTES AND QUESTIONS

1.   *Separate provision for examinations and courses.* As noted above, *supra* Section D.1, Congress enacted a separate provision mandating that courses and examinations be offered "in a place and manner accessible to persons with disabilities or offer alternative accessible arrangements for such individuals." 42 U.S.C. § 12189. Is there a reason that Congress might have been concerned that the main prohibition section of Title III ("No individual shall be discriminated against on the basis of disability in the full and equal enjoyment of the goods, services, facilities, privileges, advantages, or accommodations of any place of public accommodation by any person who owns, leases (or leases to), or operates a place of public accommodation") would not be sufficient to protect those individuals taking courses or examinations?

2.   *Preferred accommodations.* The defendant in this case argued that it was only required to provide the plaintiff with a "reasonable accommodation," and not necessarily her preferred accommodation. However, the court held that the language in the DOJ's regulation—that examinations must be "administered so as to *best ensure* that, when the examination is administered to an individual with a disability that impairs sensory . . . skills, the examination results accurately reflect the individual's aptitude or achievement level . . . rather than reflecting the individual's impaired sensory . . . skills"— is a reasonable interpretation of the statute and therefore is entitled to *Chevron* deference. Thus, the plaintiff in this case was entitled to her preferred accommodation. Recall that in the employment context, employers are not required to grant an employee's *preferred* accommodation. Other than a difference in the statutory language, is there a reason why individuals needing modifications for examinations and courses should be treated more favorably than individuals needing employment accommodations?

3.   *Deference to past accommodations.* Before the passage of the ADA, accommodations given to individuals taking licensing exams, such as the bar exam, were much less common. Even since the passage of the ADA, and the broadened definition of "disability" under the ADA Amendments Act of 2008, disputes continue to arise regarding whether particular accommodations during licensing examinations are appropriate. One issue that frequently arises is when a student received accommodations for the SAT or ACT to get into college and was accommodated throughout college only to discover that the Law School Admission Council (LSAC), who administers the LSAT, will not provide the same accommodations that the student had received. What, if any, deference or consideration should a testing agency give to the fact that

the student had received a particular accommodation to take one of the college admission exams and throughout college? For an interesting discussion of this issue, see Laura Rothstein, *Forty Years of Disability Policy in Legal Education and the Legal Profession: What Has Changed and What Are the New Issues?*, 22 AM. U. J. GENDER SOC. POL'Y & L. 519 566–70 (2014).

E. INSURANCE

FLETCHER V. TUFTS UNIVERSITY
367 F.Supp.2d 99 (D. Mass. 2005)

LINDSAY, DISTRICT JUDGE.

I. Introduction

Madeleine Fletcher ("Fletcher" or "the plaintiff") is a former employee of defendant Tufts University ("Tufts"). During the time of her employment, Tufts provided its employees, including Fletcher, with the opportunity to subscribe to a long-term disability benefits plan (the "LTD Plan" or "the Plan") issued by defendant Metropolitan Life Insurance Company ("MetLife"). Fletcher subscribed to the LTD Plan and, after being diagnosed with a debilitating mental disorder, sought and received long-term disability benefits under the Plan. Because MetLife determined that Fletcher's disability was the result of a mental illness and she was not institutionalized, MetLife terminated her long-term disability payments after two years, pursuant to the terms of the Plan. Had she suffered a physical disability, Fletcher's benefits would have continued until she reached age sixty-five.

* * *

Both defendants have moved to dismiss the amended complaint pursuant to Fed.R.Civ.P. 12(b)(6).

II. Factual Allegations

The following allegations are made in the amended complaint.

Fletcher became a professor of Spanish literature at Tufts in 1980. As noted above, Tufts provided Fletcher with long-term disability insurance pursuant to the LTD Plan.

In April of 1998, Fletcher wrote a letter to one of her classes that triggered concerns about her mental health. She was admitted to a hospital, where she was diagnosed by a psychiatrist with bipolar disorder, manic type, with psychotic features. After her release from the hospital, Fletcher was treated by two psychiatrists who concluded that she had an ongoing psychotic disorder that rendered her "grossly disabled." Tufts placed Fletcher on medical leave from September 1, 1998 through January 31, 1999.

Following her medical leave, Fletcher remained unable to work, and MetLife approved her request for disability benefits pursuant to the terms of the Plan. She received those benefits from February 28, 1999 to February 27, 2001. On February 27, 2001, the benefits were terminated, because MetLife concluded that Fletcher suffered from a mental disability and was not confined to a hospital or other institution. Under the terms of the Plan, a participant who is "disabled due to mental illness and not confined in a hospital or institution" is entitled to benefits for the lesser of twenty-four months or the maximum benefit duration otherwise applicable under the Plan. It was under this provision of the Plan that Fletcher's disability benefits were terminated.

In July of 2001, Fletcher underwent a "return to work evaluation" by a physician, Dr. Harvey Waxman. In a report dated August 1, 2001, Dr. Waxman concluded that Fletcher's continuing disability rendered her incapable of performing the essential functions of her job, and that no accommodation could be made that would allow her to work. Based on Dr. Waxman's report, Tufts informed Fletcher that she could not return to her faculty position at Tufts.

On December 10, 2001, Fletcher requested that MetLife review its decision to terminate her benefits. At some point before the plaintiff made this request, her counsel spoke to an authorized representative of MetLife who told plaintiff's counsel that MetLife "could probably" waive the sixty-day deadline for requesting a review of the benefits determination. Notwithstanding this assurance, MetLife denied as untimely the request for a review. On the same day that she sought internal review from MetLife of the decision to terminate her benefits, Fletcher also filed, with the Equal Employment Opportunity Commission ("EEOC"), charges of discrimination against Tufts and MetLife. The charges alleged violations of the ADA by both defendants. On February 20, 2002, Fletcher received "right to sue" notices from the EEOC.

Fletcher filed this lawsuit on May 20, 2002, alleging violations of Title I and Title III of the ADA by Tufts and MetLife, respectively. . . .

III. Discussion

* * *

B. *Count One: Title I of the ADA*

Title I of the ADA provides that "[n]o covered entity shall discriminate against a qualified individual with a disability because of the disability of such individual in regard to . . . employee compensation . . . and other terms, conditions and privileges of employment." 42 U.S.C. § 12112(a). In count I of the amended complaint, the plaintiff alleges that Tufts violated Title I by adopting and maintaining a long-term disability plan that discriminates against employees with mental disabilities. Specifically, Fletcher asserts that the LTD Plan discriminates against persons with mental disabilities by limiting to twenty-four months the period during which such persons are entitled to receive benefits if they are not confined in a hospital or institution, while allowing persons with physical disabilities to receive benefits until they reach the age of sixty-five irrespective of whether they are in a hospital or institution.

Tufts' response to count I of the plaintiff's claim is threefold. First, Tufts contends that the plaintiff is not a "qualified individual with a disability" under Title I of the ADA, and therefore lacks standing to sue under the statute. Second, Tufts asserts that the complaint should be dismissed as untimely. Finally, Tufts argues that, as a substantive matter, the ADA does not prohibit long-term disability plans, like the LTD Plan, from offering less coverage for mental disabilities than they offer for physical disabilities. I will address each of these issues in turn.

(1) Is the Plaintiff a "Qualified Individual" under Title I of the ADA?

Title I of the ADA prohibits discrimination against a "qualified individual with a disability because of the disability of such individual. . . ." 42 U.S.C. § 12112(a). Thus, a predicate to protection under Title I is that the claimant be a *qualified individual* with a disability.

Title I defines a "qualified individual with a disability" as "an individual with a disability who, with or without reasonable accommodation, can perform the essential functions of the employment position that such individual holds or desires." 42 U.S.C. § 12111(8). Because the plaintiff is admittedly unable to perform the essential functions of her job, even with a reasonable accommodation, Tufts argues that she is not a "qualified individual" as expressly defined by Title I. Therefore, according to Tufts, the plaintiff falls outside the protection of the ADA. While the First Circuit has not yet addressed this issue, some courts have adopted Tufts' reading of the statute.

The plaintiff contends that the defendant's interpretation of the ADA is too narrow, and that the term "qualified individual" should be read to include former employees. Her position has support in decisions of some federal courts of appeal, and from two district courts in the First Circuit. *See Castellano v. City of New York,* 142 F.3d 58, 68–70 (2d Cir.1998) (holding that the term "qualified individual" under Title I of the ADA covers *former* employees); *Ford,* 145 F.3d at 608 (allowing "disabled former employees to sue their former employers [under Title I of the ADA] regarding their disability benefits"); *Iwata v. Intel Corp.,* 349 F.Supp.2d 135, 147 (D.Mass.2004) (same); *Conners v. Maine Med. Ctr.,* 42 F.Supp.2d 34, 40–43 (D.Me.1999) (same). The absence of controlling precedent and the split of authority on this issue require me, in the context of the present dispute, to analyze whether Congress intended the term "qualified individual with a disability," in Title I of the ADA, to include formerly qualified employees who are totally disabled at the time that they seek the protection of the statute.

* * *

[T]he Second and Third circuits have held that the definition of "qualified individual with a disability" in Title I of the ADA includes former employees. *See Castellano,* 142 F.3d at 68–70; *Ford,* 145 F.3d at 608.

In *Castellano,* for example, the Second Circuit looked first to the statutory definition of the term "qualified individual with a disability," and concluded that the absence of a temporal modifier rendered that definition ambiguous. *See* 142 F.3d at 67 ("[Section 12111(8)] fails to specify *when* a potential plaintiff must have been a 'qualified individual with a disability' in the context of a claim that the provision of retirement or fringe benefits is discriminatory."). The court then sought the meaning of the term "qualified individual" in the "broader context" and "primary purpose" of the ADA. The court noted that excluding former employees from the definition of "qualified individual[s] with a disability" would undermine the purpose of other provisions of Title I of the ADA, particularly the statute's prohibition of discrimination as to fringe benefits, embodied in 42 U.S.C. § 12112(b). The court observed that "[m]any fringe benefits are paid out to those who no longer work and who are no longer able to work, and some fringe benefits are paid out to individuals precisely because they can no longer work." *Id.* at 68.

The *Castellano* court's reasoning can be restated along the following lines. Because "employees" generally are not entitled to receive disability-related fringe benefits unless they are unable to work, they frequently cannot enforce the ADA's prohibition of discrimination as to those benefits until they become former employees. Excluding former employees from the category of "qualified individuals" entitled to seek relief under the ADA would therefore effectively nullify prohibitions against discrimination in the provision of disability benefits by allowing employers to deny the benefits to a totally disabled employee at the only time the employee could claim them. Thus, the *Castellano* court recognized the "illogic inherent" in a statutory scheme interpreted to create a right to be free from discrimination in the post-employment provision of fringe benefits without also providing a corresponding mechanism by which that right could be enforced. . . .

I find the *Castellano* court's interpretation of the term "qualified individual" entirely persuasive. As suggested above, that interpretation recognizes the inherent contradiction between the ADA's broad remedial purpose and its express prohibition of discrimination as to fringe benefits, and a rule that would deny standing to a claimant of long-term disability benefits to seek a court remedy at the only time that the claimant is eligible to receive those benefits. I therefore embrace the conclusions of the Second and Third Circuits and conclude that former employees, who were able to perform the essential functions of the employment position for a period sufficient to qualify for long-term benefits and who allege that they are discriminated against with respect to long-term disability benefits on the basis of their disability, have standing to assert that claim. The plaintiff here thus is a "qualified individual" and has standing to bring the present Title I claim.

* * *

(3) Has the Plaintiff Stated a Claim Under Title I of the ADA?

By far, the most difficult issue in this case is whether the language in Title I of the ADA, barring discrimination against a qualified individual "because of the disability of such individual . . . ," 42 U.S.C. § 12112(a), prohibits a benefits package like the LTD Plan, which offers differing long-term disability benefits depending on whether one suffers from a physical or mental disability. A number of federal courts have held that such plans are not prohibited by Title I. *See, e.g., E.E.O.C. v. Staten Island Savings Bank,* 207 F.3d 144, 151–53 (2d Cir.2000); *Weyer,* 198 F.3d at 1116–18; *Kimber v. Thiokol Corp.,* 196 F.3d 1092, 1101–02 (10th Cir.1999); *Lewis v. Kmart Corp.,* 180 F.3d 166, 170 (4th Cir.1999); *Ford,* 145 F.3d at 608; *Parker v. Metropolitan Life Ins. Co.,* 121 F.3d 1006, 1018 (6th Cir.1997) (en banc); *EEOC v. CNA Ins. Cos.,* 96 F.3d 1039, 1043–45 (7th Cir.1996); *Krauel v. Iowa Methodist Med. Ctr.,* 95 F.3d 674, 678 (8th Cir.1996); *Modderno v. King,* 82 F.3d 1059, 1060–62 (D.C.Cir.1996) (interpreting Section 504 of the Rehabilitation Act of 1973); *El-Hajj v. Fortis Benefits Ins. Co.,* 156 F.Supp.2d 27, 30–32 (D.Me.2001); *Wilson,* 117 F.Supp.2d at 95–97. For these courts, an employee benefits plan that offers differing long-term disability benefits based on the nature of the condition giving rise to the disability is not discriminatory, as long as the same plan is offered to all employees. The defendants here rely on these cases in contending that the LTD does not violate the ADA. The defendants argue that the ADA does not require that benefit plans, like the one at issue, provide benefits to participants with mental disabilities that are equal to the benefits provided to participants with physical disabilities. The First Circuit, however, has not yet spoken on the matter.

Some time ago, after reviewing the law in connection with the present motions, I concluded that, despite the substantial precedent to the contrary, Title I of the ADA prohibits discrimination among classes of persons with disabilities unless those distinctions are made in a manner consistent with safe harbor provision of the ADA. Until now, however, I have not found the opportunity to set forth in detail the reasons for my conclusion. Fortunately, my colleague, Chief Judge William G. Young of this district, has written a thoughtful and thorough explication of why the ADA generally prohibits discrimination among classes of persons with disabilities. *See generally Iwata,* 349 F.Supp.2d 135. His analysis of the issues and his conclusions as to the import of Title I in a case like the present one coincide with mine. In disposing of the present motions, therefore, I adopt what Judge Young has written.

Judge Young had before him in *Iwata* a long-term disability plan that limited a participant's receipt of benefits to two years if the participant was eligible for benefits due to a mental disability and was not hospitalized. No such limitation applied to participants with physical disabilities. The plan in *Iwata* was therefore like the LTD Plan in this case. Just as Fletcher does in this case, the plaintiff in *Iwata*, who was totally disabled by reason of a mental disability, argued, among other things, that the defendants' long-term benefit plan was discriminatory under the ADA. The defendants in that case argued, as do the defendants here, that the ADA does not require the LTD to equalize benefits as between participants with physical and mental disabilities.

In ruling on the defendants' motion under Fed.R.Civ.P. 12(b)(6), Judge Young held that the plaintiff in *Iwata* had stated a claim of discrimination under Title I. In reaching that conclusion, he reviewed the language and structure of Title I, and its broad remedial purpose and legislative history, and derived from these sources the conviction that, as a general matter, Title I of the ADA prohibits disability plans that discriminate between persons with physical disabilities and those with mental disabilities. *Id.* at 147. He found further support for that view in the analysis of the issue in *Johnson v. K Mart Corp.*, 273 F.3d 1035 (11th Cir. 2001). Judge Young acknowledged that the *Johnson* opinion had been vacated pending a rehearing en banc, but observed that "the logic of the opinion is worth considering, regardless of the opinion's precedential value in the Eleventh Circuit." *Iwata*, 349 F.Supp.2d at 148.

After looking to the broad remedial purpose of the ADA and its language and legislative history, the *Johnson* court held that where a long-term disability plan provides fewer benefits for persons with mental disabilities than it provides for persons with physical disabilities, the plan, at least facially, violates Title I of the ADA. *Johnson*, 273 F.3d at 1054. The *Johnson* court's reasoning was informed by the concept of discrimination set forth in the Supreme Court's decision in *Olmstead v. L.C.*, 527 U.S. 581, 119 S.Ct. 2176 (1999). In *Olmstead*, the Supreme Court, in deciding a claim brought under Title II, ruled that in enacting the ADA, Congress intended a comprehensive definition of the term "discrimination"—a definition that includes not only a prohibition of disparate treatment that favors others against members of a protected class, but one that also prohibits disparate treatment among members of the same protected class. 527 U.S. at 598–603, 119 S.Ct. 2176. The key question in both forms of discrimination is whether an entity covered by the ADA has discriminated against an individual *because of that individual's disability*. *Id.* Both the *Johnson* court and Judge Young reasoned that the broad concept of discrimination, found by the Supreme Court to apply to claims brought under Title II of the ADA, applies to claims brought under Title I as well. *Johnson,* 273 F.3d at 1053–54; *Iwata,* 349 F.Supp.2d at 149.

Following the lead of the *Johnson* and *Iwata* courts and applying *Olmstead's* broad principle that the ADA forbids discrimination among classes of persons with disabilities, I find the present LTD Plan suspect. In the words of the *Johnson* court, the LTD Plan, "which differentiates between individuals who are totally disabled due to a mental disability and individuals who are totally disabled due to a physical disability because of a given individual's type of disability . . . [,] appears *prima facie* to distinguish among beneficiaries on a basis that constitutes a form of discrimination that contravenes Title I of the ADA." *Johnson,* 273 F.3d at 1054.

On its face, the LTD Plan seems to have no justification for the difference it makes between participants totally disabled by reason of a mental disability and those totally disabled because of a physical disability, except perhaps in an unstated premise that a mental disability is a lesser form of disability than a physical disability, and mental disabilities only rise to the seriousness of physical disabilities when the claimant must be hospitalized. (As noted earlier, the Plan provides that if the claimant with a mental disability is institutionalized, then benefits are not limited to the two-year period otherwise applicable.) While there is no evidence before me on the point, it is far from obvious that the cost of providing disability benefits to a hospitalized participant is less than the cost of providing such benefits to a non-hospitalized participant. Indeed, because disability benefits are designed to address income lost from one's work, it would not seem to matter, from the perspective of cost, whether the participant is in a hospital. Implicit in the LTD Plan then is the suggestion that if a participant is in an institution, his/her disability assumes more of the character of a "real" disability. By contrast, the Plan appears to treat the participant whose mental disability does not require that the participant be institutionalized as though he or she has a disability that is less significant than either the hospitalized participant with a total mental disability or any participant with a total physical disability. Judge Young offered a possible explanation for this phenomenon: "[T]here appears to be a widespread practice of limiting disability benefits for mental illness, possibly based on assumptions that mental illness is 'less real' than physical disability, or that recovery therefrom is more a matter of will than in the case of physical disability." *Iwata,* 349 F.Supp.2d at 155. If the LTD Plan's distinction between classes of persons with disabilities is based on such stereotypes or is otherwise arbitrary, Title I, considered in the light of *Olmstead,* would condemn the Plan as applied to Fletcher.

On the other hand, as Judge Young reasoned in *Iwata,* one might well argue that plans like the one at issue here are not discriminatory because they apply equally to all employees and simply offer more protection against certain risks than against others. *Id.* In other words, a disability plan lawfully may provide less coverage for one kind of disability than for another if the difference in coverage is grounded in rational classifications of risk. Risk classification, after all, is fundamental to the business of insurance. The question then is whether there is some rational basis that justifies the distinction between what the LTD Plan offers by way of benefits to participants with physical disabilities and what it offers participants with mental disabilities. If there is such a justification, then the LTD Plan might withstand the attack that it discriminates among classes of persons with disabilities.

The ADA has a so-called safe harbor provision that is expressly applicable to Title I. That provisions states:

> (c) Insurance.
>
> Subchapters I through III of this chapter and title IV of this Act shall not be construed to prohibit or restrict—
>
> (1) an insurer, hospital or medical service company, health maintenance organization, or any agent, or entity that administers benefit plans or similar organizations from underwriting risks, classifying risks or administering such risks that are based on or not inconsistent with State law; or
>
> (2) a person or organization covered by this chapter from establishing, sponsoring, observing or administering the terms of a bona fide benefit plan that are based on underwriting risks, classifying risks or administering such risks that are based on or not inconsistent with State law; or
>
> (3) a person or organization covered by this chapter from establishing, sponsoring, observing or administering the terms of a bona fide benefit plan that is not subject to State laws that regulate insurance.
>
> Paragraphs (1), (2) and (3) shall not be used as subterfuge to evade the purposes of subchapter (sic) I and III of this chapter.

42 U.S.C. § 12201(c).

In explaining the purpose of the safe harbor provision, the House Judiciary Committee wrote:

> The Committee added this provision because it does not intend for the ADA to affect legitimate *classification of risks in insurance plans,* in accordance with state laws and regulations under which such plans are regulated. . . .
>
> Specifically, Section 5101(c)(1)[42 U.S.C. § 12201(c)(1)] makes it clear that insurers may continue to sell to and underwrite

individuals applying for life, health or other insurance on an individually underwritten basis . . . *so long as the standards used are based on sound actuarial data and not on speculation.*

Section 501(c)(2)[42 U.S.C. § 12201(c)(2)] recognizes the need for employers, and their agents, to establish and observe the terms of employee benefit plans *so long as these plans are based on legitimate underwriting or classification of risks*

* * *

In sum *ADA requests that underwriting and classification of risks be based on sound actuarial principles or be related to actual or reasonably anticipated experience.*

H.R. Rep. 101–485(III), 101st Cong. 2nd Sess.1990, *reprinted* in 1990 U.S.C.C.A.N. 445, 493–96.

Speaking specifically of differentiation in coverages and benefits, the House Report made the following observation.

Under the ADA, a person with a disability cannot be denied insurance *or be subject to different terms or conditions of insurance based on disability alone, if the disability does not impose increased risks* . . . Moreover, while a plan which limits certain kinds of coverage based on classification of risk would be allowed under [the safe harbor provision], the plan may not refuse to insure . . . *or limit the amount, extent or kind of coverage available* . . . solely because of a physical or mental impairment, *except where the refusal, limitation, or rate differential is based on sound actuarial principles or is related to actual or reasonably anticipated experience.*

H.R.Rep. No. 101–485(II), 101st Cong.2d Sess. 135–148, *reprinted in* 1990 U.S.C.C.A.N. 303, 419–20. That the safe harbor provision exists is itself further evidence that Title I prohibits discrimination among classes of persons with disabilities. See *Johnson,* 273 F.3d at 1056 ("Denial of [benefits under a long term disability plan] on the express ground that the claimant is mentally disabled is discrimination of a sort prohibited by [Title I of the ADA]—unless the ADA's safe harbor provision exempts such discrimination from liability.") The passages quoted above from the statute's legislative history serve to fortify that proposition. Differences in coverages or benefits are to be tolerated under Title I only to the extent that they are based on rational classifications of risks. If Title I permitted insurers or employers to offer different benefits to participants with mental disabilities from those offered to participants with physical disabilities, at the discretion of the employer or insurer, the safe harbor provision would hardly be necessary.

The question that now arises is who bears the burden of establishing how the LTD Plan fares under the safe harbor provision. Tufts argues that the claims of discrimination made by the plaintiff here must fail because the *plaintiff* has failed to allege that the LTD Plan is not a benefits plan that is outside of the protection of the safe harbor provision. The plaintiff counters that the burden is on the defendant to demonstrate that the LTD Plan falls within the safe harbor provision and thus is exempt from the ADA's general prohibition of discrimination. To put the matter differently, the defendants argue that the burden is on the plaintiff to plead and establish that the LTD is not sheltered by the safe harbor provision. Fletcher argues, on the other hand, that the applicability of the safe harbor provision is an affirmative defense to be asserted and established by the defendants in this case.

The First Circuit has not addressed the allocation of the burden of proof as to the applicability of the ADA's safe harbor clause. I must therefore look to the language and structure of the statute to determine where that burden lies. I start with the observation that the safe harbor provision is an exception to the general prohibition against disability-based discrimination. *Compare* 42 U.S.C. § 12112(a) *with* 42 U.S.C. § 12201(c). As a specific exception to a broad remedial statute, the safe harbor provision partakes more of the character of an affirmative defense than that of a necessary element of a plaintiff's ADA claim of discrimination.

Moreover, while the language of the safe harbor provision does not itself provide a clear answer to the allocation of the pleading burden, there is guidance in the legislative history of the ADA. As noted earlier, the House Report on the ADA states that the "ADA requires that underwriting and classification of risks be based on *sound actuarial principles or be related to actual or reasonably anticipated experience.*" H.R.Rep. No. 101–485(III), 101st Cong. 2nd Sess.1990, *reprinted in* 1990 U.S.C.C.A.N. 445, 494. Whether a benefits plan can be justified by rational underwriting principles or is based on actuarial data or reasonably anticipated experience requires knowledge of much more data than the typical plaintiff in a case of this sort is likely to have or can easily acquire. On the other hand, if such information exists, insurers like MetLife are likely to have ready access to it. Furthermore, an employer like Tufts, in exploring options among underwriters for the establishment of benefit plans, would far more likely to be able to obtain access to the relevant underwriting information and actuarial data, if it exists, than a plan participant like the plaintiff. Given that the applicability of the safe harbor provision to the LTD Plan will depend upon actuarial or other empirical data more likely to be in the possession of insurers or employers like the defendants here, it follows that such parties should bear the burden of pleading and establishing the applicability of the safe harbor provision. I conclude then that the present amended complaint is not deficient in failing to allege that the LTD is not protected by the safe harbor provision, and that the plaintiff has stated a claim for discrimination under Title I of the LTD Plan.

C. Count II: Title III of the ADA

Title III of the ADA provides that "[n]o individual shall be discriminated against on the basis of disability in the full and equal enjoyment of the goods, services . . . of any place of public accommodation. . . ." 42 U.S.C. § 12182(a). That title provides further that "[i]t shall be discriminatory to subject an individual or class of individuals on the basis of a disability . . . directly, or through contractual, licensing or other arrangements, to a denial of the opportunity of the individual or class to participate in or benefit from the goods, services, facilities, advantages or accommodations of an entity." 42 U.S.C. § 12182(b)(1)(A)(i). In addition, Title III forbids "afford[ing] an individual or class of individuals, on the basis of a disability or disabilities of such individual or class, directly, or through contractual, licensing, or other arrangements with the opportunity to participate in or benefit from a good, service, facility, privilege, advantage or accommodation that is not equal to that afforded to other individuals." 42 U.S.C. § 12182(b)(1)(A)(ii). The plaintiff argues that by offering her less coverage for her mental disability than it offered to persons with physical disabilities, defendant MetLife denied her the "full and equal enjoyment" of her benefits in violation of Title III of the ADA.

MetLife responds that Title III applies only to "places of public accommodation," and therefore does not cover benefit plans. MetLife's formulation of the scope of Title III, however, has been rejected by the First Circuit. *See Carparts Distribution Center, Inc. v. Automotive Wholesaler's Ass'n. of New England,* 37 F.3d 12, 19 (1st Cir.1994) (defining the term "public accommodation" to include access to insurance plans).

While the decision in *Carparts* involved *access* to an insurance plan, the First Circuit discussed, but left open the question whether Title III also covered the *content* of such plans. *See id.* at 19–20; *see also Tompkins v. United Healthcare of New England,* 203 F.3d 90, 95 n. 4 (1st Cir.2000) (observing that "[t]he discriminatory denial of benefits under a health care plan might, in some circumstances, state a claim under Title III of the ADA."). Lower courts in this circuit, however, have applied the reasoning in *Carparts* to the *substance* of employee benefits plans. *See Conners,* 42 F.Supp.2d at 46 ("Title III's proscription applies to the substance of, rather than merely the access to, employee benefit plans. . . ."); *Boots v. Northwestern Mutual Life Ins.,* 77 F.Supp.2d 211 (D.N.H.1999); *Doukas v. Metropolitan Life Ins. Co.,* 950 F.Supp. 422, 427 (D.N.H.1996) ("[T]his court's reading of the plain and ordinary meaning of Title III leads to the conclusion that the statute extends to an insurance company's denial of insurance."). For the reasons set forth in those decisions, I conclude that the anti-discrimination requirements of Title III extend to the content of insurance plans like the LTD Plan.

MetLife further contends that the plaintiff's Title III claim must fail as a matter of law because Title I provides the exclusive remedy for claims involving employment-related benefits. However, like its definition of "public accommodation," MetLife's position on this issue overlooks the First Circuit's decision in *Carparts,* which recognized the right of a plaintiff to challenge an employee health benefit plan under both Title I and Title III of the ADA. *See Carparts,* 37 F.3d 12 (1st Cir.1994). Thus, the plaintiff may challenge her employee benefits plan under *both* Title I *and* Title III.

* * *

IV. Conclusion

Tufts motion to dismiss count I and MetLife's motion to dismiss count II are DENIED. . . .

NOTES AND QUESTIONS

1. *Title I issue.* The court in *Fletcher* is going against the grain by holding that Title I prohibits an employer from offering a long term disability benefit plan that provides greater protection to individuals with physical disabilities than to individuals with mental disabilities. In fact, as discussed in the case above, several circuits (the Second, Fourth, Sixth, Seventh, Eighth, Tenth, and D.C. Circuits) have held that as long as benefits are offered to all employees, it does not violate the ADA to provide greater protection for some health risks over other health risks. Does the court in *Fletcher* make a persuasive argument to you regarding why it allows this claim? The employer would ultimately have the opportunity to prove that the benefit plan falls under the safe harbor provision if it is based on sound actuarial principles. Do you think that restricting long-term disability benefits for mental disabilities unless they result in hospitalization (without a similar restriction on physical disabilities) relies on sound actuarial principles?

2. *Title III's applicability.* There is also a circuit split regarding whether Title III applies to insurance plans. As discussed above in the *Gil* case, some courts have held that because Title III applies to "places" of public accommodation, it does not apply to an insurance policy (or a website). The court in *Fletcher* holds that not only does Title III apply with regard to decisions involving *access* to an insurance plan, but it also applies to decisions regarding the *content* of the insurance plans. Do you agree with the court that Congress intended the ADA to regulate insurance plans?

3. *Revisiting the access/content distinction.* The Circuits mentioned in Note 1 likely relied on the access/content distinction, first introduced in Chapter 5. Recall that the access/content distinction maintains that covered entities are not allowed to discriminate against individuals with disabilities when providing *access* to a particular benefit or service but that the ADA does not require the entities provide any particular *content.* A familiar example is that a bookstore cannot deny access to individuals who are blind (including allowing a service animal), but the bookstore is not required to stock books in

braille. Do you agree with the court in *Fletcher* that the content of the long-term disability plan can be regulated by the ADA?

F. REMEDIES

1. STATUTORY PROVISIONS

(a) In general

(1) Availability of remedies and procedures

The remedies and procedures set forth in section 2000a–3(a) of this title are the remedies and procedures this subchapter provides to any person who is being subjected to discrimination on the basis of disability in violation of this subchapter or who has reasonable grounds for believing that such person is about to be subjected to discrimination in violation of section 12183 of this title. Nothing in this section shall require a person with a disability to engage in a futile gesture if such person has actual notice that a person or organization covered by this subchapter does not intend to comply with its provisions.

(2) Injunctive relief

In the case of violations of sections 12182(b)(2)(A)(iv) and section 12183(a) of this title, injunctive relief shall include an order to alter facilities to make such facilities readily accessible to and usable by individuals with disabilities to the extent required by this subchapter. Where appropriate, injunctive relief shall also include requiring the provision of an auxiliary aid or service, modification of a policy, or provision of alternative methods, to the extent required by this subchapter.

42 U.S.C. § 12188.

This provision does not specify whether money damages are available; instead, it states that the remedies available under Title III are the remedies available under Title II of the Civil Rights Act of 1964, which applies to race discrimination in places of public accommodation. 42 U.S.C. § 2000–a(a) ("All persons shall be entitled to the full and equal enjoyment of the goods, services, facilities, privileges, advantages, and accommodations of any place of public accommodation, as defined in this section, without discrimination or segregation on the ground of race, color, religion, or national origin."). The remedies under that statute specify that plaintiffs can seek injunctive relief, but not money damages. 42 U.S.C. § 2000a–3. Why do you think Congress chose not to allow individuals with disabilities to seek damages under Title III?

2. STANDING

NAIMAN V. NEW YORK UNIVERSITY
1997 WL 249970 (S.D. N.Y., May 13, 1997)

McKENNA, D.J.

Plaintiff Alec Naiman, who is deaf, was a patient at New York University Medical Center ("NYUMC"), a medical facility operated by defendant New York University ("NYU"), on four occasions between February 9, 1993, and October 18, 1995. Naiman alleges that NYU effectively excluded him from its medical facility because it failed to provide him sufficient sign language interpreting services during his visits. He seeks monetary and injunctive relief under the Americans with Disabilities Act ("ADA"), 42 U.S.C. § 12182, the Rehabilitation Act ("RA") of 1973, as amended, 29 U.S.C. § 794, and state law.

NYU moves to dismiss Naiman's First Amended Complaint pursuant to Rule 12(b)(6) of the Federal Rules of Civil Procedure on the grounds that: (1) Naiman fails to allege a prima facie case under the ADA or the RA; . . . (3) Naiman does not have standing to seek injunctive relief; and (4) Naiman is not entitled to monetary relief under the RA because he has failed to allege that NYU's alleged violations were intentional.

For the reasons set forth below, NYU's motion to dismiss is granted in part, and denied in part.

I.   Factual Background

On February 9, 1993, and again on November 16, 1993, Naiman was seen at NYUMC for "an excruciatingly painful kidney stone attack." Despite Naiman's requests, NYUMC failed to provide Naiman with a qualified sign language interpreter. On the November 16, 1993, visit, after Naiman had been at NYUMC most of the day, NYUMC eventually presented a person with minimal ability to communicate in basic sign. This person was, in large part, unable to understand Naiman. On October 3, 1995, when Naiman was again a patient, NYUMC failed to provide him with any sign language interpreting services. During the fourth visit, on October 18, 1995, NYUMC failed to provide such services "in a timely manner."

Naiman claims that he requires a sign language interpreter to "meaningfully participate[ ] in his own medical care." Naiman also claims that NYUMC's failure to provide a qualified interpreter denied him the "effective communication" necessary to allow him to communicate with NYUMC doctors and staff. Naiman allegedly continues to suffer as a result of never knowing whether NYUMC, when rendering medical services to him, will be capable of effectively communicating with him.

II. Discussion

* * *

B. Prima Facie Case Under the ADA and the RA

[The court holds that plaintiff has stated a prima facie claim under both the ADA and the Rehabilitation Act.]

* * *

C. Standing to Seek Injunctive Relief

* * *

2. Standing

To establish that he has standing, Naiman bears the burden to establish three elements:

> . . . First, the plaintiff must have suffered an "injury in fact"—an invasion of a legally protected interest which is (a) concrete and particularized, . . . and (b) "actual or imminent, not 'conjectural' or 'hypothetical'. . . . Second, there must be a causal connection between the injury and the conduct complained of. . . . Third, it must be "likely," as opposed to merely "speculative," that the injury will be "redressed by a favorable decision."

Lujan v. Defenders of Wildlife, 504 U.S. 555, 560–61, 112 S.Ct. 2130 (1992). Regarding the "injury in fact" requirement, which is the only element of standing at issue on NYU's motion, " '[p]ast exposure to illegal conduct does not in itself show a present case or controversy regarding injunctive relief . . . if unaccompanied by any continuing, present adverse effects." *City of Los Angeles v. Lyons,* 461 U.S. 95, 102, 103 S.Ct. 1660 (1983). Thus, in order for Naiman to have standing to seek injunctive relief against NYU, he must allege facts sufficient to demonstrate a "real or immediate threat that [he] will be wronged again."

NYU argues that the four incidents alleged in the complaint, which NYU describes as "intermittent visits to the emergency room over a period of years," are insufficient to demonstrate a real or immediate threat that Naiman will be wronged again. NYU contends that Naiman has failed to set forth sufficient facts in his complaint to show that "the bouts of pain he has suffered are very likely to be repeated and to necessitate emergency attention at NYU Medical Center."

The instant case is distinguishable from the cases NYU cites in favor of dismissal. In the majority of those cases there was but a single allegedly discriminatory incident, and thus the plaintiffs failed to show that they were likely to be harmed again. *See Lyons,* 461 U.S. at 111–12 (plaintiff did not have standing to seek injunctive relief against city for allegedly illegal choke-hold performed by arresting officer); *O'Brien v. Werner Bus Lines,*

Inc., 1996 WL 82484 (E.D.Pa.1996) (blind plaintiff did not have standing to seek injunctive relief against bus company that refused to allow plaintiff's guide dog onto bus, where company, among other things, issued public apology, provided plaintiff with free bus tickets, and directed its bus drivers to admit guide dogs onto buses); *Hoepfl v. Barlow,* 906 F.Supp. 317 (E.D.Va.1995) (prospective surgical patient with AIDS did not have standing to seek injunctive relief against doctor who said that he would not touch AIDS patient with ten-foot pole, where doctor later said he would conduct the surgery and plaintiff received surgery from different doctor); *Aikins v. St. Helena Hosp.,* 843 F.Supp. 1329 (N.D.Cal.1994) (deaf plaintiff did not have standing to seek injunctive relief against hospital, which failed to provide effective communication to plaintiff, who arrived in emergency room because of husband's fatal cardiac arrest).

. . . Naiman's allegation of four visits to NYUMC in which NYUMC failed to provide him with effective communication are sufficient, for pleading purposes, to demonstrate that, if Naiman were to go to NYUMC again, it would again fail to provide him with effective communication. However, this is not enough to satisfy Naiman's burden to demonstrate standing to seek injunctive relief. Naiman must also show a "real or immediate threat" that he will require the services of NYUMC in the future.[4] Although the Court concludes that Naiman's First Amended Complaint fails to allege facts sufficient to demonstrate standing to seek injunctive relief against NYU, the Court grants Naiman leave to amend the complaint within thirty days of the date of this Memorandum and Order to satisfy his pleading burden.

D. Monetary Damages Under the Rehabilitation Act

Although there is still some disagreement as to the scope of available remedies under the RA, most courts agree that compensatory damages are available. *See DeLeo v. City of Stamford,* 919 F.Supp. 70, 73 n. 3 (D.Conn.1995). *DeLeo* also upheld plaintiff's claim for punitive damages under the RA. *Id.* at 74.

NYU argues that compensatory damages are available under the RA only for intentional discrimination. Assuming that intent is a prerequisite for monetary relief under the RA, Naiman's allegation that he requested a qualified interpreter, which was not provided, coupled with the absence of any allegation that NYU attempted to provide Naiman with effective communication, sufficiently alleges intent.

---

[4] Although not exhaustive nor necessarily dispositive, such allegations (if they can be made on the facts) might include whether Naiman suffers from a recurring medical condition and the reasons why NYUMC, as opposed to some other hospital, is the facility which Naiman would go to in an emergency.

III. Conclusion

For the reasons set forth above, NYU's motion to dismiss the First Amended Complaint is granted with respect to that part of the First Amended Complaint seeking injunctive relief. Naiman is granted leave to replead his claim for injunctive relief within thirty days of the date of this Memorandum and Order. Naiman has withdrawn his claim for monetary damages under the ADA. In all other respects, NYU's motion to dismiss is denied.

NOTES AND QUESTIONS

1. *Revisiting* Aikins. Recall that a case discussed above, *Aikins v. St. Helena Hospital,* 843 F.Supp. 1329 (N.D. Cal. 1994), involved similar facts—a deaf individual seeking interpreter services at a hospital. The difference in that case was that the plaintiff herself was not being treated in the hospital. She was there because her husband had a heart attack. In that case, the court held that the plaintiff had not sufficiently alleged standing. Especially because her husband had passed away while in the hospital, the court held that Aikins could not prove (at least on the facts alleged) that she suffered a real threat of requiring that hospital's services in the future. But the court did give the plaintiff the opportunity to amend her complaint to try to establish standing. After reading *Naiman,* do you think the plaintiff in *Aikins* will be able to amend her complaint to successfully allege standing? Why or why not?

2. *Real or immediate threat.* Proving standing often requires the plaintiff to prove a "real or immediate threat" that the plaintiff will be wronged again. This is often the most difficult element for plaintiffs to meet in order to establish standing. In *Naiman,* the plaintiff had visited the hospital four times over a period of three years, and the court held that even though his four visits established that, if he were to go again, he would likely experience ineffective communication, the four visits *alone* did not establish that he will again require the services of the hospital. The court gave him leave to amend his complaint to sufficiently allege that fact. What might he claim to establish this fact? More broadly, does this seem like a strange requirement to you? If the plaintiff can establish that the hospital violated the ADA by refusing to have available interpreter services, does it make sense that the only way the plaintiff's request for injunctive relief (forcing the hospital to have available such services all of the time) will be granted is if he can establish that he will likely use the hospital's services again? When ADA claims are brought against retail stores or restaurants, it is fairly easy for a plaintiff to allege that it is likely that he will again visit that store or restaurant (unless it is far from the plaintiff's home). But this is harder to allege with respect to hospital services unless the plaintiff has a chronic condition that causes frequent trips to emergency rooms. Thus, the only way the plaintiff can guarantee that the hospital will have an interpreter available if he needs hospital services again is if he can point to some evidence that he will definitely need hospital services again. Winning the case depends on him convincing the court that he will

definitely fall ill again and need the services of the emergency room. Should the standing requirement be this onerous?

3. SERIAL LITIGATION

MOLSKI V. EVERGREEN DYNASTY CORP.
500 F.3d 1047 (9th Cir. 2007)

PER CURIAM:

This appeal presents two orders of the district court for our review. The first order declared Jarek Molski a vexatious litigant and ordered that Molski obtain leave of the court before filing any claims under Title III of the Americans with Disabilities Act ("ADA") in the United States District Court for the Central District of California. The second order sanctioned the law firm representing Molski, Thomas E. Frankovich, a Professional Law Corporation ("the Frankovich Group"), by requiring it to obtain leave of the court before filing any claims under Title III of the ADA in the Central District of California. We dismiss two of the defendants-appellees from this appeal for lack of jurisdiction. As to the remaining parties, we hold that the district court acted within its sound discretion in entering the pre-filing orders against Molski and against the Frankovich Group, and we affirm the orders of the district court.

I

Molski, who is paralyzed from the chest down, needs a wheelchair to get around. He has filed about 400 lawsuits in the federal courts within the districts in California. Molski lives in Woodland Hills, California, but frequently travels. According to Molski's amended complaint in this case, during his travels, he stopped at the Mandarin Touch Restaurant in Solvang, California on January 25, 2003. After finishing his meal, Molski decided to use the restroom. Molski was able to pass through the narrow restroom door, but there was not enough clear space to permit him to access the toilet from his wheelchair. Molski then exited the restroom, and in the course of doing so, got his hand caught in the restroom door, "causing trauma" to his hand. Molski's amended complaint also alleged that Mandarin Touch contained other accessibility barriers "too numerous to list."

Asserting claims under the ADA and California law, Molski, along with co-plaintiff Disability Rights Enforcement, Education Services: Helping You Help Others ("DREES"), a non-profit corporation, sought injunctive relief, attorneys' fees and costs, and damages. Specifically, the complaint sought "daily damages of not less than $4,000/day . . . for each day after [Molski's] visit until such time as the restaurant is made fully accessible" as well as punitive damages and pre-judgment interest. The amended complaint named as defendants Mandarin Touch Restaurant, Evergreen Dynasty Corp., and Brian and Kathy McInerney.

Shortly after the defendants answered the complaint, Mandarin Touch and Evergreen Dynasty filed a motion for an order (1) declaring Molski a vexatious litigant; (2) requiring Molski to obtain the court's permission before filing any more complaints under the ADA; and (3) imposing monetary sanctions against Molski and his counsel, Thomas E. Frankovich. Defendants Brian and Kathy McInerney did not join the motion. In a published order, the district court granted the motion in part, declaring Molski a vexatious litigant and granting the defendants' request for a pre-filing order. *Molski v. Mandarin Touch Rest.,* 347 F.Supp.2d 860, 868 (C.D.Cal.2004) [hereinafter *Mandarin Touch I*].

In determining that Molski was a vexatious litigant, the district court applied the five factors set forth in the opinion of the United States Court of Appeals for the Second Circuit in *Safir v. United States Lines, Inc.,* 792 F.2d 19, 24 (2d Cir.1986). Those factors are: (1) the litigant's history of litigation and in particular whether it entailed vexatious, harassing, or duplicative suits; (2) the litigant's motive in pursuing the litigation, for example, whether the litigant had a good faith expectation of prevailing; (3) whether the litigant is represented by counsel; (4) whether the litigant has caused unnecessary expense to the parties or placed a needless burden on the courts; and (5) whether other sanctions would be adequate to protect the courts and other parties. *Id.*

The district court first noted that Molski had an extensive history of litigation. *Mandarin Touch I,* 347 F.Supp.2d at 864. While acknowledging that the fact that a plaintiff has filed a large number of suits, standing alone, does not warrant a pre-filing order, the district court noted that a large volume of suits might indicate an intent to harass defendants into agreeing to cash settlements. The district court also noted that Molski's complaints were all textually and factually similar. While again not entirely dispositive, the district court surmised that boilerplate complaints might indicate an intent to harass defendants.

Against this background, the district court's reasoning made clear that the most important consideration was its specific finding that the allegations in Molski's numerous and similar complaints were "contrived and not credible." The court stressed that Molski often filed multiple complaints against separate establishments asserting that Molski had suffered identical injuries at each establishment on the same day. The district court pointed out that Molski had filed thirteen separate complaints for essentially identical injuries allegedly sustained during one five-day period in May 2003. In particular, Molski had alleged that, at each establishment, he injured his "upper extremities" while transferring himself to a non-ADA-compliant toilet. The district court explicitly found that, in making these duplicitous injury claims, Molski had "plainly lied" in his filings to the court because the district court "simply [did] not believe that Molski suffered 13 nearly identical injuries, generally to the same part of his body, in the course of performing the same activity, over a five-day period."

Applying the second *Safir* factor, the district court concluded that Molski's motivation in bringing numerous suits alleging both violations of the ADA and California state civil rights laws was to extract cash settlements from defendants. Although the ADA grants private plaintiffs like Molski only the rights to seek injunctive relief, attorneys' fees, and costs, the California state civil rights laws amplify the scope of relief available under federal law by also permitting the recovery of money damages. *Compare* 42 U.S.C. §§ 2000a–3(a), 12188(a)(1), *with* Cal. Civ.Code §§ 51(f), 52(a), 54(c), 54.3(a). The district court acknowledged that raising multiple claims in one suit is, in and of itself, not vexatious. However, because Molski had tried on the merits only one of his approximately 400 suits and had settled all the others, the district court concluded that Molski's consistent approach was to use the threat of money damages under California law to extract cash settlements and move on to his next case.

Applying the third factor from *Safir,* the district court found that Molski had been represented by counsel in every suit he filed. The court wrote that "courts are generally protective of *pro se* litigants," but reasoned that "this same protection does not apply to litigants represented by counsel," and concluded that this factor also weighed in favor of issuing a pre-filing order.

Under the fourth *Safir* factor, the district court determined that the large number of vexatious claims Molski had filed had placed an undue burden on the courts.

Finally, applying the fifth factor from *Safir,* the district court found that the only effective way to protect the courts and other parties from future vexatious litigation by Molski was by entering a pre-filing order. Accordingly, the district court held that, "[b]efore filing any new litigation alleging violations of Title III of the ADA in the United States District Court for the Central District of California, Molski[must] file a motion for leave to file a complaint." The court required that Molski "submit a copy of this order and a copy of the proposed filing with every motion for leave."

In the same order, the district court denied the motion of Evergreen Dynasty and Mandarin Touch for sanctions as pre-mature. Finally, the district court issued an order to show cause why it should not impose a pre-filing sanction on Molski's attorneys, the Frankovich Group.

About three months later, the district court issued a published memorandum decision regarding that order to show cause. *See Molski v. Mandarin Touch Rest.,* 359 F.Supp.2d 924 (C.D.Cal.2005) [hereinafter *Mandarin Touch II*]. The district court imposed a pre-filing order on the Frankovich Group similar to the order that it had imposed on Molski. In its decision, the district court first observed that in 2004 the Frankovich

Group filed at least 223 nearly identical lawsuits in the Northern and Central Districts of California, that the complaints all stated an ADA claim and the same four claims under California state law, that the damages requested in each case were identical and that, other than superficial alteration of the names and facts, the complaints were textually identical down to the typos. The district court also noted that plaintiffs represented by the Frankovich Group would often file multiple complaints regarding similar or identical injuries sustained at multiple establishments on a single day. The district court noted that one-third of the suits were against ethnic restaurants and commented that "such establishments are seen as easy prey for coercive claims."

Supplementing its findings from its decision accompanying the pre-filing order entered against Molski, the district court found that the Frankovich Group had filed sixteen lawsuits on Molski's behalf alleging injuries sustained over a four-day period from May 20, 2003 to May 23, 2003, all alleging that Molski suffered injuries to his upper extremities as a result of transfers or negotiating barriers. The district court also noted that, on thirty-seven occasions in 2004 alone, Molski alleged that he had been injured two or more times on the same day. On nineteen occasions, Molski alleged that he had been injured three or more times in one day. And, on nine occasions in 2004, Molski alleged that he suffered four or more injuries in one day.

Additionally, the district court discussed what it characterized as an "astonishing" letter the Frankovich Group had sent to defendants in at least two cases after suing them. The letter described itself as "friendly advice" and counseled the unrepresented defendant against hiring a lawyer. The letter warned that a defense attorney would embark on a "billing expedition" and that the defendant's money would be best spent on settlement and remediation of the ADA violations, rather than hiring a defense attorney. The letter also advised the defendant that its insurance policy might cover the claim. Finally, the letter advised the defendant that it had no bona fide defense to the lawsuit.

Relying on its inherent power to levy sanctions, the district court ordered

> that The Frankovich Group, as presently constituted, and as it may hereafter be constituted, including shareholders, associates and employees, is required to file a motion requesting leave of court before filing any new complaints alleging violations of Title III of the Americans with Disabilities Act in the United States District Court for the Central District of California. Such a motion must include a copy of this order.

Id. at 926.

As the basis for its sanction, the court first emphasized the ethics rules violations contained in the letter discussed above. For example, the letter offered legal advice to an unrepresented party whose interests conflicted with the interests of the Frankovich Group's clients. *Id.* (citing Model Rules of Prof'l Conduct R. 4.3).

Next, the district court found that many of the claims of bodily injury in complaints filed by the Frankovich Group were "contrived." The court found in particular that "the rate of physical injury defies common sense," noting that the plaintiffs alleged similar injuries sustained in a similar fashion at different businesses on the same day. The court noted that the similar injuries did not excuse the existence of accessibility barriers, but that its finding that the injury claims were contrived was "merely a recognition of the fact that reasonable people, once injured, tend to take affirmative steps to avoid similar physical injuries, rather than repeat that same activity 400 times (or five times in the same day)."

The district court also criticized the practice of the Frankovich Group of waiting one year before filing their complaints, in order to maximize the damages threatened and to intimidate the small businesses against whom the Frankovich Group frequently filed its suits.

Finally, the district court found that the high settlement rate in cases brought by the Frankovich Group, coupled with the volume of cases filed, showed a pattern of extortion.

In addition to imposing a pre-filing order on the Frankovich Group, the district court requested that the California state bar investigate the Frankovich Group's practices and consider disciplinary action. In the same order, the district court dismissed the plaintiffs' state law claims, declining to exercise supplemental jurisdiction over them.

On August 31, 2005, the district court, in a third published order, granted the defendants summary judgment on Molski's ADA claim for lack of standing. *Molski v. Mandarin Touch Rest.*, 385 F.Supp.2d 1042, 1044 (C.D.Cal.2005). Because Molski's ADA claim was the final claim remaining in the case, the district court also entered an order dismissing with prejudice the plaintiffs' case in its entirety. (The district court had already dismissed DREES's ADA claim for lack of standing in an unpublished order filed on February 9, 2005.)

On September 13, 2005, Molski and DREES filed their notice of appeal. The notice provided that the plaintiffs were appealing four rulings of the district court: (1) the December 2004 order declaring Molski a vexatious litigant; (2) the February 2005 order dismissing DREES's ADA claim for lack of standing; (3) the March 2005 order sanctioning the Frankovich Group; and (4) the August 2005 order granting the defendants summary judgment on Molski's ADA claim for lack of standing and dismissing the case.

* * *

III

... Brian and Kathy McInerney ask us to dismiss them from this appeal because they were not parties to the motion that led to the pre-filing orders entered against Molski and the Frankovich Group. [The court dismisses Brian and Kathy McInerney from the appeal for lack of jurisdiction.]

IV

We next address whether the district court erred in declaring Molski a vexatious litigant and in entering a pre-filing order against him. Two district courts in our circuit disagree about whether Molski's frequent litigation is vexatious. In this case, the Central District of California deemed Molski a vexatious litigant. *See Mandarin Touch I,* 347 F.Supp.2d at 868. However, the Northern District of California has denied a motion to declare Molski a vexatious litigant in that district. *See Molski v. Rapazzini Winery,* 400 F.Supp.2d 1208, 1212 (N.D.Cal.2005). We review a pre-filing order entered against a vexatious litigant for abuse of discretion.

The All Writs Act, 28 U.S.C. § 1651(a), provides district courts with the inherent power to enter pre-filing orders against vexatious litigants. However, such pre-filing orders are an extreme remedy that should rarely be used. Courts should not enter pre-filing orders with undue haste because such sanctions can tread on a litigant's due process right of access to the courts. A court should enter a pre-filing order constraining a litigant's scope of actions in future cases only after a cautious review of the pertinent circumstances.

Nevertheless, "[f]lagrant abuse of the judicial process cannot be tolerated because it enables one person to preempt the use of judicial time that properly could be used to consider the meritorious claims of other litigants." *De Long [v. Hennessey],* 912 F.2d [1144,] 1148 [(9th Cir. 1990)]. Thus, in *De Long,* we outlined four factors for district courts to examine before entering pre-filing orders. First, the litigant must be given notice and a chance to be heard before the order is entered. Second, the district court must compile "an adequate record for review." Third, the district court must make substantive findings about the frivolous or harassing nature of the plaintiff's litigation. Finally, the vexatious litigant order "must be narrowly tailored to closely fit the specific vice encountered."

* * *

The first factor under *De Long* is whether Molksi [sic] was given notice and an opportunity to be heard before the district court entered the pre-filing order. This is a core requirement of due process. *De Long,* 912 F.2d at 1147. In this case, Molski had fair notice of the possibility that he might be declared a vexatious litigant and have a pre-filing order entered against him because the district court's order was prompted by a motion filed by the defendants and served on Molski's counsel. Also, Molski had the opportunity to oppose the motion, both in writing and at a hearing.

The second factor of the *De Long* standard is whether the district court created an adequate record for review. "An adequate record for review should include a listing of all the cases and motions that led the district court to conclude that a vexatious litigant order was needed." *De Long*, 912 F.2d at 1147. The record before the district court contained a complete list of the cases filed by Molski in the Central District of California, along with the complaints from many of those cases. Although the district court's decision entering the pre-filing order did not list every case filed by Molski, it did outline and discuss many of them. The district court supplemented its findings in *Mandarin Touch I* with a further discussion of Molski's litigation history in *Mandarin Touch II*. The district court compiled a record adequate for review of its order.

The third factor set forth by *De Long* gets to the heart of the vexatious litigant analysis, inquiring whether the district court made " 'substantive findings as to the frivolous or harassing nature of the litigant's actions.' " *De Long*, 912 F.2d at 1148. To decide whether the litigant's actions are frivolous or harassing, the district court must "look at 'both the number and content of the filings as indicia' of the frivolousness of the litigant's claims." "An injunction cannot issue merely upon a showing of litigiousness. The plaintiff's claims must not only be numerous, but also be patently without merit."

Molski concedes that he has filed numerous claims. However, Molski contends that his suits were not vexatious because they had merit. As the district court observed, it is likely that many of the businesses Molski sued were not in compliance with the ADA. *Mandarin Touch I*, 347 F.Supp.2d at 865. However, while Molski's complaints may have stated a legitimate claim for relief, it was not clearly erroneous for the district court to find that the claims of injury contained in those complaints were patently without merit. Because many of the violations Molski challenged were similar, it would have been reasonable for Molski's complaints to contain similar allegations of barriers to entry, inadequate signage, and so on. However, it is very unlikely that Molski suffered the same injuries, often multiple times in one day, performing the same activities—transferring himself from his wheelchair to the toilet or negotiating accessibility obstacles. Common sense dictates that Molski would have figured out some way to avoid repetitive injury-causing activity; even a young child who touches a hot stove quickly learns to avoid pain by not repeating the conduct. The district court's conclusion that Molski "plainly lied" in making his injury allegations was not clearly erroneous.

In light of the district court's finding that Molski did not suffer the injuries he claimed, it was not clearly erroneous for the district court to conclude that the large number of complaints filed by Molski containing false or exaggerated allegations of injury were vexatious.

The district court's determination that Molski harassed defendants into cash settlements was justified by its findings regarding Molski's litigation strategy. California law provides that a plaintiff who suffers discrimination based on his or her disability may recover up to three times the amount of actual damages for each offense, and that, at a minimum, the plaintiff must recover damages of not less than $4000. Cal. Civ.Code § 52(a). Thus, Molski usually sought damages of not less than $4000 for each day that a facility did not comply with the ADA. Because Molski would often wait to file suit until a full year elapsed since his visit to the defendants' establishments, defendants often faced claims for statutory damages of over one million dollars. While Molski's claim for daily damages might have been legally justified, it was not clearly erroneous for the district court to find that Molski's litigation strategy evidenced an intent to harass businesses into cash settlements.[6]

The district court also did not err when it inferred an intent to harass defendants into settlement from the fact that Molski had tried on the merits only one of his roughly 400 ADA cases and the fact that Molski and the Frankovich Group targeted ethnic restaurants viewed as easy prey for coercive claims.

Frivolous litigation is not limited to cases in which a legal claim is entirely without merit. It is also frivolous for a claimant who has some measure of a legitimate claim to make false factual assertions. Just as bringing a completely baseless claim is frivolous, so too a person with a measured legitimate claim may cross the line into frivolous litigation by asserting facts that are grossly exaggerated or totally false. In an adversary system, we do not fault counsel or client for putting their best arguments forward, and it is likely the unusual case in which a finding of frivolous litigation follows in the train of a legitimate legal claim. It is a question of degree where the line falls between aggressive advocacy of legitimate claims and the frivolous assertion of false allegations. In this case, the district court,

---

[6] We note that there was a substantial disconnect between the magnitude of injuries Molski suffered and the amount of damages he sought to recover. For example, in this case, in a declaration submitted to the district court, Molski admitted that the injury he suffered at Mandarin Touch—scraping his hand on the door frame—was "not a big injury." Nonetheless, Molski claimed damages of "not less than $4,000" for each of the 363 days that elapsed between when he visited Mandarin Touch on January 25, 2003, and when he filed his complaint on January 23, 2004. Molski thus made a damage claim of no less than $1,452,000 on the day he filed his complaint, with that amount growing by the day. Even if Molski could claim statutory minimum damages in an amount far greater than any actual injury he suffered, Molski's claims of damages far in excess of the injuries he suffered are not entirely irrelevant to determining whether his litigation was vexatious.

By seeking damages of *not less than* $4000 per day, Molski would claim actual damages beyond those to which he was arguably entitled under the California statutes.... Also, there existed a possibility that the district court would reject the notion that Molski could recover daily damages, and that Molski would be forced to seek, for the most part, actual damages. Additionally, Molski's complaints usually sought punitive damages. In all of those situations, to recover actual or punitive damages, Molski would need to prove a corresponding injury. Because he claimed damages far in excess of his actual injuries, his exaggerated claims of damages support a pre-filing order to the extent that he sought to recover more than the statutory minimum of damages.

looking at the allegations of hundreds of lawsuits, made a decision that Molski's baseless and exaggerated claims of injuries exceeded any legitimacy and were made for the purpose of coercing settlement. We cannot on this record conclude that the district court's factual determinations were clearly erroneous or that the district court erroneously reached the legal conclusion that Molski's litigation was vexatious.

The fourth and final factor in the *De Long* standard is that the pre-filing order must be narrowly tailored to the vexatious litigant's wrongful behavior. In *De Long,* we held overbroad an order preventing the plaintiff from filing any suit in a particular district court. . . . Here, by contrast, the district court's order is much narrower—it only prevents Molski from filing actions under Title III of the ADA in the Central District of California. The order thus appropriately covers only the type of claims Molski had been filing vexatiously—ADA claims. The order also does not prevent Molski from filing any ADA complaints, it merely subjects Molski's complaints to an initial screening review by a district judge. The order is narrowly tailored because it will not deny Molski access to courts on any ADA claim that is not frivolous, yet it adds a valuable layer of protection, which we think was warranted, for the courts and those targeted by Molski's claims.

In summary, we reemphasize that the simple fact that a plaintiff has filed a large number of complaints, standing alone, is not a basis for designating a litigant as "vexatious." We also emphasize that the textual and factual similarity of a plaintiff's complaints, standing alone, is not a basis for finding a party to be a vexatious litigant. Accessibility barriers can be, and often are, similar in different places of public accommodation, and there is nothing inherently vexatious about using prior complaints as a template.

As we discussed above, the ADA does not permit private plaintiffs to seek damages, and limits the relief they may seek to injunctions and attorneys' fees. We recognize that the unavailability of damages reduces or removes the incentive for most disabled persons who are injured by inaccessible places of public accommodation to bring suit under the ADA. *See* Samuel R. Bagenstos, *The Perversity of Limited Civil Rights Remedies: The Case of "Abusive" ADA Litigation,* 54 U.C.L.A. L.Rev. 1, 5 (2006). As a result, most ADA suits are brought by a small number of private plaintiffs who view themselves as champions of the disabled. District courts should not condemn such serial litigation as vexatious as a matter of course. For the ADA to yield its promise of equal access for the disabled, it may indeed be necessary and desirable for committed individuals to bring serial litigation advancing the time when public accommodations will be compliant with the ADA. But as important as this goal is to disabled individuals and to the public, serial litigation can become vexatious when, as here, a large number of nearly-identical complaints contain factual allegations that are contrived, exaggerated, and defy common sense. False or grossly exaggerated claims of injury, especially when made with the intent to coerce settlement, are at odds with our system of justice, and Molski's history of litigation warrants the need for a pre-filing review of his claims.

We acknowledge that Molski's numerous suits were probably meritorious in part—many of the establishments he sued were likely not in compliance with the ADA. On the other hand, the district court had ample basis to conclude that Molski trumped up his claims of injury. The district court could permissibly conclude that Molski used these lawsuits and their false and exaggerated allegations as a harassing device to extract cash settlements from the targeted defendants because of their noncompliance with the ADA. In light of these conflicting considerations and the relevant standard of review, we cannot say that the district court abused its discretion in declaring Molski a vexatious litigant and in imposing a pre-filing order against him.

V

The final issue in this case is whether the district court erred in imposing a pre-filing order against the Frankovich Group. We review the district court's imposition of sanctions against an attorney for abuse of discretion.

The district court in this case sanctioned the Frankovich Group with a pre-filing order pursuant to its inherent power to regulate abusive or bad-faith litigation. *Mandarin Touch II,* 359 F.Supp.2d at 928. "This inherent power derives from the lawyer's role as an officer of the court which granted admission." The Supreme Court has cautioned that, because of the potency of attorney sanction orders, courts must exercise their inherent sanctioning authority with restraint and sound discretion. *Chambers,* 501 U.S. at 45, 111 S.Ct. 2123.

As a procedural matter, before imposing sanctions on an attorney, the district court must afford the attorney notice and an opportunity to be heard. As a substantive matter, justifications for imposing a pre-filing sanction on an attorney "include the attorney's willful abuse of the judicial process, bad faith conduct during litigation, or filing frivolous papers." Violations of ethics rules can also serve as a ground for imposing sanctions. Additionally, the sanction imposed must be tailored to curtail the attorney's particular misconduct.

In this case, the district court afforded the Frankovich Group notice and an opportunity to be heard before imposing its sanction. On December 10, 2004, the district court issued an order to show cause why the court should not impose a pre-filing order on the Frankovich Group for its role in facilitating Molski's litigation. The Frankovich Group responded to the order in writing, and on February 7, 2005, the district court conducted a hearing on the order. These proceedings provided the Frankovich Group the notice and opportunity to be heard that due process requires.

The district court also did not abuse its discretion in making the substantive determination that a pre-filing order was justified based on the conduct of the Frankovich Group. As discussed above, Molski's complaints repeatedly alleged injuries that the district court found to be contrived and untrue. Also, the claims of injuries often were inconsistent with the barriers alleged. For example, complaints filed by the Frankovich Group would allege bodily injury suffered as a result of inadequate signage or the lack of an accessible parking space.

In light of the similarity and exaggerated nature of the frequent injuries Molski alleged, we concluded above that the district court's findings regarding the lack of veracity in Molski's complaints were not clearly erroneous and that the district court was within its discretion in imposing a pre-filing order on Molski. When a client stumbles so far off the trail, we naturally should wonder whether the attorney for the client gave inadequate or improper advice. That the Frankovich Group filed numerous complaints containing false factual allegations, thereby enabling Molski's vexatious litigation, provided the district court with sufficient grounds on which to base its discretionary imposition of sanctions.

The district court also emphasized that the letter that the Frankovich Group sent to the defendants in at least two cases may have violated multiple ethics rules. While we do not rely on the possible ethical violations as a ground for affirming the sanction imposed on the Frankovich Group, we note that Frankovich Group's decision to send letters that many might view as intimidating to unrepresented defendants was, at best, a questionable exercise of professional judgment. The letters gave legal advice to unrepresented parties whose interests conflicted with the interests of the Frankovich Group, and this advice quite possibly ran afoul of relevant ethical rules. *See* Model Rules of Prof'l Conduct R. 4.3 ("The lawyer shall not give legal advice to an unrepresented person, other than the advice to secure counsel, if the lawyer knows or reasonably should know that the interests of such a person are or have a reasonable possibility of being in conflict with the interests of the client.").

Additionally, the letters advised the defendant that it had no bona fide defense to the ADA action, when in fact this might not be true in a particular case. For example, the ADA requires the removal of barriers in certain structures only when "such removal is readily achievable." 42 U.S.C. § 12182(b)(2)(A)(iv). This possibly false statement of law may have violated ethics provisions regarding a lawyer's candor to third parties. *See* Model Rules of Prof'l Conduct R. 4.1(a) (providing that "[i]n the course of representing a client a lawyer shall not knowingly . . . make a false statement of material fact or law to a third person.")

. . . [B]ecause the district court was within its discretion in sanctioning the Frankovich Group based on the questionable allegations of physical injury in the complaints they filed, we need not rely on the possible ethics rules violations as a ground for affirming the district court's sanction.

Finally, we hold that the district court's pre-filing sanction is sufficiently tailored to combat the Frankovich Group's practice of repetitive litigation based on false allegations of injury. The sanction requires the Frankovich Group to seek leave of the court before filing any more ADA complaints in the Central District of California, and requires that the district court's order in this case accompany the Frankovich Group's motion for leave. Functionally, the sanction ensures that a judge will initially determine whether the factual allegations in future complaints are colorable. The order will protect against the extracting of possibly unjustified settlements from uncounseled small-business defendants intimidated by the spectre of a federal complaint coupled with a coercive and misleading communication from a law firm. However, the order does not make it impossible for the Frankovich Group to pursue meritorious ADA litigation in the district court. Moreover, . . . the Frankovich Group only used abusive litigation tactics in connection with litigation under the ADA. The pre-filing order rightly applies only to complaints asserting claims for relief under the ADA. For these reasons, we hold that the pre-filing order imposed in this case is adequately tailored to punish the past sanctionable conduct of the Frankovich Group, and, more importantly, to protect the courts and the public from any future misconduct by that law firm. Lawyers are required to give their clients' interests zealous advocacy, and while the pre-filing order in this case will not stand in the way of advocacy for legitimate claims, it will help to ensure that the services of the Frankovich Group are used in support of valid claims and not as a device to encourage settlement of unwarranted or exaggerated claims. We affirm the district court's order imposing sanctions on the Frankovich Group.

ORDER

All judges on the panel have voted to deny Plaintiff/ Appellant's Petition for Panel Rehearing, and so that petition is DENIED.

The full court has been advised of Plaintiff/Appellant's Petition for Rehearing En Banc, and a judge of this court requested a vote on whether this case should be reheard en banc; however, a majority of the non-recused active judges of the court did not vote in favor of en banc consideration. Fed. R.App. P. 35. Accordingly, the Petition for Rehearing En Banc is also DENIED. No further petitions for rehearing or rehearing en banc shall be considered.

BERZON, CIRCUIT JUDGE, with whom KOZINSKI, CHIEF JUDGE, and PREGERSON, REINHARDT, HAWKINS, MCKEOWN, WARDLAW, W. FLETCHER, and PAEZ, CIRCUIT JUDGES, join, dissenting from the denial of rehearing en banc:

Pre-filing orders infringe the fundamental right to access the courts. They are properly reserved for extreme situations where there is absolutely no possibility that the allegations could support judicial relief *and* filing the suit is a burden on both the court and the opposing party-a costly exercise in futility. Under those circumstances, less draconian sanctions will not suffice. Because, by any measure, this is not such a case, I respectfully dissent from the denial of rehearing en banc.

* * *

II.

The panel opinion pays lip service to the long-standing and constitutionally-based principle that "[a]n injunction cannot issue merely upon a showing of litigiousness. The plaintiff's claims must not only be numerous, but also be patently without merit." Yet, neither the panel nor the district court contend that all or most of Molski's hundreds of ADA claims actually lack merit. In fact, both expressly concede that they are probably meritorious. Instead, the panel relies on the district court's finding that Molski's *claims of injury . . . were patently without merit,"* and concludes this is enough to make the litigation frivolous.

As an initial matter, the district court's conclusion that Molski fabricated many allegations of injury, which was affirmed by the panel, simply cannot meet our standard for factual frivolousness. To be frivolous, factual allegations must be "wholly fanciful" or "conflicting with facts of which the district court may take judicial notice." *Franklin v. Murphy,* 745 F.2d 1221, 1228 (9th Cir.1984).

The district court and the panel relied solely upon the similarity and multitude of Molski's injuries: Numerous complaints alleged that he incurred physical injuries while attempting to overcome non-ADA-compliant public accommodations. The panel asserts that "it is very unlikely that Molski suffered the same injuries, often multiple times in one day, performing the same activities-transferring himself from his wheelchair to the toilet or negotiating accessibility obstacles. Common sense dictates that Molski would have figured out some way to avoid repetitive injury-causing activity; even a young child who touches a hot stove quickly learns to avoid pain by not repeating the conduct." On this reasoning, the panel concludes that the district court's finding that Molski "plainly lied" in his injury allegations was not clearly erroneous.

But the similarity of these injuries alone does not lead to the conclusion that the allegations are patently false. First, as the panel concedes, "[b]ecause many of the violations Molski challenged were similar, it would have been reasonable for Molski's complaints to contain similar allegations of barriers to entry, inadequate signage, and so on." In addition, Molski provided a reasonable explanation for the similarity of his injuries and the injurious nature of seemingly small acts. As another district court explained, in rejecting the district court's analysis here and declining to find Molski a vexatious litigant:

> Molski explains that, as a paraplegic, he relies entirely on his upper extremities and the strain of the improper transfers to the toilet are real injuries to him. Even though the pain might be short-lived, the cumulative effect of the multiple injuries is to wear down his upper extremities, joints, and shoulders. Molski also frequently injures his buttocks when forced to transfer to a toilet that is not configured in compliance with the ADA. Molski explains that, because he sits on his buttocks all day, bruises on his buttocks do not heal quickly or easily. . . .

> Molski supports the veracity of his claims of injury with a declaration from his treating physician, Dr. Thomas Lyle Hedge. . . . Dr. Hedge declares that Molksi [sic] has suffered "repetitive, continuous and cumulative" trauma/physical injury to the upper extremities from confronting architectural barriers such as unpaved pathways and toilets without proper grab bars or at an improper height.

Molski v. Rapazzini Winery, 400 F.Supp.2d 1208, 1210–11 (N.D.Cal.2005). Given this explanation, the factual allegations of injury here were simply not "wholly fanciful," *Franklin,* 745 F.2d at 1228, even if the incremental nature of the alleged injury was not spelled out.

But even if Molski's allegations of injury *were* meritless, the pre-filing order would not be justified: The allegations of injury are entirely irrelevant to Molski's ADA causes of action; past actual injury is not necessary to bring a claim under Title III of the ADA. *Molski v. M.J. Cable, Inc.,* 481 F.3d 724, 730 (9th Cir.2007). Allegations of injury are not necessary either to sue for statutory damages under California's Unruh Act. *Botosan v. Paul McNally Realty,* 216 F.3d 827, 835 (9th Cir.2000). The panel appears to so recognize, but suggests that there are some scenarios under which Molski might want to pursue actual rather than statutory damages under state law, so the allegations of physical injury "are not entirely irrelevant." That may be. But the tangential connection of the physical injury allegation to the potential for success in the cases certainly makes it difficult to characterize the complaints as a whole as frivolous in any ordinary sense of that term.

The panel's other complaints similarly fail to justify a prefiling order. The panel complains that Molski sought daily statutory damages under California law, yet recognizes that these claims "might have been legally justified" because of a split among district courts on the issue. The panel also relies upon the fact that Molski often waited a year before filing suit, which greatly increased the statutory damages claim. But this conduct is permitted under the statute; if there is a problem created by the statutory scheme, the appropriate fix is legislative, not judicial.

In sum: The panel justifies its ruling by relying on assertedly false claims of injury that would be relevant only under California law and on permissible litigation strategies that increase Molski's damages claim under California law. Not only do these reasons entirely fail to justify the extreme sanction of a pre-filing order, they are also exclusively concerned with Molski's claims under state law. Yet the prefiling order enjoins Molski from filing only *federal ADA claims*. . . . At the very least, the pre-filing order should restrict Molski's ability to file access claims only under California law. What we have here, in other words, is not a "close[ ] fit" but a grotesquely oversized pre-filing order, going far beyond the only "vice[s] encountered" in the complaints, none of which have anything at all to do with the allegations of ADA violations.

III.

I recognize that some of the tactics used by Molski and the Frankovich Group are cause for concern. But there are ample avenues for addressing any concerns raised by this case-avenues that do not involve one judge, acting alone, imposing a pre-filing order that covers an entire district.

Let me emphasize the impact of the district court's decision: *One judge* has determined that Molski and the Frankovich Group are forbidden to file ADA complaints without prior approval in the *entire Central District*. That judge has not in any way specified what standards will be used in deciding which cases may be filed and which may not. Other judges in that district may disagree with the imposition of the pre-filing order-in fact, a majority may. Yet, they have no say at all in the matter. The likelihood of internal disagreement is highlighted by the fact that a judge in the Northern District has determined, on a similar record, that Molski should *not* be subjected to a pre-filing order. *Molski v. Rapazzini Winery*, 400 F.Supp.2d at 1209–12. So Molski can now bring ADA suits in the Northern District seeking to assure access in places of public accommodation, but cannot do so in the Central District without subjecting himself to prescreening by a single judge.

* * *

IV.

At bottom, the panel may be uncomfortable with ADA litigation that it suspects is being brought to induce settlement. This concern with serial access litigation is shared by many, rightly or wrongly. But the phenomenon is a creature of our federal and state statutes and cannot justify the issuing of prefiling orders that enjoin meritorious lawsuits. Moreover, while self-interest surely drives serial access litigation in part, the reason there *can* be so many lawsuits about access to public accommodations is that there are so many violations of the laws that seek to assure access, and so many disabled people are thwarted from participating equally in the activities of everyday life. I fear that the panel's opinion may be widely used to restrict critical private enforcement of civil rights laws by other litigants and lawyers. This case should have been heard en banc to prevent that result.

* * *

NOTES AND QUESTIONS

1. *The debate over notice.* Some businesses believe that it is unfair for an individual with a disability to sue them without giving them notice of the accessibility violations in their places of business and giving them an opportunity to remedy the deficiencies. In fact, bills to require notice have been proposed in Congress several times, most recently in 2017, where the bill passed in the House. *See, e.g.,* ADA Education & Reform Act of 2017, H.R. 620, 115th Congress (2017–18). This bill would amend the ADA to state that a claim based on the failure to remove architectural barriers may not be commenced unless (1) the person aggrieved has provided to the owner or operator of the place of public accommodation a written notice specific enough to allow the identification of the barrier; and (2) for 60 days after receipt of notice the owner or operator fails to provide to the person aggrieved a written description outlining improvements that will be made to remove the barrier. However, if the removal of the barrier requires additional time (beyond the 60 days), the owner or operator is only required to make "substantial progress in removing the barrier . . . ." *Id.*

Proponents of the bill argue that many businesses (especially smaller businesses who do not have easy access to attorneys) are not aware that they are not in compliance with the ADA. For some of these businesses, the very detailed accessibility guidelines are too complicated for them to navigate. Proponents also argue that a notice requirement would promote voluntary compliance with the ADA, which is preferable to clogging the courts with ADA Title III lawsuits. On the other hand, why should a plaintiff with a disability be required to do the background work of identifying the specific facts that constitute the alleged violation, as would be required under these notice acts? After all, the ADA has been in existence for 30 years as of this writing; thus, no business can claim that it is unaware of the ADA's requirements. This notice requirement would also allow businesses to delay complying with the ADA's accessibility requirements until they get notice that they are in violation of the Act. In the meantime, many individuals with disabilities might have been injured or deterred by inaccessible businesses but if they do not have access to a lawyer, they wouldn't put the business on notice. Which side of this debate do you agree with? Should plaintiffs be required to put a business on notice of the ADA violations before filing suit under Title III?

2. *The debate over serial litigation.* Because there are no damages available under Title III, very few individuals with disabilities have an incentive to bring a lawsuit against a business that is not in compliance with the ADA. Finding an attorney to take the case is often difficult, and unless the attorney is willing to pursue the litigation on a contingency basis, most

individual plaintiffs cannot afford to pay for the fees or costs associated with litigating the case. Thus, it has become fairly common for an individual with a disability and a lawyer to team up and file many lawsuits against businesses that are in violation of the ADA's accessibility requirements. The *Molski* case above illustrates the debate over this practice. On the one hand, it seems unlikely that Molski injured himself the exact same way several times in one day at different restaurants; and thus, perhaps some of the injuries were fabricated or at least exaggerated. On the other hand, all of the cases clearly had merit. These restaurants or other places of public accommodation were in violation of the ADA. Without serial litigators like Molski, most of these businesses would continue to operate in violation of the ADA and individuals with disabilities would either be deterred from visiting those places or might try to enter and injure themselves because of the inaccessible features of the business. What do you think about this issue? Should courts try to deter serial litigation by requiring serial litigants like Molski to get permission of the court before filing any ADA Title III lawsuits? Or is serial litigation the only practical way to get businesses to remedy Title III violations in light of the unavailability of damages?

3. *Other* Molski *cases.* As you likely gathered from the *Molski* decision above, there are several reported decisions where Molski is the plaintiff. In at least one of these cases, the court used the fact that Molski is a serial litigant to hold that Molski lacks standing to sue. *See, e.g.,* Molski v. Kahn Winery, 405 F.Supp.2d 1160 (C.D. Cal. 2005). Basically, the court stated that when demonstrating that he was likely to return to the business and therefore suffer injury again, Molski's credibility was undermined by his litigation history. *Id.* at 1168–69. But not all courts have ruled against Molski. For instance, in *Molski v. M.J. Cable, Inc.*, 481 F.3d 724 (9th Cir. 2007), the court held that the district court below had abused its discretion when it denied Molski's motion for a new trial. The district court had reasoned that when the jury answered "no" to the question of whether the defendant had failed to identify and remove architectural barriers at the defendant's restaurant, the jury must have determined that Molski was not an individual under the ADA; rather, because of his litigiousness, he was a "business." *Id.* at 731–32. The Ninth Circuit disagreed with this theory and concluded that the record provides no evidence in support of the jury verdict; thus, the district court abused its discretion in denying Molski's motion for a new trial. *Id.* at 734.

4. *Improving compliance with Title III.* One thing that becomes obvious from reading the *Molski* decision is how many businesses are not in compliance with Title III. Regardless of whether you think serial litigation should be encouraged or not, is there another solution to improve compliance with Title III? Is private litigation the best way to improve compliance? Although no business should be able to claim that it is unaware of the ADA, it is true that the ADA's accessibility guidelines are very technical and confusing, especially to a non-lawyer. Can you think of a way to educate businesses about their ADA obligations that does not involve private litigation?

4. STATUTE OF LIMITATIONS

Title III of the ADA does not contain a statute of limitations period. Thus, the courts apply the statute of limitations of the most analogous state law. *See, e.g.,* Pickern v. Holiday Quality Foods, Inc., 293 F.3d 1133 (9th Cir. 2002) (applying California's one-year statute of limitations for personal injury actions); Scherr v. Marriott International, Inc., 703 F.3d 1069, 1075 (7th Cir. 2013) (applying Illinois's two-year statute of limitation period for personal injury actions). One issue that sometimes arises is whether the plaintiff must personally encounter physical barriers in a place of public accommodation during the limitations period if the plaintiff is already aware that those barriers exist. Title III has a specific provision stating that it does not require a "person with a disability to engage in a futile gesture if such person has actual notice that a person or organization . . . does not intend to comply" with the ADA. 42 U.S.C. § 12188(a)(1). Thus, in *Pickern,* 293 F.3d at 1136–37, the court stated that the plaintiff was not required to re-enter defendant's grocery store once he was aware that barriers existed and he had alleged that those barriers deterred him from re-entering the store.

CHAPTER 7

EDUCATION

■ ■ ■

A. HIGHER EDUCATION

1. INTRODUCTION/STATUTORY COVERAGE

Three different statutory provisions are potentially applicable in cases of disability discrimination in higher education.

Section 504 of the Rehabilitation Act provides:

> No otherwise qualified handicapped individual in the United States, as defined in section 706(7) of this title, shall, solely by reason of his handicap, be excluded from the participation in, be denied the benefits of, or be subjected to discrimination under any program or activity receiving Federal financial assistance. . . .

29 U.S.C. § 794. Thus, because all institutions of higher education receive *some* federal financial assistance, this statute applies in virtually *all* higher education cases.

Title II of the ADA, which applies to all state-run higher education institutions, provides:

> [N]o qualified individual with a disability shall, by reason of such disability, be excluded from participation in or be denied the benefits of the services, programs, or activities of a public entity, or be subjected to discrimination by any such entity. . . .

42 U.S.C. § 12132.

Title III of the ADA, which applies to privately owned institutions of higher education, provides:

> No individual shall be discriminated against on the basis of disability in the full and equal enjoyment of the goods, services, facilities, privileges, advantages, or accommodations of any place of public accommodation by any person who owns, leases (or leases to), or operates a place of public accommodation.

42 U.S.C. § 12182. Educational institutions are included in the definition of places of "public accommodation." 42 U.S.C. § 12181(7)(J) (defining public accommodation to include: "a nursery, elementary, secondary, undergraduate, or postgraduate private school, or other place of education").

Because the Rehabilitation Act was enacted seventeen years before the ADA, some of the cases you will read in the higher education section of this chapter will be cases decided under the Rehabilitation Act.

2. ADMISSIONS

a. Pre-Admission Inquiries

Department of Education regulations provide that a post-secondary institution "may not make preadmission inquiry as to whether an applicant for admission is a handicapped person but, after admission, may make inquiries on a confidential basis as to handicaps that may require accommodation." 34 C.F.R. § 104.42(b)(4). However, there is a "preadmission inquiry exception," which provides:

> (c) Preadmission inquiry exception. When a recipient is taking remedial action to correct the effects of past discrimination pursuant to § 104.6(a) or when a recipient is taking voluntary action to overcome the effects of conditions that resulted in limited participation in its federally assisted program or activity pursuant to § 104.6(b), the recipient may invite applicants for admission to indicate whether and to what extent they are handicapped, *Provided*, That:
>
>> (1) The recipient states clearly on any written questionnaire used for this purpose or makes clear orally if no written questionnaire is used that the information requested is intended for use solely in connection with its remedial action obligations or its voluntary action efforts; and
>>
>> (2) The recipient states clearly that the information is being requested on a voluntary basis, that it will be kept confidential, that refusal to provide it will not subject the applicant to any adverse treatment, and that it will be used only in accordance with this part.

34 C.F.R. § 104.42(c).

b. Qualified Individual with a Disability

For most academic programs at institutions of higher education, a student's physical disability is usually irrelevant to the admission decision. For instance, the fact that a student uses a wheelchair is irrelevant for most academic programs that only involve classroom learning. The institution will have to provide accommodations, but they will likely not be difficult or onerous to provide. However, with respect to some academic programs, a physical or mental disability might have an effect on whether the individual is considered a "qualified individual with a disability." The following case addresses that issue.

SOUTHEASTERN COMMUNITY COLLEGE V. DAVIS
442 U.S. 397, 99 S.Ct. 2361 (1979)

JUSTICE POWELL delivered the opinion of the Court.

This case presents a matter of first impression for this Court: Whether § 504 of the Rehabilitation Act of 1973, which prohibits discrimination against an "otherwise qualified handicapped individual" in federally funded programs "solely by reason of his handicap," forbids professional schools from imposing physical qualifications for admission to their clinical training programs.

I

Respondent, who suffers from a serious hearing disability, seeks to be trained as a registered nurse. During the 1973–1974 academic year she was enrolled in the College Parallel program of Southeastern Community College, a state institution that receives federal funds. Respondent hoped to progress to Southeastern's Associate Degree Nursing program, completion of which would make her eligible for state certification as a registered nurse. In the course of her application to the nursing program, she was interviewed by a member of the nursing faculty. It became apparent that respondent had difficulty understanding questions asked, and on inquiry she acknowledged a history of hearing problems and dependence on a hearing aid. She was advised to consult an audiologist.

On the basis of an examination at Duke University Medical Center, respondent was diagnosed as having a "bilateral, sensori-neural hearing loss." A change in her hearing aid was recommended, as a result of which it was expected that she would be able to detect sounds "almost as well as a person would who has normal hearing." But this improvement would not mean that she could discriminate among sounds sufficiently to understand normal spoken speech. Her lipreading skills would remain necessary for effective communication: "While wearing the hearing aid, she is well aware of gross sounds occurring in the listening environment. However, she can only be responsible for speech spoken to her, when the talker gets her attention and allows her to look directly at the talker."

Southeastern next consulted Mary McRee, Executive Director of the North Carolina Board of Nursing. On the basis of the audiologist's report, McRee recommended that respondent not be admitted to the nursing program. In McRee's view, respondent's hearing disability made it unsafe for her to practice as a nurse. In addition, it would be impossible for respondent to participate safely in the normal clinical training program, and those modifications that would be necessary to enable safe participation would prevent her from realizing the benefits of the program: "To adjust patient learning experiences in keeping with [respondent's] hearing limitations could, in fact, be the same as denying her full learning to meet the objectives of your nursing programs."

* * *

[After] Respondent [appealed the denial of her admission, she] filed suit in the United States District Court for the Eastern District of North Carolina, alleging both a violation of § 504 of the Rehabilitation Act of 1973, and a denial of equal protection and due process. After a bench trial, the District Court entered judgment in favor of Southeastern. It confirmed the findings of the audiologist that even with a hearing aid respondent cannot understand speech directed to her except through lipreading, and further found:

> "[I]n many situations such as an operation room intensive care unit, or post-natal care unit, all doctors and nurses wear surgical masks which would make lip reading impossible. Additionally, in many situations a Registered Nurse would be required to instantly follow the physician's instructions concerning procurement of various types of instruments and drugs where the physician would be unable to get the nurse's attention by other than vocal means." . . .

Based on these findings, the District Court concluded that respondent was not an "otherwise qualified handicapped individual" protected against discrimination by § 504. In its view, "[o]therwise qualified, can only be read to mean otherwise able to function sufficiently in the position sought in spite of the handicap, if proper training and facilities are suitable and available." Because respondent's disability would prevent her from functioning "sufficiently" in Southeastern's nursing program, the court held that the decision to exclude her was not discriminatory within the meaning of § 504.

On appeal, the Court of Appeals for the Fourth Circuit reversed. 574 F.2d 1158 (1978). It did not dispute the District Court's findings of fact, but held that the court had misconstrued § 504. In light of administrative regulations that had been promulgated while the appeal was pending, see 42 Fed.Reg. 22676 (1977), the appellate court believed that § 504 required Southeastern to "reconsider plaintiff's application for admission to the nursing program without regard to her hearing ability." It concluded that the District Court had erred in taking respondent's handicap into account in determining whether she was "otherwise qualified" for the program, rather than confining its inquiry to her "academic and technical qualifications." The Court of Appeals also suggested that § 504 required "affirmative conduct" on the part of Southeastern to modify its program to accommodate the disabilities of applicants, "even when such modifications become expensive."

Because of the importance of this issue to the many institutions covered by § 504, we granted certiorari. We now reverse.

II

As previously noted, this is the first case in which this Court has been called upon to interpret § 504. . . . Section 504 by its terms does not compel educational institutions to disregard the disabilities of handicapped individuals or to make substantial modifications in their programs to allow disabled persons to participate. Instead, it requires only that an "otherwise qualified handicapped individual" not be excluded from participation in a federally funded program "solely by reason of his handicap," indicating only that mere possession of a handicap is not a permissible ground for assuming an inability to function in a particular context.

The court below, however, believed that the "otherwise qualified" persons protected by § 504 include those who would be able to meet the requirements of a particular program in every respect except as to limitations imposed by their handicap. Taken literally, this holding would prevent an institution from taking into account any limitation resulting from the handicap, however disabling. It assumes, in effect, that a person need not meet legitimate physical requirements in order to be "otherwise qualified." We think the understanding of the District Court is closer to the plain meaning of the statutory language. An otherwise qualified person is one who is able to meet all of a program's requirements in spite of his handicap.

The regulations promulgated by the Department of HEW to interpret § 504 reinforce, rather than contradict, this conclusion. According to these regulations, a "[q]ualified handicapped person" is, "[w]ith respect to postsecondary and vocational education services, a handicapped person who meets the academic and technical standards requisite to admission or participation in the [school's] education program or activity. . . ." 45 CFR § 84.3(k)(3) (1978). An explanatory note states:

"The term 'technical standards' refers to *all* nonacademic admissions criteria that are essential to participation in the program in question." 45 CFR pt. 84, App. A, p. 405.

A further note emphasizes that legitimate physical qualifications may be essential to participation in particular programs. We think it clear, therefore, that HEW interprets the "other" qualifications which a handicapped person may be required to meet as including necessary physical qualifications.

III

The remaining question is whether the physical qualifications Southeastern demanded of respondent might not be necessary for participation in its nursing program. It is not open to dispute that, as Southeastern's Associate Degree Nursing program currently is constituted, the ability to understand speech without reliance on lipreading is necessary for patient safety during the clinical phase of the program. As the District Court found, this ability also is indispensable for many of the functions that a registered nurse performs.

Respondent contends nevertheless that § 504, properly interpreted, compels Southeastern to undertake affirmative action that would dispense with the need for effective oral communication. First, it is suggested that respondent can be given individual supervision by faculty members whenever she attends patients directly. Moreover, certain required courses might be dispensed with altogether for respondent. It is not necessary, she argues, that Southeastern train her to undertake all the tasks a registered nurse is licensed to perform. Rather, it is sufficient to make § 504 applicable if respondent might be able to perform satisfactorily some of the duties of a registered nurse or to hold some of the positions available to a registered nurse.

Respondent finds support for this argument in portions of the HEW regulations discussed above. In particular, a provision applicable to postsecondary educational programs requires covered institutions to make "modifications" in their programs to accommodate handicapped persons, and to provide "auxiliary aids" such as sign-language interpreters. Respondent argues that this regulation imposes an obligation to ensure full participation in covered programs by handicapped individuals and, in particular, requires Southeastern to make the kind of adjustments that would be necessary to permit her safe participation in the nursing program.

We note first that on the present record it appears unlikely respondent could benefit from any affirmative action that the regulation reasonably could be interpreted as requiring. Section 84.44(d)(2), for example, explicitly excludes "devices or services of a personal nature" from the kinds of auxiliary aids a school must provide a handicapped individual. Yet the only evidence in the record indicates that nothing less than close, individual attention by a nursing instructor would be sufficient to ensure patient safety if respondent took part in the clinical phase of the nursing program. Furthermore, it also is reasonably clear that § 84.44(a) does not encompass the kind of curricular changes that would be necessary to accommodate respondent in the nursing program. In light of respondent's inability to function in clinical courses without close supervision, Southeastern, with prudence, could allow her to take only academic classes. Whatever benefits respondent might realize from such a course of study, she would not receive even a rough equivalent of the training a nursing program normally gives. Such a fundamental alteration in the nature of a program is far more than the "modification" the regulation requires.

* * *

IV

We do not suggest that the line between a lawful refusal to extend affirmative action and illegal discrimination against handicapped persons always will be clear. It is possible to envision situations where an insistence on continuing past requirements and practices might arbitrarily deprive genuinely qualified handicapped persons of the opportunity to participate in a covered program. Technological advances can be expected to enhance opportunities to rehabilitate the handicapped or otherwise to qualify them for some useful employment. Such advances also may enable attainment of these goals without imposing undue financial and administrative burdens upon a State. Thus, situations may arise where a refusal to modify an existing program might become unreasonable and discriminatory. Identification of those instances where a refusal to accommodate the needs of a disabled person amounts to discrimination against the handicapped continues to be an important responsibility of HEW.

In this case, however, it is clear that Southeastern's unwillingness to make major adjustments in its nursing program does not constitute such discrimination. The uncontroverted testimony of several members of Southeastern's staff and faculty established that the purpose of its program was to train persons who could serve the nursing profession in all customary ways. This type of purpose, far from reflecting any animus against handicapped individuals is shared by many if not most of the institutions that train persons to render professional service. It is undisputed that respondent could not participate in Southeastern's nursing program unless the standards were substantially lowered. Section 504 imposes no requirement upon an educational institution to lower or to effect substantial modifications of standards to accommodate a handicapped person.[12]

One may admire respondent's desire and determination to overcome her handicap, and there well may be various other types of service for which she can qualify. In this case, however, we hold that there was no violation of § 504 when Southeastern concluded that respondent did not qualify for admission to its program. Nothing in the language or history of § 504 reflects an intention to limit the freedom of an educational institution to require reasonable physical qualifications for admission to a clinical

---

[12] Respondent contends that it is unclear whether North Carolina law requires a registered nurse to be capable of performing all functions open to that profession in order to obtain a license to practice, although McRee, the Executive Director of the State Board of Nursing, had informed Southeastern that the law did so require. Respondent further argues that even if she is not capable of meeting North Carolina's present licensing requirements, she still might succeed in obtaining a license in another jurisdiction.

Respondent's argument misses the point. Southeastern's program, structured to train persons who will be able to perform all normal roles of a registered nurse, represents a legitimate academic policy, and is accepted by the State. In effect, it seeks to ensure that no graduate will pose a danger to the public in any professional role in which he or she might be cast. Even if the licensing requirements of North Carolina or some other State are less demanding, nothing in the Act requires an educational institution to lower its standards.

training program. Nor has there been any showing in this case that any action short of a substantial change in Southeastern's program would render unreasonable the qualifications it imposed.

V

Accordingly, we reverse the judgment of the court below, and remand for proceedings consistent with this opinion.

NOTES AND QUESTIONS

1. *Defining "otherwise qualified."* The Court in *Davis* defined otherwise qualified as follows: "An otherwise qualified person is one who is able to meet all of a program's requirements in spite of his handicap." In doing so, the Court disagreed with the lower court's definition of "otherwise qualified"—"able to meet the requirements of a particular program in every respect except as to limitations imposed by their handicap." Which side do you think has the better interpretation?

2. *Reasonable modifications.* Do you read the Court in *Davis* as requiring an institution to consider offering reasonable modifications to an individual with a disability? Or does the definition of otherwise qualified— "able to meet all of a program's requirements in spite of his handicap"—seem to preclude the requirement that an institution must consider reasonable modifications? In response to Davis's argument that the statute requires the institution to take affirmative action to dispense with the need for oral communication in all cases, the Court merely stated that the types of modifications contemplated by the implementing regulations to Section 504 would not help Davis effectively perform as a nursing student. The Court stated:

> In light of respondent's inability to function in clinical courses without close supervision, Southeastern, with prudence, could allow her to take only academic classes. Whatever benefits respondent might realize from such a course of study, she would not receive even a rough equivalent of the training a nursing program normally gives. Such a fundamental alteration in the nature of a program is far more than the "modification" the regulation requires.

This might suggest that the school does not have to modify its program for a student with a disability. But the Court further elaborated:

> Technological advances can be expected to enhance opportunities to rehabilitate the handicapped or otherwise to qualify them for some useful employment. Such advances also may enable attainment of these goals without imposing undue financial and administrative burdens upon a State. Thus, situations may arise where a refusal to modify an existing program might become unreasonable and discriminatory.... Section 504 imposes no requirement upon an educational institution to lower or to effect substantial modifications of standards to accommodate a handicapped person.

Do you read the quoted language as requiring institutions to consider modifications? For several years, this was a point of contention among courts.

Some courts interpreted the above language to mean that deference should be given to the institution "without imposing any requirement to seek feasible alternative methods of accommodating the essential feature of a program to a given disability." Wynne v. Tufts University School of Medicine, 932 F.2d 19, 23 (1st Cir. 1991) (citing with disapproval Doe v. New York University, 666 F.2d 761 (2d Cir. 1981) and Doe v. Region 13 Mental Health-Mental Retardation Comm'n, 704 F.2d 1402 (5th Cir. 1983)). As explained by the court in *Wynne*, the "arguably absolutist principles of *Davis*—a handicapped person must be able to meet *all* requirements of an institution; and there is no affirmative action obligation on an institution—were meaningfully qualified by the Court in *Alexander v. Choate*. . . ." *Id.* The Court in *Alexander*, which was reproduced in Chapter 5, signaled its awareness of criticism that the *Davis* Court seemed to obscure the difference between a remedial policy for the victims of past discrimination and the elimination of existing obstacles against those with disabilities. *Id.* at 24 (citing Alexander v. Choate, 469 U.S. 287, 300, 105. S.Ct. 712 (1985)). As was made clear by the Court in *Alexander*, "to assure meaningful access, reasonable accommodations in the grantee's program or benefit may have to be made." *Alexander*, 469 U.S. at 301, 105 S.Ct. at 720. Thus, *Alexander* is sometimes thought as clarifying what the *Davis* Court arguably meant all along—that in considering whether someone is "otherwise qualified" under Section 504, the court must consider not just the person's current ability to meet the requirements of the program, but whether the person might be able to meet the current requirements if given a reasonable accommodation. *Wynne*, 932 F.2d at 24.

3. *Professional academic programs.* Most professional academic programs endeavor to train students in *all* aspects of the profession. Generally speaking, medical schools want their graduates to be able to perform surgeries (even if the prospective doctor plans on being a psychiatrist); nursing schools expect their graduates to be able to assist in surgeries (even though there are plenty of nursing jobs that do not involve surgery); and law schools want to train their law graduates in all aspects of law practice (even if the would-be law graduate does not plan on becoming a practicing lawyer). Why is this the case? Is it because the professional school is certifying to the public the ability of the graduate to know and accomplish everything that the professional school traditionally teaches? For instance, if a pregnant woman goes into labor in the middle of a restaurant, does she expect that any doctor in the restaurant will be able to successfully deliver her baby? And if the only doctor in the restaurant says that he never learned how to deliver a baby in medical school, would that say something about the quality of the medical school program from which he graduated? And yet, most professionals specialize. You would not want a doctor who normally delivers babies to operate on a brain tumor. Frankly, nor would you expect that a doctor fresh out of medical school is qualified to operate on a brain tumor. Most lawyers specialize too, although it is perhaps more likely for a lawyer to cross over to a different area of law on occasion (an employment attorney might occasionally take on a landlord/tenant dispute, for instance).

All of this raises the following question: what should be the goal of professional academic programs (for simplicity's sake, let us limit this to medical schools, nursing schools, and law schools)? Should the goal to be to train professionals who are physically and mentally capable of performing the full array of skills and tasks that might be required of a professional in that field? Or should the institution be willing to let individuals with disabilities have variations of the academic program, if necessary? Should we allow a blind man attend medical school if he plans on using his medical degree to become a psychiatrist? *See* Ohio Civil Rights Commission v. Case Western Reserve University, 666 N.E.2d 1376 (Ohio 1996) (holding that the trial court abused its discretion in finding that the prospective medical student, who was completely blind, was otherwise qualified for admission to Case Western's medical school with reasonable accommodations). *But see* Argenyi v. Creighton U., 703 F.3d 441 (8th Cir. 2013) (reversing the lower court's grant of summary judgment in favor of the medical school, holding that the medical school did not sufficiently accommodate the plaintiff's hearing impairment); Palmer College of Chiropractic v. Davenport Civil Rights Commission, 850 N.W.2d 326 (Iowa 2014) (finding in favor of a visually impaired student who was denied accommodations by the defendant chiropractic school).

4. *Discrimination when qualifications are not at issue.* Unlike the employment context, it is rare to see a claim in the higher education context where the applicant is denied admission based on alleged bias regarding the applicant's disability. Part of the reason for this scarcity of cases is because the vast majority of admissions decisions are made on a paper file alone, where an applicant's disability is not apparent or relevant. But in smaller academic programs (and smaller colleges), applicants might be interviewed before admission, which might result in the discovery or disclosure of a disability, and a subsequent denial of admission. In these cases, courts generally will apply the familiar *McDonnell Douglas* burden-shifting framework that we encountered in Chapter 3, where the fact-finder has to determine if the denial of admission was because of the disability or for another legitimate reason. For instance, in *Sjöstrand v. Ohio State University*, 750 F.3d 596 (6th Cir. 2014), the plaintiff's application for a Ph.D. program in school psychology was rejected after she disclosed her Crohn's disease. Overturning a grant of summary judgment to the university, the court found several issues of material fact regarding what motivated the rejection of the plaintiff's application, including: (1) both interviewers devoted half of the plaintiff's interview to a discussion of her disability; (2) one of the decision makers failed to return her call for two weeks and gave vague answers about why she was rejected; (3) her GPA was the highest in the applicant pool; and (4) there were factual disputes regarding all of the university's alleged reasons for rejecting her application. *Id.* at 599–601.

Of course, *Sjöstrand* is likely an outlier. Because of the multi-factored admissions policies of most institutions of higher education, few plaintiffs will succeed in such discrimination claims. For instance, in *Power v. University of North Dakota School of Law*, 954 F.3d 1047 (8th Cir. 2020), the court affirmed summary judgment for the law school when it denied the plaintiff's application.

The plaintiff's application included average scores for the law school's incoming class, but his letters of recommendation were several years old and he mentioned in his application that he had previously withdrawn from two other law schools and his work history included 18 different jobs. The admissions committee voted to reject his application. Subsequently, the plaintiff sent a letter indicating that he withdrew from the other law schools because of his bipolar disorder but that he now had his disability under control. Nevertheless, the law school did not change its decision to reject the plaintiff's application. *Id.* at 1051. In the analysis of his claim under the *McDonnell Douglas* framework, the law school gave as its reason for rejecting his application that "it would be fair to say that on review of the application we did not think [Power was] a good fit to complete our program of the study of law." The law school also emphasized that the admissions committee always weighs scores, previous courses of study, recommendation letters, and other considerations. *Id.* at 1053. The court held that the plaintiff could not prove that the law school's decision was pretextual, rejecting the plaintiff's arguments to the contrary—(1) that the application process was subjective; and (2) that the law school accepted applicants with lower scores than the plaintiff's. In part based on the deference afforded to academic decisions (discussed in the next section) the court held that the plaintiff had not proven that the decision to reject plaintiff was discriminatory. *Id.* at 1053–55.

Based on this discussion, if you were giving advice to a prospective student about whether or not to disclose a disability in their application (perhaps in a personal statement), what advice would you give the student and why? What are the pros and cons of making such a disclosure?

3. DISMISSAL/ACADEMIC DEFERENCE

Institutions of higher education are required to provide reasonable modifications to students as long as those modifications do not fundamentally alter the academic program of the institution. *See, e.g.,* 42 U.S.C. § 12182(b)(2)(A)(ii) (requiring reasonable modifications under Title III of the ADA); 42 U.S.C. § 12131(2) (defining "qualified individual with a disability" under Title II as an "an individual with a disability who, with or without reasonable modifications to rules, policies or practices, . . . meets the essential eligibility requirements for the receipt of services or the participation in programs or activities provided by a public entity").

Generally, reasonable modifications for institutions of higher education include modifications to exams or other tools of assessment (including extra time and a distraction-free exam room); note-takers; modified academic schedule; modified course books or other classroom materials; and modifications to the institution's academic requirements. The next three cases involve the relatively common scenario where a student with a disability has been dismissed for academic reasons and is requesting to have the dismissal reversed as an accommodation for the student's disability.

ZUKLE V. REGENTS OF THE UNIVERSITY OF CALIFORNIA

166 F.3d 1041 (9th Cir. 1999)

O'SCANNLAIN, CIRCUIT JUDGE:

We must decide whether a medical school violated the Americans with Disabilities Act or the Rehabilitation Act when it dismissed a learning disabled student for failure to meet the school's academic standards.

I

Sherrie Lynn Zukle entered the University of California, Davis School of Medicine ("Medical School") in the fall of 1991 for a four year course of study. The first two years comprise the "basic science" or "pre-clinical" curriculum, consisting of courses in the function, design and processes of the human body. The final two years comprise the "clinical curriculum." In the third year, students take six consecutive eight-week clinical clerkships. During the fourth year, students complete clerkships of varying lengths in more advanced areas. Most clerkships involve treating patients in hospitals or clinics, and oral and written exams.

From the beginning, Zukle experienced academic difficulty. During her first quarter, she received "Y" grades in Anatomy and Biochemistry.[1] Upon reexamination, her Biochemistry grade was converted to a "D." She did not convert her Anatomy grade at that time. In her second quarter, she received a "Y" grade in Human Physiology, which she converted to a "D" upon reexamination.

In April 1992, the Medical School referred Zukle to the Student Evaluation Committee ("SEC"). Although subject to dismissal pursuant to the Medical School's bylaws, Zukle was allowed to remain in school. The SEC (1) placed Zukle on academic probation, (2) required her to retake Anatomy and Biochemistry, (3) required her to be tested for a learning disability, and (4) placed her on a "split curriculum," meaning that she was given three years to complete the pre-clinical program, instead of the usual two years. Zukle continued to experience academic difficulty. For the spring quarter of 1992 (while on academic probation) she received a "Y" grade in Neurobiology. In the fall, she received a "Y" grade in Medical Microbiology and in the winter she received a "Y" in Principles of Pharmacology. In total, Zukle received eight "Y" grades during the pre-clinical portion of her studies. Five were converted to "C" after reexamination, two to "D" and one to "F."

In November 1992, Zukle was tested for a learning disability. The results received in January 1993, revealed that Zukle suffered from a reading disability which "affects visual processing as it relates to reading

---

[1] Medical School assigns letter grades of A, B, C, D, F, I and Y to measure academic performance. A "Y" grade in a pre-clinical course is provisional; it means that a student has earned a failing grade but will be or has been permitted to retake the exam. However, a "Y" grade in a clinical clerkship indicates unsatisfactory performance in a major portion of that clerkship and may not be converted until the student repeats that portion of the clerkship.

comprehension and rate when under timed constraints." In short, it takes Zukle longer to read and to absorb information than the average person.... Christine O'Dell, Coordinator of the University's Learning Disability Resource Center, ... recommended that the Medical School make various accommodations for Zukle's disability and recommended various techniques for Zukle to try to increase her reading comprehension. The Medical School offered all of these accommodations to Zukle.

After completing the pre-clinical portion of Medical School, Zukle took the United States Medical Licensing Exam, Part I ("USMLE") in June 1994. Shortly thereafter, she began her first clinical clerkship, OB-GYN. During this clerkship, Zukle learned that she had failed the USLME. The Medical School allowed Zukle to interrupt her OB-GYN clerkship to take a six-week review course to prepare to retake the USMLE, for which the Medical School paid.

Before leaving school to take the USMLE review course offered in southern California, Zukle asked Donal A. Walsh, the Associate Dean of Curricular Affairs, if she could rearrange her clerkship schedule. At this point, Zukle had completed the first half of her OB-GYN clerkship. She asked Dean Walsh if, instead of completing the second half of her OB-GYN clerkship upon return from retaking the USMLE, she could start the first half of a Family Practice Clerkship, and then repeat the OB-GYN clerkship in its entirety at a later date. Zukle testified that she made this request because she was concerned about how far behind she would be when she returned from the USMLE review course. She further asserted that she thought that if she started the Family Practice clerkship (which apparently requires less reading than the OB-GYN clerkship), she would be able to read for her upcoming Medicine clerkship at night. Zukle testified that Dean Walsh . . . initially approved her request. Later, however, Dean Walsh denied Zukle's request and informed her that she had to complete the OB-GYN clerkship before beginning another clerkship.

In September 1994, Zukle took and passed the USMLE on her second attempt. She returned to the Medical School and finished her OB-GYN clerkship. Without requesting any accommodations, she began her Medicine clerkship. During this clerkship, she learned that she had earned a "Y" grade in her OB-GYN clerkship. Because of this grade, Zukle was automatically placed back on academic probation.

Two weeks before the Medicine written exam, Zukle contacted her advisor, Dr. Joseph Silva, and expressed concern that she had not completed the required reading. Dr. Silva offered to speak with Dr. Ruth Lawrence, the Medicine Instructor of Record, on Zukle's behalf. According to Zukle, she then spoke with Dr. Lawrence in person and requested time off from the clerkship to prepare for the exam. Dr. Lawrence denied Zukle's request. Zukle passed the written exam, but failed the Medicine clerkship because of unsatisfactory clinical performance. On Zukle's grade sheet, Dr.

Lawrence rated Zukle as unsatisfactory in clinical problem solving skills; data acquisition, organization and recording; and skill/ability at oral presentations. Dr. Lawrence also reported negative comments from the people who worked with Zukle during the clerkship. Because Zukle had earned a failing grade while on academic probation, she was again subject to dismissal pursuant to the Medical School's bylaws.

* * *

On January 17, 1995, the Promotions Board met to consider Zukle's case. The Promotions Board voted to dismiss Zukle from the Medical School for "failure to meet the academic standards of the School of Medicine." According to Dr. Lewis, who was a member of the Promotions Board and was present when it reached its decision, "the Promotions Board considered Plaintiff's academic performance throughout her tenure at the medical school and determined that it demonstrated an incapacity to develop or use the skills and knowledge required to competently practice medicine."

In June 1995, Zukle appealed her dismissal to an *ad hoc* Board on Student Dismissal composed of faculty and students ("the Board"). Zukle appeared before the Board on November 12, 1995, and requested that her dismissal be reconsidered and that she be given extra time to prepare prior to some of her clerkships to accommodate her disability. The Board also heard testimony from Dr. Silva, who spoke favorably on her behalf, Dr. Ernest Lewis, Associate Dean of Student Affairs. . . . When asked about Zukle's request to remain in Medical School on a decelerated schedule, Dean Lewis testified:

> There is a certain point when everyone has to be able to respond in the same time frame. A physician does not have extra time when in the ER, for example. Speed of appropriate reaction to crisis is essential.

The Board on Student Dismissal voted unanimously to uphold the Promotions Board's decision of dismissal.

[Zukle filed a lawsuit challenging her dismissal from medical school. The defendant filed a motion for summary judgment, which the district court granted. Zukle appealed.] . . .

II

Zukle claims that she was dismissed from the Medical School in violation of Title II of the ADA and section 504 of the Rehabilitation Act. Title II of the ADA provides, in relevant part:

> no qualified individual with a disability shall, by reason of such disability, be excluded from participation in or be denied the benefits of the services, programs, or activities of a public entity, or be subjected to discrimination by any such entity.

42 U.S.C. § 12132. Title II prohibits discrimination by state and local agencies, which includes publicly funded institutions of higher education.

Title II of the ADA was expressly modeled after Section 504 of the Rehabilitation Act, which provides:

> No otherwise qualified individual with a disability . . . shall, solely by reason of her or his disability, be excluded from the participation in, be denied the benefits of, or be subjected to discrimination under any program or activity receiving Federal financial assistance. . . .

To make out a prima facie case under either the ADA or Rehabilitation Act Zukle must show that (1) she is disabled under the Act; (2) she is "otherwise qualified" to remain a student at the Medical School, i.e., she can meet the essential eligibility requirements of the school, with or without reasonable accommodation; (3) she was dismissed solely because of her disability; and (4) the Medical School receives federal financial assistance (for the Rehabilitation Act claim), or is a public entity (for the ADA claim).

The Regents do not dispute that Zukle is disabled and that the Medical School receives federal financial assistance and is a public entity. The Regents argue, however, that Zukle was not "otherwise qualified" to remain at the Medical School. Zukle responds that she *was* "otherwise qualified" with the aid of reasonable accommodations and that the Medical School failed reasonably to accommodate her.

A

The ADA defines a "qualified individual with a disability" as one who "meets the essential eligibility requirements . . . for participation in [a given] program[] provided by a public entity" "*with or without reasonable modifications* to rules, policies, or practices. . . ." In the school context, the implementing regulations of the Rehabilitation Act define an otherwise qualified individual as an individual who, although disabled, "meets the academic and technical standards requisite to admission or participation in the [school's] education program or activity." 34 C.F.R. § 104.3(k)(3).

However, . . . the ADA's implementing regulations require a public entity to "make reasonable modifications in policies, practices, or procedures when the modifications are necessary to avoid discrimination on the basis of disability, unless the public entity can demonstrate that making the modifications would fundamentally alter the nature of the services, program, or activity." The Supreme Court has made clear that an educational institution is not required to make fundamental or substantial modifications to its program or standards; it need only make reasonable ones.

B

In order to evaluate Zukle's claim, we must clarify the burdens of production and persuasion in cases of this type. The district court correctly noted that we have not previously addressed the allocation of the burdens of production and persuasion for the "otherwise qualified"—"reasonable accommodation" prong for a prima facie case in the school context. . . .

[W]e hold that the plaintiff-student bears the initial burden of producing evidence that she is otherwise qualified. This burden includes the burden of producing evidence of the existence of a reasonable accommodation that would enable her to meet the educational institution's essential eligibility requirements. The burden then shifts to the educational institution to produce evidence that the requested accommodation would require a fundamental or substantial modification of its program or standards. The school may also meet its burden by producing evidence that the requested accommodations, regardless of whether they are reasonable, would not enable the student to meet its academic standards. However, the plaintiff-student retains the ultimate burden of persuading the court that she is otherwise qualified.

C

Before turning to the merits of Zukle's claims, we must decide whether we should accord deference to academic decisions made by the school in the context of an ADA or Rehabilitation Act claim, an issue of first impression in this circuit.

In *Regents of the Univ. of Michigan v. Ewing*, the Supreme Court analyzed the issue of the deference a court should extend to an educational institution's decision in the due process context. *See* 474 U.S. 214 (1985). In *Ewing*, the plaintiff-medical student challenged his dismissal from medical school as arbitrary and capricious in violation of his substantive due process rights. The Court held that:

> When judges are asked to review the substance of a genuinely academic decision, such as this one, they should show great respect for the faculty's professional judgment. Plainly, they may not override it unless it is such a substantial departure from accepted academic norms as to demonstrate that the person or committee responsible did not actually exercise professional judgment.

Id. at 225, 106 S.Ct. 507.

While the Court made this statement in the context of a due process violation claim, a majority of circuits have extended judicial deference to an educational institution's academic decisions in ADA and Rehabilitation Act cases. These courts noted the limited ability of courts, "as contrasted to that of experienced educational administrators and professionals," to determine whether a student "would meet reasonable standards for academic and professional achievement established by a university," and have concluded that " '[c]ourts are particularly ill-equipped to evaluate academic performance.' "

We agree . . . that an educational institution's academic decisions are entitled to deference. Thus, while we recognize that the ultimate determination of whether an individual is otherwise qualified must be made by the court, we will extend judicial deference "to the evaluation made by the institution itself, absent proof that its standards and its application of them serve no purpose other than to deny an education to handicapped persons."

Deference is also appropriately accorded an educational institution's determination that a reasonable accommodation is not available. Therefore, we agree with the First Circuit that "a court's duty is to first find the basic facts, giving due deference to the school, and then to evaluate whether those facts add up to a professional, academic judgment that reasonable accommodation is not available." *Wynne I*, 932 F.2d at 27–28.

We recognize that extending deference to educational institutions must not impede our obligation to enforce the ADA and the Rehabilitation Act. Thus, we must be careful not to allow academic decisions to disguise truly discriminatory requirements. The educational institution has a "real obligation . . . to seek suitable means of reasonably accommodating a handicapped person and to submit a factual record indicating that it conscientiously carried out this statutory obligation." *Wynne I*, 932 F.2d at 25–26. Once the educational institution has fulfilled this obligation, however, we will defer to its academic decisions.

III

Having answered several preliminary questions, we now turn to the ultimate question—did Zukle establish a prima facie case of discrimination under the ADA or the Rehabilitation Act? As noted before, only the "otherwise qualified" prong of the prima facie case requirements is disputed by the parties. Zukle argues that she was otherwise qualified to remain at the Medical School, with the aid of the three accommodations she requested. The Medical School argues that Zukle's requested accommodations were not reasonable because they would have required a fundamental or substantial modification of its program.

Zukle bears the burden of pointing to the existence of a reasonable accommodation that would enable her to meet the Medical School's essential eligibility requirements. Once she meets this burden, the Medical School must show that Zukle's requested accommodation would fundamentally alter the nature of the school's program.

* * *

The evidence is undisputed that the Medical School offered Zukle all of the accommodations that it normally offers learning disabled students. . . . [S]he was offered double time on exams, notetaking services and textbooks on audio cassettes. Further, Zukle was allowed to retake courses, proceed on a decelerated schedule and remain at the Medical School despite being subject to dismissal under the Medical School's bylaws.

Even with these accommodations, Zukle consistently failed to achieve passing grades in her courses. Though Zukle was on a decelerated schedule, she continued to receive "Y" grades in her pre-clinical years and failed the USMLE on her first attempt. Further, although she was able to remedy some of her failing grades in her pre-clinical years, she was only able to do so by retaking exams. Moreover, she received a "Y" grade in her first clinical clerkship, automatically placing her on academic probation, and an "F" in her second. Because Zukle received a failing grade while on academic probation, she was subject to dismissal pursuant to the Medical School's bylaws. Clearly, Zukle could not meet the Medical School's essential eligibility requirements without the additional accommodations she requested.

The issue, then, is whether the ADA and Rehabilitation Act required the Medical School to provide Zukle with those additional accommodations. . . .

A

Zukle claims that the Medical School should have granted her request to modify her schedule by beginning the first half of the Family Practice Clerkship instead of finishing the second half of her OB-GYN clerkship when she returned from retaking the USMLE. She proposed that she would then begin the Medicine clerkship, and finish Family Practice and OB-GYN at a later time.

The Regents presented evidence that granting this request would require a substantial modification of its curriculum. While the Medical School has granted some students reading time prior to the commencement of a clerkship, Dean Walsh testified that once a clerkship begins "all students are expected to complete the reading and other requirements of the clerkship, including night call and ward care, and to prepare themselves for the written exam which is given only at the end of the 8-week clerkship." Zukle's request would have entailed interrupting her OB-GYN clerkship, and starting the Medicine clerkship before finishing the Family Practice clerkship. Thus, by the time Zukle began the Medicine clerkship she would have had two uncompleted clerkships.

Dean Walsh testified that the only time the Medical School allows a student to begin a clerkship, interrupt it, and then return to that clerkship at a later point is when a student has failed the USMLE and needs time off to study. However, the student is still required to return to the same clerkship. Given that no student had been allowed to rearrange her clerkships in the manner Zukle requested and that Zukle's request would entail Zukle interrupting two courses to complete them at some later date, we have little difficulty concluding that this would be a substantial alteration of the Medical School's curriculum.

. . . We defer to the Medical School's academic decision to require students to complete courses once they are begun and conclude, therefore, that this requested accommodation was not reasonable.

B

Two weeks before the scheduled written exam in her Medicine clerkship, Zukle asked Dr. Silva, her advisor, if she could have more time to prepare for the exam because she was behind in the readings. Zukle testified that she specifically requested to leave the hospital early every day so that she could spend more time preparing for the written exam in Medicine. Dr. Silva and Zukle spoke with the Instructor of Record in Zukle's Medicine clerkship, Dr. Lawrence. Dr. Lawrence told Zukle that she could not excuse her from the in-hospital part of the clerkship. . . .

The Medical School presented uncontradicted evidence that giving Zukle reduced clinical time would have fundamentally altered the nature of the Medical School curriculum. The Medical School presented the affidavit of Dean Lewis in which he explained the significance of the clinical portion of the Medical School curriculum:

> The third-year clinical clerkships are designed to simulate the practice of medicine. . . . Depending on the specialty and the setting, students are generally required to be "on call" at the hospital through an evening and night one or more times each week. Other than these call nights, students remain at the hospital or clinic during day time hours on a schedule similar to that expected of clinicians. . . . Releasing a student from a significant number of scheduled hours during the course of a rotation would compromise the clerkship's curricular purpose, i.e. the simulation of medical practice.

We defer to the Medical School's academic decision that the in-hospital portion of a clerkship is a vital part of medical education and that allowing a student to be excused from this requirement would sacrifice the integrity of its program. Thus, we conclude that neither the ADA nor the Rehabilitation Act require the Medical School to make this accommodation.

* * *

C

Finally, after she was dismissed, Zukle requested that the *ad hoc* Board place her on a decelerated schedule during the clinical portion of her studies. Specifically, Zukle sought eight weeks off before each clerkship to read the assigned text for that clerkship in its entirety.

Zukle presented evidence that the Medical School regularly allowed students to proceed on a decelerated schedule. Indeed, Zukle herself was allowed an extra year to complete the pre-clinical curriculum. However, no student had been provided the specific accommodation that Zukle requested, i.e., taking eight weeks off between clerkships. Furthermore, simply because the Medical School had granted other students' requests to proceed on a decelerated schedule, does not mean that Zukle's request was reasonable. The reasonableness of Zukle's request must be evaluated in light of Zukle's particular circumstances.

We agree with the district court that the Board's denial of Zukle's request to proceed on a decelerated schedule was a "rationally justifiable conclusion." The Board noted that, even on a decelerated schedule during the pre-clinical phase, Zukle experienced severe academic difficulties: Zukle earned deficient grades in five courses and failed the USMLE exam on her first attempt even though she had taken several pre-clinical courses twice. . . . Given Zukle's unenviable academic record, allowing her to remain in Medical School on a decelerated schedule would have lowered the Medical School's academic standards, which it was not required to do to accommodate Zukle.

IV

In conclusion, we are persuaded that Zukle failed to establish that she could meet the essential eligibility requirements of the Medical School with the aid of reasonable accommodations. Accordingly, she failed to establish a prima facie case of disability discrimination under the ADA or the Rehabilitation Act.

WONG V. REGENTS OF THE UNIVERSITY OF CALIFORNIA

192 F.3d 807 (9th Cir. 1999)

KRAVITCH, CIRCUIT JUDGE:

Plaintiff-appellant Andrew H.K. Wong appeals the district court's order granting summary judgment in favor of defendant-appellee Regents of the University of California ("the University") on Wong's claim that the University discriminated against him in violation of Title II of the Americans with Disabilities Act, 42 U.S.C. § 12132 ("the ADA") and section 504 of the Rehabilitation Act, 29 U.S.C. § 794. . . . The district court ruled that summary judgment was appropriate. . . .

I. FACTS

After excelling in his undergraduate and master's degree programs, Wong entered the School of Medicine at the University of California at Davis in the fall of 1989. . . .

Wong completed the first two years of medical school on a normal schedule and with a grade point average slightly above a "B"; he also passed the required national board examination immediately following the second year. He began his third year on schedule, enrolling in the Surgery clerkship in the summer of 1991 and, upon its conclusion, in the Medicine clerkship. When he was approximately four weeks into the Medicine clerkship, Wong learned that he had failed Surgery. In accordance with school policy, Wong appeared before the Student Evaluation Committee ("SEC"), a body that meets with students having academic problems and makes recommendations to another group, the Promotions Board, which ultimately decides what action, if any, the school should take with respect to that student. The Promotions Board placed Wong on academic probation, decided that he should repeat the Surgery clerkship, and recommended that he continue in the Medicine clerkship at least until the midterm evaluation. Wong withdrew from the Medicine clerkship in November 1991 when his midterm evaluation showed significant problems with his performance to that point. Wong's instructor of record then assigned a senior resident to work with Wong one-on-one, focusing upon taking patient histories and making oral presentations. These sessions continued through the winter of 1992.

In March 1992, Dr. Ernest Lewis, associate dean of student affairs, granted Wong's request to take time off from school to be with his father, who had just been diagnosed with lung cancer. Wong spent at least some of this time doing extra reading in preparation for his upcoming clerkships, Psychiatry and Pediatrics. He returned to school in July 1992 and between July and December passed clerkships in Psychiatry (with a "B"), Pediatrics ("C+"), and Obstetrics/Gynecology ("C"). Wong generally received positive comments on his final evaluation forms for these courses. Instructors noted that he was "competent," "prompt," "enthusiastic," "a very hard worker," and "an extremely pleasant student who related exceptionally well with the staff"; they also stated that he had "a good fund of knowledge," "contributed meaningfully to the discussions at hand," "made astute observations of patients," and "did a good job of presenting on [gynecology] rounds." Evaluators also observed, however, that Wong "seem[ed] to have difficulty putting things together" and "limited abilities to effectively communicate his thoughts," and they recommended that he work on "organizational skills" and "setting priorities."

Wong re-enrolled in the Medicine clerkship in January 1993. Three weeks later, his father died, an event that by all accounts had a devastating impact on Wong. He continued in the Medicine clerkship for a brief period of time, but after his midterm evaluation showed a borderline performance in the first half of the clerkship, Wong, with Dean Lewis's approval, withdrew from the course and left the Davis campus to be closer to his family, who lived in the San Francisco area. . . . When Wong returned to the School of Medicine at Davis in the summer of 1993, he again enrolled in Medicine. He asserts that although he did not feel prepared for this course and attempted to drop it, Dean Lewis did not permit the withdrawal, and he ultimately failed the class, triggering another appearance before the SEC and Promotions Board.

The Promotions Board adopted strict conditions for Wong to remain a student in the School of Medicine: it required him to take only reading electives for the next three quarters; to meet again with the SEC and Dean Lewis following that period to assess his progress; and, assuming he received approval to re-enter the clerkship program, to repeat the entire third year, including the courses he already had passed. During the meeting with the Promotions Board, Wong stated that he thought he might have a learning disability and learned from members of the Promotions Board about the University's Disability Resource Center ("DRC"). DRC staff members and doctors to whom they referred Wong administered a battery of tests and concluded that Wong has a disability that affects the way he processes verbal information and expresses himself verbally.[7]

When Dean Lewis learned the results of the tests, he referred Wong to Dr. Margaret Steward, a psychologist and School of Medicine faculty member, so that she could counsel him regarding coping skills and help him determine what accommodations would allow him to complete his courses successfully. . . . Dr. Steward reported to Dean Lewis in a memorandum that "[t]here is no doubt that [Wong] will need extra time to complete the clerkship years." In the same memorandum, she also specifically recommended giving Wong extra time to read before his next two clerkships, Medicine and Surgery; in a later memorandum, she informed Dean Lewis that she had discussed with Wong that he needed to pass the Medicine clerkship to provide "empirical support" for extra reading time before his next clerkship and that "if he passes Medicine that he needs to anticipate extra time in order to complete the clerkship years." Finally, Dr. Steward recommended that Dean Lewis assign Wong an "SLD [Student Learning Disability] advisor" with whom he could meet to review strategies for coping with his disability. Dean Lewis never appointed this advisor. Wong also contends (and the University does not dispute) that Dr. Steward told him that the School of Medicine "would set up a learning disability resource team to ensure that Wong received adequate accommodations," but the school never did so.

---

[7] One of the evaluations divided Wong's disability into two categories: "[r]eceptive language" and "[e]xpressive language." According to this description, Wong's problem with receptive language stems from his need to slow down information that others give him verbally by repeating their words to himself. Wong does not listen to the parts of the speaker's communication that occur while he is processing the previous message. With respect to expressive language, Wong sometimes cannot find the words he needs to express his thoughts quickly; to compensate, he uses gestures or substitutes generic words for technical terms. Both aspects of the disability can result in significant miscommunication and anxiety, and having to deal with new, technical, or "not-quite-mastered" information exacerbates the problem.

After completing the requisite three quarters of elective reading under the supervision of a faculty member, Wong planned to retake the Medicine clerkship in July 1994. After attending orientation, however, he felt unprepared for the course and asked for another eight weeks off for additional reading. Dean Lewis granted this request, although he noted that he did not know how the extra time would help Wong. In September 1994, Wong took and passed Medicine, earning a "B" and receiving overwhelmingly positive comments on his grade report, including observations of his "excellent fund of knowledge," "excellent retention of new material," and compassionate manner with patients as he performed effective physical exams and formulated diagnoses. The instructor noted some difficulty in making verbal presentations, including uncertainty and taking extra time to answer, but concluded that Wong was a "solid third year medical student" who performed satisfactorily "in all areas of the clerkship." Wong then received eight weeks off to read in preparation for his Surgery clerkship, which commenced in January 1995 and in which he earned a "B." The comments on his grade report were similar to those for the preceding clerkship: generally positive remarks mitigated by reference to his need for time and a calm setting to make good oral presentations. The instructor of record concluded:

> [T]he department was very pleased with [Wong]'s performance on the clerkship. We thought that he had turned in a solid performance and that he had improved markedly over the past year. We think that he has everything it takes to become a safe and effective physician.

Before completing the Surgery clerkship, Wong contacted Dean Lewis's office and requested eight weeks off to read for his next clerkship, Pediatrics. Dean Lewis denied this request through the registrar; he has offered several different reasons for this decision, giving rise to an issue of fact on this point. In an October 1997 deposition, Dean Lewis stated that he received Wong's request through the registrar, who told him that Wong wanted time off for reading but also asked to intersperse fourth year electives with his remaining third year clerkships because he wanted to graduate on time without having to take the core clerkships in straight succession. According to Dean Lewis's testimony, he did not grant Wong's request because Wong needed to finish his third year before proceeding to fourth year courses and because giving Wong time off to read would keep him from graduating the following year. Wong denies that he pressed for permission to take fourth year courses in order to keep from delaying his graduation date; he contends that he only mentioned this alternative after Dean Lewis denied his request for eight weeks off to read for Pediatrics and told Wong that he must take courses in succession for the remainder of the year.

In the same deposition, Dean Lewis also explained his denial of Wong's request for reading time as follows: Wong already had received time off before the previous two clerkships and had passed the Pediatrics clerkship three years earlier. For these reasons, Dean Lewis opined that Wong did not need the extra time for this Pediatrics clerkship. In the course of this explanation, however, Dean Lewis again mentioned his belief that Wong wanted to graduate on time; furthermore, Dean Lewis acknowledged that Pediatrics, as well as Obstetrics/Gynecology and Psychiatry, which he expected Wong to take in succession following Pediatrics, had become much more rigorous and demanding over the past few years. Wong concurred in Dean Lewis's evaluation of the relative difficulty of the 1995 Pediatrics course as compared to the 1992 Pediatrics course.

Finally, in his December 1997 declaration, Dean Lewis repeated as reasons for denying Wong's requested accommodation that he already had granted Wong a significant amount of time off for additional reading and directed studies and that Wong previously had passed Pediatrics (and the next scheduled clerkship, Obstetrics/Gynecology) with no accommodation. Lewis also advanced a third set of explanations: "In that he was presumed to have previously read the material for those courses, I decided that allowing additional time off to read before repeating those clerkships would have been unreasonable, unfair to other students and contrary to the purposes of the curriculum."

Wong received a "Y" grade in the Pediatrics clerkship. . . . At the time Wong learned of his unsatisfactory performance in Pediatrics, he already had begun his Obstetrics/Gynecology clerkship. A preliminary report from his instructor in that course stated that for the first two weeks, Wong's performance had been "borderline" and "lower than expected." This evaluation particularly noted that Wong did not communicate effectively and seemed unsure of himself when examining patients, causing them to react with anger or anxiety.

Wong's "Y" grade in Pediatrics triggered another appearance before the SEC and Promotions Board. In a letter to the Promotions Board, Wong attributed his poor performance in the pediatric ward to a flu-like virus that affected him during the first two weeks of the clerkship. He stated that during this time, he was extremely ill, once requiring IV fluids, and that he fell behind in his reading which affected his performance in the wards. Wong also mentioned being preoccupied with his mother's health; she recently had been diagnosed with cancer. Wong contends that Dean Lewis's refusal to grant him an eight-week reading period prior to this clerkship also contributed to his failing grade; he did not tell the Promotions Board about the refused accommodation because, according to Wong, Dean Lewis ordered him not to mention that issue, an allegation that the University has not disputed.

The SEC recommended dismissal from the School of Medicine, and the Promotions Board concurred. . . . After a discussion, it was . . . approved to recommend Mr. Wong['s dismissal] for failure to meet the academic standards of the School of Medicine. "The Dean of the School of Medicine accepted this recommendation and dismissed Wong on May 17, 1995. . . .

II. DISCUSSION

. . . The dispute focuses upon the second element [of the prima facie case]: the University argues that Wong was not qualified because he could not satisfy the academic standards of the School of Medicine, even with reasonable accommodation.

. . . Wong argues that, viewing the evidence in his favor, he has created an issue of fact as to whether allowing him eight weeks of additional reading time between the Surgery and Pediatrics clerkships was a reasonable modification of the School of Medicine's academic program. If extra reading time was reasonable, Wong contends, the evidence shows that he was qualified to continue in the School of Medicine because when granted that accommodation, he met the school's standards. . . .

A. *Standards of Review*

* * *

In this case, we must consider another standard of review as well: the degree of deference (if any) with which we should treat an educational institution's decisions involving its academic standards and curriculum. . . . [I]n the realm of the ADA and Rehabilitation Act, we [recently] concluded, as most other circuits have, "that an educational institution's academic decisions are entitled to deference." *Zukle,* 166 F.3d at 1047. . . .

This deference is not absolute, however: courts still hold the final responsibility for enforcing the Acts, including determining whether an individual is qualified, with or without accommodation, for the program in question. We must ensure that educational institutions are not "disguis[ing] truly discriminatory requirements" as academic decisions; to this end, "[t]he educational institution has a 'real obligation . . . to seek suitable means of reasonably accommodating a handicapped person *and to submit a factual record indicating that it conscientiously carried out this statutory obligation.*'" Subsumed within this standard is the institution's duty to make itself aware of the nature of the student's disability; to explore alternatives for accommodating the student; and to exercise professional judgment in deciding whether the modifications under consideration would give the student the opportunity to complete the program without fundamentally or substantially modifying the school's standards. We defer to the institution's academic decisions only after we determine that the school "has fulfilled this obligation." *Zukle,* 166 F.3d at 1048. Keeping these standards in mind, we examine the two issues in contention: whether the accommodation Wong requested was reasonable and whether, with accommodation, he was "qualified" to continue his studies at the School of Medicine.

B.   *Reasonable Accommodation*

A public entity must "make reasonable modifications in policies, practices, or procedures when the modifications are necessary to avoid discrimination on the basis of disability." The Acts do not require an academic institution "to make fundamental or substantial modifications to its programs or standards," however. . . .

. . . In a case involving assessment of the standards of an academic institution, however, we abstain from an in-depth, *de novo* analysis of suggested accommodations that the school rejected if the institution demonstrates that it conducted such an inquiry itself and concluded that the accommodations were not feasible or would not be effective. We do not defer to the academic institution's decision in the present case because the record that the University presented falls short of this requirement.

Dean Lewis's denial of Wong's requested accommodation is not entitled to deference because the University failed to present us with a record undisputedly showing that Dean Lewis investigated the proposed accommodation to determine whether the School of Medicine feasibly could implement it (or some alternative modification) without substantially altering the school's standards. First, Dean Lewis rejected Wong's request for an eight-week reading period before the Pediatrics clerkship without informing himself of Wong's need for accommodation of his learning disability. Despite Dr. Steward's earlier statement to Dean Lewis to the effect that Wong was certain to need additional time to finish the third-year clerkships, Dean Lewis failed to discuss Wong's proposal with any of the professionals who had worked with Wong to pinpoint his disability and help him develop skills to cope with it. . . .

[T]he fact that [Dean Lewis] simply passed messages to Wong through the registrar stating his decision to deny Wong's request—without consulting Wong or any person at the University whose job it was to formulate appropriate accommodations—strikes us as a conspicuous failure to carry out the obligation "conscientiously" to explore possible accommodations.

Second, the evidence creates real doubts that Dean Lewis gave any consideration to the effect the proposed accommodation might have upon the School of Medicine's program requirements or academic standards at the time he denied Wong's request. In his October 1997 deposition, Dean Lewis stated that he denied Wong's requested accommodation because (1) Wong wanted to graduate on time, and (2) Wong already had taken Pediatrics and had received a significant amount of time off for reading, and Dean Lewis therefore did not believe Wong needed additional time off. Neither of these reasons is relevant to the School of Medicine's curriculum or standards. Only in a declaration dated two months after this deposition did Dean Lewis assert that he denied the requested accommodation because it was "contrary to the purposes of the curriculum." A jury reasonably could find that Dean Lewis did not formulate this final rationale for denying the accommodation until long after Wong's dismissal from the School of Medicine. Such after-the-fact justification obviously does not satisfy the University's obligation to present "undisputed facts" showing that it conscientiously considered whether possible modification would fundamentally or substantially alter the school's standards when it decided that it could not reasonably accommodate the disabled student. We therefore do not defer to the institution's decision; we examine the rejection of Wong's request for an eight-week reading period *de novo*.

. . . Our analysis focuses upon whether this evidence shows as a matter of law that the proposed accommodation is unreasonable; we conclude for the reasons discussed below that the evidence creates an issue of fact as to the reasonableness of granting Wong an eight-week reading period prior to his Pediatrics clerkship.

First, Dr. Steward, the Coordinator of the Student Learning Disability Resource Teams and a member of the medical school faculty, informed Dean Lewis soon after Wong's diagnosis that Wong certainly would need additional time to complete the clerkship portion of the curriculum. Dr. Steward also stated that if Wong passed the Medicine clerkship after receiving additional reading time, that success would provide empirical support for Wong to receive the same accommodation for his next clerkship. . . .

Second, the School of Medicine had granted Wong this same accommodation for his two previous clerkships. An institution's past decision to make a concession to a disabled individual does not obligate it to continue to grant that accommodation in the future, nor does it render the accommodation reasonable as a matter of law. The fact that the school previously made the exact modification for the Surgery and Medicine clerkships that Wong requested for the Pediatrics clerkship, however, is certainly persuasive evidence from which a jury could conclude that the accommodation was reasonable. . . .

Third, that Wong had earned "B's" and received generally positive comments in the Medicine and Surgery clerkships for which Dean Lewis granted him eight weeks of reading time indicates that it may have been reasonable for Wong to continue receiving this same accommodation. . . .

Our holding that Wong has created an issue of fact as to the reasonableness of an eight-week reading period between clerkships does not conflict with our opinion in *Zukle,* in which we decided that the plaintiff did not create an issue of fact as to the reasonableness of the same accommodation that Wong requested. In *Zukle,* we reached the conclusion that a disabled medical student's requested decelerated schedule for clerkships was not a reasonable accommodation only after determining that a deferential standard of review was appropriate. We noted that the Promotions Board had considered the plaintiff's previous failure to perform adequately even when granted a decelerated schedule. . . . Here, however, Wong has presented evidence that when granted the decelerated schedule, his performance drastically improved, and that the University failed to consider fully the effect of this modification on its program and on his abilities.

* * *

C. *Qualified Individual*

. . . For purposes of resolving the summary judgment issue, Wong concedes that he is not qualified to continue in the School of Medicine without reasonable accommodation; the issue we must consider, therefore, is whether, with the accommodation of time off between clerkships for additional reading, Wong has created an issue of fact that he could satisfy the school's academic standards.

Again, our analysis begins with a determination of whether we defer to the University's decision to dismiss Wong for "failure to meet the academic standards of the School of Medicine." We will not defer to a school's decision if the ostensibly professional, academic judgment "disguise[s] truly discriminatory requirements." Moreover, the academic institution bears the burden of presenting us with a factual record that shows it conscientiously considered all pertinent and appropriate information in making its decision. Far from demonstrating a conscientious effort to consider all relevant factors in deciding that Wong could not meet the school's academic requirements even with reasonable accommodation, the record contains evidence that the University eschewed its obligation to consider possible modifications it could make (or could have made) in the program to accommodate Wong and the past and potential effects of such accommodations (and lack thereof) on Wong's performance.

The University has not disputed Wong's assertion that Dean Lewis instructed him not to mention the requested accommodation—or Dean Lewis's denial of it—to the Promotions Board. In fact, the record contains evidence that at least two Promotions Board members believed that Dean Lewis *had* given Wong accommodations and erroneously believed that Wong had been unable to perform adequately even with those modifications. These same two individuals also identified Wong's failure of the Pediatrics clerkship as the determining factor in their decision to dismiss him. . . . The University has presented no evidence that the Promotions Board considered the fact that in his previous two clerkships, Wong had performed well after receiving an eight-week reading period as an accommodation but that in the Pediatrics clerkship, Wong performed poorly after failing to receive the same accommodation.

This failure to take Wong's disability and need for accommodation into account shows that the school's system for evaluating a learning disabled student's abilities and its own duty to make its program accessible to such individuals fell short of the standards we require to grant deference to an academic institution's decision-making process. We therefore analyze whether Wong has created an issue of fact with respect to his qualifications *de novo*.

Wong has produced enough evidence that he could meet the University's eligibility requirements to shift the burden of production to the University: his final grade sheets from the Medicine and Surgery clerkships for which he received the accommodation show that he received satisfactory grades and generally positive comments from his evaluators. The University argues, however, that an examination of Wong's entire academic record demonstrates that he did not have the capacity to become an effective physician. . . . For the reasons discussed below, however, we cannot say as a matter of law that he was unqualified to continue participating in the medical program.

Most importantly, a comparison of Wong's final grade sheets from his 1991 Surgery and 1993 Medicine clerkships (which he failed and for which he received no accommodation) and his 1994 Medicine and 1995 Surgery clerkships (which he passed with grades of "B" and for which he received eight weeks of reading time prior to starting) show a marked improvement, not only in Wong's performance on written and oral examinations, *but also in his performance in the clinical setting*. For example, the final grade sheet for the 1993 Medicine clerkship reported that Wong's clinical performance was "below that expected" because, for example, he could not collect data from patients and use it to formulate a diagnosis; his oral presentations were problematic; and he had difficulty with interpersonal interactions. In contrast, his 1994 Medicine clerkship evaluation stated that his clinical performance was "satisfactory in all areas." It noted some difficulty with verbal presentations, including taking a little extra time or repeating a question, but stated that he nonetheless answered questions satisfactorily. Significantly, this grade sheet reported excellent performance in two areas with which Wong earlier had struggled: interpersonal relationships (both with patients and with other professionals) and synthesizing a diagnosis while taking a patient's history.

Wong's poor performance in the 1995 Pediatrics clerkship for which he did not receive the accommodation he requested mimicked his earlier failures. The comments he received regarding his clinical performance were similar to the assessments of his work in the 1993 Medicine and 1991 Surgery clerkships: he could not synthesize information; his oral presentation skills were poor; and he lacked confidence. From all of this evidence, a reasonable jury could discern a pattern: Wong failed when he did not have extra time to prepare before a clerkship, but with the modified schedule, he succeeded in all areas of the clerkship.

* * *

III. CONCLUSION

Faculty members and administrators of a professional school are unquestionably in the best position to set standards for the institution and to establish curricular requirements that fulfill the school's purpose of training students for the work that lies ahead of them. However, "extending deference to educational institutions must not impede our obligation to enforce the ADA and the Rehabilitation Act.... The educational institution has a 'real obligation . . . to seek suitable means of reasonably accommodating a handicapped person and to submit a factual record indicating that it conscientiously carried out this statutory obligation.' " Here, school administrators accepted the recommendation of a faculty member (and learning disability services coordinator) to grant Wong the schedule modification he requested for two courses, and Wong performed well with this accommodation. The School of Medicine did not present any evidence that during this time period, it believed that Wong's decelerated schedule impeded his attainment of the goals of the program or lowered the school's academic standards. Then, however, for reasons about which there is a dispute of fact, the school refused to continue granting Wong the accommodation and dismissed him when he could not perform satisfactorily without it.

. . . We will not sanction an academic institution's decision to refuse to accommodate a disabled student and subsequent dismissal of that student when the record contains facts from which a reasonable jury could conclude that the school made those decisions for arbitrary reasons unrelated to its academic standards.

[Reversed and remanded].

NOTES AND QUESTIONS

1. *Academic deference.* As the court discussed in *Zukle* and *Wong*, it had to determine how much deference to give to the institution's decisions. In the due process context involving the dismissal of a medical student, the Supreme Court held that judges should show great respect for the genuinely academic decisions made by the faculty while using their professional judgment. Courts should not override an academic decision unless it is such a "substantial departure from accepted norms as to demonstrate that the person or committee responsible did not actually exercise professional judgment." Regents of the Univ. of Michigan v. Ewing, 474 U.S. 214, 225, 106 S.Ct. 507 (1985). The idea is that courts are particularly ill-equipped to evaluate academic performance.

The first case to decide how this judicial deference concept applied in the disability context was *Wynne v. Tufts University School of Medicine*, 932 F.2d

19 (1st Cir. 1991) (en banc). The plaintiff, Stephen Wynne, had difficulty with the multiple-choice questions that were commonly used in his first-year examinations in medical school, and he failed eight out of fifteen first-year classes, subsequently failing his Biochemistry exam a total of three times. An evaluation revealed he had a learning disability that affected his ability to process information required for multiple-choice questions. After he was dismissed from medical school, he filed suit, arguing that the medical school's failure to give him an alternative to written multiple choice examinations was discriminatory in violation of Section 504 of the Rehabilitation Act. The medical school argued that Wynne's proposed modification would be a fundamental alteration of the medical school program. *Id.* at 21–22.

The court was called upon to decide how to apply the *Ewing*-type deference in the context of a statute prohibiting disability discrimination. The court stated that the "same principle of respect for academic decisionmaking applies but with two qualifications." *Id.* at 25. First, there is a "real obligation on the academic institution to seek suitable means of reasonably accommodating" a disabled student and to "submit a factual record indicating that it conscientiously carried out this statutory obligation." *Id.* at 25–26. Second, if the institution submits undisputed facts "demonstrating that the relevant officials within the institution considered alternative means, their feasibility, cost and effect on the academic program, and came to a rationally justifiable conclusion that the available alternatives would result either in lowering academic standards or requiring substantial program alteration, the court could rule as a matter of law that the institution had met its duty of seeking reasonable accommodation." *Id.* at 26. The *Wynne I* court remanded the case for a determination of whether Tufts Medical School had met its burden "of demonstrating that its determination that no reasonable way existed to accommodate Wynne's inability to perform adequately on written multiple-choice examinations was a reasoned, professional academic judgment, not a mere ipse dixit." *Id.* at 27.

On appeal after remand, the First Circuit had to decide whether, in fact, Tufts had reached "a rationally justifiable conclusion that accommodating plaintiff would lower academic standards or otherwise unduly affect its program." Wynne v. Tufts Univ. Sch. of Med., 976 F.2d. 791, 793 (1st Cir. 1992). The Court considered voluminous documents that Tufts produced after remand which discussed, among other things, why biochemistry is important to a medical school curriculum, why multiple choice testing was the fairest means of evaluating the subject matter, "what thought [the university] had given to different methods of testing proficiency in biochemistry," and "why it eschewed alternatives to multiple-choice testing, particularly with respect to make-up examinations." *Id.* at 794. The First Circuit concluded that Tufts had successfully "demythologized the institutional thought processes leading to its determination that it could not deviate from its wanted format to accommodate Wynne's professed disability." *Id.* Tufts met its burden of proving that the modification would constitute a fundamental alteration because it showed that its officials had decided "rationally, if not inevitably, that no further accommodation could be made without imposing an undue (and injurious) hardship on the academic program." *Id.* at 796.

As mentioned in *Zukle*, other circuits have followed the approach in *Wynne*. Do you think the court's conclusion that the Medical School's decision deserved deference in *Zukle* but not in *Wong* was correct? More broadly, why should institutions of higher education be given this broad deference? As we saw in the employment context, an employer's assertion of the essential functions of a job is given some weight, but is only one of several factors that courts should consider in determining the essential functions of the job. Is a court more well-equipped to determine the essential functions of a job that the judge has never encountered than it is to determine whether a particular academic modification would fundamentally alter an academic program? If so, why?

2. *Comparing* Zukle *and* Wong. As discussed in the note above, the court gives deference to the Medical School's decision in *Zukle* but refuses to give deference to the Medical School's decision in *Wong*. Do you think that the decision regarding whether or not to grant deference to the institution's decision was the controlling factor in this case? Or are the factual circumstances surrounding Zukle's experience in medical school and Wong's experience sufficiently different to explain the difference in the results of the opinions?

3. *Withdrawn accommodations.* Note the court's language in *Wong*:

> An institution's past decision to make a concession to a disabled individual does not obligate it to continue to grant that accommodation in the future, nor does it render the accommodation reasonable as a matter of law. The fact that the school previously made the exact modification for the Surgery and Medicine clerkships that Wong requested for the Pediatrics clerkship, however, is certainly persuasive evidence from which a jury could conclude that the accommodation was reasonable.

In the employment context, Professor Porter has identified a phenomenon known as "withdrawn accommodations." Nicole Buonocore Porter, *Withdrawn Accommodations*, 63 DRAKE L. REV. 885 (2015). This occurs when a covered entity (either an employer, or in this case, an educational institution) provides a particular accommodation and then later decides to stop providing the accommodation. Courts vary in what weight they give the fact that an entity had previously provided an accommodation and then withdrew it.

How should this issue be resolved in the educational context? Do you agree with the court in *Wong* that the fact that the school had previously approved the modifications to his clerkship schedule is relevant to the determination of whether it should have provided the modification for the rest of his clerkships? Is there a legitimate reason the school might have refused the same modification that it had previously allowed?

HALPERN V. WAKE FOREST UNIVERSITY HEALTH SCIENCES

669 F.3d 454 (4th Cir. 2012)

FLOYD, CIRCUIT JUDGE:

Appellant Ronen Halpern brought an action alleging that his dismissal from medical school for unprofessional behavior violated the Rehabilitation Act of 1973, 29 U.S.C. § 794, and the Americans with Disabilities Act (ADA), 42 U.S.C. § 12182. The district court granted summary judgment in favor of Appellee Wake Forest University Health Sciences (Wake Forest or the Medical School). Halpern filed this timely appeal. Because we agree with the district court that, with or without a reasonable accommodation, Halpern was not "otherwise qualified" to participate in the Medical School's program, we affirm.

I.

A.

Halpern was enrolled in Wake Forest's Doctor of Medicine program from July 2004 to March 2009. As at most medical schools, Wake Forest's curriculum is designed as a four-year program. During the first two years, students take classes to acquire knowledge in core areas, and for the last two years, students participate in rotations in different clinical environments. Prior to beginning these rotations, students must pass Step One of the United States Medical Licensure Examination (the Step One Exam).

The Medical School's Student Bulletin outlines the seven fundamental educational goals of its curriculum. One of these is that students establish "[p]rofessional [a]ttitudes and [b]ehavior." The Bulletin instructs that to satisfy this goal, students must demonstrate, prior to graduating, their respect for and ability to work with other health care professionals, adherence to the highest standards of integrity, ability to admit mistakes and lack of knowledge, and other identified aspects of professional behavior.

B.

Halpern has been diagnosed with Attention Deficit Hyperactivity Disorder (ADHD) and anxiety disorder—not otherwise specified, both of which he treats with prescription medications. He received his ADHD diagnosis while he was an undergraduate student at Emory University, and Emory provided accommodations for this disability. Upon matriculating at Wake Forest in July 2004, Halpern failed to disclose his ADHD diagnosis, and he did not request any disability-related accommodations.

Halpern's difficulties with professionalism began almost immediately after his arrival at the Medical School and continued throughout the first two years of his enrollment. In August 2004, Academic Computing staff reported that Halpern had acted in a "very abusive" manner that was "far and beyond worse" than anything they had experienced with other students. Dr. Joseph Ernest, then-Associate Dean of Student Services, met with Halpern and convinced him to apologize for his behavior so as to "set[ ] a more professional standard for his interactions" with Academic Computing.

During the fall of his second year of medical school, Halpern was absent from a small group session without notice. He falsely represented to faculty members inquiring into his absence that he had given advance notice to the group facilitators that he would not be present. When confronted, he retorted that he "got more out of" a different small group session that he had opted to attend without permission "than any . . . lecture, small group, or . . . class assignment to date." Subsequently, he was late to a lecture but signed the attendance sheet as though he had arrived on time. Faculty members contacted him regarding the discrepancy, and he replied that he was already "well aware of" the issues discussed. Halpern now attributes his conduct during this period to side effects of his ADHD medication.

Halpern experienced a severe reaction to this medication during the spring of his second year of school. He first informed the Medical School of a potential problem in March 2006, when he asked to postpone his Step One Exam. After Halpern presented a doctor's note explaining that he was suffering an adverse reaction to medication, the Medical School approved Halpern's request to delay the exam until May 2006. In May, Halpern asked to delay the exam further . . . and received an additional medical postponement. He successfully took the Step One Exam in June 2006.

From June 2006 to August 2006, Halpern participated in an internal medicine clinical rotation. It is undisputed his performance in this rotation was deficient. His evaluation indicates he had numerous problems, including a below-average fund of medical knowledge and difficulty forming differential diagnoses. His "largest obstacle," however, "was his frequent lapses in professionalism": He was resistant to feedback, lacked interpersonal skills, and was absent without permission for more than one week. Additionally, Halpern failed to use an electronic log system, and he resisted efforts to help correct what he insisted was a technical problem, claiming that he had "more important things to do, like see patients." Academic Computing staff ultimately concluded that he was refusing to enter the necessary data, thereby preventing staff and faculty from recording feedback on his performance. After failing this rotation, Halpern met with Dr. Ernest and revealed that he had not slept in twelve days. Shortly thereafter, Halpern went on medical leave to address the severe side effects of his medications.

Halpern returned to the Medical School in February 2007. During conversations with Dr. Ernest discussing his return to rotations, Halpern indicated that he might seek accommodations for his medication-related insomnia, but he did not reveal his ADHD diagnosis. Dr. Ernest suggested that Halpern meet with each clerkship director prior to beginning a rotation to discuss their policy regarding absences, but he noted that some of the accommodations Halpern wanted—including the ability to call out of work without prior notice if he had been unable to sleep—likely would be infeasible. Dr. Ernest explained that, like practicing physicians, medical students were expected to provide advance notice of absences whenever possible and to coordinate coverage for patient care. Halpern reports that he felt discouraged from seeking an accommodation, and he failed to submit a formal request for any accommodation. In this meeting with Dr. Ernest, Halpern signed an acknowledgement that he was on "Academic or Professional Probation" as a result of failing a rotation.

Halpern resumed clinical rotations in April 2007. From April 2007 to October 2008, he successfully completed ten clinical rotations. The evaluations for these rotations show he received either passing or honors marks in the "Patient Rapport/Professionalism" category, and many of the comments regarding his performance were positive. But, these records also reveal several incidents of unprofessional behavior in connection with his rotations. His neurology evaluation noted he missed a required lecture with the clerkship director. He also failed to appear for a family medicine examination in October 2007 and did not respond when paged. Although Dr. Ernest recommended that the family medicine faculty give him a failing grade for this exam, they permitted him to take it at a later date. The evaluation of his obstetrics/gynecology (OB/GYN) rotation was particularly critical. The evaluator reported Halpern had difficulty with constructive criticism and recommended that he "[b]e more humble," "accept feedback graciously," and "[r]ealize that rules apply to [him] as well as everyone else."

His interaction with staff members revealed more, and more acute, problems with professionalism. In April 2007, shortly after his return from medical leave, he paced back and forth in the financial aid office for forty-five minutes stating that someone should give him a scholarship to become a trauma surgeon. The financial aid director reported this bizarre behavior made her "very nervous."

In December 2007, Halpern requested, for the first time, an accommodation for his ADHD—specifically, testing accommodations for a surgery examination. He emailed this request to Dr. Ernest. Although Dr. Ernest informed him that the school required him to meet with a faculty member prior to receiving accommodations, he repeatedly sought to receive accommodations without first attending such a meeting. Halpern neglected to produce documentation of his disability until the day of the exam; nevertheless, the Medical School provided the requested accommodations.

Halpern failed to respond in October 2008 to repeated requests from student services staff that he review the "Dean's Letter" to be mailed out with his residency applications. Several hours after the deadline to respond had passed, he appeared at the student services office, "rude[ly]" insisting that the letter contained numerous errors and expressing disbelief that the staff member responsible for the letter was not there.

Finally, in November 2008, Halpern failed to send letters of appreciation to scholarship donors, despite numerous reminders. Although typically this would not have resulted in expulsion, because Halpern was on probation due to his failure of the internal medicine rotation, the Medical School referred his file to the Student Progress and Promotions Committee (SPPC), which makes disciplinary recommendations to the Medical School's dean. A student may appeal the SPPC's recommendation to the Academic Appeals Committee, but the dean of the Medical School makes the ultimate determination regarding discipline.

Halpern appeared before the SPPC in December 2008. During this appearance, he maintained that his medical condition did not affect his ability to "perform optimally in the medical curriculum." He further asserted his belief that the incidents of unprofessionalism "were isolated" and that he had "addressed them." After reviewing his records, the SPPC voted to recommend Halpern's dismissal based on a pattern of unprofessional behavior.

Halpern appealed to the Academic Appeals Committee through a letter to Associate Dean of Education, Dr. K. Patrick Ober. Halpern wrote that he was aware of his "behavioral tendencies"—including excessive defensiveness, intolerance of others, and rudeness—which he attributed both to his ADHD and to cultural differences between Israel, where he grew up, and the United States. Halpern suggested a "special remediation" plan including a comprehensive assessment by a treatment team, participation in a program for distressed physicians, continuing treatment by his psychiatrist, and "strict probation." He also submitted letters from his psychiatrist, Dr. Doreen Hughes, who ascribed his behavior to ADHD, an anxiety disorder, and childhood exposure to trauma, family modeling, and first-hand accounts of the Holocaust. After reviewing these materials and Halpern's record, the Academic Appeals Committee upheld the SPPC's recommendation.

Halpern then appealed to the Dean of the Medical School, Dr. William Applegate. Dr. Applegate considered and rejected alternatives to dismissal, including Halpern's suggested plan. Dr. Applegate explained that he believed, in light of the pattern of behavior Halpern engaged in both before and after his medical leave, Halpern inevitably would revert to unprofessional conduct. Particularly concerning was Halpern's treatment of staff members. While Halpern might be able to control his behavior towards other physicians, Dr. Applegate worried that the incidents with Medical School staff indicated he would treat nonphysician health care providers in a disrespectful and unprofessional manner. Such an attitude would undermine the team-centered approach to health care that Wake Forest sought to instill and would have a deleterious effect on patient care. Concluding that no accommodation could adequately alleviate these concerns, Dr. Applegate adopted the SPPC's recommendation of dismissal.

C.

Halpern brought suit ..., alleging that his dismissal violated the Rehabilitation Act and ADA because the Medical School failed to make reasonable accommodations for his disability. The district court . . . granted summary judgment in favor of Wake Forest on the ground that Halpern was not "otherwise qualified" as a medical student because demonstrating professionalism was a fundamental aspect of the Medical School's program. The court further held that Halpern's proposed accommodation—obtaining therapeutic treatment, participating in a distressed physicians program, and continuing as a student on strict probation—was unreasonable "because of the uncertainty of the duration and the prospects for success of such behavior modification efforts."

II.

* * *

A.

* * *

To the extent possible, we construe the ADA and Rehabilitation Act to impose similar requirements. Thus, despite the different language these statutes employ, they require a plaintiff to demonstrate the same elements to establish liability. In the context of a student excluded from an educational program, to prove a violation of either Act, the plaintiff must establish that (1) he has a disability, (2) he is otherwise qualified to participate in the defendant's program, and (3) he was excluded from the program on the basis of his disability. . . .

Wake Forest concedes that Halpern has satisfied the first element. His ADHD and anxiety disorder constitute disabilities giving rise to protection under the Rehabilitation Act and ADA. Accordingly, we consider whether the district court erred in determining as a matter of law that Halpern was not "otherwise qualified" to participate in the Medical School's program.

B.

A "qualified" individual is one "who, with or without reasonable modifications to rules, policies, or practices, ... meets the essential eligibility requirements" for participation in a program or activity. A plaintiff asserting a violation of the ADA or Rehabilitation Act bears the burden to establish that he is qualified. To determine whether a plaintiff has satisfied this burden, a court must decide whether he has presented sufficient evidence to show (1) that he could satisfy the essential eligibility requirements of the program, i.e., those requirements " 'that bear more than a marginal relationship to the [program] at issue,' and (2) if not, whether 'any reasonable accommodation by the [defendant] would enable' " the plaintiff to meet these requirements.

The parties dispute whether we should accord deference to the Medical School's professional judgment regarding Halpern's ability to satisfy the School's essential eligibility requirements. In the context of due-process challenges, the Supreme Court has held that a court should defer to a school's professional judgment regarding a student's academic or professional qualifications. *See Regents of the Univ. of Mich. v. Ewing*, 474 U.S. 214, 225, 106 S.Ct. 507 (1985).

Based on these cases, our sister circuits have overwhelmingly extended some level of deference to schools' professional judgments regarding students' qualifications when addressing disability discrimination claims. . . . And we have observed in dicta that, in general, "great deference to a school's determination of the qualifications of a hopeful student" is appropriate "because courts are particularly ill-equipped to evaluate academic performance."

Because we are likewise at a comparative disadvantage in determining whether Halpern is qualified to continue in the Doctor of Medicine program and whether his proposed accommodations would effect substantial modifications to the Medical School's program, we accord great respect to Wake Forest's professional judgments on these issues. But, in doing so, we must take care "not to allow academic decisions to disguise truly discriminatory requirements," so we assiduously review the record to ensure that the educational institution has "conscientiously carried out [its] statutory obligation" to provide reasonable accommodations to persons with disabilities.

Adopting an appropriately deferential view, we find that professionalism was an essential requirement of the Medical School's program and that, without an accommodation, Halpern could not satisfy this requirement. Throughout the period of Halpern's enrollment at Wake Forest, the Medical School identified professionalism as a fundamental goal of its educational program, and it required that students demonstrate professional behavior and attitudes prior to graduating. The Student Bulletin explicated different aspects of professional behavior that the school sought to instill, such as the ability to collaborate with others and to admit mistakes gracefully. As Dr. Applegate explained in his affidavit, the Medical School emphasized professionalism based on evidence that inappropriate and disruptive behavior by physicians increases adverse patient outcomes.

Halpern does not dispute that the Medical School's professionalism requirement is essential. Instead, he maintains that because he received passing marks in professionalism in his clinical rotations after returning from medical leave, a question of fact exists as to whether he satisfied the requirement. This argument, however, fails to take into account Halpern's treatment of staff both before and after his medical leave. We accept Dr. Applegate's reasonable inference that Halpern's unprofessional treatment of staff, in contrast with his behavior towards faculty, suggests that he would interact poorly with health care providers who are not physicians, thereby undermining the team approach to health care. Halpern's contention also ignores the instances of unprofessional conduct reflected in his clinical evaluations, such as his resistance to constructive criticism during his OB/GYN rotation and failure to appear for a family medicine exam. Although, in isolation, these may not have warranted his evaluators giving him failing grades in professionalism, the school reasonably considered them as part of an ongoing pattern of unprofessional behavior.

Halpern's own admissions support the conclusion that without an accommodation he is unqualified to participate in the Doctor of Medicine program. In his letters appealing the SPPC's recommendation of dismissal, Halpern acknowledged his problematic behavioral tendencies. He did not argue that the professionalism requirement was nonessential or that he should be exempted. Instead, he requested the opportunity to undergo treatment and demonstrate he could satisfy the School's professionalism standards. Similarly, when deposed, he conceded that his past behavior had been perceived as rude, and he stated that the Medical School should not permit him to become a doctor if he was rude or hostile.

In light of the extensive evidence of Halpern's unprofessional behavior—both before and after his medical leave—and the potential for such behavior to undermine patient care, we have no difficulty concluding that, absent an accommodation, Halpern was not "otherwise qualified" for the Medical School's program. Therefore, we next consider whether there was a reasonable accommodation available by which Halpern would have become qualified.

C.

Federal law mandates that federal grantees and public accommodations make "reasonable," but not "substantial" or "fundamental," modifications to accommodate persons with disabilities. A modification "is not reasonable if it either imposes undue financial and administrative burdens ... or requires a fundamental alteration in the nature of the program." A modification to "an essential aspect" of the program constitutes a "fundamental alteration" and, therefore, is an unreasonable accommodation. Although determination of the reasonableness of a proposed modification is often fact-specific, a court may grant summary judgment in favor of a defendant if the plaintiff fails to present evidence from which a jury may infer that the accommodation is "reasonable on its face, *i.e.*, ordinarily or in the run of cases," or if the defendant establishes as a matter of law that the proposed modification will cause "undue hardship in the particular circumstances."

As discussed above, we find that the requirement that students demonstrate professional behavior is an essential aspect of Wake Forest's Doctor of Medicine program. Accordingly, Halpern could not reasonably seek to avoid or lessen the professionalism requirement; rather, he must show that a reasonable accommodation would have permitted him to satisfy this criterion. He contends that his proposed special remediation plan, which included ongoing psychiatric treatment, participation in a program for distressed physicians, and continuing in the Medical School on strict probation, constituted a reasonable accommodation for his disability through which he could have met Wake Forest's standards for professionalism. We disagree. For the following reasons, we conclude that Halpern's proposed special remediation plan was unreasonable on its face and, as a result, that the district court properly granted summary judgment in favor of Wake Forest.

First, Halpern's request for an accommodation was untimely. The school was not obligated to accommodate Halpern's disability until he "provided a proper diagnosis . . . and requested specific accommodation." Halpern failed to inform Wake Forest that he was disabled until December 2007, and when he did so, he requested only testing accommodations. Even when he appeared before the SPPC, he maintained that his medical conditions did not impact his ability to participate in the Medical School. He suggested, for the first time, that his behavioral problems were manifestations of a disability in his letter to Dr. Ober appealing the SPPC's recommendation of dismissal.

We have previously observed that "misconduct—even misconduct related to a disability—is not itself a disability" and may be a basis for dismissal. By the time Halpern requested that the Medical School implement his special remediation plan, he had already engaged in numerous unprofessional acts that warranted his dismissal, including acting abusively towards staff, multiple unexcused absences, repeated failure to meet deadlines, and tardiness. Thus, Halpern sought not a disability accommodation, but "a second chance to better control [his] treatable medical condition." This, however, "is not a cause of action under the ADA." A school, if informed that a student has a disability with behavioral manifestations, may be obligated to make accommodations to help the student avoid engaging in misconduct. But, the law does not require the school to ignore misconduct that has occurred because the student subsequently asserts it was the result of a disability. Halpern's argument that he was owed an opportunity to continue at the Medical School and correct his misbehavior is, therefore, without merit.

Second, the indefinite duration and uncertain likelihood of success of Halpern's proposed accommodation renders it unreasonable. . . . [T]he

Rehabilitation Act and ADA do not obligate a school to permit a student to continue in an educational program with the hope that at some unknown time in the future he will be able to satisfy the program's essential requirements. At the time Halpern proposed the special remediation plan, he had already delayed his graduation by one year due to his medical leave, and he was seeking to further extend his medical education to have an opportunity to demonstrate his ability to behave professionally. Neither Halpern nor his expert could specify a time at which his treatment would be complete; indeed, they acknowledged there was no guarantee Halpern's treatment plan would be successful. Consequently, it was unreasonable to demand that Wake Forest wait to determine if and when the plan would enable Halpern to meet its professionalism standards.

Finally, we reject Halpern's argument that even if his proposed accommodation was unreasonable, Wake Forest violated the ADA by failing to engage in an "interactive process to identify a reasonable accommodation." An interactive effort to identify an accommodation would not have corrected the untimeliness of Halpern's request or erased his record of prior misconduct. Dr. Applegate's affidavit indicates that he carefully considered alternatives to dismissal, but, because Halpern had consistently reverted to unprofessional conduct even after the Medical School's officials attempted to intervene, he was unable to identify any accommodation that could ensure Halpern would not engage in such behavior as a practicing physician. Thus, he concluded that all possible accommodations permitting Halpern to remain in the program would be unreasonable because they would allow Halpern to graduate with a medical degree.

. . . Where a professional school has reasonably determined based on an identifiable pattern of prior conduct that a student is unfit to join his chosen profession, federal law does not obligate the school to allow that student to remain in and graduate from its educational program. As the evidence in the record amply justifies Dr. Applegate's conclusion, we find that the Medical School did not violate the Rehabilitation Act or the ADA.

III.

Because, with or without reasonable accommodations, Halpern is unqualified for Wake Forest's Doctor of Medicine program, we affirm the district court's grant of summary judgment.

NOTES AND QUESTIONS

1. *Lack of professionalism as grounds for dismissal.* Do you agree with the medical school's decision that the plaintiff's lack of professionalism warranted his dismissal from medical school? Is the concept of "professionalism" too amorphous in nature to be considered an essential qualification of the medical school program? Have you ever encountered doctors who were unprofessional, maybe those who barked orders at nurses

and other staff? If your answer was yes, does this mean that Wake Forest should not have the right to demand more from its medical students? Law schools do not have an exact equivalent to the clinical settings employed by medical schools. Most law students participate in only one clinical or externship experience. If a law student behaved "unprofessionally" in that environment, perhaps treating the law school clinical staff or the court staff rudely, do you think that behavior would lead to the law student's dismissal? If not, does that say something negative about how law schools treat issues of professionalism?

2. *Duration.* As one of the reasons for rejecting plaintiff's claim, the court states "the indefinite duration and uncertain likelihood of success of Halpern's proposed accommodation renders it unreasonable. . . ." In redacted portions of the opinion, the court cites to a similar rule in the employment context, where courts have held that employers do not have to wait indefinitely for an employee's disability-related restrictions to get better. This rule is often applied in the context of a leave of absence but is also applied in cases where an employee cannot pass a particular test or requirement of the job. Halpern was asking to remain a student while he tried treatment for his disability. It is perhaps easy to understand why the school was opposed to that option. But what if Halpern had asked for an additional leave from medical school to see if therapy for his disability would be effective? Would that have been a reasonable accommodation?

3. *Misconduct.* The court correctly states how most courts handle misconduct issues—even if the misconduct is caused by a disability, educational institutions do not have to ignore the behavior. This is the same rule that applies in the employment context. *See, e.g.,* Tyndall v. Nat'l Educ. Ctrs., Inc. of California, 31 F.3d 209, 214–15 (4th Cir. 1994) (finding the dismissal of an employee for attendance problems did not constitute discrimination, even if her disability caused her absences); Little v. FBI, 1 F.3d 255, 259 (4th Cir. 1993) (holding that the plaintiff could be terminated for intoxication, although it was related to alcoholism, a disability). Should this be the rule? In other words, if Halpern's disability *caused* his unprofessional behavior, does the medical school have an obligation to accommodate him by excusing this misconduct, at least initially? Or is this just a matter of poor timing on the part of the plaintiff? If he had told the medical school and his instructors that he had a disability that might sometimes cause him to behave unprofessionally, and he had asked for an accommodation to help him control his unprofessional behavior, arguably the school would have been obligated to accommodate him, if possible. But because he waited until after he behaved inappropriately, he is out of luck. Does this rule make sense? Do you think that Halpern knew or even suspected that his behavior was related to his ADHD and the medications he was taking to treat it? If not, then does it seem unfair to require him to ask for an accommodation when he is not aware that he needed an accommodation? Is there any way around this dilemma?

4. WAIVER OF DEGREE REQUIREMENTS

GUCKENBERGER V. BOSTON UNIVERSITY
("GUCKENBERGER I")
974 F.Supp. 106 (D. Mass. 1997)

SARIS, DISTRICT JUDGE.

INTRODUCTION

This is a class action brought by students with Attention Deficit Hyperactivity Disorder ("ADHD"), Attention Deficit Disorder ("ADD"), and learning disorders (collectively "learning disabilities") against Boston University ("BU") under the Americans with Disabilities Act ("ADA"), 42 U.S.C.A. § 12101 *et seq.* and the Rehabilitation Act, 29 U.S.C.A. § 794. . . . The class claims that BU discriminates against the learning-disabled by: (1) establishing unreasonable, overly-burdensome eligibility criteria for qualifying as a disabled student; (2) failing to provide reasonable procedures for evaluation and review of a student's request for accommodations; and (3) instituting an across-the-board policy precluding course substitutions in foreign language and mathematics. . . .

Particularly with respect to the issue of course substitution, this class action concerns the interplay between the rights of learning-disabled students to reasonable accommodation and the rights of institutions of higher education to establish and enforce academic standards.

* * *

After a two-week bench trial, and an evaluation of the witnesses and evidence in this case, I have made numerous findings of fact and conclusions of law.

* * *

FINDINGS OF FACT

I. *BU's Recruitment of the Learning Disabled*

BU is one of the largest private universities in the United States, with 20,000 students, 2,000 faculty members, and fifteen undergraduate and graduate colleges that offer 150 separate degree-granting programs. The College of Arts and Sciences is the largest college in the university. It has longstanding course requirements, including one semester of mathematics and four semesters of a foreign language. Degree requirements at all of BU's colleges are approved by the Provost, the President, and the Board of Trustees.

Before 1995, BU was a leader among educational institutions in seeking to provide comprehensive services to students with diagnosed learning disabilities. The university recruited learning-disabled enrollees by establishing the Learning Disabilities Support Services ("LDSS"), a renowned accommodations program that functioned as a unit within BU's Disability Services office ("DSO"). LDSS was often described as a "model program." Through LDSS, the university declared a commitment to enabling students with learning disabilities to reach their maximum academic potential. For example, LDSS promotional brochures offered learning-disabled students various complimentary accommodations including notetaking assistance, and extended time on examinations. . . .

Before 1995, not only did LDSS often authorize in-class notetakers, tape-recorded textbooks, and time and one half on final examinations for students with documented learning disabilities (the so-called "vanilla" accommodations), but LDSS staff also occasionally recommended that disabled students receive a course substitution for required mathematics and foreign language classes. For example, students who received an LDSS recommendation for a math substitution were allowed to take classes such as Anthropology 245 ("Anthropology of Money"), Economics 320 ("Economics of Less Developed Regions"), or Geography 100 ("Introduction to Environmental Science") instead of the required math curriculum. Similarly, learning-disabled students who received a foreign language exemption might opt instead for one of several foreign culture courses including Art History 226 ("Arts of Japan") or History 292 ("African Colonial History").

In developing lists of "approved" course substitutions and recommending waivers of math and foreign language requirements for certain students, LDSS worked with the heads of the various academic departments at the College of Liberal Arts ("CLA") (now called the College of Arts and Sciences) ("CAS"). However, neither LDSS nor CLA notified or sought the approval of the President, Provost, or any other member of BU's central administration. Eighty-eight students requested foreign language waivers at CLA during academic years 1992–1993 and 1993–1994. On average, BU granted approximately 10 to 15 requests for course substitutions a year.

Prior to 1995, the process of applying for accommodations, including course substitutions, from BU was relatively straightforward. A learning-disabled student submitted to LDSS a description of her need for accommodation, a statement of her accommodations history, and a current medical or psycho-educational evaluation (one that had been conducted within three years of entering the university). Once the student's documentation was filed, members of the LDSS staff determined whether accommodation was appropriate. In 1995, LDSS was permanently staffed with a full-time director, two assistant coordinators and a secretary, and it also employed several part-time learning disabilities specialists. Several of these administrators had specific training in special education and in the provision of accommodations to post-secondary students with learning disabilities.

If LDSS granted a student's request for accommodation, the student would be notified. An LDSS staff member would also write letters, referred to as "accommodations letters," to the student's faculty members and to the dean of the student's particular school explaining the student's disability and recommending that the student be provided with the listed accommodations. Students were responsible for distributing these letters to their professors, and for meeting with their instructors to arrange the provision of in-class and exam accommodations.

The results of LDSS's "marketing" to students with learning disabilities were pronounced. In academic year 1990–1991, 42 students who self-identified as learning disabled applied, 24 were accepted and two enrolled. Four years later, 348 such students applied, 233 accepted and 94 enrolled. In late 1995, 429 learning-disabled students applied to the university. As its reputation developed, BU was recommended by guidance counselors and college manuals as a desirable academic setting the learning disabled. Between 1990 and 1996, hundreds of students with learning disabilities came to BU and registered for academic accommodations and/or comprehensive services through LDSS. By the 1995–1996 school year, BU had approximately 480 learning disabled students.

II. *Westling Orders Change*

Current BU president Jon Westling became the university's provost (i.e., its chief academic officer) in 1985. A graduate of Reed College and a Rhodes Scholar, Westling has spent a total of 23 years at BU. He has served as both an administrator and as a teacher in the humanities core curriculum at the CLA. Westling holds no graduate degrees.

In the spring of 1995, Provost Westling discovered that LDSS and CLA had been allowing students with learning disabilities to substitute other classes for the mathematics and foreign language coursework that was otherwise a long-standing prerequisite to obtaining a baccalaureate degree in the College of Arts and Sciences. Chagrined that LDSS was facilitating alterations of the core curriculum without university approval, Westling assigned his assistant and troubleshooter, Craig Klafter, a Ph.D in Modern History, to research learning disabilities in general and LDSS's process of granting accommodations in particular. Confronting LDSS-director Loring Brinckerhoff, Klafter sought proof of the existence of a disability that prevented a student from learning a foreign language. Brinckerhoff referred Klafter to a book that he had co-authored concerning learning disabilities in post-secondary education. After reading Brinckerhoff's book and other secondary materials, Klafter determined that there was no scientific proof of the existence of a learning disability that prevents the successful study of math or foreign language.

As a result of Klafter's investigation, in June of 1995 Westling informed W. Norman Johnson, BU's Vice President and Dean of Students, and the College of Liberal Arts that the university was to cease granting course substitutions, "effective immediately." In addition, Westling told Johnson to direct LDSS to send all accommodation letters to the Provost's office for review before they were distributed to the students or faculty. Westling made the decision to end the course substitution practice without convening any committees or panels, and without speaking to any experts on learning disabilities or to any faculty members on the importance of math and foreign language to the liberal arts curriculum. With the course substitution "bee" in his academic bonnet, Westling decided to become personally involved with the accommodations evaluation process, even though he had no expertise or experience in diagnosing learning disabilities or in fashioning appropriate accommodations.

III. *"Somnolent Samantha"*

At around the time that Westling ordered the first changes in the accommodations practice at BU, he also began delivering speeches denouncing the zealous advocacy of "the learning disabilities movement." In [his] addresses, Westling questioned the rapidly increasing number of children being diagnosed with learning disorders, and accused learning-disabilities advocates of fashioning "fugitive" impairments that are not supported in the scientific and medical literature. Although Westling's orations recognized a need to "endorse the profoundly humane goal of addressing the specific needs of individuals with specific impairments," his public addresses resonated with a dominant theme: that "the learning disability movement is a great mortuary for the ethics of hard work, individual responsibility, and pursuit of excellence, and also for genuinely humane social order."

At the beginning of one such speech . . . , Westling introduced a student named Samantha, who was, he said, a freshman in one of his classes at BU. Westling recounted how Samantha approached him on the first day of class and how, "shyly yet assertively," she presented a letter addressed to him from the Disability Services office.

> The letter explained that Samantha had a learning disability "in the area of auditory processing" and would need the following accommodations: "time and one-half on all quizzes, tests, and examinations;" double-time on any mid-term or final examination; examinations in a room separate from other students; copies of my lecture notes; and a seat at the front of the class. Samantha, I was also informed, might fall asleep in my class, and I should be particularly concerned to fill her in on any material she missed while dozing.

Westling's speech went on to name the student "Somnolent Samantha" and to label her "an unwitting casualty of the culture wars." To Westling, Samantha exemplified those students who, placated by the promise of accommodation rather than encouraged to work to achieve their fullest potential, had become "sacrificial victims to the triumph of the therapeutic." Throughout his twenty-page address, Westling reiterated the view that, by "seiz[ing] on the existence of some real disabilities and conjur[ing] up other alleged disabilities in order to promote a particular vision of human society," the learning disabilities movement cripples allegedly disabled students who could overcome their academic difficulties "with concentrated effort," demoralizes non-disabled students who recognize hoaxes performed by their peers, and "wreak [s] educational havoc." In closing, Westling remarked:

> The policies that have grown out of learning disabilities ideology leach our sense of humanity. We are taught not that mathematics is difficult for us but worth pursuing, but that we are ill. Samantha, offered the pillow of learning disability on which to slumber, was denied, perhaps forever, access to a dimension of self-understanding.

Westling fabricated the student named Samantha to illustrate his point regarding students with learning disorders. Remarkably, at trial, Westling admitted not only that such a student never existed, but that his description of her did not even represent a prototype of the learning-disabled students he had encountered. Rather, Somnolent Samantha represented Westling's belief—fuelled mostly by popular press and anecdotal accounts—that students with learning disabilities were often fakers who undercut academic rigor.

... Even though Westling has referred to students with learning disabilities as "draft dodgers" and has repeatedly voiced his concern that students without established learning disorders might be faking a disability to gain an educational advantage, to date, there has not been a single documented instance at BU in which a student has been found to have fabricated a learning disorder in order to claim eligibility for accommodations.

IV. *The Twenty-Eight Files*

By the fall semester of the 1995–1996 academic year, BU was at a bureaucratic impasse. LDSS head Loring Brinckerhoff was ignoring Westling's directives, and LDSS was continuing the practice of approving course substitutions and granting accommodations without Westling's involvement. Although Dean Johnson had specifically conveyed Westling's orders to Brinckerhoff in a memo dated June 29, 1995, LDSS issued 58 accommodations letters (some of which allowed course substitutions) to students between July and September of 1995 without seeking Westling's approval.

Irate that his mandates were being disregarded, in October of 1995, Westling directly ordered that all of the accommodations letters that LDSS had prepared but that had not yet been picked up by the affected students be delivered to his office. At the time, LDSS held 28 such letters. Westling also requested that he be given access to the documentation files for each of the students who were the subject of the 28 letters.

After receiving the letters and files, Westling and his staff reviewed the documentation to determine if the students' evaluations actually supported LDSS's recommended accommodations. Specifically, when reviewing the files, the provost's office looked for current evaluations done by credentialed evaluators, clear diagnoses, an evaluator's recommendation listing specific accommodations, and an LDSS recommendation that was consistent with the recommendations made by the student's evaluator. None of the provost office staff members who were involved in this review had any expertise in learning disabilities.

In a letter dated November 2, 1995, Westling communicated his analysis of the letters and files to Brinckerhoff's supervisor, the director of the Office of Disability Services, William P. ("Kip") Opperman. Of the 28 files, Westling determined that, "[i]n all but a few cases, the requested accommodations [were] not supported by the attached documentation." With respect to several of the students, Westling reached the reasonable conclusion that there was actually "insufficient information" to determine whether or not students were entitled to accommodation because the documentation provided by LDSS was not current, did not support the requested accommodation, or was missing. For example, in regard to one student, Westling states that the testing psychologist "does not say [the student] is incapable of learning a foreign language," only that the student " 'has had a history of difficulty with foreign language.' " Rather than authorizing a course substitution as LDSS had done, Westling remarks that the student should be "encouraged to avail himself of the tutoring available to him through the University." With respect to other students, Westling incorrectly determined that the documentation did not support a claim of learning disability.

After describing in detail the perceived shortcomings of each file, Westling's letter to Kip Opperman concludes: . . . "I strongly advise you to take the corrective actions indicated in this letter."

Among the "corrective actions" Westling suggests throughout the letter are: (1) that students "be required to provide *current* evaluations" in light of federal guidelines stating that evaluations that are more than three years old are unreliable; (2) that the evaluations provide actual test results that support the tester's conclusions; (3) that "[i]ndividuals who provide evaluations of learning disabilities should be physicians, clinical psychologists or licensed psychologists and must have a record of reputable practice"; (4) that all requests for accommodation contain an analysis by LDSS staff, an academic history of the student, and the student's academic status at BU; and (5) that LDSS "should not misinform students that course substitutions for foreign language or mathematics requirements are available." Although Westling had no evidence that learning disabilities changed or abated after students finished high school, he mandated that BU students provide current evaluations (i.e., those that are less than three years old) on the basis of regulations promulgated by the Department of Education for grades kindergarten through twelve. In establishing standards for the credentials of evaluators, Westling relied on consultations with doctors at BU's School of Medicine that Klafter sought in late 1995.

[A]s a result of Westling's correspondence, Brinckerhoff sent a letter on behalf of LDSS to most of the 28 students whose files Westling had reviewed, denying the student's request for accommodation and informing the student of his right to appeal the decision to the Provost. . . .

LDSS staff members later told several worried students to disregard Brinckerhoff's letter denying accommodations; however, no formal letter or statement retracting the denial of accommodations was ever issued.

V. *Chaos*

On December 4, 1995, Brinckerhoff sent a form letter to all BU students who had previously registered with LDSS. The letter, which purported "to inform [students] of recent policy changes at LD Support Services," stated that the following requirements must be fulfilled by January 8, 1996, if students were to remain eligible for accommodations through LDSS:

(1) Students whose documentation was more than three years old "must be reevaluated in order to continue to receive services and accommodations through the LDSS office;"

(2) Students must submit to LDSS documentation of a learning disability that has been prepared by "a licensed psychologist, clinical psychologist, neuropsychologist, or reputable physician;" and

(3) Students seeking accommodations for the spring semester of 1996 must provide LDSS with a high school transcript, a college transcript, and a current BU course schedule including course numbers, course descriptions, and the names and addresses of the professors.

Brinckerhoff distributed the letter to students just prior to final examinations for the fall semester of 1995. He did not forward a copy of the letter to Westling for his approval; nor did he check that it accurately conveyed Westling's policy directives. When Westling learned of the letter, he requested that Norm Johnson issue a statement retracting some of the requirements for accommodation that Brinckerhoff had articulated.

. . . [T]hree weeks after Brinckerhoff's correspondence, Johnson sent a letter to the learning-disabled students at BU. Johnson's letter . . . sought "to correct a significant error in Dr. Brinckerhoff's letter" regarding the need for reevaluation. Although Brinckerhoff's letter stated that students with old documentation must be retested if they were to continue to receive assistance from LDSS, Johnson maintained (without explanation) that "[n]o such reevaluation will be necessary in order to continue receiving services from Learning Disability Support Services." Johnson also expressed his "regret" that students "were notified of these proposed changes during the examination period," and he apologized "for any inconvenience."

Throughout the first semester of the 1995–1996 school year, learning-disabled students, parents and professors received mixed and inconsistent messages from university administrators regarding the requirements for seeking and receiving academic accommodations at BU. As a result of the confusing and chaotic climate occasioned by BU's new accommodations policy, there was a substantial reduction in the number of students with self-identified learning disabilities who have attended BU since 1995. Whereas 94 students with self-proclaimed learning disabilities enrolled at BU in 1994, the number of such students had dropped to 71 by the 1996–1997 academic year.

VI. *Resignation, Reorganization, and Restructure*

Early in 1996, several members of the disability services office resigned, including Brinckerhoff and Opperman, and the Provost's office became the primary decision maker in determining whether a student was to receive an accommodation for a learning disability. In evaluating requests for reasonable accommodations, the Provost's office consulted with specialists like neuropsychologists or the remaining staff at LDSS. With the LDSS office virtually unstaffed, the university undertook to restructure the entire disability services department. Instead of having a self-contained unit within the disability services office to evaluate the accommodations requests of learning-disabled students, the new Office of Disability Services ("DS") was structured to manage accommodations for all students with disabilities, whether physical, mental, or in learning.

* * *

VII. *Present Accommodations Process*

In January of 1997, BU hired Dr. Lorraine Wolf as the new clinical director for learning disability support services. Before being appointed, Wolf was a practicing neuropsychologist and an assistant professor of Clinical Psychology at Columbia University. . . .

At present, students with documented learning disabilities at BU may request accommodations such as reduced course loads, use of special computer technology, books on tape, extra time on examinations in a distraction-free environment, and note takers. BU's eligibility requirements for receiving such accommodations are summarized as follows:

(1) Learning-disabled students must be tested for a learning disorder by a physician, licensed clinical psychologist or a person with a doctorate degree in neuropsychology, educational or child psychology, or another appropriate specialty. The evaluator must have at least three years' experience in diagnosing learning disorders.

(2) Documentation must be current, as it is recognized by BU for only three years after the date of the evaluation. A learning-disabled student whose documentation is too old at the time he matriculates, or whose documentation "expires" during his time at BU, must be reevaluated (including retesting). If retesting is deemed unnecessary by the student's evaluator, the evaluator is required to fill in a form explaining why it is not "medically necessary."

The procedure for requesting and receiving an accommodation for a learning disability at BU is as follows. First, a student requesting accommodations submits an application to the DS office. Wolf reviews the submitted documentation and makes a determination regarding the accommodations that are appropriate for the student. Then, the student's file and Wolf's recommendations are forwarded to the President's Office. Klafter reviews each student's documentation for consistency and, when necessary, discusses with university faculty and administrators how the recommended accommodation will affect a particular academic program or course of study. If the President's Office accepts Wolf's accommodation recommendations, as is mostly the case, the DS office notifies the student. Generally within two weeks of the request, the DS office also generates accommodations letters to be given to the affected faculty members.

As of April 1997, the President's office endorsed most of Wolf's recommendations for a grant or denial of a request for accommodations due to a learning disability. In several situations, Westling consulted with Wolf and with the relevant department head and denied a requested accommodation where he believed the request was inconsistent with academic standards. For example, Westling rejected a request for a notetaker by a learning-disabled ROTC student in a course on manufacturing engineering; however, he authorized the student's use of a tape-recorder. In other situations, despite initial hesitation, Westling agreed to a notetaker for a student studying social work and a calculator for a student in a math course. In the Wolf era, the interaction between the President's Office and DS in evaluating student files focuses on determining which modifications of academic requirements are appropriate for a given learning-disabled student, rather than on ascertaining the nature and extent of a student's learning disability.

BU admits that it has yet to articulate a single, specific process for students to follow if their request for accommodation is denied. In this litigation, the university takes the position that either the appeal to President Westling or the university's Section 504 grievance procedure is adequate to address student concerns.

* * *

IX. *Learning Disorders, ADD, and ADHD—A Primer*

Seven expert witnesses testified at trial about the nature, diagnosis, and accommodation of the conditions known as learning disorders, ADD, and ADHD. . . .

A. *The Disabilities*

1. *Dyslexia*

Dyslexia has been traditionally defined as an "unexpected difficulty learning to read despite intelligence, motivation and education." . . .

[One expert] describes the disorder as a neurobiological condition that "interfere[s] with a normally intelligent [person's] ability to acquire speech, reading, or other cognitive skills." Dyslexia, the most common learning disorder, is a reading disability that is the result of a phonological processing deficit, or "decoding" problem. A dyslexic's ability to break down written words into their basic linguistic units is impaired. However, her higher-level cognitive comprehension abilities—vocabulary, reasoning, concept formation, and general intelligence—may remain intact despite the deficit in phonological processing. About 80 percent of people with learning disabilities have dyslexia. If an individual has a learning disability that makes phonological processing difficult, that individual will have a difficulty with any aspect of learning that involves language, including the acquisition of proficiency in a foreign language.

2. *Attention Deficit Disorder ("ADD")/Attention Deficit Hyperactivity Disorder ("ADHD")*

ADD and ADHD, as described in volume four of the *Diagnostical Statistical Manual* of the American Psychiatric Association ("DSM–IV"), have the following diagnostic feature: "a persistent pattern of inattention and/or hyperactivity-impulsivity that is more frequent and severe than is typically observed in individuals at a comparable level of development." An individual who has the chronic disorder classified as ADHD has neurological problems that involve inattention, hyperactivity, and impulsivity. ADD, which is a subtype of ADHD, is manifest only as a problem with attention. The DSM–IV's diagnostic criteria require that some hyperactive, impulsive or inattentive symptoms that caused impairment were present before age 7 years, and that the symptoms are not better accounted for by another mental disorder. Although ADD and ADHD may interfere with a student's ability to perform effectively, they are not technically learning disabilities, in that the person's ability to acquire basic academic skills is not compromised.

Approximately three percent of the young adult population demonstrates symptoms of ADD or ADHD. According to Professor Rachel Klein, who has performed a longitudinal study, ADD and ADHD have a relatively high rate of permanent, spontaneous remission as a person moves from adolescence into adulthood. . . . Klein also testified that "there are a fair number of instances in which there is considerable question about the accuracy of the diagnosis of ADHD in college-age students."

B. *The Diagnoses*

Over the last decade, there has been a steady growth in the number of students identifying themselves as learning disabled, but this growth is now flattening out. Some experts attribute this growth to: (1) the enactment of the Individuals with Disabilities Education Act in 1975, which requires public school districts to identify students with learning disabilities; (2) the increasing awareness of the existence of learning disabilities among educators, researchers and the public at large; and (3) the passage of the Americans with Disabilities Act. The number of students with learning disabilities at colleges and universities hovers at about two per cent.

The DSM–IV now has a section on learning disorders. . . . The DSM–IV provides: "Learning disorders are diagnosed when the individual's achievement on individually administered, standardized tests in reading, mathematics, or written expression is substantially below that expected for age, schooling, and level of intelligence." The American Psychiatric Association defines "substantially below" as a discrepancy of more than 2 standard deviations between achievement and I.Q. . . .

By contrast, ADD and ADHD diagnoses involve a clinical evaluation and can include psychological testing that costs up to $1,200. Evaluators make assessments on the individual that take into account behavioral reports from sources such as the person himself, his parents, teachers, spouses, and friends. As a result, ADD/ADHD is both underdiagnosed and overdiagnosed, and normal behavioral problems in children are sometimes misdiagnosed as ADD or ADHD, especially in young boys.

C. *Possibility for Change*

Once diagnosed, learning disorders and ADD/ADHD have significantly different possibilities of change or remission. Although ADD/ADHD have a high rate of remission as a person enters adulthood, specific learning disorders do not disappear over time. Some individuals with language-based learning disorders such as dyslexia may learn to overcome their processing problems; however, reading can occur only "at a great cost in time." Other dyslexics may never learn to decode, but may accomplish reading by struggling to recognize words in context. As opposed to individuals with ADHD, after a person with a learning disorder reaches adulthood (age 18), there is no significant change in his cognitive abilities.

* * *

CONCLUSIONS OF LAW

I. *Discrimination Claims under the ADA and Section 504*

The plaintiff class claims that BU discriminates against students with learning disabilities in violation of the Americans with Disabilities Act ("ADA"), and the Rehabilitation Act of 1973 ("Section 504").

A. *The Laws*

* * *

The ADA defines discrimination to include: (1) the use of criteria that unnecessarily "screen out" or "tend to screen out" individuals with disabilities from the use and enjoyment of goods and services, (2) the failure to make nonfundamental, reasonable modifications of "policies, practices or procedures" when such modification is necessary to accommodate disabled persons, and (3) the failure to take necessary steps "to ensure that no individual with a disability is excluded, denied services, segregated or otherwise treated differently than other individuals." 42 U.S.C. § 12182(b)(2) (defining "discrimination" under the ADA). . . .

B. *Documentation Requirements*

Plaintiffs argue that BU's new accommodations policy makes it unnecessarily difficult for students to document their learning disabilities when requesting accommodation.

[Eds. Note: The court decided that BU's requirement to have students tested by a "physician, licensed psychologist, or an evaluator who has a doctorate degree in neuropsychology, education, or another appropriate field" was unduly restrictive. The court stated:

> Many students with long histories of learning disorders in elementary and high school were tested by trained, experienced professionals whose credentials do not match BU's criteria but were deemed acceptable by the student's secondary school, and are acceptable under the guidelines set forth by the Association for Higher Education and Disabilities ("AHEAD"). BU's policy raises a high hurdle because it seemingly requires students with current testing to be retested if the evaluation has not been performed by a person with credentials accepted to BU.

The court also decided that BU did not have a good reason for having this policy. The court stated:

> The record is sparse on the point. While concerns about improving the quality of documentation of learning disabilities are valid, there is no evidence that reports or testing by those evaluators with masters degrees are worse than those by Ph.D.'s, nor is there

evidence that a Ph.D. gets better training than a person with a masters in the specific standardized testing that must be conducted to diagnose learning disabilities. Indeed, the AHEAD guidelines list "educational psychologists" and "learning disabilities specialists" among the professionals who may have the experience that qualifies them to diagnose learning disabilities.

However, with respect to diagnosing ADD and ADHD, the court determined that BU could legitimately require an evaluation by a physician or someone with a Ph.D.:

> These conditions are primarily identified through clinical evaluations rather than through standardized testing, and a well-trained eye is essential for proper diagnosis. Defendants' expert Professor Klein testified credibly that an evaluator with a Ph.D. or an M.D. is more likely to distinguish between ADD/ADHD and medical or psychological conditions that present comparable symptoms. The Court is persuaded that, in regard to ADD/ADHD, a doctorate level of training is "necessary" within the meaning of the federal law.

With respect to BU's requirement that individuals need to be retested every three years, the court determined that this requirement violated the ADA because it "screened out or tended to screen out" individuals with disabilities by making it much more difficult for them to receive their needed accommodations. As the court described:

> Based on the evidence, I easily find that this initial "currency" requirement imposed significant additional burdens on disabled students. For example, Elizabeth Guckenberger testified that her retesting process took four days and cost $800.00. Jill Cutler's retesting took four hours and cost $650.00. Dean Robert Shaw testified that the evaluations could cost up to $1,000 and involve multiple visits. Cutler's tearful testimony was particularly compelling with respect to the emotional impact of the retesting because it was a poignant reminder that she was not "normal." BU's initial requirement mandating retesting for students with learning disabilities screened out or tended to screen out the learning disabled within the meaning of the federal law.

As to the university's defense that such currency was required, the court noted:

> Because every expert who testified agreed that there is no demonstrable change in a specific learning disorder, such as dyslexia, after an individual reaches age 18, BU has failed to demonstrate that the three-year retesting requirement, as initially written, was necessary for students who had been diagnosed with specific learning disorders.

> . . . Defendants have produced no peer reviewed literature or scientific testimony that provides evidence for the idea that a person's learning disability will show any change after adulthood, or that a student's test scores will show significant change during the course of their college career. . . . Moreover, no other college or university in the United States or Canada requires retesting after age 18, and the AHEAD guidelines call for retesting every five years once an individual reaches adulthood.

However, with respect to ADD and ADHD, the court determined that retesting is essential because the symptoms of ADD and ADHD change in different environments, are often treated with medication, and these disorders often remit from adolescence to adulthood. End of Eds. Note]

* * *

D. *Course Substitutions*

1. *The Competing Contentions*

Plaintiffs claim that BU's blanket refusal to authorize course substitutions for students with learning disabilities amounts to a failure to modify the university's practices to prevent discrimination as required by federal law. Specifically, the class argues that, because many learning-disabled students have extreme difficulty in taking and passing courses in mathematics and foreign language, allowing course substitutions for those class members is a reasonable accommodation, and, thus, BU's refusal to authorize such a modification is discriminatory.

BU asserts that its refusal of course substitutions is consistent with the law because exemptions of this nature would amount to a fundamental alteration of its academic liberal arts program, a course of study that has been in place for over a century. Also, BU emphasizes that it provides special programs for students with foreign language and math difficulties (like an oral enhancement program and one-on-one tutoring) in addition to the classroom accommodations that are available in any other course.

2. *The Legal Framework*

. . . The ADA specifically defines discrimination to include:

> a failure to make reasonable modifications in policies, practices or procedures, when such modifications are necessary to afford such goods, services, facilities, privileges, advantages, or accommodations to individuals with disabilities, unless the entity can demonstrate that making such modifications would fundamentally alter the nature of such goods, services, facilities, privileges, advantages, or accommodations.

42 U.S.C. § 12182(b)(2)(A)(ii). The regulations implementing Section 504 also require an educational institution that receives federal funding to

"make such modifications to its academic requirements as are necessary to ensure that such requirements do not have the effect of discriminating, on the basis of handicap, against a qualified handicapped applicant or student." 34 C.F.R. § 104.44. However, the regulations further explain that "academic requirements that the recipient can demonstrate are essential to the program of instruction being pursued by such student . . . will not be regarded as discriminatory within the meaning of this section." *Id.*

Significantly, with regard to academic institutions, the regulations interpreting Section 504 provide that reasonable modifications "may include changes in the length of time permitted for the completion of degree requirements, *substitution of specific courses required for the completion of degree requirements,* and adaptation of the manner in which specific courses are conducted." 34 C.F.R. § 104.44. The appendix to the regulations elaborates:

> Paragraph (a) of § 104.44 requires that a recipient make certain adjustments to academic requirements and practices that discriminate or have the effect of discriminating on the basis of handicap. . . . For example, an institution might permit an otherwise qualified handicapped student who is deaf to substitute an art appreciation or music history course for a required course in music appreciation or could modify the manner in which the music appreciation course is conducted for the deaf student. *It should be stressed that academic requirements that can be demonstrated by the recipient to be essential to its program of instruction or to particular degrees need not be changed.*

34 C.F.R. § 104, app. A ¶ 31. . . .

In the reasonable modifications context, the plaintiff has the initial burden of proving "that a modification was requested and that the requested modification is [generally] reasonable," that is, "in the run of cases." "If the plaintiff meets this burden, the defendant must make the requested modification unless the defendant pleads and meets its burden of proving that the requested modification would fundamentally alter the nature of the public accommodation."

3.   *The Analysis*

Turning to the instant case, the Court must first consider whether plaintiffs have met their burden of establishing that course substitutions in math and foreign language are, generally, "reasonable" accommodations.

The plaintiffs are aided substantially in satisfying their initial burden by the mere fact that the administrative regulations interpreting Section 504 and the ADA specifically provide that modifying academic requirements to allow course substitutions may be a reasonable means of accommodating the disabled. In addition, plaintiffs offered evidence at trial to support their contention that a course substitution is reasonable, at least in regard to BU's foreign language requirements. . . . On all of the evidence, the Court is persuaded that plaintiffs have demonstrated that requesting a course substitution in foreign language for students with demonstrated language disabilities is a reasonable modification.

With respect to math course substitutions, however, . . . plaintiffs have not demonstrated that a request for a course substitution in mathematics is a reasonable modification of BU's degree requirements.

Because plaintiffs have established that the request for a course substitution in foreign language is reasonable, the burden now shifts to BU to demonstrate that the requested course substitution would fundamentally alter the nature of its liberal arts degree program.

Fortunately, in determining which modifications amount to a "fundamental alteration," the Court does not write on a clean blackboard. Two related First Circuit cases provide invaluable assistance in evaluating a university's burden of supporting its conclusion that a requested modification by a learning disabled student of an academic requirement would fundamentally alter the nature of the program. *See Wynne v. Tufts Univ. Sch. of Med.,* 932 F.2d 19 (1st Cir.1991) (en banc). . . .

. . . The Court stressed that, while deference need be given to the institutional decisionmakers in deciding whether an accommodation is possible, "there is a real obligation on the academic institution to seek suitable means of reasonably accommodating a handicapped person." *Id.* at 25. Specifically, it found that

> [i]f the institution submits undisputed facts demonstrating that the relevant officials within the institution considered alternative means, their feasibility, cost and effect on the academic program, and came to a rationally justifiable conclusion that the available alternative would result either in lowering academic standards or requiring substantial program alteration, the court could rule as a matter of law that the institution had met its duty of seeking reasonable accommodation.

Even more than the dispute over the format of a test in the *Wynne* cases, the degree requirements that are at issue in the instant litigation go to the heart of academic freedom. Universities have long been considered to have the freedom to determine "what may be taught, how it shall be taught, and who may be admitted to study."

Based on a review of the relevant cases, I conclude that a university can refuse to modify academic degree requirements—even course requirements that students with learning disabilities cannot satisfy—as long it "undertake[s] a diligent assessment of the available options," and makes "a professional, academic judgment that reasonable accommodation is simply not available." *Id.* at 27–28. That is to say, neither the ADA nor the

Rehabilitation Act require a university to provide course substitutions that the university rationally concludes would alter an essential part of its academic program. Accordingly, plaintiffs' front-line of attack against any across-the-board policy precluding course substitutions under the ADA and Rehabilitation Act fails.

4. *Westling's Ipse Dixit*

As a fallback, the plaintiff class argues: (1) that in the circumstances of this case, BU's refusal to modify its liberal arts degree requirements flunks the *Wynne*-test because Westling was motivated by discriminatory animus in declining to modify the academic standards in question, and (2) that BU refused to modify its math and foreign language requirements as an accommodation for the learning disabled without making a diligent, reasoned, academic judgment.

Based on my review of the record, plaintiffs prevail on both of these arguments. A substantial motivating factor in Westling's decision not to consider degree modifications was his unfounded belief that learning disabled students who could not meet degree requirements were unmotivated (like "Somnolent Samantha") or disingenuous. Although Westling was also inspired by a genuine concern for academic standards, his course substitution prohibition was founded, in part, on uninformed stereotypes. Relying only on popular press accounts that suggested learning disabilities were being unfairly exaggerated and misdiagnosed, Westling provided no concrete evidence that any BU student faked a learning disability to get out of a course requirement.

Even though Westling may have had a good faith (even passionate) belief in the value of foreign languages to a liberal arts program, the Court finds that he did not dispassionately determine whether the benefits of attaining that proficiency are outweighed by the costs to the learning disabled student. Westling made the decision not to modify the mathematics and foreign language requirements for students with learning disabilities without consulting any experts on learning disabilities. Nor did Westling discuss the importance of foreign language to BU's liberal arts curriculum with any of the relevant BU department heads, professors or officials. Indeed, the only deliberation that took place regarding academic adjustments as accommodations for the learning disabled was Westling's consultation with Klafter about whether scientific evidence supports the existence of a learning disability that prevents foreign language proficiency. Westling's reliance on discriminatory stereotypes, together with his failure to consider carefully the effect of course substitutions on BU's liberal arts programs and to consult with academics and experts in learning disabilities, constitutes a failure of BU's obligation to make a rational judgment that course substitutions would fundamentally alter the course of study. Although BU ultimately has the right to decline to modify its degree requirements—and that decision will be given great deference—

it must do so after reasoned deliberations as to whether modifications would change the essential academic standards of its liberal arts curriculum.

* * *

ORDER OF JUDGMENT

1. The Court orders BU to cease and desist implementing its current policy of requiring that students with learning disorders (not ADD or ADHD) who have current evaluations by trained professionals with masters degrees and sufficient experience be completely retested by professionals who have medical degrees, or doctorate degrees, or licensed clinical psychologists in order to be eligible for reasonable accommodations.

2. The Court orders BU to propose, within 30 days of the receipt of this order, a deliberative procedure for considering whether modification of its degree requirement in foreign language would fundamentally alter the nature of its liberal arts program. Such a procedure shall include a faculty committee set up by the College of Arts and Sciences to examine its degree requirements and to determine whether a course substitution in foreign languages would fundamentally alter the nature of the liberal arts program. . . . BU shall report back to the Court by the end of the semester concerning its decision and the reasons. . . .

GUCKENBERGER V. BOSTON UNIVERSITY ("GUCKENBERGER II")

8 F.Supp.2d 82 (D. Mass. 1998)

MEMORANDUM AND ORDER ON THE ISSUE OF COURSE SUBSTITUTIONS

SARIS, DISTRICT JUDGE.

INTRODUCTION

. . . The Court issued its findings of fact, conclusions of law, and order of judgment on August 15, 1997, after a ten-day bench trial. In paragraph two of its order, the Court required BU to propose and to implement a "deliberative procedure" for considering whether course substitutions for the foreign language requirement of BU's College of Arts and Sciences (the "College") would "fundamentally alter the nature" of BU's undergraduate liberal arts degree. BU, using the College's existing Dean's Advisory Committee to consider the issue, decided that course substitutions would constitute such a fundamental alteration. Plaintiffs challenge that determination. After hearing, the Court holds that BU has complied with the order.

BACKGROUND

A. Procedural History

As part of a wholesale attack on BU's policies toward the learning disabled, plaintiffs alleged that BU's refusal to allow learning disabled students at the College to satisfy its foreign language requirement by completing selected non-language courses constituted a violation of federal and state discrimination law. . . . The Court rejected plaintiffs' sweeping argument that "any across-the-board policy precluding course substitutions" violates discrimination law. . . .

Plaintiffs were successful, however, in pressing an inquiry into reasonable accommodation. Based on an administrative regulation that course substitutions "might" be a reasonable means of accommodating the disabled, 34 C.F.R. Pt. 104, App. A ¶ 31, and evidence introduced at trial, the Court held that plaintiffs had "demonstrated that requesting a course substitution in foreign language for students with demonstrated language disabilities is a reasonable modification." Therefore, the burden of demonstrating "that the requested course substitution would fundamentally alter the nature of [BU's] liberal arts degree program" shifted to the University.

The Court determined, for two reasons, that BU had failed to meet its burden at trial of demonstrating why it should not have to accommodate plaintiffs' request. First, BU's president, defendant Jon Westling, had been substantially motivated by uninformed stereotypes (as reflected in the "Somnolent Samantha" metaphor) when he made the decision to deny the request. Second, President Westling did not engage in any form of "reasoned deliberation as to whether modifications would change the essential academic standards of [the College's] liberal arts curriculum." . . .

B. BU's Deliberative Procedure

The Court considers the following facts to be undisputed.

On October 6, 1997, the Court approved the use of the existing Dean's Advisory Committee (the "Committee") of the College as the mechanism for deliberating the issue of course substitutions for the foreign language requirement in accordance with the Court's order. In the course of normal business, the Committee "is charged by the by-laws of the College with advising the Dean on issues involving academic standards." During the relevant time period, the Committee was composed of eleven faculty members of the College, including professors of mathematics, English, philosophy, natural sciences, engineering and foreign languages. The Committee is normally chaired by Dennis D. Berkey, who is the Dean of the College and the Provost of BU. However, Dean Berkey removed himself as chairman of proceedings relating to course substitutions because of his role in the "central administration" of BU. In his place, Associate Professor of Mathematics Paul Blanchard assumed the role of Acting Chairman.

The Committee convened to consider the issue of course substitutions on seven occasions. In keeping with its practice for general business, the Committee meetings were closed to interested parties and the public, with two exceptions. The first meeting on this issue was attended by [the attorneys] for BU, who "set out the Committee's responsibilities as outlined in the Court's decision." Also, several College students addressed the Committee at the November 14, 1997 meeting. Their involvement was directed by the Court at a October 6, 1997 hearing and was solicited through notice posted on an internet bulletin board and an advertisement published in BU's student newspaper. . . . Neither President Westling nor his direct staff had any involvement with the Committee proceedings, and the Committee did not officially seek any other input from non-members.

The Committee kept minutes of four of its seven meetings. No minutes were recorded during the first two meetings, but, following the Court's order to do so at the October 6 hearing, minutes were kept for all but the last of the remaining meetings.

. . . [T]he Committee . . . submitted [its report] to President Westling in accordance with the BU by-laws. Its final recommendation was:

> After extensive review and deliberation, the [Committee's] professional and academic judgment is that the conjunction of the foregoing considerations (which we have merely summarized here) entails but one conclusion: the foreign language requirement is fundamental to the nature of the liberal arts degree at Boston University. The [Committee] therefore recommends against approving course substitutions for any student as an alternative to fulfilling the foreign language requirement.

Two days later, President Westling, in a letter to Dean Berkey, accepted the recommendation of the Committee. . . .

DISCUSSION

A. *The Test*

The First Circuit crafted the following test for evaluating the decision of an academic institution with respect to the availability of reasonable accommodations for the learning disabled:

> If the institution submits undisputed facts demonstrating that the relevant officials within the institution considered alternative means, their feasibility, cost and effect on the academic program, and came to a rationally justifiable conclusion that the available alternatives would result either in lowering academic standards or requiring substantial program alteration, the court could rule as a matter of law that the institution had met its duty of seeking reasonable accommodation.

Wynne I, 932 F.2d at 26. "[T]he point is not whether a [university] is 'right' or 'wrong' in making program-related decisions. Such absolutes rarely apply in the context of subjective decisionmaking, particularly in a scholastic setting."

B.   *Basic Facts Showing Reasoned Deliberation*

The Court's first task under this test is "to find the basic facts, giving due deference to the school. . . ." Those "basic facts" must include showings of the following: (1) an "indication of who took part in the decision [and] when it was made;" (2) a "discussion of the unique qualities" of the foreign language requirement as it now stands; and (3) "a consideration of possible alternatives" to the requirement. As these elements suggest, the required showing of undisputed facts refers to the "consideration" of the request by BU and not, as plaintiffs suggest, to a broad-ranging consensus of expert or university opinion on the value of foreign languages to a liberal arts curriculum.

The Court concludes that BU has presented sufficient undisputed essential facts, satisfying each of the three aspects of *Wynne*'s requirements. First, the Committee, made up of eminent members of the College faculty, deliberated this issue over the course of two months. The eleven Committee members include four department chairmen and represent diverse disciplines beyond the foreign languages. Though it would have been better to have kept minutes of all seven meetings, the four meetings provide the Court with sufficient insight to allow the Court to review the procedure that BU followed and to "demythologize[ ] the institutional thought processes. . . ." BU took pains to insulate President Westling from the process to remove any concerns about his earlier comments which, in substantial part, necessitated this remedy. . . .

Second, the Committee had vigorous discussions of the "unique qualities" of the foreign language requirement and its importance to the liberal arts curriculum. Its members rallied around an articulated defense, highlighted throughout the Report, of the rigorous foreign language requirement of the College. In both the Minutes and the Report, the Committee mentioned technical educational gains from the learning of foreign languages, such as enhancing an ability to read foreign literature in its original form and laying a "foundation" for other areas of academic concentration. For example, some members at the October 8 meeting believed it was important to be immersed in ancient Greek and Latin to understand Greek and Roman cultures. Another Committee member waxed "that someone who can read in French would realize that Madame Bovary dies in the imperfect tense, something we don't have in the English language, and it makes for a very different understanding of the novel."

Additionally, the Committee repeatedly emphasized its view that foreign language study uniquely contributed to the College's emphasis on multiculturalism: "A mind cooped up within a single culture is not liberally educated, and knowledge of a foreign language is essential to countering parochialism of outlook and knowledge." The Committee also portrayed foreign language study as part of a broader liberal arts education which, in its view, contemplates "some competence in thinking in diverse areas of knowledge." Commenting on the specific contribution of foreign language learning to liberal arts, the Committee reported that "[e]ncountering a foreign culture in and through the complexities of its verbal structures and representations poses a unique challenge to familiar idioms, settled habits of mind, and securities of knowledge."

Third, the Committee "explained what thought it had given to different methods" of meeting the requirement and "why it eschewed alternatives" to meeting the requirement. The minutes indicate that alternatives were discussed in at least four of the Committee's meetings. . . . One dissenting member suggested an alternative proposal whereby a "student would select courses from a faculty approved list that focus on the language, culture, history, literature, and art of countries where the language is spoken." . . . Additionally, the objections of several students were noted at length.

As a whole, the Committee concluded that "[n]o content course taught in English can substitute fully for the insider access to other cultures—with its attendant invitation to thoroughgoing critical self-awareness—that is the hallmark of foreign language study." The Committee acknowledged that some students, both learning disabled and not, will "struggle" with the rigorous requirement, but nonetheless concluded "that no other goal could serve the same purpose within the [College] curriculum."

Furthermore, the Committee discussed the College's existing accommodations of learning disabled students attempting to fulfill the foreign language requirement, a consideration that weighs in BU's favor in this analysis. The College allows all its students to satisfy the foreign language requirement in a variety of ways, including a free "Foreign Language Enhancement Program" that provides one-on-one instruction to learning disabled students navigating the required sequences of language classes. Learning disabled students are allowed spelling accommodations in language classes, and student tutoring is provided by the foreign language department at no cost to students. BU provides for additional time on tests, a reading track for French and Spanish, distraction-free testing, distribution of lecture notes in advance, and replacement of written with oral exams.

C. Professional, Academic Judgment

Having found undisputed facts of a reasoned deliberation, the Court must "evaluate whether those facts add up to a professional, academic judgment that reasonable accommodation is simply not available." *Wynne I*, 932 F.2d at 27–28. In the unique context of academic curricular decision-making, the courts may not override a faculty's professional judgment "unless it is such a substantial departure from accepted academic norms as to demonstrate that the person or committee responsible did not actually exercise professional judgment."

This standard is in keeping with the policy of judicial deference to academic decision making. The Court previously indicated that BU's decision would be given "great deference" so long as it occurred "after reasoned deliberations as to whether modifications would change the essential academic standards of its liberal arts curriculum." Such deference is appropriate in this arena, because "[w]hen judges are asked to review the substance of a genuinely academic decision, . . . they should show great respect for the faculty's professional judgment." *Wynne I,* 932 F.2d at 25. While, of course, "academic freedom does not embrace the freedom to discriminate," the First Circuit has observed that "[w]e are a society that cherishes academic freedom and recognizes that universities deserve great leeway in their operations."

Plaintiffs attack the academic judgment of the Committee in three ways. First, they argue that BU's decision does mark "a substantial departure from accepted academic norms" because a majority of other colleges and universities—including Princeton, Harvard, Yale, Columbia, Dartmouth, Cornell and Brown—either do not have a general foreign language requirement or permit course substitutions for foreign languages. . . . The evidence that BU is only among a handful of schools of higher education in its decision to deny course substitutions in language requirements is relevant to an evaluation of its decision to deny a reasonable accommodation. However, a court should not determine that an academic decision is a "substantial departure from accepted academic norms" simply by conducting a head-count of other universities. This approach is particularly inappropriate in the protean area of a liberal arts education. The liberal arts curriculum cannot be fit into a cookie cutter mold, unlike the medical school curriculum in *Wynne,* where no one disputed that mastery of biochemistry was necessary.

* * *

This Court concludes that so long as an academic institution rationally, without pretext, exercises its deliberate professional judgment not to permit course substitutions for an academic requirement in a liberal arts curriculum, the ADA does not authorize the courts to intervene even if a majority of other comparable academic institutions disagree.

Second, plaintiffs challenge the substance of the Committee's conclusions and analysis. Specifically, they argue that there are sixteen "material facts" in dispute, such as the following: (1) the two year (four semester) foreign language requirement is not "sufficient to permit the vast majority of students to read major works of literature in a foreign language," thus debunking the *Madame Bovary* line of argument as involving an imperfect logic, not an imperfect tense; (2) a "foreign language requirement does not provide students with educational benefits regarding a foreign culture;" (3) there is "no particular thinking process involved in learning a foreign language that is distinct from any other type of learning;" and (4) BU's "foreign language requirement does not address ethnocentrism among students."

... While plaintiffs have submitted affidavits of ... other academics who strongly disagree with BU's conclusions and label them as "trite," "idealistic" or "cliches," these issues raise the kinds of academic decisions that universities—not courts—are entrusted with making.

[Eds. Note: The court also dismissed the plaintiffs' third argument that BU's report does not meet the minimum accepted standards of academic study and inquiry because the committee did not refer to outside experts.]

* * *

Plaintiffs' vigorous attacks on BU's submission generally overstate the Court's level of scrutiny at this stage of litigation. My opinion as to the value of foreign languages in a liberal arts curriculum is not material so long as the requirements of *Wynne* have been met. Despite plaintiffs' attempts to pull truly academic policy debates into the courtroom, the facts "essential" to this order are actually undisputed: BU implemented a deliberative procedure by which it considered in a timely manner both the importance of the foreign language requirement to this College and the feasibility of alternatives. . . .

BU's deliberations and conclusions pass muster under *Wynne*. The Court has no cause to doubt the academic qualifications and professionalism of the eleven members of the Committee. There is no evidence that the Committee's decision was mere lip service to the Court's order or was tainted by pretext, insincerity, or bad faith, beyond plaintiffs' unsubstantiated speculation that President Westling's bias infected the Committee. . . .

The Court concludes that the Committee's judgment that "a person holding a liberal arts degree from Boston University ought to have some experience studying a foreign language," is "rationally justifiable" and represents a professional judgment with which the Court should not interfere. Therefore, the Court concludes as a matter of law that BU has not violated its duty to provide reasonable accommodations to learning disabled students under the ADA by refusing to provide course substitutions.

NOTES AND QUESTIONS

1. *Westling's hostility towards learning disabilities.* What was your reaction to Westling's hostility towards those with learning disabilities? Although perhaps not expressed as vehemently or offensively as Westling did, do you think his viewpoint is shared by others? Have you ever heard anyone express skepticism about learning disabilities? To the extent others share

Westling's view, what do you think accounts for it? Does it have something to do with the difficulty in diagnosing learning disabilities? Westling refers to students with learning disabilities as "fakers" and "draft dodgers." Are learning disabilities easier to "fake" than other disabilities?

2. *Course substitutions.* Did your undergraduate institution have a foreign language requirement? Although it is much more common now, it was relatively rare in the 1990s, when this case was decided. Does the court give sufficient weight to the fact that so few schools required foreign language, and of those who did, most allowed course substitutions for those who had learning disabilities? During the deliberations that led to the committee voting against course substitutions for the foreign language requirement, one committee member stated: "someone who can read in French would realize that Madame Bovary dies in the imperfect tense, something we don't have in the English language, and it makes for a very different understanding of the novel." The plaintiff's response to this is: "the two year (four semester) foreign language requirement is not 'sufficient to permit the vast majority of students to read major works of literature in a foreign language,' thus debunking the *Madame Bovary* line of argument as involving an imperfect logic, not an imperfect tense." Who has the better argument?

3. *Academic deference.* The *Guckenberger* cases illustrate the importance of academic deference. As long as the institution has a reasoned, deliberative procedure and considers alternatives to the academic requirements, the court will not second-guess its academic judgment. In giving deference to BU in *Guckenberger II*, the court gives some weight to the fact that the committee was insulated from the bias and judgment of Westling. Do you think this was true? Even for those members who were tenured, full professors, many decisions—including decisions regarding grants, sabbaticals, awards, etc.—must be approved by the provost and the president. Because the names of the members of the committee were public, is it possible that some of those members might worry about retribution from Westling if they did not vote the way he wanted? If so, do you think the committee felt obligated to vote consistently with Westling's beliefs? Does the court give sufficient attention to this possibility?

B. PRIMARY/SECONDARY EDUCATION

1. INDIVIDUALS WITH DISABILITIES EDUCATION ACT ("IDEA")

Most of the history and statutory requirements of the IDEA are discussed in detail in the *Rowley* opinion, immediately below. One of the provisions that is not discussed is the definition of disability. Chapter 2 discussed the definition of disability under the ADA, which is the same definition that is used in Section 504 of the Rehabilitation Act. However, the IDEA has its own definition of disability.

As defined in the statute, a "child with a disability" is a child

(i)   with intellectual disabilities, hearing impairments (including deafness), speech or language impairments, visual impairments (including blindness), serious emotional disturbance (referred to in this chapter as "emotional disturbance"), orthopedic impairments, autism, traumatic brain injury, other health impairments, or specific learning disabilities, and

(ii) who, by reason thereof, needs special education and related services.

20 U.S.C. § 1401(3)(A). The regulations promulgated under the IDEA require that, for each of the conditions, it must "adversely affect a child's educational performance" in order to qualify as a disability under the IDEA. 34 C.F.R. § 300.8(c).

a.   Free Appropriate Public Education

BOARD OF EDUCATION OF THE HENDRICK HUDSON CENTRAL SCHOOL DISTRICT, WESTCHESTER COUNTY v. ROWLEY
458 U.S. 176, 102 S.Ct. 3034 (1982)

JUSTICE REHNQUIST delivered the opinion of the Court.

This case presents a question of statutory interpretation. Petitioners contend that the Court of Appeals and the District Court misconstrued the requirements imposed by Congress upon States which receive federal funds under the Education of the Handicapped Act. We agree and reverse the judgment of the Court of Appeals.

I

The Education of the Handicapped Act (Act), 20 U.S.C. § 1401 *et seq.*, provides federal money to assist state and local agencies in educating handicapped children, and conditions such funding upon a State's compliance with extensive goals and procedures. The Act represents an ambitious federal effort to promote the education of handicapped children, and was passed in response to Congress' perception that a majority of handicapped children in the United States "were either totally excluded from schools or [were] sitting idly in regular classrooms awaiting the time when they were old enough to 'drop out.'" The Act's evolution and major provisions shed light on the question of statutory interpretation which is at the heart of this case.

Congress first addressed the problem of educating the handicapped in 1966 when it amended the Elementary and Secondary Education Act of 1965 to establish a grant program "for the purpose of assisting the States in the initiation, expansion, and improvement of programs and projects . . . for the education of handicapped children." That program was repealed in 1970 by the Education of the Handicapped Act, Part B of which established a grant program similar in purpose to the repealed legislation. Neither the 1966 nor the 1970 legislation contained specific guidelines for state use of the grant money; both were aimed primarily at stimulating the States to develop educational resources and to train personnel for educating the handicapped.

Dissatisfied with the progress being made under these earlier enactments, and spurred by two District Court decisions holding that handicapped children should be given access to a public education, Congress in 1974 greatly increased federal funding for education of the handicapped and for the first time required recipient States to adopt "a goal of providing full educational opportunities to all handicapped children." Pub.L. 93–380, 88 Stat. 579, 583 (1974 statute). The 1974 statute was recognized as an interim measure only, adopted "in order to give the Congress an additional year in which to study what if any additional Federal assistance [was] required to enable the States to meet the needs of handicapped children." The ensuing year of study produced the Education for All Handicapped Children Act of 1975.

In order to qualify for federal financial assistance under the Act, a State must demonstrate that it "has in effect a policy that assures all handicapped children the right to a free appropriate public education." 20 U.S.C. § 1412(1). . . . States receiving money under the Act must provide education to the handicapped by priority, first "to handicapped children who are not receiving an education" and second "to handicapped children . . . with the most severe handicaps who are receiving an inadequate education," § 1412(3), and "to the maximum extent appropriate" must educate handicapped children "with children who are not handicapped." § 1412(5). The Act broadly defines "handicapped children" to include "mentally retarded, hard of hearing, deaf, speech impaired, visually handicapped, seriously emotionally disturbed, orthopedically impaired, [and] other health impaired children, [and] children with specific learning disabilities." § 1401(1).

The "free appropriate public education" required by the Act is tailored to the unique needs of the handicapped child by means of an "individualized educational program" (IEP). § 1401(18). The IEP, which is prepared at a meeting between a qualified representative of the local educational agency, the child's teacher, the child's parents or guardian, and, where appropriate, the child, consists of a written document containing

(A) a statement of the present levels of educational performance of such child, (B) a statement of annual goals, including short-term instructional objectives, (C) a statement of the specific educational services to be provided to such child, and the extent to which such child will be able to participate in regular educational programs, (D) the projected date for initiation and anticipated duration of such services, and (E) appropriate objective criteria and evaluation procedures and schedules for determining, on at least an annual basis, whether instructional objectives are being achieved. § 1401(19).

Local or regional educational agencies must review, and where appropriate revise, each child's IEP at least annually. § 1414(a)(5).

In addition to the state plan and the IEP already described, the Act imposes extensive procedural requirements upon States receiving federal funds under its provisions. Parents or guardians of handicapped children must be notified of any proposed change in "the identification, evaluation, or educational placement of the child or the provision of a free appropriate public education to such child," and must be permitted to bring a complaint about "any matter relating to" such evaluation and education. §§ 1415(b)(1)(D) and (E).[6] Complaints brought by parents or guardians must be resolved at "an impartial due process hearing," and appeal to the state educational agency must be provided if the initial hearing is held at the local or regional level. §§ 1415(b)(2) and (c). Thereafter, "[a]ny party aggrieved by the findings and decision" of the state administrative hearing has "the right to bring a civil action with respect to the complaint . . . in any State court of competent jurisdiction or in a district court of the United States without regard to the amount in controversy." § 1415(e)(2).

Thus, although the Act leaves to the States the primary responsibility for developing and executing educational programs for handicapped children, it imposes significant requirements to be followed in the discharge of that responsibility. Compliance is assured by provisions permitting the withholding of federal funds upon determination that a participating state or local agency has failed to satisfy the requirements of the Act, §§ 1414(b)(2)(A), 1416, and by the provision for judicial review. At present, all States except New Mexico receive federal funds under the portions of the Act at issue today.

II

This case arose in connection with the education of Amy Rowley, a deaf student at the Furnace Woods School in the Hendrick Hudson Central School District, Peekskill, N.Y. Amy has minimal residual hearing and is an excellent lipreader. During the year before she began attending Furnace Woods, a meeting between her parents and school administrators resulted in a decision to place her in a regular kindergarten class in order to determine what supplemental services would be necessary to her

---

    6 The requirements that parents be permitted to file complaints regarding their child's education, and be present when the child's IEP is formulated, represent only two examples of Congress' effort to maximize parental involvement in the education of each handicapped child. In addition, the Act requires that parents be permitted "to examine all relevant records with respect to the identification, evaluation, and educational placement of the child, and . . . to obtain an independent educational evaluation of the child." § 1415(b)(1)(A). . . .

education. Several members of the school administration prepared for Amy's arrival by attending a course in sign-language interpretation, and a teletype machine was installed in the principal's office to facilitate communication with her parents who are also deaf. At the end of the trial period it was determined that Amy should remain in the kindergarten class, but that she should be provided with an FM hearing aid which would amplify words spoken into a wireless receiver by the teacher or fellow students during certain classroom activities. Amy successfully completed her kindergarten year.

As required by the Act, an IEP was prepared for Amy during the fall of her first-grade year. The IEP provided that Amy should be educated in a regular classroom at Furnace Woods, should continue to use the FM hearing aid, and should receive instruction from a tutor for the deaf for one hour each day and from a speech therapist for three hours each week. The Rowleys agreed with parts of the IEP, but insisted that Amy also be provided a qualified sign-language interpreter in all her academic classes in lieu of the assistance proposed in other parts of the IEP. Such an interpreter had been placed in Amy's kindergarten class for a 2-week experimental period, but the interpreter had reported that Amy did not need his services at that time. The school administrators likewise concluded that Amy did not need such an interpreter in her first-grade classroom. They reached this conclusion after consulting the school district's Committee on the Handicapped, which had received expert evidence from Amy's parents on the importance of a sign-language interpreter, received testimony from Amy's teacher and other persons familiar with her academic and social progress, and visited a class for the deaf.

When their request for an interpreter was denied, the Rowleys demanded and received a hearing before an independent examiner. After receiving evidence from both sides, the examiner agreed with the administrators' determination that an interpreter was not necessary because "Amy was achieving educationally, academically, and socially" without such assistance. The examiner's decision was affirmed on appeal by the New York Commissioner of Education on the basis of substantial evidence in the record. Pursuant to the Act's provision for judicial review, the Rowleys then brought an action in the United States District Court for the Southern District of New York, claiming that the administrators' denial of the sign-language interpreter constituted a denial of the "free appropriate public education" guaranteed by the Act.

The District Court found that Amy "is a remarkably well-adjusted child" who interacts and communicates well with her classmates and has "developed an extraordinary rapport" with her teachers. It also found that "she performs better than the average child in her class and is advancing easily from grade to grade," but "that she understands considerably less of what goes on in class than she could if she were not deaf" and thus "is not learning as much, or performing as well academically, as she would without her handicap," This disparity between Amy's achievement and her potential led the court to decide that she was not receiving a "free appropriate public education," which the court defined as "an opportunity to achieve [her] full potential commensurate with the opportunity provided to other children." According to the District Court, such a standard "requires that the potential of the handicapped child be measured and compared to his or her performance, and that the resulting differential or 'shortfall' be compared to the shortfall experienced by nonhandicapped children." The District Court's definition arose from its assumption that the responsibility for "giv[ing] content to the requirement of an 'appropriate education'" had "been left entirely to the [federal] courts and the hearing officers."

A divided panel of the United States Court of Appeals for the Second Circuit affirmed. The Court of Appeals "agree[d] with the [D]istrict [C]ourt's conclusions of law," and held that its "findings of fact [were] not clearly erroneous."

We granted certiorari to review the lower courts' interpretation of the Act. Such review requires us to consider two questions: What is meant by the Act's requirement of a "free appropriate public education"? And what is the role of state and federal courts in exercising the review granted by 20 U.S.C. § 1415? We consider these questions separately.

III

A

This is the first case in which this Court has been called upon to interpret any provision of the Act. As noted previously, the District Court and the Court of Appeals concluded that "[t]he Act itself does not define 'appropriate education,'" but leaves "to the courts and the hearing officers" the responsibility of "giv[ing] content to the requirement of an 'appropriate education.'" Petitioners contend that the definition of the phrase "free appropriate public education" used by the courts below overlooks the definition of that phrase actually found in the Act. Respondents agree that the Act defines "free appropriate public education," but contend that the statutory definition is not "functional" and thus "offers judges no guidance in their consideration of controversies involving 'the identification, evaluation, or educational placement of the child or the provision of a free appropriate public education.'" The United States, appearing as *amicus curiae* on behalf of respondents, states that "[a]lthough the Act includes definitions of a 'free appropriate public education' and other related terms, the statutory definitions do not adequately explain what is meant by 'appropriate.'"

We are loath to conclude that Congress failed to offer any assistance in defining the meaning of the principal substantive phrase used in the Act. It is beyond dispute that, contrary to the conclusions of the courts below, the Act does expressly define "free appropriate public education":

> The term 'free appropriate public education' means *special education* and *related services* which (A) have been provided at public expense, under public supervision and direction, and without charge, (B) meet the standards of the State educational agency, (C) include an appropriate preschool, elementary, or secondary school education in the State involved, and (D) are provided in conformity with the individualized education program required under section 1414(a)(5) of this title. § 1401(18) (emphasis added).

"Special education," as referred to in this definition, means "specially designed instruction, at no cost to parents or guardians, to meet the unique needs of a handicapped child, including classroom instruction, instruction in physical education, home instruction, and instruction in hospitals and institutions." § 1401(16). "Related services" are defined as "transportation, and such developmental, corrective, and other supportive services ... as may be required to assist a handicapped child to benefit from special education." § 1401(17).

Like many statutory definitions, this one tends toward the cryptic rather than the comprehensive, but that is scarcely a reason for abandoning the quest for legislative intent. Whether or not the definition is a "functional" one, as respondents contend it is not, it is the principal tool which Congress has given us for parsing the critical phrase of the Act. We think more must be made of it than either respondents or the United States seems willing to admit.

According to the definitions contained in the Act, a "free appropriate public education" consists of educational instruction specially designed to meet the unique needs of the handicapped child, supported by such services as are necessary to permit the child "to benefit" from the instruction. Almost as a checklist for adequacy under the Act, the definition also requires that such instruction and services be provided at public expense and under public supervision, meet the State's educational standards, approximate the grade levels used in the State's regular education, and comport with the child's IEP. Thus, if personalized instruction is being provided with sufficient supportive services to permit the child to benefit from the instruction, and the other items on the definitional checklist are satisfied, the child is receiving a "free appropriate public education" as defined by the Act.

Other portions of the statute also shed light upon congressional intent. Congress found that of the roughly eight million handicapped children in the United States at the time of enactment, one million were "excluded entirely from the public school system" and more than half were receiving an inappropriate education. In addition, as mentioned in Part I, the Act requires States to extend educational services first to those children who are receiving no education and second to those children who are receiving an "inadequate education." § 1412(3). When these express statutory findings and priorities are read together with the Act's extensive procedural requirements and its definition of "free appropriate public education," the face of the statute evinces a congressional intent to bring previously excluded handicapped children into the public education systems of the States and to require the States to adopt *procedures* which would result in individualized consideration of and instruction for each child.

Noticeably absent from the language of the statute is any substantive standard prescribing the level of education to be accorded handicapped children. Certainly the language of the statute contains no requirement like the one imposed by the lower courts—that States maximize the potential of handicapped children "commensurate with the opportunity provided to other children." That standard was expounded by the District Court without reference to the statutory definitions or even to the legislative history of the Act. Although we find the statutory definition of "free appropriate public education" to be helpful in our interpretation of the Act, there remains the question of whether the legislative history indicates a congressional intent that such education meet some additional substantive standard. For an answer, we turn to that history.

B

(i)

As suggested in Part I, federal support for education of the handicapped is a fairly recent development. Before passage of the Act some States had passed laws to improve the educational services afforded handicapped children, but many of these children were excluded completely from any form of public education or were left to fend for themselves in classrooms designed for education of their nonhandicapped peers. As previously noted, the House Report begins by emphasizing this exclusion and misplacement, noting that millions of handicapped children "were either totally excluded from schools or [were] sitting idly in regular classrooms awaiting the time when they were old enough to 'drop out.'" One of the Act's two principal sponsors in the Senate urged its passage in similar terms:

> While much progress has been made in the last few years, we can take no solace in that progress until all handicapped children are, in fact, receiving an education. The most recent statistics provided by the Bureau of Education for the Handicapped estimate that . . . 1.75 million handicapped children do not receive any educational services, and 2.5 million handicapped children are not receiving

an appropriate education. 121 Cong.Rec. 19486 (1975) (remarks of Sen. Williams).

This concern, stressed repeatedly throughout the legislative history, confirms the impression conveyed by the language of the statute: By passing the Act, Congress sought primarily to make public education available to handicapped children. But in seeking to provide such access to public education, Congress did not impose upon the States any greater substantive educational standard than would be necessary to make such access meaningful. Indeed, Congress expressly "recognize[d] that in many instances the process of providing special education and related services to handicapped children is not guaranteed to produce any particular outcome." Thus, the intent of the Act was more to open the door of public education to handicapped children on appropriate terms than to guarantee any particular level of education once inside.

Both the House and the Senate Reports attribute the impetus for the Act and its predecessors to two federal-court judgments rendered in 1971 and 1972. As the Senate Report states, passage of the Act "followed a series of landmark court cases establishing in law the right to education for all handicapped children." The first case, *Pennsylvania Assn. for Retarded Children v. Commonwealth*, 334 F.Supp. 1257 (Ed Pa.1971) and 343 F.Supp. 279 (1972) (*PARC*), was a suit on behalf of retarded children challenging the constitutionality of a Pennsylvania statute which acted to exclude them from public education and training. The case ended in a consent decree which enjoined the State from "deny[ing] to any mentally retarded child *access* to a free public program of education and training." 334 F.Supp., at 1258 (emphasis added).

PARC was followed by *Mills v. Board of Education of District of Columbia*, 348 F.Supp. 866 (D.C.1972), a case in which the plaintiff handicapped children had been excluded from the District of Columbia public schools. The court's judgment, quoted in S.Rep., at 6, provided that

> no [handicapped] child eligible for a publicly supported education in the District of Columbia public schools shall be *excluded* from a regular school assignment by a Rule, policy, or practice of the Board of Education of the District of Columbia. . . .

Mills and *PARC* both held that handicapped children must be given *access* to an adequate, publicly supported education. Neither case purports to require any particular substantive level of education. Rather, like the language of the Act, the cases set forth extensive procedures to be followed in formulating personalized educational programs for handicapped children. See 348 F.Supp., at 878–883; 334 F.Supp., at 1258–1267. The fact that both *PARC* and *Mills* are discussed at length in the legislative Reports suggests that the principles which they established are the principles which, to a significant extent, guided the drafters of the Act. Indeed, immediately after discussing these cases the Senate Report describes the

1974 statute as having "incorporated the major principles of the right to education cases." Those principles in turn became the basis of the Act, which itself was designed to effectuate the purposes of the 1974 statute.

That the Act imposes no clear obligation upon recipient States beyond the requirement that handicapped children receive some form of specialized education is perhaps best demonstrated by the fact that Congress, in explaining the need for the Act, equated an "appropriate education" to the receipt of some specialized educational services. The Senate Report states: "[T]he most recent statistics provided by the Bureau of Education for the Handicapped estimate that of the more than 8 million children . . . with handicapping conditions requiring special education and related services, only 3.9 million such children are receiving an appropriate education." This statement, which reveals Congress' view that 3.9 million handicapped children were "receiving an appropriate education" in 1975, is followed immediately in the Senate Report by a table showing that 3.9 million handicapped children were "served" in 1975 and a slightly larger number were "unserved." . . .

It is evident from the legislative history that the characterization of handicapped children as "served" referred to children who were receiving some form of specialized educational services from the States, and that the characterization of children as "unserved" referred to those who were receiving no specialized educational services. . . . * * * By characterizing the 3.9 million handicapped children who were "served" as children who were "receiving an appropriate education," the Senate and House Reports unmistakably disclose Congress' perception of the type of education required by the Act: an "appropriate education" is provided when personalized educational services are provided.

(ii)

Respondents contend that "the goal of the Act is to provide each handicapped child with an equal educational opportunity." We think, however, that the requirement that a State provide specialized educational services to handicapped children generates no additional requirement that the services so provided be sufficient to maximize each child's potential "commensurate with the opportunity provided other children." Respondents and the United States correctly note that Congress sought "to provide assistance to the States in carrying out their responsibilities under . . . the Constitution of the United States to provide equal protection of the laws." But we do not think that such statements imply a congressional intent to achieve strict equality of opportunity or services.

The educational opportunities provided by our public school systems undoubtedly differ from student to student, depending upon a myriad of factors that might affect a particular student's ability to assimilate information presented in the classroom. The requirement that States provide "equal" educational opportunities would thus seem to present an entirely unworkable standard requiring impossible measurements and comparisons. Similarly, furnishing handicapped children with only such services as are available to nonhandicapped children would in all probability fall short of the statutory requirement of "free appropriate public education"; to require, on the other hand, the furnishing of every special service necessary to maximize each handicapped child's potential is, we think, further than Congress intended to go. Thus to speak in terms of "equal" services in one instance gives less than what is required by the Act and in another instance more. The theme of the Act is "free appropriate public education," a phrase which is too complex to be captured by the word "equal" whether one is speaking of opportunities or services.

* * *

The District Court and the Court of Appeals thus erred when they held that the Act requires New York to maximize the potential of each handicapped child commensurate with the opportunity provided nonhandicapped children. Desirable though that goal might be, it is not the standard that Congress imposed upon States which receive funding under the Act. Rather, Congress sought primarily to identify and evaluate handicapped children, and to provide them with access to a free public education.

(iii)

Implicit in the congressional purpose of providing access to a "free appropriate public education" is the requirement that the education to which access is provided be sufficient to confer some educational benefit upon the handicapped child. It would do little good for Congress to spend millions of dollars in providing access to a public education only to have the handicapped child receive no benefit from that education. The statutory definition of "free appropriate public education," in addition to requiring that States provide each child with "specially designed instruction," expressly requires the provision of "such . . . supportive services . . . as may be required to assist a handicapped child *to benefit* from special education." § 1401(17). We therefore conclude that the "basic floor of opportunity" provided by the Act consists of access to specialized instruction and related services which are individually designed to provide educational benefit to the handicapped child.

The determination of when handicapped children are receiving sufficient educational benefits to satisfy the requirements of the Act presents a more difficult problem. The Act requires participating States to educate a wide spectrum of handicapped children, from the marginally hearing-impaired to the profoundly retarded and palsied. It is clear that the benefits obtainable by children at one end of the spectrum will differ dramatically from those obtainable by children at the other end, with infinite variations in between. One child may have little difficulty competing successfully in an academic setting with nonhandicapped children while another child may encounter great difficulty in acquiring even the most basic of self-maintenance skills. We do not attempt today to establish any one test for determining the adequacy of educational benefits conferred upon all children covered by the Act. Because in this case we are presented with a handicapped child who is receiving substantial specialized instruction and related services, and who is performing above average in the regular classrooms of a public school system, we confine our analysis to that situation.

The Act requires participating States to educate handicapped children with nonhandicapped children whenever possible. When that "mainstreaming" preference of the Act has been met and a child is being educated in the regular classrooms of a public school system, the system itself monitors the educational progress of the child. Regular examinations are administered, grades are awarded, and yearly advancement to higher grade levels is permitted for those children who attain an adequate knowledge of the course material. The grading and advancement system thus constitutes an important factor in determining educational benefit. Children who graduate from our public school systems are considered by our society to have been "educated" at least to the grade level they have completed, and access to an "education" for handicapped children is precisely what Congress sought to provide in the Act.

C

When the language of the Act and its legislative history are considered together, the requirements imposed by Congress become tolerably clear. Insofar as a State is required to provide a handicapped child with a "free appropriate public education," we hold that it satisfies this requirement by providing personalized instruction with sufficient support services to permit the child to benefit educationally from that instruction. Such instruction and services must be provided at public expense, must meet the State's educational standards, must approximate the grade levels used in the State's regular education, and must comport with the child's IEP. In addition, the IEP, and therefore the personalized instruction, should be formulated in accordance with the requirements of the Act and, if the child is being educated in the regular classrooms of the public education system, should be reasonably calculated to enable the child to achieve passing marks and advance from grade to grade.

IV

A

As mentioned in Part I, the Act permits "[a]ny party aggrieved by the findings and decision" of the state administrative hearings "to bring a civil action" in "any State court of competent jurisdiction or in a district court of the United States without regard to the amount in controversy." § 1415(e)(2). . . . In reviewing the complaint, the Act provides that a court "shall receive the record of the [state] administrative proceedings, shall hear additional evidence at the request of a party, and, basing its decision on the preponderance of the evidence, shall grant such relief as the court determines is appropriate." § 1415(e)(2).

The parties disagree sharply over the meaning of these provisions, petitioners contending that courts are given only limited authority to review for state compliance with the Act's procedural requirements and no power to review the substance of the state program, and respondents contending that the Act requires courts to exercise *de novo* review over state educational decisions and policies. We find petitioners' contention unpersuasive, for Congress expressly rejected provisions that would have so severely restricted the role of reviewing courts. . . .

But although we find that this grant of authority is broader than claimed by petitioners, we think the fact that it is found in § 1415, which is entitled "Procedural safeguards," is not without significance. When the elaborate and highly specific procedural safeguards embodied in § 1415 are contrasted with the general and somewhat imprecise substantive admonitions contained in the Act, we think that the importance Congress attached to these procedural safeguards cannot be gainsaid. It seems to us no exaggeration to say that Congress placed every bit as much emphasis upon compliance with procedures giving parents and guardians a large measure of participation at every stage of the administrative process as it did upon the measurement of the resulting IEP against a substantive standard. We think that the congressional emphasis upon full participation of concerned parties throughout the development of the IEP, as well as the requirements that state and local plans be submitted to the Secretary for approval, demonstrates the legislative conviction that adequate compliance with the procedures prescribed would in most cases assure much if not all of what Congress wished in the way of substantive content in an IEP.

Thus the provision that a reviewing court base its decision on the "preponderance of the evidence" is by no means an invitation to the courts to substitute their own notions of sound educational policy for those of the school authorities which they review. The very importance which Congress has attached to compliance with certain procedures in the preparation of an IEP would be frustrated if a court were permitted simply to set state decisions at nought. The fact that § 1415(e) requires that the reviewing court "receive the records of the [state] administrative proceedings" carries with it the implied requirement that due weight shall be given to these proceedings. And we find nothing in the Act to suggest that merely because Congress was rather sketchy in establishing substantive requirements, as opposed to procedural requirements for the preparation of an IEP, it intended that reviewing courts should have a free hand to impose substantive standards of review which cannot be derived from the Act itself. In short, the statutory authorization to grant "such relief as the court determines is appropriate" cannot be read without reference to the obligations, largely procedural in nature, which are imposed upon recipient States by Congress.

Therefore, a court's inquiry in suits brought under § 1415(e)(2) is twofold. First, has the State complied with the procedures set forth in the Act? And second, is the individualized educational program developed through the Act's procedures reasonably calculated to enable the child to receive educational benefits? If these requirements are met, the State has complied with the obligations imposed by Congress and the courts can require no more.

B

In assuring that the requirements of the Act have been met, courts must be careful to avoid imposing their view of preferable educational methods upon the States. The primary responsibility for formulating the education to be accorded a handicapped child, and for choosing the educational method most suitable to the child's needs, was left by the Act to state and local educational agencies in cooperation with the parents or guardian of the child. . . .

We previously have cautioned that courts lack the "specialized knowledge and experience" necessary to resolve "persistent and difficult questions of educational policy." *San Antonio Independent School Dist. v. Rodriguez*, 411 U.S., at 42, 93 S.Ct., at 1301. We think that Congress shared that view when it passed the Act. As already demonstrated, Congress' intention was not that the Act displace the primacy of States in the field of education, but that States receive funds to assist them in extending their educational systems to the handicapped. Therefore, once a court determines that the requirements of the Act have been met, questions of methodology are for resolution by the States.

* * *

VI

Applying these principles to the facts of this case, we conclude that the Court of Appeals erred in affirming the decision of the District Court. Neither the District Court nor the Court of Appeals found that petitioners had failed to comply with the procedures of the Act, and the findings of neither court would support a conclusion that Amy's educational program failed to comply with the substantive requirements of the Act. On the contrary, the District Court found that the "evidence firmly establishes that Amy is receiving an 'adequate' education, since she performs better than the average child in her class and is advancing easily from grade to grade." In light of this finding, and of the fact that Amy was receiving personalized instruction and related services calculated by the Furnace Woods school administrators to meet her educational needs, the lower courts should not have concluded that the Act requires the provision of a sign-language interpreter. Accordingly, the decision of the Court of Appeals is reversed, and the case is remanded for further proceedings consistent with this opinion.

JUSTICE WHITE, with whom JUSTICE BRENNAN and JUSTICE MARSHALL join, dissenting.

In order to reach its result in this case, the majority opinion contradicts itself, the language of the statute, and the legislative history. Both the majority's standard for a "free appropriate education" and its standard for judicial review disregard congressional intent.

I

The majority first turns its attention to the meaning of a "free appropriate public education."

* * *

I agree that the language of the Act does not contain a substantive standard beyond requiring that the education offered must be "appropriate." However, if there are limits not evident from the face of the statute on what may be considered an "appropriate education," they must be found in the purpose of the statute or its legislative history. The Act itself announces it will provide a "*full* educational opportunity to all handicapped children." 20 U.S.C. § 1412(2)(A). This goal is repeated throughout the legislative history, in statements too frequent to be " 'passing references and isolated phrases.' " These statements elucidate the meaning of "appropriate." According to the Senate Report, for example, the Act does "guarantee that handicapped children are provided *equal* educational opportunity." This promise appears throughout the legislative history. Indeed, at times the purpose of the Act was described as tailoring each handicapped child's educational plan to enable the child "to achieve his or her maximum potential." Senator Stafford, one of the sponsors of the Act, declared: "We can all agree that education [given a handicapped child] should be equivalent, at least, to the one those children who are not handicapped receive." The legislative history thus directly supports the conclusion that the Act intends to give handicapped children an educational opportunity commensurate with that given other children.

The majority opinion announces a different substantive standard, that "Congress did not impose upon the States any greater substantive educational standard than would be necessary to make such access meaningful." While "meaningful" is no more enlightening than "appropriate," the Court purports to clarify itself. Because Amy was provided with *some* specialized instruction from which she obtained *some* benefit and because she passed from grade to grade, she was receiving a meaningful and therefore appropriate education.

This falls far short of what the Act intended. . . . It would apparently satisfy the Court's standard of "access to specialized instruction and related services which are individually designed to provide educational benefit to the handicapped child," for a deaf child such as Amy to be given a teacher with a loud voice, for she would benefit from that service. The Act requires more. It defines "special education" to mean "specifically designed instruction, at no cost to parents or guardians, to *meet the unique needs* of a handicapped child. . . ." § 1401(16) (emphasis added). Providing a teacher with a loud voice would not meet Amy's needs and would not satisfy the Act. The basic floor of opportunity is instead, as the courts below recognized, intended to eliminate the effects of the handicap, at least to the extent that the child will be given an equal opportunity to learn if that is reasonably possible. Amy Rowley, without a sign-language interpreter, comprehends less than half of what is said in the classroom—less than half of what normal children comprehend. This is hardly an equal opportunity to learn, even if Amy makes passing grades.

* * *

II

The Court's discussion of the standard for judicial review is as flawed as its discussion of a "free appropriate public education." According to the Court, a court can ask only whether the State has "complied with the procedures set forth in the Act" and whether the individualized education program is "reasonably calculated to enable the child to receive educational benefits." Both the language of the Act and the legislative history, however, demonstrate that Congress intended the courts to conduct a far more searching inquiry.

* * *

The legislative history shows that judicial review is not limited to procedural matters and that the state educational agencies are given first, but not final, responsibility for the content of a handicapped child's education. . . . The deliberate change in the review provision is an unusually clear indication that Congress intended courts to undertake substantive review instead of relying on the conclusions of the state agency.

* * *

Under the judicial review provisions of the Act, neither the District Court nor the Court of Appeals was bound by the State's construction of what an "appropriate" education means in general or by what the state authorities considered to be an appropriate education for Amy Rowley. Because the standard of the courts below seems to me to reflect the congressional purpose and because their factual findings are not clearly erroneous, I respectfully dissent.

NOTES AND QUESTIONS

1.   *What does a "free appropriate public education" require?* The majority and the dissent have very different interpretations of what a school district is required to provide in order to meet the minimum substantive standard for a "free appropriate public education." The majority defines the standard as not requiring anything more than special-education services that allow the child to "benefit" from the education, as long as the rest of the IDEA requirements are met. The dissent interprets the statute as requiring special-education services that would give the child with the disability an "equal opportunity to learn." Both opinions point to evidence in the legislative history to support their interpretations. Which side do you think has the better argument as a matter of statutory interpretation?

2.   Rowley *from a policy perspective.* Is the majority correct that an equal education standard would be unworkable? As a practical matter, what would that mean? The dissent states: "The basic floor of opportunity is instead, as the courts below recognized, intended to eliminate the effects of the handicap, at least to the extent that the child will be given an equal opportunity to learn if that is reasonably possible." In the case of Amy Rowley, it appears reasonably possible to give her an equal opportunity to learn, through the sign language interpreter. But would the dissent's standard be difficult to apply in other cases? For instance, suppose a child has an intellectual disability. What would be required to give that child an equal opportunity to learn? Is the lower court's standard helpful in answering this question? The lower court used a "potential maximizing" standard: "an opportunity to achieve [her] full potential commensurate with the opportunity provided to other children." How would a court figure out what is required to maximize a child's potential? Most children who are not disabled do not get an education that is uniquely suited to meet their needs and maximize their potential. Why should this be the standard for disabled children? Or do you agree with the majority that it should *not* be the standard?

3.   *The facts of* Rowley. With regard to Amy Rowley, do you think the education services she was given (the FM hearing aid, tutor, and speech therapist, but without the sign language interpreter) were enough to allow her to "benefit" from the education? Is the dissent correct that a loud-speaking teacher would be sufficient to meet the majority's standard because Amy would "benefit" from a loud-speaking teacher? The district court noted that Amy missed about half of what was said in class. And yet, presumably because she was a smart child, she still managed to pass kindergarten. Do you think Amy's claim that she needed a sign language interpreter would have been more successful if she were older and therefore had a more difficult time learning the material because she was missing half of what was going on in the classroom? Or perhaps if she were not as smart, and therefore struggled more than she did, would she have been given a sign language interpreter? If so, does this seem like the right result? Should she receive fewer special-education services because she is smart?

4. *Hearing impairments in the classroom.* Imagine being hearing impaired in law school (assuming you are not). Even if you were good at reading lips, do you think you would be able to survive law school without a sign language interpreter? As long as you sit in the middle and front of the classroom, and as long as your professor does not turn her back to you to write on the board, you might be able to lip-read well enough to understand what the professor is saying. But what about when other students speak? You probably would not be able to read their lips and the professor is unlikely to repeat everything the student said. Instead, you might see the professor saying "Yes, that's exactly right!" but have no idea what the other student said that is "exactly right." Kindergarten and first-grade are obviously not the same as law school, but even kindergarten teachers sometimes call on students to participate, and a student with a hearing impairment and no sign language interpreter is likely to miss much of what happens in the classroom.

5. *Amy Rowley's story.* For a fascinating story about this case from Amy's perspective, see *Rowley Revisited: A Personal Narrative*, 37 J.L. & EDUC. 311 (2008). In this essay, she recounts what it was like to grow up during the litigation of this case, and describes her experience trying to understand what was going on in class as a deaf student. One particularly compelling passage is Amy's description of why she did not respond to the interpreter that the school had provided on a trial basis during her kindergarten year. She states:

> One day this man shows up in my class. I know he is the interpreter because my mom has told me he will be coming. But I am scared. I don't know what an interpreter is. I have never seen one before. I am only five, and I don't know what I am supposed to do with him. He also looks scary. He is very tall to anyone who is little like me, and he is wearing standard interpreter attire of all black clothes. But I don't know that white interpreters wear dark colors to contrast with their skin color. No one in kindergarten is wearing all black so there must be something wrong with him. I am even more scared. I am only so eager to walk away and keep myself occupied with other doings. Once in a while I quickly steal a glance at him and see him signing. I wonder why. I did not understand that he was signing what the teacher was saying.

Id. at 316–17. To the extent that you thought that Amy did not need a sign language interpreter because the trial interpreter reported that she did not need him, does this narrative change your mind? Finally, for those who like happy endings to stories, Amy Rowley appears to be having a successful career—at last check, she was an Associate Professor and Coordinator of the American Sign Language Program in the Modern Languages and Literatures department at California State University—East Bay.

ENDREW F. v. DOUGLAS COUNTY SCHOOL DISTRICT RE-1
137 S.Ct. 988 (2017)

CHIEF JUSTICE ROBERTS delivered the opinion of the Court.

Thirty-five years ago, this Court held that the Individuals with Disabilities Education Act establishes a substantive right to a "free appropriate public education" for certain children with disabilities. *Board of Ed. of Hendrick Hudson Central School Dist., Westchester Cty. v. Rowley,* 458 U.S. 176, 102 S.Ct. 3034 (1982). We declined, however, to endorse any one standard for determining "when handicapped children are receiving sufficient educational benefits to satisfy the requirements of the Act." That "more difficult problem" is before us today.

I

A

[A history of the IDEA's provisions is omitted.]

* * *

B

This Court first addressed the FAPE requirement in *Rowley.* Plaintiff Amy Rowley was a first grader with impaired hearing. Her school district offered an IEP under which Amy would receive instruction in the regular classroom and spend time each week with a special tutor and a speech therapist. The district proposed that Amy's classroom teacher speak into a wireless transmitter and that Amy use an FM hearing aid designed to amplify her teacher's words; the district offered to supply both components of this system. But Amy's parents argued that the IEP should go further and provide a sign-language interpreter in all of her classes. Contending that the school district's refusal to furnish an interpreter denied Amy a FAPE, Amy's parents initiated administrative proceedings, then filed a lawsuit under the Act. *Rowley,* 458 U.S., at 184–185, 102 S.Ct. 3034.

The District Court agreed that Amy had been denied a FAPE. The court acknowledged that Amy was making excellent progress in school: She was "perform [ing] better than the average child in her class" and "advancing easily from grade to grade." *Id.,* at 185, 102 S.Ct. 3034. At the same time, Amy "under[stood] considerably less of what goes on in class than she could if she were not deaf." Concluding that "it has been left entirely to the courts and the hearings officers to give content to the requirement of an 'appropriate education,'" the District Court ruled that Amy's education was not "appropriate" unless it provided her "an opportunity to achieve [her] full potential commensurate with the opportunity provided to other children." *Rowley,* 458 U.S., at 185–186, 102 S.Ct. 3034. The Second Circuit agreed with this analysis and affirmed.

In this Court, the parties advanced starkly different understandings of the FAPE requirement. Amy's parents defended the approach of the lower courts, arguing that the school district was required to provide instruction and services that would provide Amy an "equal educational opportunity" relative to children without disabilities. The school district, for its part, contended that the IDEA "did not create substantive individual rights"; the FAPE provision was instead merely aspirational.

Neither position carried the day. On the one hand, this Court rejected the view that the IDEA gives "courts *carte blanche* to impose upon the States whatever burden their various judgments indicate should be imposed." *Rowley*, 458 U.S., at 190, n. 11, 102 S.Ct. 3034. After all, the statutory phrase "free appropriate public education" was expressly defined in the Act, even if the definition "tend[ed] toward the cryptic rather than the comprehensive." *Id.*, at 188, 102 S.Ct. 3034. This Court went on to reject the "equal opportunity" standard adopted by the lower courts, concluding that "free appropriate public education" was a phrase "too complex to be captured by the word 'equal' whether one is speaking of opportunities or services." *Id.*, at 199, 102 S.Ct. 3034. The Court also viewed the standard as "entirely unworkable," apt to require "impossible measurements and comparisons" that courts were ill suited to make. *Id.*, at 198, 102 S.Ct. 3034.

On the other hand, the Court also rejected the school district's argument that the FAPE requirement was actually no requirement at all. Instead, the Court carefully charted a middle path. Even though "Congress was rather sketchy in establishing substantive requirements" under the Act, the Court nonetheless made clear that the Act guarantees a substantively adequate program of education to all eligible children. We explained that this requirement is satisfied, and a child has received a FAPE, if the child's IEP sets out an educational program that is "reasonably calculated to enable the child to receive educational benefits." For children receiving instruction in the regular classroom, this would generally require an IEP "reasonably calculated to enable the child to achieve passing marks and advance from grade to grade." *Id.*, at 204, 102 S.Ct. 3034.

In view of Amy Rowley's excellent progress and the "substantial" suite of specialized instruction and services offered in her IEP, we concluded that her program satisfied the FAPE requirement. *Id.*, at 202, 102 S.Ct. 3034. But we went no further. Instead, we expressly "confine[d] our analysis" to the facts of the case before us. Observing that the Act requires States to "educate a wide spectrum" of children with disabilities and that "the benefits obtainable by children at one end of the spectrum will differ dramatically from those obtainable by children at the other end," we declined "to establish any one test for determining the adequacy of educational benefits conferred upon all children covered by the Act."

C

Petitioner Endrew F. was diagnosed with autism at age two. Autism is a neurodevelopmental disorder generally marked by impaired social and communicative skills, "engagement in repetitive activities and stereotyped movements, resistance to environmental change or change in daily routines, and unusual responses to sensory experiences." 34 C.F.R. § 300.8(c)(1)(i) (2016). A child with autism qualifies as a "[c]hild with a disability" under the IDEA, and Colorado (where Endrew resides) accepts IDEA funding. § 1401(3)(A). Endrew is therefore entitled to the benefits of the Act, including a FAPE provided by the State.

Endrew attended school in respondent Douglas County School District from preschool through fourth grade. Each year, his IEP Team drafted an IEP addressed to his educational and functional needs. By Endrew's fourth grade year, however, his parents had become dissatisfied with his progress. Although Endrew displayed a number of strengths—his teachers described him as a humorous child with a "sweet disposition" who "show[ed] concern[ ] for friends"—he still "exhibited multiple behaviors that inhibited his ability to access learning in the classroom." Endrew would scream in class, climb over furniture and other students, and occasionally run away from school. He was afflicted by severe fears of commonplace things like flies, spills, and public restrooms. As Endrew's parents saw it, his academic and functional progress had essentially stalled: Endrew's IEPs largely carried over the same basic goals and objectives from one year to the next, indicating that he was failing to make meaningful progress toward his aims. His parents believed that only a thorough overhaul of the school district's approach to Endrew's behavioral problems could reverse the trend. But in April 2010, the school district presented Endrew's parents with a proposed fifth grade IEP that was, in their view, pretty much the same as his past ones. So his parents removed Endrew from public school and enrolled him at Firefly Autism House, a private school that specializes in educating children with autism.

Endrew did much better at Firefly. The school developed a "behavioral intervention plan" that identified Endrew's most problematic behaviors and set out particular strategies for addressing them. Firefly also added heft to Endrew's academic goals. Within months, Endrew's behavior improved significantly, permitting him to make a degree of academic progress that had eluded him in public school.

In November 2010, some six months after Endrew started classes at Firefly, his parents again met with representatives of the Douglas County School District. The district presented a new IEP. Endrew's parents considered the IEP no more adequate than the one proposed in April, and rejected it. They were particularly concerned that the stated plan for addressing Endrew's behavior did not differ meaningfully from the plan in his fourth grade IEP, despite the fact that his experience at Firefly suggested that he would benefit from a different approach.

In February 2012, Endrew's parents filed a complaint with the Colorado Department of Education seeking reimbursement for Endrew's tuition at Firefly. To qualify for such relief, they were required to show that the school district had not provided Endrew a FAPE in a timely manner prior to his enrollment at the private school. See § 1412(a)(10)(C)(ii). Endrew's parents contended that the final IEP proposed by the school district was not "reasonably calculated to enable [Endrew] to receive educational benefits" and that Endrew had therefore been denied a FAPE. *Rowley,* 458 U.S., at 207, 102 S.Ct. 3034. An Administrative Law Judge (ALJ) disagreed and denied relief.

Endrew's parents sought review in Federal District Court. Giving "due weight" to the decision of the ALJ, the District Court affirmed. The court acknowledged that Endrew's performance under past IEPs "did not reveal immense educational growth." But it concluded that annual modifications to Endrew's IEP objectives were "sufficient to show a pattern of, at the least, minimal progress." Because Endrew's previous IEPs had enabled him to make this sort of progress, the court reasoned, his latest, similar IEP was reasonably calculated to do the same thing. In the court's view, that was all *Rowley* demanded.

The Tenth Circuit affirmed. The Court of Appeals recited language from *Rowley* stating that the instruction and services furnished to children with disabilities must be calculated to confer "*some* educational benefit." 798 F.3d, at 1338 (quoting *Rowley,* 458 U.S., at 200, 102 S.Ct. 3034; emphasis added by Tenth Circuit). The court noted that it had long interpreted this language to mean that a child's IEP is adequate as long as it is calculated to confer an "educational benefit [that is] merely . . . more than *de minimis.*" 798 F.3d, at 1338. Applying this standard, the Tenth Circuit held that Endrew's IEP had been "reasonably calculated to enable [him] to make *some* progress." Accordingly, he had not been denied a FAPE.

We granted certiorari.

II

A

The Court in *Rowley* declined "to establish any one test for determining the adequacy of educational benefits conferred upon all children covered by the Act." 458 U.S., at 202, 102 S.Ct. 3034. The school district, however, contends that *Rowley* nonetheless established that "an IEP need not promise any particular *level* of benefit," so long as it is " 'reasonably calculated' to provide *some* benefit, as opposed to *none.*"

The district relies on several passages from *Rowley* to make its case. It points to our observation that "any substantive standard prescribing the level of education to be accorded" children with disabilities was "[n]oticeably absent from the language of the statute." 458 U.S., at 189, 102 S.Ct. 3034. The district also emphasizes the Court's statement that the Act requires States to provide access to instruction "sufficient to confer *some* educational benefit," reasoning that any benefit, however minimal, satisfies this mandate. Finally, the district urges that the Court conclusively adopted a "some educational benefit" standard when it wrote that "the intent of the Act was more to open the door of public education to handicapped children . . . than to guarantee any particular level of education." *Id.*, at 192, 102 S.Ct. 3034.

These statements in isolation do support the school district's argument. But the district makes too much of them. Our statement that the face of the IDEA imposed no explicit substantive standard must be evaluated alongside our statement that a substantive standard was "implicit in the Act. " *Rowley*, 458 U.S., at 193, n. 15, 102 S.Ct. 3034. Similarly, we find little significance in the Court's language concerning the requirement that States provide instruction calculated to "confer some educational benefit." The Court had no need to say anything more particular, since the case before it involved a child whose progress plainly demonstrated that her IEP was designed to deliver more than adequate educational benefits. The Court's principal concern was to correct what it viewed as the surprising rulings below: that the IDEA effectively empowers judges to elaborate a federal common law of public education, and that a child performing *better* than most in her class had been denied a FAPE. The Court was not concerned with precisely articulating a governing standard for closer cases. And the statement that the Act did not "guarantee any particular level of education" simply reflects the unobjectionable proposition that the IDEA cannot and does not promise "any particular [educational] outcome." *Id.*, at 192, 102 S.Ct. 3034. No law could do that—for any child.

More important, the school district's reading of these isolated statements runs headlong into several points on which *Rowley* is crystal clear. For instance—just after saying that the Act requires instruction that is "sufficient to confer some educational benefit"—we noted that "[t]he determination of when handicapped children are receiving *sufficient* educational benefits . . . presents a . . . difficult problem." *Id.*, at 200, 202, 102 S.Ct. 3034. And then we expressly declined "to establish any one test for determining the *adequacy* of educational benefits" under the Act. *Id.*, at 202, 102 S.Ct. 3034. It would not have been "difficult" for us to say when educational benefits are sufficient if we had just said that *any* educational benefit was enough. And it would have been strange to refuse to set out a test for the adequacy of educational benefits if we had just done exactly that. We cannot accept the school district's reading of *Rowley*.

B

While *Rowley* declined to articulate an overarching standard to evaluate the adequacy of the education provided under the Act, the decision and the statutory language point to a general approach: To meet its substantive obligation under the IDEA, a school must offer an IEP reasonably calculated to enable a child to make progress appropriate in light of the child's circumstances.

The "reasonably calculated" qualification reflects a recognition that crafting an appropriate program of education requires a prospective judgment by school officials. The Act contemplates that this fact-intensive exercise will be informed not only by the expertise of school officials, but also by the input of the child's parents or guardians. Any review of an IEP must appreciate that the question is whether the IEP is *reasonable,* not whether the court regards it as ideal.

The IEP must aim to enable the child to make progress. After all, the essential function of an IEP is to set out a plan for pursuing academic and functional advancement. See §§ 1414(d)(1)(A)(i)(I)–(IV). This reflects the broad purpose of the IDEA, an "ambitious" piece of legislation enacted "in response to Congress' perception that a majority of handicapped children in the United States 'were either totally excluded from schools or [were] sitting idly in regular classrooms awaiting the time when they were old enough to "drop out." ' " *Rowley,* 458 U.S., at 179, 102 S.Ct. 3034 (quoting H.R.Rep. No. 94–332, p. 2 (1975)). A substantive standard not focused on student progress would do little to remedy the pervasive and tragic academic stagnation that prompted Congress to act.

That the progress contemplated by the IEP must be appropriate in light of the child's circumstances should come as no surprise. A focus on the particular child is at the core of the IDEA. The instruction offered must be *"specially* designed" to meet a child's *"unique* needs" through an "[*i*]*ndividualized* education program." §§ 1401(29), (14). An IEP is not a form document. It is constructed only after careful consideration of the child's present levels of achievement, disability, and potential for growth. §§ 1414(d)(1)(A)(i)(I)–(IV), (d)(3)(A)(i)–(iv). As we observed in *Rowley,* the IDEA "requires participating States to educate a wide spectrum of handicapped children," and "the benefits obtainable by children at one end of the spectrum will differ dramatically from those obtainable by children at the other end, with infinite variations in between." 458 U.S., at 202, 102 S.Ct. 3034.

Rowley sheds light on what appropriate progress will look like in many cases. There, the Court recognized that the IDEA requires that children with disabilities receive education in the regular classroom "whenever possible." When this preference is met, "the system itself monitors the educational progress of the child." *Id.,* at 202–203, 102 S.Ct. 3034. "Regular examinations are administered, grades are awarded, and yearly advancement to higher grade levels is permitted for those children who attain an adequate knowledge of the course material." *Id.*, at 203, 102 S.Ct. 3034. Progress through this system is what our society generally means by an "education." And access to an "education" is what the IDEA promises. Accordingly, for a child fully integrated in the regular classroom, an IEP typically should, as *Rowley* put it, be "reasonably calculated to enable the child to achieve passing marks and advance from grade to grade." *Id.*, at 203–204, 102 S.Ct. 3034.

This guidance is grounded in the statutory definition of a FAPE. One of the components of a FAPE is "special education," defined as "specially designed instruction . . . to meet the unique needs of a child with a disability." §§ 1401(9), (29). In determining what it means to "meet the unique needs" of a child with a disability, the provisions governing the IEP development process are a natural source of guidance: It is through the IEP that "[t]he 'free appropriate public education' required by the Act is tailored to the unique needs of" a particular child. *Id.*, at 181, 102 S.Ct. 3034.

The IEP provisions reflect *Rowley*'s expectation that, for most children, a FAPE will involve integration in the regular classroom and individualized special education calculated to achieve advancement from grade to grade. Every IEP begins by describing a child's present level of achievement, including explaining "how the child's disability affects the child's involvement and progress in the general education curriculum." § 1414(d)(1)(A)(i)(I)(aa). It then sets out "a statement of measurable annual goals . . . designed to . . . enable the child to be involved in and make progress in the general education curriculum," along with a description of specialized instruction and services that the child will receive. §§ 1414(d)(1)(A)(i)(II), (IV). The instruction and services must likewise be provided with an eye toward "progress in the general education curriculum." § 1414(d)(1)(A)(i)(IV)(bb). Similar IEP requirements have been in place since the time the States began accepting funding under the IDEA.

The school district protests that these provisions impose only procedural requirements—a checklist of items the IEP must address—not a substantive standard enforceable in court. But the procedures are there for a reason, and their focus provides insight into what it means, for purposes of the FAPE definition, to "meet the unique needs" of a child with a disability. §§ 1401(9), (29). When a child is fully integrated in the regular classroom, as the Act prefers, what that typically means is providing a level of instruction reasonably calculated to permit advancement through the general curriculum.[2]

---

[2] This guidance should not be interpreted as an inflexible rule. We declined to hold in *Rowley,* and do not hold today, that "every handicapped child who is advancing from grade to grade . . . is automatically receiving a [FAPE]." *Board of Ed. of Hendrick Hudson Central School Dist., Westchester Cty. v. Rowley,* 458 U.S. 176, 203, n. 25, 102 S.Ct. 3034 (1982).

EDUCATION

Rowley had no need to provide concrete guidance with respect to a child who is not fully integrated in the regular classroom and not able to achieve on grade level. That case concerned a young girl who was progressing smoothly through the regular curriculum. If that is not a reasonable prospect for a child, his IEP need not aim for grade-level advancement. But his educational program must be appropriately ambitious in light of his circumstances, just as advancement from grade to grade is appropriately ambitious for most children in the regular classroom. The goals may differ, but every child should have the chance to meet challenging objectives.

Of course this describes a general standard, not a formula. But whatever else can be said about it, this standard is markedly more demanding than the "merely more than *de minimis*" test applied by the Tenth Circuit. It cannot be the case that the Act typically aims for grade-level advancement for children with disabilities who can be educated in the regular classroom, but is satisfied with barely more than *de minimis* progress for those who cannot.

When all is said and done, a student offered an educational program providing "merely more than *de minimis*" progress from year to year can hardly be said to have been offered an education at all. For children with disabilities, receiving instruction that aims so low would be tantamount to "sitting idly . . . awaiting the time when they were old enough to 'drop out.'" *Rowley,* 458 U.S., at 179, 102 S.Ct. 3034. The IDEA demands more. It requires an educational program reasonably calculated to enable a child to make progress appropriate in light of the child's circumstances.

C

Endrew's parents argue that the Act goes even further. In their view, a FAPE is "an education that aims to provide a child with a disability opportunities to achieve academic success, attain self-sufficiency, and contribute to society that are substantially equal to the opportunities afforded children without disabilities."

This standard is strikingly similar to the one the lower courts adopted in *Rowley,* and it is virtually identical to the formulation advanced by Justice Blackmun in his separate writing in that case. See 458 U.S., at 185–186, 102 S.Ct. 3034; *id.,* at 211, 102 S.Ct. 3034 (opinion concurring in judgment) ("[T]he question is whether Amy's program . . . offered her an opportunity to understand and participate in the classroom that was substantially equal to that given her non-handicapped classmates"). But the majority rejected any such standard in clear terms. *Id.,* at 198, 102 S.Ct. 3034 ("The requirement that States provide 'equal' educational opportunities would . . . seem to present an entirely unworkable standard requiring impossible measurements and comparisons"). Mindful that Congress (despite several intervening amendments to the IDEA) has not materially changed the statutory definition of a FAPE since *Rowley* was decided, we decline to interpret the FAPE provision in a manner so plainly at odds with the Court's analysis in that case.

D

We will not attempt to elaborate on what "appropriate" progress will look like from case to case. It is in the nature of the Act and the standard we adopt to resist such an effort: The adequacy of a given IEP turns on the unique circumstances of the child for whom it was created. This absence of a bright-line rule, however, should not be mistaken for "an invitation to the courts to substitute their own notions of sound educational policy for those of the school authorities which they review." *Rowley,* 458 U.S., at 206, 102 S.Ct. 3034.

At the same time, deference is based on the application of expertise and the exercise of judgment by school authorities. The Act vests these officials with responsibility for decisions of critical importance to the life of a disabled child. The nature of the IEP process, from the initial consultation through state administrative proceedings, ensures that parents and school representatives will fully air their respective opinions on the degree of progress a child's IEP should pursue. By the time any dispute reaches court, school authorities will have had a complete opportunity to bring their expertise and judgment to bear on areas of disagreement. A reviewing court may fairly expect those authorities to be able to offer a cogent and responsive explanation for their decisions that shows the IEP is reasonably calculated to enable the child to make progress appropriate in light of his circumstances.

The judgment of the United States Court of Appeals for the Tenth Circuit is vacated, and the case is remanded for further proceedings consistent with this opinion.

NOTES AND QUESTIONS

1.   *The Court's standard in* Endrew F. The Court states that the FAPE requirement under the IDEA "requires an educational program reasonably calculated to enable a child to make progress appropriate in light of the child's circumstances." Although the Court makes clear that the standard articulated by the Tenth Circuit in *Endrew F.* (anything more than a *de minimis* educational benefit) is inadequate, the standard is still fairly vague. Instead of fighting over what "some educational benefit" means, parents and school districts will likely be arguing over what "appropriate progress" means. Could the Court have announced a more definitive standard? Or does the nature of an IEP (an *individualized* education program) make it impossible to arrive at any bright-line rule?

2.   *The circuit split that preceded* Endrew F. Although the Court does not discuss it, a circuit split had developed in the courts regarding what standard should be used when a parent challenges an IEP. Recall that *Rowley* had stated that the IEP had to provide "some educational benefit." Some courts, like the

Tenth Circuit in *Endrew F.*, only required a school district to prove that it was offering an IEP that provided anything more than a *de minimis* benefit to the child with a disability. *See, e.g.,* Endrew F. ex rel. Joseph F. v. Douglas County School Dist. Re-1, 789 F.3d 1329, 1338 (10th Cir. 2015); O.S. v. Fairfax Cty. Sch. Bd., 804 F.3d 354, 359 (4th Cir. 2015); D.B. ex rel. Elizabeth B. v. Esposito, 675 F.3d 26, 34–35 (1st Cir. 2012); M.B. ex rel. Berns v. Hamilton Se. Sch., 668 F.3d 851, 862 (7th Cir. 2011); JSK by and through JK v. Hendry Cty. Sch. Bd., 941 F.2d 1563, 1572–73 (11th Cir. 1991).

Other circuits had adopted a higher standard, requiring school districts to provide an IEP that offered a "meaningful educational benefit." *See, e.g.,* Deal v. Hamilton Cty. Bd. of Educ., 392 F.3d 840, 862 (6th Cir. 2004); Polk v. Cent. Susquehanna Intermediate Unit 16, 853 F.2d 171, 183 (3d Cir. 1988). Yet the Court in *Endrew F.* does not address or even mention the "meaningful educational benefit" standard used by the Sixth and Third circuits. Do you think that the standard that the Court arrives at in *Endrew F.*—an educational program "reasonably calculated to enable a child to make progress appropriate in light of the child's circumstances—is significantly different from the "meaningful educational benefit" standard used by the Sixth and Third Circuits?

3. *The meaning of footnote 2.* In *Endrew F.*, the Court stated that, when a child is being mainstreamed, providing a FAPE "typically means . . . providing a level of instruction reasonably calculated to permit advancement through the general curriculum." The Court then dropped a footnote and explained: "This guidance should not be interpreted as an inflexible rule. We declined to hold in *Rowley,* and do not hold today, that 'every handicapped child who is advancing from grade to grade . . . is automatically receiving a [FAPE].' " What do you think the Court meant by this footnote? In other words, when might a child who is fully mainstreamed and successfully advancing from grade to grade be held to *not* be receiving a FAPE?

4. *Content vs. implementation. Endrew F.* dealt with the content of an IEP—whether the IEP as written was appropriate. A separate issue is presented when dealing with implementation—whether a school has appropriately implemented the IEP. *See* L.J. by N.N.J. v. School Board of Broward County, 927 F.3d 1203 (11th Cir. 2019). In this case, an issue arose when L.J. transitioned from elementary school to middle school. The history of this case is very lengthy and complicated, with several complaints and several decisions by the ALJ and the courts. But the crux of the plaintiff's complaint is that the school failed to properly implement the plaintiff's elementary school IEP during the child's 7th and 8th grade years in middle school. The reason the elementary school IEP is at issue is because of a provision in the IDEA, the "stay put" provision (discussed *infra* Section B.1.d), which requires schools to keep in place the last IEP anytime a plaintiff is challenging a new IEP. So the middle school was required to implement an IEP that was designed for elementary school. *Id.* at 1209. The court in this case noted that *Endrew F.* dealt with claims regarding the IEP *as written*. But, even when an IEP as written satisfies the IDEA, a school can violate its obligation to provide a FAPE

if it fails to implement the IEP *in practice*. That is the issue that was before the court in this case. *Id*. at 1211.

In announcing the appropriate standard in these failure-to-implement cases, the court held that a plaintiff

> must demonstrate that the school has materially failed to implement a child's IEP. And to do that, the plaintiff must prove more than a minor or technical gap between the plan and reality; *de minimis* shortfalls are not enough. A material implementation failure occurs only when a school has failed to implement substantial or significant provisions of a child's IEP.

Id. at 1211.

The court justified its announced standard with four arguments. First, the FAPE statutory language requires that the special education and related services must be provided "in conformity with" the IEP. *Id*. at 1212 (citing 20 U.S.C. § 1401(9)). The court stated that "in conformity with" suggests "general agreement or congruence, not perfect adherence." *Id*. Nothing in the text, according to the court, requires holding schools to "perfect implementation." *Id*. Second, the court argued that children develop quickly so there must be flexibility in the child's IEP. *Id*. Third, the court stated that requiring perfect implementation is inconsistent with the recognition that the IEP is a plan, not a contract. *Id*. at 1212–13. And fourth, the parties here (as in many other cases) were disputing the implementation of a "stay-put" IEP, and it might be literally impossible to fulfill an old IEP in a new setting. *Id*. at 1213.

When implementing this "material failure to implement" standard, the court stated that lack of educational progress is evidence of a material failure but should not be dispositive. *Id*. at 1214. Furthermore, schools must be given some leeway when implementing a stay-put IEP, especially when the child has transitioned from one educational level to another. Finally, courts should view the implementation as a whole in light of the IEP's overall goals. *Id*. at 1215. The court took pains to distinguish *Endrew F.*, noting that the standard announced in *Endrew F.* is particularly inapt in implementation cases where a school is operating under a stay-put IEP. Here, the school proposed a new IEP when L.J. moved to middle school but was required to implement an old IEP from elementary school when L.J.'s mother challenged the proposed replacement. Thus, "it would make little sense to force a school to implement an IEP it believes is outdated, and then force the school to defend that same IEP as fully appropriate for the child." *Id*. at 1216. What do you think about the "material failure" standard the court announced in this case? Does it ameliorate some or all of the progress made in *Endrew F.* that requires schools to provide an education that allows the child to make "appropriate progress"? Justify your response.

5. *Providing a FAPE during a pandemic.* During the spring of 2020, when schools across the country shut down due to the global pandemic, COVID-19, special education teachers and administrators had to figure out how to implement IEPs during the shut-down. And as this edition is being

written, schools are experiencing closures during the fall of 2020 and possibly beyond. How does a school implement an IEP if the school shuts down? Or if children with disabilities cannot attend in person because they are at high risk of complications from COVID-19? The Department of Education attempted to answer these questions in a Q&A guidance released in March 2020. *See* Questions and Answers on Providing Services to Children with Disabilities During the Coronavirus Disease 2019 Outbreak, March 2020, https://sites.ed. gov/idea/files/qa-covid-19-03-12-2020.pdf. The basic takeaway from the Q&A is that, if schools are continuing to provide educational services to non-disabled students during a closure, they must do so for students with disabilities to the maximum extent possible. The temporal period that would trigger a required review of the IEP is 10 consecutive school days. In other words, if a school closes down for more than 10 days (but is still providing services to non-disabled children) or if a child must stay home for more than 10 days due to illness or risk of illness from COVID-19, the school must consider and implement appropriate changes to the child's IEP.

b.   Mainstreaming (Least Restrictive Environment)

SACRAMENTO CITY UNIFIED SCHOOL DISTRICT V. RACHEL H.

14 F.3d 1398 (9th Cir. 1994)

SNEED, CIRCUIT JUDGE:

The Sacramento Unified School District ("the District") timely appeals the district court's judgment in favor of Rachel Holland ("Rachel") and the California State Department of Education. The court found that the appropriate placement for Rachel under the Individuals with Disabilities Act ("IDEA") was full-time in a regular second grade classroom with some supplemental services. The District contends that the appropriate placement for Rachel is half-time in special education classes and half-time in a regular class. We affirm the judgment of the district court.

I.

FACTS AND PRIOR PROCEEDINGS

Rachel Holland is now 11 years old and is mentally retarded. She was tested with an I.Q. of 44. She attended a variety of special education programs in the District from 1985–89. Her parents sought to increase the time Rachel spent in a regular classroom, and in the fall of 1989, they requested that Rachel be placed full-time in a regular classroom for the 1989–90 school year. The District rejected their request and proposed a placement that would have divided Rachel's time between a special education class for academic subjects and a regular class for non-academic activities such as art, music, lunch, and recess. The district court found that this plan would have required moving Rachel at least six times each day between the two classrooms. The Hollands instead enrolled Rachel in a regular kindergarten class at the Shalom School, a private school. Rachel remained at the Shalom School in regular classes and at the time the district court rendered its opinion was in the second grade.

... Although the IEP is required to be reviewed annually, *see* 20 U.S.C. § 1401a(20)(B), because of the dispute between the parties, Rachel's IEP has not been reviewed since January 1990.[3]

The Hollands appealed the District's placement decision to a state hearing officer pursuant to 20 U.S.C. § 1415(b)(2). They maintained that Rachel best learned social and academic skills in a regular classroom and would not benefit from being in a special education class. The District contended Rachel was too severely disabled to benefit from full-time placement in a regular class. The hearing officer concluded that the District had failed to make an adequate effort to educate Rachel in a regular class pursuant to the IDEA. The officer found that (1) Rachel had benefitted from her regular kindergarten class—that she was motivated to learn and learned by imitation and modeling; (2) Rachel was not disruptive in a regular classroom; and (3) the District had overstated the cost of putting Rachel in regular education—that the cost would not be so great that it weighed against placing her in a regular classroom. The hearing officer ordered the District to place Rachel in a regular classroom with support services, including a special education consultant and a part-time aide.

The District appealed this determination to the district court. . . . The court affirmed the decision of the hearing officer that Rachel should be placed full-time in a regular classroom.

In considering whether the District proposed an appropriate placement for Rachel, the district court examined the following factors: (1) the educational benefits available to Rachel in a regular classroom, supplemented with appropriate aids and services, as compared with the educational benefits of a special education classroom; (2) the non-academic benefits of interaction with children who were not disabled; (3) the effect of Rachel's presence on the teacher and other children in the classroom; and (4) the cost of mainstreaming Rachel in a regular classroom.

1. *Educational Benefits*

The district court found the first factor, educational benefits to Rachel, weighed in favor of placing her in a regular classroom. Each side presented expert testimony which is summarized in the margin. The court noted that the District's evidence focused on Rachel's limitations but did not establish that the educational opportunities available through special education

---

[3]   The 1990 IEP objectives include: speaking in 4- or 5-word sentences; repeating instructions of complex tasks; initiating and terminating conversations; stating her name, address and phone number; participating in a safety program with classmates; developing a 24-word sight vocabulary; counting to 25; printing her first and last names and the alphabet; playing cooperatively; participating in lunch without supervision; and identifying upper and lower case letters and the sounds associated with them.

were better or equal to those available in a regular classroom. Moreover, the court found that the testimony of the Hollands' experts was more credible because they had more background in evaluating children with disabilities placed in regular classrooms and that they had a greater opportunity to observe Rachel over an extended period of time in normal circumstances. The district court also gave great weight to the testimony of Rachel's current teacher, Nina Crone, whom the court found to be an experienced, skillful teacher. Ms. Crone stated that Rachel was a full member of the class and participated in all activities. Ms. Crone testified that Rachel was making progress on her IEP goals: She was learning one-to-one correspondence in counting, was able to recite the English and Hebrew alphabets, and was improving her communication abilities and sentence lengths.

The district court found that Rachel received substantial benefits in regular education and that all of her IEP goals could be implemented in a regular classroom with some modification to the curriculum and with the assistance of a part-time aide.

2. *Non-academic Benefits*

The district court next found that the second factor, non-academic benefits to Rachel, also weighed in favor of placing her in a regular classroom. The court noted that the Hollands' evidence indicated that Rachel had developed her social and communications skills as well as her self-confidence from placement in a regular class, while the District's evidence tended to show that Rachel was not learning from exposure to other children and that she was isolated from her classmates. The court concluded that the differing evaluations in large part reflected the predisposition of the evaluators. The court found the testimony of Rachel's mother and her current teacher to be the most credible. These witnesses testified regarding Rachel's excitement about school, learning, and her new friendships and Rachel's improved self-confidence.

3. *Effect on the Teacher and Children in the Regular Class*

The district court next addressed the issue of whether Rachel had a detrimental effect on others in her regular classroom. The court looked at two aspects: (1) whether there was detriment because the child was disruptive, distracting or unruly, and (2) whether the child would take up so much of the teacher's time that the other students would suffer from lack of attention. The witnesses of both parties agreed that Rachel followed directions and was well-behaved and not a distraction in class. The court found the most germane evidence on the second aspect came from Rachel's second grade teacher, Nina Crone, who testified that Rachel did not interfere with her ability to teach the other children and in the future would require only a part-time aide. Accordingly, the district court determined that the third factor, the effect of Rachel's presence on the teacher and other children in the classroom weighed in favor of placing her in a regular classroom.

4.   *Cost*

Finally, the district court found that the District had not offered any persuasive or credible evidence to support its claim that educating Rachel in a regular classroom with appropriate services would be significantly more expensive than educating her in the District's proposed setting.

The District contended that it would cost $109,000 to educate Rachel full-time in a regular classroom. This figure was based on the cost of providing a full-time aide for Rachel plus an estimated $80,000 for school-wide sensitivity training. The court found that the District did not establish that such training was necessary. Further, the court noted that even if such training were necessary, there was evidence from the California Department of Education that the training could be had at no cost. Moreover, the court found it would be inappropriate to assign the total cost of the training to Rachel when other children with disabilities would benefit. In addition, the court concluded that the evidence did not suggest that Rachel required a full-time aide.

In addition, the court found that the District should have compared the cost of placing Rachel in a special class of approximately 12 students with a full-time special education teacher and two full-time aides and the cost of placing her in a regular class with a part-time aide. The District provided no evidence of this cost comparison.

The court also was not persuaded by the District's argument that it would lose significant funding if Rachel did not spend at least 51% of her time in a special education class. The court noted that a witness from the California Department of Education testified that waivers were available if a school district sought to adopt a program that did not fit neatly within the funding guidelines. The District had not applied for a waiver.

By inflating the cost estimates and failing to address the true comparison, the District did not meet its burden of proving that regular placement would burden the District's funds or adversely affect services available to other children. Therefore, the court found that the cost factor did not weigh against mainstreaming Rachel.

The district court concluded that the appropriate placement for Rachel was full-time in a regular second grade classroom with some supplemental services and affirmed the decision of the hearing officer.

IV.

DISCUSSION

* * *

B. *Mainstreaming Requirements of the IDEA*

1. *The Statute*

The IDEA provides that each state must establish:

> [P]rocedures to assure that, to the maximum extent appropriate, children with disabilities . . . are educated with children who are not disabled, and that special classes, separate schooling, or other removal of children with disabilities from the regular educational environment occurs only when the nature or severity of the disability is such that education in regular classes with the use of supplementary aids and services cannot be achieved satisfactorily. . . .

20 U.S.C. § 1412(5)(B).

This provision sets forth Congress's preference for educating children with disabilities in regular classrooms with their peers.

* * *

3. *Test for Determining Compliance with the IDEA's Mainstreaming Requirement*

We have not adopted or devised a standard for determining the presence of compliance with 20 U.S.C. § 1412(5)(B). The Third, Fifth and Eleventh Circuits use what is known as the *Daniel R.R.* test. *Daniel R.R.*, 874 F.2d at 1048.[5] The Fourth, Sixth and Eighth Circuits apply the *Roncker* test. *Roncker v. Walter*, 700 F.2d 1058, 1063 (6th Cir.), *cert. denied*, 464 U.S. 864, 104 S.Ct. 196 (1983).[6]

Although the district court relied principally on *Daniel R.R.* and *Greer*, it did not specifically adopt the *Daniel R.R.* test over the *Roncker* test. Rather, it employed factors found in both lines of cases in its analysis. The result was a four-factor balancing test in which the court considered (1) the educational benefits of placement full-time in a regular class; (2) the non-

---

[5]   First, the court must determine "whether education in the regular classroom, with the use of supplemental aids and services, can be achieved satisfactorily. . . ." *Daniel R.R.*, 874 F.2d at 1048. If the court finds that education cannot be achieved satisfactorily in the regular classroom, then it must decide "whether the school has mainstreamed the child to the maximum extent appropriate." *Id.*

Factors the courts consider in applying the first prong of this test are (1) the steps the school district has taken to accommodate the child in a regular classroom; (2) whether the child will receive an educational benefit from regular education; (3) the child's overall educational experience in regular education; and (4) the effect the disabled child's presence has on the regular classroom. *Daniel R.R.*, 874 F.2d at 1048–49.

[6]   According to the court in *Roncker*: "[W]here the segregated facility is considered superior, the court should determine whether the services which make that placement superior could be feasibly provided in a non-segregated setting. If they can, the placement in the segregated school would be inappropriate under the Act." 700 F.2d at 1063.

Courts are to (1) compare the benefits the child would receive in special education with those she would receive in regular education; (2) consider whether the child would be disruptive in the non-segregated setting; and (3) consider the cost of mainstreaming. *Id.*

academic benefits of such placement; (3) the effect Rachel had on the teacher and children in the regular class; and (4) the costs of mainstreaming Rachel. This analysis directly addresses the issue of the appropriate placement for a child with disabilities under the requirements of 20 U.S.C. § 1412(5)(B). Accordingly, we approve and adopt the test employed by the district court.

4.   *The District's Contentions on Appeal*

The District strenuously disagrees with the district court's findings that Rachel was receiving academic and non-academic benefits in a regular class and did not have a detrimental effect on the teacher or other students. It argues that the court's findings were contrary to the evidence of the state Diagnostic Center and that the court should not have been persuaded by the testimony of Rachel's teacher, particularly her testimony that Rachel would need only a part-time aide in the future. The district court, however, conducted a full evidentiary hearing and made a thorough analysis. The court found the Hollands' evidence to be more persuasive. Moreover, the court asked Rachel's teacher extensive questions regarding Rachel's need for a part-time aide. We will not disturb the findings of the district court.

The District is also not persuasive on the issue of cost. The District now claims that it will lose up to $190,764 in state special education funding if Rachel is not enrolled in a special education class at least 51% of the day. However, the District has not sought a waiver pursuant to California Education Code § 56101. This section provides that (1) any school district may request a waiver of any provision of the Education Code if the waiver is necessary or beneficial to the student's IEP, and (2) the Board may grant the waiver when failure to do so would hinder compliance with federal mandates for a free appropriate education for children with disabilities.

... We affirm the judgment of the district court. While we cannot determine what the appropriate placement is for Rachel at the present time, we hold that the determination of the present and future appropriate placement for Rachel should be based on the principles set forth in this opinion and the opinion of the district court.

HARTMANN V. LOUDOUN COUNTY BOARD OF EDUCATION
118 F.3d 996 (4th Cir. 1997)

WILKINSON, CHIEF JUDGE:

Roxanna and Joseph Hartmann brought suit on behalf of their disabled son Mark against the Loudoun County Board of Education under the Individuals With Disabilities Education Act (IDEA), 20 U.S.C. § 1400 *et seq*. The Hartmanns alleged that the Board had failed to ensure that Mark was educated with non-handicapped children "to the maximum extent appropriate" as required by the IDEA's mainstreaming provision, 20 U.S.C. § 1412(5)(B). The district court agreed, rejecting the findings of both the local hearing officer and the state review officer. The Board appeals, contending that the court's decision is contrary to the law and the evidence in the record. We agree. As Supreme Court precedent makes clear, the IDEA does not grant federal courts a license to substitute their own notions of sound educational policy for those of local school authorities, or to disregard the findings developed in state administrative proceedings. Upon careful review of the record, however, we are forced to conclude that this is precisely what has occurred in this case. Accordingly, we reverse and remand with directions to dismiss.

I.

Mark Hartmann is an eleven-year-old autistic child. Autism is a developmental disorder characterized by significant deficiencies in communication skills, social interaction, and motor control. Mark is unable to speak and suffers severe problems with fine motor coordination. Mark's writing ability is extremely limited; he does not write by hand and can consistently type only a few words such as "is" and "at" by himself on a keyboard device known as a Canon communicator. The parties agree that Mark's greatest need is to develop communication skills.

Mark spent his pre-school years in various programs for disabled children. In kindergarten, he spent half his time in a self-contained program for autistic children and half in a regular education classroom at Butterfield Elementary in Lombard, Illinois. Upon entering first grade, Mark received speech and occupational therapy one-on-one, but was otherwise included in the regular classroom at Butterfield full-time with an aide to assist him.

After Mark's first-grade year, the Hartmanns moved to Loudoun County, Virginia, where they enrolled Mark at Ashburn Elementary for the 1993–1994 school year. Based on Mark's individualized education program (IEP) from Illinois, the school placed Mark in a regular education classroom. To facilitate Mark's inclusion, Loudoun officials carefully selected his teacher, hired a full-time aide to assist him, and put him in a smaller class with more independent children. Mark's teacher, Diane Johnson, read extensively about autism, and both Johnson and Mark's aide, Suz Leitner, received training in facilitated communication, a special communication technique used with autistic children. Mark received five hours per week of speech and language therapy with a qualified specialist, Carolyn Clement. Halfway through the year, Virginia McCullough, a special education teacher, was assigned to provide Mark with three hours of instruction a week and to advise Mark's teacher and aide.

* * *

Mark engaged in daily episodes of loud screeching and other disruptive conduct such as hitting, pinching, kicking, biting, and removing his clothing. These outbursts not only required Diane Johnson and Leitner to calm Mark and redirect him, but also consumed the additional time necessary to get the rest of the children back on task after the distraction.

Despite these efforts, by the end of the year Mark's IEP team concluded that he was making no academic progress in the regular classroom. In Mark's May 1994 IEP, the team therefore proposed to place Mark in a class specifically structured for autistic children at Leesburg Elementary. Leesburg is a regular elementary school which houses the autism class in order to facilitate interaction between the autistic children and students who are not handicapped. The Leesburg class would have included five autistic students working with a special education teacher and at least one full-time aide. Under the May IEP, Mark would have received only academic instruction and speech in the self-contained classroom, while joining a regular class for art, music, physical education, library, and recess. The Leesburg program also would have permitted Mark to increase the portion of his instruction received in a regular education setting as he demonstrated an improved ability to handle it.

The Hartmanns refused to approve the IEP, claiming that it failed to comply with the mainstreaming provision of the IDEA, which states that "to the maximum extent appropriate," disabled children should be educated with children who are not handicapped. 20 U.S.C. § 1412(5)(B). The county initiated due process proceedings, and on December 14, 1994, the local hearing officer upheld the May 1994 IEP. She found that Mark's behavior was disruptive and that despite the "enthusiastic" efforts of the county, he had obtained no academic benefit from the regular education classroom. On May 3, 1995, the state review officer affirmed the decision, adopting both the hearing officer's findings and her legal analysis. The Hartmanns then challenged the hearing officer's decision in federal court.

* * *

The district court reversed the hearing officer's decision. The court rejected the administrative findings and concluded that Mark could receive significant educational benefit in a regular classroom and that "the Board simply did not take enough appropriate steps to try to include Mark in a regular class." The court made little of the testimony of Mark's Loudoun County instructors, and instead relied heavily on its reading of Mark's experience in Illinois and Montgomery County. While the hearing officer had addressed Mark's conduct in detail, the court stated that "[g]iven the strong presumption for inclusion under the IDEA, disruptive behavior should not be a significant factor in determining the appropriate educational placement for a disabled child." Loudoun County now appeals.

II.

The IDEA embodies important principles governing the relationship between local school authorities and a reviewing district court. Although section 1415(e)(2) provides district courts with authority to grant "appropriate" relief based on a preponderance of the evidence, 20 U.S.C. § 1415(e)(2), that section "is by no means an invitation to the courts to substitute their own notions of sound educational policy for those of the school authorities which they review." [*Rowley*]. Absent some statutory infraction, the task of education belongs to the educators who have been charged by society with that critical task. Likewise, federal courts must accord "due weight" to state administrative proceedings. *Id.* Administrative findings in an IDEA case "are entitled to be considered *prima facie* correct," and "the district court, if it is not going to follow them, is required to explain why it does not."

These principles reflect the IDEA's recognition that federal courts cannot run local schools. Local educators deserve latitude in determining the individualized education program most appropriate for a disabled child. The IDEA does not deprive these educators of the right to apply their professional judgment. . . .

In this same vein, the IDEA's mainstreaming provision establishes a presumption, not an inflexible federal mandate. Under its terms, disabled children are to be educated with children who are not handicapped only "to the maximum extent appropriate." 20 U.S.C. § 1412(5)(B). Section 1412(5)(B) explicitly states that mainstreaming is not appropriate "when the nature or severity of the disability is such that education in regular classes with the use of supplementary aids and services cannot be achieved satisfactorily." 20 U.S.C. § 1412(5)(B).

III.

The district court's ruling strayed generally from the aforementioned principles. It diverged in particular from our decision in *DeVries v. Fairfax County Sch. Bd.*, 882 F.2d 876 (4th Cir.1989). In *DeVries,* we held that mainstreaming is not required where (1) the disabled child would not receive an educational benefit from mainstreaming into a regular class; (2) any marginal benefit from mainstreaming would be significantly outweighed by benefits which could feasibly be obtained only in a separate instructional setting; or, (3) the disabled child is a disruptive force in a regular classroom setting. *Id.* at 879. Although the district court failed to mention *DeVries,* its opinion suggests that none of these three categories describes Mark's situation. The district court found that Mark could receive substantial educational benefit in a regular classroom, that his disruptive behavior was not sufficient to justify a more segregated instructional setting, and that the Leesburg program would not have been an appropriate placement. After careful examination of the record, however, we are forced to conclude that the district court's decision fails to account for the administrative findings and is not supported by the evidence based on a correct application of the law. In effect, the court simply substituted its own judgment regarding Mark's proper educational program for that of local school officials.

A.

In finding that Mark could receive an educational benefit in a regular classroom, the district court disregarded both the hearing officer's finding and the overwhelming evidence that Mark made no academic progress in the regular second grade classroom at Ashburn. Mark's teacher testified, for example, that he was unable to retain skills: "once we thought he mastered [a math skill] and we left it alone and went onto another concept, if we went back to review, it seemed that he had forgotten." She confessed, "I felt like he lost a year in my classroom." Other Loudoun County personnel testified to the same effect. His speech therapist, for instance, stated that "[t]he only gain that I saw him make was in the one to one setting." The supervisor for the county's program for autistic students likewise concluded, "I think there has been no progress academically in the inclusive settings;" "I think we're wasting his time." The hearing officer accordingly found that "Mark made no measurable academic progress attributable to his placement in the regular classroom."

* * *

The district court acknowledged the testimony of Mark's second grade teacher regarding his lack of progress, but asserted that the hearing officer's conclusions were erroneous because the officer failed to give due weight to the testimony of Cathy Thornton, Mark's private tutor during second grade, and to Mark's first grade experience in Illinois. To the contrary, the administrative decisions took careful note of both. The hearing officer fully credited Thornton's testimony, finding that Mark made progress with both her and his speech therapist. The officer went further, however, and observed that both the tutoring and speech instruction occurred in a one-to-one setting outside of the regular class. In light of Mark's failure to progress in the regular classroom, the officer drew the only reasonable inference from this evidence, namely that separate instruction was precisely what Mark needed to make educational progress. As to Mark's experience in Illinois, the state review officer explained that the Illinois assessment of Mark's capabilities was flawed:

> [I]t became clear during the course of the second grade that Mark's academic skills were not as advanced as the Illinois school system thought. Mark cannot read and cannot add, yet the Illinois teachers thought he was reading at first grade level and progressing in the first grade math workbook. . . . Mark apparently did not make the academic progress in first grade the records forwarded to Loudoun County from Illinois indicated. . . .

While the district court opinion references the hearing officer's decision, its failure to address the administrative findings noted above simply does not reflect the teachings of *Rowley* and *Doyle* that state proceedings must command considerable deference in federal courts.

The district court also relied heavily on Mark's subsequent performance in the Montgomery County schools during fourth grade. While Montgomery County personnel did make some conclusory statements asserting that Mark made progress, the evidence is inconclusive at best. The district court pointed to math skills Mark demonstrated at the end of fourth grade, for example, but Mark was pulled out of the regular class for math instruction, just as Loudoun County had recommended. Any progress he made in math therefore simply supports the conclusion that separate, one-on-one instruction is appropriate for Mark. Mark also continued to receive speech therapy one-on-one, and his special education teacher in Montgomery County admitted that the county had no reliable method for assessing Mark's reading ability.

Finally, the district court pointed to perceived improvement in Mark's social skills due to interaction with his non-disabled peers. Any such benefits, however, cannot outweigh his failure to progress academically in the regular classroom. The mainstreaming provision represents recognition of the value of having disabled children interact with non-handicapped students. The fact that the provision only creates a presumption, however, reflects a congressional judgment that receipt of such social benefits is ultimately a goal subordinate to the requirement that disabled children receive educational benefit. Here the evidence clearly supports the judgment of the local education officials and the administrative hearing officers that Mark's educational progress required significant instruction outside of the regular classroom setting.

B.

The district court attributed Mark's lack of progress in Loudoun County to the county's alleged failure to make reasonable efforts to accommodate him in the regular classroom. We interpret this as a ruling that the county failed to provide the supplementary aids and services contemplated by the IDEA's mainstreaming provision. 20 U.S.C. § 1412(5)(B).

The district court's conclusion is remarkable in light of the extensive measures taken on Mark's behalf. The hearing officer found that Loudoun personnel were "enthusiastic" about including Mark at Ashburn, a description fully supported by the record. The Ashburn principal deliberately reduced the size of Mark's class and ensured that it was composed of students who were more independent and had higher level skills. Mark's teacher was selected because of her excellent teaching abilities, and the county hired a full-time, one-on-one aide for Mark. Mark received a full hour of speech and language instruction daily. Frank Johnson, the supervisor of the county's program for autistic children, provided assistance in behavior management throughout the year. Halfway through the year, the school's efforts increased when Virginia McCullough began providing special education services directly to Mark as well as advising Mark's teacher and aide. Inclusion specialists Gail

Mayfield and Jamie Ruppmann consulted with the school during the fall, and Mark's teacher sought advice from other experts whose names were provided to her by the school or the Hartmanns. The teacher testified that she met constantly with Mark's aide, his speech therapist, the IEP team, and others to work on Mark's program—daily at the beginning of the year and at least twice a week throughout.

The district court nonetheless found the county's efforts insufficient. The court relied primarily on its conclusion that the Loudoun educators involved with Mark had inadequate training and experience to work with an autistic child. The court found the credentials of two groups to be lacking. Neither the special education professionals nor the regular education instructors were deemed properly qualified. The conclusion that Mark had inadequately trained personnel developing and implementing his program, however, is irreconcilable with either the law or the record.

As to special education personnel, the district court concedes that the individuals working with Mark during the first half of the year, Mary Kearney and Jamie Ruppmann, were fully competent to assist him. Kearney led Mark's IEP team, while Ruppmann provided consultation services. In addition to serving as the county Director of Special Education, Kearney had participated in the Virginia Systems Change Project, a two-year state program on mainstreaming which involved selected schools from across the state. Ruppmann is an experienced, highly qualified consultant.

During the second half of the year, Frank Johnson led the IEP team, and Virginia McCullough provided Mark with special education services. The district court rejected their qualifications, asserting, for example, that Johnson's credentials were clearly inadequate because they were inferior to those of Kearney and Ruppmann. However, in addition to serving as the supervisor of Loudoun County's program for autistic children, Johnson had a special education masters degree, did graduate work with an autistic child, worked directly with approximately ten autistic children as a teacher, and had attended special education courses and seminars relating to autism throughout his professional career. Both McCullough's early childhood degree program and her work in Loudoun County focused specifically on integrating children with disabilities into the regular classroom.

To dismiss Johnson's and McCullough's qualifications is to adopt exactly the sort of potential-maximizing standard rejected by the Supreme Court in *Rowley*. We think the Court's admonition that the IDEA does not require "the furnishing of every special service necessary to maximize each handicapped child's potential," *Rowley*, 458 U.S. at 199, 102 S.Ct. at 3047 encompasses the notion that the IDEA likewise does not require special education service providers to have every conceivable credential relevant to every child's disability. Not all school systems will have the resources to hire top-notch consultants, nor will every school have the good fortune to have personnel who were involved in a major state program related to the needs of every disabled child. We note that in Virginia, there is no certification for autism. Furthermore, at the time of the trial, Loudoun County had eleven autistic children in a total school population of approximately 20,000 students. In this light, Johnson's experience teaching ten autistic children was substantial. Johnson and McCullough were clearly qualified to work with Mark as special educators, even accepting the district court's assertion that Ruppmann and Kearney had better credentials.

The suggestion that the regular education instructors, Mark's teacher and aide, were not adequately qualified also does not survive close scrutiny. Diane Johnson was an experienced professional properly certified under state law, and Virginia law does not require teaching assistants to be certified. Furthermore, Johnson and Leitner both obtained special training to work with Mark. Both received in-service instruction and attended an outside seminar on inclusion of disabled children in the regular classroom. They also were trained in facilitated communication, a special communication method used with Mark in Illinois.

To demand more than this from regular education personnel would essentially require them to become special education teachers trained in the full panoply of disabilities that their students might have. Virginia law does not require this, nor does the IDEA. First, such a requirement would fall afoul of *Rowley*'s admonition that the IDEA does not guarantee the ideal educational opportunity for every disabled child. Furthermore, when the IDEA was passed, "Congress' intention was not that the Act displace the primacy of States in the field of education, but that States receive funds to assist them in extending their educational systems to the handicapped." The IDEA "expressly incorporates State educational standards." We can think of few steps that would do more to usurp state educational standards and policy than to have federal courts re-write state teaching certification requirements in the guise of applying the IDEA.

In sum, we conclude that Loudoun County's efforts on behalf of Mark were sufficient to satisfy the IDEA's mainstreaming directive.

C.

The district court also gave little or no weight to the disruptive effects of Mark's behavior in the classroom, stating that "[g]iven the strong presumption for inclusion under the IDEA, disruptive behavior should not be a significant factor in determining the appropriate educational placement for a disabled child." This statement simply ignores *DeVries*, where we specifically held that mainstreaming is inappropriate when "the handicapped child is a disruptive force in the non-segregated setting." 882 F.2d at 879. In this case, disruptive behavior was clearly an issue. The hearing officer summarized:

[Mark's] misbehaviors include continual vocalization, especially whining, screeching and crying when unhappy or frustrated, hitting, pinching, kicking, biting, sucking the leg of a chair, rolling on the floor, and removing his shoes and clothing. Mark is a big strong child who cannot be easily restrained when he engages in injurious behaviors such as hitting, kicking, pinching and biting. His continual vocalizations are distracting and make it difficult for other children to stay on task. When Jamie Ruppmann observed Mark in his classroom, she observed two instances of significant disruption, in which he threw himself on the floor. She noted that in each instance it took about five to eight minutes to get Mark settled down. His loud screeching outbursts, which occur daily, take the attention of the teacher and the aide to redirect him; these outbursts also take the other children off task and they then have to be redirected. Mark hits and pinches others several times a day.

While the hearing officer did not find Mark's disruptive behavior by itself to be dispositive, the attention she gave to Mark's conduct was entirely appropriate, indeed required, under *DeVries*.

* * *

IV.

This is not a case which either the local educational authorities or the reviewing administrative officers took lightly. We have sketched in great detail the efforts that Loudoun County made to provide Mark Hartmann with a suitable education. Furthermore, the administrative review process could not have been more thorough. The hearing officer heard testimony from eighteen witnesses over a two month period and made detailed factual findings regarding all aspects of Mark's educational experience. The officer's analysis carefully incorporated those findings and specifically addressed the evidence the Hartmanns presented in support of their position. The district court, however, set all this extensive effort and review at nought. The court failed to mention, let alone discuss, critical administrative findings inconsistent with its conclusions. While making much of the credentials and credibility of witnesses endorsing full inclusion, the court gave little or no attention to the testimony of Loudoun professionals. In some instances the court, without listening to local educators, discounted their views despite the fact that the hearing officer had found them credible. One Loudoun official was dismissed outright as "a philosophical opponent of inclusion" for daring to state that he saw no evidence that Mark had progressed in the regular classroom.

The IDEA encourages mainstreaming, but only to the extent that it does not prevent a child from receiving educational benefit. The evidence in this case demonstrates that Mark Hartmann was not making academic progress in a regular education classroom despite the provision of adequate supplementary aids and services. Loudoun County properly proposed to place Mark in a partially mainstreamed program which would have addressed the academic deficiencies of his full inclusion program while permitting him to interact with nonhandicapped students to the greatest extent possible. This professional judgment by local educators was deserving of respect. The approval of this educational approach by the local and state administrative officers likewise deserved a deference from the district court which it failed to receive. In rejecting reasonable pedagogical choices and disregarding well-supported administrative findings, the district court assumed an educational mantle which the IDEA did not confer. Accordingly, the judgment must be reversed, and the case remanded with directions to dismiss it.

NOTES AND QUESTIONS

1. *The integration presumption.* Why do you think mainstreaming is such an important goal of the IDEA? What are some of the benefits of integrating students with disabilities? These two cases involved parents wanting to mainstream their children and the school districts refusing. But what if the parents are *against* mainstreaming because they believe that a specialized program would be more effective for their child? How should courts weigh the parents' interests in *not* mainstreaming their children against the presumption in favor of integration? For an interesting discussion of the mainstreaming debate, see Ruth Colker, *The Disability Integration Presumption: Thirty Years Later*, 154 U. PA. L. REV. 789 (2006).

2. *Comparing* Rachel H. *and* Hartmann. What do you think accounts for the different result in these two cases? The courts in both cases spend some time discussing the educational benefits these students receive from being in the regular classroom, and Rachel certainly seems to derive more educational benefit than Mark. Is that what causes the difference in results? Or do you think the main difference is the level of disruption caused by these two students? Rachel appears to cause virtually no disruption whereas Mark's outbursts in class are significantly disruptive. Finally, do you think that the reaction of the students' teachers influenced the courts' decisions? For instance, Rachel's teacher seemed to be exceptionally skilled at getting the most out of Rachel while still managing the rest of the classroom. If Rachel had a less talented and dedicated teacher, might the result in the case have been different? And if so, is the statute and its procedural mechanism working as intended?

3. *Effect on other students.* Just as in the employment context where one employee's right to a reasonable accommodation might cause burdens on other employees, integrating students with disabilities into the regular classroom can sometimes affect the learning experience of other students. The court in *Hartmann* considered Mark's negative effect on other students and the classroom experience to be very significant in determining that Mark should not be mainstreamed. Although we understand why the Hartmanns want what

they believe to be best for their son, can you also imagine how you might feel if your child was being hit, pinched, or bitten by Mark? How *should* courts balance the interests of students with disabilities and non-disabled students when those interests conflict? Does the court give adequate attention to this potential conflict between disabled students and their non-disabled classmates?

c.   Related Services

CEDAR RAPIDS COMMUNITY SCHOOL DISTRICT V. GARRET F.

526 U.S. 66, 119 S.Ct. 992 (1999)

JUSTICE STEVENS delivered the opinion of the Court.

The Individuals with Disabilities Education Act (IDEA), 84 Stat. 175, as amended, was enacted, in part, "to assure that all children with disabilities have available to them . . . a free appropriate public education which emphasizes special education and related services designed to meet their unique needs." 20 U.S.C. § 1400(c). Consistent with this purpose, the IDEA authorizes federal financial assistance to States that agree to provide disabled children with special education and "related services." The question presented in this case is whether the definition of "related services" in § 1401(a)(17)[1] requires a public school district in a participating State to provide a ventilator-dependent student with certain nursing services during school hours.

I

Respondent Garret F. is a friendly, creative, and intelligent young man. When Garret was four years old, his spinal column was severed in a motorcycle accident. Though paralyzed from the neck down, his mental capacities were unaffected. He is able to speak, to control his motorized wheelchair through use of a puff and suck straw, and to operate a computer with a device that responds to head movements. Garret is currently a student in the Cedar Rapids Community School District (District), he attends regular classes in a typical school program, and his academic performance has been a success. Garret is, however, ventilator dependent,[2]

---

[1] "The term 'related services' means transportation, and such developmental, corrective, and other supportive services (including speech pathology and audiology, psychological services, physical and occupational therapy, recreation, including therapeutic recreation, social work services, counseling services, including rehabilitation counseling, and medical services, except that such medical services shall be for diagnostic and evaluation purposes only) as may be required to assist a child with a disability to benefit from special education, and includes the early identification and assessment of disabling conditions in children."

20 U.S.C. § 1401(a)(17). . . .

[2] In his report in this case, the Administrative Law Judge explained: "Being ventilator dependent means that [Garret] breathes only with external aids, usually an electric ventilator,

and therefore requires a responsible individual nearby to attend to certain physical needs while he is in school.[3]

During Garret's early years at school his family provided for his physical care during the schoolday. When he was in kindergarten, his 18-year-old aunt attended him; in the next four years, his family used settlement proceeds they received after the accident, their insurance, and other resources to employ a licensed practical nurse. In 1993, Garret's mother requested the District to accept financial responsibility for the health care services that Garret requires during the schoolday. The District denied the request, believing that it was not legally obligated to provide continuous one-on-one nursing services.

Relying on both the IDEA and Iowa law, Garret's mother requested a hearing before the Iowa Department of Education. An Administrative Law Judge (ALJ) received extensive evidence concerning Garret's special needs, the District's treatment of other disabled students, and the assistance provided to other ventilator-dependent children in other parts of the country. In his 47-page report, the ALJ found that the District has about 17,500 students, of whom approximately 2,200 need some form of special education or special services. Although Garret is the only ventilator-dependent student in the District, most of the health care services that he needs are already provided for some other students. "The primary difference between Garret's situation and that of other students is his dependency on his ventilator for life support." . . .

[T]he ALJ explained that applicable federal regulations distinguish between "school health services," which are provided by a "qualified school nurse or other qualified person," and "medical services," which are provided by a licensed physician. See 34 C.F.R. §§ 300.16(a), (b)(4), (b)(11) (1998). The District must provide the former, but need not provide the latter (except, of course, those "medical services" that are for diagnostic or evaluation purposes, 20 U.S.C. § 1401(a)(17)). . . . The ALJ thus concluded that the IDEA required the District to bear financial responsibility for all of the services in dispute, including continuous nursing services.

---

and occasionally by someone else's manual pumping of an air bag attached to his tracheotomy tube when the ventilator is being maintained. This later procedure is called ambu bagging."

[3] "He needs assistance with urinary bladder catheterization once a day, the suctioning of his tracheotomy tube as needed, but at least once every six hours, with food and drink at lunchtime, in getting into a reclining position for five minutes of each hour, and ambu bagging occasionally as needed when the ventilator is checked for proper functioning. He also needs assistance from someone familiar with his ventilator in the event there is a malfunction or electrical problem, and someone who can perform emergency procedures in the event he experiences autonomic hyperreflexia. Autonomic hyperreflexia is an uncontrolled visceral reaction to anxiety or a full bladder. Blood pressure increases, heart rate increases, and flushing and sweating may occur. Garret has not experienced autonomic hyperreflexia frequently in recent years, and it has usually been alleviated by catheterization. He has not ever experienced autonomic hyperreflexia at school. Garret is capable of communicating his needs orally or in another fashion so long as he has not been rendered unable to do so by an extended lack of oxygen."

The District challenged the ALJ's decision in Federal District Court, but that court approved the ALJ's IDEA ruling and granted summary judgment against the District. The Court of Appeals affirmed. . . . The Court of Appeals read our opinion in *Irving Independent School Dist. v. Tatro,* 468 U.S. 883, 104 S.Ct. 3371 (1984), to provide a two-step analysis of the "related services" definition in § 1401(a)(17)—asking first, whether the requested services are included within the phrase "supportive services"; and second, whether the services are excluded as "medical services." The Court of Appeals succinctly answered both questions in Garret's favor. The Court found the first step plainly satisfied, since Garret cannot attend school unless the requested services are available during the schoolday. As to the second step, the court reasoned that *Tatro* "established a bright-line test: the services of a physician (other than for diagnostic and evaluation purposes) are subject to the medical services exclusion, but services that can be provided in the school setting by a nurse or qualified layperson are not."

In its petition for certiorari, the District challenged only the second step of the Court of Appeals' analysis. The District pointed out that some federal courts have not asked whether the requested health services must be delivered by a physician, but instead have applied a multifactor test that considers, generally speaking, the nature and extent of the services at issue. See, *e.g., Neely v. Rutherford County School,* 68 F.3d 965, 972–973 (C.A.6 1995); *Detsel v. Board of Ed. of Auburn Enlarged City School Dist.,* 820 F.2d 587, 588 (CA2 1987) *(per curiam).* We granted the District's petition to resolve this conflict.

II

The District contends that § 1401(a)(17) does not require it to provide Garret with "continuous one-on-one nursing services" during the schoolday, even though Garret cannot remain in school without such care. However, the IDEA's definition of "related services," our decision in *Irving Independent School Dist. v. Tatro,* 468 U.S. 883, 104 S.Ct. 3371 (1984), and the overall statutory scheme all support the decision of the Court of Appeals.

The text of the "related services" definition, see n. 1, *supra,* broadly encompasses those supportive services that "may be required to assist a child with a disability to benefit from special education." As we have already noted, the District does not challenge the Court of Appeals' conclusion that the in-school services at issue are within the covered category of "supportive services." As a general matter, services that enable a disabled child to remain in school during the day provide the student with "the meaningful access to education that Congress envisioned." *Tatro,* 468 U.S., at 891, 104 S.Ct. 3371.

This general definition of "related services" is illuminated by a parenthetical phrase listing examples of particular services that are included within the statute's coverage. § 1401(a)(17). "[M]edical services" are enumerated in this list, but such services are limited to those that are "for diagnostic and evaluation purposes." The statute does not contain a more specific definition of the "medical services" that are excepted from the coverage of § 1401(a)(17).

The scope of the "medical services" exclusion is not a matter of first impression in this Court. In *Tatro* we concluded that the Secretary of Education had reasonably determined that the term "medical services" referred only to services that must be performed by a physician, and not to school health services. 468 U.S., at 892–894, 104 S.Ct. 3371. Accordingly, we held that a specific form of health care (clean intermittent catheterization) that is often, though not always, performed by a nurse is not an excluded medical service. We referenced the likely cost of the services and the competence of school staff as justifications for drawing a line between physician and other services, but our endorsement of that line was unmistakable. It is thus settled that the phrase "medical services" in § 1401(a)(17) does not embrace all forms of care that might loosely be described as "medical" in other contexts, such as a claim for an income tax deduction.

The District does not ask us to define the term so broadly. Indeed, the District does not argue that any of the items of care that Garret needs, considered individually, could be excluded from the scope of 20 U.S.C. § 1401(a)(17). It could not make such an argument, considering that one of the services Garret needs (catheterization) was at issue in *Tatro,* and the others may be provided competently by a school nurse or other trained personnel. As the ALJ concluded, most of the requested services are already provided by the District to other students, and the in-school care necessitated by Garret's ventilator dependency does not demand the training, knowledge, and judgment of a licensed physician. While more extensive, the in-school services Garret needs are no more "medical" than was the care sought in *Tatro.*

Instead, the District points to the combined and continuous character of the required care, and proposes a test under which the outcome in any particular case would "depend upon a series of factors, such as [1] whether the care is continuous or intermittent, [2] whether existing school health personnel can provide the service, [3] the cost of the service, and [4] the potential consequences if the service is not properly performed."

The District's multifactor test is not supported by any recognized source of legal authority. The proposed factors can be found in neither the text of the statute nor the regulations that we upheld in *Tatro.* Moreover, the District offers no explanation why these characteristics make one service any more "medical" than another. The continuous character of certain services associated with Garret's ventilator dependency has no apparent relationship to "medical" services, much less a relationship of equivalence.

Continuous services may be more costly and may require additional school personnel, but they are not thereby more "medical." Whatever its imperfections, a rule that limits the medical services exemption to physician services is unquestionably a reasonable and generally workable interpretation of the statute. Absent an elaboration of the statutory terms plainly more convincing than that which we reviewed in *Tatro,* there is no good reason to depart from settled law.

Finally, the District raises broader concerns about the financial burden that it must bear to provide the services that Garret needs to stay in school. The problem for the District in providing these services is not that its staff cannot be trained to deliver them; the problem, the District contends, is that the existing school health staff cannot meet all of their responsibilities and provide for Garret at the same time. Through its multifactor test, the District seeks to establish a kind of undue-burden exemption primarily based on the cost of the requested services. The first two factors can be seen as examples of cost-based distinctions: Intermittent care is often less expensive than continuous care, and the use of existing personnel is cheaper than hiring additional employees. The third factor-the cost of the service-would then encompass the first two. The relevance of the fourth factor is likewise related to cost because extra care may be necessary if potential consequences are especially serious.

The District may have legitimate financial concerns, but our role in this dispute is to interpret existing law. Defining "related services" in a manner that *accommodates* the cost concerns Congress may have had, is altogether different from using cost *itself* as the definition. Given that § 1401(a)(17) does not employ cost in its definition of "related services" or excluded "medical services," accepting the District's cost-based standard as the sole test for determining the scope of the provision would require us to engage in judicial lawmaking without any guidance from Congress. It would also create some tension with the purposes of the IDEA. The statute may not require public schools to maximize the potential of disabled students commensurate with the opportunities provided to other children, see *Rowley,* 458 U.S., at 200, 102 S.Ct. 3034; and the potential financial burdens imposed on participating States may be relevant to arriving at a sensible construction of the IDEA, see *Tatro,* 468 U.S., at 892, 104 S.Ct. 3371. But Congress intended "to open the door of public education" to all qualified children and "require[d] participating States to educate handicapped children with nonhandicapped children whenever possible." *Rowley,* 458 U.S., at 192, 202, 102 S.Ct. 3034.

This case is about whether meaningful access to the public schools will be assured, not the level of education that a school must finance once access is attained. It is undisputed that the services at issue must be provided if Garret is to remain in school. Under the statute, our precedent, and the purposes of the IDEA, the District must fund such "related services" in order to help guarantee that students like Garret are integrated into the public schools.

The judgment of the Court of Appeals is accordingly

Affirmed.

JUSTICE THOMAS, with whom JUSTICE KENNEDY joins, dissenting.

The majority, relying heavily on our decision in *Irving Independent School Dist. v. Tatro,* 468 U.S. 883, 104 S.Ct. 3371 (1984), concludes that the Individuals with Disabilities Education Act (IDEA), 20 U.S.C. § 1400 *et seq.,* requires a public school district to fund continuous, one-on-one nursing care for disabled children. Because *Tatro* cannot be squared with the text of IDEA, the Court should not adhere to it in this case. Even assuming that *Tatro* was correct in the first instance, the majority's extension of it is unwarranted and ignores the constitutionally mandated rules of construction applicable to legislation enacted pursuant to Congress' spending power.

I

As the majority recounts, IDEA authorizes the provision of federal financial assistance to States that agree to provide, *inter alia,* "special education and related services" for disabled children. § 1401(a)(18). In *Tatro, supra,* we held that this provision of IDEA required a school district to provide clean intermittent catheterization to a disabled child several times a day. In so holding, we relied on Department of Education regulations, which we concluded had reasonably interpreted IDEA's definition of "related services" to require school districts in participating States to provide "school nursing services" (of which we assumed catheterization was a subcategory) but not "services of a physician." *Id.,* at 892–893, 104 S.Ct. 3371. This holding is contrary to the plain text of IDEA, and its reliance on the Department of Education's regulations was misplaced.

A

Before we consider whether deference to an agency regulation is appropriate, "we first ask whether Congress has 'directly spoken to the precise question at issue. If the intent of Congress is clear, that is the end of the matter; for the court, as well as the agency, must give effect to the unambiguously expressed intent of Congress.'" *National Credit Union Admin. v. First Nat. Bank & Trust Co.,* 522 U.S. 479, 499–500, 118 S.Ct. 927 (1998) (quoting *Chevron U.S.A. Inc. v. Natural Resources Defense Council, Inc.,* 467 U.S. 837, 842–843, 104 S.Ct. 2778 (1984)).

Unfortunately, the Court in *Tatro* failed to consider this necessary antecedent question before turning to the Department of Education's regulations implementing IDEA's related services provision. The Court instead began "with the regulations of the Department of Education, which," it said, "are entitled to deference." *Tatro, supra,* at 891–892, 104 S.Ct. 3371. The Court need not have looked beyond the text of IDEA, which expressly indicates that school districts are not required to provide medical services, except for diagnostic and evaluation purposes. 20 U.S.C. § 1401(a)(17). The majority asserts that *Tatro* precludes reading the term "medical services" to include "all forms of care that might loosely be described as 'medical.'" The majority does not explain, however, why "services" that are "medical" in nature are not "medical services." Not only is the definition that the majority rejects consistent with other uses of the term in federal law, it also avoids the anomalous result of holding that the services at issue in *Tatro* (as well as in this case), while not "medical services," would nonetheless qualify as medical care for federal income tax purposes.

The primary problem with *Tatro,* and the majority's reliance on it today, is that the Court focused on the provider of the services rather than the services themselves. We do not typically think that automotive services are limited to those provided by a mechanic, for example. Rather, anything done to repair or service a car, no matter who does the work, is thought to fall into that category. Similarly, the term "food service" is not generally thought to be limited to work performed by a chef. The term "medical" similarly does not support *Tatro*'s provider-specific approach, but encompasses services that are "of, *relating to, or concerned with* physicians *or* with the practice of medicine." See Webster's Third New International Dictionary 1402 (1986).

IDEA's structure and purpose reinforce this textual interpretation. Congress enacted IDEA to increase the *educational* opportunities available to disabled children, not to provide medical care for them. As such, where Congress decided to require a supportive service—including speech pathology, occupational therapy, and audiology—that appears "medical" in nature, it took care to do so explicitly. See § 1401(a)(17). Congress specified these services precisely because it recognized that they would otherwise fall under the broad "medical services" exclusion. Indeed, when it crafted the definition of related services, Congress could have, but chose not to, include "nursing services" in this list.

* * *

II

Assuming that *Tatro* was correctly decided in the first instance, it does not control the outcome of this case. Because IDEA was enacted pursuant to Congress' spending power, *Rowley, supra,* at 190, n. 11, 102 S.Ct. 3034, our analysis of the statute in this case is governed by special rules of construction. We have repeatedly emphasized that, when Congress places conditions on the receipt of federal funds, "it must do so unambiguously." *Pennhurst State School and Hospital v. Halderman,* 451 U.S. 1, 17, 101

S.Ct. 1531 (1981). This is because a law that "condition[s] an offer of federal funding on a promise by the recipient . . . amounts essentially to a contract between the Government and the recipient of funds." *Gebser v. Lago Vista Independent School Dist.*, 524 U.S. 274, 286, 118 S.Ct. 1989 (1998). As such, "[t]he legitimacy of Congress' power to legislate under the spending power . . . rests on whether the State voluntarily and knowingly accepts the terms of the 'contract.' There can, of course, be no knowing acceptance if a State is unaware of the conditions or is unable to ascertain what is expected of it." *Pennhurst, supra,* at 17, 101 S.Ct. 1531. It follows that we must interpret Spending Clause legislation narrowly, in order to avoid saddling the States with obligations that they did not anticipate.

The majority's approach in this case turns this Spending Clause presumption on its head. We have held that, in enacting IDEA, Congress wished to require "States to educate handicapped children with nonhandicapped children whenever possible," *Rowley, supra,* at 202, 102 S.Ct. 3034. Congress, however, also took steps to limit the fiscal burdens that States must bear in attempting to achieve this laudable goal. These steps include requiring States to provide an education that is only "appropriate" rather than requiring them to maximize the potential of disabled students, see 20 U.S.C. § 1400(c); *Rowley, supra,* at 200, 102 S.Ct. 3034, recognizing that integration into the public school environment is not always possible, see § 1412(5), and clarifying that, with a few exceptions, public schools need not provide "medical services" for disabled students, §§ 1401(a)(17) and (18).

For this reason, we have previously recognized that Congress did not intend to "impos[e] upon the States a burden of unspecified proportions and weight" in enacting IDEA. *Rowley, supra,* at 190, n. 11, 102 S.Ct. 3034. These federalism concerns require us to interpret IDEA's related services provision, consistent with *Tatro,* as follows: Department of Education regulations require districts to provide disabled children with health-related services that school nurses can perform as part of their normal duties. This reading of *Tatro,* although less broad than the majority's, is equally plausible and certainly more consistent with our obligation to interpret Spending Clause legislation narrowly. . . .

Unlike clean intermittent catheterization, however, a school nurse cannot provide the services that respondent requires and continue to perform her normal duties. To the contrary, because respondent requires continuous, one-on-one care throughout the entire schoolday, all agree that the district must hire an additional employee to attend solely to respondent. This will cost a minimum of $18,000 per year. Although the majority recognizes this fact, it nonetheless concludes that the "more extensive" nature of the services that respondent needs is irrelevant to the question whether those services fall under the medical services exclusion. This approach disregards the constitutionally mandated principles of construction applicable to Spending Clause legislation and blindsides unwary States with fiscal obligations that they could not have anticipated.

For the foregoing reasons, I respectfully dissent.

NOTES AND QUESTIONS

1.   *Defining "medical services."* The Court in *Garret F.* was following the rule announced in *Irving Independent School Dist. v. Tatro,* where the Court had concluded that the "Secretary of Education had reasonably determined that the term 'medical services' referred only to services that must be performed by a physician, and not to school health services." 468 U.S. at 892–94, 104 S.Ct. 3371. Do you think that was a reasonable line for the Secretary of Education to draw? If not, do you agree with the majority that it should follow the *Tatro* precedent anyway for *stare decisis* purposes? Or does the dissent have the better argument?

2.   *Other exclusions from "related services."* As the Court stated in *Garret F.* and *Tatro,* excluded medical services are services that must be performed by a physician (other than services for evaluation and diagnostic purposes). One court held that long-term psychiatric care is excluded as a "related service" even though the services received at the institution are not necessarily always (or even often) provided by a physician. *See* Mary T. v. School Dist. of Philadelphia, 575 F.3d 235, 248 (3d Cir. 2009). The court reasoned that, unlike the *Garret* case, the services received by the student did not allow her to remain in school. *See also* Butler v. Evans, 225 F.3d 887, 894–95 (7th Cir. 2000) (stating that the school district was not required to reimburse parents of a child with a disability for the child's hospitalization for psychiatric care).

3.   *Should there be an undue hardship defense for "related services"?* The dissent points out that the expense for Garret's services would be about $18,000 per year. Is that an unreasonably high expense to place on a school district? Is it odd to you that the school district in *Garret F* has to pay for one-on-one, continuous nursing services for Garret, but the school district in *Rowley* does not have to pay for Rowley to have a sign language interpreter, which would have cost about $15,000 per year? *See* Lou Ann Walker, *Though Deaf, Amy Rowley Is a Good Student—Too Good, Says the Supreme Court,* PEOPLE, July 19, 1982, http://www.people.com/people/archive/article/0,,200826 75,00.html (providing the cost of the interpreter). Can the answer to this question be found in the access/content distinction explored in Chapter 5?

d.   Discipline/Stay-Put Provision

HONIG V. DOE
484 U.S. 305, 108 S.Ct. 592 (1988)

JUSTICE BRENNAN delivered the opinion of the Court.

As a condition of federal financial assistance, the Education of the Handicapped Act requires States to ensure a "free appropriate public education" for all disabled children within their jurisdictions. In aid of this goal, the Act establishes a comprehensive system of procedural safeguards designed to ensure parental participation in decisions concerning the education of their disabled children and to provide administrative and judicial review of any decisions with which those parents disagree. Among these safeguards is the so-called "stay-put" provision, which directs that a disabled child "shall remain in [his or her] then current educational placement" pending completion of any review proceedings, unless the parents and state or local educational agencies otherwise agree. 20 U.S.C. § 1415(e)(3). Today we must decide whether, in the face of this statutory proscription, state or local school authorities may nevertheless unilaterally exclude disabled children from the classroom for dangerous or disruptive conduct growing out of their disabilities. In addition, we are called upon to decide whether a district court may, in the exercise of its equitable powers, order a State to provide educational services directly to a disabled child when the local agency fails to do so.

I

In the Education of the Handicapped Act (EHA or the Act), 20 U.S.C. § 1400 *et seq.,* Congress sought "to assure that all handicapped children have available to them . . . a free appropriate public education which emphasizes special education and related services designed to meet their unique needs, [and] to assure that the rights of handicapped children and their parents or guardians are protected." § 1400(c). When the law was passed in 1975, Congress had before it ample evidence that such legislative assurances were sorely needed: 21 years after this Court declared education to be "perhaps the most important function of state and local governments," *Brown v. Board of Education,* 347 U.S. 483, 493, 74 S.Ct. 686, 691 (1954), congressional studies revealed that better than half of the Nation's 8 million disabled children were not receiving appropriate educational services. § 1400(b)(3). Indeed, one out of every eight of these children was excluded from the public school system altogether, § 1400(b)(4); many others were simply "warehoused" in special classes or were neglectfully shepherded through the system until they were old enough to drop out. Among the most poorly served of disabled students were emotionally disturbed children: Congressional statistics revealed that for the school year immediately preceding passage of the Act, the educational needs of 82 percent of all children with emotional disabilities went unmet.

Although these educational failings resulted in part from funding constraints, Congress recognized that the problem reflected more than a lack of financial resources at the state and local levels. Two federal-court decisions, which the Senate Report characterized as "landmark," demonstrated that many disabled children were excluded pursuant to state statutes or local rules and policies, typically without any consultation with, or even notice to, their parents. See *Mills v. Board of Education of District of Columbia,* 348 F.Supp. 866 (DC 1972); *Pennsylvania Assn. for Retarded Children v. Pennsylvania,* 334 F.Supp. 1257 (ED Pa.1971), and 343 F.Supp. 279 (1972) (*PARC*). Indeed, by the time of the EHA's enactment, parents had brought legal challenges to similar exclusionary practices in 27 other States.

In responding to these problems, Congress did not content itself with passage of a simple funding statute. Rather, the EHA confers upon disabled students an enforceable substantive right to public education in participating States, see *Board of Education of Hendrick Hudson Central School Dist. v. Rowley,* 458 U.S. 176, 102 S.Ct. 3034 (1982), and conditions federal financial assistance upon a State's compliance with the substantive and procedural goals of the Act. Accordingly, States seeking to qualify for federal funds must develop policies assuring all disabled children the "right to a free appropriate public education," and must file with the Secretary of Education formal plans mapping out in detail the programs, procedures, and timetables under which they will effectuate these policies. 20 U.S.C. §§ 1412(1), 1413(a). Such plans must assure that, "to the maximum extent appropriate," States will "mainstream" disabled children, *i.e.,* that they will educate them with children who are not disabled, and that they will segregate or otherwise remove such children from the regular classroom setting "only when the nature or severity of the handicap is such that education in regular classes ... cannot be achieved satisfactorily." § 1412(5).

The primary vehicle for implementing these congressional goals is the "individualized educational program" (IEP), which the EHA mandates for each disabled child. Prepared at meetings between a representative of the local school district, the child's teacher, the parents or guardians, and, whenever appropriate, the disabled child, the IEP sets out the child's present educational performance, establishes annual and short-term objectives for improvements in that performance, and describes the specially designed instruction and services that will enable the child to meet those objectives. § 1401(19). The IEP must be reviewed and, where necessary, revised at least once a year in order to ensure that local agencies tailor the statutorily required "free appropriate public education" to each child's unique needs. § 1414(a)(5).

Envisioning the IEP as the centerpiece of the statute's education delivery system for disabled children, and aware that schools had all too often denied such children appropriate educations without in any way consulting their parents, Congress repeatedly emphasized throughout the Act the importance and indeed the necessity of parental participation in both the development of the IEP and any subsequent assessments of its effectiveness. Accordingly, the Act establishes various procedural safeguards that guarantee parents both an opportunity for meaningful input into all decisions affecting their child's education and the right to seek review of any decisions they think inappropriate. These safeguards include the right to examine all relevant records pertaining to the identification, evaluation, and educational placement of their child; prior written notice whenever the responsible educational agency proposes (or refuses) to change the child's placement or program; an opportunity to present complaints concerning any aspect of the local agency's provision of a free appropriate public education; and an opportunity for "an impartial due process hearing" with respect to any such complaints. §§ 1415(b)(1), (2).

At the conclusion of any such hearing, both the parents and the local educational agency may seek further administrative review and, where that proves unsatisfactory, may file a civil action in any state or federal court. §§ 1415(c), (e)(2). In addition to reviewing the administrative record, courts are empowered to take additional evidence at the request of either party and to "grant such relief as [they] determine[ ] is appropriate." § 1415(e)(2). The "stay-put" provision at issue in this case governs the placement of a child while these often lengthy review procedures run their course. It directs that:

> "During the pendency of any proceedings conducted pursuant to [§ 1415], unless the State or local educational agency and the parents or guardian otherwise agree, the child shall remain in the then current educational placement of such child...." § 1415(e)(3).

The present dispute grows out of the efforts of certain officials of the San Francisco Unified School District (SFUSD) to expel two emotionally disturbed children from school indefinitely for violent and disruptive conduct related to their disabilities. In November 1980, respondent John Doe assaulted another student at the Louise Lombard School, a developmental center for disabled children. Doe's April 1980 IEP identified him as a socially and physically awkward 17-year-old who experienced considerable difficulty controlling his impulses and anger. Among the goals set out in his IEP was "[i]mprovement in [his] ability to relate to [his] peers [and to] cope with frustrating situations without resorting to aggressive acts." Frustrating situations, however, were an unfortunately prominent feature of Doe's school career: physical abnormalities, speech difficulties, and poor grooming habits had made him the target of teasing and ridicule as early as the first grade; his 1980 IEP reflected his continuing difficulties with peers, noting that his social skills had deteriorated and that he could tolerate only minor frustration before exploding.

On November 6, 1980, Doe responded to the taunts of a fellow student in precisely the explosive manner anticipated by his IEP: he choked the student with sufficient force to leave abrasions on the child's neck, and kicked out a school window while being escorted to the principal's office afterwards. Doe admitted his misconduct and the school subsequently suspended him for five days. Thereafter, his principal referred the matter to the SFUSD Student Placement Committee (SPC or Committee) with the recommendation that Doe be expelled. On the day the suspension was to end, the SPC notified Doe's mother that it was proposing to exclude her child permanently from SFUSD and was therefore extending his suspension until such time as the expulsion proceedings were completed. The Committee further advised her that she was entitled to attend the November 25 hearing at which it planned to discuss the proposed expulsion.

After unsuccessfully protesting these actions by letter, Doe brought this suit against a host of local school officials and the State Superintendent of Public Instructions. Alleging that the suspension and proposed expulsion violated the EHA, he sought a temporary restraining order canceling the SPC hearing and requiring school officials to convene an IEP meeting. The District Judge granted the requested injunctive relief and further ordered defendants to provide home tutoring for Doe on an interim basis; shortly thereafter, she issued a preliminary injunction directing defendants to return Doe to his then current educational placement at Louise Lombard School pending completion of the IEP review process. Doe reentered school on December 15, 5 1/2 weeks, and 24 school-days, after his initial suspension.

Respondent Jack Smith was identified as an emotionally disturbed child by the time he entered the second grade in 1976. School records prepared that year indicated that he was unable "to control verbal or physical outburst[s]" and exhibited a "[s]evere disturbance in relationships with peers and adults." Further evaluations subsequently revealed that he had been physically and emotionally abused as an infant and young child and that, despite above average intelligence, he experienced academic and social difficulties as a result of extreme hyperactivity and low self-esteem. Of particular concern was Smith's propensity for verbal hostility; one evaluator noted that the child reacted to stress by "attempt [ing] to cover his feelings of low self worth through aggressive behavior[,] . . . primarily verbal provocations."

Based on these evaluations, SFUSD placed Smith in a learning center for emotionally disturbed children. His grandparents, however, believed that his needs would be better served in the public school setting and, in September 1979, the school district acceded to their requests and enrolled him at A.P. Giannini Middle School. His February 1980 IEP recommended placement in a Learning Disability Group, stressing the need for close supervision and a highly structured environment. Like earlier evaluations, the February 1980 IEP noted that Smith was easily distracted, impulsive, and anxious; it therefore proposed a half-day schedule and suggested that the placement be undertaken on a trial basis.

At the beginning of the next school year, Smith was assigned to a full-day program; almost immediately thereafter he began misbehaving. School officials met twice with his grandparents in October 1980 to discuss returning him to a half-day program; although the grandparents agreed to the reduction, they apparently were never apprised of their right to challenge the decision through EHA procedures. The school officials also warned them that if the child continued his disruptive behavior—which included stealing, extorting money from fellow students, and making sexual comments to female classmates—they would seek to expel him. On November 14, they made good on this threat, suspending Smith for five days after he made further lewd comments. His principal referred the matter to the SPC, which recommended exclusion from SFUSD. As it did in John Doe's case, the Committee scheduled a hearing and extended the suspension indefinitely pending a final disposition in the matter. On November 28, Smith's counsel protested these actions on grounds essentially identical to those raised by Doe, and the SPC agreed to cancel the hearing and to return Smith to a half-day program at A.P. Giannini or to provide home tutoring. Smith's grandparents chose the latter option and the school began home instruction on December 10; on January 6, 1981, an IEP team convened to discuss alternative placements.

After learning of Doe's action, Smith sought and obtained leave to intervene in the suit. The District Court subsequently entered summary judgment in favor of respondents on their EHA claims and issued a permanent injunction. In a series of decisions, the District Judge found that the proposed expulsions and indefinite suspensions of respondents for conduct attributable to their disabilities deprived them of their congressionally mandated right to a free appropriate public education, as well as their right to have that education provided in accordance with the procedures set out in the EHA. The District Judge therefore permanently enjoined the school district from taking any disciplinary action other than a 2- or 5-day suspension against any disabled child for disability-related misconduct, or from effecting any other change in the educational placement of any such child without parental consent pending completion of any EHA proceedings. In addition, the judge barred the State from authorizing unilateral placement changes and directed it to establish an EHA compliance-monitoring system or, alternatively, to enact guidelines governing local school responses to disability-related misconduct. Finally, the judge ordered the State to provide services directly to disabled children when, in any individual case, the State determined that the local educational agency was unable or unwilling to do so.

On appeal, the Court of Appeals for the Ninth Circuit affirmed the orders with slight modifications. *Doe v. Maher*, 793 F.2d 1470 (1986). Agreeing with the District Court that an indefinite suspension in aid of expulsion constitutes a prohibited "change in placement" under § 1415(e)(3), the Court of Appeals held that the stay-put provision admitted of no "dangerousness" exception and that the statute therefore rendered invalid those provisions of the California Education Code permitting the indefinite suspension or expulsion of disabled children for misconduct arising out of their disabilities. The court concluded, however, that fixed suspensions of up to 30 schooldays did not fall within the reach of § 1415(e)(3), and therefore upheld recent amendments to the state Education Code authorizing such suspensions. Lastly, the court affirmed that portion of the injunction requiring the State to provide services directly to a disabled child when the local educational agency fails to do so.

Petitioner Bill Honig, California Superintendent of Public Instruction, sought review in this Court, claiming that the Court of Appeals' construction of the stay-put provision conflicted with that of several other Courts of Appeals which had recognized a dangerousness exception, compare *Doe v. Maher, supra* (case below), with *Jackson v. Franklin County School Board,* 765 F.2d 535, 538 (CA5 1985); *Victoria L. v. District School Bd. of Lee County, Fla.,* 741 F.2d 369, 374 (CA11 1984); *S-1 v. Turlington,* 635 F.2d 342, 348, n. 9 (CA5 1981), and that the direct services ruling placed an intolerable burden on the State. We granted certiorari to resolve these questions and now affirm.

* * *

III

The language of § 1415(e)(3) is unequivocal. It states plainly that during the pendency of any proceedings initiated under the Act, unless the state or local educational agency and the parents or guardian of a disabled child otherwise agree, "the child *shall* remain in the then current educational placement." § 1415(e)(3) (emphasis added). Faced with this clear directive, petitioner asks us to read a "dangerousness" exception into the stay-put provision on the basis of either of two essentially inconsistent assumptions: first, that Congress thought the residual authority of school officials to exclude dangerous students from the classroom too obvious for comment; or second, that Congress inadvertently failed to provide such authority and this Court must therefore remedy the oversight. Because we cannot accept either premise, we decline petitioner's invitation to rewrite the statute.

Petitioner's arguments proceed, he suggests, from a simple, commonsense proposition: Congress could not have intended the stay-put provision to be read literally, for such a construction leads to the clearly unintended, and untenable, result that school districts must return violent or dangerous students to school while the often lengthy EHA proceedings run their course. We think it clear, however, that Congress very much meant to strip schools of the *unilateral* authority they had traditionally employed to exclude disabled students, particularly emotionally disturbed students, from school. In so doing, Congress did not leave school administrators powerless to deal with dangerous students; it did, however, deny school officials their former right to "self-help," and directed that in the future the removal of disabled students could be accomplished only with the permission of the parents or, as a last resort, the courts.

As noted above, Congress passed the EHA after finding that school systems across the country had excluded one out of every eight disabled children from classes. In drafting the law, Congress was largely guided by the recent decisions in *Mills v. Board of Education of District of Columbia,* 348 F.Supp. 866 (1972), and *PARC,* 343 F.Supp. 279 (1972), both of which involved the exclusion of hard-to-handle disabled students. *Mills* in particular demonstrated the extent to which schools used disciplinary measures to bar children from the classroom. There, school officials had labeled four of the seven minor plaintiffs "behavioral problems," and had excluded them from classes without providing any alternative education to them or any notice to their parents. After finding that this practice was not limited to the named plaintiffs but affected in one way or another an estimated class of 12,000 to 18,000 disabled students, the District Court enjoined future exclusions, suspensions, or expulsions "on grounds of discipline."

Congress attacked such exclusionary practices in a variety of ways. It required participating States to educate *all* disabled children, regardless of the severity of their disabilities, 20 U.S.C. § 1412(2)(C), and included within the definition of "handicapped" those children with serious emotional disturbances. § 1401(1). It further provided for meaningful parental participation in all aspects of a child's educational placement, and barred schools, through the stay-put provision, from changing that placement over the parent's objection until all review proceedings were completed. Recognizing that those proceedings might prove long and tedious, the Act's drafters did not intend § 1415(e)(3) to operate inflexibly, and they therefore allowed for interim placements where parents and school officials are able to agree on one. Conspicuously absent from § 1415(e)(3), however, is any emergency exception for dangerous students. This absence is all the more telling in light of the injunctive decree issued in *PARC,* which permitted school officials unilaterally to remove students in " 'extraordinary circumstances.' " 343 F.Supp., at 301. Given the lack of any similar exception in *Mills,* and the close attention Congress devoted to these "landmark" decisions, we can only conclude that the omission was intentional; we are therefore not at liberty to engraft onto the statute an exception Congress chose not to create.

Our conclusion that § 1415(e)(3) means what it says does not leave educators hamstrung. The Department of Education has observed that, "[w]hile the [child's] placement may not be changed [during any complaint proceeding], this does not preclude the agency from using its normal procedures for dealing with children who are endangering themselves or others." Comment following 34 CFR § 300.513 (1987). Such procedures may include the use of study carrels, timeouts, detention, or the restriction of privileges. More drastically, where a student poses an immediate threat to the safety of others, officials may temporarily suspend him or her for up to 10 schooldays.[8] This authority, which respondent in no way disputes, not only ensures that school administrators can protect the safety of others by promptly removing the most dangerous of students, it also provides a "cooling down" period during which officials can initiate IEP review and seek to persuade the child's parents to agree to an interim placement. And in those cases in which the parents of a truly dangerous child adamantly refuse to permit any change in placement, the 10-day respite gives school officials an opportunity to invoke the aid of the courts under § 1415(e)(2), which empowers courts to grant any appropriate relief.

Petitioner contends, however, that the availability of judicial relief is more illusory than real, because a party seeking review under § 1415(e)(2) must exhaust time-consuming administrative remedies, and because under the Court of Appeals' construction of § 1415(e)(3), courts are as bound by the stay-put provision's "automatic injunction" as are schools. It is true that judicial review is normally not available under § 1415(e)(2) until all administrative proceedings are completed, but as we have previously noted, parents may bypass the administrative process where exhaustion would be futile or inadequate. While many of the EHA's procedural safeguards protect the rights of parents and children, schools can and do seek redress through the administrative review process, and we have no reason to believe that Congress meant to require schools alone to exhaust in all cases, no matter how exigent the circumstances. The burden in such cases, of course, rests with the school to demonstrate the futility or inadequacy of administrative review, but nothing in § 1415(e)(2) suggests that schools are completely barred from attempting to make such a showing. Nor do we think that § 1415(e)(3) operates to limit the equitable powers of district courts such that they cannot, in appropriate cases, temporarily enjoin a dangerous disabled child from attending school. As the EHA's legislative history makes clear, one of the evils Congress sought

---

[8]   The Department of Education has adopted the position first espoused in 1980 by its Office of Civil Rights that a suspension of up to 10 school-days does not amount to a "change in placement" prohibited by § 1415(e)(3). U.S. Dept. of Education, Office of Special Education Programs, Policy Letter (Feb. 26, 1987), Ed. for Handicapped L.Rep. 211:437 (1987). The EHA nowhere defines the phrase "change in placement," nor does the statute's structure or legislative history provide any guidance as to how the term applies to fixed suspensions. Given this ambiguity, we defer to the construction adopted by the agency charged with monitoring and enforcing the statute. Moreover, the agency's position comports fully with the purposes of the statute: Congress sought to prevent schools from permanently and unilaterally excluding disabled children by means of indefinite suspensions and expulsions; the power to impose fixed suspensions of short duration does not carry the potential for total exclusion that Congress found so objectionable. Indeed, despite its broad injunction, the District Court in *Mills v. Board of Education of District of Columbia*, 348 F.Supp. 866 (DC 1972), recognized that school officials could suspend disabled children on a short-term, temporary basis. Because we believe the agency correctly determined that a suspension in excess of 10 days does constitute a prohibited "change in placement," we conclude that the Court of Appeals erred to the extent it approved suspensions of 20 and 30 days' duration.

to remedy was the unilateral exclusion of disabled children by *schools,* not courts, and one of the purposes of § 1415(e)(3), therefore, was "to prevent *school* officials from removing a child from the regular public school classroom over the parents' objection pending completion of the review proceedings." The stay-put provision in no way purports to limit or pre-empt the authority conferred on courts by § 1415(e)(2); indeed, it says nothing whatever about judicial power.

In short, then, we believe that school officials are entitled to seek injunctive relief under § 1415(e)(2) in appropriate cases. In any such action, § 1415(e)(3) effectively creates a presumption in favor of the child's current educational placement which school officials can overcome only by showing that maintaining the child in his or her current placement is substantially likely to result in injury either to himself or herself, or to others. In the present case, we are satisfied that the District Court, in enjoining the state and local defendants from indefinitely suspending respondent or otherwise unilaterally altering his then current placement, properly balanced respondent's interest in receiving a free appropriate public education in accordance with the procedures and requirements of the EHA against the interests of the state and local school officials in maintaining a safe learning environment for all their students.

IV

We believe the courts below properly construed and applied § 1415(e)(3), except insofar as the Court of Appeals held that a suspension in excess of 10 schooldays does not constitute a "change in placement." We therefore affirm the Court of Appeals' judgment on this issue as modified herein. Because we are equally divided on the question whether a court may order a State to provide services directly to a disabled child where the local agency has failed to do so, we affirm the Court of Appeals' judgment on this issue as well.

Affirmed.

NOTES AND QUESTIONS

1. *No dangerousness exception.* Do you agree with the Court that Congress did not intend to include a dangerousness exception to the stay-put provision? Does this make it unduly difficult for schools to appropriately manage misbehaving children? Is obtaining injunctive relief a viable safety valve for school districts that are attempting to deal with extremely unruly students?

2. *Statutory amendments.* After the Court's decision in *Honig,* Congress amended and reauthorized the IDEA in 1990, 1997, and 2004. The 1997 and 2004 amendments contain specific provisions regarding the discipline of students with disabilities. The statute has several provisions that apply to disciplining students with disabilities:

- Codifying the decision in *Honig v. Doe*, suspensions or changes in placement of up to ten days do not violate the stay-put provision. 20 U.S.C. § 1415(k)(1)(B).

- In order to suspend a child or change the placement of a child for more than ten days, the school must conduct a manifestation determination to determine if the misconduct was caused by the child's disability. If it is determined that the behavior was not caused by the disability, the school may apply regular discipline procedures that it would apply to non-disabled students. However, if the manifestation determination concludes that the behavior was caused by the disability, the child must be put back to their original placement unless the parents and the school agree otherwise. 20 U.S.C. § 1415(k)(1)(C), (E), (F).

- The school can remove a student to an interim alternative educational setting for not more than 45 school days without regard to the result of the manifestation determination in three instances—if the child: (1) carries or possesses a weapon to or at school; (2) knowingly possesses or uses illegal drugs, or sells or solicits the sale of a controlled substance; or (3) has inflicted serious bodily injury on another person while at school, on school premises, or at a school function. 20 U.S.C. § 1415(k)(1)(G)(i)–(iii).

3.   *After the discipline amendments.* Although the 2004 Amendments implemented significant change to the disciplinary provisions of the IDEA, school districts throughout the country are still required to make difficult decisions in light of the inherent conflict between educating students with disabilities and maintaining a safe environment for all students, teachers, and administrators. Following the Amendments, teachers and administrators are afforded more discretion in disciplining students with disabilities if those students engage in certain forms of misconduct identified by the statute. Yet, many teachers and school administrators nonetheless claim that the Amendments do not enable them to adequately handle students with disabilities who are violent or seriously disruptive. Arguably the most debated issue resulting from the Amendments involves the elimination of the manifestation determination requirement when a student with a disability engages in the type of misbehavior included within the new version of Section 1415(k)(1)(G). While proponents of this change argue its purpose is to ensure the safety of students and teachers, others argue that this particular Amendment seems inconsistent with the IDEA's original mission of ensuring children with disabilities receive equal access to educational opportunities. What do you think? Did the Amendments go far enough, too far, or achieve the right result?

e. Private School Reimbursement

FLORENCE COUNTY SCHOOL DISTRICT FOUR V. CARTER
510 U.S. 7, 114 S.Ct. 361 (1993)

JUSTICE O'CONNOR delivered the opinion of the Court.

I

Respondent Shannon Carter was classified as learning disabled in 1985, while a ninth grade student in a school operated by petitioner Florence County School District Four. School officials met with Shannon's parents to formulate an individualized education program (IEP) for Shannon, as required under IDEA. 20 U.S.C. §§ 1401(a)(18) and (20), 1414(a)(5). The IEP provided that Shannon would stay in regular classes except for three periods of individualized instruction per week, and established specific goals in reading and mathematics of four months' progress for the entire school year. Shannon's parents were dissatisfied, and requested a hearing to challenge the appropriateness of the IEP. See § 1415(b)(2). Both the local educational officer and the state educational agency hearing officer rejected Shannon's parents' claim and concluded that the IEP was adequate. In the meantime, Shannon's parents had placed her in Trident Academy, a private school specializing in educating children with disabilities. Shannon began at Trident in September 1985 and graduated in the spring of 1988.

Shannon's parents filed this suit in July 1986, claiming that the school district had breached its duty under IDEA to provide Shannon with a "free appropriate public education," § 1401(a)(18), and seeking reimbursement for tuition and other costs incurred at Trident. After a bench trial, the District Court ruled in the parents' favor. The court held that the school district's proposed educational program and the achievement goals of the IEP "were wholly inadequate" and failed to satisfy the requirements of the Act. The court further held that "[a]lthough [Trident Academy] did not comply with all of the procedures outlined in [IDEA]," the school "provided Shannon an excellent education in substantial compliance with all the substantive requirements" of the statute. The court found that Trident "evaluated Shannon quarterly, not yearly as mandated in [IDEA], it provided Shannon with low teacher-student ratios, and it developed a plan which allowed Shannon to receive passing marks and progress from grade to grade." The court also credited the findings of its own expert, who determined that Shannon had made "significant progress" at Trident and that her reading comprehension had risen three grade levels in her three years at the school. The District Court concluded that Shannon's education was "appropriate" under IDEA, and that Shannon's parents were entitled to reimbursement of tuition and other costs.

The Court of Appeals for the Fourth Circuit affirmed. 950 F.2d 156 (1991). The court agreed that the IEP proposed by the school district was inappropriate under IDEA. It also rejected the school district's argument that reimbursement is never proper when the parents choose a private school that is not approved by the State or that does not comply with all the terms of IDEA. According to the Court of Appeals, neither the text of the Act nor its legislative history imposes a "requirement that the private school be approved by the state in parent-placement reimbursement cases." To the contrary, the Court of Appeals concluded, IDEA's state-approval requirement applies only when a child is placed in a private school by public school officials. Accordingly, "when a public school system has defaulted on its obligations under the Act, a private school placement is 'proper under the Act' if the education provided by the private school is 'reasonably calculated to enable the child to receive educational benefits.'" *Id.,* at 163.

The court below recognized that its holding conflicted with *Tucker v. Bay Shore Union Free School Dist.,* 873 F.2d 563, 568 (1989), in which the Court of Appeals for the Second Circuit held that parental placement in a private school cannot be proper under the Act unless the private school in question meets the standards of the state education agency. We granted certiorari to resolve this conflict among the Courts of Appeals.

II

In *School Comm. of Burlington v. Department of Ed. of Mass.,* 471 U.S. 359, 369, 105 S.Ct. 1996, 2002 (1985), we held that IDEA's grant of equitable authority empowers a court "to order school authorities to reimburse parents for their expenditures on private special education for a child if the court ultimately determines that such placement, rather than a proposed IEP, is proper under the Act." Congress intended that IDEA's promise of a "free appropriate public education" for disabled children would normally be met by an IEP's provision for education in the regular public schools or in private schools chosen jointly by school officials and parents. In cases where cooperation fails, however, "parents who disagree with the proposed IEP are faced with a choice: go along with the IEP to the detriment of their child if it turns out to be inappropriate or pay for what they consider to be the appropriate placement." *Id.,* at 370, 105 S.Ct., at 2003. For parents willing and able to make the latter choice, "it would be an empty victory to have a court tell them several years later that they were right but that these expenditures could not in a proper case be reimbursed by the school officials." Because such a result would be contrary to IDEA's guarantee of a "free appropriate public education," we held that "Congress meant to include retroactive reimbursement to parents as an available remedy in a proper case."

As this case comes to us, two issues are settled: (1) the school district's proposed IEP was inappropriate under IDEA, and (2) although Trident did not meet the § 1401(a)(18) requirements, it provided an education otherwise proper under IDEA. This case presents the narrow question whether Shannon's parents are barred from reimbursement because the private school in which Shannon enrolled did not meet the § 1401(a)(18) definition of a "free appropriate public education." We hold that they are not, because § 1401(a)(18)'s requirements cannot be read as applying to parental placements.

Section 1401(a)(18)(A) requires that the education be "provided at public expense, under public supervision and direction." Similarly, § 1401(a)(18)(D) requires schools to provide an IEP, which must be designed by "a representative of the local educational agency," 20 U.S.C. § 1401(a)(20), and must be "establish[ed]," "revise[d]," and "review[ed]" by the agency, § 1414(a)(5). These requirements do not make sense in the context of a parental placement. In this case, as in all *Burlington* reimbursement cases, the parents' rejection of the school district's proposed IEP is the very reason for the parents' decision to put their child in a private school. In such cases, where the private placement has necessarily been made over the school district's objection, the private school education will not be under "public supervision and direction." Accordingly, to read the § 1401(a)(18) requirements as applying to parental placements would effectively eliminate the right of unilateral withdrawal recognized in *Burlington*. Moreover, IDEA was intended to ensure that children with disabilities receive an education that is both appropriate and free. *Burlington, supra,* at 373, 105 S.Ct., at 2004. To read the provisions of § 1401(a)(18) to bar reimbursement in the circumstances of this case would defeat this statutory purpose.

Nor do we believe that reimbursement is necessarily barred by a private school's failure to meet state education standards. Trident's deficiencies, according to the school district, were that it employed at least two faculty members who were not state-certified and that it did not develop IEP's. As we have noted, however, the § 1401(a)(18) requirements—including the requirement that the school meet the standards of the state educational agency, § 1401(a)(18)(B)—do not apply to private parental placements. Indeed, the school district's emphasis on state standards is somewhat ironic. As the Court of Appeals noted, "it hardly seems consistent with the Act's goals to forbid parents from educating their child at a school that provides an appropriate education simply because that school lacks the stamp of approval of the same public school system that failed to meet the child's needs in the first place." Accordingly, we disagree with the Second Circuit's theory that "a parent may not obtain reimbursement for a unilateral placement if that placement was in a school that was not on [the State's] approved list of private" schools. *Tucker*, 873 F.2d, at 568. Parents' failure to select a program known to be approved by the State in favor of an unapproved option is not itself a bar to reimbursement.

Furthermore, although the absence of an approved list of private schools is not essential to our holding, we note that parents in the position of Shannon's have no way of knowing at the time they select a private school whether the school meets state standards. South Carolina keeps no publicly available list of approved private schools, but instead approves private school placements on a case-by-case basis. In fact, although public school officials had previously placed three children with disabilities at Trident, Trident had not received blanket approval from the State. South Carolina's case-by-case approval system meant that Shannon's parents needed the cooperation of state officials before they could know whether Trident was state-approved. As we recognized in *Burlington,* such cooperation is unlikely in cases where the school officials disagree with the need for the private placement. 471 U.S., at 372, 105 S.Ct., at 2004.

III

The school district also claims that allowing reimbursement for parents such as Shannon's puts an unreasonable burden on financially strapped local educational authorities. The school district argues that requiring parents to choose a state approved private school if they want reimbursement is the only meaningful way to allow States to control costs; otherwise States will have to reimburse dissatisfied parents for any private school that provides an education that is proper under the Act, no matter how expensive it may be.

There is no doubt that Congress has imposed a significant financial burden on States and school districts that participate in IDEA. Yet public educational authorities who want to avoid reimbursing parents for the private education of a disabled child can do one of two things: give the child a free appropriate public education in a public setting, or place the child in an appropriate private setting of the State's choice. This is IDEA's mandate, and school officials who conform to it need not worry about reimbursement claims.

Moreover, parents who, like Shannon's, "unilaterally change their child's placement during the pendency of review proceedings, without the consent of state or local school officials, do so at their own financial risk." *Burlington, supra,* at 373–374, 105 S.Ct., at 2004–2005. They are entitled to reimbursement *only* if a federal court concludes both that the public placement violated IDEA and that the private school placement was proper under the Act.

Finally, we note that once a court holds that the public placement violated IDEA, it is authorized to "grant such relief as the court determines is appropriate." 20 U.S.C. § 1415(e)(2). Under this provision, "equitable considerations are relevant in fashioning relief," *Burlington,* 471 U.S., at 374, 105 S.Ct., at 2005, and the court enjoys "broad discretion" in so doing. Courts fashioning discretionary equitable relief under IDEA must consider all relevant factors, including the appropriate and reasonable level of reimbursement that should be required. Total reimbursement will not be appropriate if the court determines that the cost of the private education was unreasonable.

Accordingly, we affirm the judgment of the Court of Appeals.

NOTES AND QUESTIONS

1. *The* Burlington *rule.* As the Court noted in *Florence County*, in *School Comm. of Burlington v. Department of Ed. of Mass.,* 471 U.S. 359, 369, 105 S.Ct. 1996, 2002 (1985), the Court held that IDEA's grant of equitable authority empowers a court "to order school authorities to reimburse parents for their expenditures on private special education for a child if the court ultimately determines that such placement, rather than a proposed IEP, is proper under the Act." The rationale for the rule in *Burlington* is that, if cooperation in developing the IEP fails, parents are left with a difficult choice—to keep their child in an educational environment that they believe is inadequate, or, if financially able, to pay for what they believe to be an appropriate placement in a private school. As the Court noted in *Burlington,* for parents able to place the child in a private school, "it would be an empty victory to have a court tell them several years later that they were right" but that these expenditures were not reimbursable. *Burlington,* 471 U.S. at 370.

2. *Justifying the reimbursement rule.* As discussed in the note above, the Court in *Florence County* provides justification for the reimbursement rule. But does the Court adequately address the criticisms? One such criticism is simply the financial burden of forcing the school district to pay for private school tuition, which can be very expensive. The Court in *Florence County* notes that the district court has "broad discretion" to fashion remedies and thus can limit the amount of reimbursement, presumably if the private school tuition is egregiously costly. But even more modest private school tuition is likely to exceed what it would cost the school district to educate the child in the public school. Of course, as the Court points out, the school district can avoid the expense of private school tuition simply by developing an adequate IEP in the first place. However, in at least some of the cases, the school district officials sincerely believe that the IEP it is proposing is not only adequate but in the best interests of the child. Does the reimbursement rule give wealthy parents too much power to coerce school districts into giving them what they want by threatening to move their child to an expensive private school? And does the reimbursement rule unfairly provide an advantage to wealthy parents because they can afford to take the chance on a private placement, whereas less wealthy parents are often forced to leave their child in the inadequate placement and perhaps try to challenge it through the due process provisions of the Act? Are you comfortable with the inequities built into the reimbursement rule? Is there another way of fashioning a rule regarding private school placements that would not cause the same inequities?

3. *1997 Reauthorization of the IDEA.* In 1997, Congress added a provision that specifically addressed private school reimbursement.

(C) Payment for education of children enrolled in private schools without consent of or referral by the public agency

(i) In general

Subject to subparagraph (A), this subchapter does not require a local educational agency to pay for the cost of education, including special education and related services, of a child with a disability at a private school or facility if that agency made a free appropriate public education available to the child and the parents elected to place the child in such private school or facility.

(ii) Reimbursement for private school placement

If the parents of a child with a disability, who previously received special education and related services under the authority of a public agency, enroll the child in a private elementary school or secondary school without the consent of or referral by the public agency, a court or a hearing officer may require the agency to reimburse the parents for the cost of that enrollment if the court or hearing officer finds that the agency had not made a free appropriate public education available to the child in a timely manner prior to that enrollment.

(iii) Limitation on reimbursement

The cost of reimbursement described in clause (ii) may be reduced or denied if—

> **(aa)** at the most recent IEP meeting that the parents attended prior to removal of the child from the public school, the parents did not inform the IEP Team that they were rejecting the placement proposed by the public agency to provide a free appropriate public education to their child, including stating their concerns and their intent to enroll their child in a private school at public expense; or

> **(bb)** 10 business days (including any holidays that occur on a business day) prior to the removal of the child from the public school, the parents did not give written notice to the public agency of the information described in item (aa);

>> **(II)** if, prior to the parents' removal of the child from the public school, the public agency informed the parents, through the notice requirements described in section 1415(b)(3) of this title, of its intent to evaluate the child (including a statement of the purpose of the evaluation that was appropriate and reasonable), but the parents did not make the child available for such evaluation; or

>> **(III)** upon a judicial finding of unreasonableness with respect to actions taken by the parents. . . .

20 U.S.C. § 1412(a)(10)(C).

4. *Forest Grove School District v. T.A.* The reimbursement provision above allows reimbursement for private school tuition for parents of a child with a disability "who previously received special education and related services under the authority of a public agency." 20 U.S.C. § 1412(a)(10)(C)(ii). The issue in *Forest Grove School District v. T.A.,* 557 U.S. 230, 129 S.Ct. 2484 (2009) was what result should follow if the child had been denied the provision of special-education services and the parents enrolled the child in the private school before the child received any special education services in the public school? Are the parents precluded from seeking reimbursement? This case involved a child who had difficulty in school from the very beginning. However, when the parents finally sought help in his freshman year, the school psychologist evaluated him and determined that he did not need any further testing for learning disabilities and that he did not qualify for special education services. Eventually, his parents sought private professional advice, and he was diagnosed with ADHD and a number of disabilities related to learning and memory. Advised by the private specialist that he would do better in a structured, learning residential environment, the parents enrolled him in a private school. The parents then gave notice to the school district about the private placement and sought to have him qualified for special education services in the public school, but the school district once again determined that, because his ADHD did not have a sufficiently adverse impact on his educational performance, he was not eligible for special education services and the district refused to provide him with an IEP.

In the administrative review process, the hearing officer agreed with the parents that the child was eligible for special education services and that the school district had failed to provide a FAPE and ordered reimbursement for the private school tuition. The school district sought judicial review, and the district court accepted the hearing officer's findings of facts but set aside the reimbursement award after finding that the 1997 Amendments categorically barred reimbursement of private-school tuition for students who had not "previously received special education and related services under the authority of a public agency." The Court of Appeals for the Ninth Circuit reversed and remanded.

The Supreme Court, relying on the broad grant of discretion to fashion remedies under the IDEA (discussed in *Burlington* and *Florence County*), held that unless the 1997 Amendments specifically repealed the reimbursement rule in *Burlington*, the Court should be able to award reimbursement in this case. The Court did not find any indication that § 1412(a)(10)(C)(ii) (quoted above) was intended to preclude reimbursement in this case. The Court noted that failing to provide special-education services at all was just as serious of a violation (if not more serious) as providing inadequate services. As the Court stated:

> [B]y immunizing a school district's refusal to find a child eligible for special-education services no matter how compelling the child's need, the School District's interpretation of § 1412(a)(10)(C) would produce a rule bordering on the irrational. It would be particularly strange for

the Act to provide a remedy, as all agree it does, when a school district offers a child inadequate special-education services but to leave parents without relief in the more egregious situation in which the school district unreasonably denies a child access to such services altogether.

Forest Grove School District v. T.A., 557 U.S. 230, 245 129 S.Ct. 2484, 2495 (2009).

f.   Procedures and Remedies

SCHAFFER V. WEAST
546 U.S. 49, 126 S.Ct. 528 (2005)

JUSTICE O'CONNOR delivered the opinion of the Court.

The Individuals with Disabilities Education Act (IDEA or Act), 84 Stat. 175, as amended, 20 U.S.C. § 1400 *et seq.*, is a Spending Clause statute that seeks to ensure that "all children with disabilities have available to them a free appropriate public education," § 1400(d)(1)(A). Under IDEA, school districts must create an "individualized education program" (IEP) for each disabled child. § 1414(d). If parents believe their child's IEP is inappropriate, they may request an "impartial due process hearing." § 1415(f). The Act is silent, however, as to which party bears the burden of persuasion at such a hearing. We hold that the burden lies, as it typically does, on the party seeking relief.

I

A

Congress first passed IDEA as part of the Education of the Handicapped Act in 1970, 84 Stat. 175, and amended it substantially in the Education for All Handicapped Children Act of 1975, 89 Stat. 773. At the time the majority of disabled children in America were "either totally excluded from schools or sitting idly in regular classrooms awaiting the time when they were old enough to 'drop out,'" H.R.Rep. No. 94–332, p. 2 (1975). IDEA was intended to reverse this history of neglect. . . .

IDEA is "frequently described as a model of 'cooperative federalism.'" It "leaves to the States the primary responsibility for developing and executing educational programs for handicapped children, [but] imposes significant requirements to be followed in the discharge of that responsibility." *Board of Ed. of Hendrick Hudson Central School Dist., Westchester Cty. v. Rowley,* 458 U.S. 176, 183, 102 S.Ct. 3034 (1982). . . .

The core of the statute, however, is the cooperative process that it establishes between parents and schools. The central vehicle for this collaboration is the IEP process. State educational authorities must identify and evaluate disabled children, §§ 1414(a)–(c), develop an IEP for each one, § 1414(d)(2), and review every IEP at least once a year, § 1414(d)(4). Each IEP must include an assessment of the child's current educational performance, must articulate measurable educational goals, and must specify the nature of the special services that the school will provide. § 1414(d)(1)(A).

Parents and guardians play a significant role in the IEP process. They must be informed about and consent to evaluations of their child under the Act. § 1414I(3). Parents are included as members of "IEP teams." § 1414(d)(1)(B). They have the right to examine any records relating to their child, and to obtain an "independent educational evaluation of the[ir] child." § 1415(b)(1). They must be given written prior notice of any changes in an IEP, § 1415(b)(3), and be notified in writing of the procedural safeguards available to them under the Act, § 1415(d)(1). If parents believe that an IEP is not appropriate, they may seek an administrative "impartial due process hearing." § 1415(f). School districts may also seek such hearings, as Congress clarified in the 2004 amendments. They may do so, for example, if they wish to change an existing IEP but the parents do not consent, or if parents refuse to allow their child to be evaluated. As a practical matter, it appears that most hearing requests come from parents rather than schools.

Although state authorities have limited discretion to determine who conducts the hearings, § 1415(f)(1), and responsibility generally for establishing fair hearing procedures, § 1415(a), Congress has chosen to legislate the central components of due process hearings. It has imposed minimal pleading standards, requiring parties to file complaints setting forth "a description of the nature of the problem," § 1415(b)(7)(B)(ii), and "a proposed resolution of the problem to the extent known and available . . . at the time," § 1415(b)(7)(B)(iii). At the hearing, all parties may be accompanied by counsel, and may "present evidence and confront, cross-examine, and compel the attendance of witnesses." §§ 1415(h)(1)–(2). After the hearing, any aggrieved party may bring a civil action in state or federal court. § 1415(i)(2). Prevailing parents may also recover attorney's fees. § 1415(i)(3)(B). Congress has never explicitly stated, however, which party should bear the burden of proof at IDEA hearings.

B

This case concerns the educational services that were due, under IDEA, to petitioner Brian Schaffer. Brian suffers from learning disabilities and speech-language impairments. From prekindergarten through seventh grade he attended a private school and struggled academically. In 1997, school officials informed Brian's mother that he needed a school that could better accommodate his needs. Brian's parents contacted respondent Montgomery County Public Schools System (MCPS) seeking a placement for him for the following school year.

MCPS evaluated Brian and convened an IEP team. The committee generated an initial IEP offering Brian a place in either of two MCPS middle schools. Brian's parents were not satisfied with the arrangement, believing that Brian needed smaller classes and more intensive services. The Schaffers thus enrolled Brian in another private school, and initiated a due process hearing challenging the IEP and seeking compensation for the cost of Brian's subsequent private education.

In Maryland, IEP hearings are conducted by administrative law judges (ALJs). After a 3-day hearing, the ALJ deemed the evidence close, held that the parents bore the burden of persuasion, and ruled in favor of the school district. The parents brought a civil action challenging the result. The United States District Court for the District of Maryland reversed and remanded, after concluding that the burden of persuasion is on the school district. *Brian S. v. Vance,* 86 F.Supp.2d 538 (D.Md. 2000). Around the same time, MCPS offered Brian a placement in a high school with a special learning center. Brian's parents accepted, and Brian was educated in that program until he graduated from high school. The suit remained alive, however, because the parents sought compensation for the private school tuition and related expenses.

Respondents appealed to the United States Court of Appeals for the Fourth Circuit. While the appeal was pending, the ALJ reconsidered the case, deemed the evidence truly in "equipoise," and ruled in favor of the parents. The Fourth Circuit vacated and remanded the appeal so that it could consider the burden of proof issue along with the merits on a later appeal. The District Court reaffirmed its ruling that the school district has the burden of proof. 240 F.Supp.2d 396 (D.Md.2002). On appeal, a divided panel of the Fourth Circuit reversed. Judge Michael, writing for the majority, concluded that petitioners offered no persuasive reason to "depart from the normal rule of allocating the burden to the party seeking relief." 377 F.3d 449, 453 (C.A.4 2004). We granted certiorari to resolve the following question: At an administrative hearing assessing the appropriateness of an IEP, which party bears the burden of persuasion?

II

A

... When we are determining the burden of proof under a statutory cause of action, the touchstone of our inquiry is, of course, the statute. The plain text of IDEA is silent on the allocation of the burden of persuasion. We therefore begin with the ordinary default rule that plaintiffs bear the risk of failing to prove their claims. McCormick § 337, at 412 ("The burdens of pleading and proof with regard to most facts have been and should be assigned to the plaintiff who generally seeks to change the present state of affairs and who therefore naturally should be expected to bear the risk of failure of proof or persuasion").

Thus, we have usually assumed without comment that plaintiffs bear the burden of persuasion regarding the essential aspects of their claims. For example, Title VII of the Civil Rights Act of 1964, 42 U.S.C. § 2000e *et seq.,* does not directly state that plaintiffs bear the "ultimate" burden of persuasion, but we have so concluded. In numerous other areas, we have presumed or held that the default rule applies. Congress also expressed its approval of the general rule when it chose to apply it to administrative proceedings under the Administrative Procedure Act, 5 U.S.C. § 556(d).

The ordinary default rule, of course, admits of exceptions. See McCormick § 337, at 412–415. For example, the burden of persuasion as to certain elements of a plaintiff's claim may be shifted to defendants, when such elements can fairly be characterized as affirmative defenses or exemptions. Under some circumstances this Court has even placed the burden of persuasion over an entire claim on the defendant. But while the normal default rule does not solve all cases, it certainly solves most of them. Decisions that place the *entire* burden of persuasion on the opposing party at the *outset* of a proceeding—as petitioners urge us to do here—are extremely rare. Absent some reason to believe that Congress intended otherwise, therefore, we will conclude that the burden of persuasion lies where it usually falls, upon the party seeking relief.

B

* * *

Petitioners . . . contend that we should take instruction from the lower court opinions of *Mills v. Board of Education,* 348 F.Supp. 866 (D.D.C.1972), and *Pennsylvania Association for Retarded Children v. Pennsylvania,* 334 F.Supp. 1257 (E.D.Pa.1971) (hereinafter *PARC*). IDEA's drafters were admittedly guided "to a significant extent" by these two landmark cases. *Rowley,* 458 U.S., at 194, 102 S.Ct. 3034. As the court below noted, however, the fact that Congress "took a number of the procedural safeguards from *PARC* and *Mills* and wrote them directly into the Act" does not allow us to "conclude . . . that Congress intended to adopt the ideas that it failed to write into the text of the statute." 377 F.3d, at 455.

Petitioners also urge that putting the burden of persuasion on school districts will further IDEA's purposes because it will help ensure that children receive a free appropriate public education. In truth, however, very few cases will be in evidentiary equipoise. Assigning the burden of persuasion to school districts might encourage schools to put more resources into preparing IEPs and presenting their evidence. But IDEA is silent about whether marginal dollars should be allocated to litigation and administrative expenditures or to educational services. Moreover, there is reason to believe that a great deal is already spent on the administration of the Act. Litigating a due process complaint is an expensive affair, costing schools approximately $8,000-to-$12,000 per hearing. See Department of Education, J. Chambers, J. Harr, & A. Dhanani, What Are We Spending on Procedural Safeguards in Special Education 1999–2000, p. 8 (May 2003). Congress has also repeatedly amended the Act in order to reduce its administrative and litigation-related costs. For example, in 1997 Congress mandated that States offer mediation for IDEA disputes. In 2004, Congress added a mandatory "resolution session" prior to any due process hearing. It also made new findings that "[p]arents and schools should be given expanded opportunities to resolve their disagreements in positive and constructive ways," and that "[t]eachers, schools, local educational agencies, and States should be relieved of irrelevant and unnecessary paperwork burdens that do not lead to improved educational outcomes."

Petitioners in effect ask this Court to assume that every IEP is invalid until the school district demonstrates that it is not. The Act does not support this conclusion. IDEA relies heavily upon the expertise of school districts to meet its goals. It also includes a so-called "stay-put" provision, which requires a child to remain in his or her "then-current educational placement" during the pendency of an IDEA hearing. § 1415(j). Congress could have required that a child be given the educational placement that a parent requested during a dispute, but it did no such thing. Congress appears to have presumed instead that, if the Act's procedural requirements are respected, parents will prevail when they have legitimate grievances. See Rowley, supra, at 206, 102 S.Ct. 3034 (noting the "legislative conviction that adequate compliance with the procedures prescribed would in most cases assure much if not all of what Congress wished in the way of substantive content in an IEP").

Petitioners' most plausible argument is that "[t]he ordinary rule, based on considerations of fairness, does not place the burden upon a litigant of establishing facts peculiarly within the knowledge of his adversary." But this "rule is far from being universal, and has many qualifications upon its application." Greenleaf's Lessee v. Birth, 6 Pet. 302, 312 (1832); see also McCormick § 337, at 413 ("Very often one must plead and prove matters as to which his adversary has superior access to the proof"). School districts have a "natural advantage" in information and expertise, but Congress addressed this when it obliged schools to safeguard the procedural rights of parents and to share information with them. As noted above, parents have the right to review all records that the school possesses in relation to their child. § 1415(b)(1). They also have the right to an "independent educational evaluation of the[ir] child." The regulations clarify this entitlement by providing that a "parent has the right to an independent educational evaluation at public expense if the parent disagrees with an evaluation obtained by the public agency." 34 CFR § 300.502(b)(1) (2005). IDEA thus ensures parents access to an expert who can evaluate all the materials that the school must make available, and who can give an independent opinion. They are not left to challenge the government without a realistic opportunity to access the necessary evidence, or without an expert with the firepower to match the opposition.

Additionally, in 2004, Congress added provisions requiring school districts to answer the subject matter of a complaint in writing, and to provide parents with the reasoning behind the disputed action, details about the other options considered and rejected by the IEP team, and a description of all evaluations, reports, and other factors that the school used in coming to its decision. § 615I(2)(B)(i)(I) of IDEA. Prior to a hearing, the parties must disclose evaluations and recommendations that they intend to rely upon. 20 U.S.C. § 1415(f)(2). IDEA hearings are deliberately informal and intended to give ALJs the flexibility that they need to ensure that each side can fairly present its evidence. IDEA, in fact, requires state authorities to organize hearings in a way that guarantees parents and children the procedural protections of the Act. See § 1415(a). Finally, and perhaps most importantly, parents may recover attorney's fees if they prevail. § 1415(i)(3)(B). These protections ensure that the school bears no unique informational advantage.

III

Finally, respondents and several States urge us to decide that States may, if they wish, override the default rule and put the burden always on the school district. Several States have laws or regulations purporting to do so, at least under some circumstances. Because no such law or regulation exists in Maryland, we need not decide this issue today. Justice BREYER contends that the allocation of the burden ought to be left *entirely* up to the States. But neither party made this argument before this Court or the courts below. We therefore decline to address it.

We hold no more than we must to resolve the case at hand: The burden of proof in an administrative hearing challenging an IEP is properly placed upon the party seeking relief. In this case, that party is Brian, as represented by his parents. But the rule applies with equal effect to school districts: If they seek to challenge an IEP, they will in turn bear the burden of persuasion before an ALJ. The judgment of the United States Court of Appeals for the Fourth Circuit is, therefore, affirmed.

THE CHIEF JUSTICE took no part in the consideration or decision of this case.

JUSTICE GINSBURG, dissenting.

When the legislature is silent on the burden of proof, courts ordinarily allocate the burden to the party initiating the proceeding and seeking relief. As the Fourth Circuit recognized, however, "other factors," prime among them "policy considerations, convenience, and fairness," may warrant a different allocation. 377 F.3d 449, 452 (C.A.4 2004). The Court has followed the same counsel. See *Alaska Dept. of Environmental Conservation v. EPA,* 540 U.S. 461, 494, n. 17, 124 S.Ct. 983 (2004) ("No 'single principle or rule . . . solve[s] all cases and afford[s] a general test for ascertaining the incidence' of proof burdens.") For reasons well stated by Circuit Judge Luttig, dissenting in the Court of Appeals, 377 F.3d, at 456–459, I am persuaded that "policy considerations, convenience, and fairness" call for assigning the burden of proof to the school district in this case.

. . . Under typical civil rights and social welfare legislation, the complaining party must allege and prove discrimination or qualification for statutory benefits. The IDEA is atypical in this respect: It casts an affirmative, beneficiary-specific obligation on providers of public education. School districts are charged with responsibility to offer to each disabled child an individualized education program (IEP) suitable to the child's special needs. 20 U.S.C. §§ 1400(d)(1), 1412(a)(4), 1414(d). The proponent of the IEP, it seems to me, is properly called upon to demonstrate its adequacy.

Familiar with the full range of education facilities in the area, and informed by "their experiences with other, similarly-disabled children," 377 F.3d, at 458 (Luttig, J., dissenting), "the school district is . . . in a far better position to demonstrate that it has fulfilled [its statutory] obligation than the disabled student's parents are in to show that the school district has failed to do so," *id.*, at 457.

Understandably, school districts striving to balance their budgets, if "[l]eft to [their] own devices," will favor educational options that enable them to conserve resources. Saddled with a proof burden in administrative "due process" hearings, parents are likely to find a district-proposed IEP "resistant to challenge." Placing the burden on the district to show that its plan measures up to the statutorily mandated "free appropriate public education," 20 U.S.C. § 1400(d)(1)(A), will strengthen school officials' resolve to choose a course genuinely tailored to the child's individual needs.

The Court acknowledges that "[a]ssigning the burden of persuasion to school districts might encourage schools to put more resources into preparing IEPs." Curiously, the Court next suggests that resources spent on developing IEPs rank as "administrative expenditures" not as expenditures for "educational services." Costs entailed in the preparation of suitable IEPs, however, are the very expenditures necessary to ensure each child covered by the IDEA access to a free appropriate education. These outlays surely relate to "educational services." Indeed, a carefully designed IEP may ward off disputes productive of large administrative or litigation expenses.

This case is illustrative. Not until the District Court ruled that the school district had the burden of persuasion did the school design an IEP that met Brian Schaffer's special educational needs. Had the school district, in the first instance, offered Brian a public or private school placement equivalent to the one the district ultimately provided, this entire litigation and its attendant costs could have been avoided.

Notably, nine States, as friends of the Court, have urged that placement of the burden of persuasion on the school district best comports with the IDEA's aim. If allocating the burden to school districts would saddle school systems with inordinate costs, it is doubtful that these States would have filed in favor of petitioners. Cf. Brief for United States as *Amicus Curiae* Supporting Appellees Urging Affirmance in No. 00–1471(CA4), p. 12 ("Having to carry the burden of proof regarding the adequacy of its proposed IEP . . . should not substantially increase the workload for the school.").

One can demur to the Fourth Circuit's observation that courts "do not automatically assign the burden of proof to the side with the bigger guns," 377 F.3d, at 453, for no such reflexive action is at issue here. It bears emphasis that "the vast majority of parents whose children require the benefits and protections provided in the IDEA" lack "knowledge[e] about the educational resources available to their [child]" and the "sophisticat[ion]" to mount an effective case against a district-proposed IEP. *Id.,* at 458 (Luttig, J., dissenting). In this setting, "the party with the 'bigger guns' also has better access to information, greater expertise, and an affirmative obligation to provide the contested services." 377 F.3d, at 458 (Luttig, J., dissenting). Policy considerations, convenience, and fairness, I think it plain, point in the same direction. Their collective weight warrants a rule requiring a school district, in "due process" hearings, to explain persuasively why its proposed IEP satisfies the IDEA's standards. I would therefore reverse the judgment of the Fourth Circuit.

NOTES AND QUESTIONS

1. *Does* Schaffer *stack the deck against parents and their disabled children?* Several scholars criticized *Schaffer. See, e.g.,* Kelly D. Thomason, *The Costs of a "Free" Education: The Impact of* Schaffer v. Weast *and* Arlington v. Murphy *on Litigation Under the IDEA,* 57 DUKE L.J. 457 (2007) (criticizing the *Schaffer* decision and the *Arlington v. Murphy* decision discussed in the note below); Nicole Thompson, *The Great Burden on American Disabled Students: The Aftermath of* Schaffer v. Weast, 4 MOD. AM. 21 (2008) (same); Jordan L. Wilson, *Missing the Big IDEA: The Supreme Court Loses Sight of the Policy Behind the Individuals with Disabilities Education Act in* Schaffer v. Weast, 44 HOUS. L. REV. 161 (2007) (arguing that the Court came to the right conclusion but only because the parents in the *Schaffer* case were asking for a more restrictive environment for their child; in cases where the school is seeking the more restrictive environment, the school district should bear the burden of proof). *But see* Jennifer M. Burns, Schaffer v. Weast: *Why the Complaining Party Should Bear the Burden of Proof in an Administrative Hearing to Determine the Validity of an IEP Under IDEA,* 29 HAMLINE L. REV. 567 (2006) (arguing in favor of the decision). Is all of this commentary (mostly student-written notes) warranted, given how rare it is for the evidence to truly be in equipoise? In other words, how often will this decision have practical significance?

2.   *Expert fees.* The IDEA allows for the award of "reasonable attorneys' fees as part of the costs" to parents who prevail in an action under the IDEA. 20 U.S.C. § 1415(i)(3)(B). In *Arlington Central School District v. Murphy*, 548 U.S. 291, 126 S.Ct. 2455 (2006), the Court had to decide whether this fee-shifting provision authorizes prevailing parents to recover fees for services rendered by experts in IDEA actions. The Court, in an opinion authored by Justice Alito, held that it does not. The Court relied on the fact that the IDEA is spending-clause legislation; thus, when significant costs are placed on the states, notice should be given, and here, according to the Court, no notice was given that states could be liable for the costs of expert fees. Unlike the burden of proof issue, which will be result-changing in a very small number of cases, the decision in *Murphy* is much more significant. Given the deference provided to school districts and state hearing officers under *Rowley* and its progeny, parents will need to hire their own experts to challenge the IEP proposed by the school district. The decision in *Murphy* makes it much more difficult to do so, except for the wealthiest of parents. For instance, in *Murphy*, the parents spent $29,350 for an educational consultant to assist throughout the IDEA proceedings. Many parents would not be able to afford those fees. Does this decision swing the pendulum too far in favor of school districts? Or do you agree with the Court that school districts should not have to bear the burden of expensive fees charged by the parents' experts?

Even if the *Schaffer* decision alone is not often outcome-determinative, one commentator noted that the combination of the *Schaffer* and *Murphy* decisions has had the effect of increasing judicial outcomes in favor of school districts. *See* Perry A. Zirkel, *Legal Currency in Special Education Law: Top Ten for School Leaders*, 262 ED. LAW. REP. 1, at *5 (2011). Other commentators have argued that the combination of the *Schaffer* and *Murphy* decisions, along with the highly individualized standard set in *Endrew F.*, will make it very difficult for low-income parents to challenge inadequate IEPs. *See* Claire Raj & Emily Suski, Endrew F.'s *Unintended Consequences*, 46 J. L. & EDUC. 499 (2017). As explained by the authors, the individualized standard of *Endrew F.*—that the IEP must be "reasonably calculated to enable a child to make progress appropriate in light of the child's circumstances"—will further entrench the disparities between low and high-income children with disabilities. *Id.* at 500.

> [T]he *Endrew F.* decision virtually requires parents of children with disabilities to marshal substantial resources, including expert opinions, if they disagree with the IEP offered by their child's school. Yet, in *Arlington*, the Court concluded that parents have no right to reimbursement for expert services if they prevail in IDEA litigation against the school district beyond the statutory rate for travel reimbursement for witnesses. In *Schaffer*, the Court announced that the burden of proof will be on the moving party—typically the parents—in any challenges to the IEP. If parents do not have the resources to independently locate and pay for experts and other costs of proving IEPs inadequate, shouldering the burden of proof to

successfully traverse the *Endrew F.* middle ground will be a difficult, if not impossible, task.

Id. What do you think of this argument?

2. ADA AND REHABILITATION ACT IN PRIMARY/SECONDARY EDUCATION

FRY V. NAPOLEAN COMMUNITY SCHOOLS
137 S.Ct. 743 (2017)

JUSTICE KAGAN delivered the opinion of the Court.

The Individuals with Disabilities Education Act (IDEA or Act), 20 U.S.C. § 1400 *et seq.*, ensures that children with disabilities receive needed special education services. One of its provisions, § 1415(*l*), addresses the Act's relationship with other laws protecting those children. Section 1415(*l*) makes clear that nothing in the IDEA "restrict[s] or limit[s] the rights [or] remedies" that other federal laws, including antidiscrimination statutes, confer on children with disabilities. At the same time, the section states that if a suit brought under such a law "seek[s] relief that is also available under" the IDEA, the plaintiff must first exhaust the IDEA's administrative procedures. In this case, we consider the scope of that exhaustion requirement. We hold that exhaustion is not necessary when the gravamen of the plaintiff's suit is something other than the denial of the IDEA's core guarantee—what the Act calls a "free appropriate public education." § 1412(a)(1)(A).

I

A

The IDEA offers federal funds to States in exchange for a commitment: to furnish a "free appropriate public education"—more concisely known as a FAPE—to all children with certain physical or intellectual disabilities. As defined in the Act, a FAPE comprises "special education and related services"—both "instruction" tailored to meet a child's "unique needs" and sufficient "supportive services" to permit the child to benefit from that instruction. §§ 1401(9), (26), (29); see *Board of Ed. of Hendrick Hudson Central School Dist., Westchester Cty. v. Rowley,* 458 U.S. 176, 203, 102 S.Ct. 3034 (1982). An eligible child, as this Court has explained, acquires a "substantive right" to such an education once a State accepts the IDEA's financial assistance. *Smith v. Robinson,* 468 U.S. 992, 1010, 104 S.Ct. 3457 (1984).

Under the IDEA, an "individualized education program," called an IEP for short, serves as the "primary vehicle" for providing each child with the promised FAPE. (Welcome to—and apologies for—the acronymic world of federal legislation.) Crafted by a child's "IEP Team"—a group of school officials, teachers, and parents—the IEP spells out a personalized plan to meet all of the child's "educational needs." §§ 1414(d)(1)(A)(i)(II)(bb), (d)(1)(B). Most notably, the IEP documents the child's current "levels of academic achievement," specifies "measurable annual goals" for how she can "make progress in the general education curriculum," and lists the "special education and related services" to be provided so that she can "advance appropriately toward [those] goals." §§ 1414(d)(1)(A)(i)(I), (II), (IV)(aa).

Because parents and school representatives sometimes cannot agree on such issues, the IDEA establishes formal procedures for resolving disputes. To begin, a dissatisfied parent may file a complaint as to any matter concerning the provision of a FAPE with the local or state educational agency (as state law provides). That pleading generally triggers a "[p]reliminary meeting" involving the contending parties, § 1415(f)(1)(B)(i); at their option, the parties may instead (or also) pursue a full-fledged mediation process, see § 1415(e). Assuming their impasse continues, the matter proceeds to a "due process hearing" before an impartial hearing officer. Any decision of the officer granting substantive relief must be "based on a determination of whether the child received a [FAPE]." § 1415(f)(3)(E)(i). If the hearing is initially conducted at the local level, the ruling is appealable to the state agency. Finally, a parent unhappy with the outcome of the administrative process may seek judicial review by filing a civil action in state or federal court.

Important as the IDEA is for children with disabilities, it is not the only federal statute protecting their interests. Of particular relevance to this case are two antidiscrimination laws—Title II of the Americans with Disabilities Act (ADA), 42 U.S.C. § 12131 *et seq.*, and § 504 of the Rehabilitation Act, 29 U.S.C. § 794—which cover both adults and children with disabilities, in both public schools and other settings. Title II forbids any "public entity" from discriminating based on disability; Section 504 applies the same prohibition to any federally funded "program or activity." 42 U.S.C. §§ 12131–12132; 29 U.S.C. § 794(a). A regulation implementing Title II requires a public entity to make "reasonable modifications" to its "policies, practices, or procedures" when necessary to avoid such discrimination. 28 C.F.R. § 35.130(b)(7) (2016); see, *e.g., Alboniga v. School Bd. of Broward Cty.,* 87 F.Supp.3d 1319, 1345 (S.D.Fla.2015) (requiring an accommodation to permit use of a service animal under Title II). In similar vein, courts have interpreted § 504 as demanding certain "reasonable" modifications to existing practices in order to "accommodate" persons with disabilities. *Alexander v. Choate,* 469 U.S. 287, 299–300, 105 S.Ct. 712 (1985); see, *e.g., Sullivan v. Vallejo City Unified School Dist.,* 731 F.Supp. 947, 961–962 (E.D.Cal.1990) (requiring an accommodation to permit use of a service animal under § 504). And both statutes authorize individuals to seek redress for violations of their substantive guarantees by bringing suits for injunctive relief or money damages.

This Court first considered the interaction between such laws and the IDEA in *Smith v. Robinson,* 468 U.S. 992, 104 S.Ct. 3457. The plaintiffs there sought "to secure a 'free appropriate public education' for [their] handicapped child." But instead of bringing suit under the IDEA alone, they appended "virtually identical" claims (again alleging the denial of a "free appropriate public education") under § 504 of the Rehabilitation Act and the Fourteenth Amendment's Equal Protection Clause. The Court held that the IDEA altogether foreclosed those additional claims: With its "comprehensive" and "carefully tailored" provisions, the Act was "the exclusive avenue" through which a child with a disability (or his parents) could challenge the adequacy of his education.

Congress was quick to respond. In the Handicapped Children's Protection Act of 1986, 100 Stat. 796, it overturned *Smith*'s preclusion of non-IDEA claims while also adding a carefully defined exhaustion requirement. Now codified at 20 U.S.C. § 1415(*l*), the relevant provision of that statute reads:

> "Nothing in [the IDEA] shall be construed to restrict or limit the rights, procedures, and remedies available under the Constitution, the [ADA], title V of the Rehabilitation Act [including § 504], or other Federal laws protecting the rights of children with disabilities, except that before the filing of a civil action under such laws seeking relief that is also available under [the IDEA], the [IDEA's administrative procedures] shall be exhausted to the same extent as would be required had the action been brought under [the IDEA]."

The first half of § 1415(*l*) (up until "except that") "reaffirm[s] the viability" of federal statutes like the ADA or Rehabilitation Act "as separate vehicles," no less integral than the IDEA, "for ensuring the rights of handicapped children." According to that opening phrase, the IDEA does not prevent a plaintiff from asserting claims under such laws even if, as in *Smith* itself, those claims allege the denial of an appropriate public education (much as an IDEA claim would). But the second half of § 1415(*l*) (from "except that" onward) imposes a limit on that "anything goes" regime, in the form of an exhaustion provision. According to that closing phrase, a plaintiff bringing suit under the ADA, the Rehabilitation Act, or similar laws must in certain circumstances—that is, when "seeking relief that is also available under" the IDEA—first exhaust the IDEA's administrative procedures. The reach of that requirement is the issue in this case.

B

Petitioner E.F. is a child with a severe form of cerebral palsy, which "significantly limits her motor skills and mobility." When E.F. was five years old, her parents—petitioners Stacy and Brent Fry—obtained a trained service dog for her, as recommended by her pediatrician. The dog, a goldendoodle named Wonder, "help[s E.F.] to live as independently as possible" by assisting her with various life activities. In particular, Wonder aids E.F. by "retrieving dropped items, helping her balance when she uses her walker, opening and closing doors, turning on and off lights, helping her take off her coat, [and] helping her transfer to and from the toilet."

But when the Frys sought permission for Wonder to join E.F. in kindergarten, officials at Ezra Eby Elementary School refused the request. Under E.F.'s existing IEP, a human aide provided E.F. with one-on-one support throughout the day; that two-legged assistance, the school officials thought, rendered Wonder superfluous. In the words of one administrator, Wonder should be barred from Ezra Eby because all of E.F.'s "physical and academic needs [were] being met through the services/programs/ accommodations" that the school had already agreed to. Later that year, the school officials briefly allowed Wonder to accompany E.F. to school on a trial basis; but even then, "the dog was required to remain in the back of the room during classes, and was forbidden from assisting [E.F.] with many tasks he had been specifically trained to do." And when the trial period concluded, the administrators again informed the Frys that Wonder was not welcome. As a result, the Frys removed E.F. from Ezra Eby and began homeschooling her.

In addition, the Frys filed a complaint with the U.S. Department of Education's Office for Civil Rights (OCR), charging that Ezra Eby's exclusion of E.F.'s service animal violated her rights under Title II of the ADA and § 504 of the Rehabilitation Act. Following an investigation, OCR agreed. The office explained in its decision letter that a school's obligations under those statutes go beyond providing educational services: A school could offer a FAPE to a child with a disability but still run afoul of the laws' ban on discrimination. And here, OCR found, Ezra Eby had indeed violated that ban, even if its use of a human aide satisfied the FAPE standard. OCR analogized the school's conduct to "requir[ing] a student who uses a wheelchair to be carried" by an aide or "requir[ing] a blind student to be led [around by a] teacher" instead of permitting him to use a guide dog or cane. Regardless whether those—or Ezra Eby's—policies denied a FAPE, they violated Title II and § 504 by discriminating against children with disabilities.

In response to OCR's decision, school officials at last agreed that E.F. could come to school with Wonder. But after meeting with Ezra Eby's principal, the Frys became concerned that the school administration "would resent [E.F.] and make her return to school difficult." Accordingly, the Frys found a different public school, in a different district, where administrators and teachers enthusiastically received both E.F. and Wonder.

C

The Frys then filed this suit in federal court against the local and regional school districts in which Ezra Eby is located, along with the school's principal (collectively, the school districts). The complaint alleged that the school districts violated Title II of the ADA and § 504 of the Rehabilitation

Act by "denying [E.F.] equal access" to Ezra Eby and its programs, "refus[ing] to reasonably accommodate" E.F.'s use of a service animal, and otherwise "discriminat[ing] against [E.F.] as a person with disabilities." According to the complaint, E.F. suffered harm as a result of that discrimination, including "emotional distress and pain, embarrassment, [and] mental anguish." In their prayer for relief, the Frys sought a declaration that the school districts had violated Title II and § 504, along with money damages to compensate for E.F.'s injuries.

The District Court granted the school districts' motion to dismiss the suit, holding that § 1415(*l*) required the Frys to first exhaust the IDEA's administrative procedures. A divided panel of the Court of Appeals for the Sixth Circuit affirmed on the same ground. In that court's view, § 1415(*l*) applies if "the injuries [alleged in a suit] relate to the specific substantive protections of the IDEA." 788 F.3d 622, 625 (2015). And that means, the court continued, that exhaustion is necessary whenever "the genesis and the manifestations" of the complained-of harms were "educational" in nature. *Id.*, at 627. On that understanding of § 1415(*l*), the Sixth Circuit held, the Frys' suit could not proceed: Because the harms to E.F. were generally "educational"—most notably, the court reasoned, because "Wonder's absence hurt her sense of independence and social confidence at school"—the Frys had to exhaust the IDEA's procedures. Judge Daughtrey dissented, emphasizing that in bringing their Title II and § 504 claims, the Frys "did not allege the denial of a FAPE" or "seek to modify [E.F.'s] IEP in any way." *Id.*, at 634.

We granted certiorari to address confusion in the courts of appeals as to the scope of § 1415(*l*)'s exhaustion requirement. We now vacate the Sixth Circuit's decision.

II

Section 1415(*l*) requires that a plaintiff exhaust the IDEA's procedures before filing an action under the ADA, the Rehabilitation Act, or similar laws when (but only when) her suit "seek[s] relief that is also available" under the IDEA. We first hold that to meet that statutory standard, a suit must seek relief for the denial of a FAPE, because that is the only "relief" the IDEA makes "available." We next conclude that in determining whether a suit indeed "seeks" relief for such a denial, a court should look to the substance, or gravamen, of the plaintiff's complaint.

A

In this Court, the parties have reached substantial agreement about what "relief" the IDEA makes "available" for children with disabilities—and about how the Sixth Circuit went wrong in addressing that question. The Frys maintain that such a child can obtain remedies under the IDEA for decisions that deprive her of a FAPE, but none for those that do not. So in the Frys' view, § 1415(*l*)'s exhaustion requirement can come into play only when a suit concerns the denial of a FAPE—and not, as the Sixth Circuit held, when it merely has some articulable connection to the education of a child with a disability. The school districts, for their part, also believe that the Sixth Circuit's exhaustion standard "goes too far" because it could mandate exhaustion when a plaintiff is "seeking relief that is *not* in substance available" under the IDEA. And in particular, the school districts acknowledge that the IDEA makes remedies available only in suits that "directly implicate[ ]" a FAPE—so that only in those suits can § 1415(*l*) apply. For the reasons that follow, we agree with the parties' shared view: The only relief that an IDEA officer can give—hence the thing a plaintiff must seek in order to trigger § 1415(*l*)'s exhaustion rule—is relief for the denial of a FAPE.

We begin, as always, with the statutory language at issue, which (at risk of repetition) compels exhaustion when a plaintiff seeks "relief" that is "available" under the IDEA. . . . So to establish the scope of § 1415(*l*), we must identify the circumstances in which the IDEA enables a person to obtain redress (or, similarly, to access a benefit).

That inquiry immediately reveals the primacy of a FAPE in the statutory scheme. In its first section, the IDEA declares as its first purpose "to ensure that all children with disabilities have available to them a free appropriate public education." § 1400(d)(1)(A). That principal purpose then becomes the Act's principal command: A State receiving federal funding under the IDEA must make such an education "available to all children with disabilities." § 1412(a)(1)(A). The guarantee of a FAPE to those children gives rise to the bulk of the statute's more specific provisions. For example, the IEP—"the centerpiece of the statute's education delivery system"—serves as the "vehicle" or "means" of providing a FAPE. *Rowley,* 458 U.S., at 181, 102 S.Ct. 3034. And finally, as all the above suggests, the FAPE requirement provides the yardstick for measuring the adequacy of the education that a school offers to a child with a disability: Under that standard, this Court has held, a child is entitled to "meaningful" access to education based on her individual needs. *Rowley,* 458 U.S., at 192, 102 S.Ct. 3034.

The IDEA's administrative procedures test whether a school has met that obligation—and so center on the Act's FAPE requirement. As noted earlier, any decision by a hearing officer on a request for substantive relief "shall" be "based on a determination of whether the child received a free appropriate public education." § 1415(f)(3)(E)(i). Or said in Latin: In the IDEA's administrative process, a FAPE denial is the *sine qua non.* Suppose that a parent's complaint protests a school's failure to provide some accommodation for a child with a disability. If that accommodation is needed to fulfill the IDEA's FAPE requirement, the hearing officer must order relief. But if it is not, he cannot—even though the dispute is between a child with a disability and the school she attends. There might be good reasons, unrelated to a FAPE, for the school to make the requested accommodation. Indeed, another federal law (like the ADA or Rehabilitation Act) might *require* the accommodation on one of those alternative grounds. But still, the hearing officer cannot provide the requested relief. His role, under the IDEA, is to enforce the child's "substantive right" to a FAPE. And that is all.

For that reason, § 1415(*l*)'s exhaustion rule hinges on whether a lawsuit seeks relief for the denial of a free appropriate public education. If a lawsuit charges such a denial, the plaintiff cannot escape § 1415(*l*) merely by bringing her suit under a statute other than the IDEA—as when, for example, the plaintiffs in *Smith* claimed that a school's failure to provide a FAPE also violated the Rehabilitation Act. Rather, that plaintiff must first submit her case to an IDEA hearing officer, experienced in addressing exactly the issues she raises. But if, in a suit brought under a different statute, the remedy sought is not for the denial of a FAPE, then exhaustion of the IDEA's procedures is not required. After all, the plaintiff could not get any relief from those procedures: A hearing officer, as just explained, would have to send her away empty-handed. And that is true even when the suit arises directly from a school's treatment of a child with a disability—and so could be said to relate in some way to her education. A school's conduct toward such a child—say, some refusal to make an accommodation—might injure her in ways unrelated to a FAPE, which are addressed in statutes other than the IDEA. A complaint seeking redress for those other harms, independent of any FAPE denial, is not subject to § 1415(*l*)'s exhaustion rule because, once again, the only "relief" the IDEA makes "available" is relief for the denial of a FAPE.

B

Still, an important question remains: How is a court to tell when a plaintiff "seeks" relief for the denial of a FAPE and when she does not? Here, too, the parties have found some common ground: By looking, they both say, to the "substance" of, rather than the labels used in, the plaintiff's complaint. And here, too, we agree with that view: What matters is the crux—or, in legal-speak, the gravamen—of the plaintiff's complaint, setting aside any attempts at artful pleading.

That inquiry makes central the plaintiff's own claims, as § 1415(*l*) explicitly requires. The statutory language asks whether a lawsuit in fact "seeks" relief available under the IDEA—not, as a stricter exhaustion statute might, whether the suit "could have sought" relief available under the IDEA (or, what is much the same, whether any remedies "are" available under that law). In effect, § 1415(*l*) treats the plaintiff as "the master of the claim": She identifies its remedial basis—and is subject to exhaustion or not based on that choice. A court deciding whether § 1415(*l*) applies must therefore examine whether a plaintiff's complaint—the principal instrument by which she describes her case—seeks relief for the denial of an appropriate education.

But that examination should consider substance, not surface. The use (or non-use) of particular labels and terms is not what matters. The inquiry, for example, does not ride on whether a complaint includes (or, alternatively, omits) the precise words(?) "FAPE" or "IEP." After all, § 1415(*l*)'s premise is that the plaintiff is suing under a statute *other than* the IDEA, like the Rehabilitation Act; in such a suit, the plaintiff might see no need to use the IDEA's distinctive language—even if she is in essence contesting the adequacy of a special education program. And still more critically, a "magic words" approach would make § 1415(*l*)'s exhaustion rule too easy to bypass. . . . Section 1415(*l*) is not merely a pleading hurdle. It requires exhaustion when the gravamen of a complaint seeks redress for a school's failure to provide a FAPE, even if not phrased or framed in precisely that way.

In addressing whether a complaint fits that description, a court should attend to the diverse means and ends of the statutes covering persons with disabilities—the IDEA on the one hand, the ADA and Rehabilitation Act (most notably) on the other. The IDEA, of course, protects only "children" (well, really, adolescents too) and concerns only their schooling. § 1412(a)(1)(A). And as earlier noted, the statute's goal is to provide each child with meaningful access to education by offering individualized instruction and related services appropriate to her "unique needs." § 1401(29). By contrast, Title II of the ADA and § 504 of the Rehabilitation Act cover people with disabilities of all ages, and do so both inside and outside schools. And those statutes aim to root out disability-based discrimination, enabling each covered person (sometimes by means of reasonable accommodations) to participate equally to all others in public facilities and federally funded programs. In short, the IDEA guarantees individually tailored educational services, while Title II and § 504 promise non-discriminatory access to public institutions. That is not to deny some overlap in coverage: The same conduct might violate all three statutes— which is why, as in *Smith,* a plaintiff might seek relief for the denial of a FAPE under Title II and § 504 as well as the IDEA. But still, the statutory differences just discussed mean that a complaint brought under Title II and § 504 might instead seek relief for simple discrimination, irrespective of the IDEA's FAPE obligation.

One clue to whether the gravamen of a complaint against a school concerns the denial of a FAPE, or instead addresses disability-based discrimination, can come from asking a pair of hypothetical questions. First, could the plaintiff have brought essentially the same claim if the alleged conduct had occurred at a public facility that was *not* a school—say, a public theater or library? And second, could an *adult* at the school—say, an employee or visitor—have pressed essentially the same grievance? When the answer to those questions is yes, a complaint that does not expressly allege the denial of a FAPE is also unlikely to be truly about that subject; after all, in those other situations there is no FAPE obligation and yet the same basic suit could go forward. But when the answer is no, then the complaint probably does concern a FAPE, even if it does not explicitly say so; for the FAPE requirement is all that explains why only a child in the school setting (not an adult in that setting or a child in some other) has a viable claim.

Take two contrasting examples. Suppose first that a wheelchair-bound child sues his school for discrimination under Title II (again, without mentioning the denial of a FAPE) because the building lacks access ramps. In some sense, that architectural feature has educational consequences, and a different lawsuit might have alleged that it violates the IDEA: After all, if the child cannot get inside the school, he cannot receive instruction there; and if he must be carried inside, he may not achieve the sense of independence conducive to academic (or later to real-world) success. But is the denial of a FAPE really the gravamen of the plaintiff's Title II complaint? Consider that the child could file the same basic complaint if a municipal library or theater had no ramps. And similarly, an employee or visitor could bring a mostly identical complaint against the school. That the claim can stay the same in those alternative scenarios suggests that its essence is equality of access to public facilities, not adequacy of special education. And so § 1415(*l*) does not require exhaustion.

But suppose next that a student with a learning disability sues his school under Title II for failing to provide remedial tutoring in mathematics. That suit, too, might be cast as one for disability-based discrimination, grounded on the school's refusal to make a reasonable accommodation; the complaint might make no reference at all to a FAPE or an IEP. But can anyone imagine the student making the same claim against a public theater or library? Or, similarly, imagine an adult visitor or employee suing the school to obtain a math tutorial? The difficulty of transplanting the complaint to those other contexts suggests that its essence—even though not its wording—is the provision of a FAPE, thus bringing § 1415(*l*) into play.

A further sign that the gravamen of a suit is the denial of a FAPE can emerge from the history of the proceedings. In particular, a court may consider that a plaintiff has previously invoked the IDEA's formal procedures to handle the dispute—thus starting to exhaust the Act's remedies before switching midstream. Recall that a parent dissatisfied with her child's education initiates those administrative procedures by filing a complaint, which triggers a preliminary meeting (or possibly mediation) and then a due process hearing. A plaintiff's initial choice to pursue that process may suggest that she is indeed seeking relief for the denial of a FAPE—with the shift to judicial proceedings prior to full exhaustion reflecting only strategic calculations about how to maximize the prospects of such a remedy. Whether that is so depends on the facts; a court may conclude, for example, that the move to a courtroom came from a late-acquired awareness that the school had fulfilled its FAPE obligation and that the grievance involves something else entirely. But prior pursuit of the IDEA's administrative remedies will often provide strong evidence that the substance of a plaintiff's claim concerns the denial of a FAPE, even if the complaint never explicitly uses that term.

III

The Court of Appeals did not undertake the analysis we have just set forward. As noted above, it asked whether E.F.'s injuries were, broadly speaking, "educational" in nature. 788 F.3d, at 627 (reasoning that the "value of allowing Wonder to attend [school] with E.F. was educational" because it would foster "her sense of independence and social confidence," which is "the sort of interest the IDEA protects"). That is not the same as asking whether the gravamen of E.F.'s complaint charges, and seeks relief for, the denial of a FAPE. And that difference in standard may have led to a difference in result in this case. Understood correctly, § 1415(*l*) might not require exhaustion of the Frys' claim. We lack some important information on that score, however, and so we remand the issue to the court below.

The Frys' complaint alleges only disability-based discrimination, without making any reference to the adequacy of the special education services E.F.'s school provided. The school districts' "refusal to allow Wonder to act as a service dog," the complaint states, "discriminated against [E.F.] as a person with disabilities . . . by denying her equal access" to public facilities. The complaint contains no allegation about the denial of a FAPE or about any deficiency in E.F.'s IEP. More, it does not accuse the school even in general terms of refusing to provide the educational instruction and services that E.F. needs. As the Frys explained in this Court: The school districts "have said all along that because they gave [E.F.] a one-on-one [human] aide, that all of her . . . educational needs were satisfied. And we have not challenged that, and it would be difficult for us to challenge that." The Frys instead maintained, just as OCR had earlier found, that the school districts infringed E.F.'s right to equal access—even if their actions complied in full with the IDEA's requirements.

And nothing in the nature of the Frys' suit suggests any implicit focus on the adequacy of E.F.'s education. Consider, as suggested above, that the Frys could have filed essentially the same complaint if a public library or theater had refused admittance to Wonder. Or similarly, consider that an adult visitor to the school could have leveled much the same charges if prevented from entering with his service dog. In each case, the plaintiff would challenge a public facility's policy of precluding service dogs (just as a blind person might challenge a policy of barring guide dogs) as violating Title II's and § 504's equal access requirements. The suit would have nothing to do with the provision of educational services. From all that we know now, that is exactly the kind of action the Frys have brought.

But we do not foreclose the possibility that the history of these proceedings might suggest something different. As earlier discussed, a plaintiff's initial pursuit of the IDEA's administrative remedies can serve as evidence that the gravamen of her later suit is the denial of a FAPE, even though that does not appear on the face of her complaint. The Frys may or may not have sought those remedies before filing this case: None of the parties here have addressed that issue, and the record is cloudy as to the relevant facts. Accordingly, on remand, the court below should establish whether (or to what extent) the Frys invoked the IDEA's dispute resolution process before bringing this suit. And if the Frys started down that road, the court should decide whether their actions reveal that the gravamen of their complaint is indeed the denial of a FAPE, thus necessitating further exhaustion.

With these instructions and for the reasons stated, we vacate the judgment of the Court of Appeals and remand the case for further proceedings consistent with this opinion.

It is so ordered.

[Concurring opinion is omitted.]

NOTES AND QUESTIONS

1. *Overlapping claims under the IDEA, ADA, and Section 504 of the Rehabilitation Act.* Although most claims related to educating children with disabilities are brought under the IDEA, parents sometimes bring claims under Section 504 of the Rehabilitation Act or the ADA. As Professor Mark Weber discusses, one reason parents might bring a claim under Section 504 is because they want to seek compensatory damages (which are generally unavailable under the IDEA). *See* Mark C. Weber, *A New Look at Section 504 and the ADA in Special Education Cases*, 16 TEX. J. ON C.L. & C.R. 1 (2010) (noting, however, that successful damages claims are relatively rare under Section 504). But Section 504 also applies to any child with a disability who is not eligible for special education services under the IDEA but might need accommodations in school. In these cases, schools develop "504 plans," which are agreements (usually more informal than IEPs) regarding what services or accommodations the child needs. Parents might also bring Section 504 claims to seek the modification of standards for participation in athletic programs.

Finally, as demonstrated in *Ellenberg v. New Mexico Military Institute*, 478 F.3d 1262 (10th Cir. 2007), the IDEA is not an anti-discrimination statute; thus, when the plaintiff in that case was denied admission to a unique military-like secondary school because of her disability, her claims were properly brought under Section 504 and the ADA—not under the IDEA. Similarly, as the Court noted in *Fry*, even though the plaintiff could have challenged the denial of her request to have her service dog with her at school as a failure to provide her with a FAPE, it instead brought the claim under Title II of the ADA and Section 504 of the Rehabilitation Act, arguing that the school district discriminated against her by failing to provide her a reasonable modification—allowing her service dog. Although the issue in *Fry* was one of exhaustion—when are plaintiffs required to exhaust their remedies under the IDEA before bringing claims under the ADA or Section 504—the *Fry* case also demonstrates another possible application of Section 504 and the ADA. The Frys were not contesting the IEP developed for the child; instead, they were only contesting the school's failure to allow in Wonder, the child's service dog.

2.   *Exhaustion and* Fry. As held in *Fry*, in determining whether a plaintiff is required to exhaust their remedies under the IDEA, courts should look at the gravamen of the complaint—what is the essence of the complaint? Is it challenging whether the school provided the student with a FAPE or is it more akin to a discrimination claim that could be brought by anyone trying to bring a service dog into a school? The Court states that when making the determination regarding the gravamen of the complaint, courts should ask two questions: (1) could the complaint have been brought against the school by an adult with a disability if the school had refused to allow the adult to bring in her service dog; and (2) could the child have brought the same complaint against another governmental entity that refused to allow in the service dog? If courts answer both questions in the affirmative, then it is likely that the gravamen of the complaint is not the failure to provide a FAPE under the IDEA and exhaustion is not necessary. What do you think of the Court's test? Do you think the two questions will help courts decide future exhaustion issues?

3.   *Ehlena and Wonder's Story.* For a story that is bound to pull on a few heart strings (and includes pictures of Wonder), see Michale J. Steinberg, *Ehlena and Wonder the Service Dog's Incredible Journey to the Supreme Court,* ACLU.org (Oct. 27, 2016), https://www.aclu.org/blog/disability-rights/ disability-rights-and-education/ehlena-and-wonder-service-dogs-incredible. There is lots to love about this story (especially if you're a dog lover) but perhaps the best part of this story is the happy ending for the plaintiff. Not only did she win the case before the Supreme Court, but perhaps more importantly, the new school E.F. attended welcomed Wonder with open arms, even creating an ID badge for him and putting his picture in the yearbook under "staff."

INDEX

References are to Pages

ACCESSIBILITY
Government Services (ADA Title II), this index
Public Accommodations (ADA Title III), this index

ACTUAL DISABILITY
Generally, 23–69
ADA Amendments Act of 2008 (ADAAA)
    Generally, 51–70
    HIV, 33
    Major bodily functions, 60–61
    Major life activities, below
    Mitigating measures, below
    Pre-amendments narrowing of definition of disability, 34–50
    Short-term impairments, 60
    Summary of statutory provisions, 51–53
Defining disability
    Generally, 23–32
    ADA Amendments Act (ADAAA), above
    Pre-amendments narrowing of definition, 34–50
DOT certification, 44
Hierarchy of impairments, 45
HIV, 33
Major bodily functions, 60–61
Major life activities
    Generally, 19
    ADAAA, 53
    HIV, 33
Minority group approach, 46–47
Mitigating measures
    Generally, 20
    Employer's obligation, effect of mitigating measures rule, 45–46
    Summary of ADAAA provisions, 51
Per se disability, 33
Pre-amendments narrowing of definition, 34–50
Short-term impairments, 60
Statutory definition, 23

ADA AMENDMENTS ACT OF 2008 (ADAAA)
Generally, 51–70
Actual Disability, this index
Broad construction, 51
Case outcomes, empirical examination, 82–87

Enactment, 1, 20
Major life activities, 53
Mitigating measures. Actual Disability, this index
Post-ADAAA summary, 82–87
Regarded as disabled
    Generally, 74
    New "regarded as" prong, 80
    Pre-Amendments interpretation, 70–74
    Reasonable accommodations, 81
    Transitory and minor exception, 80–81
Short-term impairments, 60
Substantially limits, 52–53
Summary of statutory provisions, 51–53

ADMINISTRATIVE ENFORCEMENT, 322–323

ADMISSIONS
Higher Education, this index

ALCOHOL USE
Employment Discrimination, this index
Record of claim, completion of rehabilitation program, 70

AMERICANS WITH DISABILITIES ACT
Generally, 18–21
Actual Disability, this index
Amendments act
    Actual Disability, this index
    ADA Amendments Act of 2008 (ADAAA), this index
Definition of disability
    Generally, 19–20
    Actual Disability, this index
    Record of disability, 69–70
    Regarded as disabled, below
Education
    Higher Education, this index
    Primary and Secondary Education, this index
Employment Discrimination, this index
Enactment of ADA and ADAAA, 1, 4
Government Services (ADA Title II), this index
Higher Education, this index
Major life activities. Actual Disability, this index
Minority group approach, 46–47

683

Primary and Secondary Education, this
index
Public Accommodations (ADA Title III),
this index
Record of disability, 69–70
Regarded as disabled
Generally, 70–82
Major life activity of working, 73–74
Pre-Amendments interpretation, 70–
74
Proving, 73–74
Substantial limitation
Generally, 19
ADAAA, 52–53

ARBITRATION
Employment discrimination claims, 325

ASSOCIATIONAL DISCRIMINATION
Employment Discrimination, this index

ATTENDANCE POLICIES
Employment Discrimination, this index

ATTORNEYS
Bar exam, testing accommodations, 478 et
seq.
Licensure, ADA Title II, 407–416

**BLIND AND VISUALLY IMPAIRED
PERSONS**
Jury service, blind *vs.* deaf, 366

BURDEN OF PROOF
Employment Discrimination, this index
Individuals with Disabilities Education Act
(IDEA), 668

CIVIC PARTICIPATION
Government services (ADA Title II), 361–
367

CIVIL RIGHTS MODEL, 6

COLLEGES AND UNIVERSITIES
Higher Education, this index

CONSTITUTIONAL STATUS
Levels of scrutiny, equal protection
analysis, 7
Rational basis, 18

DAMAGES
ADA and Rehabilitation Act, 670–671
ADA Title II, 417
Caps on amounts, 324
Employment discrimination, 323–324

**DEAF AND HEARING IMPAIRED
PERSONS**
Classroom, hearing impairments in, 608
Interpreter services, provision by hospital,
446
Jury service, blind *vs.* deaf, 366

DEFINITION OF DISABILITY
Generally, 19–20
Actual Disability, this index
Americans with Disabilities Act, this index
Individuals with Disabilities Education Act
(IDEA), 592–593
Record of disability, 69–70
Regarded as disabled, 70–82

DIRECT THREAT
Employment Discrimination, this index

DISABILITY RIGHTS MOVEMENT
Brief history, 2–4

DISPARATE IMPACT
Drug and alcohol use, 251–252
Employment discrimination, 299–301
Government services (ADA Title II), 346
Jury trial, disparate treatment *vs.*
disparate impact cases, 323

DRUG USE
Employment Discrimination, this index
Record of claim, completion of
rehabilitation program, 70

EDUCATION
Generally, 525 et seq.
Higher Education, this index
Primary and Secondary Education, this
index

ELEVENTH AMENDMENT IMMUNITY
ADA Title II, 349
Family and Medical Leave Act (FMLA),
320

EMPLOYMENT DISCRIMINATION
Generally, 20–21, 89 et seq.
Alcohol use. Drug and alcohol use, below
Arbitration alternative, 325
Asking disability-related questions, 293–
294
Associational discrimination
Generally, 257–279
Categories, 279
Misconduct, 270
Reasonable accommodations, 279
Attendance policies
Leaves of absence, 162–163
Working from home, 178–179
Burden of proof
Burden-shifting framework, 89–90
Direct threat to health or safety of
others, 234
Qualification standards *vs.* qualified
individual, 217
Vacant position, reassignment to, 143
Business necessity standard, 294
But for *vs.* mixed motive, 103–104
Circumstantial evidence, 101–102
Cost of reasonable accommodations, 127
Counting employees, payroll method, 321
Covered employers, 321

Decline in employment of persons with disabilities, 326
Deference to employer judgment, essential functions, 113–114
Deferral jurisdictions, time limits for filing charge, 322
Direct threat to health or safety of others
  Generally, 218–235
  Burden of proof, 234
  Defenses, dueling, 234
  Health care workers, 233–234
  Public health authorities, role of, 233
  Risk to self, 234
  Statutory language and EEOC regulation, 218–219
  Subjective vs. objective inquiry, 233
Disparate impact claims, 299–301
Doctor's notes explaining absence from work, 294
Drug and alcohol use
  Generally, 237–253
  Disparate impact claims, 252
  Drug testing, 252
  Formerly addicted persons, 252
EEOC enforcement, 322–323
Essential functions
  Deference to employer judgment, 113–114
  Defined, 104
  Qualification standards distinguished, 113, 217–218
  When work is performed, 183
Exhaustion of remedies, 325
Family and Medical Leave Act, this index
Genetic Information Nondiscrimination Act (GINA), 295
Harassment, 301–302
Intentional discrimination, remedies, 323–324
Investigation of charge by EEOC, 322
Job-relatedness standard, 294
Judicial estoppel, qualified individual with disability, 114–119
Jurisdiction of ADA and Rehabilitation Act, 321–322
Leaves of absence
  EEOC guidance, 162
  Indefinite leave, 162
  Overlap with FMLA, 162–163
Medical examinations and inquiries
  Generally, 280–295
  Asking disability-related questions, 293–294
  Doctor's notes explaining absence from work, 294
  Genetic Information Nondiscrimination Act (GINA), 295
  Psychological and personality testing, 294
  Statutory provisions, 280–281
  Temporal categories, 282–283

Mental impairments
  Generally, 253–279
  Physical impairments compared, 257
Mixed motive vs. but for, 103–104
Prima facie case, plaintiff's
  Generally, 89–104
  Burden-shifting framework, 89–90
  But for vs. mixed motive, 103–104
  Circumstantial evidence, 101–102
Private litigation enforcement, 323
Psychological and personality testing, 294
Punitive damages, intentional discrimination, remedies, 323–324
Qualification standards
  Generally, 206–218
  Burden of proof, qualification standards vs. qualified individual, 217
  Statutory language, 206
  Vision, uncorrected, 218
Qualified individual with disability
  Generally, 104–119
  Deference to employer judgment, 113–114
  Essential functions, 104, 113–114
  Individualized inquiry, 113
  Judicial estoppel, 114–119
  Marginal functions, 113
  Qualified, defined, 104
  Reasonable accommodation, 113
Reasonable accommodation mandate
  Generally, 119–192
  Affirmative actions vs. anti-discrimination, 183–185
  Costs, role of, 127
  Effectiveness of change or modification, 128
  Employer reluctance to hire persons with disabilities, 326
  Equal treatment vs. special treatment, 185
  High-cost accommodations, 205
  Interactive process, 185–192
  Other employees, accommodations affecting, 130
  Qualified individual with disability, 113
  Reasonable, defined, 128–130
  Record of disability, entitlement to reasonable accommodations, 70
  Regarded as disabled, 81
  Statutory language and EEOC regulations, 119–120
  Statutory provisions, 89
  Undue hardship
    Generally, 128–129, 193–206
    EEOC guidance, 193
    High-cost accommodations, 205
    Reasonable accommodation vs. undue hardship, 206
    Statutory language, 193

Vacant position, reassignment to, below

Working from home, 178–179

Reasonable cause finding by EEOC, 322

Remedies, 323–324

Retaliatory acts, 287–298

Right to sue letter, 323

Statutes of limitation, 325

Statutory provisions, 89

Stigma or insensitivity, 128

Time limits for filing charge, 322

Undue hardship. Reasonable accommodation mandate, above

Vacant position, reassignment to

Generally, 131–148

Affirmative action, reassignment as, 148

Burden of proof, 143

Collective bargaining agreements, 143

Preferential treatment, 142–143, 183–185

Reasonable accommodation *vs.* undue hardship, 143

Seniority, benefits of, 142

Vision, uncorrected, 218

Working from home, 178–179

EQUAL EMPLOYMENT OPPORTUNITY COMMISSION (EEOC)

Enforcement of discrimination claims, 322–323

Leaves of absence, EEOC guidance, 162

Reasonable accommodation regulations, 120

Right to sue letter, 323

Time limits for filing charge, 322

Undue hardship, EEOC guidance, 193

EQUAL PROTECTION

Levels of scrutiny, 7

ESSENTIAL FUNCTIONS

Employment Discrimination, this index

ESTOPPEL

Judicial estoppel, qualified individual with disability, 114–119

EXAMINATIONS AND COURSES

Generally, 476–489

Deference to past accommodations, 488–489

Preferred accommodations, 488

Statutory provisions and regulations, 476–477

Testing accommodation, 478 et seq.

EXAMINATIONS, MEDICAL

Employment Discrimination, this index

EXHAUSTION OF REMEDIES

Employment discrimination, 325

EXPERT FEES

IDEA and ADA, 669

FAMILY AND MEDICAL LEAVE ACT (FMLA)

Generally, 302–321

Accrued paid leave, substitution of, 304

ADA, interplay with, 320–321

Covered employers, 303

Designating leave as FMLA leave, 319

Eleventh Amendment immunity, 320

Eligibility for FMLA leave, 303

Incapacity, proof of, 318

Leave of absence, overlap with FMLA, 162–163

Light duty assignment, offer of, 319

Medical certificate to support leave request, 303–304

Notice of need for leave, 303

Private right of action, 304

Providing care for family member, 319

Reinstatement after leave, 304, 319

Serious health conditions, 301–302, 318

Statute of limitations on FMLA claims, 304

Statutory provisions, 302

Workers' compensation, interplay with, 319

GENETIC INFORMATION NONDISCRIMINATION ACT (GINA)

Employment discrimination, 295

GOLF CARTS

Use in tournament, 421 et seq.

GOVERNMENT SERVICES (ADA TITLE II)

Generally, 21, 329–417

Access/content distinction, 338–347

Accessibility

Generally, 382–397

Alterations, 385

Alternate means of access, 385

Administrative complaints, 416–417

Attorney licensure, 407–416

Background, 329–330

Civic participation, 361–367

Coverage

Generally, 330–338

Eleventh Amendment immunity, 338

Prisons, 333

Public employment claims, 338

Quasi-public entities, 333

Termination of parental rights, state court proceedings, 334

Damages claims, 417

De-institutionalization, 360–361

Direct threat of harm defense, 381

Discriminatory intent, prerequisite for recovery of damages, 417

Disparate impact claims, 347

Eleventh Amendment immunity, 338

Enforcement, 416–417

Facility access, 385

Integration, 347–361

Jury service, 366–367

Licensing rules
> Generally, 397–416
> Attorney licensure, 407–416
> Mental health diagnosis *vs.* conduct, 416

Prisons, applicability of Title II, 333

Private enforcement action, 417

Public employment claims, 338

Punitive damages, prohibition, 417

Quasi-public entities, applicability of Title II, 333

Rehabilitation Act and Title II
> Generally, 381
> Statutory synchronicity, 416

Remedies, 416–417

Statutory language, 329–330

Termination of parental rights, state court proceedings, 334

Zoning
> Generally, 367–382
> Alteration of policies, 381
> Mental health clinic, 367–375
> Methadone clinic, 375
> Reasonable modification, 381
> Variances, 382

HARASSMENT

Employment discrimination, 301–302

HEARING IMPAIRMENTS

Deaf and Hearing Impaired Persons, this index

HIGHER EDUCATION
> Generally, 525–591

Admissions
> Generally, 526–535
> Otherwise qualified, defined, 532
> Pre-admission inquiries, 526
> Professional academic programs, 533–534
> Qualified individual with disability
>> Generally, 526–535
>> Otherwise qualified, defined, 532
>> Reasonable modifications, 532–533
> Reasonable modifications, 532–533

Course substitutions, 591

Dismissal/academic deference
> Generally, 535–566, 591
> Lack of professionalism as grounds for dismissal, 565–566
> Misconduct, 566
> Withdrawn accommodations, 556

Duration of proposed accommodation, 566

Learning disabilities, 590–591

Misconduct issues, 566

Otherwise qualified, defined, 532

Pre-admission inquiries, 526

Professional academic programs, 533–534

Professionalism, lack of, as grounds for dismissal, 565–566

Reasonable modifications, 532–533, 535

Statutory coverage, 525–526

Waiver of degree requirements
> Generally, 567–591
> Course substitutions, 591
> Learning disabilities, 590–591

Withdrawn accommodations, 556

HISTORICAL BACKGROUND

Disability rights movement, 2–4

INDIVIDUALS WITH DISABILITIES EDUCATION ACT (IDEA)
> Generally, 591–670

Primary and Secondary Education, this index

INTERPRETATION

Models of disability interpretation, 5–7

JURISDICTION

ADA and Rehabilitation Act, 321–322

EEOC, exclusive jurisdiction, 322–323

JURY SERVICE

Automatic exclusion upon request, 367

Blind *vs.* deaf, 366

Targeted exclusion, 367

JURY TRIAL

Disparate treatment *vs.* disparate impact cases, 323

LEAVES OF ABSENCE, 162–163

LICENSES AND PERMITS

Licensing rules, ADA Title II, 397–416

LONG-TERM DISABILITY INSURANCE

Physical *vs.* mental disabilities, 489–501

MAJOR LIFE ACTIVITIES

Actual Disability, this index

MEDICAL EXAMINATIONS AND INQUIRIES

Employment Discrimination, this index

MENTAL HEALTH

Employment Discrimination, this index

Professional licensing, diagnosis *vs.* conduct, 416

Zoning, mental health clinic (ADA Title II), 367–375

METHADONE CLINIC

Zoning (ADA Title II), 375

MITIGATING MEASURES

Actual Disability, this index

MODELS OF DISABILITY INTERPRETATION
> Generally, 5–7

Civil rights model, 6

PRIMARY AND SECONDARY EDUCATION
Generally, 591–670
ADA and Rehabilitation Act (Section 504)
Generally, 670–680
Compensatory damage claims, 670–671
Overlapping claims, 680–681
Discipline of students with disabilities, 643–653
Expert witness fees, ADA and IDEA, 669
Free appropriate public education, 592–608
Hearing impairments in classroom, 608
Individuals with Disabilities Education Act (IDEA)
Generally, 591–670
Burden of proof, 668
Disability, defined, 592–593
Discipline/stay-put provision, 643–653
Equal education standard, 608
Expert fees, 669
Free appropriate public education, 592–608
Mainstreaming (least restrictive environment), 609–635
Manifestation determination, 653
Medical services, defined, 643
Overlapping claims, 680
Private school reimbursement, 654–661
Procedures and remedies, 661–670
Related services, 635–643
Special education services and reimbursement for private school tuition, 660–661
Undue hardship defense for related services, 643
Integration presumption, 634
Least restrictive environment, 609–635
Mainstreaming (least restrictive environment), 609–635
Medical services, defined, 643
Overlapping claims, 680–681
Private school reimbursement, 654–661
Special education services and reimbursement for private school tuition, 660–661
Undue hardship defense for related services, 643

PRISONS
ADA Title II, applicability, 333

PRIVATE RIGHT OF ACTION
EEOC right to sue letter, 323
FMLA actions, 304
Government services (ADA Title II), 417

PRIVATE SCHOOLS
Tuition reimbursement, 654–661

PUBLIC ACCOMMODATIONS (ADA TITLE III)
Generally, 21, 419–523
Cruise ships, foreign flag, 437
Examinations and Courses, this index
Golf tournaments and golf carts, 421 et seq.
Insurance, 489–501
Interpreter services and undue hardship, 446
Necessity of proposed modification, 437–438
Notice and opportunity to remedy deficiencies, 521
Reasonable modifications, 421–446
Remedies
Generally, 501–523
Serial litigation, 506–522
Standing, 502–506
Statute of limitations, 523
Statutory provisions, 501, 512
Segway, allowing use, 437 et seq.
Serial litigation, 506–522
Standing to sue, 502–506
Statute of limitations, 523
Statutory provisions, 419–421
Testing. Examinations and Courses, this index

PUBLIC SERVICES
Government Services (ADA Title II), this index

PUBLIC-PRIVATE PARTNERSHIPS
ADA Title II, applicability, 333

PUNITIVE DAMAGES
Intentional discrimination, 323–324
Prohibition, ADA Title II, 417

QUALIFICATION STANDARDS
Employment Discrimination, this index

QUALIFIED INDIVIDUAL WITH DISABILITY
Employment Discrimination, this index

QUASI-PUBLIC ENTITIES
ADA Title II, applicability, 333

REASONABLE ACCOMMODATIONS
Employment Discrimination, this index

REASSIGNMENT
Vacant positions. Employment Discrimination, this index

REGARDED AS DISABLED
Generally, 70–82
ADAAA and post-ADAAA, 74–82
Pre-Amendments interpretation, 70–74

REHABILITATION ACT (SECTION 504)
Generally, 3
Damages, ADA and Rehabilitation Act, 670–671

Government Services (ADA Title II), this
index
Primary and Secondary Education, this
index

REMEDIES
Employment discrimination, 323–324
Government services (ADA Title II), 416–
417
Individuals with Disabilities Education Act
(IDEA), 661–670
Public Accommodations (ADA Title III),
this index

RETALIATION CLAIMS
But for causation, 298
Elements of claim, 297–298

STANDING TO SUE
Public accommodations (ADA Title III),
502–506

STATUTES OF LIMITATION
Employment discrimination, 325
Family and Medical Leave Act (FMLA)
claims, 304
Public accommodations (ADA Title III), 523

STIGMA
Employment discrimination, 128
Psychological damage, 5

TERMINATION OF PARENTAL
RIGHTS
State court proceedings, applicability of
ADA Title II, 334

TESTING
Examinations and Courses, this index

UNDUE HARDSHIP
IDEA, related services, 643
Interpreter services, 446
Reasonable accommodations. Employment
Discrimination, this index

UNIVERSITIES AND COLLEGES
Higher Education, this index

VACANT POSITIONS
Reassignment. Employment
Discrimination, this index

VISION
Qualification standards, uncorrected
vision, 218

ZONING
Government Services (ADA Title II), this
index